REA's Test Prep Bo  Best!

(a sample of the <u>hundreds of letters</u> REA receives each year)

“ This [REA] study guide was a tremendous help and I credit it with giving me the tools to help me pass the TASP. ”

Student, Austin, TX

“ My students report your chapters of review as the most valuable single resource they used for review and preparation. ”

Teacher, American Fork, UT

“ Your book was such a better value and was so much more complete than anything your competition has produced (and I have them all!). ”

Teacher, Virginia Beach, VA

“ Compared to the other books that my fellow students had, your book was the most useful in helping me get a great score. ”

Student, North Hollywood, CA

“ Your book was responsible for my success on the exam, which helped me get into the college of my choice... I will look for REA the next time I need help. ”

Student, Chesterfield, MO

“ Just a short note to say thanks for the great support your book gave me in helping me pass the test... I'm on my way to a B.S. degree because of you! ”

Student, Orlando, FL

(more on next page)

(continued from front page)

"I just wanted to thank you for helping me get a great score on the AP U.S. History exam... Thank you for making great test preps!"

Student, Los Angeles, CA

"Your *Fundamentals of Engineering Exam* book was the absolute best preparation I could have had for the exam, and it is one of the major reasons I did so well and passed the FE on my first try."

Student, Sweetwater, TN

"I used your book to prepare for the test and found that the advice and the sample tests were highly relevant... Without using any other material, I earned very high scores and will be going to the graduate school of my choice."

Student, New Orleans, LA

"What I found in your book was a wealth of information sufficient to shore up my basic skills in math and verbal... The practice tests were challenging and the answer explanations most helpful. It certainly is the *Best Test Prep for the GRE*!"

Student, Pullman, WA

"I really appreciate the help from your excellent book. Please keep up the great work."

Student, Albuquerque, NM

"I am writing to thank you for your test preparation... your book helped me immeasurably and I have nothing but praise for your *GRE* preparation."

Student, Benton Harbor, MI

(more on back page)

The Best Test Preparation for the

TASP®

Texas Academic Skills Program™

Ellen Conner, M.A.
English Instructor
Clear Lake High School, Houston, Texas

Jocelyn Chadwick-Joshua, Ph.D.
Co-Chair of the Writing Committee for TASP
Director of Graduate Rhetoric and Director of Developmental Writing
University of North Texas, Denton, Texas

George P. Parks, Jr., Ed.M., M.A.
English Instructor
Clear Lake High School, Houston, Texas

Robert B. Truscott, M.A.
Former Assistant Director
Douglass/Cook College Writing Center
Rutgers University, New Brunswick, New Jersey

Clara Wajngurt, Ph.D.
Associate Professor of Math and Computer Science
Queensborough Community College, Bayside, New York

Research & Education Association

The Best Test Preparation for the
TASP® (Texas Academic Skills Program™)

Year 2003 Printing

Printed in the United States of America

Library of Congress Control Number 2001086297

International Standard Book Number 0-87891-893-0

Research & Education Association
61 Ethel Road West
Piscataway, New Jersey 08854

REA supports the effort to conserve and protect environmental resources by printing on recycled papers.

About Research & Education Association

Research & Education Association (REA) is an organization of educators, scientists, and engineers specializing in various academic fields. Founded in 1959 with the purpose of disseminating the most recently developed scientific information to groups in industry, government, high schools, and universities, REA has since become a successful and highly respected publisher of study aids, test preps, handbooks, and reference works.

REA's Test Preparation series includes study guides for all academic levels in almost all disciplines. Research & Education Association publishes test preps for students who have not yet completed high school, as well as high school students preparing to enter college. Students from countries around the world seeking to attend college in the United States will find the assistance they need in REA's publications. For college students seeking advanced degrees, REA publishes test preps for many major graduate school admission examinations in a wide variety of disciplines, including engineering, law, and medicine. Students at every level, in every field, with every ambition can find what they are looking for among REA's publications.

Unlike most test preparation books—which present only a few practice tests that bear little resemblance to the actual exams—REA's series presents tests that accurately depict the official exams in both degree of difficulty and types of questions. REA's practice tests are always based upon the most recently administered exams, and include every type of question that can be expected on the actual exams.

REA's publications and educational materials are highly regarded and continually receive an unprecedented amount of praise from professionals, instructors, librarians, parents, and students. Our authors are as diverse as the subject matter represented in the books we publish. They are well-known in their respective fields and serve on the faculties of prestigious high schools, colleges, and universities throughout the United States and Canada.

Acknowledgments

In addition to our authors, we would like to thank Dr. Max Fogiel, President, for his overall guidance, which brought this publication to completion; Larry B. Kling, Quality Control Manager of Books in Print, for his supervision of revisions; Catherine Battos, Editorial Assistant, for coordinating revisions; M. Slim Fayache, M.S., Leonard A. Kenner, and Andrew J. Parks for their editorial contributions; and Marty Perzan for typesetting the manuscript.

Contents

About Research & Education Association v
Study Schedule xi

Chapter 1 • *Passing the TASP* 1
About this Book 2
About the Test 2
Who takes the test and what is it used for? 2
Who administers the test? 3
When should the TASP be taken? 3
When and where is the test given? 3
Is there a registration fee? 4
How to Use this Book 4
What do I study first? 4
When should I start studying? 4
Format of the TASP 5
Sections of the TASP 6
Reading Section 6
Mathematics Section 6
Writing Section 6
About the Review Sections 7
Reading Section Review 7
Mathematics Section Review 7
Writing Section Review 7
Scoring the TASP Test 8
How do I score my practice tests? 8
Scoring the Reading and Mathematics Sections 9
Scoring the Writing Section 11
What scores do I need to pass the actual TASP? 12
When will I receive my score report and what will it look like? 12
Studying for the TASP 13
TASP Test-Taking Tips 14
The Day of the Test 14
Before the Test 14
During the Test 15
After the Test 16

Chapter 2 • *Reading Section Review* 19
The Passages 20
The Questions 21
Strategies for the Reading Section 22
A Four-Step Approach 24
Step 1: Preview 24

Step 2: Read Actively 30
Step 3: Review the Passage 35
Step 4: Answer the Questions 35
Vocabulary Enhancer 43
Similar Forms and Sounds 43
Multiple Meanings 47
Connotation and Denotation 47
Vocabulary Builder 49
Additional Vocabulary 67
Knowing Your Word Parts 85
Figures of Speech 96
Interpretation of Graphic Information Questions 97
Reading Drills Answer Key 109

Chapter 3 • *Mathematics Section Review* 115
Strategies for the Math Section 117
Arithmetic 121
Integers and Real Numbers 121
Fractions 126
Exponents 134
Order of Operations 137
Decimals 139
Percentages 145
Radicals 150
Averages 154
Arithmetic Drills Answer Key 158
Algebra 160
Operations with Polynomials 160
Simplifying Algebraic Expressions 164
Linear Equations 168
Two Linear Equations 173
Quadratic Equations 180
Absolute Value Equations 191
Inequalities 192
Ratios and Proportions 196
Algebra Drills Answer Key 200
Geometry 201
Points, Lines, and Angles 201
Regular Polygons 212
Triangles 215
Quadrilaterals 222
Circles 229
Solids 235
Coordinate Geometry 237
Geometry Drills Answer Key 242
Word Problems 244
Algebraic 244

Rate 245
Work 246
Mixture 247
Interest 249
Discount 250
Profit 252
Sets 253
Geometry 255
Measurement 256
Data Interpretation 258
Combination of Mathematical Skills 261
Word Problem Drills Answer Key 265
Detailed Explanations of Answers 267
Reference Table 285

Chapter 4 • *Writing Section Review* 287
Part I: Multiple-Choice 290
Strategies for the Multiple-Choice Subsection 291
Recognizing the Writer's Purpose and Intended Audience 293
Analyzing a Passage for Purpose and Audience 293
Determine What Essay Strategy the Writer Uses:
Explain, Inform, or Persuade 293
Consider Implications and Inferences 293
Determine the Nature of the Audience 294
Recognizing Effective Organization: Unity, Focus, and Development 296
Look for Key Sections (T) and (*t*) 296
Key Sections to Recognize 296
Determine the Type of Evidence (E) 296
Check for Logic 297
Note the Transitions 298
Recognizing Effective Sentence Structure and Mechanics 301
Test Your Skills 301
Diagnostic 301
Diagnostic Answer Key 305
Review of Standard Written English 308
Sentence Fragments 308
Run-on Sentences 308
Short Sentences/Wordiness 309
Misplaced Modifiers 311
Parallel Structure 312
Phrases and Clauses 313
Subject-Verb Agreement 318
Comparison of Adjectives 319
Pronouns 320
Conjunctions 338
The Comma 339
The Colon and Semicolon 347

Quotation Marks 351
The Apostrophe 358
Stops 361
Interjections, Dashes, and Parentheses 365
Capitalization 368
Writing Drills Answer Key 379
Part II: Writing Sample 396
Strategies for the Writing Sample 397
Appropriate, Unified, and Focused Essays: Recognizing Effective Writing 399
Why Essays Exist 399
Organization and Purposeful Development 399
Essay Writing 399
Seven Steps to Prove a Thesis 400
The Writing Process: Controlling Organization, Paragraph Development, Sentence Structure, Usage, and Mechanical Conventions 400
Composing Your Essay: Using the Writing Process 400
Writing Your Essay 402
Prewriting/Planning Time 402
Consider Your Audience 402
Control Your Point of View 402
Consider Your Support 403
Write Your Rough Draft 403
Transitions 403
Grammar 404
Providing Evidence in Your Essay 405
Organizing and Reviewing the Paragraphs 405
Paragraphing with No Evidence 405
Check for Logic 406
Polishing and Editing Your Essay 408
Polishing Checklist 408
Proofreading 408
Essay Writing Drills Answer Key 411

The Practice Tests

Practice Test 1 419
Answer Key 475
Detailed Explanations of Answers 476
Practice Test 2 527
Answer Key 585
Detailed Explanations of Answers 586
Answer Sheets 629

Study Schedule

The following study schedule will help you become thoroughly prepared for the TASP Test. Although the schedule is designed as a 12-week study program, it can be condensed if less time is available by consolidating some of the two-week blocks into one-week blocks. Be sure to set aside enough time each day for studying purposes. You may wish to study for an hour every day or, depending on your personal schedule, perhaps devote longer stretches of your weekend to the task. Keep in mind that the more time you spend studying for the TASP, the more prepared and confident you will be on the day of the exam.

Week	Activity
1-2	Read and study the introduction to the TASP on the following pages. Then, take and score Practice Test 1 to determine your strengths and weaknesses. You should have someone with good writing skills critique your essay. Any area in which you score low is an area you will need to study more thoroughly.
3	Study the Reading Section Review. Be sure to complete all drills and check your answers.
4-5	Study the Mathematics Section Review. Complete all drills and check your answers.
6-7	Study Part I of the Writing Section Review for the Multiple-Choice Subsection of the test. Begin by completing the grammar diagnostic exercise to determine your strengths and weaknesses in the use of grammar. Then, go on to complete all drills and check your answers.
8	Study Part II of the Writing Section Review for the Writing Sample Subsection of the test. Complete the drill section and write the sample essay. The essay should be read and graded by someone with strong writing skills who can offer constructive criticism. Then, compare your essay to the samples provided.
9-10	Take Practice Test 2 and, after scoring your exam, review thoroughly all of the explanations to the questions you answered incorrectly. This will help to strengthen your weaknesses. Restudy the reviews of the areas in which you are still weak.
11-12	Use this time to further review any areas of concern by continuing to study the reviews. You may want to retake the practice tests. Additional answer sheets are provided in the back of this book.

Good luck!

TASP

Texas Academic Skills Program

Passing the TASP

Chapter 1

PASSING THE TASP

About this Book

This book provides you with an accurate and complete representation of the Texas Academic Skills Program (TASP) Test. Inside you will find reviews that are designed to provide you with the information and strategies needed to pass the exam, along with two practice tests based on the format of the most recently administered TASP. You are allowed five hours to complete the actual test. The same amount of time is given to take our practice tests. The practice tests contain every type of question that you can expect to appear on the TASP. Following each test, you will find an answer key with detailed explanations designed to help you more completely understand the test material.

About the Test

Who takes the test and what is it used for?

The Texas Academic Skills Program was designed to ensure that students obtain the reading, math, and writing skills appropriate to their grade level. Nearly 240,000 students take the TASP Test each year. The test is taken by four main groups of people:

1. Students entering Texas public colleges, universities, and technical institutes (including those students transferring from out-of-state schools or from private institutions within the state of Texas)
2. Students seeking admission to public and private teacher-education programs
3. Students seeking admission to upper-level programs that require the TASP for admission
4. Students enrolled in a certificate program of 43–59 semester credit hours or the equivalent

In addition, the TASP must be passed by:

- Those seeking teacher certification through an approved alternative certification program
- Anyone teaching through the use of an emergency teaching permit who wishes to have his/her permit renewed

Exemptions from the TASP are available for those students who meet qualifying standards on the ACT, Scholastic Assessment Test (SAT), or the exit-level Texas Assessment of Academic Skills (TAAS) test. Check your eligibility with your TAAS or college admissions officer.

When taking the TASP, you do not have to take every section in one sitting. You may use the time allotted to complete all of the sections, or just one or two. But, keep in mind that you must eventually pass all three sections, and that you must wait until the next test administration to complete any sections not taken.

No Texas public college or university can deny you admission for failing the TASP; however, for any section(s) not passed, the completion of remedial course work in that subject area will be required. If you fail the TASP, don't panic! You may retake the test as many times as necessary, and you need only retake the section(s) you did not pass.

If you're thinking of taking the computer-administered TASP Test, consult the official TASP bulletin for details.

Who administers the test?

The TASP is developed and administered by the Texas Higher Education Coordinating Board (THECB), the Texas Education Agency (TEA), and National Evaluation Systems, Inc. (NES), and involves the assistance of educators throughout Texas. A test development process was designed and is implemented to ensure that the content and difficulty level of the test are appropriate.

When should the TASP be taken?

You must take the TASP before you complete nine or more college-level semester credit hours. If the school you plan to attend administers a placement test upon entry to the school, you must take the test before the end of the semester in which you will have obtained 15 or more credit hours.

If you would like, you can take the Pre-TASP Test (PTT), which is a shorter version of the TASP Test. The PTT will serve as practice for the official TASP Test and as a diagnostic test to discover your areas of weakness. For more information, contact:

State Board for Educator Certification
Attention: Pre-TASP Test
1001 Trinity St.
Austin, TX 78701
(512) 469-3000
Website: http://www.sbec.state.tx.us

When and where is the test given?

The TASP is administered on Saturday mornings six times during the year at approximately 100 locations. The test centers are located throughout the state and are primarily found at colleges and universities. It is required that you arrive at your test center no later than 8:00 a.m.

To receive information on upcoming administrations of the TASP, consult the *TASP Test Registration Bulletin*, which may be obtained from Texas public colleges, universities, and school districts or by contacting:

National Evaluation Systems, Inc.
P.O. Box 140347
Austin, TX 78714-0347
(512) 926-0469
(512) 927-5101 (for computer-administered testing)

Registration information, as well as test dates and locations, are provided in the bulletin. In addition, the registration bulletin should be consulted for information on making special testing accommodations for students with disabilities.

Is there a registration fee?

To take the TASP, you will be required to pay a registration fee. Financial assistance may be granted in certain situations. To find out if you qualify for assistance, contact your academic advisor or the financial aid officer at a college, university, or technical institute.

How to Use this Book

What do I study first?

Before you do anything else, take one of the practice tests included in this book to help determine which areas of the TASP may cause you the most difficulty. Carefully reviewing the detailed explanations of answers will help you to understand what you are doing wrong. After you have taken a practice test, you can begin studying the reviews which cover your problem areas. These reviews include the information you need to know when taking the exam.

Once you have done this, go back and study all of the remaining reviews and the test-taking tips which appear at the end of this introduction. They will be very useful in helping you brush up on your skills. Make sure to take the second practice test to further test yourself and become familiar with the format and procedures involved with taking the actual TASP.

To get the most out of your studying time, we recommend that you follow the Study Schedule appearing before this introduction. It details how you can best budget your time.

When should I start studying?

It is never too early for you to start studying for the TASP. The earlier you begin, the more time you will have to sharpen your skills. Do not procrastinate! Cramming is *not* an effective way to study, since it does not allow you the time needed to learn and review the test material.

Format of the TASP

Section	Number of Questions	Skills/Areas Covered
Reading	40–50 multiple-choice	Word and Phrase Meanings Main Ideas and Supporting Details Purpose, Point of View, and Intended Meaning Relationship of Ideas Critical Reasoning Use of Study Skills
Mathematics	40–50 multiple-choice	Fundamental Mathematics Algebra Geometry
Writing (two parts):		
Multiple-Choice Subsection	40–50 multiple-choice	Elements of Composition Sentence Structure, Usage, and Mechanics
Writing Sample Subsection	one essay of 300–600 words	Appropriateness Unity and Focus Development Organization Sentence Structure Usage Mechanical Conventions

Total Testing Time: 5 hours

All of the questions on the TASP, with the exception of the Writing Sample Subsection, will be in multiple-choice format. Each question will have four answers, lettered A through D, from which to choose. You should have plenty of time in which to complete the TASP, but be aware of the amount of time you are spending on each section so that you allow yourself time to complete the test. Keep in mind that no one will tell you when to move on to the next test, so work straight through to the end. Although speed is not very important, a steady pace should be maintained when answering the questions. Using the practice tests will help you prepare for this task.

Sections of the TASP

Reading Section

The first part of the TASP is the Reading Section, which consists of between 40 and 50 multiple-choice questions based on approximately 10 reading selections. The passages vary in length from 300 to 750 words, and present diverse topics that simulate the types of reading materials you will be exposed to as a first-year college student. The skills tested in this section are determining word and phrase meanings; understanding main ideas and supporting details; identifying the author's purpose, point-of-view, and intended meaning; analyzing relationships between ideas; using critical reasoning to evaluate passages; and completing reading assignments through the use of study skills such as organizing and summarizing information, understanding and following directions, and interpreting graphs, tables, and charts.

Mathematics Section

In the Mathematics Section, you will encounter between 40 and 50 multiple-choice questions based on fundamental mathematics, algebraic graphing and equations, algebraic operations and quadratics, and geometry and reasoning. Fundamental mathematics questions include using number concepts and computation; solving word problems that deal with integers, fractions, or decimals; and interpreting graphs, tables, and charts. Questions involving algebraic graphing and equations cover graphing numbers and the relationship between numbers; solving equations with one and two variables; and solving one- and two-variable word problems. Questions dealing with algebraic operations and quadratics require understanding operations involving algebraic expressions and solving problems involving quadratic equations. Geometry and reasoning questions comprise solving problems with geometric figures and solving problems using reasoning skills.

Writing Section

The Writing Section consists of two parts: a Multiple-Choice Subsection and a Writing Sample Subsection.

You will be presented with approximately 16 passages in the Multiple-Choice Subsection. Each passage will be followed by a number of multiple-choice questions, each referring to a numbered portion of the passage. Between 40 and 50 questions appear in all. The skills covered will include the elements of composition, sentence structure, usage, and mechanics. Questions focusing on the elements of composition will cover recognizing an essay's purpose and audience; recognizing unity, focus, and development in an essay; and recognizing effective organization. Questions dealing with sentence structure, usage, and mechanics will include recognizing sentences that are effective and recognizing edited standard written English.

In the Writing Sample Subsection, you will be required to write a 300- to 600-word, multiple-paragraph essay on a given topic. The skills you will be expected to demonstrate correctly in your writing are appropriateness, unity and focus, development, organization, sentence structure, usage, and mechanical conventions.

About the Review Sections

Our reviews are written to help you understand the concepts behind TASP Test questions. They will help prepare you for the test by teaching you what you need to know. The three reviews in this book correspond to the three sections of the actual TASP, and are complete with drills to help reinforce the subject matter. By using the reviews in conjunction with taking the practice tests, you will be able to sharpen your skills and pass the TASP Test.

Reading Section Review

This review includes strategies for the Reading Section, a four-step approach to answering each of the different types of reading questions, a vocabulary enhancer, and drills to help reinforce the review material. Studying this information and completing the drills will improve your performance and help you pass the Reading Section of the TASP. The vocabulary enhancer will not only help you to excel on the Reading Section, but it will also increase your skills for the Writing Section.

Mathematics Section Review

Covered in this review are the basics of what you need to know to pass the Mathematics Section. You will find strategies for the Mathematics Section, a review of arithmetic, algebra, geometry, and word problems, and drills to strengthen your abilities in these areas.

Writing Section Review

The Writing Section Review is divided into two parts: Part I covers the Multiple-Choice Subsection, and Part II covers the Writing Sample Subsection.

Part I of this review comprises strategies for the Multiple-Choice Subsection, reviews on recognizing the writer's purpose and intended audience, recognizing effective organization, recognizing effective sentence structure and mechanics, and a review of standard written English. As with the other reviews, this material is reinforced by drills.

In Part II, you will be armed with strategies for the Writing Sample Subsection. Also included will be review material dealing with appropriate, unified, and focused essays, writing your essay, polishing and editing your essay, and drills.

Scoring the TASP Test

How do I score my practice tests?

Use this Scoring Worksheet to track your score improvement from Practice Test 1 to Practice Test 2. The procedure which follows describes how to score the multiple-choice Reading and Mathematics Sections and the two-part Writing Section. Use this scoring information to assess your performance on the practice tests. It will give you an approximate idea of how the official test would be scored.

Scoring Worksheet

	Test 1		Test 2	
	Number Correct (Raw Score)	Percent Correct	Number Correct (Raw Score)	Percent Correct
Reading (approx. 70% is passing)	____	____	____	____
Mathematics (approx. 70% is passing)	____	____	____	____
Writing:				
Writing Sample (8, 7, 6 are passing; 5 must pass multiple-choice section; 4, 3, 2, 1, 0 are failing)				
1st Scorer	____		____	
2nd Scorer	____		____	
Total Score	____		____	
Multiple-Choice (25 out of 35 passes; counted only if you score 5 on writing sample)	____	____	____	____

Scoring the Reading and Mathematics Sections

The first thing you will do to score your practice test is to determine your number of correct answers (your raw score) for the Reading and Mathematics sections, as the two-part Writing Section is scored separately. Although each multiple-choice section on the TASP will contain between 40 and 50 questions, not all of the questions will be scored. The unscored questions are trial items that may appear on future exams. You should also bear in mind that on the actual test, questions will be weighted according to their level of difficulty (i.e., a correct answer to a relatively easy question might earn you one point, whereas a correct response to a relatively difficult one might be worth three points). The following chart identifies each TASP section and its number of scorable questions.

Section of TASP	Number of Questions in Section	Number of Scored Questions in Section
Reading	40–50	36
Mathematics	40–50	36
Writing: Multiple-Choice Subsection	40–50	35

Due to the fact that only 36 questions are scored in each of the Reading and Mathematics Sections, you should randomly discount 9 questions from each section before calculating your raw score. For example, in the Reading Section you may choose to disregard questions 4, 7, 15, 20, 27, 33, 36, 39, and 44. In the Mathematics Section you may choose to disregard questions 3, 9, 13, 17, 21, 24, 31, 38, and 41. This will leave you with the correct number of scored items for each section.

After you have determined the number of questions (out of 36) that you answered correctly on the Reading Section, use the Scoring Worksheet to record this number in the Raw Score column. Your raw score should then be converted into a percentage. To convert your raw score, refer to the Raw Score Conversion Chart. Find your number of correct answers in the column labeled Number Correct, then move to the column to the right labeled Percent Correct and find the number that corresponds to your raw score. This is your total percent correct. For example, if you have 24 correct answers, then you obtained a 67% on the Reading Section. When you have established your percentage correct, record it on the Scoring Worksheet. To pass the Reading Section, you must answer approximately 70% of the questions correctly.

You should now use the same method to determine your raw score and percentage correct for the Mathematics Section. Make sure to record your scores on the Scoring Worksheet. As with the Reading Section, you must respond correctly to approximately 70% of the questions to pass the Mathematics Section.

Raw Score Conversion Chart
Reading and Mathematics Sections
(* rounded to nearest whole number)

Number Correct	Percent Correct*	Number Correct	Percent Correct*
0	0%	19	53%
1	3%	20	56%
2	6%	21	58%
3	8%	22	61%
4	11%	23	64%
5	14%	24	67%
6	17%	25	69%
7	19%	You must score approx. 70% correct	
8	22%	26	72%
9	25%	27	75%
10	28%	28	78%
11	31%	29	81%
12	33%	30	83%
13	36%	31	86%
14	39%	32	89%
15	42%	33	92%
16	44%	34	94%
17	47%	35	97%
18	50%	36	100%

Scoring the Writing Section

The Writing Section of the TASP will be scored using a different method due to the format of this test section. Of the two subsections, the Writing Sample outweighs the Multiple-Choice Subsection when your score is tabulated. In addition, your performance on the Writing Sample will determine how the score on the Multiple-Choice Subsection will be counted.

The Writing Sample Subsection

The Writing Sample will be the first subsection to be scored. Two scorers will grade the Writing Sample, and each will assign it a score between 0 and 4. The two scores will then be added together to form a total score. For example, the first scorer may give an essay a score of 3, while the second scorer may give it a score of 4. These two scores will be added together for a total score of 7 (3 + 4 = 7).

Once your essay has been assigned a total score, it will fall into one of the following three categories:

Writing Sample Scoring Criteria

With a total score of	6, 7, 8	you automatically pass the Writing Section of the TASP, regardless of your score on the Multiple-Choice Subsection.
With a total score of	5	you will pass the Writing Section of the TASP only if you obtain 25 correct answers out of the 35 scored items on the Multiple-Choice Subsection.
With a total score of	4, 3, 2, 1, 0	you will automatically fail the Writing Section of the TASP, regardless of your score on the Multiple-Choice Subsection.

As noted in the preceding chart, your Multiple-Choice Subsection will only be graded if your Writing Sample receives a total grade of 5. If it scores above 5 or below 5, the Multiple-Choice Subsection score will not be counted.

You may want to find two people who are willing to score your essay in order to use the process described above to obtain your score. If you do, ask each one of them to assign your Writing Sample a grade between 0 and 4, with 0 being low and 4 being high. Then add the two scores together to form a total score.

Should you decide to grade your own essay, assign the essay a score between 0 and 4, then double that number. If you do score your own essay, be objective! Most of us like to think that our work is excellent, but we must learn to see where there is room for improvement. On the other hand, some people have a tendency to automatically decide that their work is poor, when it may not be at all. Try to see your writing for what it is, whether it is excellent, terrible, or average.

As your scores are determined by each scorer, record them on the Scoring Worksheet. Add them together and mark down your total score. Once you have a total score, determine where your essay falls in this table.

If you scored:	you:
6, 7, or 8	have passed the Writing Section.
5	must determine your number of correct answers in the Multiple-Choice Subsection. If you obtained at least 25 correct answers, you have passed the Writing Section.
4, 3, 2, 1, or 0	have failed the Writing Section.

The Multiple-Choice Subsection

If you scored a 5 on the Writing Sample, you must tabulate your score on the Multiple-Choice Subsection in order to determine whether or not you passed the Writing Section. To do this you must first randomly discount 10 questions, since only 35 of the 45 questions are counted as scored items. You may want to disregard questions 2, 7, 13, 18, 24, 27, 33, 36, 40, and 44. At this point, you should score your remaining questions. If you obtain 25 correct out of the 35 scored questions, then you pass the Writing Section.

Although your performance on the Writing Sample may not necessitate the scoring of your Multiple-Choice Subsection, you should score it anyway. If you are not up to par on the day of the test, passing this section may hinge upon your score on the Multiple-Choice Subsection.

What scores do I need to pass the actual TASP?

The actual TASP is scored in very much the same way as you scored your practice tests. First, your Reading and Mathematics Section raw scores are tabulated. They are then converted into scaled scores ranging from 100 to 300. This is to allow for changes in the level of difficulty from one test administration to the next. A scaled score of at least 230 must be obtained on the Reading Section and on the Mathematics Section to pass these sections. A scaled score of 230 is nearly equivalent to a 70% on one of the practice tests. Scores for the Writing Section are determined through the process used to score your practice tests.

When will I receive my score report and what will it look like?

Your score report for the TASP will arrive between three and five weeks after the test. The report will list your score for each section in addition to how well you performed on each of the major skill areas.

As previously mentioned, scores for each multiple-choice section will be expressed on a scaled score range from a low of 100 to a high of 300. As mentioned, you will need a score of at least 230 to pass each section. Your writing sample score will fall in a range from a low of 0 to a high of 8. Scoring a 6, 7, or 8 means that you pass the Writing Section regardless of your score on the multiple-choice questions. If you score a 5 on the Writing Sample, you must get at least 25 questions correct out of the 35 scored items in order to pass the Writing Section. Scoring lower than 5 on the Writing Sample will cause you to fail the Writing Section regardless of your score on the multiple-choice questions. Should you fail the writing sample, areas in which you need improvement will be explained under your score.

Once your scores are available, they will be forwarded to the institutions you requested. As per your indication, they will be sent by either Standard Delivery, Expedited Delivery, or Emergency Delivery. Consult your registration bulletin for further information regarding these delivery schedules.

Studying for the TASP

It is very important for you to choose the time and place for studying that works best for you. Some students may set aside a certain number of hours every morning to study, while others may choose to study at night before going to sleep. Other students may study during the day, while waiting on a line, or even while eating lunch. Only you can determine when and where your study time will be most effective. But, be consistent and use your time wisely. Work out a study routine and stick to it!

When you take the practice tests, try to make your testing conditions as much like the actual test as possible. Turn your television and radio off, and sit down at a quiet table free from distraction. Make sure to time yourself. Start off by setting a timer for four hours, then if you need that additional hour, reset the timer for one hour.

As you complete each practice test, score your test and thoroughly review the explanations to the questions you answered incorrectly; however, do not review too much at any one time. Concentrate on one problem area at a time by reviewing the question and explanation, and by studying our review until you are confident that you completely understand the material.

Since you will be allowed to write in your test booklet during the actual TASP Test, you may want to write in the margins and spaces of this book when practicing; however, do not make miscellaneous notes on your answer sheet. Mark your answers clearly and make sure the answer you have chosen corresponds to the question you are answering.

Keep track of your scores and mark them on the Scoring Worksheet! By doing so, you will be able to gauge your progress and discover general weaknesses in particular sections. You should carefully study the reviews that cover your areas of difficulty, as this will build your skills in those areas.

TASP Test-Taking Tips

Although you may be unfamiliar with standardized tests such as the TASP, there are many ways to acquaint yourself with this type of examination and help alleviate your test-taking anxieties. Listed below are ways to help you become accustomed to the TASP, some of which may be applied to other standardized tests as well.

Become comfortable with the format of the TASP. When you are practicing to take the TASP, simulate the conditions under which you will be taking the actual test. You should practice under the same time constraints as well. Stay calm and pace yourself. After simulating the test only a couple of times, you will boost your chances of doing well, and you will be able to sit down for the actual TASP much more confidently.

Know the directions and format for each section of the test. Familiarizing yourself with the directions and format of the different test sections will not only save you time, but will also ensure that you are familiar enough with the TASP to avoid nervousness (and the mistakes caused by being nervous).

Work on the easier questions first. If you find yourself working too long on one question, make a mark next to it in your test booklet and continue. After you have answered all of the questions that you can, go back to the ones you have skipped.

If you are unsure of an answer, guess. Remember, only correct answers will be counted in your score, so you will not be penalized for guessing. If you do guess, guess wisely. Use the process of elimination by going through each answer to a question and eliminating as many of the answer choices as possible. By eliminating two answer choices, you have given yourself a fifty-fifty chance of getting the item correct since there will only be two choices left from which to make your guess.

Be sure that you are marking your answer in the circle that corresponds to the number of the question in the test booklet. Since the multiple-choice sections are graded by machine, marking one wrong answer will throw off your score.

The Day of the Test

Before the Test

On the day of the test, you should wake up early (hopefully after a decent night's rest) and have a good breakfast. Make sure to dress comfortably, so that you are not distracted by being too hot or too cold while taking the test. Also plan to arrive at the test center early. This will allow you to collect your thoughts and relax before the test, and will also spare you the anguish that comes with being late. As an added incentive to make sure you arrive early, keep in mind that NO ONE WILL BE ALLOWED INTO THE TEST SESSION AFTER 8:00 A.M. If you arrive late, you will not receive credit or a refund.

Before you leave for the test center, make sure that you have your admission ticket and two other forms of identification, one of which **must** contain a recent photograph (i.e., driver's license, student identification card, passport, library card, Department of Public Safety identification card, current alien registration card, etc.). You will not be admitted to the test center if you do not have proper identification, and you will not be refunded or credited in any way.

You must also bring several sharpened No. 2 pencils with erasers, as none will be provided at the test center.

If you would like, you may wear a watch to the test center; however, watches with alarms, calculator functions, flashing lights, beeping sounds, etc., will not be allowed. You also cannot bring into your testing room a calculator, slide rule, notebook, or any written material such as a dictionary or textbook. Cellular phones, electronic pagers, and photographic or recording devices are also not allowed. In addition, you will not be permitted to have briefcases or packages in your testing room. Drinking, eating, and smoking are prohibited.

During the Test

When you arrive at the test center, try to sit in a seat where you feel you will be comfortable. The TASP is administered in one sitting and no breaks are given during the exam. If you need to use the rest room, you may leave the testing room, but you will not be allowed to make up any lost time. Procedures will be followed to maintain test security.

Once you enter the test center, follow all of the rules and instructions given by the test supervisor. If you do not, you risk being dismissed from the test and having your TASP scores canceled.

When all of the test materials have been passed out, the test instructor will give you directions for filling out your answer sheet. You must fill out this sheet carefully since this information will be printed on your score report. Fill out your name exactly as it appears on your identification documents and admission ticket, unless otherwise instructed.

Remember that you can write in your test booklet, as no scratch paper will be provided. Mark your answers in the appropriate spaces on the answer sheet. Each numbered row of circles will contain four circles corresponding to each answer choice for that question. Fill in darkly, completely, and in a neat manner the circle which corresponds to your answer. You can change your answer, but remember to completely erase your old answer. Only one answer should be marked. This is very important, as your answer sheet will be machine scored and stray lines or unnecessary marks may cause the machine to score your answers incorrectly.

Keep in mind that you will only be told when to begin the TASP and when the test session has ended. You will not be instructed as to when you should begin or end each individual test section (i.e., the Reading Section, the Mathematics Section, the Writing Section). Continue working through the test until all of the sections and subsections that you wish to take have been completed. After four hours have elapsed, you may have an extra hour if needed. When you have finished working, you may want to go back and check your answers.

After the Test

When you have completed the TASP sections you wish to take, you may hand in your test materials and leave. If you need the entire five hours to complete the test, your test materials will be collected at approximately 1:30 p.m., at which time you will be dismissed. Then, go home and relax! Your score report will arrive in two to three weeks.

TASP

Texas Academic Skills Program

Reading Section Review

Chapter 2

READING SECTION REVIEW

I. Strategies for the Reading Section

II. A Four-Step Approach

III. Vocabulary Enhancer

This review was developed to prepare you for the Reading Section of the TASP. You will be guided through a step-by-step approach to attacking reading passages and questions. Also included are tips to help you quickly and accurately answer the questions which will appear in this section. By studying our review, you will greatly increase your chances of achieving a passing score on the Reading Section of the TASP.

Remember, the more you know about the skills tested, the better you will perform on the test. In this section, the skills you will be tested on are

- determining what a word or phrase means;
- determining main ideas;
- recognizing supporting details;
- determining purpose;
- determining point of view;
- organizing ideas in the passage; and
- evaluating the validity of the author's argument.

To help you master these skills, we present examples of the types of questions you will encounter and explanations of how to answer them. A drill section is also provided for further practice. Even if you are sure you will perform well on this section, make sure to complete the drills, as they will help sharpen your skills.

The Passages

The eight reading passages in the Reading Section are specially designed to be on the level of the types of material that you will encounter in college textbooks. They will present you with very diverse subjects. Although you will not be expected to have prior knowledge of the information presented in the passages, you will be expected to know the fundamental reading comprehension techniques presented in this chapter. Only your ability to read and comprehend material will be tested.

The Questions

Each passage will be followed by a number of questions, with the total number appearing in the section being between 40 and 50 questions. The questions will ask you to make determinations based on what you have read. You will encounter 10 main types of questions in this test. These questions will ask you to

1. determine which of the given answer choices best expresses the main idea of the passage;
2. determine the author's purpose in writing the passage;
3. determine which fact best supports the writer's main idea;
4. know the difference between fact and opinion in a statement;
5. organize the information in the passage;
6. determine which of the answer choices best summarizes the information presented in the passage;
7. recall information from the passage;
8. analyze cause and effect relationships based on information in the passage;
9. determine the definition of a word as it is used in the passage; and
10. answer a question based on information presented in graphic form.

I. Strategies for the Reading Section

You should follow this plan of attack when answering Reading Section questions.

Before the test, this is your plan of attack:

➤ Step 1 Study our review to build your reading skills.

➤ Step 2 Make sure to study and learn the directions to save yourself time during the actual test. You should simply skim them when beginning the section. The directions will read similar to the following.

DIRECTIONS: You will encounter eight passages in this section of the test, each followed by a number of questions. Only **ONE** answer to each question is the **best** answer, although more than one answer may appear to be correct. There are between 40 and 50 multiple-choice questions in this section. Choose your answers carefully and mark them on your answer sheet. Make sure that the space you are marking corresponds to the answer you have chosen.

When reading the passage, this is your plan of attack:

➤ Step 1 Read quickly while keeping in mind that questions will follow.

➤ Step 2 Uncover the main idea or theme of the passage. Many times it is contained within the first few lines of the passage.

➤ Step 3 Uncover the main idea of each paragraph. Usually it is contained in either the first or last sentence of the paragraph.

➤ Step 4 Skim over the detailed points of the passage while circling key words or phrases. These are words or phrases such as *but, on the other hand, although, however, yet,* and *except.*

When answering the questions, this is your plan of attack:

➤ Step 1 Attack each question one at a time. Read it carefully.

➤ Step 2 If the question is asking for a general answer, such as the main idea or the purpose of the passage, answer it immediately.

➤ Step 3 If the question is asking for an answer that can only be found in a specific place in the passage, save it for last since this type of question requires you to go back to the passage and therefore takes more of your time.

➤ Step 4 For the detail-oriented questions, try to eliminate or narrow down your choices before looking for the answer in the passage.

➤ Step 5 Go back into the passage, utilizing the key words you circled, to find the answer.

➤ Step 6 Any time you cannot find the answer, use the process of elimination to the greatest extent and then guess.

Additional Tips

- Look over all the passages first and then attack the passages that seem easiest and most interesting.
- Identify and underline what sentences are the main ideas of each paragraph.
- When a question asks you to draw inferences, your answer should reflect what is implied in the passage, rather than what is directly stated.
- Use the context of the sentence to find the meaning of an unfamiliar word.
- Identify what sentences are example sentences and label them with an "E." Determine whether or not the writer is using facts or opinions.
- Circle key transitions and identify dominant patterns of organization.
- Make your final response and move on. Don't dawdle or get frustrated by the really troubling passages. If you haven't gotten answers after two attempts, answer as best you can and move on.
- If you have time at the end, go back to the passages that were difficult and review them again.

II. A Four-Step Approach

When you take the Reading Section of the TASP, you will have two tasks:

1. to read the passage and
2. to answer the questions.

Of the two, carefully reading the passage is the most important; answering the questions is based on an understanding of the passage. Here is a four-step approach to reading:

Step 1: preview,

Step 2: read actively,

Step 3: review the passage, and

Step 4: answer the questions.

You should study the following exercises and use these four steps when you complete the Reading Section of the TASP.

STEP 1: Preview

A preview of the reading passage will give you a purpose and a reason for reading; previewing is a good strategy to use in test-taking. Before beginning to read the passage (usually a four-minute activity if you preview and review), you should take about 30 seconds to look over the passage and questions. An effective way to preview the passage is to read quickly the first sentence of each paragraph, the concluding sentence of the passage, and the questions — not all the answers — following the passage. A passage is given below. Practice previewing the passage by reading the first sentence of each paragraph and the last line of the passage.

PASSAGE

1 That the area of obscenity and pornography is a difficult one for the Supreme Court is well documented. The Court's numerous attempts to define obscenity have proven unworkable and left the decision to the subjective preferences of the justices. Perhaps Justice Stewart put it best when, after refusing to define obscenity, he declared, "But I know it when I see it." Does the Court literally have to see it to know it? Specifically, what role does the fact-pattern, including the materials' medium, play in the Court's decision?

2 Several recent studies employ fact-pattern analysis in modeling the Court's decision making. These studies examine the fact-pattern or case characteristics, often with ideological and attitudinal factors, as a determinant of the decision reached by the Court. In broad terms, these studies owe their theoretical underpinnings to attitude theory. As the name suggests, attitude theory views the Court's attitudes as an explanation of its decisions.

3 These attitudes, however, do not operate in a vacuum. As Spaeth explains, "the activation of an attitude involves both an object and the situation in

which that object is encountered." The objects to which the court directs its attitudes are litigants. The situation — the subject matter of the case — can be defined in broad or narrow terms. One may define the situation as an entire area of the law (e.g., civil liberties issues). On an even broader scale the situation may be defined as the decision to grant certiorari or whether to defect from a minimum-winning coalition.

4 Defining the situation with such broad strokes, however, does not allow one to control for case content. In many specific issue areas, the cases present strikingly similar patterns. In examining the Court's search and seizure decisions, Segal found a relatively small number of situational and case characteristic variables explain a high proportion of the Court's decisions.

5 Despite Segal's success, efforts to verify the applicability of fact-pattern analysis in other issue areas and using broad-based factors have been slow in coming. Renewed interest in obscenity and pornography by federal and state governments, the academic community, and numerous antipornography interest groups indicates the Court's decisions in this area deserve closer examination.

6 The Court's obscenity and pornography decisions also present an opportunity to study the Court's behavior in an area where the Court has granted significant decision-making authority to the states. In *Miller vs. California* (1973) the Court announced the importance of local community standards in obscenity determinations. The Court's subsequent behavior may suggest how the Court will react in other areas where it has chosen to defer to the states (e.g., abortion).

QUESTIONS

1. The main idea of the passage is best stated in which of the following?

   (A) The Supreme Court has difficulty convicting those who violate obscenity laws.

   (B) The current definitions for obscenity and pornography provided by the Supreme Court are unworkable.

   (C) Fact-pattern analysis is insufficient for determining the attitude of the Court toward the issues of obscenity and pornography.

   (D) Despite the difficulties presented by fact-pattern analysis, Justice Segal found the solution in the patterns of search and seizure decisions.

2. The main purpose of the writer in this passage is to

   (A) convince the reader that the Supreme Court is making decisions about obscenity based only on their subjective views.

   (B) explain to the reader how fact-pattern analysis works with respect to cases of obscenity and pornography.

(C) define obscenity and pornography for the layperson.

(D) demonstrate the role fact-pattern analysis plays in determining the Supreme Court's attitude about cases in obscenity and pornography.

3. Of the following, which fact best supports the writer's contention that the Court's decisions in the areas of obscenity and pornography deserve closer scrutiny?

(A) The fact that a Supreme Court Justice said, "I know it when I see it."

(B) Recent studies that employ fact-pattern analysis in modeling the Court's decision-making process.

(C) The fact that attitudes do not operate in a vacuum.

(D) The fact that federal and state governments, interest groups, and the academic community show renewed interest in the obscenity and pornography decisions by the Supreme Court.

4. Among the following statements, which states an opinion expressed by the writer rather than a fact?

(A) That the area of obscenity and pornography is a difficult one for the Supreme Court is well documented.

(B) The objects to which a court directs its attitudes are the litigants.

(C) In many specific issue areas, the cases present strikingly similar patterns.

(D) The Court's subsequent behavior may suggest how the Court will react in other legal areas.

5. The list of topics below that best reflects the organization of the topics of the passage is

(A) I. The difficulties of the Supreme Court

II. Several recent studies

III. Spaeth's definition of "attitude"

IV. The similar patterns of cases

V. Other issue areas

VI. The case of *Miller vs. California*

(B) I The Supreme Court, obscenity, and fact-pattern analysis

II. Fact-pattern analyses and attitude theory

III. The definition of "attitude" for the Court

IV. The definition of "situation"

V. The breakdown in fact-pattern analysis

VI. Studying Court behavior

(C) I. Justice Stewart's view of pornography

II. Theoretical underpinnings

III. A minimum-winning coalition

IV. Search and seizure decisions

V. Renewed interest in obscenity and pornography

VI. The importance of local community standards

(D) I. The Court's numerous attempts to define obscenity

II. Case characteristics

III. The subject matter of cases

IV. The Court's proportion of decisions

V. Broad-based factors

VI. Obscenity determination

6. Which paragraph below is the best summary of the passage?

(A) The Supreme Court's decision-making process with respect to obscenity and pornography has become too subjective. Fact-pattern analyses, used to determine the overall attitude of the Court, reveal only broad-based attitudes on the part of the Court toward the situations of obscenity cases. But these patterns cannot fully account for the Court's attitudes toward case content. Research is not conclusive that fact-pattern analyses work when applied to legal areas. Renewed public and local interest suggests continued study and close examination of how the Court makes decisions. Delegating authority to the states may reflect patterns for Court decisions in other socially sensitive areas.

(B) Though subjective, the Supreme Court decisions are well documented. Fact-pattern analyses reveal the attitude of the Supreme Court toward its decisions in cases. Spaeth explains that an attitude involves both an object and a situation. For the Court, the situation may be defined as the decision to grant certiorari. Cases present strikingly similar patterns, and a small number of variables explain a high proportion of the Court's decisions. Segal has made an effort to verify the applicability of fact-pattern analysis with some success. The Court's decisions on obscenity and pornography suggest weak Court behavior, such as in *Miller vs. California.*

(C) To determine what obscenity and pornography mean to the Supreme Court, we must use fact-pattern analysis. Fact-pattern analysis reveals the ideas that the Court uses to operate in a vacuum. The litigants and the subject matter of cases is defined in broad terms (such as an entire area of law) to reveal the Court's decision-making process. Search and seizure cases reveal strikingly similar patterns, leaving the Court open to grant certiorari effectively. Renewed public interest in the Court's decisions proves how the Court will react in the future.

(D) Supreme Court decisions about pornography and obscenity are under examination and are out of control. The Court has to see the case to know it. Fact-pattern analyses reveal that the Court can only define cases in narrow terms, thus revealing individual egotism on the part of the Justices. As a result of strikingly similar patterns in search and seizure cases, the Court should be studied further for its weakness in delegating authority to state courts, as in the case of *Miller vs. California.*

7. Based on the passage, the rationale for fact-pattern analyses arises out of what theoretical groundwork?

(A) Subjectivity theory

(B) The study of cultural norms

(C) Attitude theory

(D) Cybernetics

8. Based on data in the passage, what would most likely be the major cause for the difficulty in pinning down the Supreme Court's attitude toward cases of obscenity and pornography?

(A) The personal opinions of the Court Justices

(B) The broad nature of the situations of the cases

(C) The ineffective logistics of certiorari

(D) The inability of the Court to resolve the variables presented by individual case content

9. In the context of the passage, *subjective* might be most nearly defined as

(A) personal.

(B) wrong.

(C) focussed.

(D) objective.

[Answers: 1. (C) 2. (D) 3. (D) 4. (D) 5. (B) 6. (C) 7. (C) 8. (D) 9. (A)]

By previewing the passage, you should have read the following:

- That the area of obscenity and pornography is a difficult one for the Supreme Court is well documented.
- Several recent studies employ fact-pattern analysis in modeling the Court's decision making.
- These attitudes, however, do not operate in a vacuum.
- Defining the situation with such broad strokes, however, does not allow one to control for case content.
- Despite Segal's success, efforts to verify the applicability of fact-pattern analysis in other issue areas and using broad-based factors have been slow in forthcoming.
- The Court's obscenity and pornography decisions also present an opportunity to study the Court's behavior in an area where the Court has granted significant decision-making authority to the states.
- The Court's subsequent behavior may suggest how the Court will react in other areas where it has chosen to defer to the states (e.g., abortion).

These few sentences tell you much about the entire passage.

As you begin to examine the passage, you should first determine the main idea of the passage and underline it, so that you can easily refer back to it if a question requires you to do so (see question 1). The main idea should be found in the first paragraph of the passage, and may even be the first sentence. From what you have read thus far, you now know that the main idea of this passage is that: the Supreme Court has difficulty in making obscenity and pornography decisions.

In addition, you also know that recent studies have used fact-pattern analysis in modeling the Court's decision. You have learned also that attitudes do not operate independently and that case content is important. The feasibility of using fact-pattern analysis in other areas and broad-based factors have not been quickly verified. To study the behavior of the Court in an area in which they have granted significant decision-making authority to the states, one has only to consider the obscenity and pornography decisions. In summary, the author suggests that the Court's subsequent behavior may suggest how the Court will react in those other areas in which decision-making authority has previously been granted to the states. As you can see, having this information will make the reading of the passage much easier.

You should have also looked at the stem of the question in your preview. You do not necessarily need to spend time reading the answers to each question in your preview. The stem alone can help to guide you as you read.

The stems in this case are:

1. The main idea of the passage is best stated in which of the following?
2. The main purpose of the writer in this passage is to
3. Of the following, which fact best supports the writer's contention that the Court's decisions in the areas of obscenity and pornography deserve closer scrutiny?
4. Among the following statements, which states an opinion expressed by the writer rather than a fact?
5. The list of topics below that best reflects the organization of the topics of the passage is
6. Which paragraph below is the best summary of the passage?
7. Based on the passage, the rationale for fact-pattern analyses arises out of what theoretical groundwork?
8. Based on data in the passage, what would most likely be the major cause for the difficulty in pinning down the Supreme Court's attitude toward cases of obscenity and pornography?
9. In the context of the passage, *subjective* might be most nearly defined as

STEP 2: Read Actively

After your preview, you are now ready to read actively. This means that as you read, you will be engaged in such things as underlining important words, topic sentences, main ideas, and words denoting the tone of the passage. If you think underlining can help you save time and help you remember the main ideas, feel free to use your pencil.

Read carefully the first sentence of each paragraph since this often contains the topic of the paragraph. You may wish to underline each topic sentence.

During this stage, you should also determine the writer's purpose in writing the passage (see question 2), as this will help you focus on the main points and the writer's key points in the organization of a passage. You can determine the author's purpose by asking yourself, "Does *the relationship* between the writer's main idea plus evidence the writer uses answer one of four questions":

- What is the writer's overall primary goal or objective?
- Is the writer trying primarily to persuade you by proving or using facts to make a case for an idea? (P)
- Is the writer trying only primarily to inform and enlighten you about an idea, object, or event? (I)
- Is the writer attempting primarily to amuse you? Keep you fascinated? Laughing? (A)

Read these examples and see if you can decide what the primary purpose of the following statements might be.

(A) Jogging too late in life can cause more health problems than it solves. I will allow that the benefits of jogging are many: lowered blood pressure, increased vitality, better cardiovascular health, and better muscle tone. However, an older person may have a history of injury or chronic ailments that makes jogging counterproductive. For example, the elderly jogger may have hardening of the arteries, emphysema, or undiscovered aneurysms just waiting to burst and cause stroke or death. Chronic arthritis in the joints will only be aggravated by persistent irritation and use. Moreover, for those of us with injuries sustained in our youth — such as torn Achilles' tendons or torn knee cartilage — jogging might just make a painful life more painful, cancelling out the benefits the exercise is intended to produce.

(B) Jogging is a sporting activity that exercises all the main muscle groups of the body. That the arms, legs, buttock, and torso voluntary muscles are engaged goes without question. Running down a path makes you move your upper body as well as your lower body muscles. People do not often take into account, however, how the involuntary muscle system is also put through its paces. The heart, diaphragm, even the eye and face muscles, take part as we hurl our bodies through space at speeds up to five miles per hour over distances as long as twenty-six miles.

(C) It seems to me that jogging styles are as identifying as fingerprints! People seem to be as individual in the way they run as they are in personality. Here comes the Duck, waddling down the track, little wings going twice as fast as the feet in an effort to stay upright. At about the quarter mile mark, I see the Penguin, quite natty in the latest jogging suit, body stiff as a board from neck to ankles and the ankles flexing a mile a minute to cover the yards. And down there at the half-mile post — there comes the Giraffe — a tall fellow in a spotted electric yellow outfit, whose long strides cover about a dozen yards each, and whose neck waves around under some old army camouflage hat that probably served its time in a surplus store in the Bronx rather than in Desert Storm. Once you see the animals in the jogger woods once, you can identify them from miles away just by seeing their gait. And by the way, be careful whose hoof you're stepping on, it may be mine!

In (A) the writer makes a statement that a number of people would debate and which isn't clearly demonstrated in science or common knowledge. In fact, common wisdom usually maintains the opposite thesis. Many would say that jogging improves the health of the aging — even slows down the aging process. As soon as you see a writer point to or identify *an issue open to debate* and standing in need of proof, s/he is setting out to persuade you of one side or the other. You'll notice, too, that the writer in this case takes a stand, here. It's almost as if s/he is saying, "I have concluded that . . ." But a thesis or arguable idea is only a *hypothesis* until evidence is summoned by the writer to prove it. Effective arguments are based on serious, factual, or demonstrable evidence, not opinion.

In (B) the writer is just stating a fact. This is not a matter for debate. From here, the writer's evidence is to *explain* and *describe* what is meant by the fact. S/he proceeds to *analyze* (break down into its elements) the way the different muscle groups come into play or do work when jogging, thus explaining the fact stated as a main point in the opening sentence. That jogging exercises all the muscle groups is not in question or a matter of debate. Besides taking the form of explaining how something works, what parts it is made of (for example, the basic parts of a bicycle are...), writers may show how the idea, object, or event functions. A writer may use this information to prove something. But if s/he doesn't argue to prove a debatable point, then the purpose must be either to inform (as here) or to entertain.

In (C) the writer is taking a stand, but s/he is not attempting to prove anything, merely pointing to a lighthearted observation. Moreover, all of the examples s/he uses to support the statement are either fanciful, funny, odd, or peculiar to the writer's particular vision. Joggers aren't really animals, after all.

Make sure to examine all of the facts that the author uses to support his/her main idea. This will allow you to decide whether or not the writer has made a case, and what sort of purpose s/he supports. Look for supporting details — facts, examples, illustrations, the testimony or research of experts, that are about the topic in question and *show* what the writer *says* is so. In fact, paragraphs and theses consist of *show* and *tell*. The writer *tells* you something is so or not so and then *shows* you facts, illustrations, expert testimony, or experience to back up what s/he says is or is not so. As you determine where the author's supporting details are, you may want to label them with an "S" so that you can refer back to them easily when answering questions (see question 3).

It is also important for you to be able to recognize the difference between the statements of fact presented and statements of the author's opinion. You will be tested on this skill in this section of the test (see question 4). Let's look at the following examples. In each case ask yourself if you are reading a fact or an opinion.

1. Some roses are red.
2. Roses are the most beautiful flower on earth.
3. After humans smell roses, they fall in love.
4. Roses are the worst plants to grow in your backyard.

Number 1 is a fact. All you have to do is go look at the evidence. Go to a florist. You will see that number 1 is true. A fact is anything which can be demonstrated to be true in reality or which has been demonstrated to be true in reality and is documented by others. For example, the moon is in orbit about 250,000 miles from the earth.

Number 2 is an opinion. The writer claims this as truth, but since it is an abstract quality (beauty), it remains to be seen. Others will hold different opinions. This is a matter of taste, not fact.

Number 3 is an opinion. There is probably some time-related coincidence between these two, but there is no verifiable or repeatable and observable evidence that this is always true — at least not the way it is true that if you throw a ball into the air, it will always come back down to earth if left on its own without interference. Opinions have a way of sounding absolute, are held by the writer with confidence, but are not backed up by factual evidence.

Number 4, though perhaps sometimes true, is a matter of opinion. Many variables contribute to the health of a plant in a garden: soil, temperature range, amount of moisture, number, and kinds of bugs. This is a debatable point that the writer would have to prove.

As you read, you should note the structure of the passage. There are several common structures for the passages. Some of these structures are described below.

Main Types of Paragraph Structures

1. The structure is a main idea plus supporting arguments.
2. The structure is a main idea plus examples.
3. The structure includes comparisons or contrasts.
4. There is a pro and a con structure.
5. The structure is chronological.
6. The structure has several different aspects of one idea. For example, a passage on education in the United States in the 1600s and 1700s might first define education, then describe colonial education, then give information about separation of church and state, and then outline the tax opposition and support arguments. Being able to recognize these structures will help you recognize how the author has organized the passage.

Examining the structure of the passage will help you answer questions that ask you to organize (see question 5) the information in the passage, or to summarize (see question 6) the information presented in that passage.

For example, if you see a writer using a transitional pattern that reflects a sequence moving forward in time, such as "In 1982 . . . Then, in the next five years . . . A decade later, in 1997, the xxxx will . . ." chances are the writer is telling a story, history, or the like. Writers often use transitions of classification to analyze an idea, object, or event. They may say something like, "The first part . . . Secondly . . . Thirdly . . . Finally." You may then ask yourself what is this analysis for? To explain or to persuade me of something? These transitional patterns may also help reveal the relationship of one part of a passage to another. For example, a writer may be writing "on the one hand, . . . on the other hand . . ." This should alert you to the fact that the writer is comparing two things or contrasting them. What for? Is one better than the other? Worse?

By understanding the *relationship* among the main point, transitions, and supporting information, you may more readily determine the pattern of organization as well as the writer's purpose in a given piece of writing.

As with the paragraph examples above showing the difference among possible purposes, you must look at the relationship between the facts or information presented (that's the show part) and what the writer is trying to point out to you (that's the tell part) with that data. For example, in the data given in number 6 above, the discussion presented about education in the 1600s might be used

- to prove that it was a failure (a form of argument),
- that it consisted of these elements (an analysis of the status of education during that time), or
- that education during that time was silly.

To understand the author's purpose, the main point and the evidence that supports it must be considered together to be understood. In number 6, no statement appears which controls these disparate areas of information. To be meaningful, a controlling main point is needed. You need to know that that main point is missing. You need to be able to distinguish between the writer showing data and the writer telling or making a point.

In the two paragraphs below, consider the different relationship between the same data above and the controlling statement, and how that controlling statement changes the discussion from explanation to argument:

(A) Colonial education was different than today's and consisted of several elements. Education in those days meant primarily studying the three "r's" (reading, 'riting, and 'rithmetic) and the Bible. The church and state were more closely aligned with one another — education was, after all, for the purpose of serving God better, not to make more money.

(B) Colonial "education" was really just a way to create a captive audience for the Church. Education in those days meant studying the three "r's" in order to learn God's word — the Bible — not commerce. The Church and state were closely aligned with one another, and what was good for the Church was good for the state — or else you were excommunicated, which kept you out of Heaven for sure.

The same information areas are brought up in both cases, but in (A) the writer treats it analytically (. . ."consisted of several elements" . . .), not taking any real debatable stand on the issue. What is, is. However, the controlling statement in (B) puts forth a volatile hypothesis, and then uses the same information to support that hypothesis.

STEP 3: Review the Passage

After you finish reading actively, take 10 or 20 seconds to look over the main idea and the topic sentences that you have underlined, and the key words and phrases you have marked. Now you are ready to enter Step 4 and answer the questions.

STEP 4: Answer the Questions

In Step 2, Read Actively, you gathered enough information from the passage to answer questions dealing with main idea, purpose, support, fact vs. opinion, organization, and summarization. Let's look again at these questions.

Main Idea Questions

Looking back at the questions which follow the passage, you see that question 1 is a "main idea" question:

1. The main idea of the passage is best stated in which of the following?

   (A) The Supreme Court has difficulty convicting those who violate obscenity laws.

   (B) The current definitions for obscenity and pornography provided by the Supreme Court are unworkable.

   (C) Fact-pattern analysis is insufficient for determining the attitude of the Court toward the issues of obscenity and pornography.

   (D) Despite the difficulties presented by fact-pattern analysis, Justice Segal found the solution in the patterns of search and seizure decisions.

In answering the question, you see that answer choice (C) is correct. The writer uses the second, third, fourth, and fifth paragraphs to show how fact-pattern analysis is an ineffective determinant of Court attitude toward obscenity and pornography.

Answer (A) is incorrect. Nothing is ever said directly about "convicting" persons accused of obscenity, only that the Court has difficulty defining it.

Choice (B) is also incorrect. Though it is stated as a fact by the writer, it is only used as an effect that leads the writer to examine how fact-pattern analysis does or does not work to reveal the "cause" or attitude of the Court toward obscenity and pornography.

Finally, answer choice (D) is incorrect. The statement is contrary to what Segal found when he examined search and seizure cases.

Purpose Questions

In examining question 2, you see that you must determine the author's purpose in writing the passage:

2. The main purpose of the writer in this passage is to

   (A) convince the reader that the Supreme Court is making decisions about obscenity based on their subjective views only.

   (B) explain to the reader how fact-pattern analysis works with respect to cases of obscenity and pornography.

   (C) define obscenity and pornography for the layperson.

   (D) demonstrate the role fact-pattern analysis plays in determining the Supreme Court's attitude about cases in obscenity and pornography.

Looking at the answer choices, you see that choice (D) is correct. Though the writer never states it directly, s/he summons data consistently to show that fact-pattern analysis only gives us part of the picture, or "broad strokes" about the Court's attitude, but cannot account for the attitude toward individual cases.

Choice (A) is incorrect. The writer doesn't try to convince us of this fact, but merely states it as an opinion resulting from the evidence derived from the "well-documented" background to the problem.

(B) is also incorrect. The writer does more than just explain the role of fact-pattern analysis, but rather shows how it cannot fully apply.

The passage is about the Court's difficulty in defining these terms, not the man or woman in the street. Nowhere do definitions for these terms appear. Therefore, choice (C) is incorrect.

Support Questions

Question 3 requires you to analyze the author's supporting details:

3. Of the following, which fact best supports the writer's contention that the Court's decisions in the areas of obscenity and pornography deserve closer scrutiny?

   (A) The fact that a Supreme Court Justice said, "I know it when I see it."

   (B) Recent studies that employ fact-pattern analysis in modeling the Court's decision-making process.

   (C) The fact that attitudes do not operate in a vacuum.

   (D) The fact that federal and state governments, interest groups, and the academic community show renewed interest in the obscenity and pornography decisions by the Supreme Court.

To answer this question, let's look at the answer choices. Choice (D) must be correct. In the fifth paragraph, the writer states that the "renewed interest" — a real and observable fact — from these groups "indicates the Court's decisions . . . deserve closer examination," another way of saying scrutiny.

Answer (A) is incorrect. The writer uses this remark to show how the Court cannot effectively define obscenity and pornography, relying on "subjective preferences" to resolve issues.

In addition, choice (B) is incorrect because the writer points to the data in (D), not fact-pattern analyses, to prove this.

(C), too, is incorrect. Although it is true, the writer makes this point to show how fact-pattern analysis doesn't help clear up the real-world "situation" in which the Court must make its decisions.

Fact vs. Opinion Questions

By examining question 4, you can see that you are required to know the difference between fact and opinion:

4. Among the following statements, which states an opinion expressed by the writer rather than a fact?

   (A) That the area of obscenity and pornography is a difficult one for the Supreme Court is well documented.

   (B) The objects to which a court directs its attitudes are the litigants.

   (C) In many specific issue areas, the cases present strikingly similar patterns.

   (D) The Court's subsequent behavior may suggest how the Court will react in other legal areas.

Keeping in mind that an opinion is something that cannot be proven to hold true in all circumstances, you can determine that choice (D) is correct. It is the only statement among the four for which the evidence is yet to be gathered. It is the writer's opinion that this may be a way to predict the Court's attitudes.

(A), (B), and (C) are all taken from data or documentation in existence already in the world, and are, therefore, incorrect.

Organization Questions

Question 5 asks you to organize given topics to reflect the organization of the passage:

5. The list of topics below that best reflects the organization of the topics of the passage is

   (A) I. The difficulties of the Supreme Court

   II. Several recent studies

   III. Spaeth's definition of "attitude"

   IV. The similar patterns of cases

V. Other issue areas

VI. The case of *Miller vs. California*

(B) I. The Supreme Court, obscenity, and fact-pattern analysis

II. Fact-pattern analyses and attitude theory

III. The definition of "attitude" for the Court

IV. The definition of "situation"

V. The breakdown in fact-pattern analysis

VI. Studying Court behavior

(C) I. Justice Stewart's view of pornography

II. Theoretical underpinnings

III. A minimum-winning coalition

IV. Search and seizure decisions

V. Renewed interest in obscenity and pornography

VI. The importance of local community standards

(D) I. The Court's numerous attempts to define obscenity

II. Case characteristics

III. The subject matter of cases

IV. The Court's proportion of decisions

V. Broad-based factors

VI. Obscenity determination

After examining all of the choices, you will determine that choice (B) is the correct response. These topical areas lead directly to the implied thesis that the "role" of fact-pattern analysis is insufficient for determining the attitude of the Supreme Court in the areas of obscenity and pornography. (See question 1.)

Answer (A) is incorrect because the first topic stated in the list is not the topic of the first paragraph. It is too global. The first paragraph is about the difficulties the Court has with defining obscenity and how fact-pattern analysis might be used to determine the Court's attitude and clear up the problem.

(C) is incorrect because each of the items listed in this topic list are supporting evidence or data for the real topic of each paragraph. (See the list in (B) for correct topics.) For example, Justice Stewart's statement about pornography is only cited to indicate the nature of the problem with obscenity for the Court. It is not the focus of the paragraph itself.

Finally, (D) is incorrect. As with choice (C) these are all incidental pieces of information or data used to make broader points.

Summarization Questions

To answer question 6, you must be able to summarize the passage:

6. Which paragraph below is the best summary of the passage?

   (A) The Supreme Court's decision-making process with respect to obscenity and pornography has become too subjective. Fact-pattern analyses, used to determine the overall attitude of the Court, reveal only broad-based attitudes on the part of the Court toward the situations of obscenity cases. But these patterns cannot fully account for the Court's attitudes toward case content. Research is not conclusive that fact-pattern analyses work when applied to legal areas. Renewed public and local interest suggests continued study and close examination of how the Court makes decisions. Delegating authority to the states may reflect patterns for Court decisions in other socially sensitive areas.

   (B) Though subjective, the Supreme Court decisions are well documented. Fact-pattern analyses reveal the attitude of the Supreme Court toward its decisions in cases. Spaeth explains that an attitude involves both an object and a situation. For the Court, the situation may be defined as the decision to grant certiorari. Cases present strikingly similar patterns, and a small number of variables explain a high proportion of the Court's decisions. Segal has made an effort to verify the applicability of fact-pattern analysis with some success. The Court's decisions on obscenity and pornography suggest weak Court behavior, such as in *Miller vs. California.*

   (C) To determine what obscenity and pornography mean to the Supreme Court, we must use fact-pattern analysis. Fact-pattern analysis reveals the ideas that the Court uses to operate in a vacuum. The litigants and the subject matter of cases is defined in broad terms (such as an entire area of law) to reveal the Court's decision-making process. Search and seizure cases reveal strikingly similar patterns, leaving the Court open to grant certiorari effectively. Renewed public interest in the Court's decisions proves how the Court will react in the future.

   (D) Supreme Court decisions about pornography and obscenity are under examination and are out of control. The Court has to see the case to know it. Fact-pattern analyses reveal that the Court can only define cases in narrow terms, thus revealing individual egotism on the part of the Justices. As a result of strikingly similar patterns in search and seizure cases, the Court should be studied further for its weakness in delegating authority to state courts, as in the case of *Miller vs. California.*

The paragraph that best and most accurately reports what the writer demonstrated based on the implied thesis (see question 1) is answer choice (C) which is correct.

Choice (A) is incorrect. While it reflects some of the evidence presented in the passage, the passage does not imply that all Court decisions are subjective, just the ones about pornography and obscenity. Similarly, the writer does not suggest that delegating authority to the states as in *Miller vs. California* is a sign of some weakness, but merely that it is worthy of study as a tool for predicting or identifying the Court attitude.

Response (B) is also incorrect. The writer summons information over and over to show how fact-pattern analysis cannot pin down the Court's attitude toward case content.

(D) is incorrect. Nowhere does the writer say or suggest that the justice system is "out of control" or that the justices are "egotists," only that they are liable to be reduced to being "subjective" rather than based on an identifiable shared standard.

At this point, the four remaining question types must be discussed: recall questions (see question 7), cause/effect questions (see question 8), definition questions (question 9), and definition questions. They are as follows:

Recall Questions

To answer question 7, you must be able to recall information from the passage:

7. Based on the passage, the rationale for fact-pattern analyses arises out of what theoretical groundwork?

   (A) Subjectivity theory

   (B) The study of cultural norms

   (C) Attitude theory

   (D) Cybernetics

The easiest way to answer this question is to refer back to the passage. In the second paragraph, the writer states that recent studies using fact-pattern analyses, "owe their theoretical underpinnings to attitude theory." Therefore, we can conclude that response (C) is correct.

Answer choices (A), (B), and (D) are incorrect, as they are never discussed or mentioned by the writer.

Cause/Effect Questions

Question 8 requires you to analyze a cause and effect relationship:

8. Based on data in the passage, what would most likely be the major cause for the difficulty in pinning down the Supreme Court's attitude toward cases of obscenity and pornography?

   (A) The personal opinions of the Court Justices

   (B) The broad nature of the situations of the cases

   (C) The ineffective logistics of certiorari

   (D) The inability of the Court to resolve the variables presented by individual case content

Choice (D) is correct, as it is precisely what fact-pattern analyses cannot resolve.

Response (A) is incorrect because no evidence is presented for this, only that they do make personal decisions.

Answer choice (B) is incorrect because this is one way in which fact-pattern analysis can be helpful.

Finally, (C) is only a statement about certiorari being difficult to administer, and this was never claimed about them by the writer in the first place.

Definition Questions

Returning to question 9, we can now determine an answer:

9. In the context of the passage, *subjective* might be most nearly defined as

   (A) personal.

   (B) wrong.

   (C) focussed.

   (D) objective.

Choice (A) is best. By taking in and noting the example of Justice Stewart provided by the writer, we can see that Justice Stewart's comment is an example not of right or wrong. (He doesn't talk about right or wrong. He uses the verb "know" — whose root points to *know*ledge, understanding, insight, primarily, not ethical considerations.). He probably doesn't mean focussed by this since the focus is provided by the appearance or instance of the case itself. By noting the same word ending and the appearance of the root "object" — meaning an observable thing exiting outside of ourselves in time and space, and comparing it with the root of subjective, "subject" — often pointing to something personally studied, we can begin to rule out "objective" as perhaps the opposite of "subjective." Most of the time if we are talking about people's "preferences," they are usually about taste or quality, and they are usually not a result of scientific study or clear reasoning, but arise out of a combination of personal taste and idiosyncratic intuitions. Thus, (A) becomes the most likely choice.

(C) is incorrect because the Court's focus is already in place: on obscenity and pornography.

Answer (B) is incorrect. Nothing is implied or stated about the rightness or wrongness of the decisions themselves. Rather it is the definition of obscenity that seems "unworkable."

(D) is also incorrect. Objective is the direct opposite of subjective. To reason based on the object of study is the opposite of reasoning based upon the beliefs, opinions, or ideas of the one viewing the object, rather than the evidence presented by the object itself independent of the observer.

You may not have been familiar with the word subjective, but from your understanding of the writer's intent, you should have been able to figure out what s/he was after. Surrounding words and phrases almost always offer you some clues in determining the meaning of a word. In addition, any examples that appear in the text may also provide some hints.

III. Vocabulary Enhancer

It is important to understand the meanings of all words — not just the ones you are asked to define. A good vocabulary is a strength that can help you perform well on all sections of this test. The following information will build your skills in determining the meanings of words.

Similar Forms and Sounds

The complex nature of language sometimes makes reading difficult. Words often become confusing when they have similar forms and sounds. Indeed the author may have a correct meaning in mind, but an incorrect word choice can alter the meaning of the sentence or even make it totally illogical.

NO: Martha was always part of that *cliché.*

YES: Martha was always part of that *clique.*

(A *cliché* is a trite or hackneyed expression; a *clique* is an exclusive group of people.)

NO: The minister spoke of the soul's *immorality.*

YES: The minister spoke of the soul's *immortality.*

(*Immorality* means wickedness; *immortality* means imperishable or unending life.)

NO: Where is the nearest *stationary* store?

YES: Where is the nearest *stationery* store?

(*Stationary* means immovable; *stationery* is paper used for writing.)

Below are groups of words that are often confused because of their similar forms and sounds.

1. accent – *v.* – to stress or emphasize (You must *accent* the last syllable.)

   ascent – *n.* – a climb or rise (John's *ascent* of the mountain was dangerous.)

   assent – *n.* – consent; compliance (We need your *assent* before we can go ahead with the plans.)

2. accept – *v.* – to take something offered (She *accepted* the gift.)

   except – *prep.* – other than; but (Everyone was included in the plans *except* him.)

3. advice – *n.* – opinion given as to what to do or how to handle a situation (Her sister gave her *advice* on what to say at the interview.)

   advise – *v.* – to counsel (John's guidance counselor *advised* him on which colleges to apply to.)

4. affect – *v.* – to influence (Mary's suggestion did not *affect* me.)

   effect – 1. *v.*– to cause to happen (The plan was *effected* with great success.); 2. *n.* – result (The *effect* of the medicine is excellent.)

5. allusion – *n.* – indirect reference (In the poem, there are many Biblical *allusions.*)

   illusion – *n.* – false idea or conception; belief or opinion not in accord with the facts (Greg was under the *illusion* that he could win the race after missing three weeks of practice.)

6. already – *adv.* – previously (I had *already* read that novel.)

   all ready – *adv.* + *adj.* – prepared (The family was *all ready* to leave on vacation.)

7. altar – *n.* – table or stand used in religious rites (The priest stood at the *altar.*)

   alter – *v.* – to change (Their plans were *altered* during the strike.)

8. capital – 1. *n.* – a city where the government meets (The senators had a meeting in Albany, the *capital* of New York.); 2. money used in business (They had enough *capital* to develop the industry.)

   capitol – *n.* – building in which the legislature meets (Senator Brown gave a speech at the *capitol* in Washington.)

9. choose – *v.* – to select (Which camera did you *choose*?)

   chose – (past tense, *choose.*) (Susan *chose* to stay home.)

10. cite – *v.* – to quote (The student *cited* evidence from the text.)

    site – *n.* – location (They chose the *site* where the house would be built.)

11. clothes – *n.* – garments (Because she got caught in the rain, her *clothes* were wet.)

    cloths – *n.* – pieces of material (The *cloths* were used to wash the windows.)

12. coarse – *adj.* – rough; unrefined (Sandpaper is *coarse.*)

    course – 1. *n.* – path of action (She did not know what *course* would solve the problem.); 2. passage (We took the long *course* to the lake.); 3. series of studies (We both enrolled in the physics *course.*); 4. part of a meal (She served a five *course* meal.)

13. consul – *n.* – a person appointed by the government to live in a foreign city and represent the citizenry and business interests of his native country there (The *consul* was appointed to Naples, Italy.)

    council – *n.* – a group used for discussion, advisement (The *council* decided to accept his letter of resignation.)

counsel – *v.* – to advise (Tom *counsels* Jerry on tax matters.)

14. decent – *adj.* – proper; respectable (He was very *decent* about the entire matter.)

descent – 1. *n.* – moving down (In Dante's *Inferno*, the *descent* into Hell was depicted graphically.); 2. ancestry (He is of Irish *descent.*)

15. device – 1. *n.* – plan; scheme (The *device* helped her win the race.); 2. invention (We bought a *device* that opens the garage door automatically.)

devise – *v.* – to contrive (He *devised* a plan so John could not win.)

16. emigrate – *v.* – to go away from a country (Many Japanese *emigrated* from Japan in the late 1800s.)

immigrate – *v.* – to come into a country (Her relatives *immigrated* to the United States after World War I.)

17. eminent – *n.* – prominent (He is an *eminent* member of the community.)

imminent – *adj.* – impending (The decision is *imminent.*)

immanent – *adj.* – existing within (Maggie believed that religious spirit is *immanent* in human beings.)

18. fair – 1. *adj.* – beautiful (She was a *fair* maiden.); 2. just (She tried to be *fair.*); 3. *n* – festival (There were many games at the *fair.*)

fare – *n.* – amount of money paid for transportation (The city proposed that the subway *fare* be raised.)

19. forth – *adv.* – onward (The soldiers moved *forth* in the blinding snow.)

fourth – *n., adj.* – 4th (She was the *fourth* runner-up in the beauty contest.)

20. its – possessive form of *it* (Our town must improve *its* roads.)

it's – contraction of it is (*It's* time to leave the party.)

21. later – *adj., adv.* – at a subsequent date (We will take a vacation *later* this year.)

latter – *n.* – second of the two (Susan can visit Monday or Tuesday. The *latter,* however, is preferable.)

22. lead – 1. *n.* – (led) a metal (The handgun was made of *lead.*); 2. *v.t.* – (leed) to show the way (The camp counselor *leads* the way to the picnic grounds.)

led – past tense of *lead* (#2 above) (The dog *led* the way.)

23. loose – *adj.* – free; unrestricted (The dog was let *loose* by accident.)

lose – *v.* – to suffer the loss of (He was afraid he would *lose* the race.)

24. moral – 1. *adj.* – virtuous (She is a *moral* woman with high ethical standards.); 2. *n.* – lesson taught by a story, incident, etc. (Most fables end with a *moral.*)

morale – *n.* – mental condition (After the team lost the game, their *morale* was low.)

25. of – *prep.* – from (She is *of* French descent.)

off – *adj.* – away; at a distance (The television fell *off* the table.)

26. passed – *v.* – having satisfied some requirement (He *passed* the test.)

past – 1. *adj.* – gone by or elapsed in time (His *past* deeds got him in trouble.); 2. *n.* – a period of time gone by (His *past* was shady.); 3. *prep.* – beyond (She ran *past* the house.)

27. personal – *adj.* – private (Jack was unwilling to discuss his childhood; it was too *personal.*)

personnel – *n.* – staff (The *personnel* at the department store was made up of young adults.)

28. principal – *n.* – head of a school (The *principal* addressed the graduating class.)

principle – *n.* – the ultimate source, origin, or cause of something; a law, truth (The *principles* of physics were reviewed in class today.)

29. prophecy – *n.* – prediction of the future (His *prophecy* that he would become a doctor came true.)

prophesy – *v.* – to declare or predict (He *prophesied* that we would win the lottery.)

30. quiet – *adj.* – still; calm (At night all is *quiet.*)

quite – *adv.* – really; truly (She is *quite* a good singer.)

quit – *v.* – to free oneself (Peter had little time to spare so he *quit* the chorus.)

31. respectfully – *adv.* – with respect, honor, esteem (He declined the offer *respectfully.*)

respectively – *adv.* – in the order mentioned (Jack, Susan and Jim, who are members of the club, were elected president, vice-president, and secretary *respectively.*)

32. stationary – *adj.* – immovable (The park bench is *stationary.*)

stationery – *n.* – paper used for writing (The invitations were printed on yellow *stationery.*)

33. straight – *adj.* – not curved (The road was *straight.*)

strait – 1. *adj.* – restricted; narrow; confined (The patient was put in a *strait* jacket.); 2. *n.* – narrow waterway (He sailed through the *Straits* of Magellan.)

34. than – *conj.* – used most commonly in comparisons (Maggie is older *than* I.)

    then – *adv.* – soon afterward (We lived in Boston, *then* we moved to New York.)

35. their – possessive form of *they* (That is *their* house on Tenafly Drive.)

    they're – contraction of they are (*They're* leaving for California next week.)

    there – *adv.* – at that place (Who is standing *there* under the tree?)

36. to – *prep.* – in the direction of; toward; as (She made a turn *to* the right on Norman Street.)

    too – 1. *adv.* – more than enough (She served *too* much for dinner.); 2. also (He is going to Maine *too.*)

    two – *n.* – 2; one and one (We have *two* pet rabbits).

37. weather – *n.* – the general condition of the atmosphere (The *weather* is expected to be clear on Sunday.)

    whether – *conj.* – if it be a case or fact (We don't know *whether* the trains are late.)

38. who's – contraction of who is or who has (*Who's* willing to volunteer for the night shift?)

    whose – possessive form of *who* (*Whose* book is this?)

39. your – possessive form of *you* (Is this *your* seat?)

    you're – contraction of you and are (I know *you're* going to do well on the test.)

Multiple Meanings

In addition to words that sound alike, you must be careful when dealing with words that have multiple meanings. For example:

> The boy was thrilled that his mother gave him a piece of chewing *gum.*
>
> Dentists advise people to floss their teeth to help prevent *gum* disease.

As you can see, one word can have different meanings depending on the context in which it is used.

Connotation and Denotation

Language can become even more complicated. Not only can a single word have numerous definitions and subtle meanings, it may also take on added meanings through implication. The **connotation** is the idea suggested by its place near or association with other words or phrases. The **denotation** of a word is the direct explicit meaning.

Connotation

Sometimes, you will be asked to tell the meaning of a word in the context of the paragraph. You may not have seen the word before, but from your understanding of the writer's intent, you should be able to figure out what it is s/he's after. For example, read the following paragraph:

> Paris is a beautiful city, perhaps the most beautiful on earth. Long, broad avenues are lined with seventeenth and eighteenth century apartments, office buildings, and cafes. Flowers give the city a rich and varied look. The bridges and the river lend an air of lightness and grace to the whole urban landscape.

1. In this paragraph, "rich" most nearly means

   (A) wealthy.

   (B) polluted.

   (C) colorful.

   (D) dull.

If you chose "colorful" you would be right. Although "rich" literally means "wealthy" (that is its *denotation,* its literal meaning), here the writer means more than the word's literal meaning, and seems to be highlighting the variety and color that the flowers add to the avenues, that is, richness in a figurative sense.

The writer is using a non-literal meaning, or *connotation* that we associate with the word "rich" to show what s/he means. When we think of something "rich," we usually also think of abundance, variety, color, and not merely numbers.

Denotation

Determining the denotation of a word is different from determining a word's connotation. Read this paragraph:

> Many soporifics are on the market to help people sleep. Take a glass of water and two *Sleepeze* and you get the "zzzzz" you need. *Sominall* supposedly helps you get the sleep you need so you can go on working. With *Morpho,* your head hits the pillow and you're asleep before the light goes out.

1. From this paragraph, a "soporific" is probably

   (A) a drug that stimulates you to stay awake.

   (B) a kind of sleeping bag.

   (C) a kind of bed.

   (D) a drug that helps you sleep.

What is a soporific? You can figure out what it means by looking at what is said around it. People take these "soporifics" to go to sleep, not to wake up. So it can't be (A). You can't take two beds and a glass of water to go to sleep, either. So, it can't be (C). Anyway, you might be able to identify what a soporific is because you recognize the brand names used as examples. So, it must be some sort of pill that you take to sleep. Well, pills are usually drugs of some kind. Therefore, the answer is (D).

Vocabulary Builder

Although the context in which a word appears can help you determine the meaning of the word, one sure-fire way to know a definition is to learn it. By studying the following lists of words and memorizing their definition(s), you will be better equipped to answer Reading Section questions that deal with word meanings.

To benefit most from this vocabulary list, study the words and their definitions, then answer all of the drill questions making sure to check your answers with the answer key that appears at the end of the review.

Group 1

abstract – *adj.* – not easy to understand; theoretical

acclaim – *n.* – loud approval; applause

acquiesce – *v.* – agree or consent to an opinion

adamant – *adj.* – not yielding; firm

adversary – *n.* – an enemy; foe

advocate – 1. *v.* – to plead in favor of; 2. *n.* – supporter; defender

aesthetic – *adj.* – showing good taste; artistic

alleviate – *v.* – to lessen or make easier

aloof – *adj.* – distant in interest; reserved; cool

altercation – *n.* – controversy; dispute

altruistic – *adj.* – unselfish

amass – *v.* – to collect together; accumulate

ambiguous – *adj.* – not clear; uncertain; vague

ambivalent – *adj.* – undecided

ameliorate – *v.* – to make better; to improve

amiable – *adj.* – friendly

amorphous – *adj.* – having no determinate form

anarchist – *n.* – one who believes that a formal government is unnecessary antagonism – *n.* – hostility; opposition

apathy – *n.* – lack of emotion or interest

appease – *v.* – to make quiet; to calm

apprehensive – *adj.* – fearful; aware; conscious

arbitrary – *adj.* – based on one's preference or whim

arrogant – *adj.* – acting superior to others; conceited

articulate – 1. *v.* – to speak distinctly; 2. *adj.* – eloquent; fluent; 3. *adj.* – capable of speech; 4. *v* – to hinge; to connect; 5. *v.* – to convey; to express effectively

☞ Drill 1

DIRECTIONS: Match each word in the left column with the word in the right column that is most *opposite* in meaning.

	Word			Match	
1. ____ articulate		6. ____ abstract		A. hostile	F. disperse
2. ____ apathy		7. ____ acquiesce		B. concrete	G. enthusiasm
3. ____ amiable		8. ____ arbitrary		C. selfish	H. certain
4. ____ altruistic		9. ____ amass		D. reasoned	I. resist
5. ____ ambivalent		10. ____ adversary		E. ally	J. incoherent

DIRECTIONS: Match each word in the left column with the word in the right column that is most *similar* in meaning.

	Word			Match	
11. ____ adamant		14. ____ antagonism		A. afraid	D. insistent
12. ____ aesthetic		15. ____ altercation		B. disagreement	E. hostility
13. ____ apprehensive				C. tasteful	

Group 2

assess – *v.* – to estimate the value of

astute – *adj.* – cunning; sly; crafty

atrophy – *v.* – to waste away through lack of nutrition

audacious – *adj.* – fearless; bold

augment – *v.* – to increase or add to; to make larger

austere – *adj.* – harsh; severe; strict

authentic – *adj.* – real; genuine; trustworthy

authoritarian – *adj.* – acting as a dictator; demanding obedience

banal – *adj.* – common; petty; ordinary

belittle – *v.* – to make small; to think lightly of

benefactor – *n.* – one who helps others; a donor

benevolent – *adj.* – kind; generous

benign – *adj.* – mild; harmless

biased – *adj.* – prejudiced; influenced; not neutral

blasphemous – *adj.* – irreligious; away from acceptable standards

blithe – *adj.* – happy; cheery; merry

brevity – *n.* – briefness; shortness

candid – *adj.* – honest; truthful; sincere

capricious – *adj.* – changeable; fickle

caustic – *adj.* – burning; sarcastic; harsh

censor – *v.* – to examine and delete objectionable material

censure – *v.* – to criticize or disapprove of

charlatan – *n.* – an imposter; fake

coalesce – *v.* – to combine; come together

collaborate – *v.* – to work together; cooperate

☞ Drill 2

DIRECTIONS: Match each word in the left column with the word in the right column that is most *opposite* in meaning.

	Word			Match	
1.	____ augment	6. ____ authentic		A. permit	F. malicious
2.	____ biased	7. ____ candid		B. oppose	G. neutral
3.	____ banal	8. ____ belittle		C. praise	H. mournful
4.	____ benevolent	9. ____ collaborate		D. diminish	I. unusual
5.	____ censor	10. ____ blithe		E. dishonest	J. fake

DIRECTIONS: Match each word in the left column with the word in the right column that is most *similar* in meaning.

	Word			Match	
11.	____ charlatan	14. ____ censure		A. harmless	D. imposter
12.	____ benign	15. ____ capricious		B. cunning	E. criticize
13.	____ astute			C. changeable	

Group 3

compatible – *adj.* – in agreement; harmonious

complacent – *adj.* – content; self-satisfied; smug

compliant – *adj.* – yielding; obedient

comprehensive – *adj.* – all-inclusive; complete; thorough

compromise – *v.* – to settle by mutual adjustment

concede – 1. *v.* – to acknowledge; admit; 2. to surrender; to abandon one's position

concise – *adj.* – in few words; brief; condensed

condescend – *v.* – to come down from one's position or dignity

condone – *v.* – to overlook; to forgive

conspicuous – *adj.* – easy to see; noticeable

consternation – *n.* – amazement or terror that causes confusion

consummation – *n.* – the completion; finish

contemporary – *adj.* – living or happening at the same time; modern

contempt – *n.* – scorn; disrespect

contrite – *adj.* – regretful; sorrowful

conventional – *adj.* – traditional; common; routine

cower – *v.* – crouch down in fear or shame

defamation – *n.* – any harm to a name or reputation; slander

deference – *n.* – a yielding to the opinion of another

deliberate – 1. *v.* – to consider carefully; weigh in the mind; 2. *adj.* – intentional

denounce – *v.* – to speak out against; condemn

depict – *v.* – to portray in words; present a visual image

deplete – *v.* – to reduce; to empty

depravity – *n.* – moral corruption; badness

deride – *v.* – to ridicule; laugh at with scorn

☞ Drill 3

DIRECTIONS: Match each word in the left column with the word in the right column that is most *opposite* in meaning.

Word		Match	
1. ____ deplete	6. ____ condone	A. unintentional	F. support
2. ____ contemporary	7. ____ conspicuous	B. disapprove	G. beginning
3. ____ concise	8. ____ consummation	C. invisible	H. ancient
4. ____ deliberate	9. ____ denounce	D. respect	I. virtue
5. ____ depravity	10. ____ contempt	E. fill	J. verbose

DIRECTIONS: Match each word in the left column with the word in the right column that is most *similar* in meaning.

Word		Match	
11. ____ compatible	14. ____ comprehensive	A. portray	D. thorough
12. ____ depict	15. ____ complacent	B. content	E. common
13. ____ conventional		C. harmonious	

Group 4

desecrate – *v.* – to violate a holy place or sanctuary

detached – *adj.* – separated; not interested; standing alone

deter – *v.* – to prevent; to discourage; hinder

didactic – 1. *adj.* – instructive; 2. dogmatic; preachy

digress – *v.* – stray from the subject; wander from topic

diligence – *n.* – hard work

discerning – *adj.* – distinguishing one thing from another

discord – *n.* – disagreement; lack of harmony

discriminating – 1. *v.* – distinguishing one thing from another; 2. *v.* – demonstrating bias; 3. *adj.* – able to distinguish

disdain – 1. *n.* – intense dislike; 2. *v.* – look down upon; scorn

disparage – *v.* – to belittle; undervalue

disparity – *n.* – difference in form, character, or degree

dispassionate – *adj.* – lack of feeling; impartial

disperse – *v.* – to scatter; separate

disseminate – *v.* – to circulate; scatter

dissent – *v.* – to disagree; differ in opinion

dissonance – *n.* – harsh contradiction

diverse – *adj.* – different; dissimilar

document – 1. *n.* – official paper containing information; 2. *v.*– to support; substantiate; verify

dogmatic – *adj.* – stubborn; biased; opinionated

dubious – *adj.* – doubtful; uncertain; skeptical; suspicious

eccentric – *adj.* – odd; peculiar; strange

efface – *v.* – wipe out; erase

effervescence – 1. *n.* – liveliness; spirit; enthusiasm; 2. bubbliness

egocentric – *adj.* – self-centered

☞ Drill 4

DIRECTIONS: Match each word in the left column with the word in the right column that is most *opposite* in meaning.

Word		Match	
1. ____ detached	6. ____ dubious	A. agree	F. respect
2. ____ deter	7. ____ diligence	B. certain	G. compliment
3. ____ dissent	8. ____ disdain	C. lethargy	H. sanctify
4. ____ discord	9. ____ desecrate	D. connected	I. harmony
5. ____ efface	10. ____ disparage	E. assist	J. restore

DIRECTIONS: Match each word in the left column with the word in the right column that is most *similar* in meaning.

Word		Match	
11. ____ effervescence	14. ____ document	A. violate	D. liveliness
12. ____ efface	15. ____ eccentric	B. distribute	E. odd
13. ____ disseminate		C. substantiate	

Group 5

elaboration – *n.* – act of clarifying; adding details

eloquence – *n.* – the ability to speak well

elusive – *adj.* – hard to catch; difficult to understand

emulate – *v.* – to imitate; copy; mimic

endorse – *v.* – support; to approve of; recommend

engender – *v.* – to create; bring about

enhance – *v.* – to improve; compliment; make more attractive

enigma – *n.* – mystery; secret; perplexity

ephemeral – *adj.* – temporary; brief; short-lived

equivocal – *adj.* – doubtful; uncertain

erratic – *adj.* – unpredictable; strange

erroneous – *adj.* – untrue; inaccurate; not correct

esoteric – *adj.* – incomprehensible; obscure

euphony – *n.* – pleasant sound

execute – 1. *v.* – put to death; kill; 2. to carry out; fulfill

exemplary – *adj.* – serving as an example; outstanding

exhaustive – *adj.* – thorough; complete

expedient – *adj.* – helpful; practical; worthwhile

expedite – *v.* – speed up

explicit – *adj.* – specific; definite

extol – *v.* – praise; commend

extraneous – *adj.* – irrelevant; not related; not essential

facilitate – *v.* – make easier; simplify

fallacious – *adj.* – misleading

fanatic – *n.* – enthusiast; extremist

☞ Drill 5

DIRECTIONS: Match each word in the left column with the word in the right column that is most *opposite* in meaning.

Word		Match	
1. ____ extraneous	6. ____ erratic	A. incomplete	F. eternal
2. ____ ephemeral	7. ____ explicit	B. delay	G. abridge
3. ____ exhaustive	8. ____ euphony	C. dependable	H. relevant
4. ____ expedite	9. ____ elusive	D. comprehensible	I. indefinite
5. ____ erroneous	10. ____ elaborate	E. dissonance	J. accurate

DIRECTIONS: Match each word in the left column with the word in the right column that is most *similar* in meaning.

Word		Match	
11. ____ endorse	14. ____ fallacious	A. enable	D. worthwhile
12. ____ expedient	15. ____ engender	B. recommend	E. deceptive
13. ____ facilitate		C. create	

Group 6

fastidious – *adj.* – fussy; hard to please

fervor – *n.* – passion; intensity

fickle – *adj.* – changeable; unpredictable

fortuitous – *adj.* – accidental; happening by chance; lucky

frivolity – *n.* – giddiness; lack of seriousness

fundamental – *adj.* – basic; necessary

furtive – *adj.* – secretive; sly

futile – *adj.* – worthless; unprofitable

glutton – *n.* – overeater

grandiose – *adj.* – extravagant; flamboyant

gravity – *n.* – seriousness

guile – *n.* – slyness; deceit

gullible – *adj.* – easily fooled

hackneyed – *adj.* – commonplace; trite

hamper – *v.* – interfere with; hinder

haphazard – *adj.* – disorganized; random

hedonistic – *adj.* – pleasure seeking

heed – *v.* – obey; yield to

heresy – *n.* – opinion contrary to popular belief

hindrance – *n.* – blockage; obstacle

humility – *n.* – lack of pride; modesty

hypocritical – *adj.* – two-faced; deceptive

hypothetical – *adj.* – assumed; uncertain

illuminate – *v.* – make understandable

illusory – *adj.* – unreal; false; deceptive

☞ Drill 6

DIRECTIONS: Match each word in the left column with the word in the right column that is most *opposite* in meaning.

	Word		Word		Match		Match
1.	____ heresy	6.	____ fervent	A.	predictable	F.	beneficial
2.	____ fickle	7.	____ fundamental	B.	dispassionate	G.	orthodoxy
3.	____ illusory	8.	____ furtive	C.	simple	H.	organized
4.	____ frivolity	9.	____ futile	D.	extraneous	I.	candid
5.	____ grandiose	10.	____ haphazard	E.	real	J.	seriousness

DIRECTIONS: Match each word in the left column with the word in the right column that is most *similar* in meaning.

	Word		Word		Match		Match
11.	____ glutton	14.	____ hackneyed	A.	hinder	D.	overeater
12.	____ heed	15.	____ hindrance	B.	obstacle	E.	obey
13.	____ hamper			C.	trite		

Group 7

immune – *adj.* – protected; unthreatened by

immutable – *adj.* – unchangeable; permanent

impartial – *adj.* – unbiased; fair

impetuous – 1. *adj.* – rash; impulsive; 2. forcible; violent

implication – *n.* – suggestion; inference

inadvertent – *adj.* – not on purpose; unintentional

incessant – *adj.* – constant; continual

incidental – *adj.* – extraneous; unexpected

inclined – 1. *adj.* – apt to; likely to; 2. angled

incoherent – *adj.* – illogical; rambling

incompatible – *adj.* – disagreeing; disharmonious

incredulous – *adj.* – unwilling to believe; skeptical

indifferent – *adj.* – unconcerned

indolent – *adj.* – lazy; inactive

indulgent – *adj.* – lenient; patient

inevitable – *adj.* – sure to happen; unavoidable

infamous – *adj.* – having a bad reputation; notorious

infer – *v.* – form an opinion; conclude

initiate – 1. *v.* – begin; admit into a group; 2. *n.* – a person who is in the process of being admitted into a group

innate – *adj.* – natural; inborn

innocuous – *adj.* – harmless; innocent

innovate – *v.* – introduce a change; depart from the old

insipid – *adj.* – uninteresting; bland

instigate – *v.* – start; provoke

intangible – *adj.* – incapable of being touched; immaterial

☞ Drill 7

DIRECTIONS: Match each word in the left column with the word in the right column that is most *opposite* in meaning.

Word		Match	
1. ____ immutable	6. ____ innate	A. intentional	F. changeable
2. ____ impartial	7. ____ incredulous	B. articulate	G. avoidable
3. ____ inadvertent	8. ____ inevitable	C. gullible	H. harmonious
4. ____ incoherent	9. ____ intangible	D. material	I. learned
5. ____ incompatible	10. ____ indolent	E. biased	J. energetic

DIRECTIONS: Match each word in the left column with the word in the right column that is most *similar* in meaning.

Word		Match	
11. ____ impetuous	14. ____ instigate	A. lenient	D. conclude
12. ____ incidental	15. ____ indulgent	B. impulsive	E. extraneous
13. ____ infer		C. provoke	

Group 8

ironic – *adj.* – contradictory; inconsistent; sarcastic

irrational – *adj.* – not logical

jeopardy – *n.* – danger

kindle – *v.* – ignite; arouse

languid – *adj.* – weak; fatigued

laud – *v.* – to praise

lax – *adj.* – careless; irresponsible

lethargic – *adj.* – lazy; passive

levity – *n.* – silliness; lack of seriousness

lucid – 1. *adj.* – shining; 2. easily understood

magnanimous – *adj.* – forgiving; unselfish

malicious – *adj.* – spiteful; vindictive

marred – *adj.* – damaged

meander – *v.* – wind on a course; go aimlessly

melancholy – *n.* – depression; gloom

meticulous – *adj.* – exacting; precise

minute – *adj.* – extremely small; tiny

miser – *n.* – penny pincher; stingy person

mitigate – *v.* – alleviate; lessen; soothe

morose – *adj.* – moody; despondent

negligence – *n.* – carelessness

neutral – *adj.* – impartial; unbiased

nostalgic – *adj.* – longing for the past; filled with bittersweet memories

novel – *adj.* – new

☞ Drill 8

DIRECTIONS: Match each word in the left column with the word in the right column that is most *opposite* in meaning.

Word		Match	
1. ____ irrational	6. ____ magnanimous	A. extinguish	F. ridicule
2. ____ kindle	7. ____ levity	B. jovial	G. kindly
3. ____ meticulous	8. ____ minute	C. selfish	H. sloppy
4. ____ malicious	9. ____ laud	D. logical	I. huge
5. ____ morose	10. ____ novel	E. seriousness	J. stale

DIRECTIONS: Match each word in the left column with the word in the right column that is most *similar* in meaning.

Word		Match	
11. ____ ironic	14. ____ jeopardy	A. lessen	D. carelessness
12. ____ marred	15. ____ negligence	B. damaged	E. danger
13. ____ mitigate		C. sarcastic	

Group 9

nullify – *v.* – cancel; invalidate

objective – 1. *adj.* – open-minded; impartial; 2. *n.* – goal

obscure – *adj.* – not easily understood; dark

obsolete – *adj.* – out of date; passe

ominous – *adj.* – threatening

optimist – *n.* – person who hopes for the best; sees the good side

orthodox – *adj.* – traditional; accepted

pagan – 1. *n.* – polytheist; 2. *adj.* – polytheistic

partisan – 1. *n.* – supporter; follower; 2. *adj.* – biased; one sided

perceptive – *adj.* – full of insight; aware

peripheral – *adj.* – marginal; outer

pernicious – *adj.* – dangerous; harmful

pessimism – *n.* – seeing only the gloomy side; hopelessness

phenomenon – 1. *n.* – miracle; 2. occurrence

philanthropy – *n.* – charity; unselfishness

pious – *adj.* – religious; devout; dedicated

placate – *v.* – pacify

plausible – *adj.* – probable; feasible

pragmatic – *adj.* – matter-of-fact; practical

preclude – *v.* – inhibit; make impossible

predecessor – *n.* – one who has occupied an office before another

prodigal – *adj.* – wasteful; lavish

prodigious – *adj.* – exceptional; tremendous

profound – *adj.* – deep; knowledgeable; thorough

profusion – *n.* – great amount; abundance

☞ Drill 9

DIRECTIONS: Match each word in the left column with the word in the right column that is most *opposite* in meaning.

Word		Match	
1. ____ objective	6. ____ plausible	A. scanty	F. minute
2. ____ obsolete	7. ____ preclude	B. assist	G. anger
3. ____ placate	8. ____ prodigious	C. superficial	H. pessimism
4. ____ profusion	9. ____ profound	D. biased	I. modern
5. ____ peripheral	10. ____ optimism	E. improbable	J. central

DIRECTIONS: Match each word in the left column with the word in the right column that is most *similar* in meaning.

Word		Match	
11. ____ nullify	14. ____ pernicious	A. invalidate	D. threatening
12. ____ ominous	15. ____ prodigal	B. follower	E. harmful
13. ____ partisan		C. lavish	

Group 10

prosaic – *adj.* – tiresome; ordinary

provincial – *adj.* – regional; unsophisticated

provocative – 1. *adj.* – tempting; 2. irritating

prudent – *adj.* – wise; careful; prepared

qualified – *adj.* – experienced; indefinite

rectify – *v.* – correct

redundant – *adj.* – repetitious; unnecessary

refute – *v.* – challenge; disprove

relegate – *v.* – banish; put to a lower position

relevant – *adj.* – of concern; significant

remorse – *n.* – guilt; sorrow

reprehensible – *adj.* – wicked; disgraceful

repudiate – *v.* – reject; cancel

rescind – *v.* – retract; discard

resignation – 1. *n.* – quitting; 2. submission

resolution – *n.* – proposal; promise; determination

respite – *n.* – recess; rest period

reticent – *adj.* – silent; reserved; shy

reverent – *adj.* – respectful

rhetorical – *adj.* – having to do with verbal communication

rigor – *n.* – severity

sagacious – *adj.* – wise; cunning

sanguine – 1. *adj.* – optimistic; cheerful; 2. red

saturate – *v.* – soak thoroughly; drench

scanty – *adj.* – inadequate; sparse

☞ Drill 10

DIRECTIONS: Match each word in the left column with the word in the right column that is most *opposite* in meaning.

Word		Match	
1. ____ provincial	6. ____ remorse	A. inexperienced	F. affirm
2. ____ reticent	7. ____ repudiate	B. joy	G. extraordinary
3. ____ prudent	8. ____ sanguine	C. pessimistic	H. sophisticated
4. ____ qualified	9. ____ relevant	D. unrelated	I. forward
5. ____ relegate	10. ____ prosaic	E. careless	J. promote

DIRECTIONS: Match each word in the left column with the word in the right column that is most *similar* in meaning.

Word		Match	
11. ____ provocative	14. ____ rescind	A. drench	D. severity
12. ____ rigor	15. ____ reprehensible	B. tempting	E. blameworthy
13. ____ saturate		C. retract	

Group 11

scrupulous – *adj.* – honorable; exact

scrutinize – *v.* – examine closely; study

servile – *adj.* – slavish; groveling

skeptic – *n.* – doubter

slander – *v.* – defame; maliciously misrepresent

solemnity – *n.* – seriousness

solicit – *v.* – ask; seek

stagnant – *adj.* – motionless; uncirculating

stanza – *n.* – group of lines in a poem having a definite pattern

static – *adj.* – inactive; changeless

stoic – *adj.* – detached; unruffled; calm

subtlety – 1. *n.* – understatement; 2. propensity for understatement; 3. sophistication; 4. cunning

superficial – *adj.* – on the surface; narrow-minded; lacking depth

superfluous – *adj.* – unnecessary; extra

surpass – *v.* – go beyond; outdo

sycophant – *n.* – flatterer

symmetry – *n.* – correspondence of parts; harmony

taciturn – *adj.* – reserved; quiet; secretive

tedious – *adj.* – time-consuming; burdensome; uninteresting

temper – *v.* – soften; pacify; compose

tentative – *adj.* – not confirmed; indefinite

thrifty – *adj.* – economical; pennywise

tranquility – *n.* – peace; stillness; harmony

trepidation – *n.* – apprehension; uneasiness

trivial – *adj.* – unimportant; small; worthless

☞ Drill 11

DIRECTIONS: Match each word in the left column with the word in the right column that is most *opposite* in meaning.

Word		Match	
1. ____ scrutinize	6. ____ tentative	A. frivolity	F. skim
2. ____ skeptic	7. ____ thrifty	B. enjoyable	G. turbulent
3. ____ solemnity	8. ____ tranquility	C. prodigal	H. active
4. ____ static	9. ____ solicit	D. chaos	I. believer
5. ____ tedious	10. ____ stagnant	E. give	J. confirmed

DIRECTIONS: Match each word in the left column with the word in the right column that is most *similar* in meaning.

Word		Match	
11. ____ symmetry	14. ____ subtle	A. understated	D. fear
12. ____ superfluous	15. ____ trepidation	B. unnecessary	E. flatterer
13. ____ sycophant		C. balance	

Group 12

tumid – *adj.* – swollen; inflated

undermine – *v.* – to weaken; ruin

uniform – *adj.* – consistent; unvaried; unchanging

universal – *adj.* – concerning everyone; existing everywhere

unobtrusive – *adj.* – inconspicuous; reserved

unprecedented – *adj.* – unheard of; exceptional

unpretentious – *adj.* – simple; plain; modest

vacillation – *n.* – fluctuation

valid – *adj.* – acceptable; legal

vehement – *adj.* – marked by rancor; violent; intense; excited

venerate – *v.* – to revere

verbose – *adj.* – wordy; talkative

viable – *adj.* – 1. capable of maintaining life; 2. possible; attainable

vigor – *n.* – energy; forcefulness

vilify – *v.* – to slander

virtuoso – *n.* – highly skilled artist

virulent – *adj.* – deadly; harmful; malicious

vital – *adj.* – important; spirited

volatile – *adj.* – changeable; undependable

vulnerable – *adj.* – open to attack; unprotected

wane – *v.* – to grow gradually smaller

whimsical – *adj.* – fanciful; amusing

wither – *v.* – wilt; shrivel; humiliate; cut down

zealot – *n.* – believer; enthusiast; fan

zenith – *n.* – point directly overhead in the sky

☞ Drill 12

DIRECTIONS: Match each word in the left column with the word in the right column that is most *opposite* in meaning.

Word		Match	
1. ____ uniform	6. ____ vigorous	A. amateur	F. support
2. ____ virtuoso	7. ____ volatile	B. trivial	G. constancy
3. ____ vital	8. ____ vacillation	C. visible	H. lethargic
4. ____ wane	9. ____ undermine	D. placid	I. wax
5. ____ unobtrusive	10. ____ valid	E. unacceptable	J. varied

DIRECTIONS: Match each word in the left column with the word in the right column that is most *similar* in meaning.

Word		Match	
11. ____ wither	14. ____ vehement	A. intense	D. possible
12. ____ whimsical	15. ____ virulent	B. deadly	E. shrivel
13. ____ viable		C. amusing	

Additional Vocabulary

The following words comprise additional vocabulary terms which may be found on the TASP.

abandon – 1. *v.* – to leave behind; 2. *v.* – to give something up; 3. *n.* – freedom; enthusiasm; impetuosity

abase – *v.* – to degrade; humiliate; disgrace

abbreviate – *v.* – to shorten; compress; diminish

aberrant – *adj.* – abnormal

abhor – *v.* – to hate

abominate – *v.* – to loathe; to hate

abridge – 1. *v.* – to shorten; 2. to limit; to take away

absolve – *v.* – to forgive; acquit

abstinence – *n.* – self-control; abstention; chastity

accede – *v.* – to comply with; consent to

accomplice – *n.* – co-conspirator; partner; partner-in-crime

accrue – *v.* – collect; build up

acrid – *adj.* – sharp; bitter; foul smelling

adept – *adj.* – skilled; practiced

adverse – *adj.* – negative; hostile; antagonistic; inimical

affable – *adj.* – friendly; amiable; good-natured

aghast – 1. *adj.* – astonished; amazed; 2. horrified; terrified; appalled

alacrity – 1. *n.* – enthusiasm; fervor; 2. liveliness; sprightliness

allocate – *v.* – to set aside; designate; assign

allure – 1. *v.* – to attract; entice; 2. *n.* – attraction; temptation; glamour

amiss – 1. *adj.* – wrong; awry; 2. *adv.* – wrongly; mistakenly

analogy – *n.* – similarity; correlation; parallelism; simile; metaphor

anoint – 1. *v.* – to crown; ordain; 2. to smear with oil

anonymous – *adj.* – nameless; unidentified

arduous – *adj.* – difficult; burdensome

awry – 1. *adj., adv.* – crooked(ly); uneven(ly); 2. wrong; askew

baleful – *adj.* – sinister; threatening; evil; deadly

baroque – *adj.* – extravagant; ornate

behoove – *v.* – to be advantageous; to be necessary

berate – *v.* – to scold; reprove; reproach; criticize

bereft – *adj.* – hurt by someone's death

biennial – 1. *adj.* – happening every two years; 2. *n.* – a plant which blooms every two years

blatant – 1. *adj.* – obvious; unmistakable; 2. crude; vulgar

bombastic – *adj.* – pompous; wordy; turgid

burly – *adj.* – strong; bulky; stocky

cache – 1. *n.* – stockpile; store; heap; 2. hiding place for goods

calamity – *n.* – disaster

cascade – 1. *n.* – waterfall; 2. *v.* – pour; rush; fall

catalyst – *n.* – anything which creates a situation in which change can occur

chagrin – *n.* – distress; shame

charisma – *n.* – appeal; magnetism; presence

chastise – *v.* – punish; discipline; admonish; rebuke

choleric – *adj.* – cranky; cantankerous

cohesion – *n.* – the act of holding together

colloquial – *adj.* – casual; common; conversational; idiomatic

conglomeration – *n.* – mixture; collection

connoisseur – *n.* – expert; authority (usually refers to a wine or food expert)

consecrate – *v.* – sanctify; make sacred; immortalize

craven – *adj.* – cowardly; fearful

dearth – *n.* – scarcity; shortage

debilitate – *v.* – deprive of strength

deign – *v.* – condescend; stoop

delineate – *v.* – to outline; to describe

demur – 1. *v.* – to object; 2. *n.* – objection; misgiving

derision – *n.* – ridicule; mockery

derogatory – *adj.* – belittling; uncomplimentary

destitute – *adj.* – poor; poverty-stricken

devoid – *adj.* – lacking; empty

dichotomy – *n.* – branching into two parts

disheartened – *adj.* – discouraged; depressed

diverge – *v.* – separate; split

docile – *adj.* – manageable; obedient

duress – *n.* – force; constraint

ebullient – *adj.* – showing excitement

educe – *v.* – draw forth

effervescence – *n.* – bubbliness; enthusiasm; animation

emulate – *v.* – to follow the example of

ennui – *n.* – boredom; apathy

epitome – *n.* – model; typification; representation

errant – *adj.* – wandering

ethnic – *adj.* – native; racial; cultural

evoke – *v.* – call forth; provoke

exotic – *adj.* – unusual; striking

facade – *n.* – front view; false appearance

facsimile – *n.* – copy; reproduction; replica

fathom – *v.* – comprehend; uncover

ferret – *v.* – drive or hunt out of hiding

figment – *n.* – product; creation

finite – *adj.* – measurable; limited; not everlasting

fledgling – *n.* – inexperienced person; beginner

flinch – *v.* – wince; draw back; retreat

fluency – *n.* – smoothness of speech

flux – *n.* – current; continuous change

forbearance – *n.* – patience; self-restraint

foster – *v.* – encourage; nurture; support

frivolity – *n.* – lightness; folly; fun

frugality – *n.* – thrift

garbled – *adj.* – mixed up

generic – *adj.* – common; general; universal

germane – *adj.* – pertinent; related; to the point

gibber – *v.* – speak foolishly

gloat – *v.* – brag; glory over

guile – *n.* – slyness; fraud

haggard – *adj.* – tired looking; fatigued

hiatus – *n.* – interval; break; period of rest

hierarchy – *n.* – body of people, things, or concepts divided into ranks

homage – *n.* – honor; respect

hubris – *n.* – arrogance

ideology – *n.* – set of beliefs; principles

ignoble – *adj.* – shameful; dishonorable

imbue – *v.* – inspire; arouse

impale – *v.* – fix on a stake; stick; pierce

implement – *v.* – begin; enact

impromptu – *adj.* – without preparation

inarticulate – *adj.* – speechless; unable to speak clearly

incessant – *adj.* – uninterrupted

incognito – *adj.* – unidentified; disguised; concealed

indict – *v.* – charge with a crime

inept – *adj.* – incompetent; unskilled

innuendo – *n.* – hint; insinuation

intermittent – *adj.* – periodic; occasional

invoke – *v.* – ask for; call upon

itinerary – *n.* – travel plan; schedule; course

jovial – *adj.* – cheery; jolly; playful

juncture – *n.* – critical point; meeting

juxtapose – *v.* – place side by side

knavery – *n.* – rascality; trickery

knead – *v.* – mix; massage

labyrinth – *n.* – maze

laggard – *n.* – a lazy person; one who lags behind

larceny – *n.* – theft; stealing

lascivious – *adj.* – indecent; immoral

lecherous – *adj.* – impure in thought and act

lethal – *adj.* – deadly

liaison – *n.* – connection; link

limber – *adj.* – flexible; pliant

livid – 1. *adj.* – black-and-blue; discolored; 2. enraged; irate

lucrative – *adj.* – profitable; gainful

lustrous – *adj.* – bright; radiant

malediction – *n.* – curse; evil spell

mandate – *n.* – order; charge

manifest – *adj.* – obvious; clear

mentor – *n.* – teacher

mesmerize – *v.* – hypnotize

metamorphosis – *n.* – change of form

mimicry – *n.* – imitation

molten – *adj.* – melted

motif – *n.* – theme

mundane – *adj.* – ordinary; commonplace

myriad – *adj.* – innumerable; countless

narcissistic – *adj.* – egotistical; self-centered

nautical – *adj.* – of the sea

neophyte – *n.* – beginner; newcomer

nettle – *v.* – annoy; irritate

notorious – *adj.* – infamous; renowned

obdurate – *adj.* – stubborn; inflexible

obligatory – *adj.* – mandatory; necessary

obliterate – *v.* – destroy completely

obsequious – *adj.* – slavishly attentive; servile

obstinate – *adj.* – stubborn

occult – *adj.* – mystical; mysterious

opaque – *adj.* – dull; cloudy; nontransparent

opulence – *n.* – wealth; fortune

ornate – *adj.* – elaborate; lavish; decorated

oust – *v.* – drive out; eject

painstaking – *adj.* – thorough; careful; precise

pallid – *adj.* – sallow; colorless

palpable – *adj.* – tangible; apparent

paradigm – *n.* – model; example

paraphernalia – *n.* – equipment; accessories

parochial – *adj.* – religious; narrow-minded

passive – *adj.* – submissive; unassertive

pedestrian – *adj.* – mediocre; ordinary

pensive – *adj.* – reflective; contemplative

percussion – *n.* – the striking of one object against another

perjury – *n.* – the practice of lying

permeable – *adj.* – porous; allowing to pass through

perpetual – *adj.* – enduring for all time

pertinent – *adj.* – related to the matter at hand

pervade – *v.* – to occupy the whole of

petty – *adj.* – unimportant; of subordinate standing

phlegmatic – *adj.* – without emotion or interest

phobia – *n.* – morbid fear

pittance – *n.* – small allowance

plethora – *n.* – condition of going beyond what is needed; excess; overabundance

potent – *adj.* – having great power or physical strength

privy – *adj.* – private; confidential

progeny – *n.* – children; offspring

provoke – *v.* – to stir action or feeling; arouse

pungent – *adj.* – sharp; stinging

quaint – *adj.* – old-fashioned; unusual; odd

quandary – *n.* – dilemma

quarantine – *n.* – isolation of a person to prevent spread of disease

quiescent – *adj.* – inactive; at rest

quirk – *n.* – peculiar behavior; startling twist

rabid – *adj.* – furious; with extreme anger

rancid – *adj.* – having a bad odor

rant – *v.* – to speak in a loud, pompous manner; rave

ratify – *v.* – to make valid; confirm

rationalize – *v.* – to offer reasons for; account for

raucous – *adj.* – disagreeable to the sense of hearing; harsh

realm – *n.* – an area; sphere of activity

rebuttal – *n.* – refutation

recession – *n.* – withdrawal; depression

reciprocal – *n.* – mutual; having the same relationship to each other

recluse – *n.* – solitary and shut off from society

refurbish – *v.* – to make new

regal – *adj.* – royal; grand

reiterate – *v.* – repeat; to state again

relinquish – *v.* – to let go; abandon

render – *v.* – deliver; provide; to give up a possession

replica – *n.* – copy; representation

resilient – *adj.* – flexible; capable of withstanding stress

retroaction – *n.* – an action elicited by a stimulus

reverie – *n.* – the condition of being unaware of one's surroundings; trance

rummage – *v.* – search thoroughly

rustic – *adj.* – plain and unsophisticated; homely

saga – *n.* – a legend; story

salient – *adj.* – noticeable; prominent

salvage – *v.* – rescue from loss

sarcasm – *n.* – ironic, bitter humor designed to wound

satire – *n.* – a novel or play that uses humor or irony to expose folly

saunter – *v.* – walk at a leisurely pace; stroll

savor – *v.* – to receive pleasure from; enjoy

seethe – *v.* – to be in a state of emotional turmoil; to become angry serrated – *adj.* – having a sawtoothed edge

shoddy – *adj.* – of inferior quality; cheap

skulk – *v.* – to move secretly

sojourn – *n.* – temporary stay; visit

solace – *n.* – hope; comfort during a time of grief

soliloquy – *n.* – a talk one has with oneself (esp. on stage)

somber – *adj.* – dark and depressing; gloomy

sordid – *adj.* – filthy; base; vile

sporadic – *adj.* – rarely occurring or appearing; intermittent

stamina – *n.* – endurance

steadfast – *adj.* – loyal

stigma – *n.* – a mark of disgrace

stipend – *n.* – payment for work done

stupor – *n.* – a stunned or bewildered condition

suave – *adj.* – effortlessly gracious

subsidiary – *adj.* – subordinate

succinct – *adj.* – consisting of few words; concise

succumb – *v.* – give in; yield; collapse

sunder – *v.* – break; split in two

suppress – *v.* – to bring to an end; hold back

surmise – *v.* – draw an inference; guess

susceptible – *adj.* – easily imposed; inclined

tacit – *adj.* – not voiced or expressed

tantalize – *v.* – to tempt; to torment

tarry – *v.* – to go or move slowly; delay

taut – *adj.* – stretch tightly

tenacious – *adj.* – persistently holding to something

tepid – *adj.* – lacking warmth, interest, enthusiasm; lukewarm

terse – *adj.* – concise; abrupt

thwart – *v.* – prevent from accomplishing a purpose; frustrate timorous – *adj.* – fearful

torpid – *adj.* – lacking alertness and activity; lethargic

toxic – *adj.* – poisonous

transpire – *v.* – to take place; come about

traumatic – *adj.* – causing a violent injury

trek – *v.* – to make a journey

tribute – *n.* – expression of admiration

trite – *adj.* – commonplace; overused

truculent – *adj.* – aggressive; eager to fight

turbulence – *n.* – condition of being physically agitated; disturbance

turmoil – *n.* – unrest; agitation

tycoon – *n.* – wealthy leader

tyranny – *n.* – absolute power; autocracy

ubiquitous – *adj.* – ever present in all places; universal

ulterior – *adj.* – buried; concealed

uncanny – *adj.* – of a strange nature; weird

unequivocal – *adj.* – clear; definite

unique – *adj.* – without equal; incomparable

unruly – *adj.* – not submitting to discipline; disobedient

unwonted – *adj.* – not ordinary; unusual

urbane – *adj.* – cultured; suave

usurpation – *n.* – act of taking something for oneself; seizure

usury – *n.* – the act of lending money at illegal rates of interest

utopia – *n.* – imaginary land with perfect social and political systems

vacuous – *adj.* – containing nothing; empty

vagabond – *n.* – wanderer; one without a fixed place

vagrant – 1. *n.* – homeless person; 2. *adj.* – rambling; wandering; transient

valance – *n.* – short drapery hanging over a window frame

valor – *n.* – bravery

vantage – *n.* – position giving an advantage

vaunted – *adj.* – boasted of

velocity – *n.* – speed

vendetta – *n.* – feud

venue – *n.* – location

veracious – *adj.* – conforming to fact; accurate

verbatim – *adj.* – employing the same words as another; literal

versatile – *adj.* – having many uses; multifaceted

vertigo – *n.* – dizziness

vex – *v.* – to trouble the nerves; annoy

vindicate – *v.* – to free from charge; clear

vivacious – *adj.* – animated; gay

vogue – *n.* – modern fashion

voluble – *adj.* – fluent

waft – *v.* – move gently by wind or breeze

waive – *v.* – to give up possession or right

wanton – *adj.* – unruly; excessive

warrant – *v.* – justify; authorize

wheedle – *v.* – try to persuade; coax

whet – *v.* – sharpen

wrath – *n.* – violent or unrestrained anger; fury

wry – *adj.* – mocking; cynical

xenophobia – *n.* – fear of foreigners

yoke – *n.* – harness; collar; bond

yore – *n.* – former period of time

zephyr – *n.* – a gentle wind; breeze

☞ Drill 13

DIRECTIONS: Each of the following questions provides a given word in capitalized letters followed by five word choices. Choose the word which is *opposite* in meaning to the given word.

1. AUTHENTIC:

   (A) cheap (B) competitive (C) false

   (D) biased (E) irrational

2. MISERLY:

   (A) unhappy (B) generous (C) optimistic

   (D) reticent (E) golden

3. DILIGENT:

   (A) lethargic (B) morose (C) silly

   (D) nostalgic (E) poor

4. PRECLUDE:

   (A) commence (B) include (C) produce

   (D) perpetuate (E) enable

5. EXTOL:

   (A) criticize (B) expedite (C) pay

   (D) deport (E) defer

6. DIVERSE:

   (A) solo (B) furtive (C) jovial

   (D) wrinkled (E) similar

7. DISPERSE:

   (A) despair (B) belittle (C) renew

   (D) renege (E) amass

8. ENDURING:
   (A) fallacious (B) temporal (C) dismal
   (D) minute (E) disseminating

9. BREVITY:
   (A) gravity (B) gluttony (C) cowardice
   (D) authenticity (E) verbosity

10. DEMUR:
    (A) assemble (B) bereave (C) approve
    (D) add (E) ascribe

11. UNWONTED:
    (A) perceptive (B) ordinary (C) tepid
    (D) desirable (E) qualified

12. CHASTISE:
    (A) repudiate (B) immortalize (C) endorse
    (D) virility (E) congratulate

13. INFAMOUS:
    (A) revered (B) resolute (C) obscure
    (D) contiguous (E) unknown

14. DISPASSIONATE:
    (A) resigned (B) profound (C) fanatical
    (D) torrid (E) prudent

15. SCANTY:
    (A) redundant (B) mediocre (C) calming
    (D) profuse (E) partisan

16. PROSAIC:
    (A) poetic (B) unique (C) rabid
    (D) disdainful (E) condescending

17. DIDACTIC:
    (A) dubious (B) dogmatic (C) punctual
    (D) rhetorical (E) reverent

18. COLLOQUIAL:
    (A) poetic (B) separate (D) formal
    (D) analogical (E) anonymous

19. COHESIVE:
    (A) adhesive (B) opposed (C) smooth
    (D) adverse (E) fragmented

20. OBLIGATORY:
    (A) promising (B) permissible (C) heaven
    (D) optional (E) responsible

21. OPAQUE:
    (A) permeable (B) similar (C) visible
    (D) opulent (E) translucent

22. SUNDER:
    (A) unite (B) create noise (C) oust
    (D) rise above (E) freeze

23. NARCISSISTIC:
    (A) flowery (B) detrimental (C) gentle
    (D) modest (E) polite

24. FOSTER:
    (A) destroy (B) relate (C) parent
    (D) abort (E) revere

25. LIVID:
    (A) homeless (B) bright (C) calm
    (D) elusive (E) opulent

26. SUPPRESS:
    (A) justify (B) advocate (C) free
    (D) level (E) immunize

27. DESTITUTE:
    (A) organized (B) ornate (C) moral
    (D) wealthy (E) obsequious

28. PAINSTAKING:
    (A) healthful (B) sordid (C) careless
    (D) sadistic (E) lethal

29. PAROCHIAL:
    (A) melancholy (B) blasphemous (C) sporting
    (D) irreligious (E) broad-minded

30. MANDATE:
    (A) emphasis (B) sophism (C) pinnacle
    (D) request (E) meander

31. LUCID:
    (A) obscure (B) tedious (C) calm
    (D) frightening (E) intelligent

32. IGNOBLE:
    (A) brave (B) honorable (C) royal
    (D) attentive (E) informal

33. PERTINENT:
    (A) respectful (B) detailed (C) dreary
    (D) blatant (E) irrelevant

34. ABSTINENCE:
    (A) indulgence (B) concurrence (C) hedonism
    (D) diligence (E) alcoholism

35. FRUGAL:

(A) unplanned (B) temperamental (C) regal
(D) ethical (E) extravagant

36. FORTUITOUS:

(A) lethargic (B) unprotected (C) weak
(D) unlucky (E) antagonistic

37. UNEQUIVOCAL:

(A) versatile (B) equal (C) noisy
(D) unclear (E) truthful

38. CONTEMPT:

(A) respect (B) pettiness (C) politeness
(D) resistance (E) compliance

39. GRAVITY:

(A) antipathy (B) derision (C) buoyancy
(D) eloquence (E) effervescence

40. AUSTERE:

(A) measurable (B) resilient (C) ornate
(D) indirect (E) destitute

41. PASSIVE:

(A) thoughtless (B) supportive (C) retentive
(D) contemporary (E) assertive

42. STAGNANT:

(A) celibate (B) active (C) effluent
(D) feminine (E) polluted

43. ADVERSE:

(A) friendly (B) quiescent (C) poetic
(D) burly (E) petty

44. CRAVEN:

(A) difficult (B) reptilian (C) pungent
(D) birdlike (E) courageous

45. HEED:

(A) adjust (B) resist (C) attend
(D) encourage (E) order

46. IMPARTIAL:

(A) biased (B) complete (C) eternal
(D) articulate (E) raucous

47. VINDICATE:

(A) remove (B) absolve (C) evoke
(D) accuse (E) ferret

48. DERISION:

(A) elimination (B) attention (C) praise
(D) entrance (E) recession

49. REPREHENSIBLE:

(A) released (B) aghast (C) awry
(D) incidental (E) commendable

50. RELEGATE:

(A) promote (B) nullify (C) include
(D) obliterate (E) placate

51. VAIN:

(A) addicted (B) modest (C) unscented
(D) abase (E) choleric

52. LAGGARD:

(A) haggard (B) lustrous (C) haphazard
(D) advanced (E) industrious

53. LABYRINTHINE:

(A) inconsistent (B) amazing (C) direct
(D) incredulous (E) mythological

54. SLANDER:

(A) praise (B) comfort (C) discipline
(D) risk (E) digress

55. PITTANCE:

(A) mound (B) plethora (C) quirk
(D) grandeur (E) phlegm

56. SOLACE:

(A) lunation (B) turmoil (C) distress
(D) valance (D) spontaneity

57. DEFERENT:

(A) current (B) constructive (C) erratic
(D) unyielding (E) applicant

58. FICKLE:

(A) bland (B) cascading (C) caustic
(D) dubious (E) faithful

59. EXOTIC:

(A) ethnic (B) diverse (C) realistic
(D) mundane (E) enigmatic

60. THWART:

(A) imprison (B) mystify (C) assist
(D) fluctuate (E) saturate

Knowing Your Word Parts

Memorization and practice are not the only ways to learn the meanings of new words. While taking this test, you will have nothing but your own knowledge and context clues to refer to when you come into contact with unfamiliar words. Even though we have provided you with a comprehensive list of words, there is a very good chance that you will come across words that you still do not know. Therefore, you will need to study our list of prefixes, roots, and suffixes in order to be prepared. Learning the meanings of these prefixes, roots, and suffixes is essential to a strong vocabulary and, therefore, to performing well on the Reading Section, as well as the entire TASP exam.

Prefix

Prefix	Meaning	Example
ab-, a-, abs-	away, from	absent – away, not present abstain – keep from doing, refrain
ad-	to, toward	adjacent – next to address – to direct towards
ante-	before	antecedent – going before in time anterior – occurring before
anti-	against	antidote – remedy to act against an evil antibiotic – substance that fights against bacteria
be-	over, thoroughly	bemoan – to mourn over belabor – to exert much labor upon
bi-	two	bisect – to divide biennial – happening every two years
cata-, cat-, cath-	down	catacombs – underground passageways catalogue – descriptive list
circum-	around	circumscribe – to draw a circle around circumspect – watchful on all sides
com-	with	combine – join together communication – to have dealing with
contra-	against	contrary – opposed contrast – to stand in opposition

Prefix	Meaning	Example
de-	down, from	decline – to bend downward decontrol – to release from government control
di-	two	dichotomy – cutting in two diarchy – system of government with two authorities
dis-, di	apart, away	discern – to distinguish as separate digress – to turn away from the subject of attention
epi-, ep-, eph-	upon, among	epidemic – happening among many people epicycle – circle whose center moves round in the circumference of a greater circle
ex-, e-	from, out	exceed – go beyond the limit emit – to send forth
extra-	outside, beyond	extraordinary – beyond or out of the common method extrasensory – beyond the senses
hyper-	beyond, over	hyperactive – over the normal activity level hypercritic – one who is critical beyond measure
hypo-	beneath, lower	hypodermic – parts beneath the skin hypocrisy – to be under a pretense of goodness
in-, il-, im-, ir-	not	inactive – not active irreversible – not reversible
in-, il-, im-, ir-	in, on, into	instill – to put in slowly impose – to lay on
inter-	among, between	intercom – to exchange conversations between people interlude – performance given between parts in a play
intra-	within	intravenous – within a vein intramural – within a single college or its students

Prefix	Meaning	Example
meta-	beyond, over, along with	metamorphosis – change over in form or nature metatarsus – part of foot beyond the flat of the foot
mis-	badly, wrongly	misconstrue – to interpret wrongly misappropriate – to use wrongly
mono-	one	monogamy – to be married to one person at a time monotone – a single, unvaried tone
multi-	many	multiple – of many parts multitude – a great number
non-	no, not	nonsense – lack of sense nonentity – not existing
ob-	against	obscene – offensive to modesty obstruct – to hinder the passage of
para-, par-	beside	parallel – continuously at equal distance apart parenthesis – sentence inserted within a passage
per-	through	persevere – to maintain an effort permeate – to pass through
poly-	many	polygon – a plane figure with many sides or angles polytheism – belief in existence of many gods
post-	after	posterior – coming after postpone – to put off till a future time
pre-	before	premature – ready before the proper time premonition – a previous warning
pro-	in favor of, forward	prolific – bringing forth offspring project – throw or cast forward

Prefix	Meaning	Example
re-	back, against	reimburse – pay back retract – to draw back
semi-	half	semicircle – half a circle semiannual – half-yearly
sub-	under	subdue – to bring under one's power submarine – travel under the surface of the sea
super-	above	supersonic – above the speed of sound superior – higher in place or position
tele-, tel-	across	telecast – transmit across a distance telepathy – communication between mind and mind at a distance
trans-	across	transpose – to change the position of two things transmit – to send from one person to another
ultra-	beyond	ultraviolet – beyond the limit of visibility ultramarine – beyond the sea
un-	not	undeclared – not declared unbelievable – not believable
uni-	one	unity – state of oneness unison – sounding together
with-	away, against	withhold – to hold back withdraw – to take away

Root

Root	Meaning	Example
act, ag	do, act, drive	activate – to make active agile – having quick motion
alt	high	altitude – height alto – highest singing voice
alter, altr	other, change	alternative – choice between two things altruism – living for the good of others

Root	Meaning	Example
am, ami	love, friend	amiable – worthy of affection amity – friendship
anim	mind, spirit	animated – spirited animosity – violent hatred
annu, enni	year	annual – every year centennial – every hundred years
aqua	water	aquarium – tank for water animals and plants aquamarine – semiprecious stone of sea-green color
arch	first, ruler	archenemy – chief enemy archetype – original pattern from which things are copied
aud, audit	hear	audible – capable of being heard audience – assembly of hearers
auto	self	automatic – self-acting autobiography – story about a person who also wrote it
bell	war	belligerent – a party taking part in a war bellicose – war-like
ben, bene	good	benign – kindly disposition beneficial – advantageous
bio	life	biotic – relating to life biology – the science of life
brev	short	abbreviate – make shorter brevity – shortness
cad, cas	fall	cadence – fall in voice casualty – loss caused by death
capit, cap	head	captain – the head or chief decapitate – to cut off the head
cede, ceed, cess	to go, to yield	recede – to move or fall back proceed – to move onward

Root	Meaning	Example
cent	hundred	century – hundred years centipede – insect with a hundred legs
chron	time	chronology – science dealing with historical dates chronicle – register of events in order of time
cide, cis	to kill, to cut	homicide – one who kills incision – a cut
clam, claim	to shout	acclaim – receive with applause proclamation – announce publicly
cogn	to know	recognize – to know again cognition – awareness
corp	body	incorporate – combine into one body corpse – dead body
cred	to trust, to believe	incredible – unbelievable credulous – too prone to believe
cur, curr, curs	to run	current – flowing body of air or water excursion – short trip
dem	people	democracy – government formed for the people epidemic – affecting all people
dic, dict	to say	dictate – to read aloud for another to transcribe verdict – decision of a jury
doc, doct	to teach	docile – easily instructed indoctrinate – to instruct
domin	to rule	dominate – to rule dominion – territory of rule
duc, duct	to lead	conduct – act of guiding induce – to overcome by persuasion
eu	well, good	eulogy – speech or writing in praise euphony – pleasantness or smoothness of sound

Root	Meaning	Example
fac, fact, fect, fic	to do, to make	factory – location of production fiction – something invented or imagined
fer	to bear, to carry	transfer – to move from one place to another refer – to direct to
fin	end, limit	infinity – unlimited finite – limited in quantity
flect, flex	to bend	flexible – easily bent reflect – to throw back
fort	luck	fortunate – lucky fortuitous – happening by chance
fort	strong	fortify – strengthen fortress – stronghold
frag, fract	break	fragile – easily broken fracture – break
fug	flee	fugitive – fleeing refugee – one who flees to a place of safety
gen	class, race	engender – to breed generic – of a general nature in regard to all members
grad, gress	to go, to step	regress – to go back graduate – to divide into regular steps
gram, graph	writing	telegram – message sent by telegraph autograph – person's handwriting or signature
ject	to throw	projectile – capable of being thrown reject – to throw away
leg	law	legitimate – lawful legal – defined by law
leg, lig, lect	to choose, gather, read	illegible – incapable of being read election – the act of choosing

Root	Meaning	Example
liber	free	liberal – favoring freedom of ideals
		liberty – freedom from restraint
log	study, speech	archaeology – study of human antiquities
		prologue – address spoken before a performance
luc, lum	light	translucent – slightly transparent
		illuminate – to light up
magn	large, great	magnify – to make larger
		magnificent – great
mal, male	bad, wrong	malfunction – to operate incorrectly
		malevolent – evil
mar	sea	marine – pertaining to the sea
		submarine – below the surface of the sea
mater, matr	mother	maternal – motherly
		matriarch – government exercised by a mother
mit, miss	to send	transmit – to send from one person or place to another
		mission – the act of sending
morph	shape	metamorphosis – a changing in shape
		anthropomorphic – having a human shape
mut	change	mutable – subject to change
		mutate – to change a vowel
nat	born	innate – inborn
		native – a person born in a place
neg	deny	negative – expressing denial
		renege – to deny
nom	name	nominate – to put forward a name
		anonymous – no name given
nov	new	novel – new
		renovate – to make as good as new

Root	Meaning	Example
omni	all	omnipotent – all powerful omnipresent – all present
oper	to work	operate – to work on something cooperate – to work with others
pass, path	to feel	pathetic – affecting the tender emotions passionate – moved by strong emotion
pater, patr	father	paternal – fatherly patriarch – government exercised by a father
ped, pod	foot	pedestrian – one who travels on foot podiatrist – foot doctor
pel, puls	to drive, to push	impel – to drive forward compulsion – irresistible force
phil	love	philharmonic – loving harmony or music philanthropist – one who loves and seeks to do good for others
port	carry	export – to carry out of the country portable – able to be carried
psych	mind	psychology – study of the mind psychiatrist – specialist in mental disorders
quer, ques, quir, quis	to ask	inquiry – to ask about question – that which is asked
rid, ris	to laugh	ridiculous – laughable derision – to mock
rupt	to break	interrupt – to break in upon erupt – to break through
sci	to know	science – systematic knowledge of physical or natural phenomena conscious – having inward knowledge
scrib, script	to write	transcribe – to write over again script – text of words

Root	Meaning	Example
sent, sens	to feel, to think	sentimental – feel great emotion sensitive – easily affected by changes
sequ, secut	to follow	sequence – connected series consecutive – following one another in unbroken order
solv, solu, solut	to loosen	dissolve – to break up absolute – without restraint
spect	to look at	spectator – one who watches inspect – to look at closely
spir	to breathe	inspire – to breathe in respiration – process of breathing
string, strict	to bind	stringent – binding strongly restrict – to restrain within bounds
stru, struct	to build	misconstrue – to interpret wrongly construct – to build
tang, ting, tact, tig	to touch	tangent – touching, but not intersecting contact – touching
ten, tent, tain	to hold	tenure – holding of office contain – to hold
term	to end	terminate – to end terminal – having an end
terr	earth	terrain – tract of land terrestrial – existing on earth
therm	heat	thermal – pertaining to heat thermometer – instrument for measuring temperature
tort, tors	to twist	contortionist – one who twists violently torsion – act of turning or twisting
tract	to pull, to draw	attract – draw toward distract – to draw away

Root	Meaning	Example
vac	empty	vacant – empty evacuate – to empty out
ven, vent	to come	prevent – to stop from coming intervene – to come between
ver	true	verify – to prove to be true veracious – truthful
verb	word	verbose – use of excess words verbatim – word for word
vid, vis	to see	video – picture phase of television vision – act of seeing external objects
vinc, vict, vang	to conquer	invincible – unconquerable victory – defeat of enemy
viv, vit	life	vital – necessary to life vivacious – lively
voc	to call	provocative – serving to excite or stimulate to action vocal – uttered by voice
vol	to wish, to will	involuntary – outside the control of will volition – the act of willing or choosing

Suffix

Suffix	Meaning	Example
-able, -ble	capable of	believable – capable of believing legible – capable of being read
-acious, -icious, -ous	full of	vivacious – full of life wondrous – full of wonder
-ant, -ent	full of	eloquent – full of eloquence expectant – full of expectation
-ary	connected with	honorary – for the sake of honor disciplinary – enforcing instruction

Suffix	Meaning	Example
-ate	to make	ventilate – to make public consecrate – to dedicate
-fy	to make	magnify – to make larger testify – to make witness
-ile	pertaining to, capable of	docile – capable of being managed easily civil – pertaining to a city or state
-ism	belief, ideal	conservationism – ideal of keeping safe sensationalism – matter, language designed to excite
-ist	doer	artist – one who creates art pianist – one who plays the piano
-ose	full of	verbose – full of words grandiose – striking, imposing
-osis	condition	neurosis – nervous condition psychosis – psychological condition
-tude	state	magnitude – state of greatness multitude – state of quantity

Figures of Speech

Figurative language helps to create imaginative and detailed writing. A figure of speech is used in the imaginative rather than the literal sense. It helps the reader to make connections between the writer's thoughts and the external world. Knowing the different types of figures of speech can help you determine the context in which a word is being used and, thereby, help you determine the meaning of that word. The following are some commonly used figures of speech.

Simile

A simile is an explicit comparison between two things. The comparison is made by using *like* and *as.*

Her hair was *like* straw.

The blanket was *as* white as snow.

Metaphor

Like the simile, the metaphor likens two things. However, *like* or *as* are not used in the comparison.

"All the world's a stage." Shakespeare

Grass is nature's blanket.

A common error is the mixed metaphor. This occurs when a writer uses two inconsistent metaphors in a single expression.

The blanket of snow clutched the earth with icy fingers.

Hyperbole

A hyperbole is a deliberate overstatement or exaggeration used to express an idea.

I have told you a thousand times not to play with matches.

Personification

Personification is the attribution of human qualities to an object, animal, or idea.

The wind laughed at their attempts to catch the flying papers.

Interpretation of Graphic Information Questions

Although graphs, charts, and tables will not play a large part on the TASP, you should be familiar with them. More than likely, you will encounter at least one passage that is accompanied by some form of graphic information. You will then be required to answer any question(s) based on the interpretation of the information presented in the graph, chart, or table.

Graphs are used to produce visual aids for given sets of information. Often, the impact of numbers and statistics is diminished by an overabundance of tedious numbers. A graph helps a reader visualize rapid or irregular information, as well as trace long periods of decline or increase. The following is a guide to reading the three principal graphic forms which you will encounter when taking the TASP test.

Line Graphs

Line graphs, like the one that follows, are used to track two elements of one or more subjects. One element is usually a time factor, over whose span the other element increases, decreases, or fluctuates. The lines which compose such a graph are composed of connected points that follow the chart through each integral stage. For example, look at the following graph.

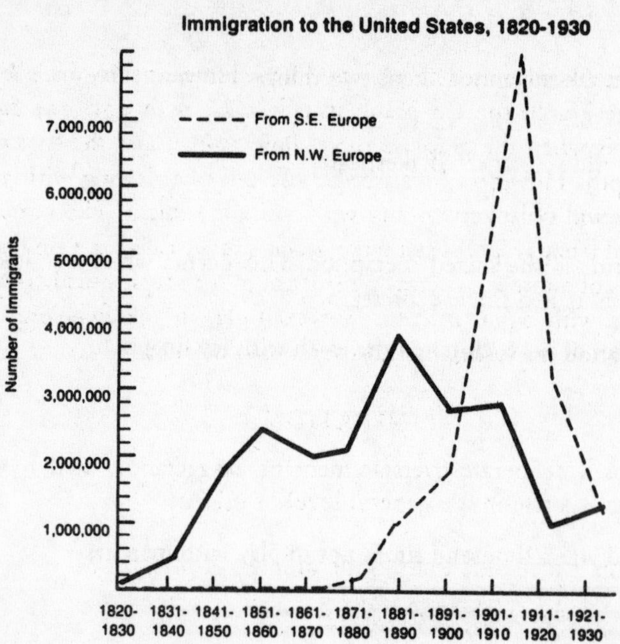

Source: Immigration and Naturalization Service of the U.S. Dept. of Justice

The average number of immigrants from 1820-1830 is represented at one point; the average number of immigrants from 1831-1840 is represented at the next. The line which connects these points is used only to ease the visual gradation between the points. It is not meant to give an accurate degree for every year between the two decades. If this were so, the line would hardly represent a straight, even progression from year to year. The sharp directness of the lines reveals otherwise. The purpose of the graph is to plot the average increases or decreases from point to point. When dealing with more than one subject, the line graph must use either different color lines (or different types of lines if the graph is black-and-white). In the graph, the dark bold line represents immigration from Northwestern Europe; the broken line represents immigration from Southeastern Europe.

To read a line graph, find the point of change that interests you. For example, if you want to trace immigration from Northwestern Europe from 1861-1870, you would find the position of the dark line on that point. Next, trace the position to the vertical information on the chart. In this instance, one would discover that approximately 2,000,000 immigrants arrived from Northwestern Europe in the period of time from 1861-1870. If wishing to discover when the number of immigrants reached 4,000,000, you would read across from 4,000,000 on the vertical side of the graph, and see that this number was reached in 1881-1890 from Northwestern Europe, and somewhere over the two decades from 1891-1910 from Southeastern Europe.

Bar Graphs

Bar graphs are likewise used to plot two dynamic elements of a subject. However, unlike a line graph, the bar graph usually deals with only one subject. The exception to this is when the graph is three-dimensional, and the bars take on the dimension of depth. However, because we will only be dealing with two-dimensional graphs, we will only be working with a single subject. The other difference between a line and a bar graph is that a bar graph usually calls for a single element to be traced in terms of another, whereas a reader of a line graph usually plots either of the two elements with equal interest. For example, in the following bar graph, inflation and deflation are being marked over a span of years.

INFLATION

Inflation is a rise in the general level of prices.

Deflation is a decline in the general level of prices.

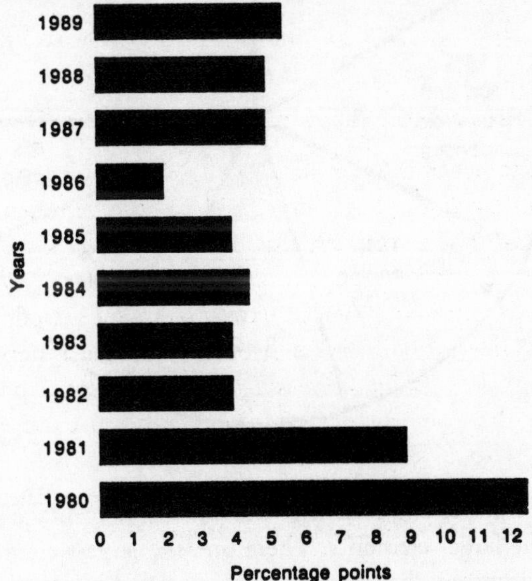

Percentage points are assigned to each year's level of prices, and that percentage decreases (deflation) from 1980 to 1981, and from 1981 to 1982. The price level is static from 1982 to 1983. The price level then increases (inflation) from 1983 to 1984. Therefore, it is obvious that the bar graph is read strictly in terms of the changes exhibited over a period of time or against some other element. A line graph, conversely, is used to plot two dynamic elements of equal interest to the reader (e.g., either number of immigrants or the particular decade in question).

To read a bar graph, simply begin at the element at the base of a bar, and trace the bar its full length. Once reaching its length, cross-reference the other element of information which matches the length of the bar.

Pie Charts

Pie charts differ greatly from line or bar graphs. Pie charts are used to help a reader visualize percentages of information with many elements to the subject. An entire "pie" represents 100% of a given quantity of information. The pie is then sliced into measurements that correspond to their respective shares of the 100%. For example, in this pie chart, Myrna's Rent occupies a slice greater than any other in the pie, because no other element equals or exceeds 25% of Myrna's Monthly Budget.

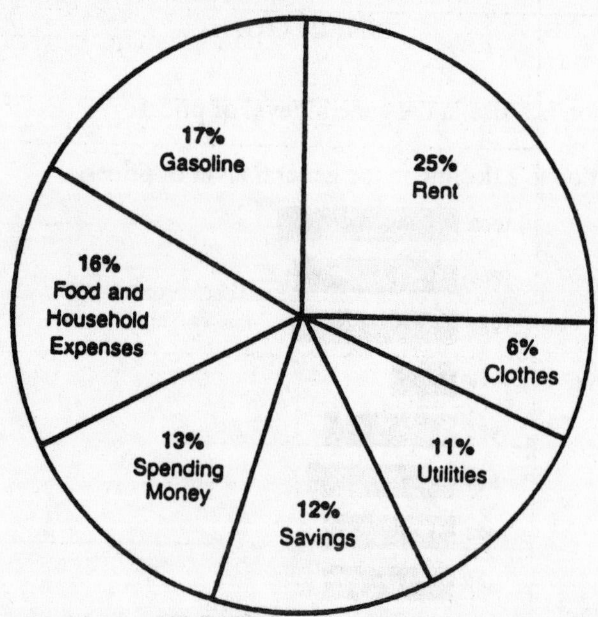

Another aspect of pie charts is that the smaller percentage elements are moved consecutively to the larger elements. Therefore, the largest element in the chart will necessarily be adjacent to the smallest element in the chart, and the line which separates them is the beginning or endpoint of the chart. From this point the chart fans out to the other elements of the chart, going from the smallest percentages to the largest.

To read a pie chart, choose the element of the subject which interests you, and compare its size to those of the other elements. In cases where the elements are similar in size, do not assume they are equal. The exact percentage of the element will be listed within that slice of the chart. For example, Myrna's Utilities, Savings, and Spending Money are all similar in size, but it is clear when reading the chart that each possesses a different value.

Reading Tables

Tables, such as the one that follows, are useful because they relate to large bodies of information within a confined area. To read a table, cross index the headings that run horizontally across the top of the table with the headings that run vertically down the left side of the table. Scanning the table for the overall information within is usually done by reading line by line as if reading regular text, while referring to the appropriate headings at the top of the table. Some tables have horizontal subheadings that clarify the separation of different areas of information.

Summary of Plant Tissues

Tissue	Location	Functions
Epidermal	Root	Protection; Increases absorption area
	Stem	Protection; Reduces H_2O loss
	Leaf	Protection; Reduces H_2O loss; Regulates gas exchange
Parenchyma	Root, stem, leaf	Storage of food and H_2O
Sclerenchyma	Stem and leaf	Support
Chlorenchyma	Leaf and young stems	Photosynthesis
Vascular a. Xylem	Root, stem, leaf	Upward transport of fluid
b. Phloem	Leaf, root, stem	Downward transport of fluid
Meristematic	Root and stem	Growth; Formation of xylem, phloem, and other tissues

To use the table above, one should simply choose a particular plant tissue and then find the appropriate information needed about that tissue through the headings listed at the top of the table. For example, the one function of chlorenchyma tissue is photosynthesis.

Helpful Hints

You should approach any graphic information you encounter as a key to a larger body of information in abbreviated form. Be sure to use the visual aids of the graphics (e.g., the size of slices on pie charts) as aids only; do not ignore the written information listed on the graph, table, etc. Note especially the title and headings so that you know exactly what it is you are looking at. Also, be aware of the source of the information, where applicable. Know what each element of the graphic information represents; this will help you compare how drastic or subtle any changes are, and over what span of time they take place. Be sure you realize what the actual numbers represent, whether it be dollars, thousands of people, millions of shares, etc. Finally, note how the graphic information relates to the text it seeks to illustrate; then, ascertain the ways in which the graphic information supports what the author has to say.

The following drills will help you to reinforce the material you have just reviewed. Carefully answer all of the questions, and check your choices against the explanations.

☞ Drill 14: Reading Comprehension

Read the passage and answer the questions that follow.

Water

1 The most important source of sediment is earth and rock material carried to the sea by rivers and streams; the same materials may also have been transported by glaciers and winds. Other sources are volcanic ash and lava, shells and skeletons of organisms, chemical precipitates formed in seawater, and particles from outer space.

2 Water is a most unusual substance because it exists on the surface of the earth in its three physical states: ice, water, and water vapor. There are other substances that might exist in a solid and liquid or gaseous state at temperatures normally found at the earth's surface, but there are fewer substances which occur in all three states.

3 Water is odorless, tasteless, and colorless. It is the only substance known to exist in a natural state as a solid, liquid, or gas on the surface of the earth. It is a universal solvent. Water does not corrode, rust, burn, or separate into its components easily. It is chemically indestructible. It can corrode almost any metal and erode the most solid rock. A unique property of water is that it expands and floats on water when frozen or in the solid state. Water has a freezing point of 0°C and a boiling point of 100°C. Water has the capacity for absorbing great quantities of heat with relatively little increase in temperature. When ***distilled***, water is a poor conductor of electricity but when salt is added, it is a good conductor of electricity.

4 Sunlight is the source of energy for temperature change, evaporation, and currents for water movement through the atmosphere. Sunlight controls the rate of photosynthesis for all marine plants, which are directly or indirectly the source of food for all marine animals. Migration, breeding, and other behaviors of marine animals are affected by light.

5 Water, as the ocean or sea, is blue because of the molecular scattering of the sunlight. Blue light, being of short wavelength, is scattered more effectively than light of longer wavelengths. Variations in color may be caused by particles suspended in the water, water depth, cloud cover, temperature, and other variable factors. Heavy concentrations of dissolved materials cause a yellowish hue, while algae will cause the water to look green. Heavy populations of plant and animal materials will cause the water to look brown.

1. Which of the following lists of topics best organizes the information in the selection?

    (A) I. Water as vapor
        II. Water as ice
        III. Water as solid

    (B) I. Properties of seawater
        II. Freezing and boiling points of water
        III. Photosynthesis
        IV. Oceans and seas

    (C) I. Water as substance
        II. Water's corrosion
        III. Water and plants
        IV. Water and algae coloration

    (D) I. Water's physical states
        II. Properties of water
        III. Effects of the sun on water
        IV. Reasons for color variation in water

2. According to the passage, what is the most unique property of water?

    (A) Water is odorless, tasteless, and colorless.

    (B) Water exists on the surface of the earth in three physical states.

    (C) Water is chemically indestructible.

    (D) Water is a poor conductor of electricity.

3. Which of the following best defines the word ***distilled*** as it is used in the last sentence of the third paragraph?

(A) Free of salt content

(B) Free of electrical energy

(C) Dehydrated

(D) Containing wine

4. The writer's main purpose in this selection is to

(A) explain the colors of water.

(B) examine the effects of the sun on water.

(C) define the properties of water.

(D) describe the three physical states of all liquids.

5. The writer of this selection would most likely agree with which of the following statements?

(A) The properties of water are found in most other liquids on this planet.

(B) Water should not be consumed in its most natural state.

(C) Water might be used to serve many different functions.

(D) Water is too unpredictable for most scientists.

Read the passage and answer the questions that follow.

The Beginnings of the Submarine

1 A submarine was first used as an offensive weapon during the American Revolutionary War. The Turtle, a one-man submersible designed by an American inventor named David Bushnell and hand-operated by a screw propeller, attempted to sink a British man-of-war in New York Harbor. The plan was to attach a charge of gunpowder to the ship's bottom with screws and explode it with a time fuse. After repeated failures to force the screws through the copper sheathing of the hull of H.M.S. Eagle, the submarine gave up and withdrew, exploding its powder a short distance from the Eagle. Although the attack was unsuccessful, it caused the British to move their blockading ships from the harbor to the outer bay.

2 On 17 February 1864, a Confederate craft, a hand-propelled submersible, carrying a crew of eight men, sank a Federal corvette that was blockading Charleston Harbor. The hit was accomplished by a torpedo suspended ahead of the Confederate Hunley as she rammed the Union frigate Housatonic, and is the first recorded instance of a submarine sinking a warship.

3 The submarine first became a major component in naval warfare during World War I, when Germany demonstrated its full potential. Wholesale sinking of Allied

shipping by the German U-boats almost swung the war in favor of the Central Powers. Then, as now, the submarine's greatest advantage was that it could operate beneath the ocean surface where detection was difficult. Sinking a submarine was comparatively easy, once it was found — but finding it before it could attack was another matter.

4 During the closing months of World War I, the Allied Submarine Devices Investigation Committee was formed to obtain from science and technology more effective underwater detection equipment. The committee developed a reasonably accurate device for locating a submerged submarine. This device was a trainable hydrophone, which was attached to the bottom of the ASW ship, and used to detect screw noises and other sounds that came from a submarine. Although the committee disbanded after World War I, the British made improvements on the locating device during the interval between then and World War II, and named it ASDIC after the committee.

5 American scientists further improved on the device, calling it SONAR, a name derived from the underlined initials of the words sound navigation and ranging.

6 At the end of World War II, the United States improved the snorkel (a device for bringing air to the crew and engines when operating submerged on diesels) and developed the Guppy (short for greater underwater propulsion power), a conversion of the fleet-type submarine of World War II fame. The superstructure was changed by reducing the surface area, streamlining every protruding object, and enclosing the periscope shears in a streamlined metal fairing. Performance increased greatly with improved electronic equipment, additional battery capacity, and the addition of the snorkel.

6. The passage implies that one of the most pressing modifications needed for the submarine was to

   (A) streamline its shape.

   (B) enlarge the submarine for accommodating more torpedoes and men.

   (C) reduce the noise caused by the submarine.

   (D) add a snorkel.

7. It is inferred that

   (A) ASDIC was formed to obtain technology for underwater detection.

   (B) ASDIC developed an accurate device for locating submarines.

   (C) the hydrophone was attached to the bottom of the ship.

   (D) ASDIC was formed to develop technology to defend U.S. shipping.

8. SONAR not only picked up the sound of submarines moving through the water but also

(A) indicated the speed at which the sub was moving.

(B) gave the location of the submarine.

(C) indicated the speed of the torpedo.

(D) placed the submarine within a specified range.

9. According to the passage, the submarine's success was due in part to its ability to

(A) strike and escape undetected.

(B) move swifter than other vessels.

(C) submerge to great depths while being hunted.

(D) run silently.

10. From the passage, one can infer

(A) David Bushnell was indirectly responsible for the sinking of the Federal corvette in Charlestown Harbor.

(B) David Bushnell invented the Turtle.

(C) the Turtle was a one-man submarine.

(D) the Turtle sank the Eagle on February 17, 1864.

Read the passage and answer the questions that follow.

Immigration

1 The influx of immigrants that America had been experiencing slowed during the conflicts with France and England, but the flow increased between 1815 and 1837, when an economic downturn sharply reduced their numbers. Thus, the overall rise in population during these years was due more to incoming foreigners than to natural increase. Most of the newcomers were from Britain, Germany, and southern Ireland. The Germans usually fared best, since they brought more money and more skills. Discrimination was common in the job market, primarily directed against the Catholics. "Irish Need Not Apply" signs were common. However, the persistent labor shortage prevented the natives from totally excluding the foreign elements. These newcomers huddled in ethnic neighborhoods in the cities, or those who could moved on West to try their hand at farming.

2 In 1790, 5% of the U.S. population lived in cities of 2,500 or more. By 1860, that figure had risen to 25%. This rapid urbanization created an array of problems.

3 The rapid growth in urban areas was not matched by the growth of services. Clean water, trash removal, housing, and public transportation all lagged behind, and the wealthy got them first. Bad water and poor sanitation produced poor health,

SOURCES OF IMMIGRATION, 1820 – 1840

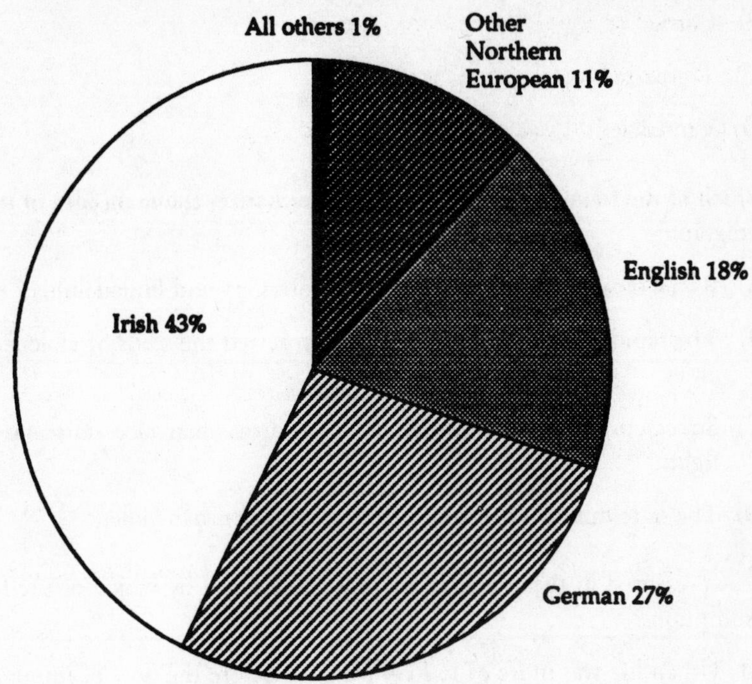

and epidemics of typhoid fever, typhus, and cholera were common. Police and fire protection were usually inadequate and the development of professional forces was resisted because of the cost and the potential for political patronage and corruption.

4 Rapid growth helped to produce a wave of violence in the cities. In New York City in 1834, the Democrats fought the Whigs with such vigor that the state militia had to be called in. New York and Philadelphia witnessed race riots in the mid-1830s, and a New York mob ***sacked*** a Catholic convent in 1834. In the 1830s, 115 major incidents of mob violence were recorded. Street crime was common in all the major cities.

11. The author's purpose for writing this essay is

    (A) to bring to light the poor treatment of immigrants.

    (B) to show the violent effects of overpopulation.

    (C) to trace the relation of immigration to the problems of rapid urban growth.

    (D) to dissuade an active life in big cities.

12. Which of the following best defines the word ***sacked*** as it is used in the last paragraph?

(A) Robbed

(B) Carried

(C) Trespassed on

(D) Vandalized

13. Which of the following statements best summarizes the main idea of the fourth paragraph?

    (A) Racial tensions caused riots in New York City and Philadelphia.

    (B) The rapid growth in urban population sewed the seeds of violence in U.S. cities.

    (C) Street crimes were far worse in urban areas than race riots and political fights.

    (D) The state militia was responsible for curbing urban violence.

14. Ideas presented in the selection are most influenced by which of the following assumptions?

    (A) Urban life was more or less controllable before the flow of immigration in 1820.

    (B) The British had more skills than the Irish.

    (C) Ethnic neighborhoods had always been a part of American society.

    (D) France and England often held conflicts.

15. According to the graph, from 1820–1840

    (A) there were more Irish immigrants than all other nationalities combined.

    (B) the combined number of immigrants from England and Germany exceeded those from Ireland.

    (C) 1% of the immigrants were from Italy.

    (D) there were an equal number of English and German immigrants.

READING DRILLS

ANSWER KEY

Drill 1
1. (J)
2. (G)
3. (A)
4. (C)
5. (H)
6. (B)
7. (I)
8. (D)
9. (F)
10. (E)
11. (D)
12. (C)
13. (A)
14. (E)
15. (B)

Drill 2
1. (D)
2. (G)
3. (I)
4. (F)
5. (A)
6. (J)
7. (E)
8. (C)
9. (B)
10. (H)
11. (D)
12. (A)
13. (B)
14. (E)
15. (C)

Drill 3
1. (E)
2. (H)
3. (J)
4. (A)
5. (I)
6. (B)
7. (C)
8. (G)
9. (F)
10. (D)
11. (C)
12. (A)
13. (E)
14. (D)
15. (B)

Drill 4
1. (D)
2. (E)
3. (A)
4. (I)
5. (J)
6. (B)
7. (C)
8. (F)
9. (H)
10. (G)
11. (D)
12. (A)
13. (B)
14. (C)
15. (E)

Drill 5
1. (H)
2. (F)
3. (A)
4. (B)
5. (J)
6. (C)
7. (I)
8. (E)
9. (D)
10. (G)
11. (B)
12. (D)
13. (A)
14. (E)
15. (C)

Drill 6
1. (G)
2. (A)
3. (E)
4. (J)
5. (C)
6. (B)
7. (D)
8. (I)
9. (F)
10. (H)
11. (D)
12. (E)
13. (A)
14. (C)
15. (B)

Drill 7

1. (F)
2. (E)
3. (A)
4. (B)
5. (H)
6. (I)
7. (C)
8. (G)
9. (D)
10. (J)
11. (B)
12. (E)
13. (D)
14. (C)
15. (A)

Drill 8

1. (D)
2. (A)
3. (H)
4. (G)
5. (B)
6. (C)
7. (E)
8. (I)
9. (F)
10. (J)
11. (C)
12. (B)
13. (A)
14. (E)
15. (D)

Drill 9

1. (D)
2. (I)
3. (G)
4. (A)
5. (J)
6. (E)
7. (B)
8. (F)
9. (C)
10. (H)
11. (A)
12. (D)
13. (B)
14. (E)
15. (C)

Drill 10

1. (H)
2. (I)
3. (E)
4. (A)
5. (J)
6. (B)
7. (F)
8. (C)
9. (D)
10. (G)
11. (B)
12. (D)
13. (A)
14. (C)
15. (E)

Drill 11

1. (F)
2. (I)
3. (A)
4. (H)
5. (B)
6. (J)
7. (C)
8. (D)
9. (E)
10. (G)
11. (C)
12. (B)
13. (E)
14. (A)
15. (D)

Drill 12

1. (J)
2. (A)
3. (B)
4. (I)
5. (C)
6. (H)
7. (D)
8. (G)
9. (F)
10. (E)
11. (E)
12. (C)
13. (D)
14. (A)
15. (B)

Drill 13

1. (C)	16. (B)	31. (A)	46. (A)
2. (B)	17. (B)	32. (B)	47. (D)
3. (A)	18. (C)	33. (E)	48. (C)
4. (E)	19. (E)	34. (A)	49. (E)
5. (A)	20. (D)	35. (E)	50. (A)
6. (E)	21. (E)	36. (D)	51. (B)
7. (E)	22. (A)	37. (D)	52. (E)
8. (B)	23. (D)	38. (A)	53. (C)
9. (E)	24. (A)	39. (E)	54. (A)
10. (C)	25. (C)	40. (C)	55. (B)
11. (B)	26. (B)	41. (E)	56. (C)
12. (E)	27. (D)	42. (B)	57. (D)
13. (A)	28. (C)	43. (A)	58. (E)
14. (C)	29. (E)	44. (E)	59. (D)
15. (D)	30. (D)	45. (B)	60. (C)

Drill 14 – Reading Comprehension

1. **(D)** The correct response is (D) because its precepts are summations of each of the composition's main paragraphs. (A) only mentions points made in the second paragraph. (B) and (C) only mention scattered points made throughout the passage, each of which does not represent a larger body of information within the passage.

2. **(B)** The second paragraph states that this is the reason that water is a most unusual substance. (A) and (C) list unusual properties of water, but are not developed in the same manner as the property stated in (B). (D) is not even correct under all circumstances.

3. **(A)** The sentence contrasts distilled water to that which contains salt, so (A) is correct. (B), (C), and (D) are not implied by the passage.

4. **(C)** The writer's didactic summary of water's properties is the only perspective found in the passage. (A) and (B) are the subjects of individual paragraphs within the passage, but hardly represent the entire passage itself. An in-depth discussion of the physical states of liquids (D) is not offered within the passage.

5. **(C)** The correct choice is (C) because of the many properties of water ascribed to it in the passage, each of which might serve one practical purpose or another. (A) and (D) are contradicted within the passage, while (B) is not implied at all by the passage.

6. **(A)** Answer (A) is correct because of the importance of streamlining mentioned in the final paragraph. (B) and (C) are not suggested in the paragraph, and (D) is secondary in importance to (A).

7. **(D)** Since it may be inferred from the general purpose of underwater detection equipment, (D) is correct. While (A) and (B) are true statements, they are not inferences. (C) is not implied in the passage.

8. **(D)** Answer (D) is correct because the "R" in SONAR stands for "Ranging." (A), (B), and (C) are neither mentioned nor implied by the passage.

9. **(A)** As was mentioned in the third sentence of the third paragraph, (A) is correct. (B), (C), and (D) are not mentioned in the passage.

10. **(A)** It may be inferred that Bushnell's invention led to the success of the later version of the submarine. (B) and (C) are true, but are not inferences because they are directly stated in the first paragraph. (D) is not a true statement; the Turtle had no direct link to the 1864 incident.

11. **(C)** Answer (C) is correct because it traces the development of the passage with the author's perspective in mind. While (A) and (B) are mentioned in the passage, they are not overriding concerns in the passage. (D) does not directly apply to the passage.

12. **(D)** The correct response is (D) because the incident is situated with other acts of violent aggression. (A) and (C) are not implied by the context of the mob riot situation. (B) is not implied at all by the paragraph.

13. **(B)** The correct answer is (B) because it represents a theme prevalent in the fourth paragraph. (A) and (D) represent individual strands within the paragraph, but do not express its main idea. (C) is not mentioned or implied in the paragraph.

14. **(A)** All of the urban difficulties mentioned in the passage stem from the rapid growth of immigration. (B) and (C) are not implied within the passage. (D) has no direct bearing on the development of the passage.

15. **(B)** The combined percentages of English and German immigrants equal 45% (Irish immigrants represent 43% of the graph). (A) is incorrect, because the Irish immigrants represent less than half of the graph. (C) is incorrect, because the graph nowhere implies that the "All Others" section of the graph is restricted to Italian immigrants. (D) is incorrect because the English and German percentages are unequal.

Mathematics Section Review

Chapter 3

MATHEMATICS SECTION REVIEW

I. Strategies for the Math Section

II. Arithmetic

III. Algebra

IV. Geometry

V. Word Problems

Are you ready to tackle the math section of the TASP? Well, the chances are that you will be, but only after reviewing the basic concepts in arithmetic, algebra, and geometry. The more familiar you are with these fundamental principles, the better you will do on the math section of the TASP. Our math review presents the various mathematical topics that will be tested on the TASP. Although these concepts may be ones with which you are already familiar, you should study our review to brush-up on your skills to ensure that you score well.

Along with a knowledge of these topics, speed and accuracy will also have a great effect upon your success. Therefore, memorize the directions in order to save time and decrease your chances of making careless mistakes. Make sure to also complete the practice drills which are provided, as they will help to strengthen your math skills so that you can quickly answer the questions.

In order to be successful on the math section of the TASP, you must also learn to relax. However, to be relaxed you must feel at ease with the test material. If you come into contact with unusual or confusing math problems, don't panic. Our math strategies can help increase your chances of answering the questions correctly. The methods that we provide consist of specific and accurate tips which illustrate for you the best way to approach particular math problems. These hints will pick up where your math knowledge leaves off. The math strategies which are presented here will help you build the confidence you need in order to score well on this section of the test.

I. Strategies for the Math Section

Before the test, this is your plan of attack:

➤ Step 1 Read and study the directions, so that you do not waste valuable time learning them on the day of the exam. This will allow you to simply skim them as you begin the test. The directions will appear similar to the following.

> **DIRECTIONS:** In this section, you will encounter between 40 and 50 multiple-choice questions. Only **ONE** answer to each question is the **best** answer, although more than one answer may appear to be correct. Choose your answers carefully and mark them on your answer sheet. Make sure that the space you are marking corresponds to the answer you have chosen. You may use the provided Reference Table in making your calculations.

If you know how to solve the problem, this is your plan of attack:

> Solve for x:
>
> $3x + 4(x + 1) = 11$
>
> (A) –1 (B) 0
>
> (C) 3/4 (D) 1

➤ Step 1 Calculate the answer as quickly as possible.

$$3x + 4x + 4 = 11$$
$$7x + 4 + (-4) = 11 + (-4)$$
$$7x = 7$$
$$x = 1$$

➤ Step 2 Find your answer among the answer choices.

The answer is (D).

If you do not know how to solve the problem, this is your plan of attack:

> A computer generates three consecutive even integers each time it is turned on. If the sum of the three numbers is 54, what is the value of the largest number?
>
> (A) 10 (B) 14
>
> (C) 20 (D) 24

➤ Step 1 Determine what the question is asking.

This question is asking you to find the largest of three even, consecutive integers.

➤ Step 2 Try to formulate an equation that solves for the unknown value using all the necessary information given in the question. Look at the answer choices and eliminate any that are obviously wrong.

Let x = the first even integer

Let $x + 2$ = the second even integer

Let $x + 4$ = the third even integer (the largest)

Therefore,

$x + (x + 2) + (x + 4) = 54$

By immediately looking at the answer choices, we see that (A) is obviously wrong since if 10 were correct, the other two numbers would be 6 and 8 which, when added together, equal only 24.

➤ Step 3 Plug in the remaining answer choices to find the correct answer.

Plugging in the other choices, we find:

If $x + 4 = 14$, then $x = 10$. Therefore, $10 + 12 + 14$ would have to equal 54. However, it only equals 36.

If $x + 4 = 20$, then $x = 16$. Therefore, $16 + 18 + 20$ would have to equal 54. It does and, therefore, (C) is the correct answer.

➤ Step 4 If you cannot formulate an equation, try to make an educated guess among the remaining answer choices.

Additional Tips

- Know all important formulas and concepts in the Mathematics Review.
- Draw sketches. This allows you to visualize exactly what the question is asking and what information you need to find.
- Always look at the answer choices before trying to work out the problem. If all the choices are in a specific format, you would want to do your work in the same format. For example, if the measurements in a problem are given in feet, but the answer choices are given in inches, you must change the feet to inches when working out the problem.
- Remember to work in only one unit and convert if more than one is presented in the problem. For example, if a problem gives numbers in

decimals and fractions, convert one in terms of the other and then work out the problem.

- Avoid lengthy computations. If a problem is taking a long time to figure out, go on to another question and come back to it if time remains.

- Do not panic if something looks unusual; it may be easy.

- Use the test booklet—draw on diagrams.

- When given specific information for a problem, immediately plug these values into your equation.

- Be suspicious of choices that seem too obvious unless it is an easy level question. Many times choices will appear that are simply repetitions of numbers used in the problem. If the question is medium or hard, the chances are that these answers are incorrect.

- After working out an equation, make sure your result is actually answering the question. Otherwise, you may have to perform some extra steps. For example, although you may solve an equation for a specific variable, this may not be the final answer. You may have to use this answer to find another quantity.

Find the greatest of three consecutive integers whose sum is 36.

(A) 11 (B) 13

(C) 15 (D) 17

Let x = the first integer

Let $x + 1$ = the second integer

Let $x + 2$ = the third integer

$$x + (x + 1) + (x + 2) = 36$$

$$3x + 3 = 36$$

$$3x = 33$$

$$x = 11$$

Although $x = 11$ and answer choice (A) is 11, this is not the correct answer. The question asks for the *greatest* of three consecutive integers. Eleven is the smallest. Therefore, 11 must be plugged into $(x + 2)$ in order to find the greatest integer which is 13.

TASP MATH TOPICS

The topics listed below should be reviewed in order to accurately answer the questions on the Math Section of the TASP. See the math review on the following pages.

ARITHMETIC

1. Integers and Real Numbers
2. Fractions
3. Exponents
4. Order of Operations
5. Decimals
6. Percentages
7. Radicals
8. Averages

ALGEBRA

1. Operations with Polynomials
2. Simplifying Algebraic Expressions
3. Linear Equations
4. Two Linear Equations
5. Quadratic Equations
6. Absolute Value Equations
7. Inequalities
8. Ratios and Proportions

GEOMETRY

1. Points, Lines, and Angles
2. Regular Polygons
3. Triangles
4. Quadrilaterals
5. Circles
6. Solids
7. Coordinate Geometry

WORD PROBLEMS

1. Algebraic
2. Rate
3. Work
4. Mixture
5. Interest
6. Discount
7. Profit
8. Sets
9. Geometry
10. Measurement
11. Data Interpretation
12. Combination of Mathematical Skills

II. Arithmetic

1. Integers and Real Numbers

Most of the numbers used in algebra belong to a set called the **real numbers** or **reals**. This set can be represented graphically by the real number line.

Given the number line below, we arbitrarily fix a point and label it with the number 0. In a similar manner, we can label any point on the line with one of the real numbers, depending on its position relative to 0. Numbers to the right of 0 are positive, while those to the left are negative. Value increases from left to right, so that if *a* is to the right of *b*, it is said to be greater than *b*.

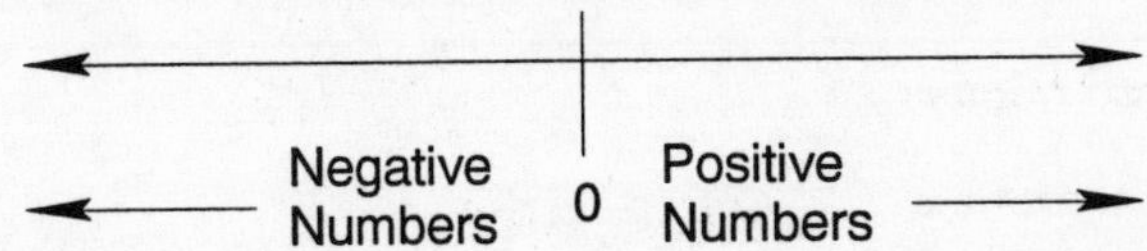

If we now divide the number line into equal segments, we can label the points on this line with real numbers. For example, the point 2 lengths to the left of 0 is – 2, while the point 3 lengths to the right of 0 is + 3 (the + sign is usually assumed, so + 3 is written simply as 3). The number line now looks like this:

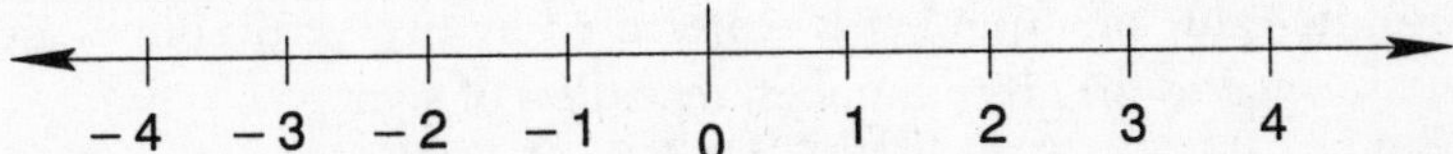

These boundary points represent the subset of the reals known as the **integers**. The set of integers is made up of both the positive and negative whole numbers:

$\{\ldots, -4, -3, -2, -1, 0, 1, 2, 3, 4, \ldots\}$.

Some subsets of integers are:

Natural Numbers or Positive Numbers—the set of integers starting with 1 and increasing:

$\mathcal{N} = \{1, 2, 3, 4, \ldots\}$.

Whole Numbers—the set of integers starting with 0 and increasing:

$\mathcal{W} = \{0, 1, 2, 3, \ldots\}$.

Negative Numbers—the set of integers starting with – 1 and decreasing:

$\mathcal{Z} = \{-1, -2, -3, \ldots\}$.

Prime Numbers—the set of positive integers greater than 1 that are divisible only by 1 and themselves:

$\{2, 3, 5, 7, 11, \ldots\}$.

Even Integers—the set of integers divisible by 2:

$\{\ldots, -4, -2, 0, 2, 4, 6, \ldots\}$.

Odd Integers—the set of integers not divisible by 2:

$\{\ldots, -3, -1, 1, 3, 5, 7, \ldots\}$.

PROBLEM

Classify each of the following numbers into as many different sets as possible. Example: real, integer ...

(1) 0 (3) $\sqrt{6}$ (5) $^2/_3$

(2) 9 (4) $^1/_2$ (6) 1.5

SOLUTION

(1) 0 is a real number and an integer.

(2) 9 is a real, natural number, and an integer.

(3) $\sqrt{6}$ is a real number.

(4) $^1/_2$ is a real number.

(5) $^2/_3$ is a real number.

(6) 1.5 is a real number and a decimal.

Absolute Value

The **absolute value** of a number is represented by two vertical lines around the number, and is equal to the given number, regardless of sign.

The absolute value of a real number A is defined as follows:

$$|A| = \begin{cases} A \text{ if } A \geq 0 \\ -A \text{ if } A < 0 \end{cases}$$

EXAMPLE

$|5| = 5, |-8| = -(-8) = 8$

Absolute values follow the given rules:

(A) $|-A| = |A|$

(B) $|A| \geq 0$, equality holding only if $A = 0$

(C) $\left|\frac{A}{B}\right| = \frac{|A|}{|B|}, B \neq 0$

(D) $|AB| = |A| \times |B|$

(E) $|A|^2 = A^2$

Absolute value can also be expressed on the real number line as the distance of the point represented by the real number from the point labeled 0.

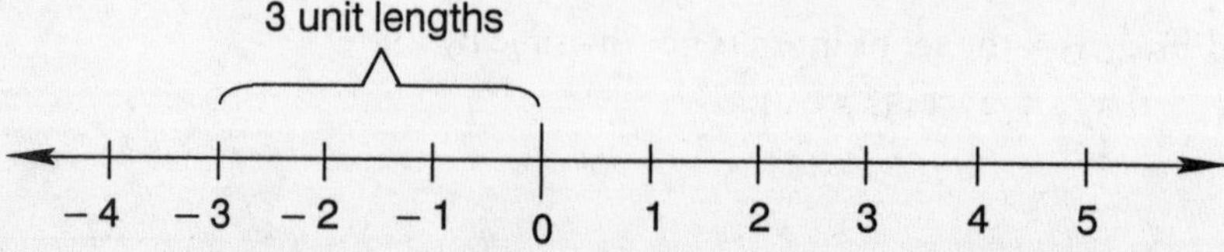

So $|-3| = 3$ because -3 is 3 units to the left of 0.

PROBLEM

Classify each of the following statements as true or false. If it is false, explain why.

(1) $|-120| > 1$

(2) $|4-12| = |4| - |12|$

(3) $|4-9| = 9-4$

(4) $|12-3| = 12-3$

(5) $|-12a| = 12|a|$

SOLUTION

(1) True

(2) False, $|4-12| = |4| - |12|$

$$|-8| = 4-12$$

$$8 \neq -8$$

In general, $|a+b| \neq |a| + |b|$

(3) True

(4) True

(5) True

PROBLEM

Find the absolute value for each of the following:

(1) 0

(2) 4

(3) $-\pi$

(4) a, where a is a real number

SOLUTION

(1) $|0| = 0$

(2) $|4| = 4$

(3) $|-\pi| = \pi$

(4) for $a > 0$, $|a| = a$

for $a = 0$, $|a| = 0$

for $a < 0$, $|a| = -a$

$$\text{i.e., } |a| = \begin{cases} a \text{ if } a > 0 \\ 0 \text{ if } a = 0 \\ -a \text{ if } a < 0 \end{cases}$$

Positive and Negative Numbers

A) **To add two numbers with like signs,** add their absolute values and write the sum with the common sign. So,

$6 + 2 = 8, (-6) + (-2) = -8$

B) **To add two numbers with unlike signs,** find the difference between their absolute values, and write the result with the sign of the number with the greater absolute value. So,

$(-4) + 6 = 2, 15 + (-19) = -4$

C) **To subtract a number *b* from another number *a*,** change the sign of *b* and add to *a*. Examples:

$10 - (3) = 10 + (-3) = 7$ (1)

$2 - (-6) = 2 + 6 = 8$ (2)

$(-5) - (-2) = (-5) + (+2) = -3$ (3)

D) **To multiply (or divide) two numbers having like signs,** multiply (or divide) their absolute values and write the result with a positive sign. Examples:

$(5)(3) = 15$ (1)

$-6 \div (-3) = 2$ (2)

E) **To multiply (or divide) two numbers having unlike signs,** multiply (or divide) their absolute values and write the result with a negative sign. Examples:

$(-2)(8) = -16$ (1)

$9 \div (-3) = -3$ (2)

According to the law of signs for real numbers, the square of a positive or negative number is always positive. This means that it is impossible to take the square root of a negative number in the real number system.

☞ Drill 1: Integers and Real Numbers

Addition

1. Simplify $4 + (-7) + 2 + (-5)$.

   (A) -6 (B) -4 (C) 0 (D) 6

2. Simplify $144 + (-317) + 213$.

   (A) -357 (B) -40 (C) 40 (D) 357

3. Simplify $|4 + (-3)| + |-2|$.

   (A) -2 (B) -1 (C) 1 (D) 3

4. What integer makes the equation $-13 + 12 + 7 + ? = 10$ a true statement?

   (A) -22 (B) -10 (C) 4 (D) 6

5. Simplify $4 + 17 + (-29) + 13 + (-22) + (-3)$.

   (A) -44 (B) -20 (C) 23 (D) 34

Subtraction

6. Simplify $319 - 428$.

   (A) -111 (B) -109 (C) -99 (D) 109

7. Simplify $91{,}203 - 37{,}904 + 1{,}073$.

   (A) 54,372 (B) 64,701 (C) 128,034 (D) 129,107

8. Simplify $|43 - 62| - |-17 - 3|$.

   (A) -39 (B) -19 (C) -1 (D) 1

9. Simplify $-(-4 - 7) + (-2)$.

   (A) -22 (B) -13 (C) -9 (D) 9

10. In the Great Smoky Mountains National Park, Mt. Le Conte rises from 1,292 feet above sea level to 6,593 feet above sea level. How tall is Mt. Le Conte?

    (A) 4,009 ft (B) 5,301 ft (C) 5,699 ft (D) 6,464 ft

Multiplication

11. Simplify $(-3) \times (-18) \times (-1)$.

    (A) -108 (B) -54 (C) -48 (D) 48

12. Simplify $|-42| \times |7|$.

    (A) -294 (B) -49 (C) 294 (D) 284

13. Simplify $(-6) \times 5 \times (-10) \times (-4) \times 0 \times 2$.

    (A) $-2{,}400$ (B) -240 (C) 0 (D) 280

14. Simplify $-|-6 \times 8|$.

(A) -48 (B) -42 (C) 2 (D) 42

15. A city in Georgia had a record low temperature of -3°F one winter. During the same year, a city in Michigan experienced a record low that was nine times the record low set in Georgia. What was the record low in Michigan that year?

(A) -31°F (B) -27°F (C) -21°F (D) -12°F

Division

16. Simplify $(-24) \div 8$.

(A) -4 (B) -3 (C) -2 (D) 3

17. Simplify $(-180) \div (-12)$.

(A) -30 (B) -15 (C) 1.5 (D) 15

18. Simplify $|-76| \div |-4|$.

(A) -21 (B) -19 (C) 13 (D) 19

19. Simplify $|216 \div (-6)|$.

(A) -36 (B) -12 (C) 36 (D) 38

20. At the end of the year, a small firm has \$2,996 in its account for bonuses. If the entire amount is equally divided among the 14 employees, how much does each one receive?

(A) \$214 (B) \$114 (C) \$170 (D) \$210

2. Fractions

The fraction, a/b, where the **numerator** is a and the **denominator** is b, implies that a is being divided by b. The denominator of a fraction can never be 0 since a number divided by 0 is not defined. If the numerator is greater than the denominator, the fraction is called an **improper fraction.** A **mixed number** is the sum of a whole number and a fraction, i.e., $4^3/_8 = 4 + {}^3/_8$.

Operations with Fractions

A) **To change a mixed number to an improper fraction,** simply multiply the whole number by the denominator of the fraction and add the numerator. This product becomes the numerator of the result and the denominator remains the same. For example,

$$5\frac{2}{3} = \frac{(5 \times 3) + 2}{3} = \frac{15 + 2}{3} = \frac{17}{3}$$

To change an improper fraction to a mixed number, simply divide the numerator by the denominator. The remainder becomes the numerator of the fractional part of the mixed number, and the denominator remains the same. For example,

$$\frac{35}{4} = 35 \div 4 = 8\frac{3}{4}$$

To check your work, change your result back to an improper fraction to see if it matches the original fraction.

B) **To find the sum of two fractions having a common denominator**, simply add together the numerators of the given fractions and put this sum over the common denominator.

$$\frac{11}{3} + \frac{5}{3} = \frac{11+5}{3} = \frac{16}{3}$$

Similarly for subtraction,

$$\frac{11}{3} - \frac{5}{3} = \frac{11-5}{3} = \frac{6}{3} = 2$$

C) **To find the sum of the two fractions having different denominators**, it is necessary to find the **lowest common denominator** (LCD) of the different denominators using a process called **factoring.**

To **factor** a number means to find two numbers that when multiplied together have a product equal to the original number. These two numbers are then said to be **factors** of the original number. For example, the factors of 6 are

(1) 1 and 6 since $1 \times 6 = 6$

(2) 2 and 3 since $2 \times 3 = 6$

Every number is the product of itself and 1. A **prime factor** is a number that does not have any factors besides itself and 1. This is important when finding the LCD of two fractions having different denominators.

To find the LCD of $^{11}/_{6}$ and $^{5}/_{16}$, we must first find the prime factors of each of the two denominators.

$6 = 2 \times 3$

$16 = 2 \times 2 \times 2 \times 2$

$\text{LCD} = 2 \times 2 \times 2 \times 2 \times 3 = 48$

Note that we do not need to repeat the 2 that appears in both the factors of 6 and 16.

Once we have determined the LCD of the denominators, each of the fractions must be converted into equivalent fractions having the LCD as a denominator.

Rewrite $^{11}/_6$ and $^5/_{16}$ to have 48 as their denominators.

$6 \times ? = 48 \qquad\qquad 16 \times ? = 48$

$6 \times 8 = 48 \qquad\qquad 16 \times 3 = 48$

If the numerator and denominator of each fraction is multiplied (or divided) by the same number, the value of the fraction will not change. This is because a fraction *b*/*b*, *b* being any number, is equal to the multiplicative identity, 1.

Therefore,

$$\frac{11}{6} \times \frac{8}{8} = \frac{88}{48} \qquad \frac{5}{16} \times \frac{3}{3} = \frac{15}{48}$$

We may now find

$$\frac{11}{6} + \frac{5}{16} = \frac{88}{48} + \frac{15}{48} = \frac{103}{48}$$

Similarly for subtraction,

$$\frac{11}{6} - \frac{5}{16} = \frac{88}{48} - \frac{15}{48} = \frac{73}{48}$$

D) **To find the product of two or more fractions,** simply multiply the numerators of the given fractions to find the numerator of the product and multiply the denominators of the given fractions to find the denominator of the product. For example,

$$\frac{2}{3} \times \frac{1}{5} \times \frac{4}{7} = \frac{2 \times 1 \times 4}{3 \times 5 \times 7} = \frac{8}{105}$$

E) **To find the quotient of two fractions,** simply invert the divisor and multiply. For example,

$$\frac{8}{9} \div \frac{1}{3} = \frac{8}{9} \times \frac{3}{1} = \frac{24}{9} = \frac{8}{3}$$

F) **To simplify a fraction** is to convert it into a form in which the numerator and denominator have no common factor other than 1. For example,

$$\frac{12}{18} = \frac{12 \div 6}{18 \div 6} = \frac{2}{3}$$

G) A **complex fraction** is a fraction whose numerator and/or denominator is made up of fractions. To simplify the fraction, find the LCD of all the fractions. Multiply both the numerator and denominator by this number and simplify.

PROBLEM

If $a = 4$ and $b = 7$, find the value of $\frac{a+\frac{a}{b}}{a-\frac{a}{b}}$.

SOLUTION

By substitution,

$$\frac{a+\frac{a}{b}}{a-\frac{a}{b}} = \frac{4+\frac{4}{7}}{4-\frac{4}{7}}$$

In order to combine the terms, we must find the LCD of 1 and 7. Since both are prime factors, the LCD = 1 × 7 = 7.

Multiplying both numerator and denominator by 7, we get

$$\frac{7\left(4+\frac{4}{7}\right)}{7\left(4-\frac{4}{7}\right)} = \frac{28+4}{28-4} = \frac{32}{24}$$

By dividing both numerator and denominator by 8, $^{32}/_{24}$ can be reduced to $^{4}/_{3}$.

☞ Drill 2: Fractions

Fractions

DIRECTIONS: Add and write the answer in simplest form.

1. $^5/_{12} + ^3/_{12} =$

   (A) $^5/_{24}$ (B) $^1/_3$ (C) $^8/_{12}$ (D) $^2/_3$

2. $^5/_8 + ^7/_8 + ^3/_8 =$

   (A) $^{15}/_{24}$ (B) $1\ ^7/_8$ (C) $^5/_6$ (D) $^7/_8$

3. $131\ ^2/_{15} + 28\ ^3/_{15} =$

   (A) $159\ ^1/_6$ (B) $159\ ^1/_5$ (C) $159\ ^1/_3$ (D) $159\ ^1/_2$

4. $3\ ^5/_{18} + 2\ ^1/_{18} + 8\ ^7/_{18} =$

   (A) $13\ ^{13}/_{18}$ (B) $13\ ^3/_4$ (C) $13\ ^7/_9$ (D) $14\ ^1/_6$

5. $17\ ^9/_{20} + 4\ ^3/_{20} + 8\ ^{11}/_{20} =$

   (A) $29\ ^{23}/_{60}$ (B) $29\ ^{23}/_{20}$ (C) $30\ ^3/_{20}$ (D) $30\ ^1/_5$

Subtract Fractions with the Same Denominator

DIRECTIONS: Subtract and write the answer in simplest form.

6. $4\,^7/_8 - 3\,^1/_8 =$

   (A) $1\,^1/_4$ (B) $1\,^3/_4$ (C) $1\,^{12}/_{16}$ (D) $1\,^7/_8$

7. $132\,^5/_{12} - 37\,^3/_{12} =$

   (A) $94\,^1/_6$ (B) $95\,^1/_{12}$ (C) $95\,^1/_6$ (D) $105\,^1/_6$

8. $19\,^1/_3 - 2\,^2/_3 =$

   (A) $16\,^2/_3$ (B) $16\,^5/_6$ (C) $17\,^1/_3$ (D) $17\,^2/_3$

9. $^8/_{21} - ^5/_{21} =$

   (A) $^1/_{21}$ (B) $^1/_7$ (C) $^3/_{21}$ (D) $^2/_7$

10. $82\,^7/_{10} - 38\,^9/_{10} =$

    (A) $43\,^4/_5$ (B) $44\,^1/_5$ (C) $44\,^2/_5$ (D) $45\,^1/_5$

Finding the LCD

DIRECTIONS: Find the lowest common denominator of each group of fractions.

11. $^2/_3$, $^5/_9$, and $^1/_6$.

    (A) 9 (B) 18 (C) 27 (D) 54

12. $^1/_2$, $^5/_6$, and $^3/_4$.

    (A) 2 (B) 4 (C) 6 (D) 12

13. $^7/_{16}$, $^5/_6$, and $^2/_3$.

    (A) 3 (B) 6 (C) 48 (D) 24

14. $^8/_{15}$, $^2/_5$, and $^{12}/_{25}$.

    (A) 5 (B) 15 (C) 25 (D) 75

15. $^2/_3$, $^1/_5$, and $^5/_6$.

    (A) 15 (B) 30 (C) 48 (D) 90

16. $^1/_3$, $^9/_{42}$, and $^4/_{21}$.

(A) 21 (B) 42 (C) 126 (D) 378

17. $^4/_9$, $^2/_5$, and $^1/_3$.

(A) 15 (B) 17 (C) 27 (D) 45

18. $^7/_{12}$, $^{11}/_{36}$, and $^1/_9$.

(A) 12 (B) 36 (C) 108 (D) 324

19. $^3/_7$, $^5/_{21}$, and $^2/_3$.

(A) 21 (B) 42 (C) 31 (D) 63

20. $^{13}/_{16}$, $^5/_8$, and $^1/_4$.

(A) 4 (B) 8 (C) 16 (D) 32

Adding Fractions with Different Denominators

DIRECTIONS: Add and write the answer in simplest form.

21. $^1/_3 + {}^5/_{12} =$

(A) $^2/_5$ (B) $^1/_2$ (C) $^9/_{12}$ (D) $^3/_4$

22. $3\,^5/_9 + 2\,^1/_3 =$

(A) $5\,^1/_2$ (B) $5\,^2/_3$ (C) $5\,^8/_9$ (D) $6\,^1/_9$

23. $12\,^9/_{16} + 17\,^3/_4 + 8\,^1/_8 =$

(A) $37\,^7/_{16}$ (B) $38\,^7/_{16}$ (C) $38\,^1/_2$ (D) $38\,^2/_3$

24. $28\,^4/_5 + 11\,^{16}/_{25} =$

(A) $39\,^2/_3$ (B) $39\,^4/_5$ (C) $40\,^9/_{25}$ (E) $40\,^{11}/_{25}$

25. $2\,^1/_8 + 1\,^3/_{16} + {}^5/_{12} =$

(A) $3\,^{35}/_{48}$ (B) $3\,^3/_4$ (C) $3\,^{19}/_{24}$ (D) $3\,^{13}/_{16}$

Subtraction with Different Denominators

DIRECTIONS: Subtract and write the answer in simplest form.

26. $8\,^9/_{12} - 2\,^2/_3 =$

(A) $6\,^1/_{12}$ (B) $6\,^1/_6$ (C) $6\,^1/_3$ (D) $6\,^7/_{12}$

27. $185\ ^{11}/_{15} - 107\ ^{2}/_{5} =$

(A) $77\ ^{2}/_{15}$ (B) $78\ ^{1}/_{5}$ (C) $78\ ^{3}/_{10}$ (D) $78\ ^{1}/_{3}$

28. $34\ ^{2}/_{3} - 16\ ^{5}/_{6} =$

(A) $17\ ^{5}/_{6}$ (B) $16\ ^{1}/_{3}$ (C) $17\ ^{1}/_{2}$ (D) 17

29. $3\ ^{11}/_{48} - 2\ ^{3}/_{16} =$

(A) $^{47}/_{48}$ (B) $1\ ^{1}/_{48}$ (C) $1\ ^{1}/_{24}$ (D) $1\ ^{8}/_{48}$

30. $81\ ^{4}/_{21} - 31\ ^{1}/_{3} =$

(A) $47\ ^{3}/_{7}$ (B) $49\ ^{6}/_{7}$ (C) $49\ ^{1}/_{6}$ (D) $49\ ^{5}/_{7}$

Multiplication

DIRECTIONS: Multiply and reduce the answer.

31. $^{2}/_{3} \times ^{4}/_{5} =$

(A) $^{6}/_{8}$ (B) $^{3}/_{4}$ (C) $^{8}/_{15}$ (D) $^{10}/_{12}$

32. $^{7}/_{10} \times ^{4}/_{21} =$

(A) $^{2}/_{15}$ (B) $^{11}/_{31}$ (C) $^{28}/_{210}$ (D) $^{1}/_{6}$

33. $5\ ^{1}/_{3} \times ^{3}/_{8} =$

(A) $^{4}/_{11}$ (B) 2 (C) $^{8}/_{5}$ (D) $5\ ^{1}/_{8}$

34. $6\ ^{1}/_{2} \times 3 =$

(A) $9\ ^{1}/_{2}$ (B) $18\ ^{1}/_{2}$ (C) $19\ ^{1}/_{2}$ (D) 20

35. $3\ ^{1}/_{4} \times 2\ ^{1}/_{3} =$

(A) $5\ ^{7}/_{12}$ (B) $6\ ^{2}/_{7}$ (C) $6\ ^{5}/_{7}$ (D) $7\ ^{7}/_{12}$

Division

DIRECTIONS: Divide and reduce the answer.

36. $^{3}/_{16} \div ^{3}/_{4} =$

(A) $^{9}/_{64}$ (B) $^{1}/_{4}$ (C) $^{6}/_{16}$ (D) $^{9}/_{16}$

37. $^{4}/_{9} \div ^{2}/_{3} =$

(A) $^{1}/_{3}$ (B) $^{1}/_{2}$ (C) $^{2}/_{3}$ (D) $^{7}/_{11}$

38. $5\,^{1}/_{4} \div ^{7}/_{10} =$

(A) $2\,^{4}/_{7}$ (B) $3\,^{27}/_{40}$ (C) $5\,^{19}/_{20}$ (D) $7\,^{1}/_{2}$

39. $4\,^{2}/_{3} \div ^{7}/_{9} =$

(A) $2\,^{24}/_{27}$ (B) 6 (C) $4\,^{14}/_{27}$ (D) $5\,^{12}/_{27}$

40. $3\,^{2}/_{5} \div 1\,^{7}/_{10} =$

(A) 2 (B) $3\,^{4}/_{7}$ (C) $4\,^{7}/_{25}$ (D) $5\,^{1}/_{10}$

Changing an Improper Fraction to a Mixed Number

DIRECTIONS: Write each improper fraction as a mixed number in simplest form.

41. $^{50}/_{4}$

(A) $10\,^{1}/_{4}$ (B) $11\,^{1}/_{2}$ (C) $12\,^{1}/_{4}$ (D) $12\,^{1}/_{2}$

42. $^{17}/_{5}$

(A) $3\,^{2}/_{5}$ (B) $3\,^{3}/_{5}$ (C) $3\,^{4}/_{5}$ (D) $4\,^{1}/_{5}$

43. $^{42}/_{3}$

(A) $10\,^{2}/_{3}$ (B) 12 (C) $13\,^{1}/_{3}$ (D) 14

44. $^{85}/_{6}$

(A) $9\,^{1}/_{6}$ (B) $10\,^{5}/_{6}$ (C) $14\,^{1}/_{6}$ (D) 12

45. $^{151}/_{7}$

(A) $19\,^{6}/_{7}$ (B) $20\,^{1}/_{7}$ (C) $21\,^{4}/_{7}$ (D) $31\,^{2}/_{7}$

Changing a Mixed Number to an Improper Fraction

DIRECTIONS: Change each mixed number to an improper fraction in simplest form.

46. $2\,^{3}/_{5}$

(A) $^{4}/_{5}$ (B) $^{6}/_{5}$ (C) $^{11}/_{5}$ (D) $^{13}/_{5}$

47. $4\,^3/_4$

(A) $^7/_4$ (B) $^{13}/_4$ (C) $^{16}/_3$ (D) $^{19}/_4$

48. $6\,^7/_6$

(A) $^{13}/_6$ (B) $^{43}/_6$ (C) $^{19}/_{36}$ (D) $^{42}/_{36}$

49. $12\,^3/_7$

(A) $^{87}/_7$ (B) $^{164}/_{14}$ (C) $^{34}/_3$ (D) $^{187}/_{21}$

50. $21\,^1/_2$

(A) $^{11}/_2$ (B) $^{22}/_2$ (C) $^{24}/_2$ (E) $^{43}/_2$

3. Exponents

When a number is multiplied by itself a specific number of times, it is said to be **raised to a power.** The way this is written is $a^n = b$, where a is the number or **base**, n is the **exponent** or **power** that indicates the number of times is to be multiplied by itself, and b is the product of this multiplication.

In the expression 3^2, 3 is the base and 2 is the exponent. This means that 3 is multiplied by itself 2 times and the product is 9.

An exponent can be either positive or negative. A negative exponent implies a fraction. Such that, if n is a positive integer

$$a^{-n} = \frac{1}{a^n},\ a \neq 0. \text{ So, } 2^{-4} = \frac{1}{2^4} = \frac{1}{16}.$$

An exponent that is 0 gives a result of 1, assuming that the base is not equal to 0.

$$a^0 = 1,\ a \neq 0$$

An exponent can also be a fraction. If m and n are positive integers,

$$a^{\frac{m}{n}} = \sqrt[n]{a^m}$$

The numerator remains the exponent of a, but the denominator tells what root to take. For example,

(1) $4^{\frac{3}{2}} = \sqrt[2]{4^3} = \sqrt{64} = 8$ (2) $3^{\frac{4}{2}} = \sqrt[2]{3^4} = \sqrt{81} = 9$

If a fractional exponent were negative, the same operation would take place, but the result would be a fraction. For example,

(1) $27^{-\frac{2}{3}} = \dfrac{1}{27^{2/3}} = \dfrac{1}{\sqrt[3]{27^2}} = \dfrac{1}{\sqrt[3]{729}} = \dfrac{1}{9}$

PROBLEM

Simplify the following expressions:

(1) -3^{-2}

(2) $(-3)^{-2}$

(3) $\frac{-3}{4^{-1}}$

SOLUTION

(1) Here the exponent applies only to 3. Since

$$x^{-y} = \frac{1}{x^y}, -3^{-2} = -(3)^{-2} = -\frac{1}{3^2} = -\frac{1}{9}$$

(2) In this case the exponent applies to the negative base. Thus,

$$(-3)^{-2} = \frac{1}{(-3)^2} = \frac{1}{(-3)(-3)} = \frac{1}{9}$$

(3) $$\frac{-3}{4^{-1}} = \frac{-3}{\left(\frac{1}{4}\right)^1} = \frac{-3}{\frac{1^1}{4^1}} = \frac{-3}{\frac{1}{4}}$$

Division by a fraction is equivalent to multiplication by that fraction's reciprocal, thus

$$\frac{-3}{\frac{1}{4}} = -3 \times \frac{4}{1} = -12 \text{ and } \frac{-3}{4^{-1}} = -12$$

General Laws of Exponents

A) $a^p a^q = a^{p+q}$

$4^2 4^3 = 4^{2+3} = 1{,}024$

B) $(a^p)^q = a^{pq}$

$(2^3)^2 = 2^6 = 64$

C) $\frac{a^p}{a^q} = a^{p-q}$

$\frac{3^6}{3^2} = 3^4 = 81$

D) $(ab)^p = a^p b^p$

$(3 \times 2)^2 = 3^2 \times 2^2 = (9)(4) = 36$

E) $\left(\frac{a}{b}\right)^p = \frac{a^p}{b^p}, b \neq 0$

$\left(\frac{4}{5}\right)^2 = \frac{4^2}{5^2} = \frac{16}{25}$

☞ Drill 3: Exponents

Multiplication

DIRECTIONS: Simplify the following expressions.

1. $4^6 \times 4^2 =$

(A) 4^4 (B) 4^8 (C) 4^{12} (D) 16^8

2. $2^2 \times 2^5 \times 2^3 =$

(A) 2^{10} (B) 4^{10} (C) 8^{10} (D) 2^{30}

3. $6^6 \times 6^2 \times 6^4 =$

(A) 18^8 (B) 18^{12} (C) 6^{12} (D) 6^{48}

4. $a^4b^2 \times a^3b =$

(A) ab (B) $2a^7b^2$ (C) $2a^{12}b$ (D) a^7b^3

5. $m^8n^3 \times m^2n \times m^4n^2 =$

(A) $3m^{16}n^6$ (B) $m^{14}n^6$ (C) $3m^{14}n^5$ (D) $3m^{14}n^5$

Division

DIRECTIONS: Simplify the following expressions.

6. $6^5 \div 6^3 =$

(A) 36 (B) 1 (C) 6 (D) 12

7. $11^8 \div 11^5 =$

(A) 1^3 (B) 11^3 (C) 11^{13} (D) 11^{40}

8. $x^{10}y^8 \div x^7y^3 =$

(A) x^2y^5 (B) x^3y^4 (C) x^3y^5 (D) x^2y^4

9. $a^{14} \div a^9 =$

(A) 1^5 (B) a^5 (C) $2a^5$ (D) a^{23}

10. $c^{17}d^{12}e^4 \div c^{12}d^8e =$

(A) $c^4d^5e^3$ (B) $c^4d^4e^3$ (C) $c^5d^8e^4$ (D) $c^5d^4e^3$

Power to a Power

DIRECTIONS: Simplify the following expressions.

11. $(3^6)^2 =$

(A) 3^4 (B) 3^8 (C) 3^{12} (D) 9^6

12. $(4^3)^5 =$

(A) 4^2 (B) 4^{15} (C) 4^8 (D) 20^3

13. $(a^4b^3)^2 =$

(A) $(ab)^9$ (B) a^8b^6 (C) $(ab)^{24}$ (D) a^6b^5

14. $(r^3p^6)^3 =$

(A) r^9p^{18} (B) $(rp)^{12}$ (C) r^6p^9 (D) $3r^3p^6$

15. $(m^6n^5q^3)^2 =$

(A) $2m^6n^5q^3$ (B) m^4n^3q (C) $m^8n^7q^5$ (D) $m^{12}n^{10}q^6$

4. Order of Operations

General Rules

In many situations, we encounter complex expressions that involve addition, subtraction, multiplication, division, raising terms to some power as well as grouping terms within parentheses and brackets. The order in which these operations should be performed is:

1. Simplify expressions in parentheses (or brackets and braces respectively) first. Always work from within parentheses outward. Absolute values rank as parentheses in the order of operations.
2. Raise all terms to the proper power if there are exponents in the expression.
3. Perform multiplication and division operations from left to right.
4. Perform addition and subtraction operations from left to right.

PROBLEM

Calculate the value of each of the following expressions:

(1) $||2-5|+6-14|$ (2) $|-5|\times 4+\frac{|-12|}{4}$

SOLUTION

(1) $||-3|+6-14| = |3+6-14| = |9-14| = |-5| = 5$

(2) $5 \times 4 + 12/4 = 20 + 3 = 23$

PROBLEM

Perform the indicated operations.

(1) $-3 + (-1)^3(-2)^2$ (2) $(-3 + 4 \times (-2)) \times (-2)$

SOLUTION

(1) $-3 + (-1)(+4) = -3 - 4 = -7$

(2) $(-3 - 8) \times (-2) = (-11) \times (-2) = 22$

☞ Drill 4: Order of Operations

1. Simplify $\frac{4+8 \times 2}{5-1}$.

   (A) 4 (B) 5 (C) 6 (D) 8

2. $96 \div 3 \div 4 \div 2 =$

   (A) 65 (B) 64 (C) 4 (D) 8

3. $3 + 4 \times 2 - 6 \div 3 =$

   (A) -1 (B) $5/3$ (C) $8/3$ (D) 9

4. $[(4 + 8) \times 3] \div 9 =$

   (A) 4 (B) 8 (C) 12 (D) 24

5. $18 + 3 \times 4 \div 3 =$

   (A) 3 (B) 5 (C) 10 (D) 22

6. $(29 - 17 + 4) \div 4 + |-2| =$

   (A) $2\,2/3$ (B) 4 (C) $4\,2/3$ (D) 6

7. $(-3) \times 5 - 20 \div 4 =$

   (A) -75 (B) -20 (C) -10 (D) $-8\,3/4$

8. $\frac{11 \times 2 + 2}{16 - 2 \times 2} =$

(A) $^{11}/_{16}$ (B) 1 (C) 2 (D) $3\ ^{2}/_{3}$

9. $|-8-4| \div 3 \times 6 + (-4) =$

(A) 20 (B) 26 (C) 32 (D) 62

10. $32 \div 2 + 4 - 15 \div 3 =$

(A) 0 (B) 7 (C) 15 (D) 23

11. $2 \times (-5)^3 \div 25 \times (-2) - 3 =$

(A) 8 (B) 17 (C) 21 (D) -9

12. $6 - 2 \times \{3 \times [(-2) - (-3)(-4)]\} =$

(A) 25 (B) -50 (C) 90 (D) -90

5. Decimals

When we divide the denominator of a fraction into its numerator, the result is a decimal. The decimal is based upon a fraction with a denominator of 10, 100, 1,000, ... and is written with a **decimal point.** Whole numbers are placed to the left of the decimal point where the first place to the left is the units place; the second to the left is the tens; the third to the left is the hundreds, etc. The fractions are placed on the right where the first place to the right is the tenths; the second to the right is the hundredths, etc.

EXAMPLE

$12\ ^{3}/_{10} = 12.3$ $4\ ^{17}/_{100} = 4.17$ $^{3}/_{100} = .03$

Since a **rational number** is of the form a/b, $b = 0$, then all rational numbers can be expressed as decimals by dividing b into a. The result is either a **terminating decimal,** meaning that b divides a with a remainder of 0 after a certain point; or **repeating decimal,** meaning that b continues to divide a so that the decimal has a repeating pattern of integers.

EXAMPLE

(A) $^{1}/_{2} = .5$

(B) $^{1}/_{3} = .333...$

(C) $^{11}/_{16} = .6875$

(D) $^{2}/_{7} = .285714285714...$

(A) and (C) are terminating decimals; (B) and (D) are repeating decimals. This explanation allows us to define **irrational numbers** as numbers whose decimal form is non-terminating and non-repeating, e.g.,

$$\sqrt{2} = 1.414\ldots$$

$$\sqrt{3} = 1.732\ldots$$

PROBLEM

Express $-{}^{10}/_{20}$ as a decimal.

SOLUTION

$$-{}^{10}/_{20} = -{}^{50}/_{100} = -.5$$

PROBLEM

Write ${}^{2}/_{7}$ as a repeating decimal.

SOLUTION

To write a fraction as a repeating decimal divide the numerator by the denominator until a pattern of repeated digits appears.

$$2 \div 7 = .285714285714\ldots$$

Identify the entire portion of the decimal which is repeated. The repeating decimal can then be written in the shortened form

$${}^{2}/_{7} = .\overline{285714}$$

Operations with Decimals

A) **To add numbers containing decimals,** write the numbers in a column making sure the decimal points are lined up, one beneath the other. Add the numbers as usual, placing the decimal point in the sum so that it is still in line with the others. It is important not to mix the digits in the tenths place with the digits in the hundredths place, and so on.

EXAMPLES

$2.558 + 6.391$

$$\begin{array}{r} 2.558 \\ +\ 6.391 \\ \hline 8.949 \end{array}$$

$57.51 + 6.2$

$$\begin{array}{r} 57.51 \\ +\ \ 6.20 \\ \hline 63.71 \end{array}$$

Similarly with subtraction,

78.54 – 21.33   7.11 – 4.2

```
  78.54          7.11
– 21.33        – 4.20
  57.21          2.91
```

Note that if two numbers differ according to the amount of digits to the right of the decimal point, zeros must be added.

.63 – .214   15.224 – 3.6891

```
  .630          15.2240
– .214        –  3.6891
  .416          11.5349
```

B) **To multiply numbers with decimals**, simply multiply as usual. Then, to figure out the number of decimal places that belong in the product, find the total number of decimal places in the numbers being multiplied.

EXAMPLES

```
   6.555   (3 decimal places)        5.32   (2 decimal places)
×    4.5   (1 decimal place)      ×   .04   (2 decimal places)
   32775                             2128
  26220                              000
  294975                             2128
 29.4975   (4 decimal places)       .2128   (4 decimal places)
```

C) **To divide numbers with decimals**, you must first make the divisor a whole number by moving the decimal point the appropriate number of places to the right. The decimal point of the dividend should also be moved the same number of places. Place a decimal point in the quotient, directly in line with the decimal point in the dividend.

EXAMPLES

12.92 ÷ 3.4   40.376 ÷ 7.21

```
          3.8                    5.6
3.4.) 12.9.2        7.21.) 40.37.6
     – 102                – 3605
       272                  4326
     – 272                – 4326
         0                     0
```

If the question asks to find the correct answer to two decimal places, simply divide until you have three decimal places and then round off. If the third decimal place is a 5 or larger, the number in the second decimal place is increased by 1. If the third decimal place is less than 5, that number is simply dropped.

PROBLEM

Find the answer to the following to 2 decimal places:

(1) $44.3 \div 3$ (2) $56.99 \div 6$

SOLUTION

(1)

$$\begin{array}{r} 14.766 \\ 3\overline{)44.300} \\ -3 \\ \hline 14 \\ -12 \\ \hline 23 \\ -21 \\ \hline 20 \\ -18 \\ \hline 20 \\ -18 \\ \hline 2 \end{array}$$

14.766 can be rounded off to 14.77

(2)

$$\begin{array}{r} 9.498 \\ 6\overline{)56.990} \\ -54 \\ \hline 29 \\ -24 \\ \hline 59 \\ -54 \\ \hline 50 \\ -48 \\ \hline 2 \end{array}$$

9.498 can be rounded off to 9.50

D) **When comparing two numbers with decimals to see which is the larger,** first look at the tenths place. The larger digit in this place represents the larger number. If the two digits are the same, however, take a look at the digits in the hundredths place, and so on.

EXAMPLES

.518 and .216

5 is larger than 2, therefore .518 is larger than .216

.723 and .726

6 is larger than 3, therefore .726 is larger than .723

☞ Drill 5: Decimals

Addition

1. 1.032 + 0.987 + 3.07 =

(A) 4.089 (B) 5.089 (C) 5.189 (D) 6.189

2. 132.03 + 97.1483 =

(A) 98.4686 (B) 110.3513 (C) 209.1783 (D) 229.1783

3. 7.1 + 0.62 + 4.03827 + 5.183 =

(A) 0.2315127 (B) 16.45433 (C) 16.94127 (D) 18.561

4. 8 + 17.43 + 9.2 =

(A) 34.63 (B) 34.86 (C) 35.63 (D) 176.63

5. 1036.173 + 289.04 =

(A) 382.6573 (B) 392.6573 (C) 1065.077 (D) 1325.213

Subtraction

6. 3.972 – 2.04 =

(A) 1.932 (B) 1.942 (C) 1.976 (D) 2.013

7. 16.047 – 13.06 =

(A) 2.887 (B) 2.987 (C) 3.041 (D) 3.141

8. 87.4 – 56.27 =

(A) 30.27 (B) 30.67 (C) 31.1 (D) 31.13

9. 1046.8 – 639.14 =

(A) 303.84 (B) 313.74 (C) 407.66 (D) 489.74

10. 10,000 – 842.91 =

(A) 9157.09 (B) 942.91 (C) 5236.09 (D) 9057.91

Multiplication

11. $1.03 \times 2.6 =$

(A) 2.18 (B) 2.678 (C) 2.78 (D) 3.38

12. $93 \times 4.2 =$

(A) 39.06 (B) 97.2 (C) 223.2 (D) 390.6

13. $0.04 \times 0.23 =$

(A) 0.0092 (B) 0.092 (C) 0.27 (D) 0.87

14. $0.0186 \times 0.03 =$

(A) 0.000348 (B) 0.000558 (C) 0.0548 (D) 0.0848

15. $51.2 \times 0.17 =$

(A) 5.29 (B) 8.534 (C) 8.704 (D) 36.352

Division

16. $123.39 \div 3 =$

(A) 31.12 (B) 41.13 (C) 401.13 (D) 411.3

17. $1428.6 \div 6 =$

(A) 0.2381 (B) 2.381 (C) 23.81 (D) 238.1

18. $25.2 \div 0.3 =$

(A) 0.84 (B) 8.04 (C) 8.4 (D) 84

19. $14.95 \div 6.5 =$

(A) 2.3 (B) 20.3 (C) 23 (D) 230

20. $46.33 \div 1.13 =$

(A) 0.41 (B) 4.1 (C) 41 (D) 410

Comparing

21. Which is the **largest** number in this set — {0.8, 0.823, 0.089, 0.807, 0.852}?

(A) 0.8 (B) 0.852 (C) 0.089 (D) 0.807

22. Which is the **smallest** number in this set — {32.98, 32.099, 32.047, 32.5, 32.304}?

    (A) 32.98 (B) 32.099 (C) 32.047 (D) 32.5

23. In which set below are the numbers arranged correctly from smallest to largest?

    (A) {0.98, 0.9, 0.993} (B) {0.113, 0.3, 0.31}
    (C) {7.04, 7.26, 7.2} (D) {0.006, 0.061, 0.06}

24. In which set below are the numbers arranged correctly from largest to smallest?

    (A) {1.018, 1.63, 1.368} (B) {4.219, 4.29, 4.9}
    (C) {0.62, 0.6043, 0.643} (D) {16.34, 16.304, 16.3}

25. Which is the **largest** number in this set — {0.87, 0.89, 0.889, 0.8, 0.987}?

    (A) 0.87 (B) 0.89 (C) 0.987 (D) 0.8

Changing a Fraction to a Decimal

26. What is $^1/_4$ written as a decimal?

    (A) 1.4 (B) 0.14 (C) 0.2 (D) 0.25

27. What is $^3/_5$ written as a decimal?

    (A) 0.3 (B) 0.35 (C) 0.6 (D) 0.65

28. What is $^7/_{20}$ written as a decimal?

    (A) 0.35 (B) 0.4 (C) 0.72 (D) 0.75

29. What is $^2/_3$ written as a decimal?

    (A) 0.23 (B) 0.33 (C) 0.5 (D) $0.\overline{6}$

30. What is $^{11}/_{25}$ written as a fraction?

    (A) 0.1125 (B) 0.25 (C) 0.4 (D) 0.44

6. Percentages

A **percent** is a way of expressing the relationship between part and whole, where whole is defined as 100%. A percent can be defined by a fraction with a denominator of 100. Decimals can also represent a percent. For instance,

56% = 0.56 = 56/100

PROBLEM

Compute the value of

(1) 90% of 400

(2) 180% of 400

(3) 50% of 500

(4) 200% of 4

SOLUTION

The symbol % means per hundred, therefore, 5% = 5/100

(1) 90% of 400 = 90/100 × 400 = 90 × 4 = 360

(2) 180% of 400 = 180/100 × 400 = 180 × 4 = 720

(3) 50% of 500 = 50/100 × 500 = 50 × 5 = 250

(4) 200% of 4 = 200/100 × 4 = 2 × 4 = 8

PROBLEM

What percent of

(1) 100 is 99.5

(2) 200 is 4

SOLUTION

(1) $99.5 = x \times 100$

$99.5 = 100x$

$.995 = x$; but this is the value of x per hundred. Therefore,

$99.5\% = x$

(2) $4 = x \times 200$

$4 = 200x$

$.02 = x$. Again, this must be changed to percent, so

$x = 2\%$

Equivalent Forms of a Number

Some problems may call for converting numbers into an equivalent or simplified form in order to make the solution more convenient.

1. Converting a fraction to a decimal:

$^1/_2 = 0.50$

Divide the numerator by the denominator.

$$\begin{array}{r} .50 \\ 2\overline{)1.00} \\ -1\,0 \\ \hline 00 \end{array}$$

2. Converting a number to a percent:

   0.50 = 50%

   Multiply by 100.

   0.50 = (0.50 × 100)% = 50%

3. Converting a percent to a decimal:

   30% = 0.30

   Divide by 100.

   30% = 30/100 = 0.30

4. Converting a decimal to a fraction:

   0.500 = $^1/_2$

   Convert .500 to 500/1000 and then simplify the fraction by dividing the numerator and denominator by common factors:

$$\frac{\not{2}\times\not{2}\times\not{5}\times\not{5}\times\not{5}}{\not{2}\times\not{2}\times 2\times\not{5}\times\not{5}\times\not{5}}$$

   and then cancel out the common numbers to get $^1/_2$.

PROBLEM

Express

(1) 1.65 as a percent

(2) 0.7 as a fraction

(3) – $^{10}/_{20}$ as a decimal

(4) $^4/_2$ as an integer

SOLUTION

(1) 1.65 × 100 = 165%

(2) 0.7 = $^7/_{10}$

(3) – $^{10}/_{20}$ = – 0.5

(4) $^4/_2$ = 2

☞ Drill 6: Percentages

Finding Percents

1. Find 3% of 80.

   (A) 0.24 (B) 2.4 (C) 24 (D) 240

2. Find 50% of 182.

   (A) 9 (B) 90 (C) 91 (D) 910

3. Find 83% of 166.

   (A) 137.78 (B) 1.377 (C) 13.778 (D) 137

4. Find 125% of 400.

   (A) 425 (B) 500 (C) 525 (D) 600

5. Find 300% of 4.

   (A) 12 (B) 120 (C) 1,200 (D) 12,000

6. Forty-eight percent of the 1,200 students at Central High are males. How many male students are there at Central High?

   (A) 57 (B) 576 (C) 580 (D) 600

7. For 35% of the last 40 days, there has been measurable rainfall. How many days out of the last 40 days have had measurable rainfall?

   (A) 14 (B) 20 (C) 25 (D) 35

8. Of every 1,000 people who take a certain medicine, 0.2% develop severe side effects. How many people out of every 1,000 who take the medicine develop the side effects?

   (A) 0.2 (B) 2 (C) 20 (D) 22

9. Of 220 applicants for a job, 75% were offered an initial interview. How many people were offered an initial interview?

   (A) 75 (B) 165 (C) 120 (D) 155

10. Find 0.05% of 4,000.

    (A) 0.05 (B) 0.5 (C) 2 (D) 20

Changing Percents to Fractions

11. What is 25% written as a fraction?

(A) $^1/_{25}$ (B) $^1/_5$ (C) $^1/_4$ (D) $^1/_3$

12. What is 33 $^1/_3$% written as a fraction?

(A) $^1/_4$ (B) $^1/_3$ (C) $^1/_2$ (D) $^2/_3$

13. What is 200% written as a fraction?

(A) $^1/_2$ (B) $^2/_1$ (C) $^{20}/_1$ (D) $^{200}/_1$

14. What is 84% written as a fraction?

(A) $^1/_{84}$ (B) $^4/_8$ (C) $^{17}/_{25}$ (D) $^{21}/_{25}$

15. What is 2% written as a fraction?

(A) $^1/_{50}$ (B) $^1/_{25}$ (C) $^1/_{10}$ (D) $^1/_4$

Changing Fractions to Percents

16. What is $^2/_3$ written as a percent?

(A) 23% (B) 32% (C) 66 $^2/_3$% (D) 57 $^1/_3$%

17. What is $^3/_5$ written as a percent?

(A) 30% (B) 35% (C) 53% (D) 60%

18. What is $^{17}/_{20}$ written as a percent?

(A) 17% (B) 70% (C) 75% (D) 85%

19. What is $^{45}/_{50}$ written as a percent?

(A) 45% (B) 50% (C) 90% (D) 95%

20. What is 1 $^1/_4$ written as a percent?

(A) 114% (B) 120% (C) 125% (D) 127%

Changing Percents to Decimals

21. What is 42% written as a decimal?

(A) 0.42 (B) 4.2 (C) 42 (D) 420

22. What is 0.3% written as a decimal?

    (A) 0.0003 (B) 0.003 (C) 0.03 (D) 0.3

23. What is 8% written as a decimal?

    (A) 0.0008 (B) 0.008 (C) 0.08 (D) 0.80

24. What is 175% written as a decimal?

    (A) 0.175 (B) 1.75 (C) 17.5 (D) 175

25. What is 35% written as a decimal?

    (A) 0.00034 (B) 0.0034 (C) 0.034 (D) 0.34

Changing Decimals to Percents

26. What is 0.43 written as a percent?

    (A) 0.0043% (B) 0.043% (C) 4.3% (D) 43%

27. What is 1 written as a percent?

    (A) 1% (B) 10% (C) 100% (D) 111%

28. What is 0.08 written as a percent?

    (A) 0.08% (B) 8% (C) 8.8% (D) 80%

29. What is 3.4 written as a percent?

    (A) 340% (B) 3.4% (C) 34% (D) 304%

30. What is 0.645 written as a percent?

    (A) 64.5% (B) 65% (C) 69% (D) 70%

7. Radicals

The **square root** of a number is a number that when multiplied by itself results in the original number. So, the square root of 81 is 9 since $9 \times 9 = 81$. However, – 9 is also a root of 81 since $(-9)(-9) = 81$. Every positive number will have two roots. Yet, the principal root is the positive one. Zero has only one square root, while negative numbers do not have real numbers as their roots.

A **radical sign** indicates that the root of a number or expression will be taken. The **radicand** is the number of which the root will be taken. The **index** tells how many times the root needs to be multiplied by itself to equal the radicand. For example,

(1) $\sqrt[3]{64}$;

3 is the index and 64 is the radicand. Since $4 \times 4 \times 4 = 64$, $\sqrt[3]{64} = 4$

(2) $\sqrt[5]{32}$;

5 is the index and 32 is the radicand. Since $2 \times 2 \times 2 \times 2 \times 2 = 32$, $\sqrt[5]{32} = 2$

Operations with Radicals

A) **To multiply two or more radicals**, we utilize the law that states

$\sqrt{a} \times \sqrt{b} = \sqrt{ab}$

Simply multiply the whole numbers as usual. Then, multiply the radicands and put the product under the radical sign and simplify. For example,

(1) $\sqrt{12} \times \sqrt{5} = \sqrt{60} = 2\sqrt{15}$

(2) $3\sqrt{2} \times 4\sqrt{8} = 12\sqrt{16} = 48$

(3) $2\sqrt{10} \times 6\sqrt{5} = 12\sqrt{50} = 60\sqrt{2}$

B) **To divide radicals**, simplify both the numerator and the denominator. By multiplying the radical in the denominator by itself, you can make the denominator a rational number. The numerator, however, must also be multiplied by this radical so that the value of the expression does not change. You must choose as many factors as necessary to rationalize the denominator. For example,

(1) $\dfrac{\sqrt{128}}{\sqrt{2}} = \dfrac{\sqrt{64} \times \sqrt{2}}{\sqrt{2}} = \dfrac{8\sqrt{2}}{\sqrt{2}} = 8$

(2) $\dfrac{\sqrt{10}}{\sqrt{3}} = \dfrac{\sqrt{10} \times \sqrt{3}}{\sqrt{3} \times \sqrt{3}} = \dfrac{\sqrt{30}}{3}$

(3) $\dfrac{\sqrt{8}}{2\sqrt{3}} = \dfrac{\sqrt{8} \times \sqrt{3}}{2\sqrt{3} \times \sqrt{3}} = \dfrac{\sqrt{24}}{2 \times 3} = \dfrac{2\sqrt{6}}{6} = \dfrac{\sqrt{6}}{3}$

C) **To add two or more radicals**, the radicals must have the same index and the same radicand. Only where the radicals are simplified can these similarities be determined.

EXAMPLE

(1) $6\sqrt{2} + 2\sqrt{2} = (6+2)\sqrt{2} = 8\sqrt{2}$

(2) $\sqrt{27} + 5\sqrt{3} = \sqrt{9}\sqrt{3} + 5\sqrt{3} = 3\sqrt{3} + 5\sqrt{3} = 8\sqrt{3}$

(3) $7\sqrt{3}+8\sqrt{2}+5\sqrt{3}=12\sqrt{3}+8\sqrt{2}$

Similarly to subtract,

(1) $12\sqrt{3}-7\sqrt{3}=(12-7)\sqrt{3}=5\sqrt{3}$

(2) $\sqrt{80}-\sqrt{20}=\sqrt{16}\sqrt{5}-\sqrt{4}\sqrt{5}=4\sqrt{5}-2\sqrt{5}=2\sqrt{5}$

(3) $\sqrt{50}-\sqrt{3}=5\sqrt{2}-\sqrt{3}$

☞ Drill 7: Radicals

Multiplication

DIRECTIONS: Multiply and simplify each answer.

1. $\sqrt{6}\times\sqrt{5}=$

   (A) $\sqrt{11}$ (B) $\sqrt{30}$ (C) $2\sqrt{5}$ (D) $3\sqrt{10}$

2. $\sqrt{3}\times\sqrt{12}=$

   (A) 3 (B) $\sqrt{15}$ (C) $\sqrt{36}$ (D) 6

3. $\sqrt{7}\times\sqrt{7}=$

   (A) 7 (B) 49 (C) $\sqrt{14}$ (D) $2\sqrt{7}$

4. $3\sqrt{5}\times2\sqrt{5}=$

   (A) $5\sqrt{5}$ (B) 25 (C) 30 (D) $5\sqrt{25}$

5. $4\sqrt{6}\times\sqrt{2}=$

   (A) $4\sqrt{8}$ (B) $8\sqrt{3}$ (C) $5\sqrt{8}$ (D) $4\sqrt{12}$

Division

DIRECTIONS: Divide and simplify the answer.

6. $\sqrt{10}\div\sqrt{2}=$

   (A) $\sqrt{8}$ (B) $2\sqrt{2}$ (C) $\sqrt{5}$ (D) $2\sqrt{5}$

7. $\sqrt{30}\div\sqrt{15}=$

   (A) $\sqrt{2}$ (B) $\sqrt{45}$ (C) $3\sqrt{5}$ (D) $\sqrt{15}$

8. $\sqrt{100} \div \sqrt{25} =$

(A) $\sqrt{4}$ (B) $5\sqrt{5}$ (C) $5\sqrt{3}$ (D) 2

9. $\sqrt{48} \div \sqrt{8} =$

(A) $4\sqrt{3}$ (B) $3\sqrt{2}$ (C) $\sqrt{6}$ (D) 6

10. $3\sqrt{12} \div \sqrt{3} =$

(A) $3\sqrt{15}$ (B) 6 (C) 9 (D) 12

Addition

DIRECTIONS: Simplify each radical and add.

11. $\sqrt{7} + 3\sqrt{7} =$

(A) $3\sqrt{7}$ (B) $4\sqrt{7}$ (C) $3\sqrt{14}$ (D) $4\sqrt{14}$

12. $\sqrt{5} + 6\sqrt{5} + 3\sqrt{5} =$

(A) $9\sqrt{5}$ (B) $9\sqrt{15}$ (C) $5\sqrt{10}$ (D) $10\sqrt{5}$

13. $3\sqrt{32} + 2\sqrt{2} =$

(A) $5\sqrt{2}$ (B) $\sqrt{34}$ (C) $14\sqrt{2}$ (D) $5\sqrt{34}$

14. $6\sqrt{15} + 8\sqrt{15} + 16\sqrt{15} =$

(A) $15\sqrt{30}$ (B) $30\sqrt{45}$ (C) $30\sqrt{15}$ (D) $15\sqrt{45}$

15. $6\sqrt{5} + 2\sqrt{45} =$

(A) $12\sqrt{5}$ (B) $8\sqrt{50}$ (C) $40\sqrt{2}$ (D) $12\sqrt{50}$

Subtraction

DIRECTIONS: Simplify each radical and subtract.

16. $8\sqrt{5} - 6\sqrt{5} =$

(A) $2\sqrt{5}$ (B) $3\sqrt{5}$ (C) $4\sqrt{5}$ (D) $14\sqrt{5}$

17. $16\sqrt{33} - 5\sqrt{33} =$

(A) $3\sqrt{33}$ (B) $33\sqrt{11}$ (C) $11\sqrt{33}$ (D) $11\sqrt{0}$

18. $14\sqrt{2} - 19\sqrt{2} =$

(A) $5\sqrt{2}$ (B) $-5\sqrt{2}$ (C) $-33\sqrt{2}$ (D) $33\sqrt{2}$

19. $10\sqrt{2} - 3\sqrt{8} =$

(A) $6\sqrt{6}$ (B) $-2\sqrt{2}$ (C) $7\sqrt{6}$ (D) $4\sqrt{2}$

20. $4\sqrt{3} - 2\sqrt{12} =$

(A) $-2\sqrt{9}$ (B) $-6\sqrt{15}$ (C) 0 (D) $6\sqrt{15}$

8. Averages

Mean

The mean is the arithmetic average. It is the sum of the variables divided by the total number of variables. For example:

$$\frac{4+3+8}{3} = 5$$

PROBLEM

Find the mean salary for four company employees who make \$5/hr., \$8/hr., \$12/hr., and \$15/hr.

SOLUTION

The mean salary is the average.

$$\frac{\$5+\$8+\$12+\$15}{4 \text{ employees}} = \frac{\$40}{4} = \$10/\text{ hr.}$$

PROBLEM

Find the mean length of five fish with lengths of 7.5 in, 7.75 in, 8.5 in, 8.5 in, 8.25 in.

SOLUTION

The mean length is the average length.

$$\frac{7.5+7.75+8.5+8.5+8.25}{5} = \frac{40.5}{5} = 8.1 \text{ in}$$

Median

The median is the middle value in a set when there is an odd number of values. There is an equal number of values larger and smaller than the median. When the set is an even number of values, the average of the two middle values is the median.

For example:

The median of (2, 3, 5, 8, 9) is 5.

The median of (2, 3, 5, 9, 10, 11) is $\frac{5+9}{2} = 7$.

Mode

The mode is the most frequently occurring value in the set of values. For example, the mode of 4, 5, 8, 3, 8, 2 would be 8, since it occurs twice while the other values occur only once.

PROBLEM

> For this series of observations find the mean, median, and mode.
>
> 500, 600, 800, 800, 900, 900, 900, 900, 900, 1000, 1100

SOLUTION

The mean is the value obtained by adding all the measurements and dividing by the number of measurements.

$$\frac{500+600+800+800+900+900+900+900+900+1000+1100}{11}$$

$$= \frac{9300}{11} = 845.45$$

The median is the observation in the middle. We have 11 observations, so here the sixth, 900, is the median.

The mode is the observation that appears most frequently. That is also 900, which has 5 appearances.

All three of these numbers are measures of central tendency. They describe the "middle" or "center" of the data.

PROBLEM

> Nine rats run through a maze. The time each rat took to traverse the maze is recorded and these times are listed below.
>
> 1 min, 2.5 min, 3 min, 1.5 min, 2 min, 1.25 min, 1 min, .9 min, 30 min
>
> Which of the three measures of central tendency would be the most appropriate in this case?

SOLUTION

We will calculate the three measures of central tendency and then compare them to determine which would be the most appropriate in describing these data.

The mean is the sum of observations divided by the number of observations. In this case

$$\frac{1+2.5+3+1.5+2+1.25+1+.9+30}{9}=\frac{43.15}{9}=4.79$$

The median is the "middle number" in an array of the observations from the lowest to the highest.

0.9, 1.0, 1.0, 1.25, 1.5, 2.0, 2.5, 3.0, 30.0

The median is the fifth observation in this array or 1.5. There are four observations larger than 1.5 and four observations smaller than 1.5.

The mode is the most frequently occurring observation in the sample. In this data set, the mode is 1.0.

mean = 4.79

median = 1.5

mode = 1.0

The mean is not appropriate here. Only one rat took more than 4.79 minutes to run the maze and this rat took 30 minutes. We see that the mean has been distorted by this one large observation.

The median or mode seems to describe this data set better and would be more appropriate to use.

☞ Drill 8: Averages

Mean

DIRECTIONS: Find the mean of each set of numbers.

1. 18, 25, and 32.

   (A) 3 (B) 25 (C) 50 (D) 75

2. 4/9, 2/3, and 5/6.

   (A) 11/18 (B) 35/54 (C) 41/54 (D) 35/18

3. 97, 102, 116, and 137.

   (A) 40 (B) 102 (C) 109 (D) 113

4. 12, 15, 18, 24, and 31.

   (A) 18 (B) 19.3 (C) 20 (D) 25

5. 7, 4, 6, 3, 11, and 14.

   (A) 5 (B) 6.5 (C) 7 (D) 7.5

Median

DIRECTIONS: Find the median value of each set of numbers.

6. 3, 8, and 6.

   (A) 3 (B) 6 (C) 8 (D) 17

7. 19, 15, 21, 27, and 12.

   (A) 19 (B) 15 (C) 21 (D) 27

8. $1\,^2/_3$, $1\,^7/_8$, $1\,^3/_4$, and $1\,^5/_6$.

   (A) $1\,^{30}/_{48}$ (B) $1\,^2/_3$ (C) $1\,^3/_4$ (D) $1\,^{19}/_{24}$

9. 29, 18, 21, and 35.

   (A) 29 (B) 18 (C) 25 (D) 35

10. 8, 15, 7, 12, 31, 3, and 28.

    (A) 7 (B) 11.6 (C) 12 (D) 14.9

Mode

DIRECTIONS: Find the mode(s) of each set of numbers.

11. 1, 3, 7, 4, 3, and 8.

    (A) 1 (B) 3 (C) 7 (D) 4

12. 12, 19, 25, and 42.

    (A) 12 (B) 19 (C) 25 (D) None

13. 16, 14, 12, 16, 30, and 28.

    (A) 6 (B) 14 (C) 16 (D) $19.\overline{3}$

14. 4, 3, 9, 2, 4, 5, and 2.

    (A) 3 and 9 (B) 5 and 9 (C) 4 and 5 (D) 2 and 4

15. 87, 42, 111, 116, 39, 111, 140, 116, 97, and 111.

    (A) 111 (B) 116 (C) 39 (D) 140

ARITHMETIC DRILLS

ANSWER KEY

Drill 1 – Integers and Real Numbers

1. (A)
2. (C)
3. (D)
4. (C)
5. (B)
6. (B)
7. (A)
8. (C)
9. (D)
10. (B)
11. (B)
12. (C)
13. (C)
14. (A)
15. (B)
16. (B)
17. (D)
18. (D)
19. (C)
20. (A)

Drill 2 – Fractions

1. (D)
2. (B)
3. (C)
4. (A)
5. (C)
6. (B)
7. (C)
8. (A)
9. (B)
10. (A)
11. (B)
12. (D)
13. (C)
14. (D)
15. (B)
16. (B)
17. (D)
18. (B)
19. (A)
20. (C)
21. (D)
22. (C)
23. (B)
24. (D)
25. (A)
26. (A)
27. (D)
28. (A)
29. (C)
30. (B)
31. (C)
32. (A)
33. (B)
34. (C)
35. (D)
36. (B)
37. (C)
38. (D)
39. (B)
40. (A)
41. (D)
42. (A)
43. (D)
44. (C)
45. (C)
46. (D)
47. (D)
48. (B)
49. (A)
50. (D)

Drill 3 – Exponents

1. (B)
2. (A)
3. (C)
4. (D)
5. (B)
6. (A)
7. (B)
8. (C)
9. (B)
10. (D)
11. (C)
12. (B)
13. (B)
14. (A)
15. (D)

Drill 4 – Order of Operations

1. (B)
2. (C)
3. (D)
4. (A)
5. (D)
6. (D)
7. (B)
8. (C)
9. (A)
10. (C)
11. (B)
12. (C)

Drill 5 – Decimals

1. (B)	9. (C)	17. (D)	25. (C)
2. (D)	10. (A)	18. (D)	26. (D)
3. (C)	11. (B)	19. (A)	27. (C)
4. (A)	12. (D)	20. (C)	28. (A)
5. (D)	13. (A)	21. (B)	29. (D)
6. (A)	14. (B)	22. (C)	30. (D)
7. (B)	15. (C)	23. (B)	
8. (D)	16. (B)	24. (D)	

Drill 6 – Percentages

1. (B)	9. (B)	17. (D)	25. (D)
2. (C)	10. (C)	18. (D)	26. (D)
3. (A)	11. (C)	19. (C)	27. (C)
4. (B)	12. (B)	20. (C)	28. (B)
5. (A)	13. (B)	21. (A)	29. (A)
6. (B)	14. (D)	22. (B)	30. (A)
7. (A)	15. (A)	23. (C)	
8. (B)	16. (C)	24. (B)	

Drill 7 – Radicals

1. (B)	6. (C)	11. (B)	16. (A)
2. (D)	7. (A)	12. (D)	17. (C)
3. (A)	8. (D)	13. (C)	18. (B)
4. (C)	9. (C)	14. (C)	19. (D)
5. (B)	10. (B)	15. (A)	20. (C)

Drill 8 – Averages

1. (B)	5. (D)	9. (C)	13. (C)
2. (B)	6. (B)	10. (C)	14. (D)
3. (D)	7. (A)	11. (B)	15. (A)
4. (C)	8. (D)	12. (D)	

III. Algebra

In algebra, letters or variables are used to represent numbers. A **variable** is defined as a placeholder, which can take on any of several values at a given time. A **constant**, on the other hand, is a symbol which takes on only one value at a given time. A **term** is a constant, a variable, or a combination of constants and variables. For example: 7.76, $3x$, xyz, $5^z/_x$, $(0.99)x^2$ are terms. If a term is a combination of constants and variables, the constant part of the term is referred to as the **coefficient** of the variable. If a variable is written without a coefficient, the coefficient is assumed to be 1.

EXAMPLES

$3x^2$	y^3
coefficient: 3	coefficient: 1
variable: x	variable: y

An **expression** is a collection of one or more terms. If the number of terms is greater than 1, the expression is said to be the sum of the terms.

EXAMPLES

$9,\ 9xy,\ 6x + x/3,\ 8yz - 2x$

An algebraic expression consisting of only one term is called a **monomial**; of two terms is called a **binomial**; of three terms is called a **trinomial**. In general, an algebraic expression consisting of two or more terms is called a **polynomial**.

1. Operations with Polynomials

A) **Addition of polynomials** is achieved by combining like terms, terms which differ only in their numerical coefficients. For example,

$$P(x) = (x^2 - 3x + 5) + (4x^2 + 6x - 3)$$

Note that the parentheses are used to distinguish the polynomials.

By using the commutative and associative laws, we can rewrite $P(x)$ as

$$P(x) = (x^2 + 4x^2) + (6x - 3x) + (5 - 3)$$

Using the distributive law, $ab + ac = a(b + c)$, yields

$$(1 + 4)x^2 + (6 - 3)x + (5 - 3)$$
$$= 5x^2 + 3x + 2$$

B) **Subtraction of two polynomials** is achieved by first changing the sign of all terms in the expression which is being subtracted and then adding this result to the other expression. For example,

$$(5x^2 + 4y^2 + 3z^2) - (4xy + 7y^2 - 3z^2 + 1)$$

$= 5x^2 + 4y^2 + 3z^2 - 4xy - 7y^2 + 3z^2 + 1$
$= (5x^2) + (4y^2 - 7y^2) + (3z^2 + 3z^2) - 4xy - 1$
$= (5x^2) + (-3y^2) + (6z^2) - 4xy - 1$

C) **Multiplication of two or more polynomials** is achieved by using the laws of exponents, the rules of signs, and the commutative and associative laws of multiplication. Begin by multiplying the coefficients and then multiply the variables according to the laws of exponents. For example,

$(y^2)\ (5)\ (6y^2)\ (yz)\ (2z^2)$
$= (1)\ (5)\ (6)\ (1)\ (2)\ (y^2)\ (y^2)\ (yz)\ (z^2)$
$= 60[(y^2)\ (y^2)\ (y)]\ [(z)\ (z^2)]$
$= 60(y^5)\ (z^3)$
$= 60y^5z^3$

D) **Multiplication of a polynomial by a monomial** is achieved by multiplying each term of the polynomial by the monomial and combining the results. For example,

$(4x^2 + 3y)\ (6xz^2)$
$= (4x^2)\ (6xz^2) + (3y)\ (6xz^2)$
$= 24x^3z^2 + 18xyz^2$

E) **Multiplication of a polynomial by a polynomial** is achieved by multiplying each of the terms of one polynomial by each of the terms of the other polynomial and combining the result. For example,

$(5y + z + 1)\ (y^2 + 2y)$
$[(5y)\ (y^2) + (5y)\ (2y)] + [(z)\ (y^2) + (z)\ (2y)] + [(1)\ (y^2) + (1)\ (2y)]$
$= (5y^3 + 10y^2) + (y^2z + 2yz) + (y^2 + 2y)$
$= (5y^3) + (10y^2 + y^2) + (y^2z) + (2yz) + (2y)$
$= 5y^3 + 11y^2 + y^2z + 2yz + 2y$

F) **Division of a monomial by a monomial** is achieved by first dividing the constant coefficients and the variable factors separately, and then multiplying these quotients. For example,

$6xyz^2 \div 2y^2z$

$$= \left(\frac{6}{2}\right)\left(\frac{x}{1}\right)\left(\frac{y}{y^2}\right)\left(\frac{z^2}{z}\right)$$

$= 3xy^{-1}z$

$$= \frac{3xz}{y}$$

G) **Division of a polynomial by a polynomial** is achieved by following the given procedure called **long division.**

Step 1: The terms of both the polynomials are arranged in order of ascending or descending powers of one variable.

Step 2: The first term of the dividend is divided by the first term of the divisor which gives the first term of the quotient.

Step 3: This first term of the quotient is multiplied by the entire divisor and the result is subtracted from the dividend.

Step 4: Using the remainder obtained from Step 3 as the new dividend, Steps 2 and 3 are repeated until the remainder is zero or the degree of the remainder is less than the degree of the divisor.

Step 5: The result is written as follows:

$$\frac{\text{dividend}}{\text{divisor}} = \text{quotient} + \frac{\text{remainder}}{\text{divisor}}$$

divisor $\neq 0$

e.g. $(2x^2 + x + 6) \div (x + 1)$

$$\begin{array}{r} 2x - 1 \\ x+1 \overline{\big)\, 2x^2 + x + 6} \\ -(2x^2 + 2x) \\ \hline -x + 6 \\ -(-x - 1) \\ \hline 7 \end{array}$$

The result is $(2x^2 + x + 6) \div (x + 1) = 2x - 1 + \dfrac{7}{x+1}$.

☞ Drill 1: Operations with Polynomials

Addition

1. $9a^2b + 3c + 2a^2b + 5c =$

(A) $19a^2bc$ (B) $11a^2b + 8c$

(C) $11a^4b^2 + 8c^2$ (D) $19a^4b^2c^2$

2. $14m^2n^3 + 6m^2n^3 + 3m^2n^3 =$

(A) $20m^2n^3$ (B) $23m^6n^9$

(C) $23m^2n^3$ (D) $32m^6n^9$

3. $3x + 2y + 16x + 3z + 6y =$

(A) $19x + 8y$ (B) $19x + 11yz$

(C) $19x + 8y + 3z$ (D) $11xy + 19xz$

4. $(4d^2 + 7e^3 + 12f) + (3d^2 + 6e^3 + 2f) =$

(A) $23d^2e^3f$ (B) $33d^2e^2f$

(C) $33d^4e^6f^2$ (D) $7d^2 + 13e^3 + 14f$

5. $3ac^2 + 2b^2c + 7ac^2 + 2ac^2 + b^2c =$

(A) $12ac^2 + 3b^2c$ (B) $14ab^2c^2$

(C) $11ac^2 + 4ab^2c$ (D) $15ab^2c^2$

Subtraction

6. $14m^2n - 6m^2n =$

(A) $20m^2n$ (B) $8m^2n$ (C) $8m$ (D) 8

7. $3x^3y^2 - 4xz - 6x^3y^2 =$

(A) $-7x^2y^2z$ (B) $3x^3y^2 - 10x^4y^2z$

(C) $-3x^3y^2 - 4xz$ (D) $-x^2y^2z - 6x^3y^2$

8. $9g^2 + 6h - 2g^2 - 5h =$

(A) $15g^2h - 7g^2h$ (B) $7g^4h^2$

(C) $7g^2 + h$ (D) $11g^2 - 7h^2$

9. $7b^3 - 4c^2 - 6b^3 + 3c^2 =$

(A) $b^3 - c^2$ (B) $-11b^2 - 3c^2$

(C) $13b^3 - c$ (D) $7b - c$

10. $11q^2r - 4q^2r - 8q^2r =$

(A) $22q^2r$ (B) q^2r

(C) $-2q^2r$ (D) $-q^2r$

Multiplication

11. $5p^2t \times 3p^2t =$

(A) $15p^2t$ (B) $15p^4t$ (C) $15p^4t^2$ (D) $8p^2t$

12. $(2r + s)\,14r =$

(A) $28rs$ (B) $28r^2 + 14sr$

(C) $16r^2 + 14rs$ (D) $28r + 14sr$

13. $(4m + p)(3m - 2p) =$

(A) $12m^2 + 5mp + 2p^2$ (B) $12m^2 - 5mp - 2p^2$

(C) $7m - p$ (D) $12m - 2p$

14. $(2a + b)(3a^2 + ab + b^2) =$

(A) $6a^3 + 5a^2b + 3ab^2 + b^3$ (B) $5a^3 + 3ab + b^3$

(C) $6a^3 + 2a^2b + 2ab^2$ (D) $3a^2 + 2a + ab + b + b^2$

15. $(6t^2 + 2t + 1)\,3t =$

(A) $9t^2 + 5t + 3$ (B) $18t^2 + 6t + 3$

(C) $9t^3 + 6t^2 + 3t$ (D) $18t^3 + 6t^2 + 3t$

Division

16. $(x^2 + x - 6) \div (x - 2) =$

(A) $x - 3$ (B) $x + 2$ (C) $x + 3$ (D) $x - 2$

17. $24b^4c^3 \div 6b^2c =$

(A) $3b^2c^2$ (B) $4b^4c^3$ (C) $4b^3c^2$ (D) $4b^2c^2$

18. $(3p^2 + pq - 2q^2) \div (p + q) =$

(A) $3p + 2q$ (B) $2q - 3p$

(C) $3p - 2q$ (D) $2q + 3p$

19. $(y^3 - 2y^2 - y + 2) \div (y - 2) =$

(A) $(y - 1)^2$ (B) $y^2 - 1$

(C) $(y + 2)(y - 1)$ (D) $(y + 1)^2$

20. $(m^2 + m - 14) \div (m + 4) =$

(A) $m - 2$ (B) $m - 3 + \frac{-2}{m+4}$

(C) $m - 3 + \frac{4}{m+4}$ (D) $m - 3$

2. Simplifying Algebraic Expressions

To factor a polynomial completely is to find the prime factors of the polynomial with respect to a specified set of numbers.

The following concepts are important while factoring or simplifying expressions.

1. The factors of an algebraic expression consist of two or more algebraic expressions which when multiplied together produce the given algebraic expression.

2. A **prime factor** is a polynomial with no factors other than itself and 1. The **least common multiple** (LCM) for a set of numbers is the smallest quantity divisible by every number of the set. For algebraic expressions the least common numerical coefficients for each of the given expressions will be a factor.

3. The **greatest common factor** (GCF) for a set of numbers is the largest factor that is common to all members of the set.

4. For algebraic expressions, the greatest common factor is the polynomial of highest degree and the largest numerical coefficient which is a factor of all the given expressions.

Some important formulae useful for the factoring of polynomials are listed below.

$$a(c + d) = ac + ad$$

$$(a + b)(a - b) = a^2 - b^2$$

$$(a + b)(a + b) = (a + b)^2 = a^2 + 2ab + b^2$$

$$(a - b)(a - b) = (a - b)^2 = a^2 - 2ab + b^2$$

$$(x + a)(x + b) = x^2 + (a + b)x + ab$$

$$(ax + b)(cx + d) = acx^2 + (ad + bc)x + bd$$

$$(a + b)(c + d) = ac + bc + ad + bd$$

$$(a + b)(a + b)(a + b) = (a + b)^3 = a^3 + 3a^2b + 3ab^2 + b^3$$

$$(a - b)(a - b)(a - b) = (a - b)^3 = a^3 - 3a^2b + 3ab^2 - b^3$$

$$(a - b)(a^2 + ab + b^2) = a^3 - b^3$$

$$(a + b)(a^2 - ab + b^2) = a^3 + b^3$$

$$(a + b + c)^2 = a^2 + b^2 + c^2 + 2ab + 2ac + 2bc$$

$$(a - b)(a^3 + a^2b + ab^2 + b^3) = a^4 - b^4$$

$$(a - b)(a^4 + a^3b + a^2b^2 + ab^3 + b^4) = a^5 - b^5$$

$$(a - b)(a^5 + a^4b + a^3b^2 + a^2b^3 + ab^4 + b^5) = a^6 - b^6$$

$$(a - b)(a^{n-1} + a^{n-2}b + a^{n-3}b^2 + \ldots + ab^{n-2} + b^{n-1}) = a^n - b^n$$

where n is any positive integer (1, 2, 3, 4, ...).

$$(a + b)(a^{n-1} - a^{n-2}b + a^{n-3}b^2 - \ldots - ab^{n-2} + b^{n-1}) = a^n + b^n$$

where n is any positive odd integer (1, 3, 5, 7, ...).

The procedure for factoring an algebraic expression completely is as follows:

Step 1: First find the greatest common factor if there is any. Then examine each factor remaining for greatest common factors.

Step 2: Continue factoring the factors obtained in Step 1 until all factors other than monomial factors are prime.

EXAMPLE

Factoring $4 - 16x^2$,

$$4 - 16x^2 = 4(1 - 4x^2) = 4(1 + 2x)(1 - 2x)$$

PROBLEM

Express each of the following as a single term.

(1) $3x^2 + 2x^2 - 4x^2$

(2) $5axy^2 - 7axy^2 - 3xy^2$

SOLUTION

(1) Factor x^2 in the expression.

$$3x^2 + 2x^2 - 4x^2 = (3 + 2 - 4)x^2 = 1x^2 = x^2$$

(2) Factor xy^2 in the expression and then factor a.

$$\begin{aligned} 5axy^2 - 7axy^2 - 3xy^2 &= (5a - 7a - 3)xy^2 \\ &= [(5 - 7)a - 3]xy^2 \\ &= (-2a - 3)xy^2 \end{aligned}$$

PROBLEM

Simplify $\dfrac{\frac{1}{x-1} - \frac{1}{x-2}}{\frac{1}{x-2} - \frac{1}{x-3}}$.

SOLUTION

Simplify the expression in the numerator by using the addition rule.

$$\frac{a}{c} + \frac{c}{d} = \frac{ab + bc}{bd}$$

Notice bd is the Least Common Denominator, LCD. We obtain

$$\frac{x - 2 - (x - 1)}{(x - 1)(x - 2)} = \frac{-1}{(x - 1)(x - 2)}$$

in the numerator.

Repeat this procedure for the expression in the denominator.

$$\frac{x - 3 - (x - 2)}{(x - 2)(x - 3)} = \frac{-1}{(x - 2)(x - 3)}$$

We now have

$$\frac{\frac{-1}{(x-1)(x-2)}}{\frac{-1}{(x-2)(x-3)}}$$

which is simplified by inverting the fraction in the denominator and multiplying it by the numerator and cancelling like terms.

$$\frac{-1}{(x-1)(x-2)} \times \frac{(x-2)(x-3)}{-1} = \frac{x-3}{x-1}$$

☞ Drill 2: Simplifying Algebraic Expressions

1. $16b^2 - 25z^2 =$

   (A) $(4b - 5z)^2$ (B) $(4b + 5z)^2$

   (C) $(4b - 5z)(4b + 5z)$ (D) $(16b - 25z)^2$

2. $x^2 - 2x - 8 =$

   (A) $(x - 4)^2$ (B) $(x - 6)(x - 2)$

   (C) $(x + 4)(x - 2)$ (D) $(x - 4)(x + 2)$

3. $2c^2 + 5cd - 3d^2 =$

   (A) $(c - 3d)(c + 2d)$ (B) $(2c - d)(c + 3d)$

   (C) $(c - d)(2c + 3d)$ (D) $(2c + d)(c + 3d)$

4. $4t^3 - 20t =$

   (A) $4t(t^2 - 5)$ (B) $4t^2(t - 20)$

   (C) $4t(t + 4)(t - 5)$ (D) $2t(2t^2 - 10)$

5. $x^2 + xy - 2y^2 =$

   (A) $(x - 2y)(x + y)$ (B) $(x - 2y)(x - y)$

   (C) $(x + 2y)(x + y)$ (D) $(x + 2y)(x - y)$

6. $5b^2 + 17bd + 6d^2 =$

   (A) $(5b + d)(b + 6d)$ (B) $(5b + 2d)(b + 3d)$

   (C) $(5b - 2d)(b - 3d)$ (D) $(5b - 2d)(b + 3d)$

7. $x^2 + x + 1 =$

   (A) $(x + 1)^2$ (B) $(x + 2)(x - 1)$

   (C) $(x - 2)(x + 1)$ (D) Not possible

8. $3z^3 + 6z^2 =$

(A) $3(z^3 + 2z^2)$ (B) $3z^2(z + 2)$

(C) $3z(z^2 + 2z)$ (D) $z^2(3z + 6)$

9. $m^2p^2 + mpq - 6q^2 =$

(A) $(mp - 2q)(mp + 3q)$ (B) $mp(mp - 2q)(mp + 3q)$

(C) $mpq(1 - 6q)$ (D) $(mp + 2q)(mp + 3q)$

10. $2h^3 + 2h^2t - 4ht^2 =$

(A) $2(h^3 - t)(h + t)$ (B) $2h(h + 2t)(h - t)$

(C) $4h(ht - t^2)$ (D) $2h(h + t) - 4ht^2$

3. Linear Equations

An **equation** is defined as a statement that two separate expressions are equal.

A **solution** to the equation is a number that makes the equation true when it is substituted for the variable. For example, in the equation $3x = 18$, 6 is the solution since $3(6) = 18$. Depending on the equation, there can be more than one solution. Equations with the same solutions are said to be **equivalent equations**. An equation without a solution is said to have a solution set that is the **empty** or **null** set and is represented by ϕ.

Replacing an expression within an equation by an equivalent expression will result in a new equation with solutions equivalent to the original equation. Given the equation below

$$3x + y + x + 2y = 15$$

by combining like terms, we get

$$3x + y + x + 2y = 4x + 3y$$

Since these two expressions are equivalent, we can substitute the simpler form into the equation to get

$$4x + 3y = 15$$

Performing the same operation to both sides of an equation by the same expression will result in a new equation that is equivalent to the original equation.

A) **Addition or subtraction**

$$y + 6 = 10$$

We can add (-6) to both sides

$$y + 6 + (-6) = 10 + (-6)$$

to get $y + 0 = 10 - 6 \rightarrow y = 4$

B) **Multiplication or division**

$$3x = 6$$

$$\frac{3x}{3} = \frac{6}{3}$$

$$x = 2$$

$3x = 6$ is equivalent to $x = 2$.

C) **Raising to a power**

$$a = x^2y$$

$$a^2 = (x^2y)^2$$

$$a^2 = x^4y^2$$

This can be applied to negative and fractional powers as well. For example,

$$x^2 = 3y^4$$

If we raise both members to the -2 power, we get

$$(x^2)^{-2} = (3y^4)^{-2}$$

$$\frac{1}{(x^2)^2} = \frac{1}{(3y^4)^2}$$

$$\frac{1}{x^4} = \frac{1}{9y^8}$$

If we raise both members to the $^1/_2$ power, which is the same as taking the square root, we get

$$(x^2)^{1/2} = (3y^4)^{1/2}$$

$$x = \sqrt{3}y^2$$

D) The **reciprocal** of both members of an equation are equivalent to the original equation. Note: The reciprocal of zero is undefined.

$$\frac{2x+y}{z} = \frac{5}{2} \qquad \frac{z}{2x+y} = \frac{2}{5}$$

PROBLEM

Solve, justifying each step, $3x - 8 = 7x + 8$.

SOLUTION

	$3x - 8 = 7x + 8$
Adding 8 to both members,	$3x - 8 + 8 = 7x + 8 + 8$
Additive inverse property,	$3x + 0 = 7x + 16$
Additive identity property,	$3x = 7x + 16$

Adding $(-7x)$ to both members,	$3x - 7x = 7x + 16 - 7x$
Commuting,	$-4x = 7x - 7x + 16$
Additive inverse property,	$-4x = 0 + 16$
Additive identity property,	$-4x = 16$
Dividing both sides by -4,	$x = {}^{16}/_{-4}$
	$x = -4$

Check: Replacing x by -4 in the original equation:

$$3x - 8 = 7x + 8$$
$$3(-4) - 8 = 7(-4) + 8$$
$$-12 - 8 = -28 + 8$$
$$-20 = -20$$

Linear Equations

A linear equation with one unknown is one that can be put into the form $ax + b = 0$, where a and b are constants, $a \neq 0$.

To solve a linear equation means to transform it into the form $x = {}^{-b}/_{a}$.

A) If the equation has unknowns on both sides of the equality, it is convenient to put similar terms on the same sides. For example,

$$4x + 3 = 2x + 9$$
$$4x + 3 - 2x = 2x + 9 - 2x$$
$$(4x - 2x) + 3 = (2x - 2x) + 9$$
$$2x + 3 = 0 + 9$$
$$2x + 3 - 3 = 0 + 9 - 3$$
$$2x = 6$$
$${}^{2x}/_{2} = {}^{6}/_{2}$$
$$x = 3$$

B) If the equation appears in fractional form, it is necessary to transform it using cross-multiplication, and then repeating the same procedure as in A), we obtain:

$$\frac{3x+4}{3} \times \frac{7x+2}{5}$$

By using cross-multiplication we would obtain

$$3(7x + 2) = 5(3x + 4)$$

This is equivalent to

$$21x + 6 = 15x + 20$$

which can be solved as in A).

$$\begin{aligned} 21x + 6 &= 15x + 20 \\ 21x - 15x + 6 &= 15x - 15x + 20 \\ 6x + 6 - 6 &= 20 - 6 \\ 6x &= 14 \\ x &= {}^{14}/_{6} \\ x &= {}^{7}/_{3} \end{aligned}$$

C) If there are radicals in the equation, it is necessary to square both sides and then apply A).

$$\begin{aligned} \sqrt{3x+1} &= 5 \\ (\sqrt{3x+1})^2 &= 5^2 \\ 3x + 1 &= 25 \\ 3x + 1 - 1 &= 25 - 1 \\ 3x &= 24 \\ x &= {}^{24}/_{3} \\ x &= 8 \end{aligned}$$

PROBLEM

Solve the equation $2(x + 3) = (3x + 5) - (x - 5)$.

SOLUTION

We transform the given equation to an equivalent equation where we can easily recognize the solution set.

$$2(x + 3) = 3x + 5 - (x - 5)$$

Distribute, $\quad 2x + 6 = 3x + 5 - x + 5$

Combine terms, $\quad 2x + 6 = 2x + 10$

Subtract $2x$ from both sides, $\quad 6 = 10$

Since $6 = 10$ is not a true statement, there is no real number which will make the original equation true. The equation is inconsistent and the solution set is ϕ, the empty set.

PROBLEM

Solve the equation $2({}^{2}/_{3}\, y + 5) + 2(y + 5) = 130$.

SOLUTION

The procedure for solving this equation is as follows:

$\frac{4}{3}y + 10 + 2y + 10 = 130,$	Distributive property
$\frac{4}{3}y + 2y + 20 = 130,$	Combining like terms
$\frac{4}{3}y + 2y = 110,$	Subtracting 20 from both sides
$\frac{4}{3}y + \frac{6}{3}y = 110,$	Converting $2y$ into a fraction with denominator 3
$\frac{10}{3}y = 110,$	Combining like terms
$y = 110 \times \frac{3}{10} = 33,$	Dividing by $\frac{10}{3}$

Check: Replace y with 33 in the original equation,

$$2(\tfrac{2}{3}(33) + 5) + 2(33 + 5) = 130$$
$$2(22 + 5) + 2(38) = 130$$
$$2(27) + 76 = 130$$
$$54 + 76 = 130$$
$$130 = 130$$

Therefore, the solution to the given equation is $y = 33$.

☞ Drill 3: Linear Equations

DIRECTIONS: Solve for the unknown.

1. $4x - 2 = 10$

   (A) -1 (B) 2 (C) 3 (D) 4

2. $7z + 1 - z = 2z - 7$

   (A) -2 (B) 0 (C) 1 (D) 2

3. $\frac{1}{3}b + 3 = \frac{1}{2}b$

   (A) $\frac{1}{2}$ (B) 2 (C) $3\frac{3}{5}$ (D) 18

4. $0.4p + 1 = 0.7p - 2$

   (A) 12 (B) 2 (C) 5 (D) 10

5. $4(3x + 2) - 11 = 3(3x - 2)$

   (A) -3 (B) -1 (C) 2 (D) 3

4. Two Linear Equations

Equations of the form $ax + by = c$, where a, b, c are constants and $a, b \neq 0$, are called **linear equations** with two unknown variables.

There are several ways to solve systems of linear equations in two variables:

Method 1: **Addition or subtraction** — If necessary, multiply the equations by numbers that will make the coefficients of one unknown in the resulting equations numerically equal. If the signs of equal coefficients are the same, subtract the equation, otherwise add.

The result is one equation with one unknown; we solve it and substitute the value into the other equations to find the unknown that we first eliminated.

Method 2: **Substitution** — Find the value of one unknown in terms of the other; substitute this value in the other equation and solve.

Method 3: **Graph** — Graph both equations. The point of intersection of the drawn lines is a simultaneous solution for the equations and its coordinates correspond to the answer that would be found analytically.

If the lines are parallel they have no simultaneous solution.

Dependent equations are equations that represent the same line; therefore, every point on the line of a dependent equation represents a solution. Since there is an infinite number of points on a line, there is an infinite number of simultaneous solutions, for example,

$$\begin{cases} 2x + y = 8 \\ 4x + 2y = 16 \end{cases}$$

The equations above are dependent. They represent the same line; all points that satisfy either of the equations are solutions of the system.

A system of linear equations is consistent if there is only one solution for the system.

A system of linear equations is inconsistent if it does not have any solutions.

Example of a consistent system. Find the point of intersection of the graphs of the equations as shown in the figure.

$$x + y = 3$$

$$3x - 2y = 14$$

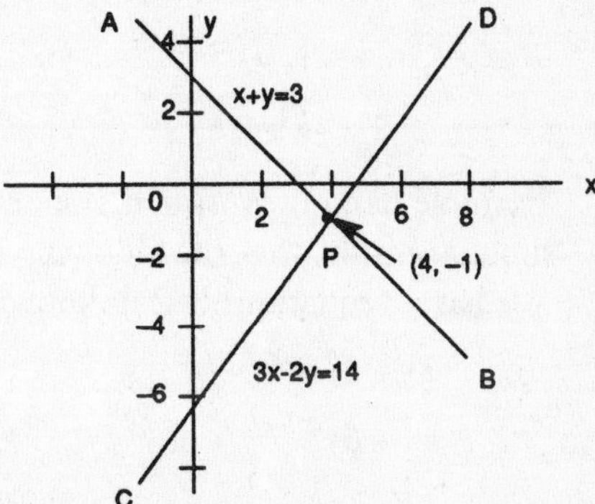

To solve these linear equations, solve for y in terms of x. The equations will be in the form $y = mx + b$, where m is the slope and b is the intercept on the y-axis.

$$\begin{aligned} x + y &= 3 \\ y &= 3 - x && \text{subtract } x \text{ from both sides} \\ 3x - 2y &= 14 && \text{subtract } 3x \text{ from both sides} \\ -2y &= 14 - 3x && \text{divide by } -2 \\ y &= -7 + {}^{3}/_{2}x \end{aligned}$$

The graphs of the linear functions, $y = 3 - x$ and $y = 7 + {}^{3}/_{2}x$, can be determined by plotting only two points. For example, for $y = 3 - x$, let $x = 0$, then $y = 3$. Let $x = 1$, then $y = 2$. The two points on this first line are (0, 3) and (1, 2). For $y = -7 + {}^{3}/_{2}x$, let $x = 0$, then $y = -7$. Let $x = 1$, then $y = -5{}^{1}/_{2}$. The two points on this second line are $(0, -7)$ and $(1, -5{}^{1}/_{2})$.

To find the point of intersection P of

$$x + y = 3 \quad \text{and} \quad 3x - 2y = 14,$$

solve them algebraically. Multiply the first equation by 2. Add these two equations to eliminate the variable y.

$$\begin{array}{rl} 2x + 2y &= 6 \\ 3x - 2y &= 14 \\ \hline 5x \qquad &= 20 \end{array}$$

Solve for x to obtain $x = 4$. Substitute this into $y = 3 - x$ to get $y = 3 - 4 = -1$. P is $(4, -1)$. AB is the graph of the first equation, and CD is the graph of the second equation. The point of intersection P of the two graphs is the only point on both lines. The coordinates of P satisfy both equations and represent the desired solution of the problem. From the graph, P seems to be the point $(4, -1)$. These coordinates satisfy both equations, and hence are the exact coordinates of the point of intersection of the two lines.

To show that $(4, -1)$ satisfies both equations, substitute this point into both equations.

$$\begin{aligned} x + y &= 3 & 3x - 2y &= 14 \\ 4 + (-1) &= 3 & 3(4) - 2(-1) &= 14 \\ 4 - 1 &= 3 & 12 + 2 &= 14 \\ 3 &= 3 & 14 &= 14 \end{aligned}$$

Example of an inconsistent system. Solve the equations $2x + 3y = 6$ and $4x + 6y = 7$ simultaneously. (See the following figure.)

We have 2 equations in 2 unknowns.

$$2x + 3y = 6 \qquad (1)$$

and

$$4x + 6y = 7 \qquad (2)$$

There are several methods to solve this problem. We have chosen to multiply each equation by a different number so that when the two equations are added, one of

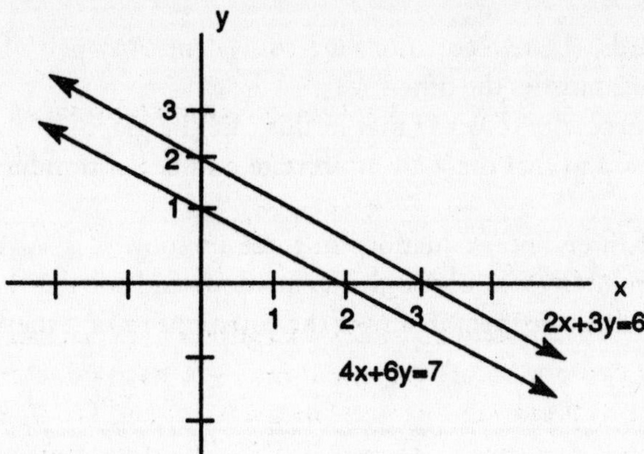

the variables drops out. Thus,

Multiplying equation (1) by 2:	$4x + 6y = 12$	(3)
Multiplying equation (2) by – 1:	$-4x - 6y = -7$	(4)
Adding equations (3) and (4):	$0 = 5$	

We obtain a peculiar result!

Actually, what we have shown in this case is that if there were a simultaneous solution to the given equations, then 0 would equal 5. But the conclusion is impossible; therefore, there can be no simultaneous solution to these two equations, hence no point satisfying both.

The straight lines which are the graphs of these equations must be parallel if they never intersect, but not identical, which can be seen from the graph of these equations (see the accompanying diagram).

Example of a dependent system. Solve the equations $2x + 3y = 6$ and $y = -(2x/3) + 2$ simultaneously.

We have 2 equations in 2 unknowns.

$$2x + 3y = 6 \quad (1)$$

and

$$y = -(2x/3) + 2 \quad (2)$$

There are several methods for solving this problem. Since equation (2) already gives us an expression for y, we use the method of substitution. Substituting $-(2x/3) + 2$ for y in the first equation:

$$2x + 3(-2x/3 + 2) = 6$$

Distributing,

$$2x - 2x + 6 = 6$$

$$6 = 6$$

Apparently we have gotten nowhere! The result $6 = 6$ is true, but indicates no solution. Actually, our work shows that no matter what real number x is, if y is determined by the second equation, then the first equation will always be satisfied.

The reason for this peculiarity may be seen if we take a closer look at the equation $y = -(2x/3) + 2$. It is equivalent to $3y = -2x + 6$ or $2x + 3y = 6$.

In other words, the two equations are equivalent. Any pair of values of x and y which satisfies one satisfies the other.

It is hardly necessary to verify that in this case the graphs of the given equations are identical lines, and that there are an infinite number of simultaneous solutions of these equations.

A system of three linear equations in three unknowns is solved by eliminating one unknown from any two of the three equations and solving them. After finding two unknowns substitute them in any of the equations to find the third unknown.

PROBLEM

Solve the system

$$2x + 3y - 4z = -8 \quad (1)$$

$$x + y - 2z = -5 \quad (2)$$

$$7x - 2y + 5z = 4 \quad (3)$$

SOLUTION

We cannot eliminate any variable from two pairs of equations by a single multiplication. However, both x and z may be eliminated from equations (1) and (2) by multiplying equation (2) by -2. Then

$$2x + 3y - 4z = -8 \quad (1)$$

$$-2x - 2y + 4z = 10 \quad (4)$$

By addition, we have $y = 2$. Although we may now eliminate either x or z from another pair of equations, we can more conveniently substitute $y = 2$ in equations (2) and (3) to get two equations in two variables. Thus, making the substitution $y = 2$ in equations (2) and (3), we have

$$x - 2z = -7 \quad (5)$$

$$7x + 5z = 8 \quad (6)$$

Multiply equation (5) by 5 and multiply equation (6) by 2. Then add the two new equations. Then $x = -1$. Substitute x in either (5) or (6) to find z.

The solution of the system is $x = -1$, $y = 2$, and $z = 3$. Check by substitution.

A system of equations, as shown below, that has all constant terms $b_1, b_2, \ldots, b_n$ equal to zero is said to be a homogeneous system.

$$\begin{cases} a_{11}x_1 + a_{12}x_2 + \ldots + a_{1n}x_m = b_1 \\ a_{21}x_1 + a_{22}x_2 + \ldots + a_{2n}x_m = b_2 \\ \vdots \qquad \vdots \qquad \vdots \qquad \vdots \\ a_{n1}x_1 + a_{n2}x_2 + \ldots + a_{nn}x_m = b_n \end{cases}$$

A homogeneous system always has at least one solution which is called the trivial solution that is $x_1 = 0$, $x_2 = 0$, …, $x_m = 0$.

For any given homogeneous system of equations, in which the number of variables is greater than or equal to the number of equations, there are non-trivial solutions.

Two systems of linear equations are said to be equivalent if and only if they have the same solution set.

PROBLEM

Solve for x and y.

$$x + 2y = 8 \quad (1)$$

$$3x + 4y = 20 \quad (2)$$

SOLUTION

Solve equation (1) for x in terms of y.

$$x = 8 - 2y \quad (3)$$

Substitute $(8 - 2y)$ for x in (2).

$$3(8 - 2y) + 4y = 20 \quad (4)$$

Solve (4) for y as follows:

Distribute: $24 - 6y + 4y = 20$

Combine like terms and then subtract 24 from both sides:

$$24 - 2y = 20$$

$$24 - 24 - 2y = 20 - 24$$

$$-2y = -4$$

Divide both sides by -2:

$$y = 2$$

Substitute 2 for y in equation (1):

$$x + 2(2) = 8$$

$$x = 4$$

Thus, our solution is $x = 4$, $y = 2$.

Check: Substitute $x = 4$, $y = 2$ in equations (1) and (2).

$$4 + 2(2) = 8$$

$$8 = 8$$

$$3(4) + 4(2) = 20$$

$$20 = 20$$

PROBLEM

Solve algebraically:	
$4x + 2y = -1$	(1)
$5x - 3y = 7$	(2)

SOLUTION

We arbitrarily choose to eliminate x first.

Multiply equation (1) by 5:	$20x + 10y = -5$	(3)
Multiply equation (2) by 4:	$20x - 12y = 28$	(4)
Subtract equation (3) – (4):	$22y = -33$	(5)
Divide equation (5) by 22:	$y = {}^{33}/_{22} = -{}^{3}/_{2}$	

To find x, substitute $y = -{}^{3}/_{2}$ in either of the original equations. If we use equation (1), we obtain $4x + 2(-{}^{3}/_{2}) = -1$, $4x - 3 = -1$, $4x = 2$, $x = {}^{1}/_{2}$.

The solution $({}^{1}/_{2}, -{}^{3}/_{2})$ should be checked in both equations of the given system.

Replacing $({}^{1}/_{2}, -{}^{3}/_{2})$ in equation (1):

$$4x + 2y = -1$$
$$4({}^{1}/_{2}) + 2(-{}^{3}/_{2}) = -1$$
$${}^{4}/_{2} - 3 = -1$$
$$2 - 3 = -1$$
$$-1 = -1$$

Replacing $({}^{1}/_{2}, -{}^{3}/_{2})$ in equation (2):

$$5x - 3y = 7$$
$$5({}^{1}/_{2}) - 3(-{}^{3}/_{2}) = 7$$
$${}^{5}/_{2} + {}^{9}/_{2} = 7$$
$${}^{14}/_{2} = 7$$
$$7 = 7$$

(Instead of eliminating x from the two given equations, we could have eliminated y by multiplying equation (1) by 3, multiplying equation (2) by 2, and then adding the two derived equations.)

☞ Drill 4: Two Linear Equations

DIRECTIONS: Find the solution set for each pair of equations.

1. $3x + 4y = -2$
   $x - 6y = -8$

   (A) (2, – 1) (B) (– 2, 1)

   (C) (– 2, – 1) (D) (1, 2)

2. $2x + y = -10$
   $-2x - 4y = 4$

   (A) (6, – 2) (B) (– 6, 2)

   (C) (– 2, 6) (D) (2, 6)

3. $6x + 5y = -4$
   $3x - 3y = 9$

   (A) (1, – 2) (B) (1, 2)

   (C) (2, – 1) (D) (– 2, 1)

4. $4x + 3y = 9$
   $2x - 2y = 8$

   (A) (– 3, 1) (B) (1, – 3)

   (C) (3, 1) (D) (3, – 1)

5. $x + y = 7$
   $x = y - 3$

   (A) (5, 2) (B) (– 5, 2)

   (C) (2, 5) (D) (– 2, 5)

6. $5x + 6y = 4$
   $3x - 2y = 1$

   (A) (3, 6) (B) (1/2, 1/4)

   (C) (– 3, 6) (D) (2, 4)

7. $x - 2y = 7$
   $x + y = -2$

(A) $(-2, 7)$ (B) $(3, -1)$

(C) $(-7, 2)$ (D) $(1, -3)$

8. $4x + 3y = 3$
$-2x + 6y = 3$

(A) $(1/2, 2/3)$ (B) $(-0.3, 0.6)$

(C) $(0.3, 0.6)$ (D) $(-0.2, 0.5)$

9. $4x - 2y = -14$
$8x + y = 7$

(A) $(0, 7)$ (B) $(2, -7)$

(C) $(7, 0)$ (D) $(-7, 2)$

10. $6x - 3y = 1$
$-9x + 5y = -1$

(A) $(1, -1)$ (B) $(2/3, 1)$

(C) $(1, 2/3)$ (D) $(-1, 1)$

---

5. Quadratic Equations

A second degree equation in x of the type $ax^2 + bx + c = 0$, $a \neq 0$, a, b, and c are real numbers, is called a **quadratic equation.**

To solve a quadratic equation is to find values of x which satisfy $ax^2 + bx + c = 0$. These values of x are called **solutions**, or **roots**, of the equation.

A quadratic equation has a maximum of two roots. Methods of solving quadratic equations:

A) **Direct solution**: Given $x^2 - 9 = 0$.

We can solve directly by isolating the variable x.

$$x^2 = 9$$

$$x = \pm 3$$

B) **Factoring**: Given a quadratic equation $ax^2 + bx + c = 0$, $a, b, c \neq 0$. To factor means to express it as the product $a(x - r_1)(x - r_2) = 0$, where r_1 and r_2 are the two roots.

Some helpful hints to remember are

a) $r_1 + r_2 = -{}^{b}/_{a}$

b) $r_1 r_2 = {}^{c}/_{a}$

Given $x^2 - 5x + 4 = 0$.

Since $r_1 + r_2 = -{}^{b}/_{a} = -{}^{(-5)}/_{1} = 5$, so the possible solutions are (3, 2), (4, 1), and (5, 0). Also, $r_1r_2 = {}^{c}/_{a} = {}^{4}/_{1} = 4$; this equation is satisfied only by the second pair, so $r_1 = 4$, $r_2 = 1$ and the factored form is $(x - 4)(x - 1) = 0$.

If the coefficient of x^2 is not 1, it is necessary to divide the equation by this coefficient and then factor.

Given $2x^2 - 12x + 16 = 0$

Dividing by 2, we obtain

$$x^2 - 6x + 8 = 0$$

Since $r_1 + r_2 = -{}^{b}/_{a} = 6$, the possible solutions are (6, 0), (5, 1), (4, 2), (3, 3). Also, $r_1r_2 = 8$, so the only possible answer is (4, 2) and the expression $x^2 - 6x + 8 = 0$ can be factored as $(x - 4)(x - 2)$.

C) **Completing the Squares:** If it is difficult to factor the quadratic equation using the previous method, we can complete the squares.

Given $x^2 - 12x + 8 = 0$.

We know that the two roots added up should be 12 because $r_1 + r_2 = -{}^{b}/_{a} = -{}^{(-12)}/_{1} = 12$. The possible roots are (12, 0), (11, 1), (10, 2), (9, 3), (8, 4), (7, 5), (6, 6).

But none of these satisfy $r_1r_2 = 8$, so we cannot use (B).

To complete the square, it is necessary to isolate the constant term.

$$x^2 - 12x = -8$$

Then take $^1/_2$ coefficient of x, square it and add to both sides.

$$x^2 - 12x + \left(\frac{-12}{2}\right)^2 = -8 + \left(\frac{-12}{2}\right)^2$$

$$x^2 - 12x + 36 = -8 + 36 = 28$$

Now we can use the previous method to factor the left side: $r_1 + r_2 = 12$, $r_1r_2 = 36$ is satisfied by the pair (6, 6), so we have

$$(x - 6)^2 = 28$$

Now extract the root of both sides and solve for x.

$$(x - 6) = \pm\sqrt{28} = \pm 2\sqrt{7}$$

$$x = \pm 2\sqrt{7} + 6$$

So the roots are

$$x = 2\sqrt{7} + 6, \quad x = -2\sqrt{7} + 6$$

PROBLEM

Solve the equation $x^2 + 8x + 15 = 0$.

SOLUTION

Since $(x + a)(x + b) = x^2 + bx + ax + ab = x^2 + (a + b)x + ab$, we may factor the given equation, $0 = x^2 + 8x + 15$, replacing $a + b$ by 8 and ab by 15. Thus,

$$a + b = 8 \quad \text{and} \quad ab = 15$$

We want the two numbers a and b whose sum is 8 and whose product is 15. We check all pairs of numbers whose product is 15:

(a) $1 \times 15 = 15$; thus, $a = 1$, $b = 15$, and $ab = 15$.

$1 + 15 = 16$; therefore, we reject these values because $a + b \neq 8$.

(b) $3 \times 5 = 15$; thus, $a = 3$, $b = 5$, and $ab = 15$.

$3 + 5 = 8$; therefore, $a + b = 8$, and we accept these values.

Hence, $x^2 + 8x + 15 = 0$ is equivalent to

$$0 = x^2 + (3 + 5)x + 3 \times 5 = (x + 3)(x + 5)$$

Hence, $x + 5 = 0$ or $x + 3 = 0$

Since the product of these two numbers is 0, one of the numbers must be 0. Hence, $x = -5$ or $x = -3$, and the solution set is $x = \{-5, -3\}$.

The student should note that $x = -5$ or $x = -3$. We are certainly not making the statement that $x = -5$ and $x = -3$. Also, the student should check that both these numbers do actually satisfy the given equations and hence are solutions.

Check: Replacing x by (-5) in the original equation:

$$\begin{aligned} x^2 + 8x + 15 &= 0 \\ (-5)^2 + 8(-5) + 15 &= 0 \\ 25 - 40 + 15 &= 0 \\ -15 + 15 &= 0 \\ 0 &= 0 \end{aligned}$$

Replacing x by (-3) in the original equation:

$$\begin{aligned} x^2 + 8x + 15 &= 0 \\ (-3)^2 + 8(-3) + 15 &= 0 \\ 9 - 24 + 15 &= 0 \\ -15 + 15 &= 0 \\ 0 &= 0 \end{aligned}$$

PROBLEM

Solve the following equations by factoring.

(1) $2x^2 + 3x = 0$ (3) $z^2 - 2z - 3 = 0$

(2) $y^2 - 2y - 3 = y - 3$ (4) $2m^2 - 11m - 6 = 0$

SOLUTION

(1) $2x^2 + 3x = 0$. Factoring out the common factor of x from the left side of the given equation,

$$x(2x + 3) = 0$$

Whenever a product $ab = 0$, where a and b are any two numbers, either $a = 0$ or $b = 0$. Then, either

$$x = 0 \text{ or } 2x + 3 = 0$$
$$2x = -3$$
$$x = -3/2$$

Hence, the solution set to the original equation $2x^2 + 3x = 0$ is $\{-3/2, 0\}$.

(2) $y^2 - 2y - 3 = y - 3$. Subtract $(y - 3)$ from both sides of the given equation.

$$y^2 - 2y - 3 - (y - 3) = y - 3 - (y - 3)$$
$$y^2 - 2y - 3 - y + 3 = y - 3 - y + 3$$
$$y^2 - 2y - \cancel{3} - y + \cancel{3} = \cancel{y} - \cancel{3} - \cancel{y} + \cancel{3}$$
$$y^2 - 3y = 0$$

Factor out a common factor of y from the left side of this equation.

$$y(y - 3) = 0$$

Thus, $y = 0$ or $y - 3 = 0$, $y = 3$.

Therefore, the solution set to the original equation $y^2 - 2y - 3 = y - 3$ is $\{0, 3\}$.

(3) $z^2 - 2z - 3 = 0$. Factor the original equation into a product of two polynomials.

$$z^2 - 2z - 3 = (z - 3)(z + 1) = 0$$

Hence,

$$(z - 3)(z + 1) = 0; \text{ and } z - 3 = 0 \text{ or } z + 1 = 0$$
$$z = 3 \qquad z = -1$$

Therefore, the solution set to the original equation $z^2 - 2z - 3 = 0$ is $\{-1, 3\}$.

(4) $2m^2 - 11m - 6 = 0$. Factor the original equation into a product of two polynomials.

$$2m^2 - 11m - 6 = (2m + 1)(m - 6) = 0$$

Thus,

$$2m + 1 = 0 \quad \text{or} \quad m - 6 = 0$$

$$2m = -1 \qquad m = 6$$

$$m = -{}^1/_2$$

Therefore, the solution set to the original equation $2m^2 - 11m - 6 = 0$ is $\{-{}^1/_2, 6\}$.

The Quadratic Formula

For a quadratic equation of a general type:

$$ax^2 + bx + c = 0$$

where $a \neq 0$, a real solution exists if and only if the discriminant, defined as

$$\Delta = b^2 - 4ac$$

is greater than or equal to zero,

i.e., $\Delta \geq 0$

In which case the quadratic formula

$$x_{1,2} = \frac{-b \pm \sqrt{\Delta}}{2a} = \frac{-b \pm \sqrt{b^2 - 4ac}}{2a}$$

gives the two roots of the equation.

If $\Delta = b^2 - 4ac = 0$, we have a double-root.

$$x_1 = x_2 = \frac{-b}{2a}$$

PROBLEM

Find the roots of the equation $x^2 + 12 - 85 = 0$.

SOLUTION

The roots of this equation may be found using the quadratic formula

$$x = \frac{-B \pm \sqrt{B^2 - 4AC}}{2A}$$

In this equation $A = 1$, $B = 12$, and $C = -85$. Hence, by the quadratic formula,

$$x = \frac{-12 + \sqrt{144 + 340}}{2} \quad \text{or} \quad x = \frac{-12 - \sqrt{144 + 340}}{2}$$

$$x = \frac{-12 + 22}{2} \quad \text{or} \quad x = \frac{-12 - 22}{2}$$

Therefore, $x = 5$ or $x = -17$. This is equivalent to the statement that the solution set is $\{-17, 5\}$.

PROBLEM

Use the quadratic formula to solve for x in the equation $x^2 - 5x + 6 = 0$.

SOLUTION

The quadratic formula,

$$x = \frac{-b \pm \sqrt{b^2 - 4ac}}{2a},$$

is used to solve equations in the form $ax^2 + bx + c = 0$. Here $a = 1$, $b = -5$, and $c = 6$. Hence,

$$x = \frac{-(-5) \pm \sqrt{(-5)^2 - 4 \times 1 \times 6}}{2 \times 1} = \frac{5 \pm \sqrt{25 - 24}}{2}$$

$$= \frac{5 \pm \sqrt{1}}{2}$$

$$= \frac{5 \pm 1}{2}$$

$$= \frac{5+1}{2} \quad \text{or} \quad \frac{5-1}{2}$$

$$= \frac{6}{2} \quad \text{or} \quad \frac{4}{2}$$

$$= 3 \quad \text{or} \quad 2$$

Thus, the roots of the equation

$$x^2 - 5x + 6 = 0$$

are $x = 3$ and $x = 2$.

Graphing Quadratic Expressions

A quadratic expression is a relation between the coordinates x and y of the form

$$y = ax^2 + bx + c; \quad a \neq 0$$

The point

$$\left(-\frac{b}{2a}, -\frac{b^2}{4a} + c\right)$$

is the vertex, or turning point, of the curve which is called a parabola. For $a > 0$ the parabola opens upward and for $a < 0$ the parabola opens downward.

The graph can also be obtained by generating a table of values (x, y) that satisfy the expression and the plot is obtained by smoothly joining the points (x, y) by a curve in the coordinate plane.

PROBLEM

> Draw the graphs of
>
> $$f(x) = x^2,\ g(x) = 3x^2,$$
>
> and also
>
> $$h(x) = {}^1/_2\, x^2$$
>
> on one set of coordinate axes.

SOLUTION

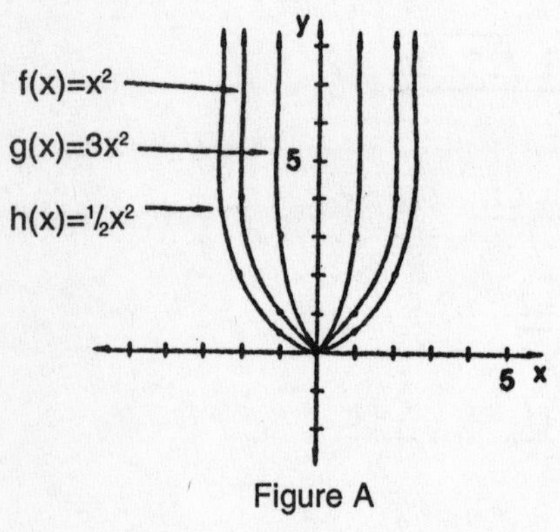

Figure A

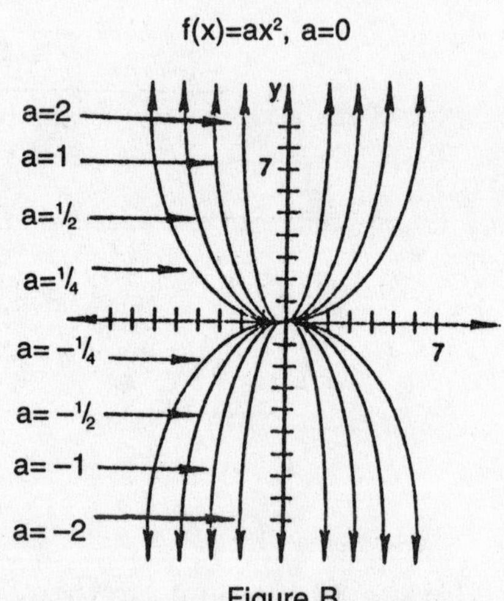

Figure B

x	0	1	−1	2	−2	3	−3
$f(x) = x^2$	0	1	1	4	4	9	9
$g(x) = 3x^2$	0	3	3	12	12	27	27
$h(x) = {}^1/_2 x^2$	0	$^1/_2$	$^1/_2$	2	2	$4^1/_2$	$4^1/_2$

We construct a composite table showing the values of each function corresponding to selected values for x.

In the example, we graphed three instances of the function

$$f(x) = ax^2,\ a > 0.$$

For different values of a, how do the graphs compare? (See figure A.) Assigning a given value to a has very little effect upon the main characteristics of the graph. The coefficient a serves as a "stretching factor" relative to the y-axis. As a increases, the two branches of the curve approach the y-axis. The curve becomes "thinner." As a decreases, the curve becomes "flatter" and approaches the x-axis.

PROBLEM

Construct the graph of $\{(x, y) \mid y = {}^1/_2\, x^2 - 2x - 3\}$.

SOLUTION

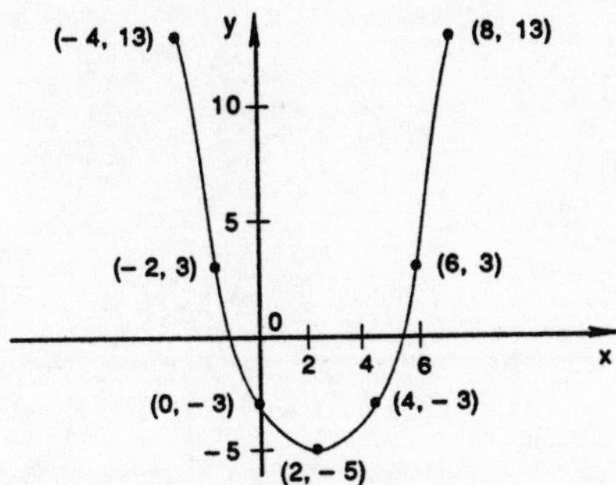

In general, the graph of the quadratic function

$$y = ax^2 + bx + c$$

is a parabola. Some of its properties are:

1. If $a > 0$, the graph opens upward.
2. If $a < 0$, the graph opens downward.

We note that $a = {}^1/_2$ in the equation

$$y = {}^1/_2\, x^2 - 2x - 3.$$

Hence, the graph is a parabola opening upward since $a > 0$. In order to determine the vertex (x_v, y_v) of the parabola, we complete the square by the following procedure:

Factor out ${}^1/_2$ from

$$y = {}^1/_2\, x^2 - 2x - 3$$

Then $\quad {}^1/_2\, x^2 - 2x - 3 = {}^1/_2(x^2 - 4x - 6)$

Complete the square of $x^2 - 4x$. This is done by taking ${}^1/_2$ of the coefficient of x and squaring it. Thus, the constant term is

$$[{}^1/_2\,(-4)]^2 = (-2)^2 = 4$$

To keep the same equation we must retain -6. Thus, we express it as $4 - 10$. Then,

$${}^1/_2\,(x^2 - 4x - 6) = {}^1/_2\,(x^2 - 4x + 4 - 10)$$

Factor $\quad (x^2 - 4x + 4)$

into $\quad (x - 2)(x - 2) = (x - 2)^2$

Then, $\quad {}^1/_2(x^2 - 4x + 4 - 10) = {}^1/_2[(x - 2)^2 - 10]$

Now, $y = \frac{1}{2}[(x-2)^2 - 10]$

Since the parabola opens upward, the vertex is the value where y is minimum. $(x-2)^2$ will always be positive since the square of a positive or of a negative number is always positive. Therefore, the minimum value of y will occur when $(x-2) = 0$. Consequently, y is least when $x - 2 = 0$ or when $x = 2$. To find y, substitute $x = 2$ into

$$\begin{aligned} y &= \tfrac{1}{2}[(x-2)^2 - 10] \\ &= \tfrac{1}{2}[(2-2)^2 - 10] \\ &= \tfrac{1}{2}[0^2 - 10] \\ &= \tfrac{1}{2}[-10] \\ &= -5 \end{aligned}$$

Hence, the vertex is $(2, -5)$.

We now assign numbers to x and calculate the corresponding y-values to obtain points on the parabola. This is done in the following table:

x	$\frac{1}{2}x^2 - 2x - 3$	y
-4	$\frac{1}{2}(-4)^2 - 2(-4) - 3$	13
-2	$\frac{1}{2}(-2)^2 - 2(-2) - 3$	3
0	$\frac{1}{2}(0)^2 - 2(0) - 3$	-3
2	$\frac{1}{2}(2)^2 - 2(2) - 3$	-5
4	$\frac{1}{2}(4)^2 - 2(4) - 3$	-3
6	$\frac{1}{2}(6)^2 - 2(6) - 3$	3
8	$\frac{1}{2}(8)^2 - 2(8) - 3$	13

The graph is shown in the accompanying figure.

☞ Drill 5: Quadratic Equations

DIRECTIONS: Solve for all values of x.

1. $x^2 - 2x - 8 = 0$

   (A) 4 and -2 (B) 4 and 8

   (C) 4 (D) -2 and 8

2. $x^2 + 2x - 3 = 0$

   (A) -3 and 2 (B) 2 and 1

   (C) 3 and 1 (D) -3 and 1

3. $x^2 - 7x = -10$

(A) – 3 and 5
(B) 2 and 5
(C) 2
(D) – 2 and – 5

4. $x^2 - 8x + 16 = 0$

(A) 8 and 2
(B) 1 and 16
(C) 4
(D) – 2 and 4

5. $3x^2 + 3x = 6$

(A) 1 and – 2
(B) 2 and 3
(C) – 3 and 2
(D) 1 and – 3

6. $x^2 + 7x = 0$

(A) 7
(B) 0 and – 7
(C) –7
(D) 0 and 7

7. $x^2 - 25 = 0$

(A) 5
(B) 5 and – 5
(C) 15 and 10
(D) – 5 and 10

8. $2x^2 + 4x = 16$

(A) 2 and – 2
(B) 8 and – 2
(C) 4 and 8
(D) 2 and – 4

9. $6x^2 - x - 2 = 0$

(A) 2 and 3
(B) 1/2 and 1/3
(C) – 1/2 and 2/3
(D) 2/3 and 3

10. $12x^2 + 5x = 3$

(A) 1/3 and – 1/4
(B) – 3/4 and 1/3
(C) 4 and 1/6
(D) 1/3 and – 4

11. Solve using the quadratic formula $6x^2 - 7x - 20 = 0$

(A) 2 and – 2
(B) 4 and – 4
(C) 5/2 and – 4/3
(D) 2 and – 1/3

12. Solve using the quadratic formula $x^2 + 5x + 6 = 0$

(A) – 2 and – 3 (B) 1/3 and – 4

(C) 2 and 3 (D) 4 and 8

13. Find the graph of $y = x^2 - 3x + 2$

(A)

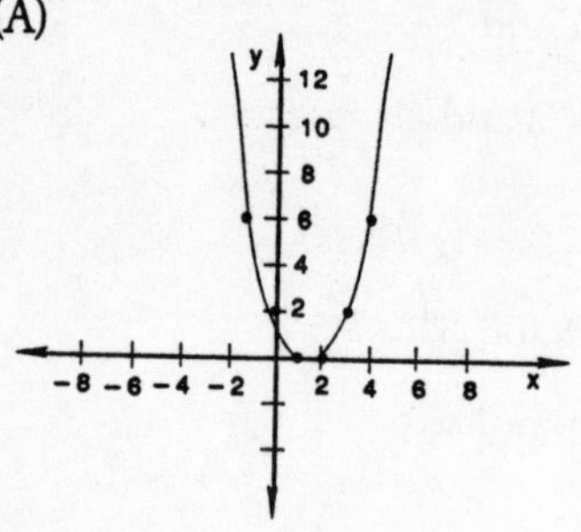

(B)

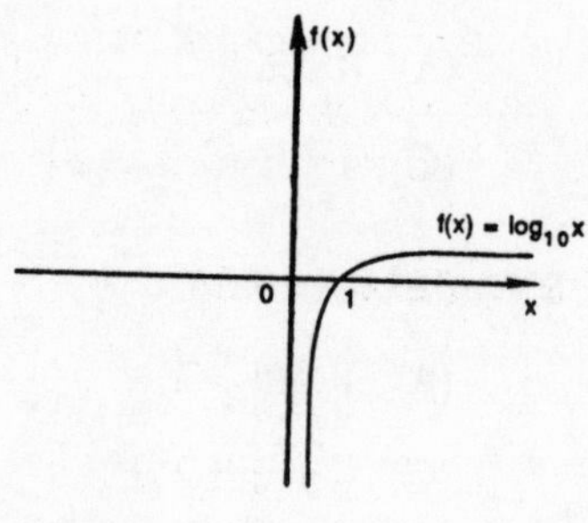

(C)

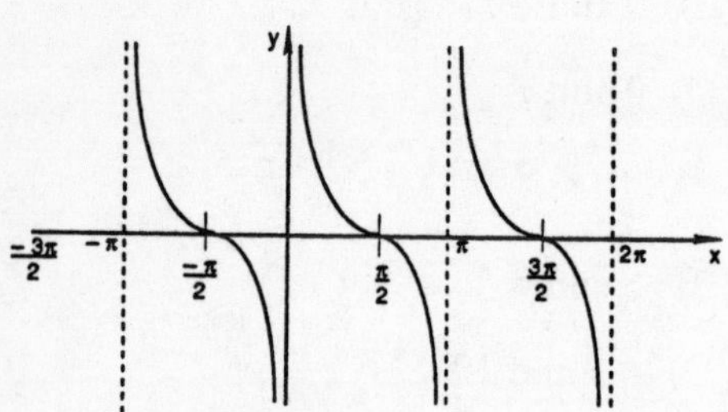

(D)

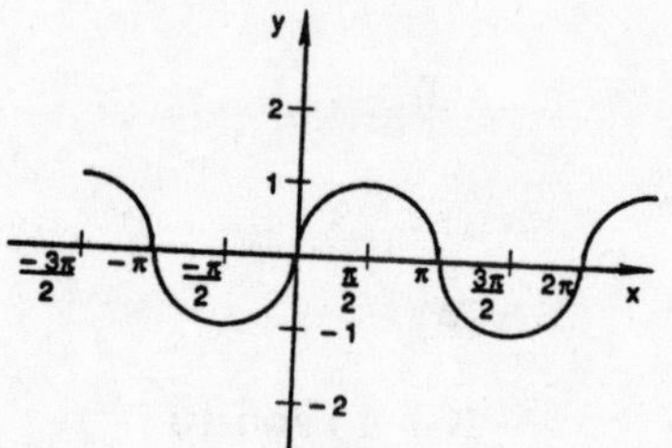

14. Find the graph of $x^2 + y - 2x = 0$

(A)

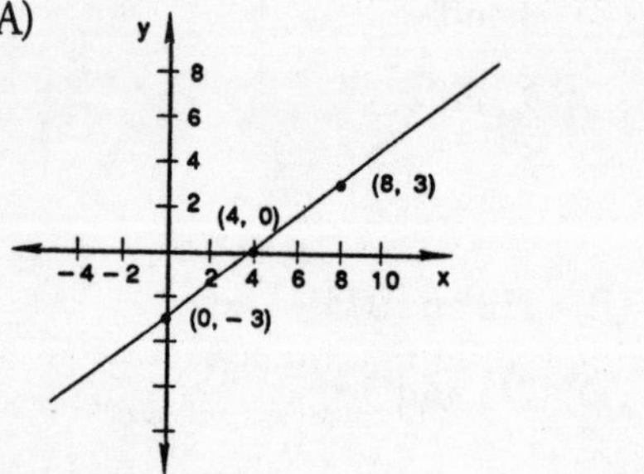

(B)

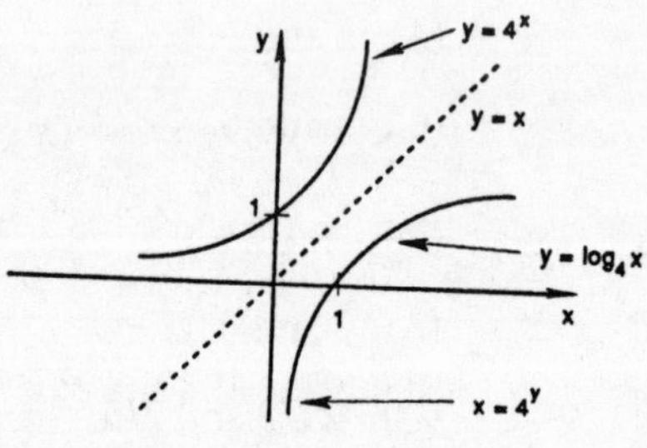

(C)

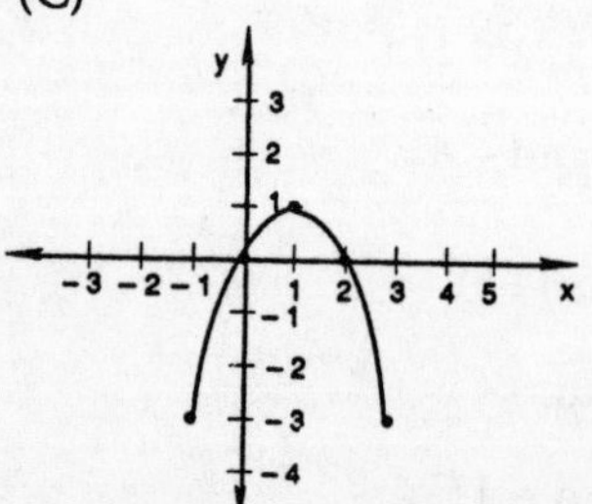

(D)

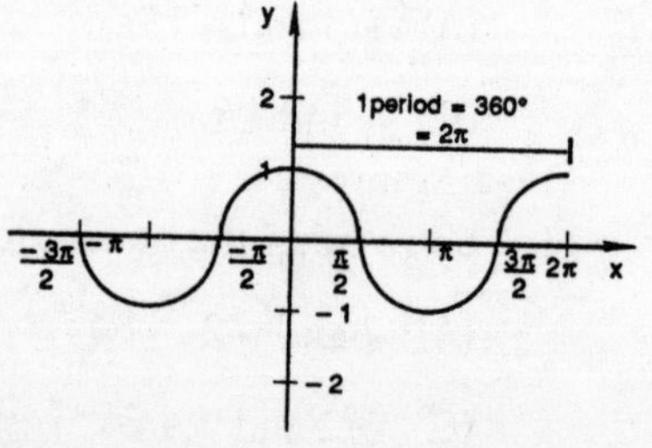

6. Absolute Value Equations

The absolute value of a, $|a|$, is defined as:

$$|a| = a \text{ when } a > 0, \; |a| = -a \text{ when } a < 0, \; |a| = 0 \text{ when } a = 0.$$

When the definition of absolute value is applied to an equation, the quantity within the absolute value symbol is considered to have two values. This value can be either positive or negative before the absolute value is taken. As a result, each absolute value equation actually contains two separate equations.

When evaluating equations containing absolute values, proceed as follows:

EXAMPLE

$|5 - 3x| = 7$ is valid if either

$$5 - 3x = 7 \quad \text{or} \quad 5 - 3x = -7$$
$$-3x = 2 \qquad\qquad -3x = -12$$
$$x = -2/3 \qquad\qquad x = 4$$

The solution set is therefore $x = (-2/3, 4)$.

Remember, the absolute value of a number cannot be negative. So, for the equation $|5x + 4| = -3$, there would be no solution.

EXAMPLE

Solve for x in $|2x - 6| = |4 - 5x|$.

There are four possibilities here. $2x - 6$ and $4 - 5x$ can be either positive or negative. Therefore,

$$2x - 6 = 4 - 5x \tag{1}$$
$$-(2x - 6) = 4 - 5x \tag{2}$$
$$2x - 6 = -(4 - 5x) \tag{3}$$
$$-(2x - 6) = -(4 - 5x) \tag{4}$$

Equations (2) and (3) result in the same solution, as do equations (1) and (4). Therefore, it is necessary to solve only for equations (1) and (2). This gives

$$2x - 6 = 4 - 5x \quad \text{or} \quad -(2x - 6) = 4 - 5x$$
$$7x = 10 \qquad\qquad -2x + 6 = 4 - 5x$$
$$x = 10/7 \qquad\qquad x = -2/3$$

The solution set is $(10/7, -2/3)$.

☞ Drill 6: Absolute Value Equations

1. $|4x - 2| = 6$

   (A) – 2 and – 1 (B) – 1 and 2

   (C) 2 (D) 1/2 and – 2

2. $|3 - 1/2y| = -7$

   (A) – 8 and 20 (B) 8 and – 20

   (C) 2 and – 5 (D) No solution

3. $2|x + 7| = 12$

   (A) – 13 and – 1 (B) – 6 and 6

   (C) – 1 and 13 (D) 6 and – 13

4. $|5x| - 7 = 3$

   (A) 2 and 4 (B) 4/5 and 3

   (C) – 2 and 2 (D) 2

5. $\left|\frac{3}{4}m\right| = 9$

   (A) 24 and – 16 (B) 4/27 and – 4/3

   (C) 4/3 and 12 (D) – 12 and 12

7. Inequalities

An inequality is a statement where the value of one quantity or expression is greater than (>), less than (<), greater than or equal to (≥), less than or equal to (≤), or not equal to (≠) that of another.

EXAMPLE

$5 > 4$

The expression above means that the value of 5 is greater than the value of 4.

A **conditional inequality** is an inequality whose validity depends on the values of the variables in the sentence. That is, certain values of the variables will make the sentence true, and others will make it false. $3 - y > 3 + y$ is a conditional inequality for the set of real numbers, since it is true for any replacement less than 0 and false for all others.

$x + 5 > x + 2$ is an **absolute inequality** for the set of real numbers, meaning that for any real value x, the expression on the left is greater than the expression on the right.

$5y < 2y + y$ is inconsistent for the set of non-negative real numbers. For any y greater than 0 the sentence is always false. A sentence is inconsistent if it is always false when its variables assume allowable values.

The solution of a given inequality in one variable x consists of all values of x for which the inequality is true.

The graph of an inequality in one variable is represented by either a ray or a line segment on the real number line.

The endpoint is not a solution if the variable is strictly less than or greater than a particular value.

EXAMPLE

$x > 2$

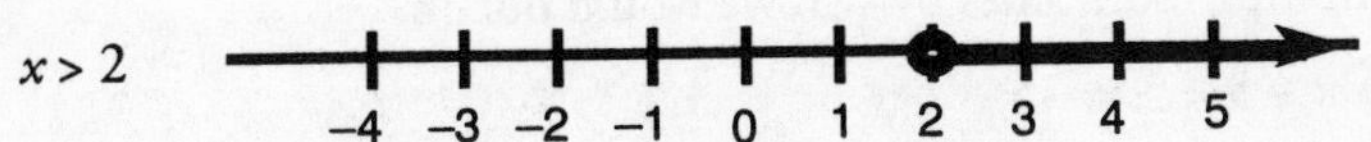

2 is not a solution and should be represented as shown.

The endpoint is a solution if the variable is either (1) less than or equal to or (2) greater than or equal to a particular value.

EXAMPLE

$5 > x \geq 2$

In this case 2 is a solution and should be represented as shown.

Properties of Inequalities

If x and y are real numbers then one and only one of the following statements is true:

$x > y$, $x = y$, or $x < y$.

This is the order property of real numbers.

If a, b, and c are real numbers:

A) If $a < b$ and $b < c$ then $a < c$.

B) If $a > b$ and $b > c$ then $a > c$.

This is the **transitive property of inequalities.**

If a, b, and c are real numbers and $a > b$ then $a + c > b + c$ and $a - c > b - c$. This is the **addition property of inequality**.

Two inequalities are said to have the same **sense** if their signs of inequality point in the same direction.

The sense of an inequality remains the same if both sides are multiplied or divided by the same positive real number.

EXAMPLE

$4 > 3$

If we multiply both sides by 5, we will obtain

$4 \times 5 > 3 \times 5$

$20 > 15$

The sense of the inequality does not change.

The sense of an inequality becomes opposite if each side is multiplied or divided by the same negative real number.

EXAMPLE

$4 > 3$

If we multiply both sides by -5, we would obtain

$4 \times -5 < 3 \times -5$

$-20 < -15$

The sense of the inequality becomes opposite.

If $a > b$ and a, b, and n are positive real numbers, then

$a^n > b^n$ and $a^{-n} < b^{-n}$

If $x > y$ and $q > p$ then $x + q > y + p$.

If $x > y > 0$ and $q > p > 0$ then $xq > yp$.

Inequalities that have the same solution set are called **equivalent inequalities.**

PROBLEM

Solve the inequality $2x + 5 > 9$.

SOLUTION

$2x + 5 + (-5) > 9 + (-5)$	Adding -5 to both sides
$2x + 0 > 9 + (-5)$	Additive inverse property
$2x > 9 + (-5)$	Additive identity property
$2x > 4$	Combining terms
$\frac{1}{2}(2x) > \frac{1}{2} \times 4$	Multiplying both sides by $\frac{1}{2}$
$x > 2$	

The solution set is

$X = \{x \mid 2x + 5 > 9\}$

$= \{x \mid x > 2\}$

(that is all x, such that x is greater than 2).

PROBLEM

Solve the inequality $4x + 3 < 6x + 8$.

SOLUTION

In order to solve the inequality $4x + 3 < 6x + 8$, we must find all values of x which make it true. Thus, we wish to obtain x alone on one side of the inequality.

Add – 3 to both sides.

$$\begin{array}{rcl} 4x + 3 & < & 6x + 8 \\ -3 & & -3 \\ \hline 4x & < & 6x + 5 \end{array}$$

Add – $6x$ to both sides.

$$\begin{array}{rcl} 4x & < & 6x + 5 \\ -6x & & -6x \\ \hline -2x & < & 5 \end{array}$$

In order to obtain x alone we must divide both sides by (– 2). Recall that dividing an inequality by a negative number reverses the inequality sign, hence

$$\frac{-2x}{-2} > \frac{5}{-2}$$

Cancelling $^{-2}/_{-2}$ we obtain, $x > -{}^{5}/_{2}$.

Thus, our solution is $\{x : x > -{}^{5}/_{2}\}$ (the set of all x such that x is greater than $-{}^{5}/_{2}$).

☞ Drill 7: Inequalities

DIRECTIONS: Find the solution set for each inequality.

1. $3m + 2 < 7$

   (A) $m \geq {}^{5}/_{3}$ (B) $m < {}^{5}/_{3}$

   (C) $m < 2$ (D) $m > 2$

2. ${}^{1}/_{2}\,x - 3 \leq 1$

   (A) $-4 \leq x \leq 8$ (B) $x \geq -8$

   (C) $x \leq 8$ (D) $2 \leq x \leq 8$

3. $-3p + 1 \geq 16$

   (A) $p \geq -5$ (B) $p \geq \frac{-17}{3}$

   (C) $p \leq \frac{-17}{3}$ (D) $p \leq -5$

4. $-6 < 2/3\ r + 6 \leq 2$

(A) $-6 < r \leq -3$

(B) $-18 < r \leq -6$

(C) $r \geq -6$

(D) $-2 < r \leq -4/3$

5. $0 < 2 - y < 6$

(A) $-4 < y < 2$

(B) $-4 < y < 0$

(C) $-4 < y < -2$

(D) $-2 < y < 4$

8. Ratios and Proportions

The ratio of two numbers x and y written $x : y$ is the fraction x / y where $y = 0$. A ratio compares x to y by dividing one by the other. Therefore, in order to compare ratios, simply compare the fractions.

A proportion is an equality of two ratios. The laws of proportion are listed below:

If $a/b = c/d$, then

$$ad = bc$$

$$b/a = d/c$$

$$a/c = b/d$$

$$(a + b)/b = (c + d)/d$$

$$(a - b)/b = (c - d)/d$$

Given a proportion $a : b = c : d$, then a and d are called extremes, b and c are called the means, and d is called the fourth proportion to a, b, and c.

PROBLEM

Solve the proportion $\frac{x+1}{4} = \frac{15}{12}$.

SOLUTION

Cross multiply to determine x; that is, multiply the numerator of the first fraction by the denominator of the second, and equate this to the product of the numerator of the second and the denominator of the first.

$$(x + 1)\ 12 = 4 \times 15$$

$$12x + 12 = 60$$

$$x = 4$$

PROBLEM

> Find the ratios of $x : y : z$ from the equations
>
> $$7x = 4y + 8z, \quad 3z = 12x + 11y.$$

SOLUTION

By transposition we have

$$7x - 4y - 8z = 0$$
$$12x + 11y - 3z = 0$$

To obtain the ratio of $x : y$, we convert the given system into an equation in terms of just x and y. z may be eliminated as follows: Multiply each term of the first equation by 3, and each term of the second equation by 8, and then subtract the second equation from the first. We thus obtain

$$\begin{array}{r} 21x - 12y - 24z = 0 \\ -(96x + 88y - 24z = 0) \\ \hline -75x - 100y \qquad = 0 \end{array}$$

Dividing each term of the last equation by 25, we obtain

$$-3x - 4y = 0$$

or $$-3x = 4y$$

Dividing both sides of this equation by 4 and by -3, we have the proportion

$$\frac{x}{4} = \frac{y}{-3}$$

We are now interested in obtaining the ratio of $y : z$. To do this we convert the given system of equations into an equation in terms of just y and z, by eliminating x as follows: Multiply each term of the first equation by 12, and each term of the second equation by 7, and then subtract the second equation from the first. We thus obtain

$$\begin{array}{r} 84x - 48y - 96z = 0 \\ -(84x + 77y - 21z = 0) \\ \hline -125y - 75z = 0 \end{array}$$

Dividing each term of the last equation by 25, we obtain

$$-5y - 3z = 0$$

or $$-3z = 5y$$

Dividing both sides of this equation by 5 and by -3, we have the proportion

$$\frac{z}{5} = \frac{y}{-3}$$

From this result and our previous result, we obtain

$$\frac{x}{4} = \frac{y}{-3} = \frac{z}{5}$$

as the desired ratios.

☞ Drill 8: Ratios and Proportions

1. Solve for n: $\frac{4}{n} = \frac{8}{5}$.

   (A) 10 (B) 8 (C) 6 (D) 2.5

2. Solve for n: $\frac{2}{3} = \frac{n}{72}$.

   (A) 12 (B) 48 (C) 64 (D) 56

3. Solve for n: $n : 12 = 3 : 4$.

   (A) 8 (B) 1 (C) 9 (D) 4

4. Four out of every five students at West High take a mathematics course. If the enrollment at West is 785, how many students take mathematics?

   (A) 628 (B) 157 (C) 705 (D) 655

5. At a factory, three out of every 1,000 parts produced are defective. In a day, the factory can produce 25,000 parts. How many of these parts would be defective?

   (A) 7 (B) 75 (C) 750 (D) 7,500

6. A summer league softball team won 28 out of the 32 games they played. What is the ratio of games won to games played?

   (A) 4 : 5 (B) 3 : 4 (C) 7 : 8 (D) 2 : 3

7. A class of 24 students contains 16 males. What is the ratio of females to males?

   (A) 1 : 2 (B) 2 : 1 (C) 2 : 3 (D) 3 : 1

8. A family has a monthly income of $1,250, but they spend $450 a month on rent. What is the ratio of the amount of income to the amount paid for rent?

   (A) 16 : 25 (B) 25 : 9 (C) 25 : 16 (D) 9 : 25

9. A student attends classes 7.5 hours a day and works a part-time job for 3.5 hours a day. She knows she must get 7 hours of sleep a night. Write the ratio of the number of free hours in this student's day to the total number of hours in a day.

(A) 1 : 3 (B) 4 : 3 (C) 8 : 24 (D) 1 : 4

10. In a survey by mail, 30 out of 750 questionnaires were returned. Write the ratio of questionnaires returned to questionnaires mailed (write in simplest form).

(A) 1 : 25 (B) 24 : 25 (C) 3 : 75 (D) 1 : 4

ALGEBRA DRILLS

ANSWER KEY

Drill 1 – Operations with Polynomials

1. (B)
2. (C)
3. (C)
4. (D)
5. (A)
6. (B)
7. (C)
8. (C)
9. (A)
10. (D)
11. (C)
12. (B)
13. (B)
14. (A)
15. (D)
16. (C)
17. (D)
18. (C)
19. (B)
20. (B)

Drill 2 – Simplifying Algebraic Expressions

1. (C)
2. (D)
3. (B)
4. (A)
5. (D)
6. (B)
7. (D)
8. (B)
9. (A)
10. (B)

Drill 3 – Linear Equations

1. (C)
2. (A)
3. (D)
4. (D)
5. (B)

Drill 4 – Two Linear Equations

1. (B)
2. (B)
3. (A)
4. (D)
5. (C)
6. (B)
7. (D)
8. (C)
9. (A)
10. (B)

Drill 5 – Quadratic Equations

1. (A)
2. (D)
3. (B)
4. (C)
5. (A)
6. (B)
7. (B)
8. (D)
9. (C)
10. (B)
11. (C)
12. (A)
13. (A)
14. (C)

Drill 6 – Absolute Value Equations

1. (B)
2. (D)
3. (A)
4. (C)
5. (D)

Drill 7 – Inequalities

1. (B)
2. (C)
3. (D)
4. (B)
5. (A)

Drill 8 – Ratios and Proportions

1. (D)
2. (B)
3. (C)
4. (A)
5. (B)
6. (C)
7. (A)
8. (B)
9. (D)
10. (A)

IV. Geometry

1. Points, Lines, and Angles

Geometry is built upon a series of undefined terms. These terms are those which we accept as known in order to define other undefined terms.

A) **Point:** Although we represent points on paper with small dots, a point has no size, thickness, or width.

B) **Line:** A line is a series of adjacent points which extends indefinitely. A line can be either curved or straight; however, unless otherwise stated, the term "line" refers to a straight line.

C) **Plane:** A plane is a collection of points lying on a flat surface, which extends indefinitely in all directions.

If *A* and *B* are two points on a line, then the **line segment** *AB* is the set of points on that line between *A* and *B* and including *A* and *B*, which are endpoints. The line segment is referred to as *AB*.

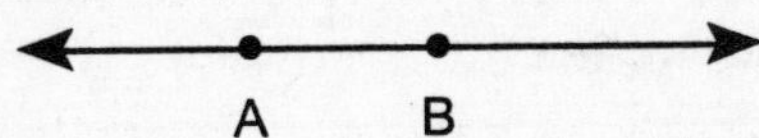

A **ray** is a series of points that lie to one side of a single endpont.

PROBLEM

How many lines can be found that contain

(1) one given point?

(2) two given points?

(3) three given points?

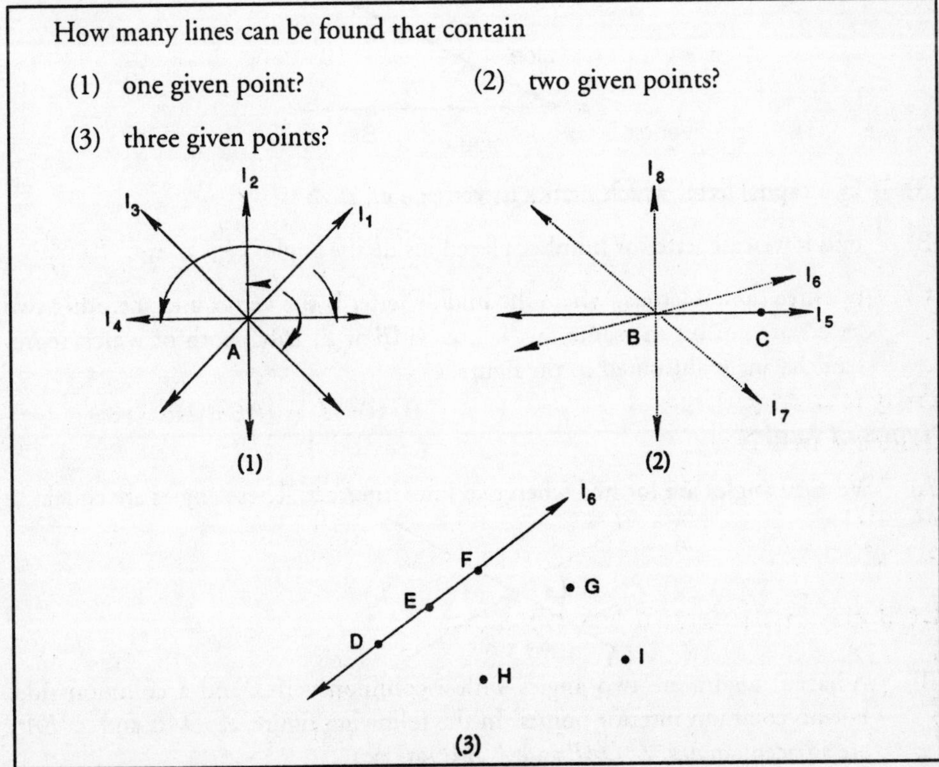

SOLUTION

(1) *Given one point A*, there are an infinite number of distinct lines that contain the given point. To see this, consider line l_1 passing through point *A*. By rotating l_1 around *A* like the hands of a clock, we obtain different lines l_2, l_3, etc. Since we can rotate l_1 in infinitely many ways, there are infinitely many lines containing *A*.

(2) *Given two distinct points B and C*, there is one and only one distinct line. To see this, consider all the lines containing point *B*; l_5, l_6, l_7, and l_8. Only l_5 contains both points *B* and *C*. Thus, there is only one line containing both points *B* and *C*. Since there is always at least one line containing two distinct points and never more than one, the line passing through the two points is said to be determined by the two points.

(3) *Given three distinct points*, there may be one line or none. If a line exists that contains the three points, such as *D*, *E*, and *F*, then the points are said to be **colinear**. If no such line exists — as in the case of points *G*, *H*, and *I*, then the points are said to be **noncolinear.**

Intersecting Lines and Angles

An **angle** is a collection of points which is the union of two rays having the same endpoint. An angle such as the one illustrated below can be referred to in any of the following ways:

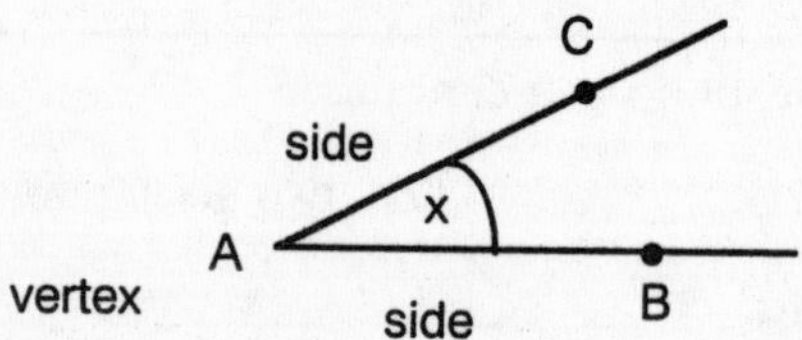

A) by a capital letter which names its vertex, i.e., ∠ *A*;

B) by a lowercase letter or number placed inside the angle, i.e., ∠ *x*;

C) by three capital letters, where the middle letter is the vertex and the other two letters are not on the same ray, i.e., ∠ *CAB* or ∠ *BAC*, both of which represent the angle illustrated in the figure.

Types of Angles

A) **Vertical angles** are formed when two lines intersect. These angles are equal.

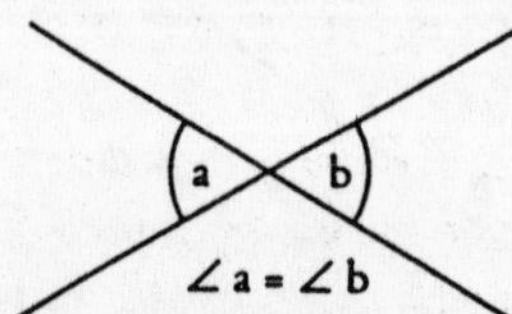

B) **Adjacent angles** are two angles with a common vertex and a common side, but no common interior points. In the following figure, ∠ *DAC* and ∠ *BAC* are adjacent angles. ∠ *DAB* and ∠ *BAC* are not.

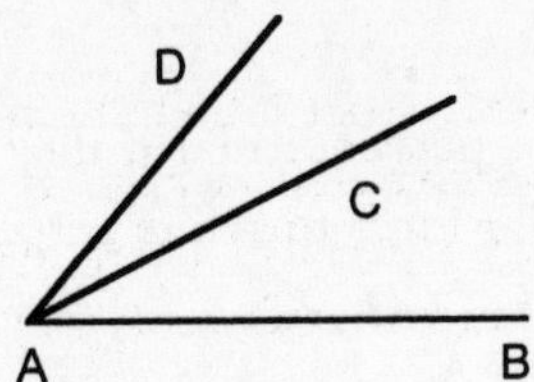

C) A **right angle** is an angle whose measure is 90°.

D) An **acute angle** is an angle whose measure is larger than 0° but less than 90°.

E) An **obtuse angle** is an angle whose measure is larger than 90° but less than 180°.

F) A **straight angle** is an angle whose measure is 180°. Such an angle is, in fact, a straight line.

G) A **reflex angle** is an angle whose measure is greater than 180° but less than 360°.

H) **Complementary angles** are two angles, the sum of the measures of which equals 90°.

I) **Supplementary angles** are two angles, the sum of the measures of which equals 180°.

J) **Congruent angles** are angles of equal measure.

PROBLEM

In the figure, we are given $\overline{AB}$ and triangle *ABC*. We are told that the measure of ∠ 1 is five times the measure of ∠ 2. Determine the measures of ∠ 1 and ∠ 2.

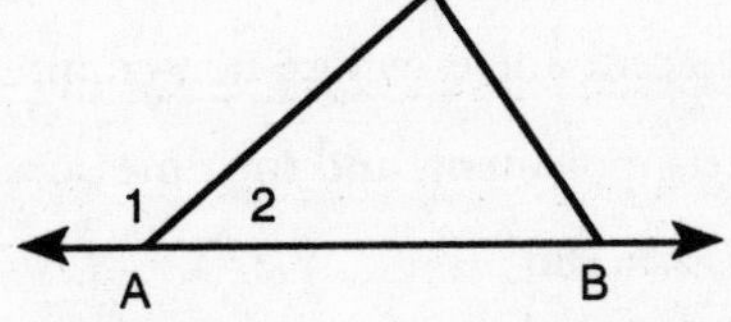

SOLUTION

Since ∠ 1 and ∠ 2 are adjacent angles whose non-common sides lie on a straight line, they are, by definition, supplementary. As supplements, their measures must sum to 180°.

If we let x = the measure of ∠ 2, then $5x$ = the measure of ∠ 1.

To determine the respective angle measures, set $x + 5x = 180$ and solve for x. $6x = 180$. Therefore, $x = 30$ and $5x = 150$.

Therefore, the measure of ∠ 1 = 150° and the measure of ∠ 2 = 30°.

Perpendicular Lines

Two lines are said to be **perpendicular** if they intersect and form right angles. The symbol for perpendicular (or is therefore perpendicular to) is $\perp$; $\overline{AB}$ is perpendicular to $\overline{CD}$ is written $\overline{AB} \perp \overline{CD}$.

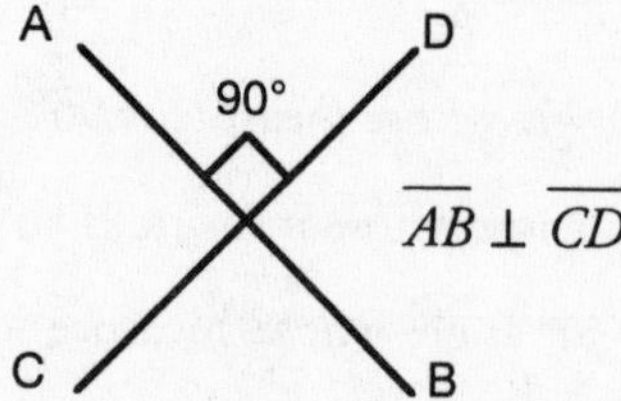

PROBLEM

> We are given straight lines $\overline{AB}$ and $\overline{CD}$ intersecting at point P. $\overline{PR} \perp \overline{AB}$ and the measure of $\angle APD$ is 170°. Find the measures of $\angle 1$, $\angle 2$, $\angle 3$, and $\angle 4$. (See figure below.)

SOLUTION

This problem will involve making use of several of the properties of supplementary and vertical angles, as well as perpendicular lines.

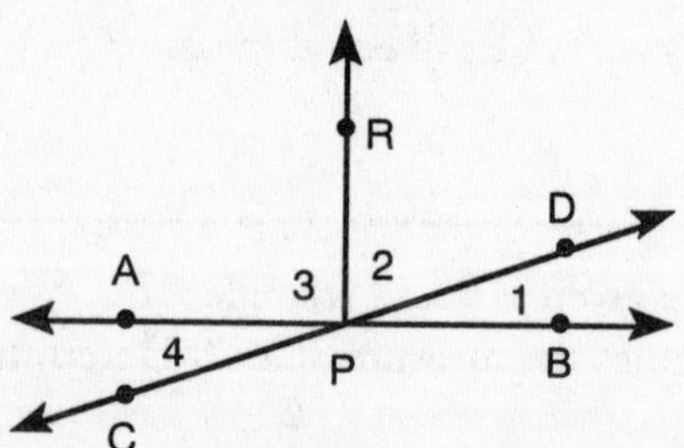

$\angle APD$ and $\angle 1$ are adjacent angles whose non-common sides lie on a straight line, $\overline{AB}$. Therefore, they are supplements and their measures sum to 180°.

$$m\angle APD + m\angle 1 = 180°$$

We know $m\angle APD = 170°$. Therefore, by substitution, $170° + m\angle 1 = 180°$. This implies $m\angle 1 = 10°$.

$\angle 1$ and $\angle 4$ are vertical angles because they are formed by the intersection of two straight lines, $\overline{CD}$ and $\overline{AB}$, and their sides form two pairs of opposite rays. As vertical angles, they are, by theorem, of equal measure. Since $m\angle 1 = 10°$, then $m\angle 4 = 10°$.

Since $\overline{PR} \perp \overline{AB}$, at their intersection the angles formed must be right angles. Therefore, $\angle 3$ is a right angle and its measure is 90°. $m\angle 3 = 90°$.

The figure shows us that $\angle APD$ is composed of $\angle 3$ and $\angle 2$. Since the measure of the whole must be equal to the sum of the measures of its parts, $m\angle APD =$

$m\angle 3 + m\angle 2$. We know the $m\angle APD = 170°$ and $m\angle 3 = 90°$; therefore, by substitution, we can solve for $m\angle 2$, our last unknown.

$$170° = 90° + m\angle 2$$

$$80° = m\angle 2$$

Therefore, $m\angle 1 = 10°$ $\quad m\angle 2 = 80°$

$m\angle 3 = 90°$ $\quad m\angle 4 = 10°$

PROBLEM

In the accompanying figure $\overline{SM}$ is the perpendicular bisector of $\overline{QR}$, and $\overline{SN}$ is the perpendicular bisector of $\overline{QP}$. Prove that $SR = SP$.

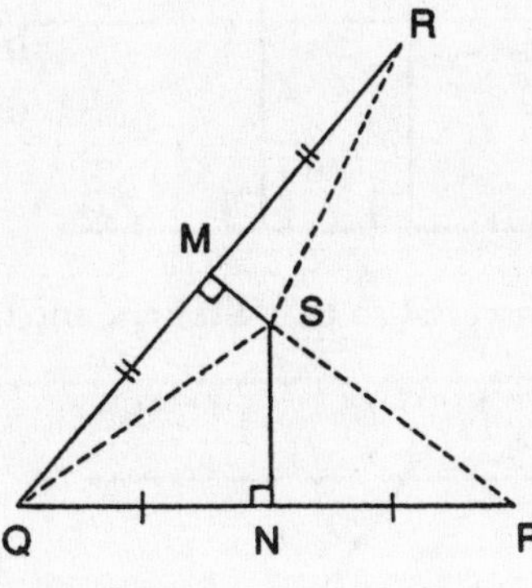

SOLUTION

Every point on the perpendicular bisector of a segment is equidistant from the endpoints of the segment.

Since point S is on the perpendicular bisector of $\overline{QR}$,

$$SR = SQ \tag{1}$$

Also, since point S is on the perpendicular bisector of $\overline{QP}$,

$$SQ = SP \tag{2}$$

By the transitive property (quantities equal to the same quantity are equal), we have

$$SR = SP \tag{3}$$

Parallel Lines

Two lines are called **parallel lines** if, and only if, they are in the same plane (coplanar) and do not intersect. The symbol for parallel, or is parallel to, is $\parallel$; $\overline{AB}$ is parallel to $\overline{CD}$ is written $\overline{AB} \parallel \overline{CD}$.

The distance between two parallel lines is the length of the perpendicular segment from any point on one line to the other line.

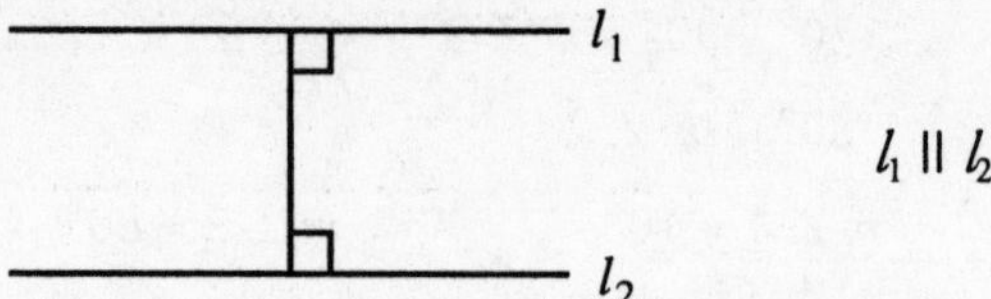

Given a line l and a point P not on line l, there is one and only one line through point P that is parallel to line l.

Two coplanar lines are either intersecting lines or parallel lines.

If two (or more) lines are perpendicular to the same line, then they are parallel to each other.

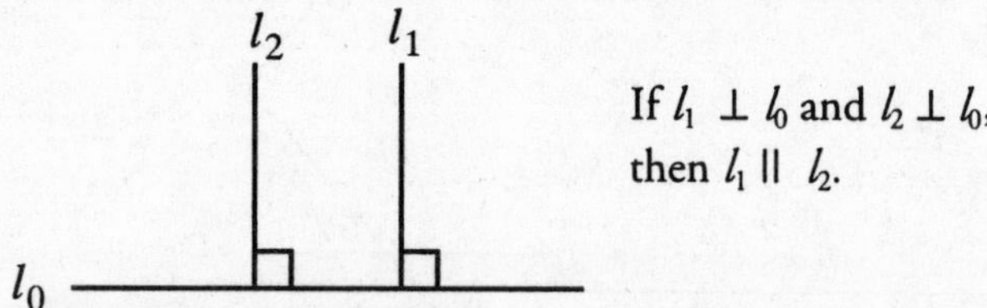

If two lines are cut by a transversal so that alternate interior angles are equal, the lines are parallel.

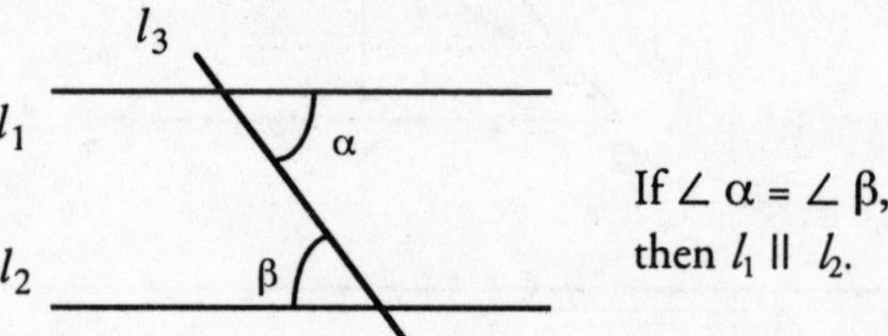

If two lines are parallel to the same line, then they are parallel to each other.

l_1

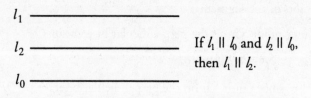

l_2 If $l_1 \parallel l_0$ and $l_2 \parallel l_0$, then $l_1 \parallel l_2$.

l_0

If a line is perpendicular to one of two parallel lines, then it is perpendicular to the other line, too.

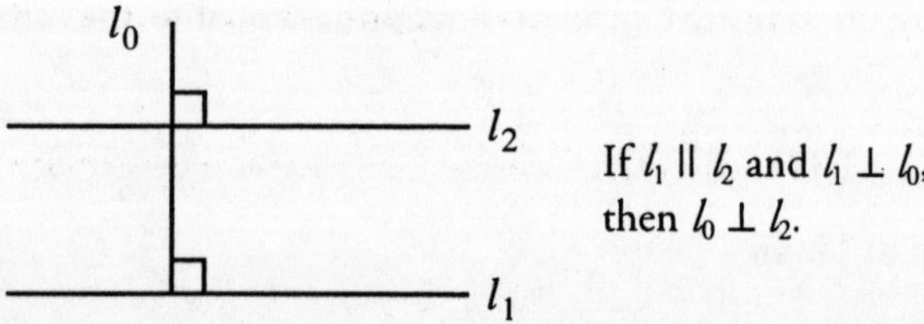

If two lines being cut by a transversal form congruent corresponding angles, then the two lines are parallel.

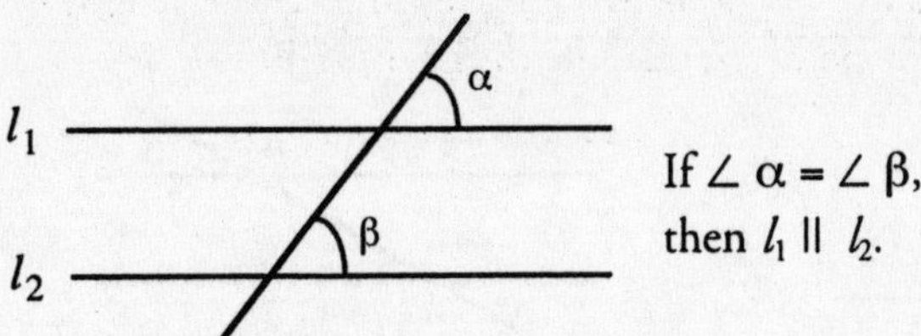

If $\angle \alpha = \angle \beta$, then $l_1 \parallel l_2$.

If two lines being cut by a transversal form interior angles on the same side of the transversal that are supplementary, then the two lines are parallel.

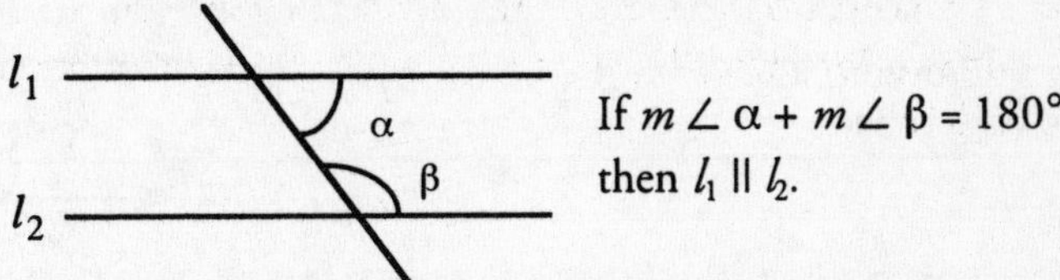

If $m\angle \alpha + m\angle \beta = 180°$, then $l_1 \parallel l_2$.

If a line is parallel to one of two parallel lines, it is also parallel to the other line.

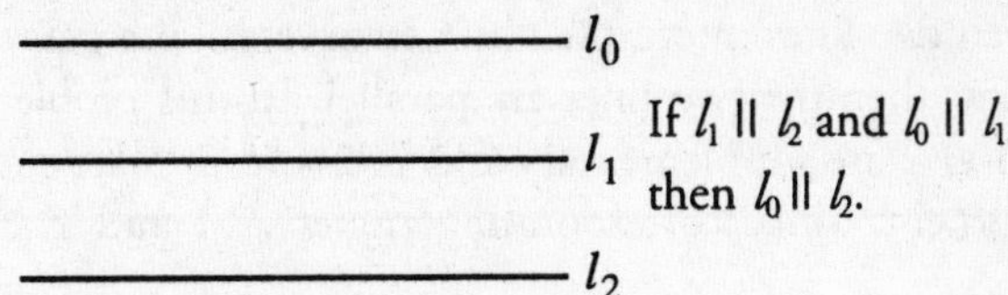

If $l_1 \parallel l_2$ and $l_0 \parallel l_1$, then $l_0 \parallel l_2$.

If two parallel lines are cut by a transversal, then:

A) The alternate interior angles are congruent.

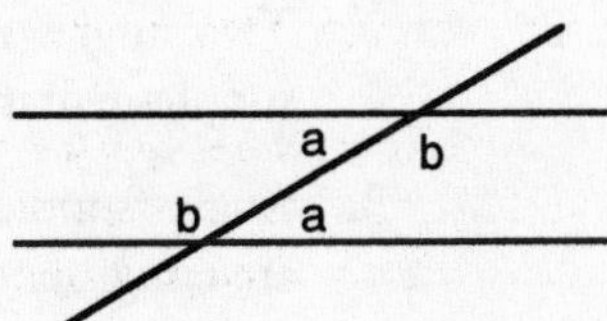

B) The corresponding angles are congruent.

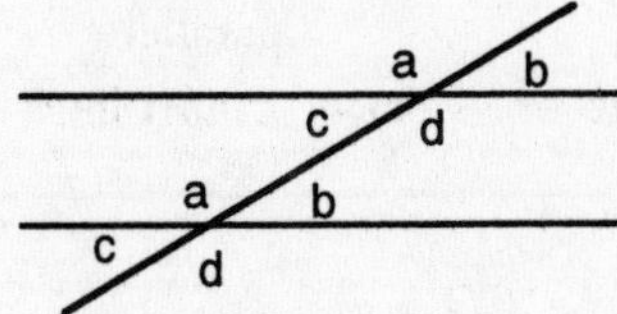

C) The consecutive interior angles are supplementary.

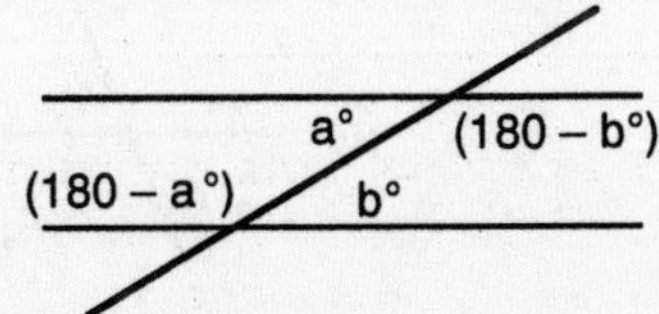

D) The alternate exterior angles are congruent.

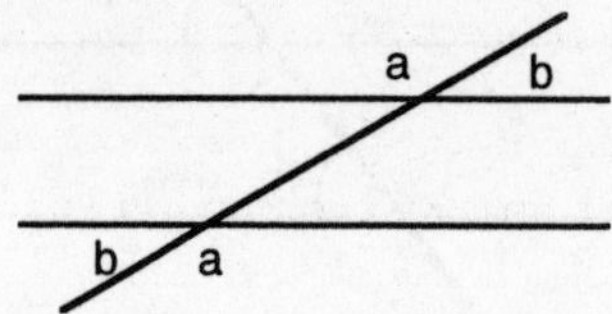

PROBLEM

Given: ∠ 2 is supplementary to ∠ 3.

Prove: $l_1 \parallel l_2$.

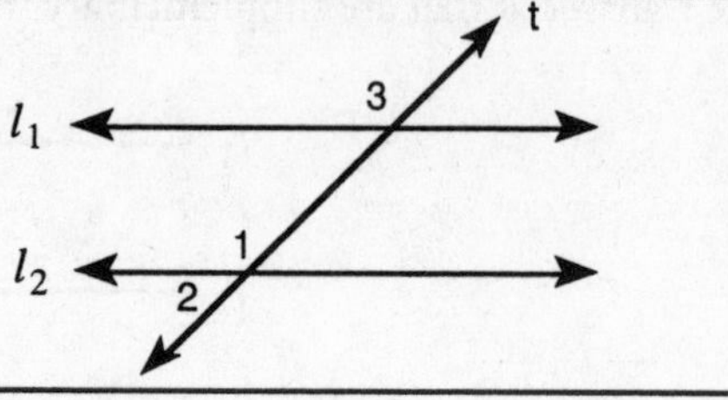

SOLUTION

Given two lines intercepted by a transversal, if a pair of corresponding angles are congruent, then the two lines are parallel. In this problem, we will show that since ∠ 1 and ∠ 2 are supplementary and ∠ 2 and ∠ 3 are supplementary, ∠ 1 and ∠ 3 are congruent. Since corresponding angles ∠ 1 and ∠ 3 are congruent, it follows $l_1 \parallel l_2$.

Statement	Reason
1. ∠ 2 is supplementary to ∠ 3.	1. Given.
2. ∠ 1 is supplementary to ∠ 2.	2. Two angles that form a linear pair are supplementary.
3. ∠ 1 ≅ ∠ 3.	3. Angles supplementary to the same angle are congruent.
4. $l_1 \parallel l_2$.	4. Given two lines intercepted by a transversal, if a pair of corresponding angles are congruent, then the two lines are parallel.

PROBLEM

If line $\overline{AB}$ is parallel to line $\overline{CD}$ and line $\overline{EF}$ is parallel to line $\overline{GH}$, prove that $m\angle 1 = m\angle 2$.

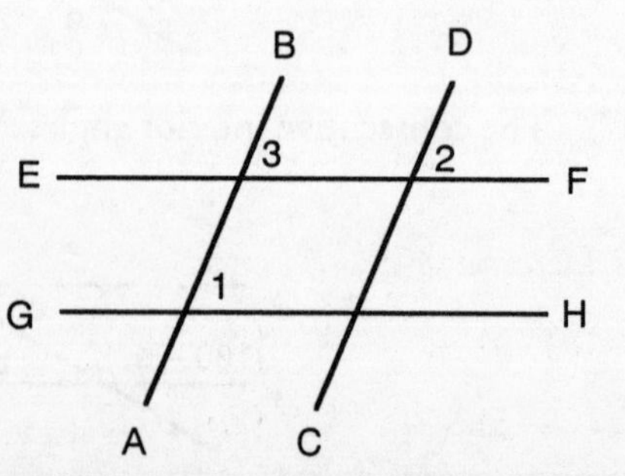

SOLUTION

To show $\angle 1 \cong \angle 2$, we relate both to $\angle 3$. Because $\overline{EF} \parallel \overline{GH}$, corresponding angles 1 and 3 are congruent. Since $\overline{AB} \parallel \overline{CD}$, corresponding angles 3 and 2 are congruent. Because both $\angle 1$ and $\angle 2$ are congruent to the same angle, it follows that $\angle 1 \cong \angle 2$.

	Statement		Reason
1.	$\overline{EF} \cong \overline{GH}$.	1.	Given.
2.	$m\angle 1 = m\angle 3$.	2.	If two parallel lines are cut by a transversal, corresponding angles are of equal measure.
3.	$\overline{AB} \parallel \overline{CD}$.	3.	Given.
4.	$m\angle 2 = m\angle 3$.	4.	If two parallel lines are cut by a transversal, corresponding angles are equal in measure.
5.	$m\angle 1 = m\angle 2$.	5.	If two quantities are equal to the same quantity, they are equal to each other.

☞ Drill 1: Points, Lines, and Angles

Intersecting Lines and Angles

1. Find a.

   (A) 38° (B) 68°

   (C) 78° (D) 90°

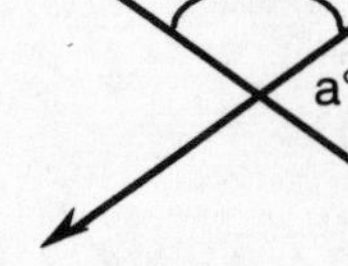

2. Find c.

   (A) 32° (B) 48°

   (C) 58° (D) 82°

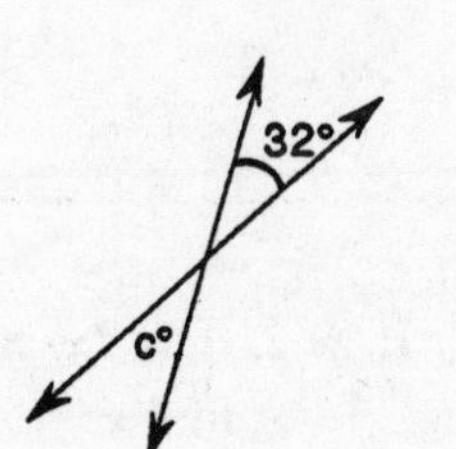

3. Determine x.

   (A) 21° (B) 23°

   (C) 51° (D) 102°

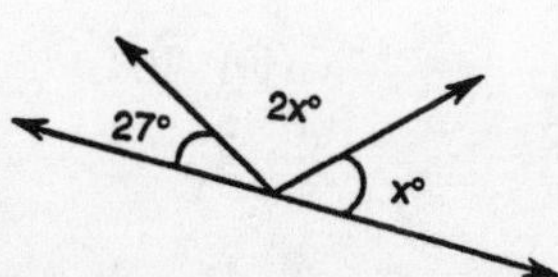

4. Find *x*.

(A) 8 (B) 11.75

(C) 21 (D) 23

5. Find *z*.

(A) 29° (B) 54°

(C) 61° (D) 88°

Perpendicular Lines

6. $\overline{BA} \perp \overline{BC}$ and $m\angle DBC = 53°$. Find $m\angle ABD$.

(A) 27° (B) 33°

(C) 37° (D) 53°

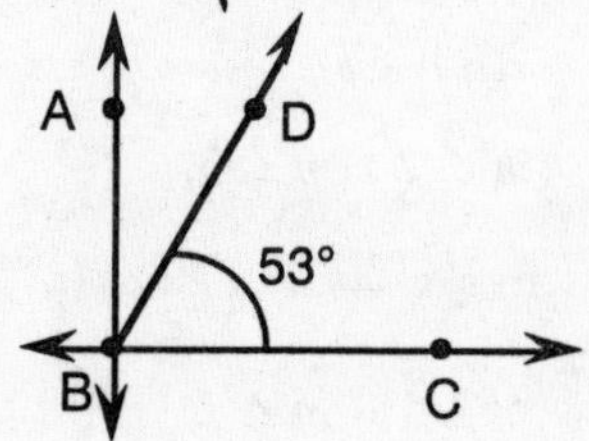

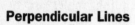

7. $m\angle 1 = 90°$. Find $m\angle 2$.

(A) 80° (B) 90°

(C) 100° (D) 135°

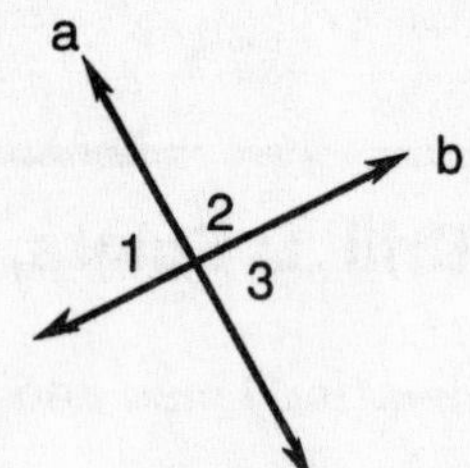

8. If $n \perp p$, which of the following statements is true?

(A) $\angle 1 \cong \angle 2$

(B) $\angle 4 \cong \angle 5$

(C) $m\angle 4 + m\angle 5 > m\angle 1 + m\angle 2$

(D) $m\angle 3 > m\angle 2$

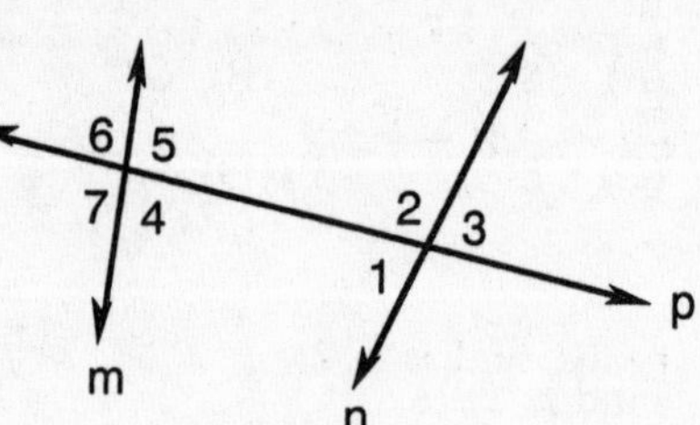

9. $\overline{CD} \perp \overline{EF}$. If $m\angle 1 = 2x$, $m\angle 2 = 30°$, and $m\angle 3 = x$, find x.

(A) 5° (B) 10°

(C) 12° (D) 20°

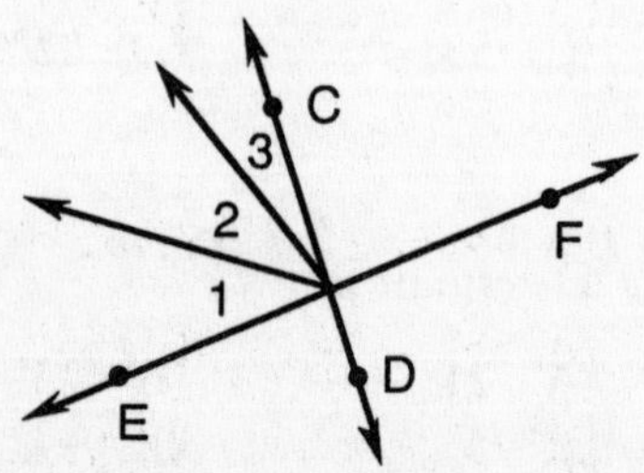

10. In the figure, $p \perp t$ and $q \perp t$. Which of the following statements is false?

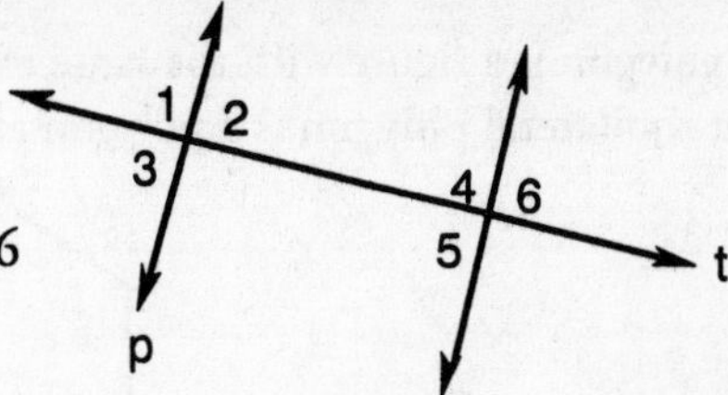

(A) $m\angle 2 > m\angle 5$

(B) $\angle 2 \cong \angle 3$

(C) $m\angle 2 + m\angle 3 = m\angle 4 + m\angle 6$

(D) $m\angle 5 + m\angle 6 = 180°$

Parallel Lines

11. If $a \parallel b$, find z.

(A) 26° (B) 32°

(C) 64° (D) 86°

12. In the figure, $p \parallel q \parallel r$. Find $m\angle 7$.

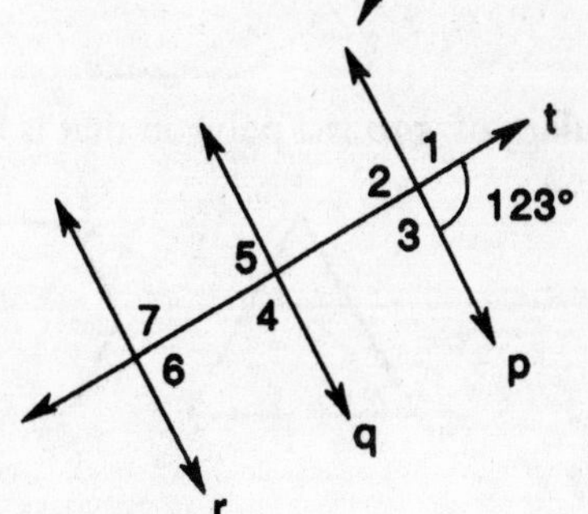

(A) 27° (B) 33°

(C) 47° (D) 57°

13. If $m \parallel n$, which of the following statements is false?

(A) $\angle 2 \cong \angle 5$

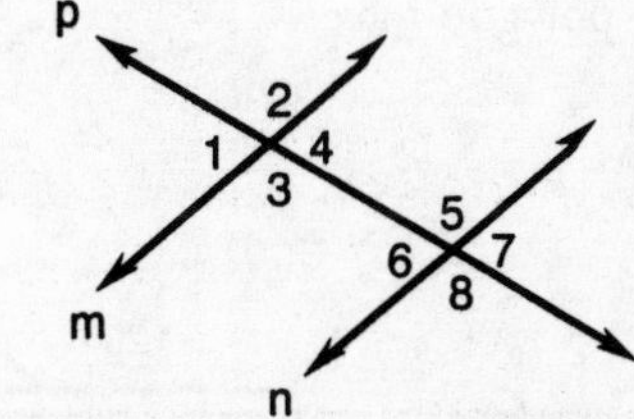

(B) $\angle 3 \cong \angle 6$

(C) $m\angle 4 + m\angle 5 = 180°$

(D) $\angle 1 \ncong \angle 8$

14. If $r \parallel s$, find $m\angle 2$.

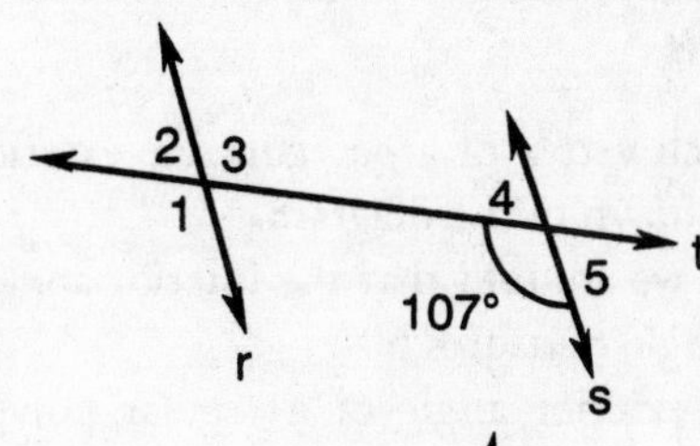

(A) 17° (B) 73°

(C) 43° (D) 67°

15. If $a \parallel b$ and $c \parallel d$, find $m\angle 5$.

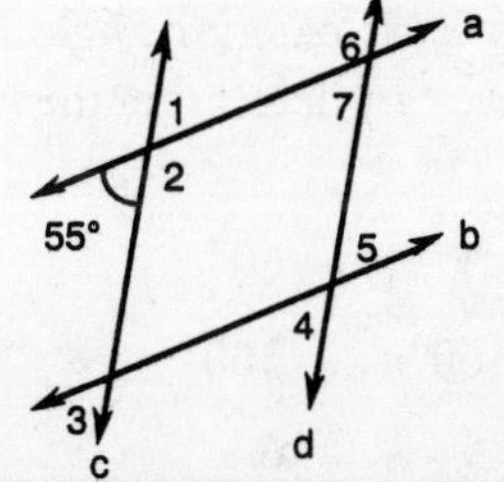

(A) 55° (B) 65°

(C) 75° (D) 95°

2. Regular Polygons

A **polygon** is a figure with the same number of sides as angles.
An **equilateral polygon** is a polygon all of whose sides are of equal measure.

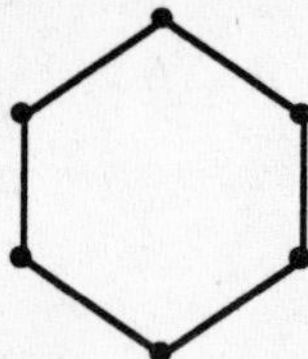

An **equiangular polygon** is a polygon all of whose angles are of equal measure.

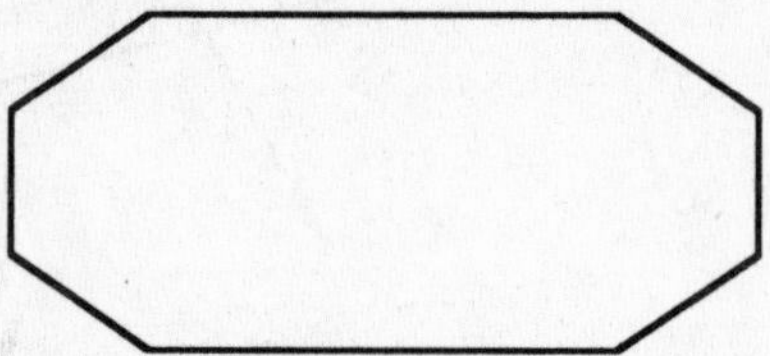

A **regular polygon** is a polygon that is both equilateral and equiangular.

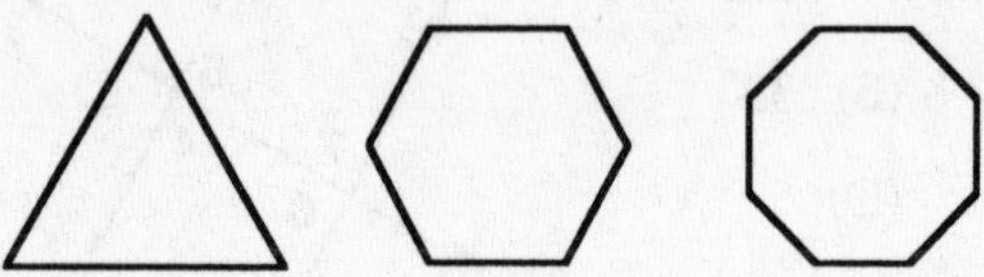

PROBLEM

Each interior angle of a regular polygon contains 120°. How many sides does the polygon have?

120° 60°

SOLUTION

At each vertex of a polygon, the exterior angle is supplementary to the interior angle, as shown in the diagram.

Since we are told that the interior angle measures 120°, we can deduce that the exterior angle measures 60°.

Each exterior angle of a regular polygon of n sides measures $^{360°}/_{n}$ degrees. We know that each exterior angle measures 60°, and, therefore, by setting $^{360°}/_{n}$ equal to 60°, we can determine the number of sides in the polygon. The calculation is as follows:

$$^{360°}/_{n} = 60°$$

$$60°n = 360°$$

$$n = 6$$

Therefore, the regular polygon, with interior angles of 120°, has 6 sides and is called a hexagon.

The area of a regular polygon can be determined by using the **apothem** and **radius** of the polygon. The apothem (a) of a regular polygon is the segment from the center of the polygon perpendicular to a side of the polygon. The radius (r) of a regular polygon is the segment joining any vertex of a regular polygon with the center of that polygon.

(A) All radii of a regular polygon are congruent.

(B) The radius of a regular polygon is congruent to a side.

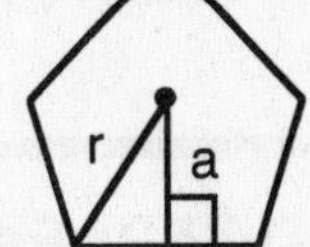

(C) All apothems of a regular polygon are congruent.

The **area** of a regular polygon equals one-half the product of the length of the apothem and the perimeter.

$$\text{Area} = {}^1/_2\ a \times p$$

PROBLEM

> Find the area of the regular polygon whose radius is 8 and whose apothem is 6.

SOLUTION

If the radius is 8, the length of a side is also 8. Therefore, the perimeter of the polygon is 40.

$$A = {}^1/_2\ a \times p$$

$$A = {}^1/_2\ (6)\ (40)$$

$$A = 120$$

PROBLEM

> Find the area of a regular hexagon if one side has length 6.

SOLUTION

Since the length of a side equals 6, the radius also equals 6 and the perimeter equals 36. The base of the right triangle, formed by the radius and apothem, is half the length of a side, or 3. Using the Pythagorean Theorem, you can find the length of the apothem.

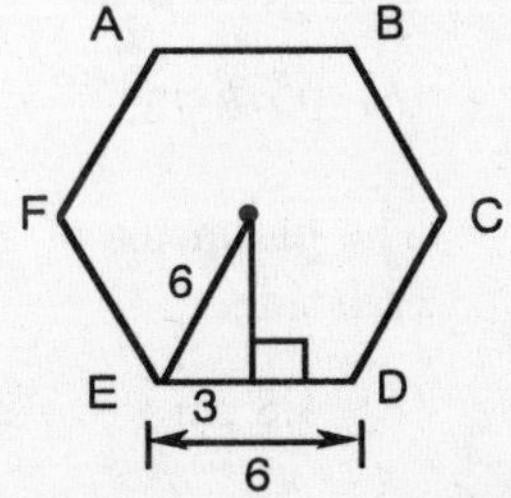

$$a^2 + b^2 = c^2$$

$$a^2 + (3)^2 = (6)^2$$

$$a^2 = 36 + 9$$

$$a^2 = 27$$

$a = 3\sqrt{3}$

The apothem equals $3\sqrt{3}$. Therefore, the area of the hexagon

$= \frac{1}{2}\, a \times p$

$= \frac{1}{2}\,(3\sqrt{3})\,(36)$

$= 54\sqrt{3}$

☞ Drill 2: Regular Polygons

1. Find the measure of an interior angle of a regular pentagon.

   (A) 55 (B) 72 (C) 90 (D) 108

2. Find the measure of an exterior angle of a regular octagon.

   (A) 40 (B) 45 (C) 135 (D) 540

3. Find the sum of the measures of the exterior angles of a regular triangle.

   (A) 90 (B) 115 (C) 360 (D) 250

4. Find the area of a square with a perimeter of 12 cm.

   (A) 9 cm^2 (B) 12 cm^2 (C) 48 cm^2 (D) 96 cm^2

5. A regular triangle has sides of 24 mm. If the apothem is $4\sqrt{3}$ mm, find the area of the triangle.

   (A) 72 mm^2 (B) $96\sqrt{3}$ mm^2 (C) 144 mm^2 (D) $144\sqrt{3}$ mm^2

6. Find the area of a regular hexagon with sides of 4 cm.

   (A) $12\sqrt{3}$ cm^2 (B) 24 cm^2 (C) $24\sqrt{3}$ cm^2 (D) 48 cm^2

7. Find the area of a regular decagon with sides of length 6 cm and an apothem of length 9.2 cm.

   (A) 55.2 cm^2 (B) 60 cm^2 (C) 138 cm^2 (D) 276 cm^2

8. The perimeter of a regular heptagon (7-gon) is 36.4 cm. Find the length of each side.

   (A) 4.8 cm (B) 5.2 cm (C) 6.7 cm (D) 7 cm

9. The apothem of a regular quadrilateral is 4 in. Find the perimeter.

   (A) 12 in (B) 16 in (C) 24 in (D) 32 in

10. A regular triangle has a perimeter of 18 cm; a regular pentagon has a perimeter of 30 cm; a regular hexagon has a perimeter of 33 cm. Which figure (or figures) have sides with the longest measure?

    (A) regular triangle

    (B) regular triangle and regular pentagon

    (C) regular pentagon

    (D) regular pentagon and regular hexagon

3. Triangles

A closed three-sided geometric figure is called a **triangle**. The points of the intersection of the sides of a triangle are called the **vertices** of the triangle.

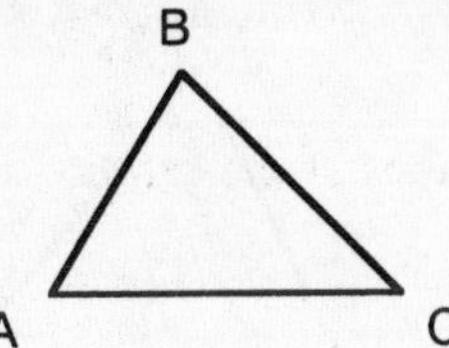

The **perimeter** of a triangle is the sum of the measures of the sides of the triangle.

A triangle with no equal sides is called a **scalene** triangle.

A triangle having at least two equal sides is called an **isosceles** triangle. The third side is called the **base** of the triangle.

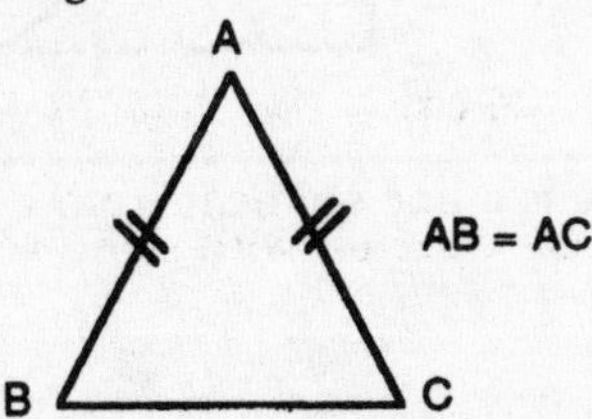

A side of a triangle is a line segment whose endpoints are the vertices of two angles of the triangle.

An interior angle of a triangle is an angle formed by two sides and includes the third side within its collection of points.

An **equilateral triangle** is a triangle having three equal sides. $AB = AC = BC$

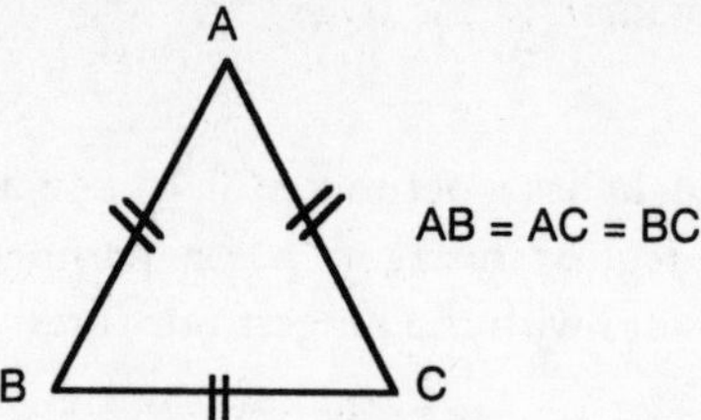

A triangle with one obtuse angle greater than 90° is called an **obtuse triangle.**

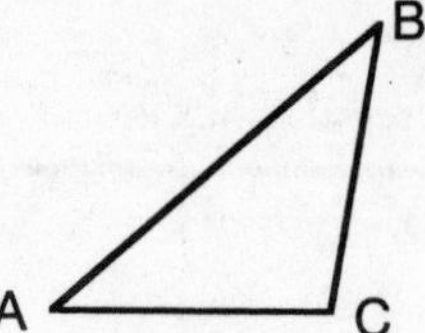

An **acute triangle** is a triangle with three acute angles (less than 90°).

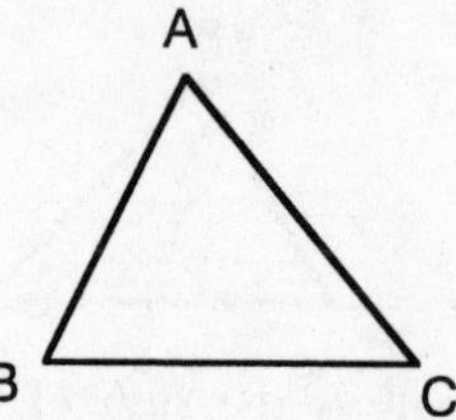

A triangle with a right angle is called a **right triangle.** The side opposite the right angle in a right triangle is called the **hypotenuse** of the right triangle. The other two sides are called arms or legs of the right triangle.

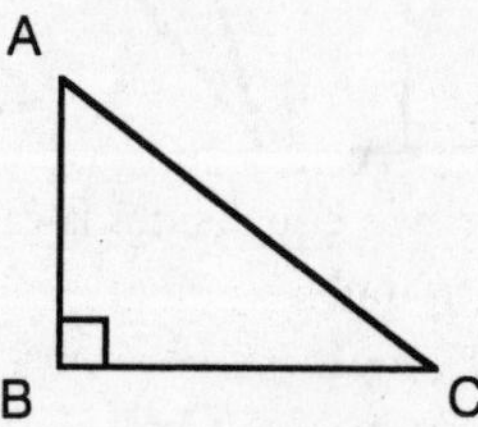

An **altitude** of a triangle is a line segment from a vertex of the triangle perpendicular to the opposite side.

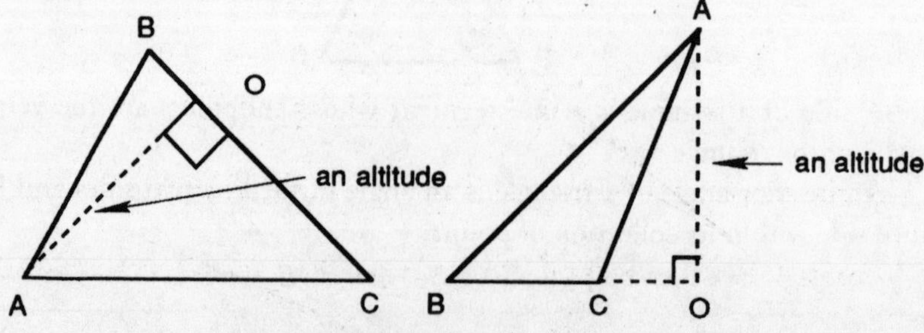

A line segment connecting a vertex of a triangle and the midpoint of the opposite side is called a **median** of the triangle.

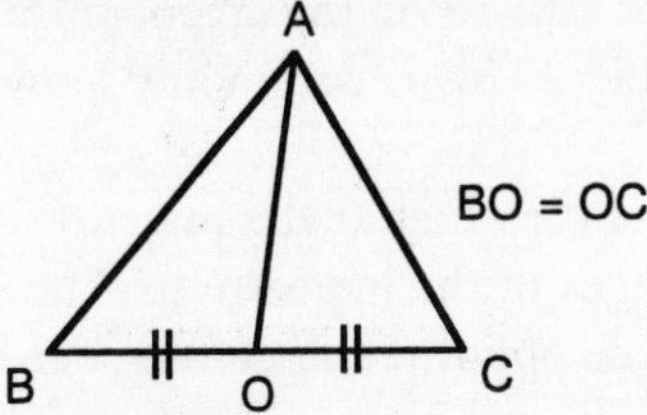

A line that bisects and is perpendicular to a side of a triangle is called a **perpendicular bisector** of that side.

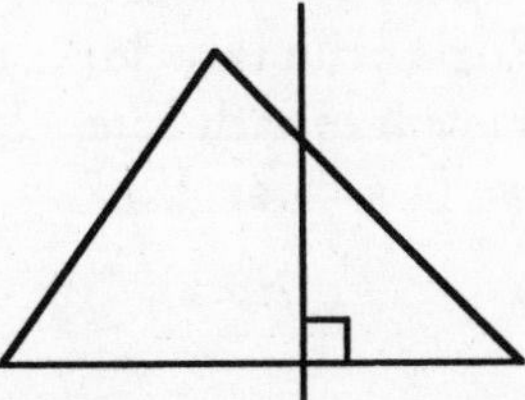

An **angle bisector** of a triangle is a line that bisects an angle and extends to the opposite side of the triangle.

A

α β

B C

$\angle \alpha = \angle \beta$

The line segment that joins the midpoints of two sides of a triangle is called a midline of the triangle.

A

D

AD = DC
BE = EC

midline: DE

B E C

An exterior angle of a triangle is an angle formed outside a triangle by one side of the triangle and the extension of an adjacent side.

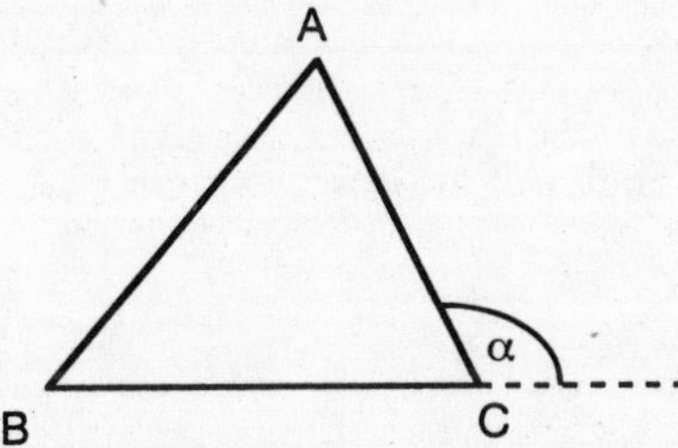

A triangle whose three interior angles have equal measure is said to be equiangular.

Two triangles are **similar** if their corresponding sides are proportional.

Three or more lines (or rays or segments) are concurrent if there exists one point common to all of them, that is, if they all intersect at the same point.

In a right triangle, the square of the hypotenuse is equal to the sum of the squares of the other two sides. This is commonly known as the Pythagorean Theorem.

In a right triangle where the other angles measure 30° and 60°, the side opposite the 30° angle is half the length of the hypotenuse. The side opposite the 60° angle is equal to the length of the side opposite the 30° angle multiplied by $\sqrt{3}$.

PROBLEM

The measure of the vertex angle of an isosceles triangle exceeds the measurement of each base angle by 30°. Find the value of each angle of the triangle.

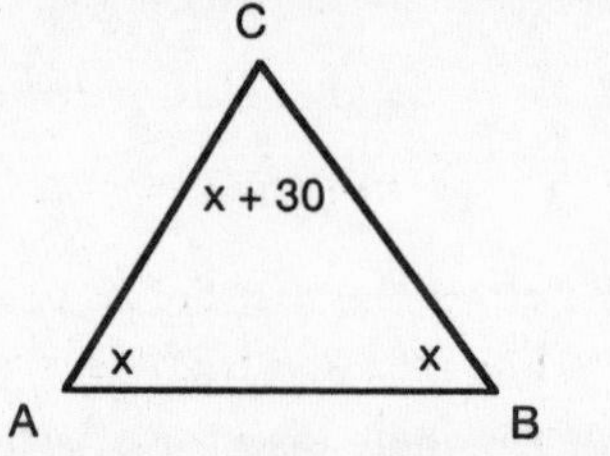

SOLUTION

We know that the sum of the values of the angles of a triangle is 180°. In an isosceles triangle, the angles opposite the congruent sides (the base angles) are, themselves, congruent and of equal value.

Therefore,

(1) Let x = the measure of each base angle.

(2) Then $x + 30$ = the measure of the vertex angle.

We can solve for x algebraically by keeping in mind the sum of all the measures will be 180°.

$$x + x + (x + 30) = 180$$
$$3x + 30 = 180$$
$$3x = 150$$
$$x = 50$$

Therefore, the base angles each measure 50°, and the vertex angle measures 80°.

PROBLEM

Prove that the base angles of an isosceles right triangle measure 45°.

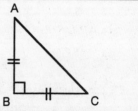

SOLUTION

As drawn in the figure, $\Delta\ ABC$ is an isosceles right triangle with base angles BAC and BCA. The sum of the measures of the angles of any triangle is 180°. For $\Delta\ ABC$, this means

$$m\angle BAC + m\angle BCA + m\angle ABC = 180° \qquad (1)$$

But $m\angle ABC = 90°$ because ABC is a right triangle. Furthermore, $m\angle BCA = m\angle BAC$, since the base angles of an isosceles triangle are congruent. Using these facts in equation (1)

$$m\angle BAC + m\angle BCA + 90° = 180°$$

or $$2m\angle BAC = 2m\angle BCA = 90°$$

or $$m\angle BAC = m\angle BCA = 45°$$

Therefore, the base angles of an isosceles right triangle measure 45°.

The area of a triangle is given by the formula $A = {}^1/_2\ bh$, where b is the length of a base, which can be any side of the triangle and h is the corresponding height of the triangle, which is the perpendicular line segment that is drawn from the vertex opposite the base to the base itself.

$$A = {}^1/_2\ bh$$
$$A = {}^1/_2\ (10)\ (3)$$
$$A = 15$$

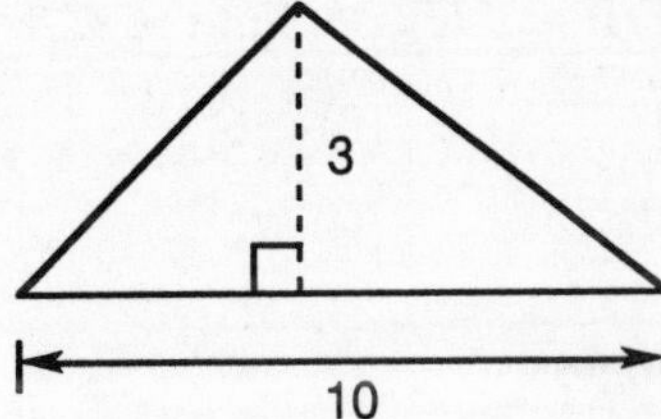

The area of a right triangle is found by taking ${}^1/_2$ the product of the lengths of its two arms.

$$A = {}^1/_2\ (5)\ (12)$$
$$A = 30$$

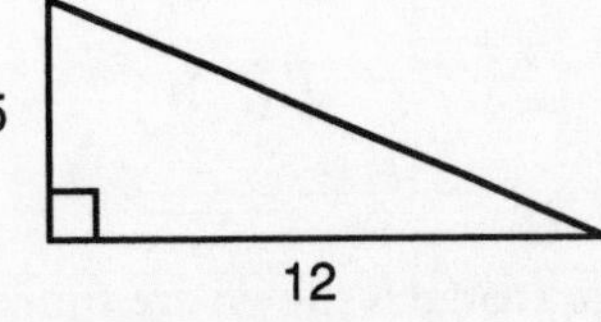

☞ Drill 3: Triangles

Angle Measures

1. In $\Delta\ PQR$, $\angle\ Q$ is a right angle. Find $m\angle R$.

   (A) 27° (B) 33°

   (C) 54° (D) 67°

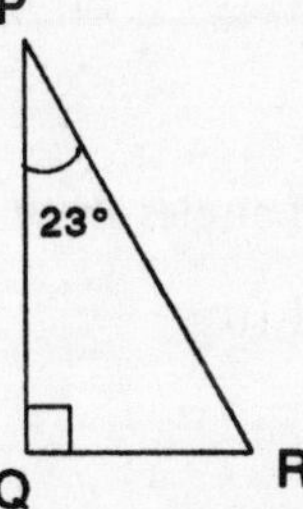

2. Δ *MNO* is isosceles. If the vertex angle, ∠ *N*, has a measure of 96°, find the measure of ∠ *M*.

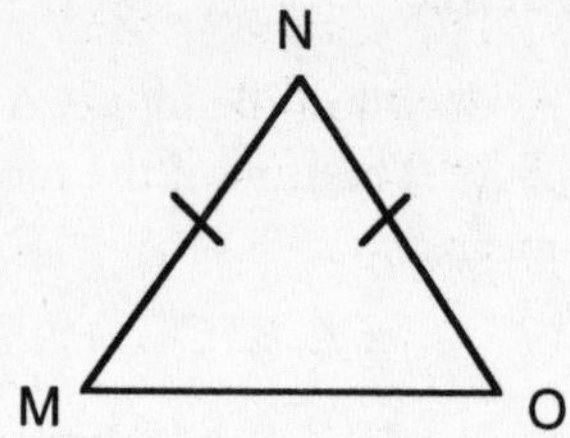

(A) 21° (B) 42°

(C) 64° (D) 84°

3. Find *x*.

(A) 15° (B) 25°

(C) 30° (D) 45°

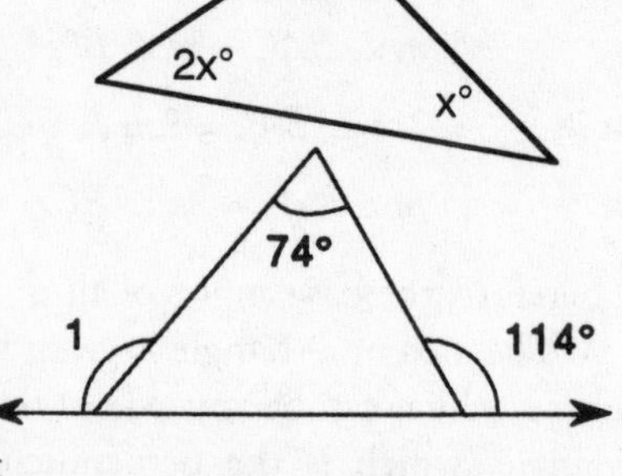

4. Find *m* ∠ 1.

(A) 140° (B) 66°

(C) 74° (D) 114°

5. Δ *ABC* is a right triangle with a right angle at *B*. Δ *BDC* is a right triangle with right angle ∠ *BDC*. If *m* ∠ *C* = 36. Find *m* ∠ *A*.

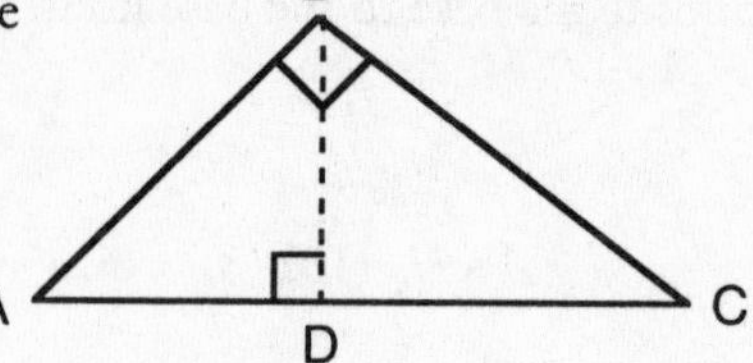

(A) 18° (B) 36°

(C) 54° (D) 72°

Similar Triangles

6. The two triangles shown are similar. Find *b*.

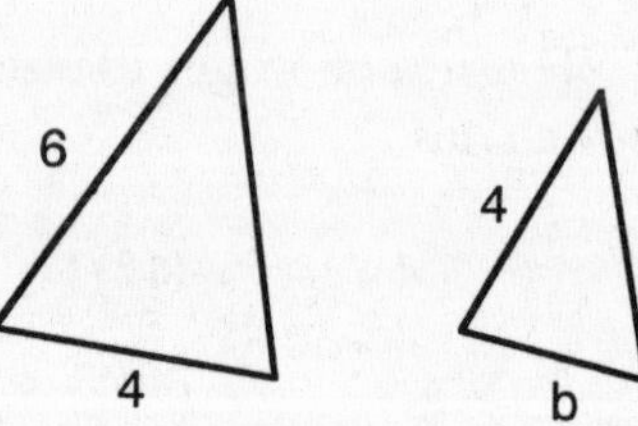

(A) $2\,^2/_3$ (B) 3

(C) 4 (D) 16

7. The two triangles shown are similar. Find *m* ∠ 1.

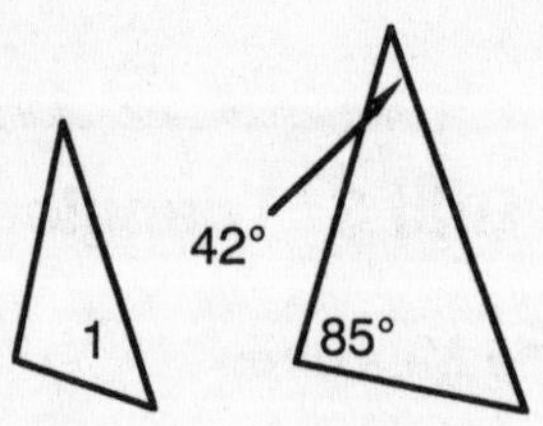

(A) 48° (B) 53°

(C) 74° (D) 127°

8. The two triangles shown are similar. Find *a* and *b*.

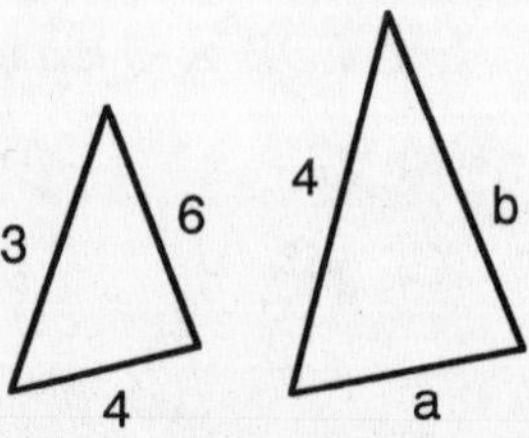

(A) 5 and 10 (B) $5\,^1/_3$ and 8

(C) $4\,^2/_3$ and $7\,^1/_3$ (D) 5 and 8

9. The perimeter of $\Delta\ LXR$ is 45 and the perimeter of $\Delta\ ABC$ is 27. If $LX = 15$, find the length of AB.

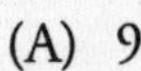

(A) 9 (B) 15

(C) 27 (D) 45

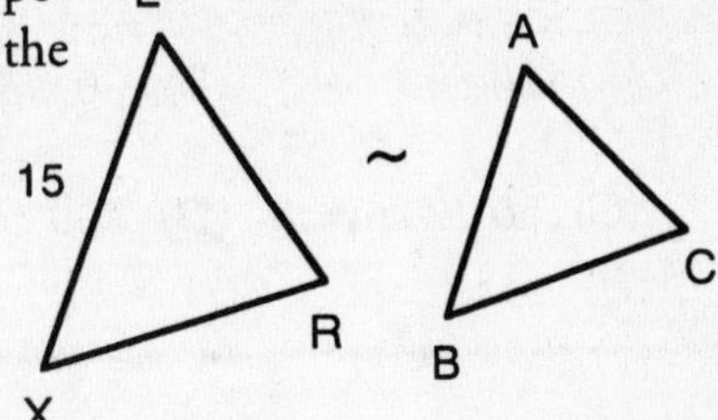

10. Find b.

(A) 9 (B) 15

(C) 20 (D) 45

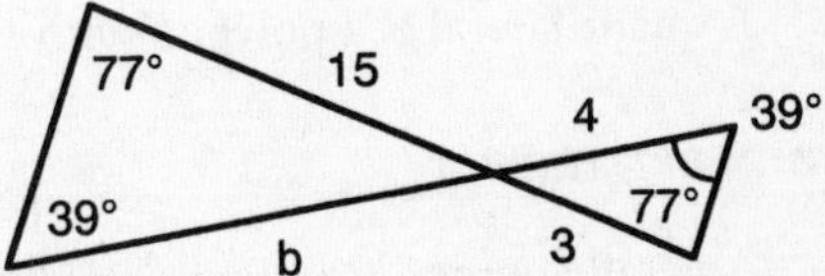

Area

11. Find the area of $\Delta\ MNO$.

(A) 22 (B) 49

(C) 56 (D) 84

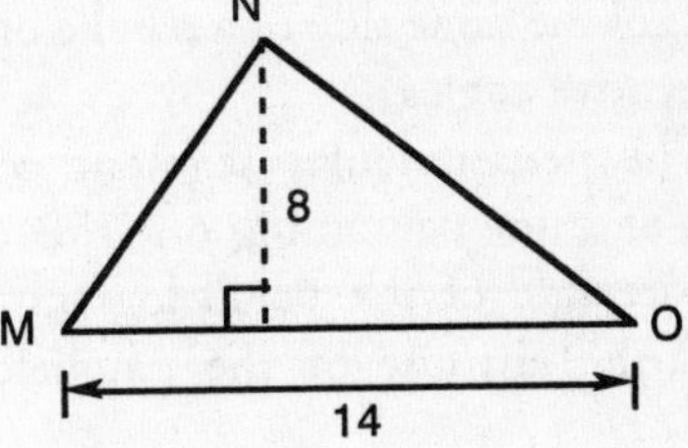

12. Find the area of $\Delta\ PQR$.

(A) 31.5 (B) 38.5

(C) 53 (D) 77

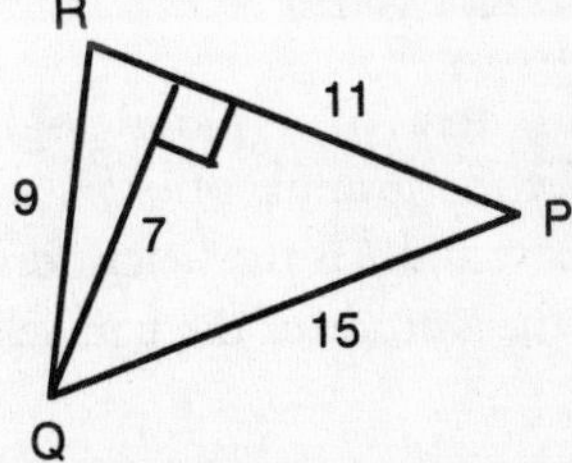

13. Find the area of $\Delta\ STU$.

(A) $4\sqrt{2}$ (B) $8\sqrt{2}$

(C) $12\sqrt{2}$ (D) $16\sqrt{2}$

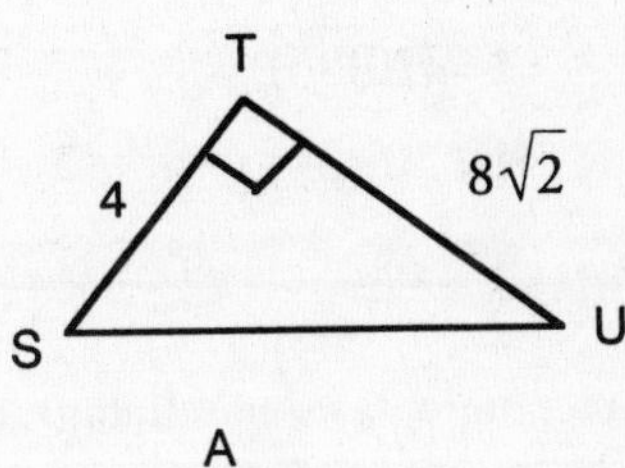

14. Find the area of $\Delta\ ABC$.

(A) 54 cm^2 (B) 81 cm^2

(C) 108 cm^2 (D) 135 cm^2

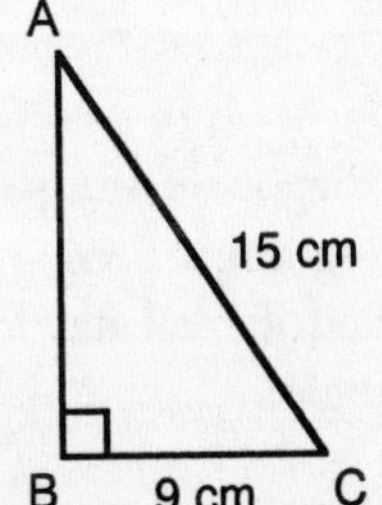

15. Find the area of Δ *XYZ*.

(A) 20 cm^2 (B) 50 cm^2

(C) $50\sqrt{2}$ cm^2 (D) 100 cm^2

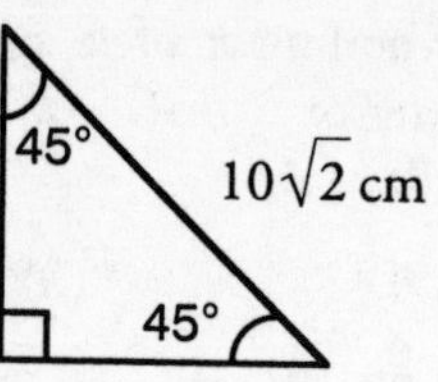

4. Quadrilaterals

A **quadrilateral** is a polygon with four sides.

Parallelograms

A **parallelogram** is a quadrilateral whose opposite sides are parallel.

Two angles that have their vertices at the endpoints of the same side of a parallelogram are called **consecutive angles**.

The perpendicular segment connecting any point of a line containing one side of the parallelogram to the line containing the opposite side of the parallelogram is called the **altitude** of the parallelogram.

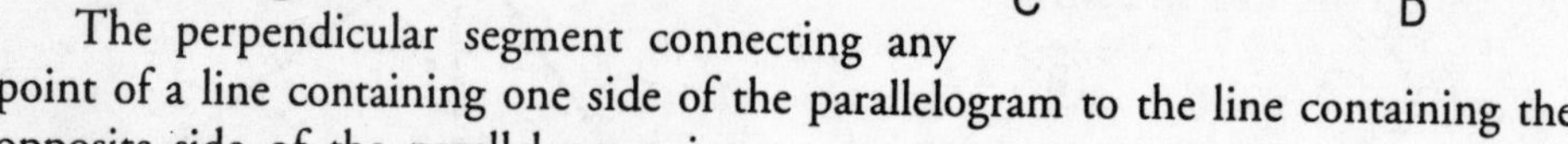

A diagonal of a polygon is a line segment joining any two non-consecutive vertices.

The area of a parallelogram is given by the formula $A = bh$, where b is the base and h is the height drawn perpendicular to that base. Note that the height equals the altitude of the parallelogram.

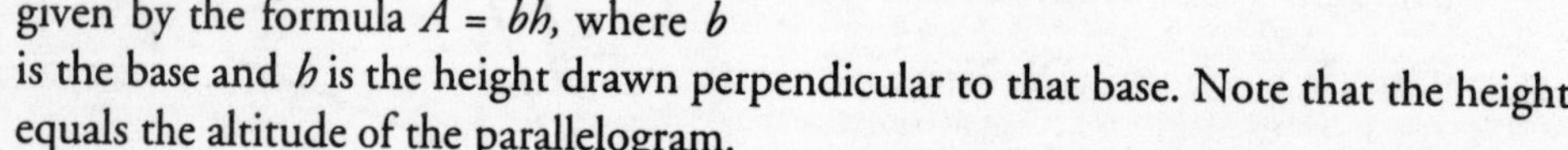

$A = bh$

$A = (10)\ (3)$

$A = 30$

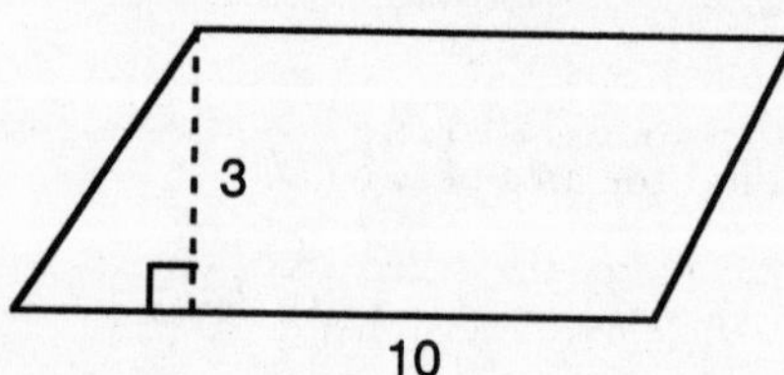

Rectangles

A rectangle is a parallelogram with right angles.

The diagonals of a rectangle are equal.

If the diagonals of a parallelogram are equal, the parallelogram is a rectangle.

If a quadrilateral has four right angles, then it is a rectangle.

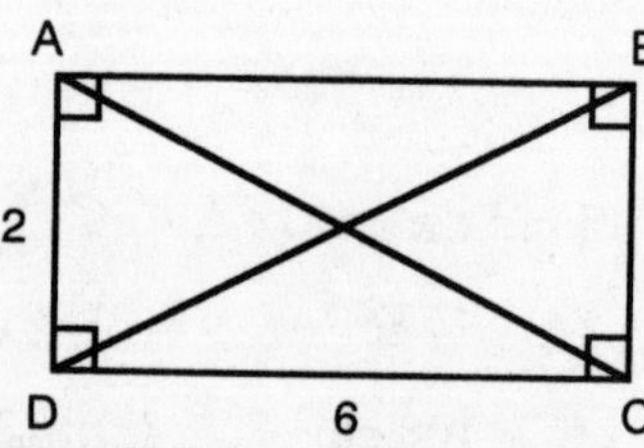

The area of a rectangle is given by the formula $A = lw$, where l is the length and w is the width.

$A = lw$

$A = (3)(10)$

$A = 30$

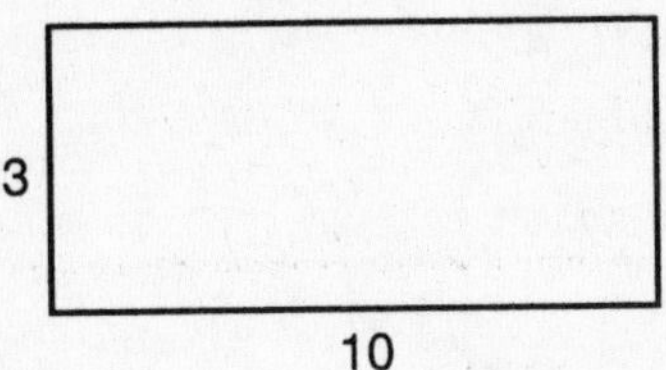

Rhombi

A rhombus is a parallelogram with two adjacent sides equal.

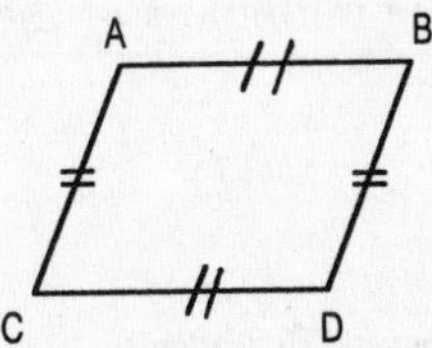

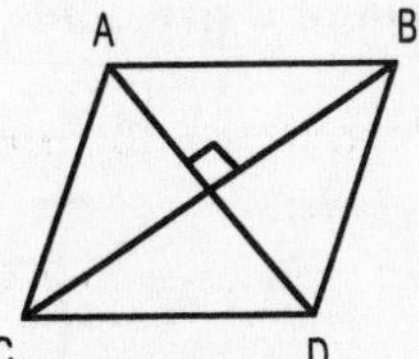

All sides of a rhombus are equal.

The diagonals of a rhombus are perpendicular to each other.

The diagonals of a rhombus bisect the angles of the rhombus.

If the diagonals of a parallelogram are perpendicular, the parallelogram is a rhombus.

If a quadrilateral has four equal sides, then it is a rhombus.

A parallelogram is a rhombus if either diagonal of the parallelogram bisects the angles of the vertices it joins.

Squares

A square is a rhombus with a right angle.

A square is an equilateral quadrilateral.

A square has all the properties of parallelograms and rectangles.

A rhombus is a square if one of its interior angles is a right angle.

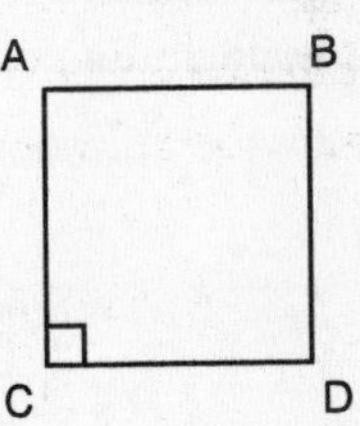

In a square, the measure of either diagonal can be calculated by multiplying the length of any side by the square root of 2.

A B C D

$AD = AB\sqrt{2}$

The area of a square is given by the formula $A = s^2$, where s is the side of the square. Since all sides of a square are equal, it does not matter which side is used.

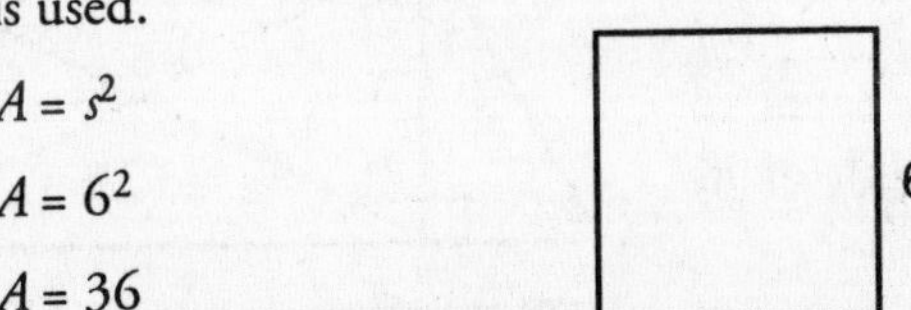

$A = s^2$

$A = 6^2$

$A = 36$

The area of a square can also be found by taking $^1/_2$ the product of the length of the diagonal squared.

$A = {}^1/_2\, d^2$

$A = {}^1/_2\, (8)^2$

$A = 32$

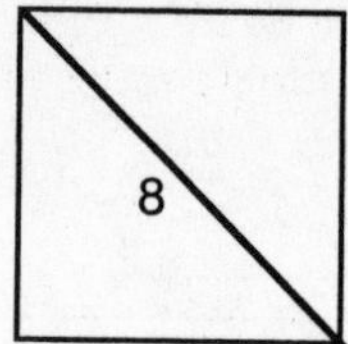

Trapezoids

A **trapezoid** is a quadrilateral with two and only two sides parallel. The parallel sides of a trapezoid are called **bases.**

The **median** of a trapezoid is the line joining the midpoints of the non-parallel sides.

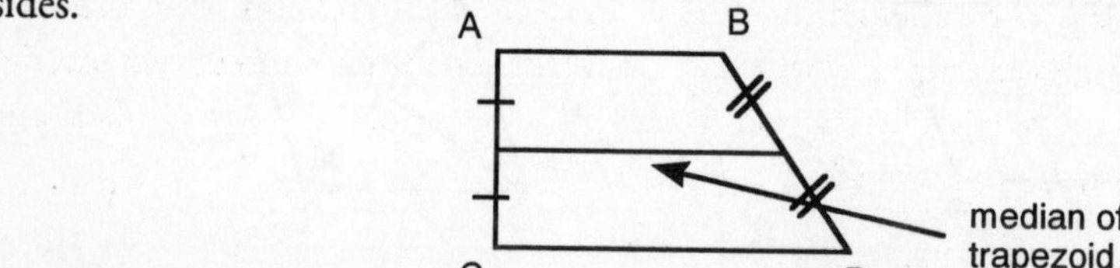

The perpendicular segment connecting any point in the line containing one base of the trapezoid to the line containing the other base is the **altitude** of the trapezoid.

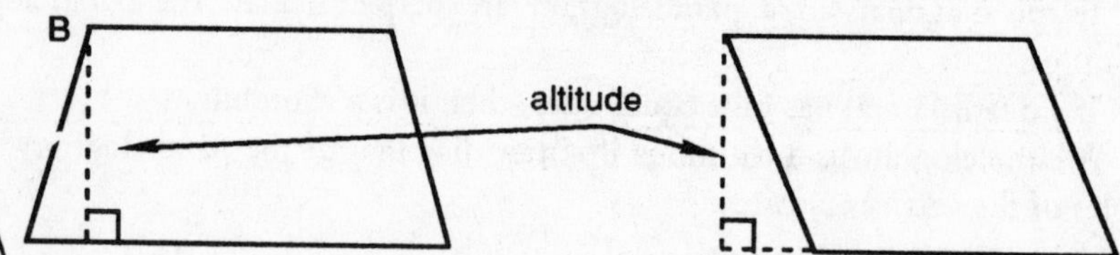

An **isosceles trapezoid** is a trapezoid whose non-parallel sides are equal. A pair of angles including only one of the parallel sides is called **a pair of base angles.**

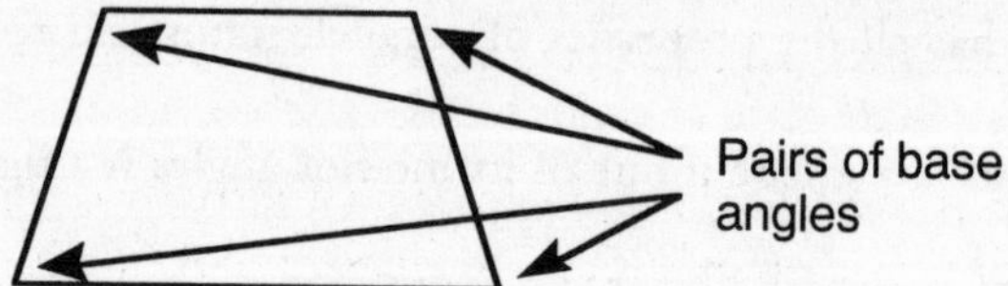

The median of a trapezoid is parallel to the bases and equal to one-half their sum.

The base angles of an isosceles trapezoid are equal.

The diagonals of an isosceles trapezoid are equal.

The opposite angles of an isosceles trapezoid are supplementary.

The area of a trapezoid is equal to one-half the product of the length of its altitude and the sum of its bases.

$A = {}^1/_2 h (b + b')$

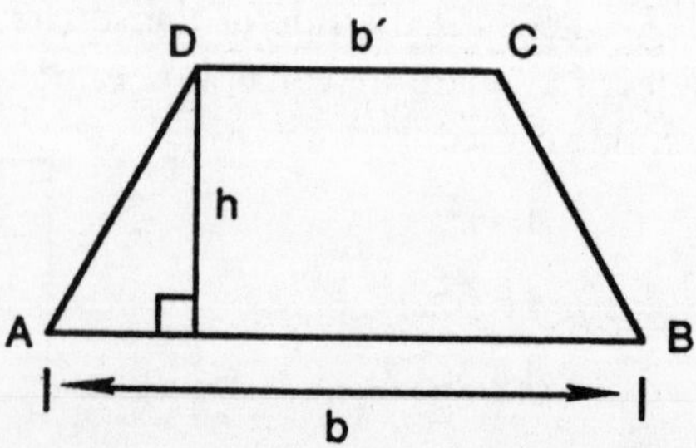

PROBLEM

Prove that all pairs of consecutive angles of a parallelogram are supplementary.

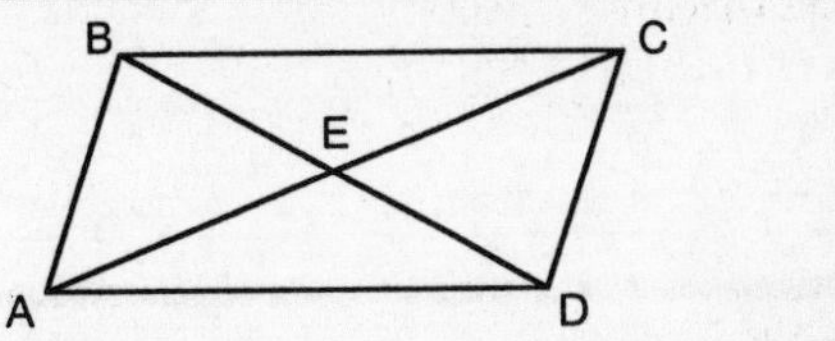

SOLUTION

We must prove that the pairs of angles $\angle$ *BAD* and $\angle$ *ADC*, $\angle$ *ADC* and $\angle$ *DCB*, $\angle$ *DCB* and $\angle$ *CBA*, and $\angle$ *CBA* and $\angle$ *BAD* are supplementary. (This means that the sum of their measures is 180°.)

Because *ABCD* is a parallelogram, $\overline{AB} \parallel \overline{CD}$. Angles *BAD* and *ADC* are consecutive interior angles, as are $\angle$ *CBA* and $\angle$ *DCB*. Since the consecutive interior angles formed by two parallel lines and a transversal are supplementary, $\angle$ *BAD* and $\angle$ *ADC* are supplementary, as are $\angle$ *CBA* and $\angle$ *DCB*.

Similarly, $\overline{AD} \parallel \overline{BC}$. Angles *ADC* and *DCB* are consecutive interior angles, as are $\angle$ *CBA* and $\angle$ *BAD*. Since the consecutive interior angles formed by two parallel lines and a transversal are supplementary, $\angle$ *CBA* and $\angle$ *BAD* are supplementary, as are $\angle$ *ADC* and $\angle$ *DCB*.

PROBLEM

In the accompanying figure, Δ *ABC* is given to be an isosceles right triangle with $\angle$ *ABC* a right angle and *AB* ≅ *BC*. Line segment $\overline{BD}$, which bisects $\overline{CA}$, is extended to *E*, so that $\overline{BD} \cong \overline{DE}$. Prove *BAEC* is a square.

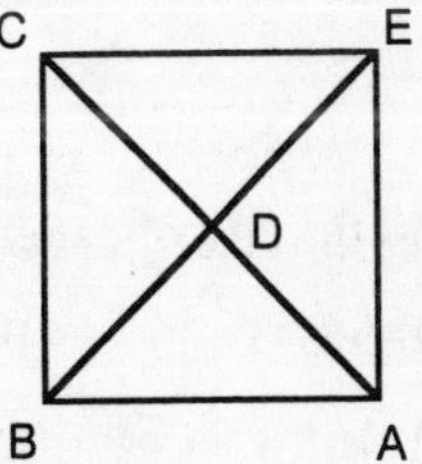

SOLUTION

A square is a rectangle in which two consecutive sides are congruent. This definition will provide the framework for the proof in this problem. We will prove that *BAEC* is a parallelogram that is specifically a rectangle with consecutive sides congruent, namely a square.

Statement	Reason
1. $\overline{BD} \cong \overline{DE}$ and $\overline{AD} \cong \overline{DC}$.	1. Given ($\overline{BD}$ bisects $\overline{CA}$).
2. *BAEC* is a parallelogram.	2. If diagonals of a quadrilateral bisect each other, then the quadrilateral is a parallelogram.
3. $\angle$ *ABC* is a right angle.	3. Given.
4. *BAEC* is a rectangle.	4. A parallelogram, one of whose angles is a right angle, is a rectangle.

5. $\overline{AB} \cong \overline{BC}$ — 5. Given.

6. *BAEC* is a square — 6. If a rectangle has two congruent consecutive sides, then the rectangle is a square.

☞ Drill 4: Quadrilaterals

Parallelograms, Rectangles, Rhombi, Squares, Trapezoids

1. In parallelogram *wxyz*, $wx = 14$, $wz = 6$, $zy = 3x + 5$, and $xy = 2y - 4$. Find x and y.

   (A) 3 and 5 (B) 4 and 5

   (C) 4 and 6 (D) 6 and 10

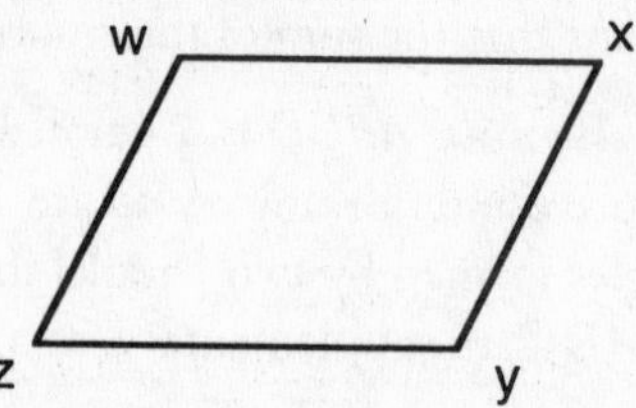

2. Quadrilateral *ABCD* is a parallelogram. If $m\angle B = (6x + 2)°$ and $m\angle D = 98°$, find x.

   (A) 12° (B) 16°

   (C) $16\,^2/_3°$ (D) 18°

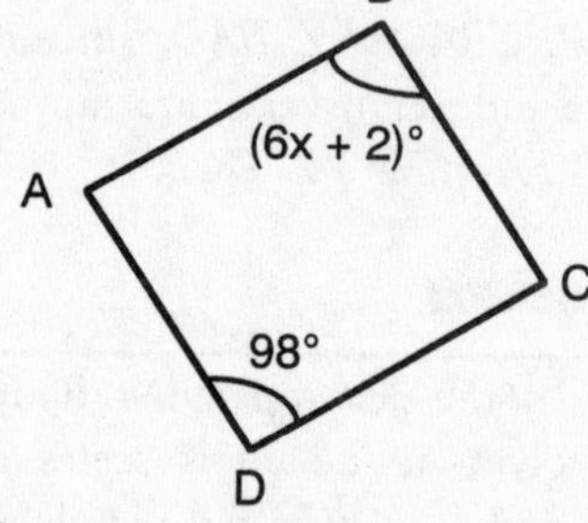

3. Find the area of parallelogram *STUV*.

   (A) 56 (B) 90

   (C) 108 (D) 162

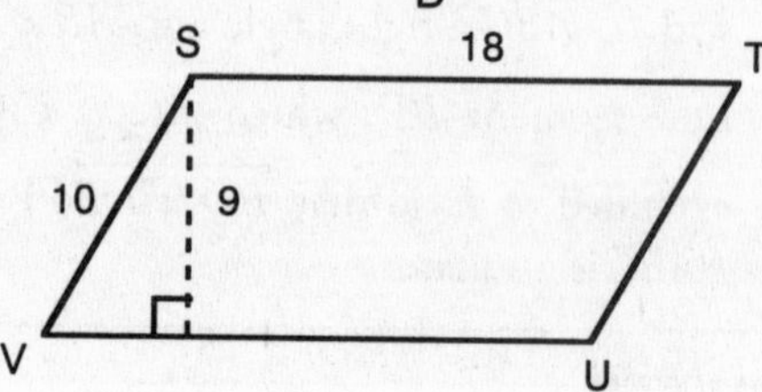

4. Find the area of parallelogram *MNOP*.

   (A) 19 (B) 32

   (C) $32\sqrt{3}$ (D) $44\sqrt{3}$

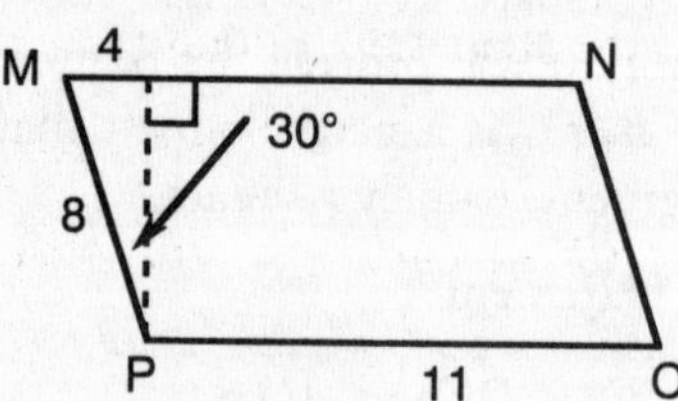

5. If the perimeter of rectangle *PQRS* is 40, find x.

   (A) 31 (B) 38

   (C) 2 (D) 44

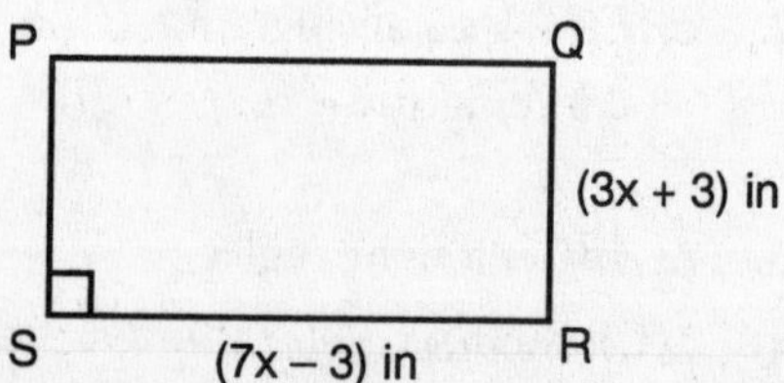

6. In rectangle $ABCD$, $AD = 6$ cm and $DC = 8$ cm. Find the length of the diagonal AC.

(A) 10 cm (B) 12 cm

(C) 20 cm (D) 28 cm

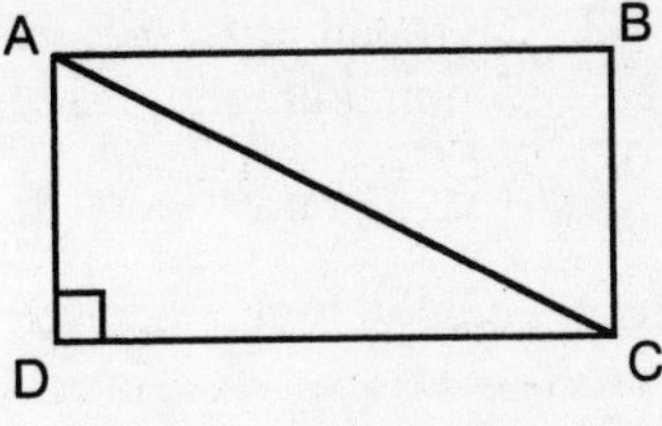

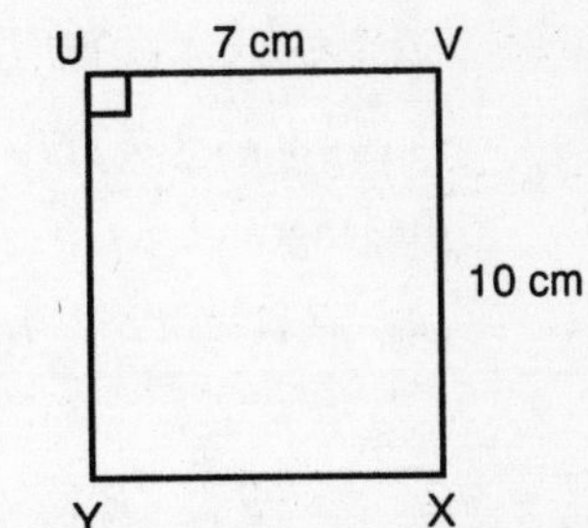

7. Find the area of rectangle $UVXY$.

(A) 17 cm^2 (B) 34 cm^2

(C) 35 cm^2 (D) 70 cm^2

8. Find x in rectangle $BCDE$ if the diagonal EC is 17 mm.

(A) 6.55 mm (B) 8 mm

(C) 8.5 mm (D) 17 mm

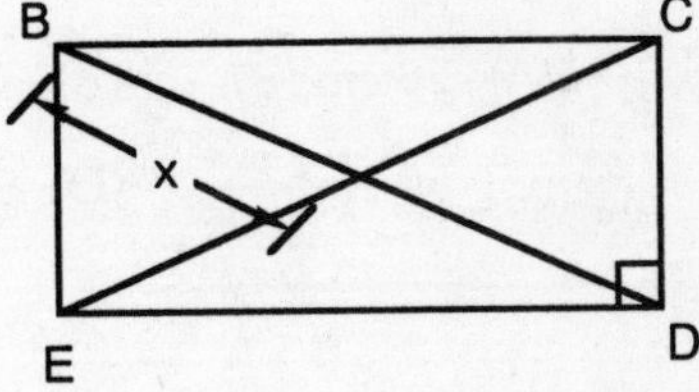

9. In rhombus $DEFG$, $DE = 7$ cm. Find the perimeter of the rhombus.

(A) 14 cm (B) 28 cm

(C) 42 cm (D) 49 cm

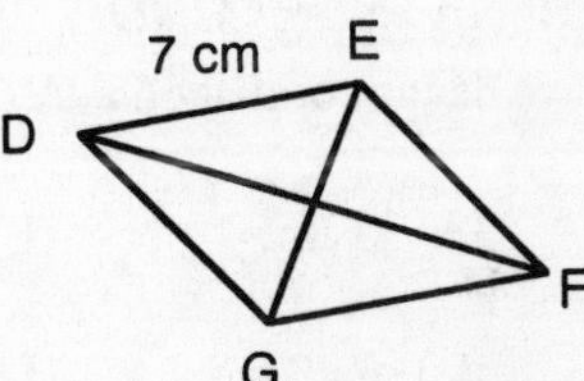

10. In rhombus $RHOM$, the diagonal $\overline{RO}$ is 8 cm and the diagonal $\overline{HM}$ is 12 cm. Find the area of the rhombus.

(A) 20 cm^2 (B) 40 cm^2

(C) 48 cm^2 (D) 68 cm^2

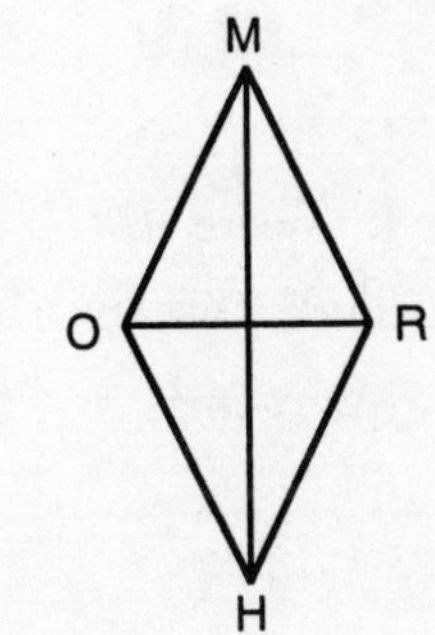

11. In rhombus $GHIJ$, $GI = 6$ cm and $HJ = 8$ cm. Find the length of GH.

(A) 3 cm (B) 4 cm

(C) 5 cm (D) $4\sqrt{3}$ cm

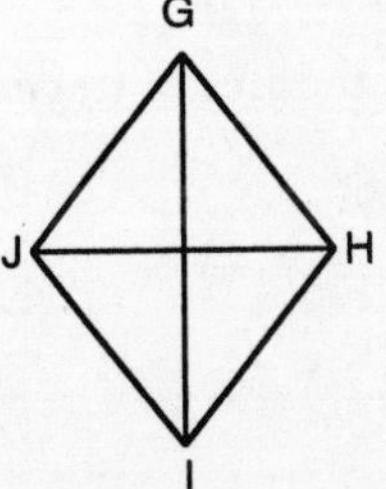

12. In rhombus *CDEF*, *CD* is 13 mm and *DX* is 5 mm. Find the area of the rhombus.

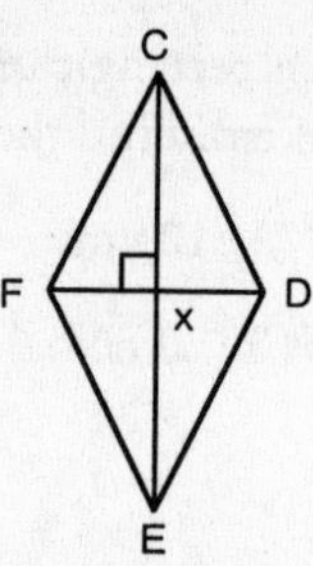

(A) 31 mm^2 (B) 60 mm^2

(C) 78 mm^2 (D) 120 mm^2

13. Quadrilateral *ATUV* is a square. If the perimeter of the square is 44 cm, find the length of $\overline{AT}$.

(A) 4 cm (B) 11 cm (C) 22 cm (D) 30 cm

14. The area of square *XYZW* is 196 cm^2. Find the perimeter of the square.

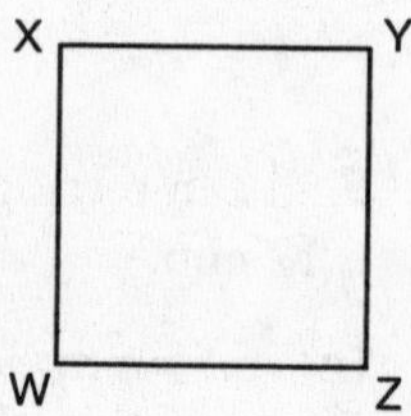

(A) 28 cm (B) 42 cm

(C) 56 cm (D) 98 cm

15. In square *MNOP*, *MN* is 6 cm. Find the length of diagonal $\overline{MO}$.

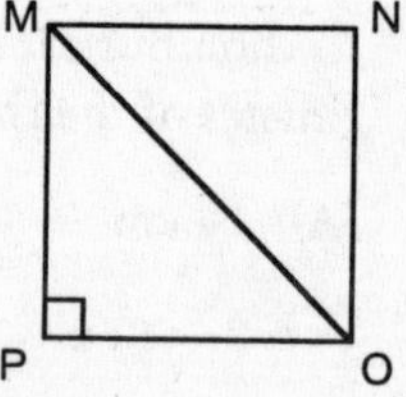

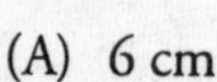
(A) 6 cm (B) $6\sqrt{2}$ cm

(C) $6\sqrt{3}$ cm (D) $6\sqrt{6}$ cm

16. In square *ABCD*, *AB* = 3 cm. Find the area of the square.

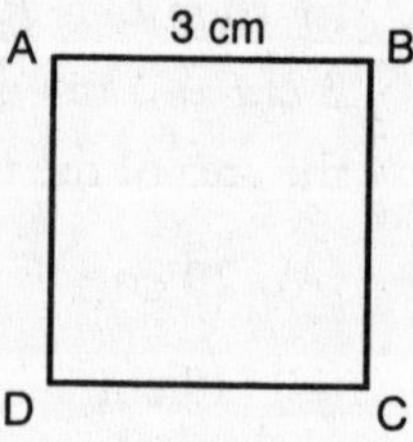

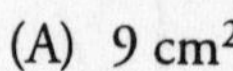
(A) 9 cm^2 (B) 12 cm^2

(C) 15 cm^2 (D) 18 cm^2

17. Find the area of trapezoid *RSTU*.

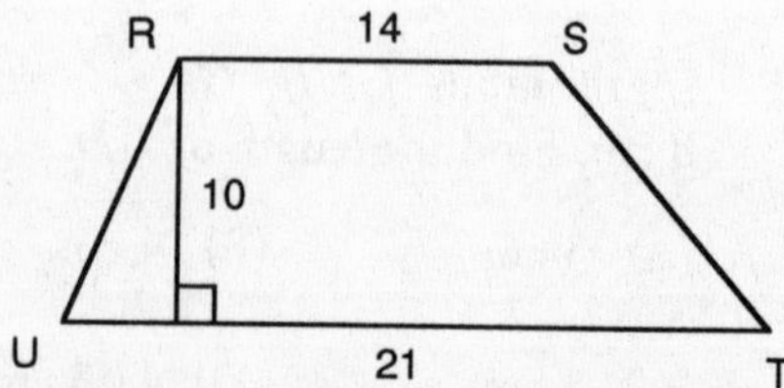

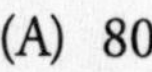
(A) 80 (B) 87.5

(C) 175 (D) 147

18. *ABCD* is an isosceles trapezoid. Find the perimeter.

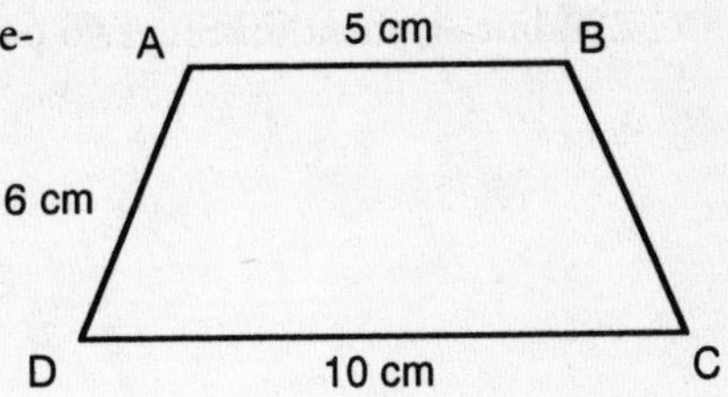

(A) 21 cm (B) 27 cm

(C) 30 cm (D) 50 cm

19. Find the area of trapezoid *MNOP*.

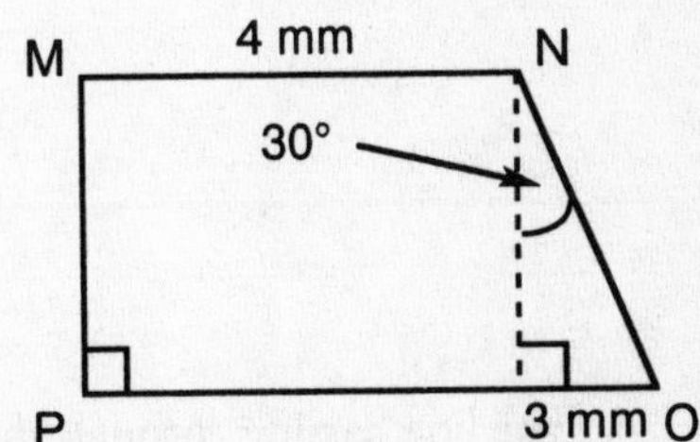

(A) $(17 + 3\sqrt{3})$ mm^2

(B) $\frac{33}{2}$ mm^2

(C) $\frac{33\sqrt{3}}{2}$ mm^2

(D) 33 mm^2

20. Trapezoid *XYZW* is isosceles. If $m\angle W = 58°$ and $m\angle Z = (4x - 6)°$, find x.

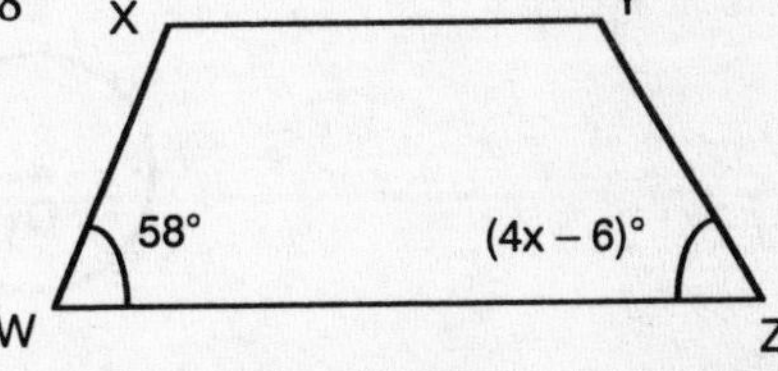

(A) 8° (B) 12°

(C) 13° (D) 16°

5. Circles

A **circle** is a set of points in the same plane equidistant from a fixed point called its center.

A **radius** of a circle is a line segment drawn from the center of the circle to any point on the circle.

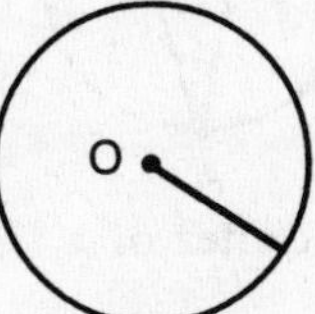

A portion of a circle is called an **arc** of the circle.

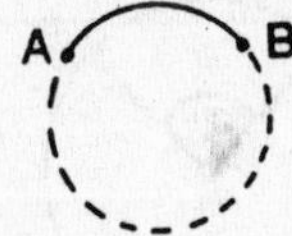

A line that intersects a circle in two points is called a **secant**.

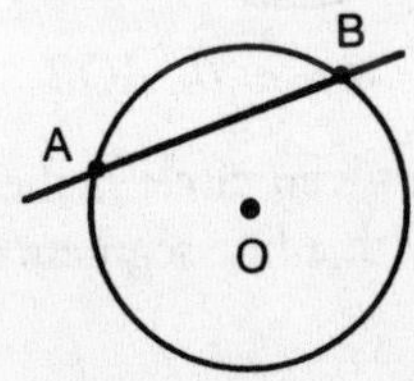

A line segment joining two points on a circle is called a **chord** of the circle.

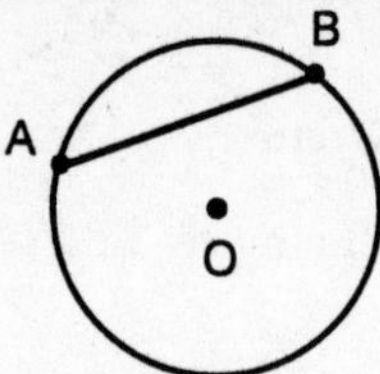

A chord that passes through the center of the circle is called a **diameter** of the circle.

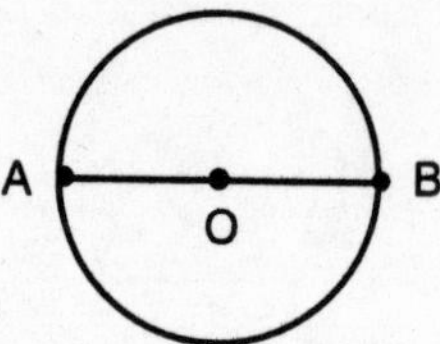

The line passing through the centers of two (or more) circles is called the **line of centers.**

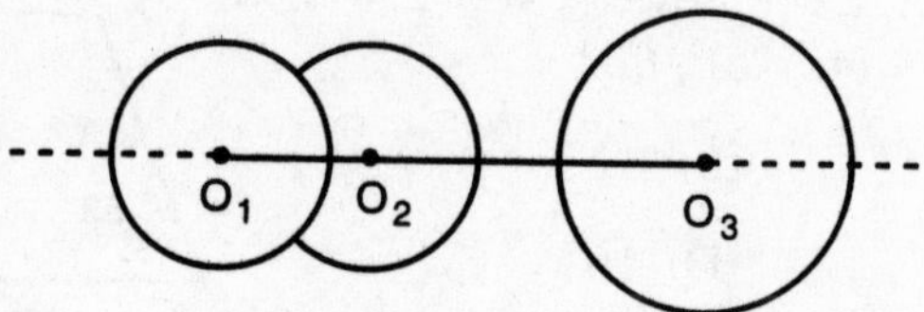

An angle whose vertex is on the circle and whose sides are chords of the circle is called an **inscribed angle.**

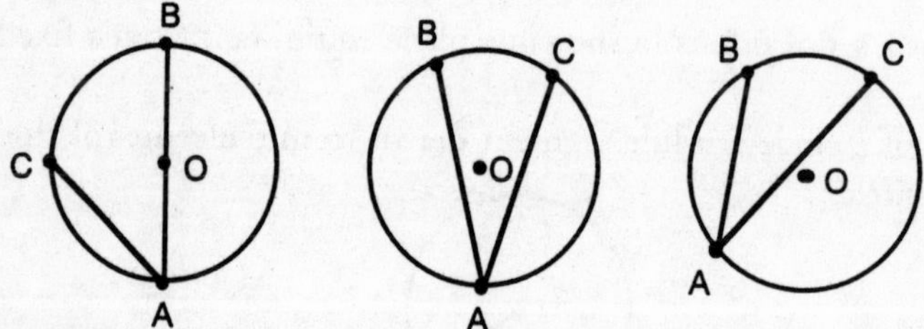

An angle whose vertex is at the center of a circle and whose sides are radii is called a **central angle.**

The measure of a minor arc is the measure of the central angle that intercepts that arc.

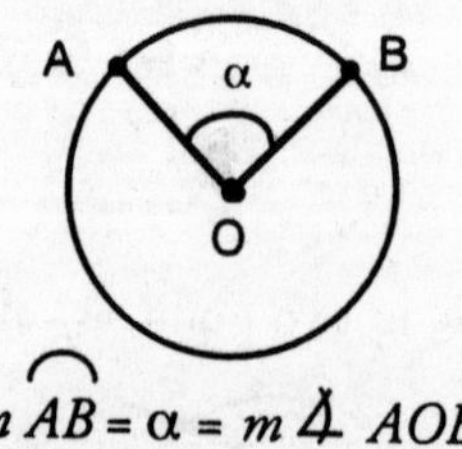

$$m\overset{\frown}{AB} = \alpha = m\measuredangle AOB$$

The distance from a point *P* to a given circle is the distance from that point to the point where the circle intersects with a line segment with endpoints at the center of the circle and point *P*.

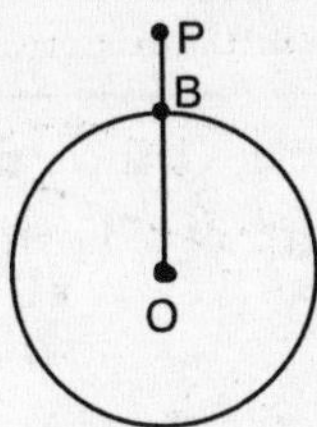

The distance of point P to the diagrammed circle with center O is the line segment PB of line segment PO.

A line that has one and only one point of intersection with a circle is called a tangent to that circle, while their common point is called a **point of tangency**.

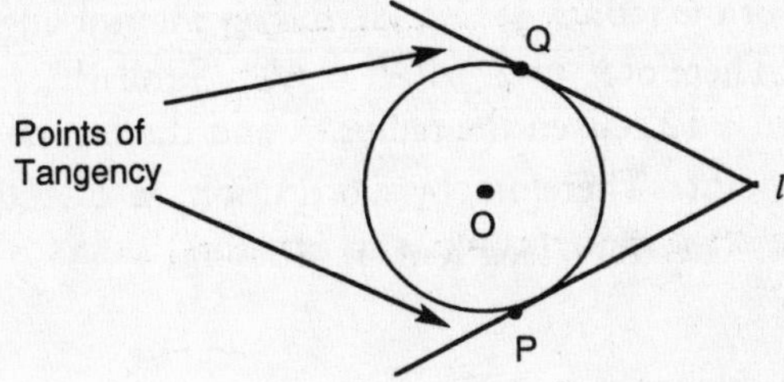

Congruent circles are circles whose radii are congruent.

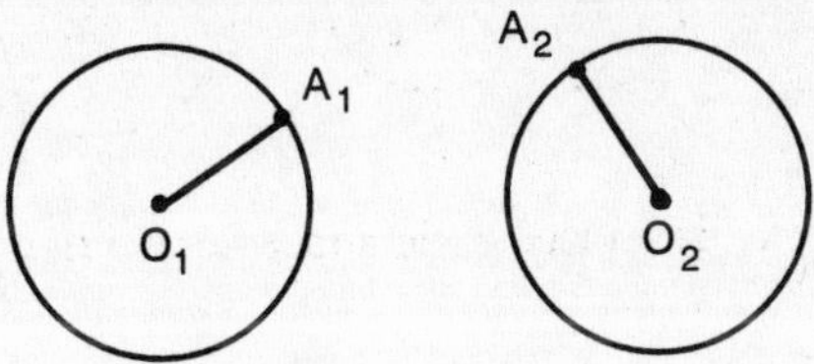

If $O_1A_1 \cong O_2A_2$, then $O_1 \cong O_2$.

The measure of a semicircle is 180°.

A **circumscribed circle** is a circle passing through all the vertices of a polygon.

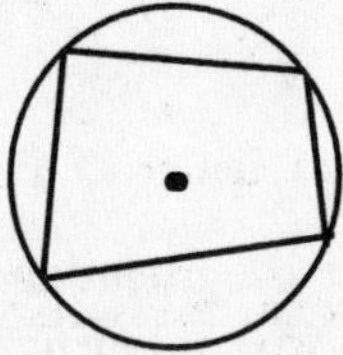

Circles that have the same center and unequal radii are called **concentric circles.**

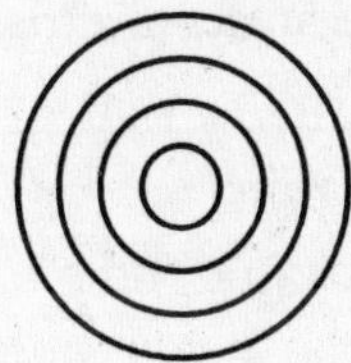

Concentric Circles

PROBLEM

A and B are points on circle Q such that $\Delta\ AQB$ is equilateral. If length of side AB = 12, find the length of arc $\overset{\frown}{AB}$.

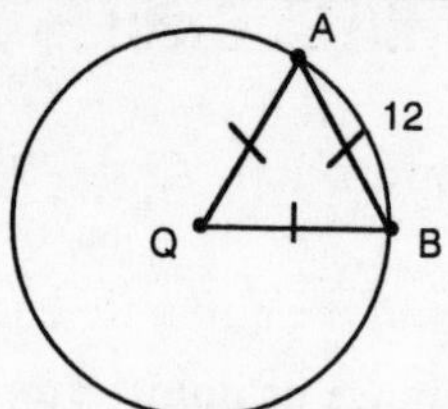

SOLUTION

To find the arc length of $\overset{\frown}{AB}$, we must find the measure of the central angle AQB and the measure of the radius $\overline{QA}$. $\angle\ AQB$ is an interior angle of the equilateral triangle $\Delta\ AQB$. Therefore, $m\angle\ AQB = 60°$. Similarly, in the equilateral $\Delta\ AQB$, $AQ = AB = QB = 12$. Given the radius, r, and the central angle, n, the arc length is given by $^{n}/_{360} \times 2\pi r$. Therefore, by substitution, $m\angle\ AQB = {}^{60}/_{360} \times 2\pi \times 12 = {}^{1}/_{6} \times 2\pi \times 12 = 4\pi$. Therefore, length of arc $\overset{\frown}{AB} = 4\pi$.

PROBLEM

In circle O, the measure of $\overset{\frown}{AB}$ is 80°. Find the measure of $\angle\ A$.

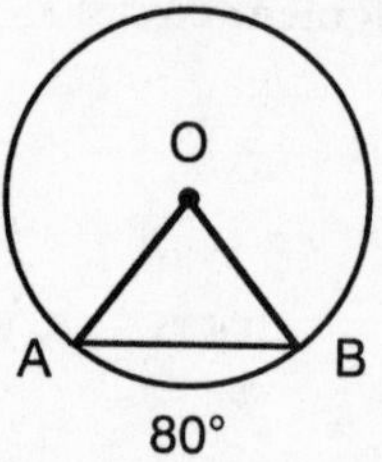

SOLUTION

The accompanying figure shows that $\overset{\frown}{AB}$ is intercepted by central angle AOB. By definition, we know that the measure of the central angle is the measure of its intercepted arc. In this case,

$$m\overset{\frown}{AB} = m\angle\ AOB = 80°$$

Radius $\overline{OA}$ and radius $\overline{OB}$ are congruent and form two sides of $\Delta\ OAB$. By a theorem, the angles opposite these two congruent sides must, themselves, be congruent. Therefore, $m\angle\ A = m\angle\ B$.

The sum of the measures of the angles of a triangle is 180°. Therefore,

$$m\angle\ A + m\angle\ B + m\angle\ AOB = 180°$$

Since $m\angle\ A = m\angle\ B$, we can write

$$m\angle\ A + m\angle\ A + 80° = 180°$$

or $$2m\angle\ A = 100°$$

or $$m\angle\ A = 50°$$

Therefore, the measure of $\angle\ A$ is 50°.

☞ Drill 5: Circles

Circumference, Area, Concentric Circles

1. Find the circumference of circle A if its radius is 3 mm.

   (A) 3π mm (B) 6π mm (C) 9π mm (D) 12π mm

2. The circumference of circle H is 20π cm. Find the length of the radius.

   (A) 10 cm (B) 20 cm (C) 10π cm (D) 15π cm

3. The circumference of circle A is how many millimeters larger than the circumference of circle B?

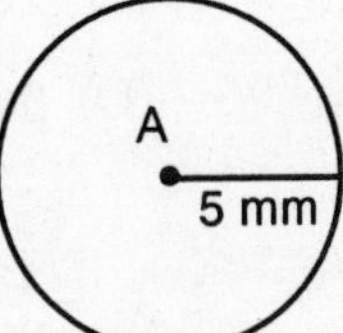

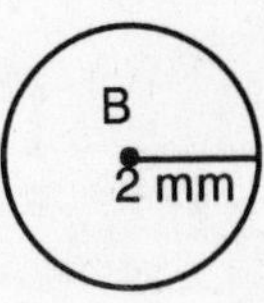

   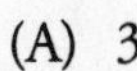

   (A) 3 (B) 6

   (C) 3π (D) 6π

4. If the diameter of circle X is 9 cm and if $\pi = 3.14$, find the circumference of the circle to the nearest tenth.

   (A) 28.3 cm (B) 14.1 cm (C) 21.1 cm (D) 24.6 cm

5. Find the area of circle I.

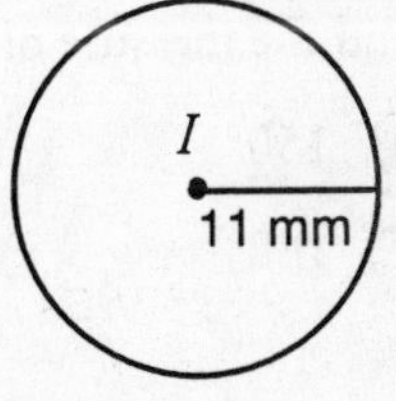

   (A) 22 mm^2 (B) 121 mm^2

   (C) 12π mm^2 (D) 132 mm^2

6. The diameter of circle Z is 27 mm. Find the area of the circle.

   (A) 91.125 mm^2 (B) 182.25 mm^2

   (C) 191.5π mm^2 (D) 182.25π mm^2

7. The area of circle B is 225π cm^2. Find the length of the diameter of the circle.

   (A) 15 cm (B) 20 cm (C) 30 cm (D) 20π cm

8. The area of circle X is 144π mm^2 while the area of circle Y is 81π mm^2. Write the ratio of the radius of circle X to that of circle Y.

   (A) 3 : 4 (B) 4 : 3 (D) 9 : 12 (D) 27 : 12

9. The circumference of circle M is 18π cm. Find the area of the circle.

   (A) 18π cm^2 (B) 81 cm^2 (C) 81π cm^2 (D) 36π cm^2

10. In two concentric circles, the smaller circle has a radius of 3 mm while the larger circle has a radius of 5 mm. Find the area of the shaded region.

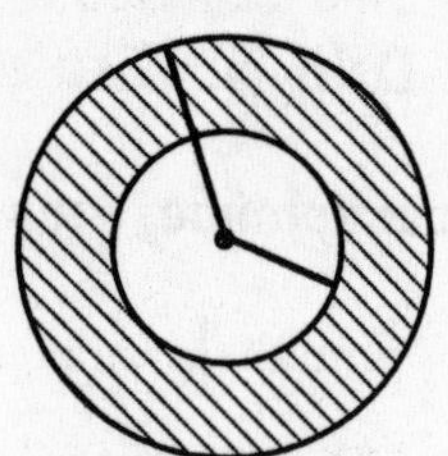

(A) 2π mm^2 (B) 8π mm^2

(C) 13π mm^2 (D) 16π mm^2

11. The radius of the smaller of two concentric circles is 5 cm while the radius of the larger circle is 7 cm. Determine the area of the shaded region.

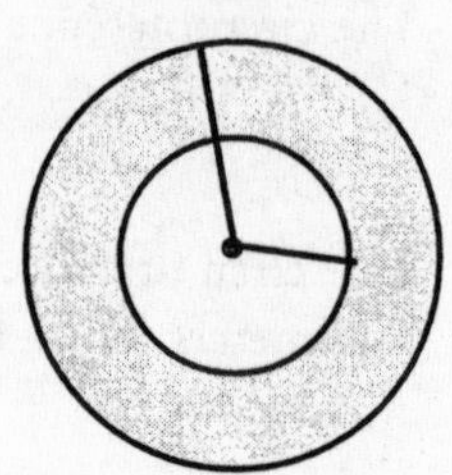

(A) 7π cm^2 (B) 24π cm^2

(C) 25π cm^2 (D) 36π cm^2

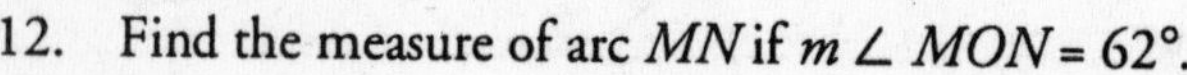

12. Find the measure of arc *MN* if $m\angle MON = 62°$.

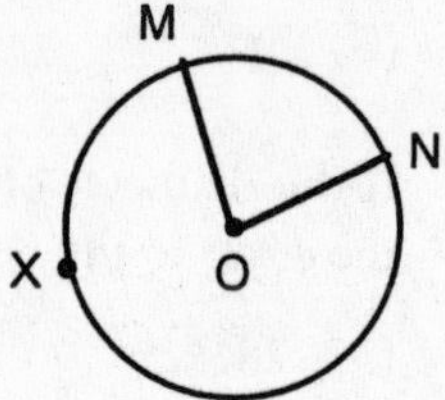

(A) 16° (B) 32°

(C) 59° (D) 62°

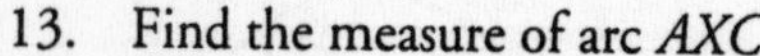

13. Find the measure of arc *AXC*.

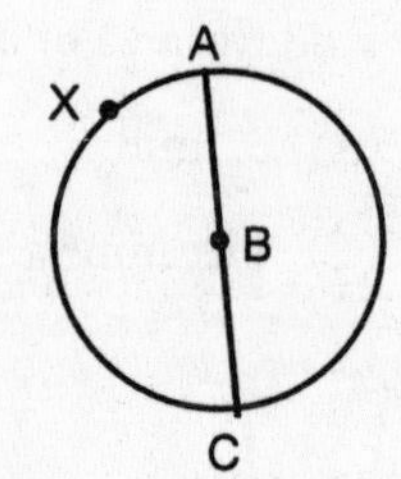

(A) 150° (B) 160°

(C) 180° (D) 270°

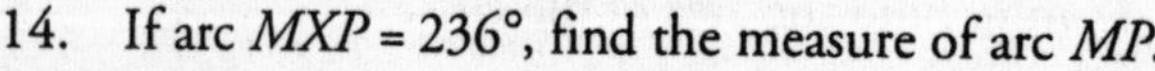

14. If arc *MXP* = 236°, find the measure of arc *MP*.

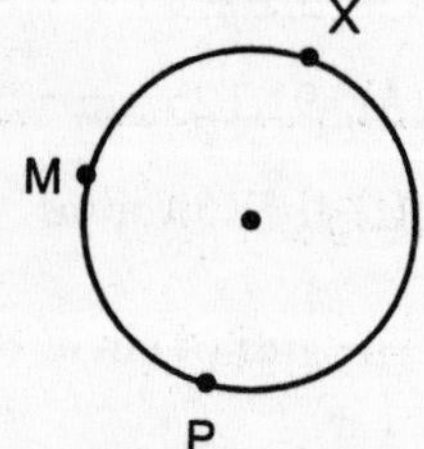

(A) 62° (B) 124°

(C) 236° (D) 270°

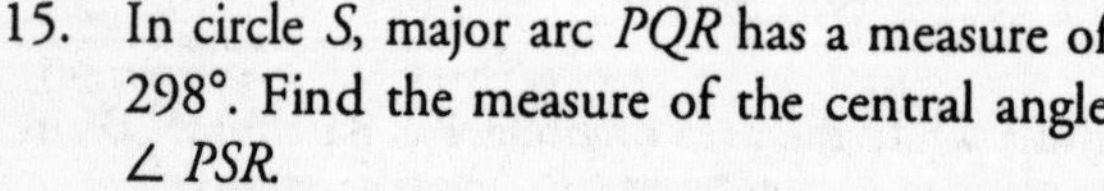

15. In circle *S*, major arc *PQR* has a measure of 298°. Find the measure of the central angle $\angle PSR$.

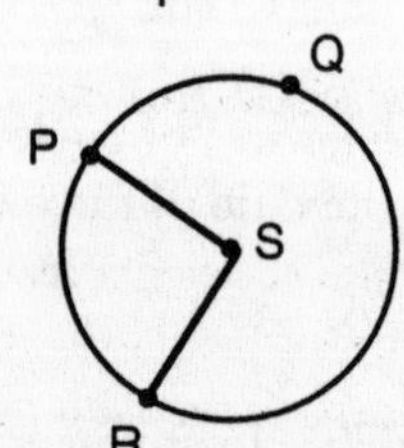

(A) 62° (B) 124°

(C) 149° (D) 298°

16. Find the measure of arc *XY* in circle *W*.

(A) 40° (B) 120°

(C) 140° (D) 180°

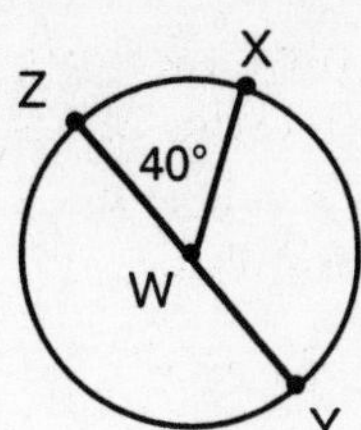

17. Find the area of the sector shown.

(A) 4 cm^2 (B) 2π cm^2

(C) 16 cm^2 (D) 8π cm^2

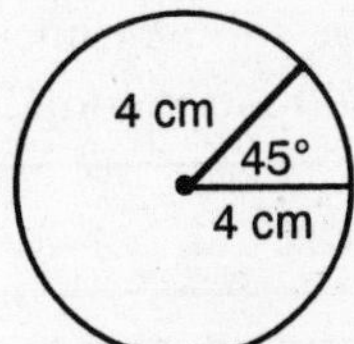

18. Find the area of the shaded region.

(A) 10 (B) 5π

(C) 25 (D) 20π

19. Find the area of the sector shown.

(A) $\frac{9\pi \text{ mm}^2}{4}$ (B) $\frac{9\pi \text{ mm}^2}{2}$

(C) 18 mm^2 (D) 6π mm^2

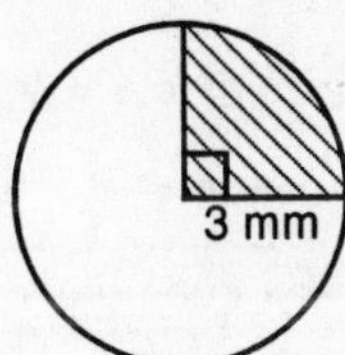

20. If the area of the square is 100 cm^2, find the area of the sector.

(A) 10π cm^2 (B) 25 cm^2

(C) 25π cm^2 (D) 100 cm^2

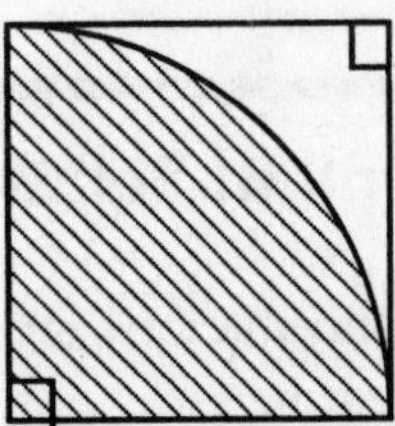

6. Solids

Solid geometry is the study of figures which consist of points not all in the same plane.

Rectangular Solids

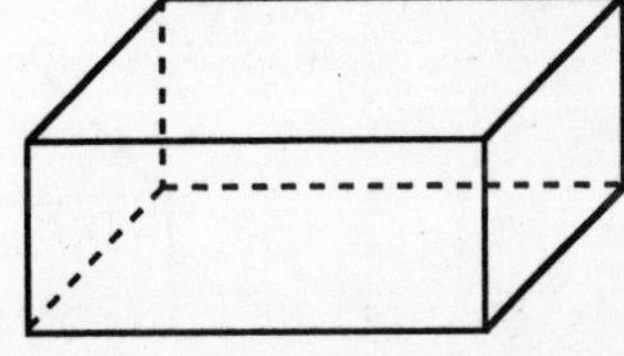

A solid with lateral faces and bases that are rectangles is called a **rectangular solid.**

The surface area of a rectangular solid is the sum of the areas of all the faces.

The volume of a rectangular solid is equal to the product of its length, width, and height.

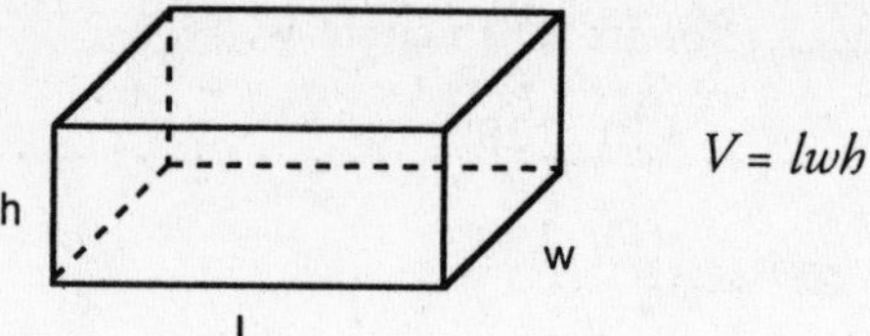

PROBLEM

What are the dimensions of a solid cube whose surface area is numerically equal to its volume?

SOLUTION

The surface area of a cube of edge length a is equal to the sum of the areas of its 6 faces. Since a cube is a regular polygon, all 6 faces are congruent. Each face of a cube is a square of edge length a. Hence, the surface area of a cube of edge length a is

$$S = 6a^2$$

The volume of a cube of edge length a is

$$V = a^3$$

We require that $A = V$, or that

$$6a^2 = a^3 \quad \text{or} \quad a = 6$$

Hence, if a cube has edge length 6, its surface area will be numerically equal to its volume.

☞ Drill 6: Solids

1. Find the total area of the rectangular prism shown.

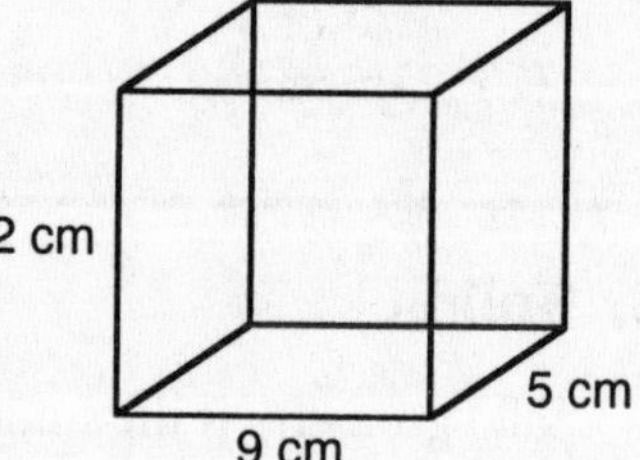

(A) 138 cm^2 (B) 336 cm^2

(C) 381 cm^2 (D) 426 cm^2

2. Find the volume of the rectangular storage tank shown.

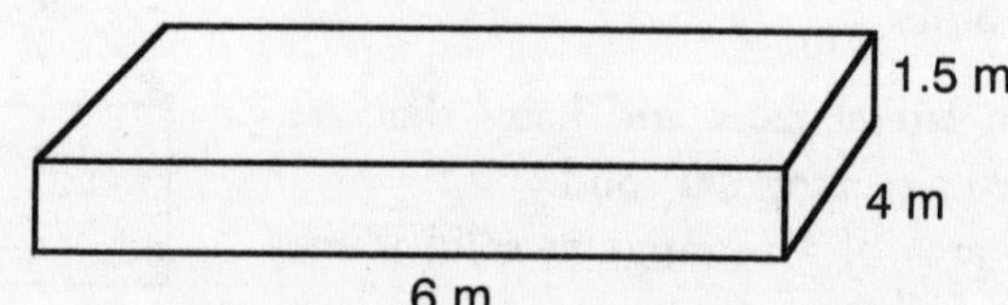

(A) 24 m^3 (B) 36 m^3 (C) 38 m^3 (D) 42 m^3

3. The lateral area of a cube is 100 cm^2. Find the length of an edge of the cube.

(A) 4 cm (B) 5 cm (C) 10 cm (D) 12 cm

7. Coordinate Geometry

Coordinate geometry refers to the study of geometric figures using algebraic principles.

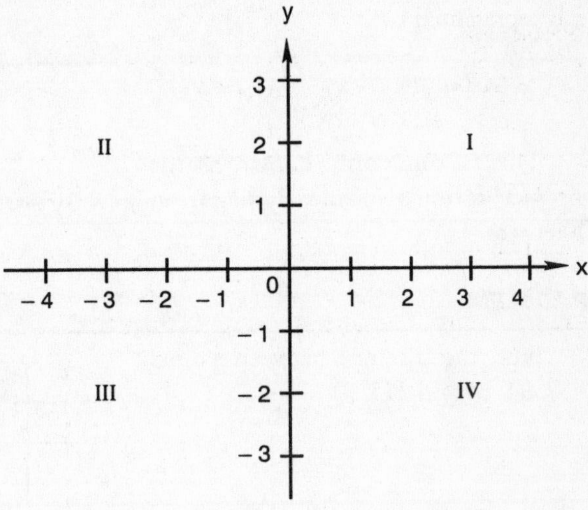

The graph shown is called the Cartesian coordinate plane. The graph consists of a pair of perpendicular lines called **coordinate axes.** The **vertical axis** is the *y*-axis and the **horizontal axis** is the *x*-axis. The point of intersection of these two axes is called the **origin**; it is the zero point of both axes. Furthermore, points to the right of the origin on the *x*-axis and above the origin on the *y*-axis represent positive real numbers. Points to the left of the origin on the *x*-axis or below the origin on the *y*-axis represent negative real numbers.

The four regions cut off by the coordinate axes are, in counterclockwise direction from the top right, called the first, second, third and fourth quadrant, respectively. The first quadrant contains all points with two positive coordinates.

In the graph shown, two points are identified by the ordered pair (x, y) of numbers. The *x*-coordinate is the first number and the *y*-coordinate is the second number.

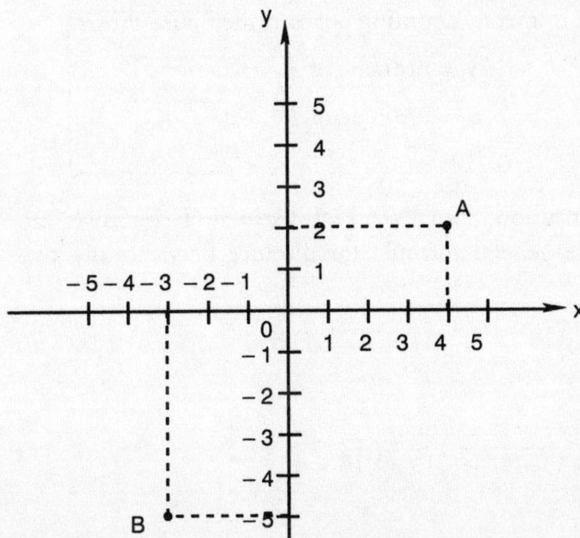

To plot a point on the graph when given the coordinates, draw perpendicular lines from the number-line coordinates to the point where the two lines intersect.

To find the coordinates of a given point on the graph, draw perpendicular lines from the point to the coordinates on the number line. The *x*-coordinate is written before the *y*-coordinate and a comma is used to separate the two.

In this case, point A has the coordinates (4, 2) and the coordinates of point B are (– 3, – 5).

For any two points A and B with coordinates (x_A, y_A) and (x_B, y_B), respectively, the distance between A and B is represented by

$$AB = \sqrt{(x_A - x_B)^2 + (y_A - y_B)^2}$$

This is commonly known as the distance formula or the **Pythagorean Theorem.**

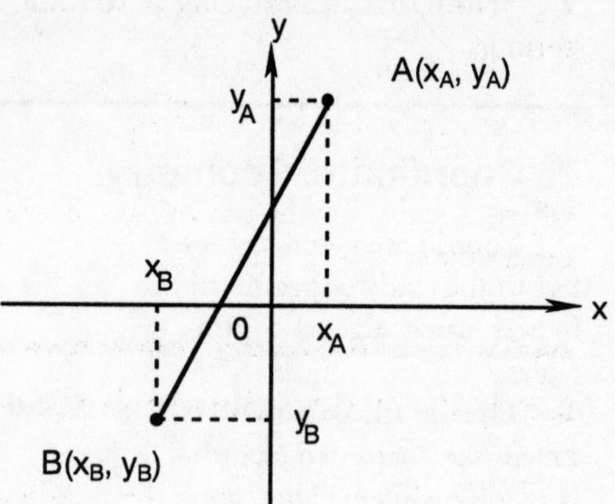

PROBLEM

Find the distance between points $A(1, 3)$ and $B(5, 3)$.

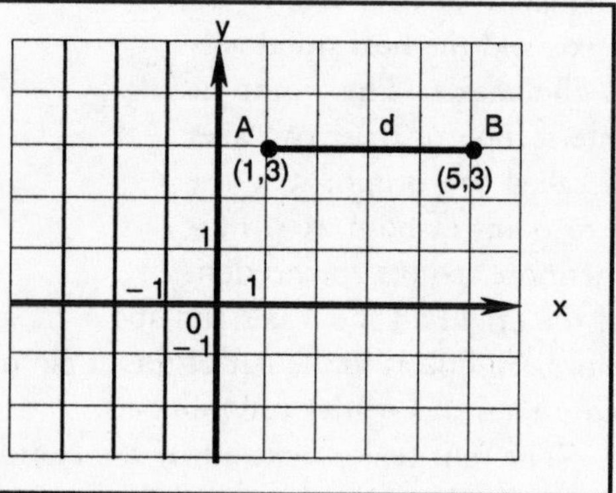

SOLUTION

In this case, where the ordinate of both points is the same, the distance between the two points is given by the absolute value of the difference between the two abscissas. In fact, this case reduces to merely counting boxes as the figure shows.

Let, x_1 = abscissa of A $\quad$ y_1 = ordinate of A

x_2 = abscissa of B $\quad$ y_2 = ordinate of B

d = the distance

Therefore, $d = | x_1 - x_2 |$. By substitution, $d = | 1 - 5 | = | -4 | = 4$. This answer can also be obtained by applying the general formula for distance between any two points

$$d = \sqrt{(x_1 - x_2)^2 + (y_1 - y_2)^2}$$

By substitution,

$$d = \sqrt{(1-5)^2 + (3-3)^2} = \sqrt{(-4)^2 + (0)^2} = \sqrt{16} = 4.$$

The distance is 4.

To find the midpoint of a segment between the two given endpoints, use the formula

$$MP = \left(\frac{x_1 + x_2}{2}, \frac{y_1 + y_2}{2}\right)$$

where x_1 and y_1 are the coordinates of one point; x_2 and y_2 are the coordinates of the other point.

☞ Drill 7: Coordinate Geometry

1. Which point shown has the coordinates (– 3, 2)?

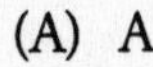
(A) A (B) B

(C) C (D) D

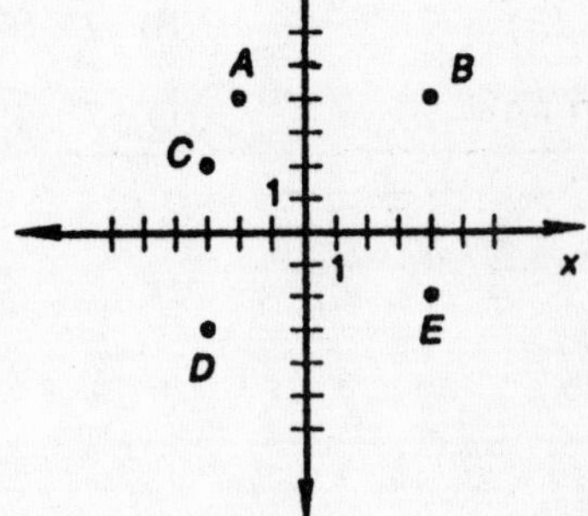

2. Name the coordinates of point A.

(A) (4, 3) (B) (3, – 4)

(C) (4, – 3) (D) (– 4, 3)

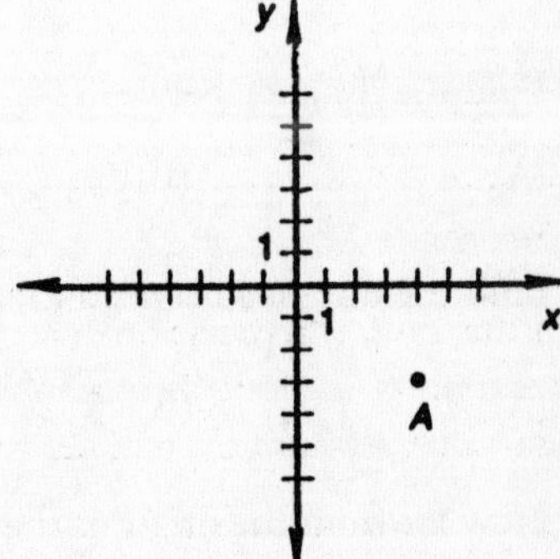

3. Which point shown has the coordinates (2.5, – 1)?

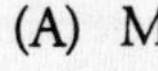
(A) M
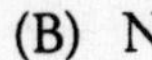
(B) N

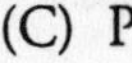
(C) P
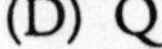
(D) Q

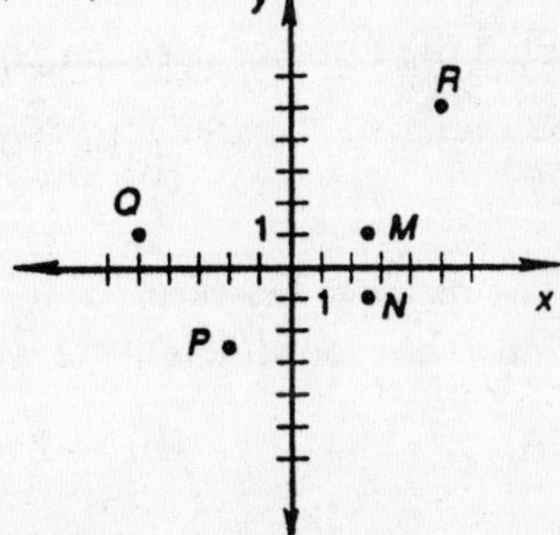

4. The correct x-coordinate for point H is what number?

(A) 3 (B) 4

(C) – 3 (D) – 5

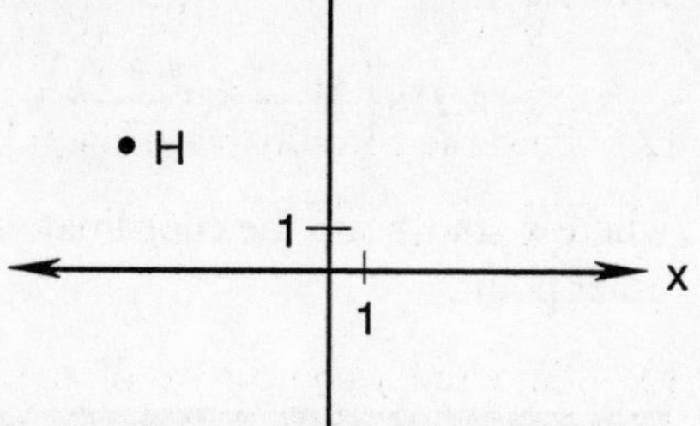

5. The correct y-coordinate for point R is what number?

(A) – 7 (B) 2

(C) – 2 (D) 7

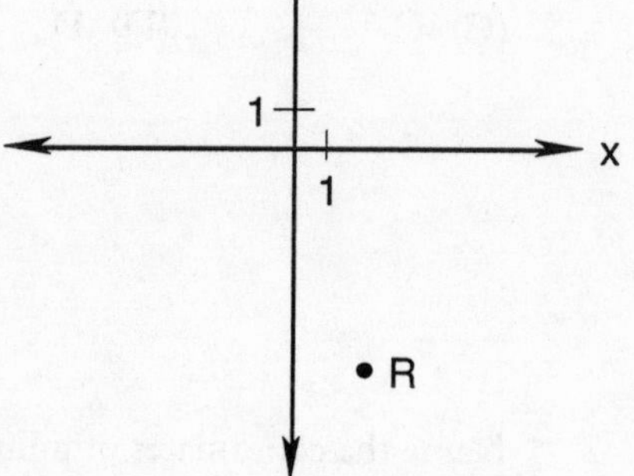

6. Find the distance between (4, – 7) and (– 2, – 7).

(A) 4 (B) 6 (C) 7 (D) 14

7. Find the distance between (3, 8) and (5, 11).

(A) 2 (B) 3 (C) $\sqrt{13}$ (D) $\sqrt{15}$

8. How far from the origin is the point (3, 4)?

(A) 3 (B) 4 (C) 5 (D) $5\sqrt{3}$

9. Find the distance between points (– 4, 2) and (3, – 5).

(A) 3 (B) $3\sqrt{3}$ (C) 7 (D) $7\sqrt{2}$

10. The distance between points A and B is 10 units. If A has coordinates (4, – 6) and B has coordinates (– 2, y), determine the value of y.

(A) 2 (B) – 2 (C) 0 (D) 1

11. Find the midpoint between the points (– 2, 6) and (4, 8).

(A) (3, 7) (B) (1, 7) (C) (3, 1) (D) (1, 1)

12. Find the coordinates of the midpoint between the points (– 5, 7) and (3, – 1).

(A) (– 4, 4) (B) (3, – 1) (C) (1, – 3) (D) (– 1, 3)

13. Find the *y*-coordinate of the midpoint of segment $\overline{AB}$ if *A* has coordinates (– 3, 7) and *B* has coordinates (– 3, – 2) is what value?

(A) 5/2 (B) 3 (C) 7/2 (D) 5

14. One endpoint of a line segment is (5, – 3). The midpoint is (– 1, 6). What is the other endpoint?

(A) (7, 3) (B) (2, 1.5) (C) (– 7, 15) (D) (– 2, 1.5)

15. The point (– 2, 6) is the midpoint for which of the following pair of points?

(A) (1, 3) and (– 5, 9) (B) (– 1, – 3) and (5, 9)

(C) (1, 4) and (5, 9) (D) (– 1, 4) and (3, – 8)

GEOMETRY DRILLS

ANSWER KEY

Drill 1 – Points, Lines, and Angles

1. (B)
2. (A)
3. (C)
4. (D)
5. (D)
6. (C)
7. (B)
8. (A)
9. (D)
10. (A)
11. (C)
12. (D)
13. (B)
14. (B)
15. (A)

Drill 2 – Regular Polygons

1. (D)
2. (B)
3. (C)
4. (A)
5. (D)
6. (C)
7. (D)
8. (B)
9. (D)
10. (B)

Drill 3 – Triangles

1. (D)
2. (B)
3. (C)
4. (A)
5. (C)
6. (A)
7. (B)
8. (B)
9. (A)
10. (C)
11. (C)
12. (B)
13. (D)
14. (A)
15. (B)

Drill 4 – Quadrilaterals

1. (A)
2. (B)
3. (D)
4. (D)
5. (C)
6. (A)
7. (D)
8. (C)
9. (B)
10. (C)
11. (C)
12. (D)
13. (B)
14. (C)
15. (B)
16. (A)
17. (C)
18. (B)
19. (C)
20. (D)

Drill 5 – Circles

1. (B)
2. (A)
3. (D)
4. (A)
5. (C)
6. (D)
7. (C)
8. (B)
9. (C)
10. (D)
11. (B)
12. (D)
13. (C)
14. (B)
15. (A)
16. (C)
17. (B)
18. (D)
19. (A)
20. (C)

Drill 6 – Solids

1. (D)	2. (B)	3. (C)

Drill 7 – Coordinate Geometry

1. (C)	5. (A)	9. (D)	13. (A)
2. (C)	6. (B)	10. (A)	14. (C)
3. (B)	7. (C)	11. (B)	15. (A)
4. (D)	8. (C)	12. (D)	

V. Word Problems

One of the main problems students have in mathematics involves solving word problems. The secret to solving these problems is being able to convert words into numbers and variables in the form of an algebraic equation.

The easiest way to approach a word problem is to read the question and ask yourself what you are trying to find. This unknown quantity can be represented by a variable.

Next, determine how the variable relates to the other quantities in the problem. More than likely, these quantities can be explained in terms of the original variable. If not, a separate variable may have to be used to represent a quantity.

Using these variables and the relationships determined among them, an equation can be written. Solve for a particular variable and then plug this number in for each relationship that involves this variable in order to find any unknown quantities.

Lastly, re-read the problem to be sure that you have answered the questions correctly and fully.

1. Algebraic

The following illustrates how to formulate an equation and solve the problem.

EXAMPLE

Find two consecutive odd integers whose sum is 36.

Let x = the first odd integer

Let $x + 2$ = the second odd integer

The sum of the two numbers is 36. Therefore,

$$x + (x + 2) = 36$$

Simplifying,

$$2x + 2 = 36$$

$$2x + 2 + (-2) = 36 + (-2)$$

$$2x = 34$$

$$x = 17$$

Plugging 17 in for x, we find the second odd integer = $(x + 2) = (17 + 2) = 19$. Therefore, we find that the two consecutive odd integers whose sum is 36 are 17 and 19, respectively.

☞ Drill 1: Algebraic

1. The sum of two numbers is 41. One number is one less than twice the other. Find the larger of the two numbers.

   (A) 13 (B) 14 (C) 21 (D) 27

2. The sum of two consecutive integers is 111. Three times the larger integer less two times the smaller integer is 58. Find the value of the smaller integer.

   (A) 55 (B) 56 (C) 58 (D) 111

3. The difference between two integers is 12. The sum of the two integers is 2. Find both integers.

   (A) 7 and 5 (B) 7 and – 5 (C) – 7 and 5 (D) 2 and 12

2. Rate

One of the formulas you will use for rate problems will be

Rate × Time = Distance

PROBLEM

If a plane travels five hours from New York to California at a speed of 600 miles per hour, how many miles does the plane travel?

SOLUTION

Using the formula rate × time = distance, multiply 600 mph × 5 hours = 3,000 miles.

The average rate at which an object travels can be solved by dividing the total distance traveled by the total amount of time.

PROBLEM

On a 40-mile bicycle trip, Cathy rode half the distance at 20 mph and the other half at 10 mph. What was Cathy's average speed on the bike trip?

SOLUTION

First you need to break down the problem. On half of the trip which would be 20 miles, Cathy rode 20 mph. Using the rate formula, $^{\text{distance}}/_{\text{rate}}$ = time, you would compute

$$\frac{20 \text{ miles}}{20 \text{ miles per hour}} = 1 \text{ hour}$$

to travel the first 20 miles. During the second 20 miles, Cathy traveled at 10 miles per hour, which would be

$$\frac{20 \text{ miles}}{10 \text{ miles per hour}} = 2 \text{ hours}$$

Thus, the average speed Cathy traveled would be $^{40}/_{3}$ = 13.3 miles per hour.

In solving for some rate problems you can use cross multiplication involving ratios to solve for x.

PROBLEM

If 2 pairs of shoes cost $52, then what is the cost of 10 pairs of shoes at this rate?

SOLUTION

$$\frac{2}{52} = \frac{10}{x}, \; 2x = 52 \times 10, \;\; x = \frac{520}{2}, \;\; x = \$260$$

☞ Drill 2: Rate

1. Two towns are 420 miles apart. A car leaves the first town traveling toward the second town at 55 mph. At the same time, a second car leaves the other town and heads toward the first town at 65 mph. How long will it take for the two cars to meet?

   (A) 2 hr (B) 3 hr (C) 3.5 hr (D) 4 hr

2. A camper leaves the campsite walking due east at a rate of 3.5 mph. Another camper leaves the campsite at the same time but travels due west. In two hours the two campers will be 15 miles apart. What is the walking rate of the second camper?

   (A) 4 mph (B) 3 mph (C) 3.25 mph (D) 3.5 mph

3. A bicycle racer covers a 75 mile training route to prepare for an upcoming race. If the racer could increase his speed by 5 mph, he could complete the same course in 3/4 of the time. Find his average rate of speed.

   (A) 15 mph (B) 15.5 mph (C) 16 mph (D) 18 mph

3. Work

In work problems, one of the basic formulas is

$$\frac{1}{x} + \frac{1}{y} = \frac{1}{z}$$

where x and y represent the number of hours it takes two objects or people to complete the work and z is the total number of hours when both are working together.

PROBLEM

Otis can seal and stamp 400 envelopes in 2 hours while Elizabeth seals and stamps 400 envelopes in 1 hour. In how many hours can Otis and Elizabeth, working together, complete a 400-piece mailing at these rates?

SOLUTION

$$\frac{1}{2}+\frac{1}{1}=\frac{1}{z},\quad \frac{1}{2}+\frac{2}{2}=\frac{3}{2},\quad \frac{3}{2}=\frac{1}{z},\quad 3z=2$$

$z = {}^2/_3$ of an hour or 40 minutes. Working together, Otis and Elizabeth can seal and stamp 400 envelopes in 40 minutes.

☞ Drill 3: Work

1. It takes Marty 3 hours to type the address labels for his club's newsletter. It only takes Pat $2^1/_4$ hours to type the same amount of labels. How long would it take them working together to complete the address labels?

   (A) $^7/_9$ hr (B) $1\ ^2/_7$ hr (C) $1\ ^4/_5$ hour (D) $2\ ^5/_8$ hr

2. It takes Troy 3 hours to mow his family's large lawn. With his little brother's help, he can finish the job in only 2 hours. How long would it take the little brother to mow the entire lawn alone?

   (A) 4 hr (B) 5 hr (C) 5.5 hr (D) 6 hr

3. A tank can be filled by one inlet pipe in 15 minutes. It takes an outlet pipe 75 minutes to drain the tank. If the outlet pipe is left open by accident, how long would it take to fill the tank?

   (A) 15.5 min (B) 15.9 min (C) 16.8 min (D) 18.75 min

4. Mixture

Mixture problems present the combination of different products and ask you to solve for different parts of the mixture.

PROBLEM

A chemist has an 18% solution and a 45% solution of a disinfectant. How many ounces of each should be used to make 12 ounces of a 36% solution?

SOLUTION

Let x = Number of ounces from the 18% solution, and

y = Number of ounces from the 45% solution.

$$x + y = 12 \quad (1)$$

$$.18x + .45y = .36(12) \quad (2)$$

Note that .18 of the first solution is pure disinfectant and that .45 of the second solution is pure disinfectant. When the proper quantities are drawn from each mixture the result is 12 ounces of mixture which is .36 pure disinfectant.

The second equation cannot be solved with two unknowns. Therefore, write one variable in terms of the other and plug it into the second equation.

$$x = 12 - y \quad (3)$$

$$.18(12 - y) + .45y = .36(12) \quad (4)$$

Simplifying,

$$2.16 - .18y + .45y = 4.32$$

$$.27y = 4.32 - 2.16$$

$$.27y = 2.16$$

$$y = 8$$

Plugging in for y in the first equation,

$$x + 8 = 12$$

$$x = 4$$

Therefore, 4 ounces of the first and 8 ounces of the second solution should be used.

PROBLEM

Clark pays \$2.00 per pound for 3 pounds of peanut butter chocolates and then decides to buy 2 pounds of chocolate covered raisins at \$2.50 per pound. If Clark mixes both together, what is the cost per pound of the mixture?

SOLUTION

The total mixture is 5 pounds and the total value of the chocolates is

$$3(\$2.00) + 2(\$2.50) = \$11.00$$

The price per pound of the chocolates is $^{\$11.00}/_{5 \text{ pounds}} = \$2.20$.

☞ Drill 4: Mixture

1. How many liters of a 20% alcohol solution must be added to 80 liters of a 50% alcohol solution to form a 45% solution?

   (A) 4 (B) 8 (C) 16 (D) 20

2. How many kilograms of water must be evaporated from 50 kg of a 10% salt solution to obtain a 15% salt solution?

   (A) 15 (B) 15.75 (C) 16 (D) $16.\overline{66}$

3. How many pounds of coffee *A* at \$3.00 a pound should be mixed with 2.5 pounds of coffee *B* at \$4.20 a pound to form a mixture selling for \$3.75 a pound?

   (A) 1 (B) 1.5 (C) 1.75 (D) 2

5. Interest

If the problem calls for computing simple interest, the interest is computed on the principal alone. If the problem involves compounded interest, then the interest on the principal is taken into account in addition to the interest earned before.

PROBLEM

How much interest will Jerry pay on his loan of \$400 for 60 days at 6% per year?

SOLUTION

Use the formula

Interest = Principal × Rate × Time ($I = P \times R \times T$)

$\$400 \times 6\%/\text{year} \times 60 \text{ days} = \$400 \times .06 \times {}^{60}/_{365}$

$= \$400 \times 0.00986 = \$3.94$

Jerry will pay \$4.00.

PROBLEM

Mr. Smith wishes to find out how much interest he will receive on \$300 if the rate is 3% compounded annually for three years.

SOLUTION

Compound interest is interest computed on both the principal and the interest it has previously earned. The interest is added to the principal at the end of every year. The interest on the first year is found by multiplying the rate by the principal. Hence, the interest for the first year is

$$3\% \times \$300 = .03 \times \$300 = \$9.00$$

The principal for the second year is now \$309, the old principal (\$300) plus the interest (\$9). The interest for the second year is found by multiplying the rate by the new principal. Hence, the interest for the second year is

$$3\% \times \$309 = .03 \times \$309 = \$9.27$$

The principal now becomes \$309 + \$9.27 = \$318.27.

The interest for the third year is found using this new principal. It is

$$3\% \times \$318.27 = .03 \times \$318.27 = \$9.55$$

At the end of the third year his principal is \$318.27 + 9.55 = \$327.82. To find how much interest was earned, we subtract his starting principal (\$300) from his ending principal (\$327.82), to obtain

$$\$327.82 - \$300.00 = \$27.82$$

☞ Drill 5: Interest

1. A man invests \$3,000, part in a 12-month certificate of deposit paying 8% and the rest in municipal bonds that pay 7% a year. If the yearly return from both investments is \$220, how much was invested in bonds?

   (A) \$80 (B) \$2,000 (C) \$220 (D) \$1,000

2. A sum of money was invested at 11% a year. Four times that amount was invested at 7.5%. How much was invested at 11% if the total annual return was \$1,025?

   (A) \$112.75 (B) \$1,025 (C) \$2,500 (D) \$3,400

3. One bank pays 6.5% a year simple interest on a savings account while a credit union pays 7.2% a year. If you had \$1,500 to invest for three years, how much more would you earn by putting the money in the credit union?

   (A) \$10.50 (B) \$31.50 (C) \$97.50 (D) \$108

6. Discount

If the discount problem asks to find the final price after the discount, first multiply the original price by the percent of discount. Then subtract this result from the original price.

If the problem asks to find the original price when only the percent of discount and the discounted price are given, simply subtract the percent of discount from 100% and divide this percent into the sale price. This will give you the original price.

PROBLEM

A popular bookstore gives 10% discount to students. What does a student actually pay for a book costing $24?

SOLUTION

10% of $24 is $2.40 and hence the student pays $24 – $2.40 = $21.60.

PROBLEM

Eugene paid $100 for a business suit. The suit's price included a 25% discount. What was the original price of the suit?

SOLUTION

Let x represent the original price of the suit and take the complement of .25 (discount price) which is .75.

$$.75x = \$100 \text{ or } x = \$133.34$$

So, the original price of the suit is $133.34.

☞ Drill 6: Discount

1. A man bought a coat marked 20% off for $156. How much had the coat cost originally?

   (A) $136 (B) $156 (C) $175 (D) $195

2. A woman saved $225 on the new sofa which was on sale for 30% off. What was the original price of the sofa?

   (A) $25 (B) $200 (C) $750 (D) $525

3. At an office supply store, customers are given a discount if they pay in cash. If a customer is given a discount of $9.66 on a total order of $276, what is the percent of discount?

   (A) 2% (B) 3.5% (C) 4.5% (D) 9.66%

7. Profit

The formula used for the profit problems is

Profit = Revenue – Cost or

Profit = Selling Price – Expenses

PROBLEM

Four high school and college friends started a business of remodeling and selling old automobiles during the summer. For this purpose they paid \$600 to rent an empty barn for the summer. They obtained the cars from a dealer for \$250 each, and it takes an average of \$410 in materials to remodel each car. How many automobiles must the students sell at \$1,440 each to obtain a gross profit of \$7,000?

SOLUTION

Total Revenues – Total Cost = Gross Profit

Revenue – [Variable Cost + Fixed Cost] = Gross Profit

Let a = number of cars

Revenue = \$1,440a

[Variable Cost = (\$250 + 410)a]

[Fixed Cost = \$600]

The desired gross profit is \$7,000.

Using the equation for the gross profit,

$$1{,}440a - [660a + 600] = 7{,}000$$

$$1{,}440a - 660a - 600 = 7{,}000$$

$$780a = 7{,}000 + 600$$

$$780a = 7{,}600$$

$$a = 9.74$$

or to the nearest car, $a = 10$.

PROBLEM

A glass vase sells for \$25. The net profit is 7%, and the operating expenses are 39%. Find the gross profit on the vase.

SOLUTION

The gross profit is equal to the net profit plus the operating expenses. The net profit is 7% of the selling cost; thus, it is equal to 7% × \$25 = .07 × \$25 = \$1.75.

The operating expenses are 39% of the selling price, thus equal to 39% × \$25 = .39 × \$25 = \$9.75.

\$1.75	net profit
+ \$9.75	operating expenses
\$11.50	gross profit

☞ Drill 7: Profit

1. An item cost a store owner \$50. She marked it up 40% and advertised it at that price. How much profit did she make if she later sold it at 15% off the advertised price?

   (A) \$7.50 (B) \$9.50 (C) \$10.50 (D) \$39.50

2. An antique dealer makes a profit of 115% on the sale of an oak desk. If the desk cost her \$200, how much profit did she make on the sale?

   (A) \$230 (B) \$315 (C) \$430 (D) \$445

3. As a graduation gift, a young man was given 100 shares of stock worth \$27.50 apiece. Within a year the price of the stock had risen by 8%. How much more were the stocks worth at the end of the first year than when they were given to the young man?

   (A) \$110 (B) \$220 (C) \$1,220 (D) \$2,750

8. Sets

A **set** is any collection of well-defined objects called elements.

A set which contains only a finite number of elements is called a **finite set**; a set which contains an infinite number of elements is called an **infinite set**. Often the sets are designated by listing their elements. For example: $\{a, b, c, d\}$ is the set which contains elements a, b, c, and d. The set of positive integers is $\{1, 2, 3, 4, \ldots\}$.

Venn diagrams can represent sets. These diagrams are circles which help to visualize the relationship between members or objects of a set.

PROBLEM

In a certain Broadway show audition, it was asked of 30 performers if they knew how to either sing or dance, or both. If 20 auditioners said they could dance and 14 said they could sing, how many could sing and dance?

SOLUTION

Divide the 30 people into 3 sets: those who dance, those who sing, and those who dance and sing. S is the number of people who both sing and dance. So $20 - S$ represents the number of people who dance and $14 - S$ represents the number of people who sing.

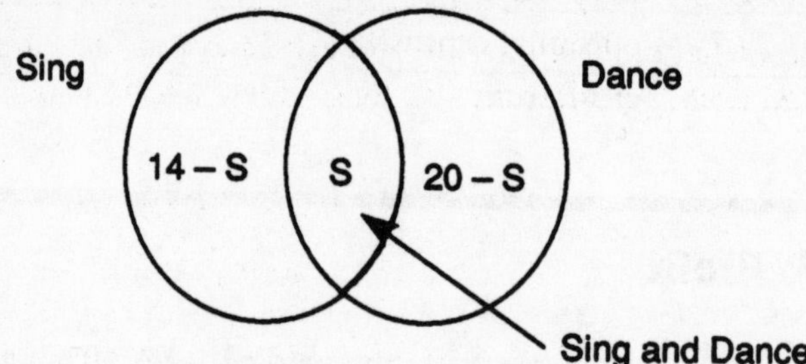

The equation for this problem is as follows:

$$(20 - S) + S + (14 - S) = 30$$
$$20 + 14 - 30 = S$$
$$34 - 30 = S$$
$$4 = S$$

So, 4 people in the audition both sing and dance.

☞ Drill 8: Sets

1. In a small school there are 147 sophomores. Of this number, 96 take both Biology and Technology I. Eighty-three take both Chemistry and Technology I. How many students are taking Technology I?

   (A) 32 (B) 51 (C) 64 (D) 83

2. In a survey of 100 people, 73 owned only stocks. Six of the people invested in both stocks and bonds. How many people owned bonds only?

   (A) 6 (B) 21 (C) 73 (D) 94

3. On a field trip, the teachers counted the orders for a snack and sent the information in with a few people. The orders were for 77 colas only and 39 fries only. If there were 133 orders, how many were for colas and fries?

   (A) 17 (B) 56 (C) 77 (D) 95

9. Geometry

PROBLEM

A boy knows that his height is 6 ft. and his shadow is 4 ft. long. At the same time of day, a tree's shadow is 24 ft. long. How high is the tree?

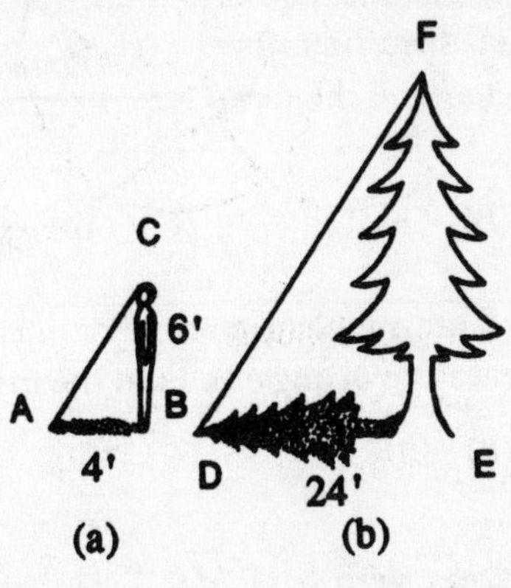

SOLUTION

Show that $\Delta\ ABC \approx \Delta\ DEF$, and then set up a proportion between the known sides *AB* and *DE*, and the sides *BC* and *EF*.

First, assume that both the boy and the tree are ⊥ to the earth. Then, $\overline{BC} \perp \overline{BA}$ and $\overline{EF} \perp \overline{ED}$. Hence,

$$\angle\ ABC \cong \angle\ DEF$$

Since it is the same time of day, the rays of light from the sun are incident on both the tree and the boy at the same angle, relative to the earth's surface. Therefore,

$$\angle\ BAC \cong \angle\ EDF$$

We have shown, so far, that 2 pairs of corresponding angles are congruent. Since the sum of the angles of any triangle is 180°, the third pair of corresponding angles is congruent (i.e., $\angle\ ACB \cong \angle\ DFE$). By the Angle Angle Angle (A.A.A.) Theorem,

$$\angle\ ABC \approx \angle\ DEF$$

By definition of similarity,

$$\frac{FE}{CB} = \frac{ED}{BA}$$

$CB = 6'$, $ED = 24'$, and $BA = 4'$. Therefore,

$$FE = (6')\ (24'/4') = 36'$$

☞ Drill 9: Geometry

1. ΔPQR is a scalene triangle. The measure of $\angle P$ is 8 more than twice the measure of $\angle R$. The measure of $\angle Q$ is two less than three times the measure of $\angle R$. Determine the measure of $\angle Q$.

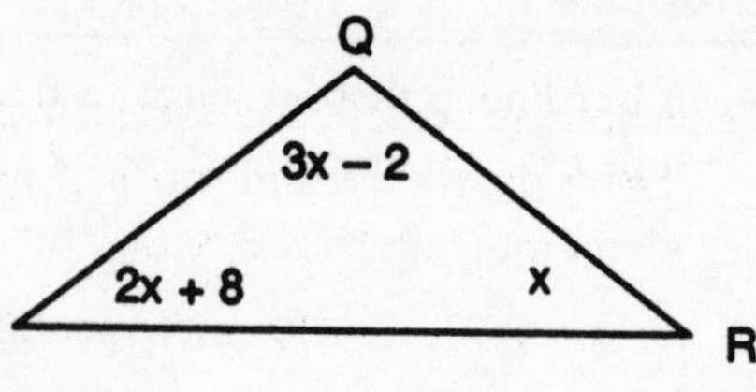

(A) 29 (B) 53 (C) 60 (D) 85

2. Angle A and angle B are supplementary. The measure of angle B is 5 more than four times the measure of angle A. Find the measure of angle B.

(A) 35 (B) 125 (C) 140 (D) 145

3. Triangle RUS is isosceles with base $\overline{SU}$. Each leg is 3 less than 5 times the length of the base. If the perimeter of the triangle is 60 cm, find the length of a leg.

(A) 6 (B) 12 (C) 27 (D) 30

10. Measurement

When measurement problems are presented in either metric or English units which involve conversion of units, the appropriate data will be given in the problem.

PROBLEM

The Eiffel Tower is 984 feet high. Express this height in meters, in kilometers, in centimeters, and in millimeters.

SOLUTION

A meter is equivalent to 39.370 inches. In this problem, the height of the tower in feet must be converted to inches and then the inches can be converted to meters. There are 12 inches in 1 foot. Therefore, feet can be converted to inches by using the factor 12 inches/1 foot.

$$984 \text{ feet} \times 12 \text{ inches}/1 \text{ foot} = 118 \times 10^2 \text{ inches}$$

Once the height is found in inches, this can be converted to meters by the factor 1 meter/39.370 inches.

$$11{,}808 \text{ inches} \times 1 \text{ meter}/39.370 \text{ inches} = 300 \text{ m}$$

Therefore, the height in meters is 300 m.

There are 1,000 meters in one kilometer. Meters can be converted to kilometers by using the factor 1 km/1,000 m.

$$300 \text{ m} \times 1 \text{ km}/1{,}000 \text{ m} = .300 \text{ km}$$

As such, there are .300 kilometers in 300 m.

There are 100 centimeters in 1 meter, thus meters can be converted to centimeters by multiplying by the factor 100 cm/1 m.

$$300 \text{ m} \times 100 \text{ cm}/1 \text{ m} = 300 \times 10^2 \text{ cm}$$

There are 30,000 centimeters in 300 m.

There are 1,000 millimeters in 1 meter; therefore, meters can be converted to millimeters by the factor 1,000 mm/1m.

$$300 \text{ m} \times 1{,}000 \text{ mm}/1 \text{ m} = 300 \times 10^3 \text{ mm}$$

There are 300,000 millimeters in 300 meters.

PROBLEM

The unaided eye can perceive objects which have a diameter of 0.1 mm. What is the diameter in inches?

SOLUTION

From a standard table of conversion factors, one can find that 1 inch = 2.54 cm. Thus, centimeters can be converted to inches by multiplying by 1 inch/2.54 cm. Here, one is given the diameter in mm, which is .1 cm. Millimeters are converted to centimeters by multiplying the number of millimeters by .1 cm/1 mm. Solving for centimeters, you obtain

$$0.1 \text{ mm} \times .1 \text{ cm}/1 \text{ mm} = .01 \text{ cm}$$

Solving for inches:

$$0.01 \text{ cm} \times {}^{1 \text{ inch}}/_{2.54 \text{ cm}} = 3.94 \times 10^{-3} \text{ inches.}$$

☞ Drill 10: Measurement

1. A brick walkway measuring 3 feet by 11 feet is to be built. The bricks measure 4 inches by 6 inches. How many bricks will it take to complete the walkway?

   (A) 132 (B) 198 (C) 330 (D) 1,927

2. A wall to be papered is three times as long as it is wide. The total area to be covered is 192 ft^2. Wallpaper comes in rolls that are 2 feet wide by 8 feet long. How many rolls will it take to cover the wall?

   (A) 8 (B) 12 (C) 16 (D) 24

3. A bottle of medicine containing 2 kg is to be poured into smaller containers that hold 8 grams each. How many of these smaller containers can be filled from the 2 kg bottle?

(A) 0.5 (B) 1 (C) 5 (D) 250

11. Data Interpretation

Some of the problems test ability to apply information given in graphs and tables.

PROBLEM

In which year was the least number of bushels of wheat produced?

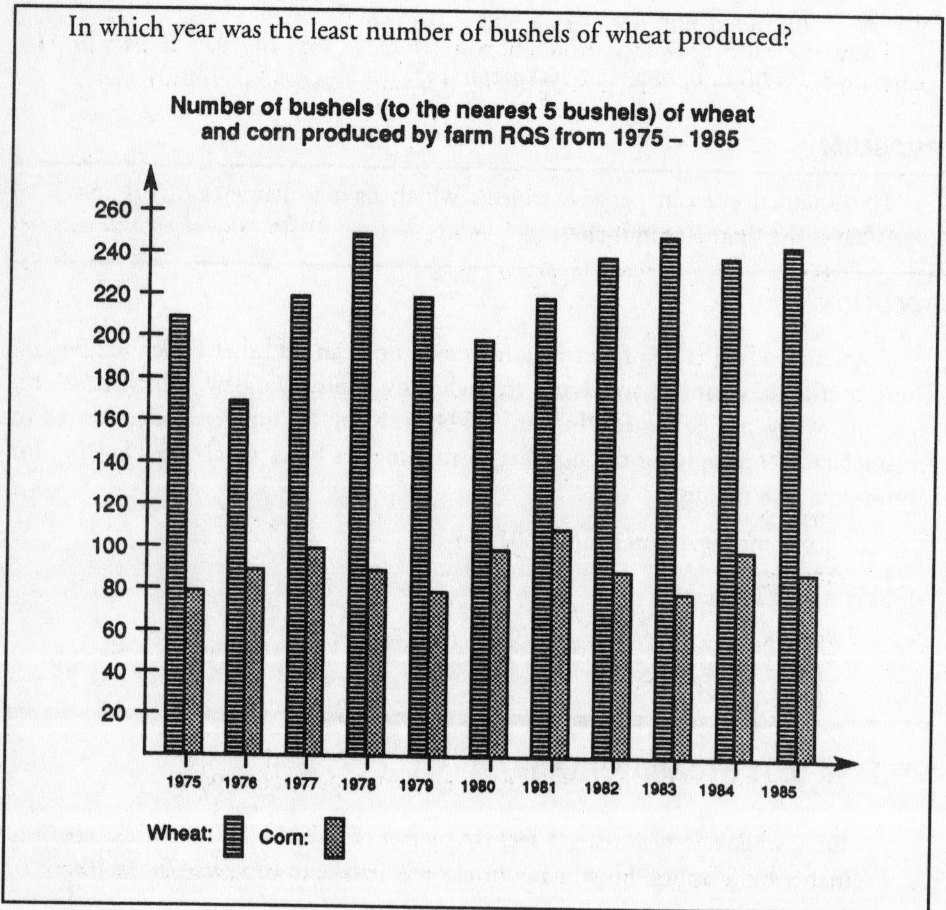

SOLUTION

By inspection of the graph, we find that the shortest bar representing wheat production is the one representing the wheat production for 1976. Thus, the least number of bushels of wheat was produced in 1976.

PROBLEM

What was the ratio of wheat production in 1985 to that of 1975?

SOLUTION

From the graph representing wheat production, the number of bushels of wheat produced in 1975 is equal to 210 bushels. This number can be found by locating the bar on the graph representing wheat production in 1975 and then drawing a horizontal line from the top of that bar to the vertical axis. The point where this horizontal line meets the vertical axis represents the number of bushels of wheat produced in 1975. This number on the vertical axis is 210. Similarly, the graph indicates that the number of bushels of wheat produced in 1985 is equal to 245 bushels.

Thus, the ratio of wheat production in 1985 to that of 1975 is 245 to 210, which can be written as $^{245}/_{210}$. Simplifying this ratio to its simplest form yields

$$\frac{245}{210} = \frac{5\times7\times7}{2\times3\times5\times7} = \frac{7}{2\times3} = \frac{7}{6} \text{ or } 7:6$$

☞ Drill 11: Data Interpretation

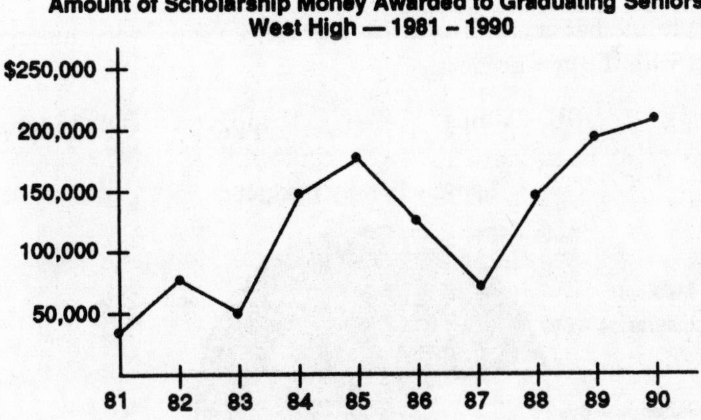

1. What was the approximate amount of scholarship money awarded in 1985?

   (A) $150,000 (B) $155,000 (C) $165,000 (D) $175,000

2. By how much did the scholarship money increase between 1987 and 1988?

   (A) $25,000 (B) $30,000 (C) $75,000 (D) $55,000

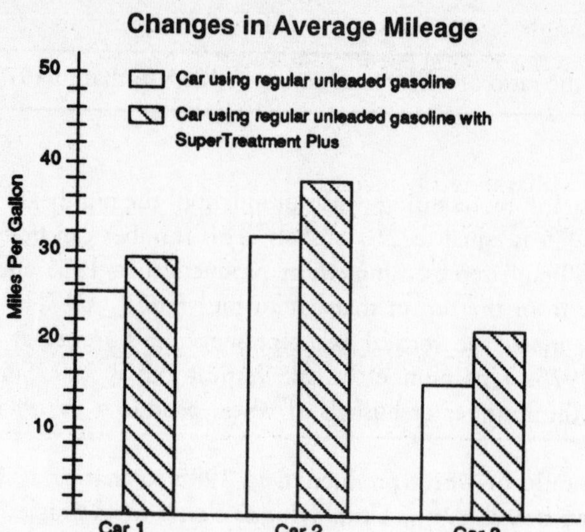

3. By how much did the mileage increase for Car 2 when the new product was used?

   (A) 5 mpg (B) 6 mpg (C) 7 mpg (D) 10 mpg

4. Which car's mileage increased the most in this test?

   (A) Cars 2 and 3 (B) Car 2 (C) Car 3 (D) Cars 1 and 2

5. According to the bar graph, if your car averages 25 mpg, what mileage might you expect with the new product?

   (A) 21 mpg (B) 29 mpg (C) 31 mpg (D) 35 mpg

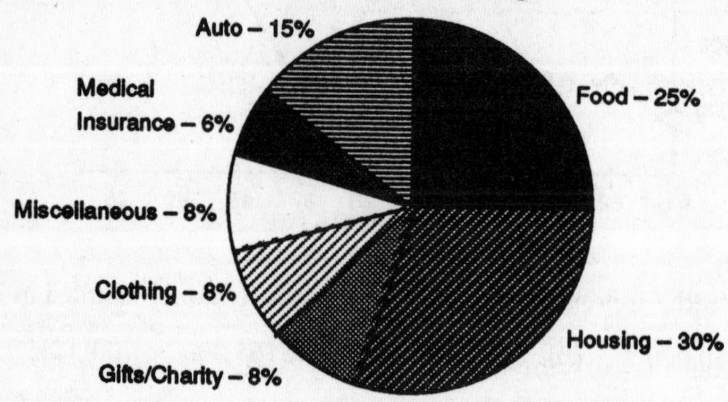

6. Using the budget shown, a family with an income of $1,500 a month would plan to spend what amount on housing?

   (A) $300 (B) $375 (C) $450 (D) $490

7. In this sample family budget, how does the amount spent on an automobile compare to the amount spent on housing?

(A) $^1/_3$ (B) $^1/_2$ (C) $^2/_3$ (D) $1^1/_2$

8. A family with a monthly income of $1,240 spends $125 a month on clothing. By what amount do they exceed the sample budget?

(A) $1.00 (B) $5.20 (C) $10.00 (D) $25.80

CALORIE CHART — BREADS

Bread	Amount	Calories
French Bread	2 oz	140
Bran Bread	1 oz	95
Whole Wheat	1 oz	115
Oatmeal Bread	0.5 oz	55
Raisin Bread	1 oz	125

9. One dieter eats two ounces of french bread. A second dieter eats two ounces of bran bread. The second dieter has consumed how many more calories than the first dieter?

(A) 40 (B) 45 (C) 50 (D) 55

10. One ounce of whole wheat bread has how many more calories than an ounce of oatmeal bread?

(A) 5 (B) 15 (C) 60 (D) 75

12. Combination of Mathematical Skills

The mathematics review of this book has provided a vast amount of information about solving math problems. For the most part, these reviews and their accompanying drill questions have involved the use of one particular type of math skill. These skills are very important, but some problems may ask you to combine these individual skills to answer a question.

If questions should arise that require using more than one math skill, do not panic. The problem may seem overwhelming at first, but just approach it one step at a time. Do not be intimidated by the question. Read it carefully because there will probably be a lot of information given.

Two examples of this type of problem and step-by-step instructions on how to solve them are given on the next page. The mathematical skills involved in solving them were discussed previously in this chapter. If you have difficulty following the examples, or have problems with the drill questions, go back and study further the chapters which discuss the math skills involved.

When tackling questions involving a combination of math skills, try to separate the problem into smaller parts that you can solve one at a time. Make sure that you fully understand the question being asked. Many times wrong answer choices will be given that can be derived at a point during the solution that falls short of actually answering the question.

If you want to, read the examples and try to work them out yourself before reading the step-by-step solution. Drill questions are also provided to help build your understanding of the problems involving multiple mathematical skills.

PROBLEM

The product of two consecutive negative integers is 156. Find the sum of the two integers.

SOLUTION

Let x represent the first negative integer, and $x + 1$ represent the second negative integer.

The product of the two numbers is represented by $x(x + 1)$. Therefore the equation is

$$x(x + 1) = 156$$

Using the distributive law on the left side, we get:

$$x^2 + x = 156$$

Transposing the 156 to the left side, we get a second degree equation (highest exponent of the x variable is 2) of the form:

$$\begin{array}{rr} x^2 + x \quad\;\; = & 156 \\ -156 & -156 \\ \hline x^2 + x - 156 = & 0 \end{array}$$

Now find two numbers whose product is –156 (the constant term on the left side) and whose sum is +1 (the coefficient of the x, the first degree term). The two numbers are +13 and –12. Therefore,

$$x^2 + x - 156 = 0$$

is solved by factoring the left side of the equation as:

$$(x + 13)\,(x - 12) = 0.$$

Set each of the factors equal to 0, since a product of two numbers is equal to zero if either one, or both numbers are zero. This means:

$$\begin{array}{rr} x + 13 = & 0 \\ -13 & -13 \\ \hline x = & -13 \end{array} \qquad \text{or} \qquad \begin{array}{rr} x - 12 = & 0 \\ +12 & +12 \\ \hline x = & 12 \end{array}$$

(negative) (positive)

Since the problem calls for two consecutive negative integers, we have $x = -13$ as the first solution to the problem. In this case the other consecutive negative integer is

$$x + 1 = -13 + 1 = -12.$$

Therefore the sum of the two negative integers is $-13 + (-12) = -25$.

PROBLEM

An experienced painter paints a living room twice as fast as his son. Working together, the father and son can paint the living room in four hours. Determine how long it would take the father, working alone, to paint the living room and find its square.

SOLUTION

We use the equation

(Rate of work per hour) (Time worked in hours) = Fraction of living room painted.

Let x = time it takes the son.

Let $^1/_2\, x$ = time it takes his father.

The sum of the parts of the task completed by each person equals 1. Then

$$\frac{4}{\frac{1}{2}x} + \frac{4}{x} = 1$$

or

$$\frac{8}{x} + \frac{4}{x} = 1$$

$$8 + 4 = x$$

$$12 = x$$

Therefore, the son takes 12 hours, and the father takes 6 hours.

To find the square of a number, multiply it by itself:

$$6 \times 6 = 36.$$

☞ Drill 12: Combination of Mathematical Skills

1. The sum of 3 times an integer and four times the next consecutive integer is -17. Find the product of the integers.

   (A) -5 (B) -3 (C) -2 (D) 6

2. A number is 14 more than another number. The sum of three times the larger number and twice the smaller number is 87. Find the square of the larger number.

   (A) 592 (B) 529 (C) 1,024 (D) 81

3. The length of a rectangle is 12 inches more than the width. Find the area of the rectangle if the perimeter is 92 inches.

   (A) 400 sq. in. (B) 17 sq. in. (C) 520 sq. in. (D) 493 sq. in.

4. Jane leaves for her evening walk traveling at 4 miles per hour. Two hours later, her husband Lee leaves the house following the same route and jogs at 6 miles per hour. How many minutes will it take Lee to catch up to Jane?

   (A) 60 (B) 240 (C) 4 (D) 200

5. The sum of twice the smallest and three times the largest of three consecutive even integers is 72. Find the sum of the first and third integer.

   (A) 28 (B) 26 (C) 30 (D) 12

WORD PROBLEM DRILLS

ANSWER KEY

Drill 1 – Algebraic

1. (D) 2. (A) 3. (B)

Drill 2 – Rate

1. (C) 2. (A) 3. (A)

Drill 3 – Work

1. (B) 2. (D) 3. (D)

Drill 4 – Mixture

1. (C) 2. (D) 3. (B)

Drill 5 – Interest

1. (B) 2. (C) 3. (B)

Drill 6 – Discount

1. (D) 2. (C) 3. (B)

Drill 7 – Profit

1. (B) 2. (A) 3. (B)

Drill 8 – Sets

1. (A) 2. (B) 3. (A)

Drill 9 – Geometry

1. (D) 2. (D) 3. (C)

Drill 10 – Measurement

1. (B) 2. (B) 3. (D)

Drill 11 – Data Interpretation

1.	(D)	5.	(B)	9.	(C)
2.	(C)	6.	(C)	10.	(A)
3.	(B)	7.	(B)		
4.	(A)	8.	(D)		

Drill 12 – Combination of Mathematical Skills

1.	(D)	3.	(D)	5.	(A)
2.	(B)	4.	(B)		

DETAILED EXPLANATIONS OF ANSWERS

Drill 1 – Algebraic

1. **(D)** Let x and y represent the two numbers. Since their sum is 41, one equation is $x + y = 41$.

Then if one of the two numbers, say x, is one less than twice the other, the second equation can be written $x = 2y - 1$.

So the two equations are

$$x + y = 41$$

and $$x = 2y - 1$$

Solve the first equation for x.

$$x = 41 - y$$

Substitute $(41 - y)$ for x in the second equation.

$$41 - y = 2y - 1$$

Solve for y.

$$41 - y = 2y - 1$$
$$42 - y = 2y$$
$$42 = 3y$$
$$14 = y$$

Then if $y = 14$ and $x + y = 41$, $x = 27$.

Check: $27 + 14 = 41$ $\qquad$ $27 = 2(14) - 1$

$41 = 41$ $\qquad$ $27 = 28 - 1$

$27 = 27$

2. **(A)** If a represents the smaller integer, then its consecutive integer is represented by $a + 1$. So the first equation becomes

$$a + (a + 1) = 111$$

Three times the larger integer is $3(a + 1)$ while two times the smaller integer is $2a$. "Less" indicates subtraction, so the second equation becomes

$$3(a + 1) - 2a = 58$$

Solve this equation for a.

$$3(a + 1) - 2a = 58$$

$$3a + 3 - 2a = 58$$
$$a + 3 = 58$$
$$a = 55$$

Since a represented the smaller integer, we have answered the question.

Check: $55 + (55 + 1) = 111$ $\quad$ $3(55 + 1) - 2(55) = 58$

$55 + 56 = 111$ $\quad$ $168 - 110 = 58$

$111 = 111$ $\quad$ $58 = 58$

3. **(B)** Let X and Y represent two integers.

"Difference" indicates subtraction, so the first equation can be written as $X - Y = 12$.

"Sum" indicates addition, so the second equation is $X + Y = 2$.

Solve these two equations simultaneously by adding them together. (The Y's are eliminated.)

$$X - Y = 12$$
$$X + Y = 2$$
$$2X = 14$$

Solve for X by dividing both sides by 2.

$$X = 7$$

Then substitute X into either one of the two original equations to find Y.

$$7 - Y = 12$$
$$-Y = 5$$
$$Y = -5$$

Check: $7 - (-5) = 12$ $\quad$ $7 + (-5) = 2$

$7 + 5 = 12$ $\quad$ $2 = 2$

$12 = 12$

Drill 2 – Rate

1. **(C)** For a problem such as this, a diagram, a chart, and the formula $D = RT$ are necessary.

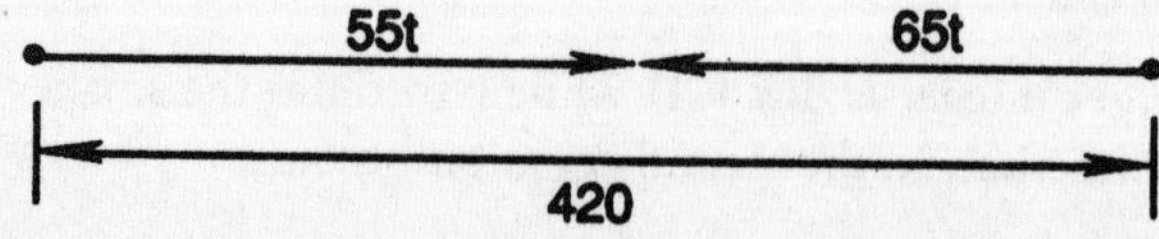

As the diagram indicates, this is an addition problem. The distance covered by the first car must be added to the distance covered by the second car to obtain the distance between the two cities.

The chart uses the three parts of the equation $D = RT$. Since the time is the unknown in this problem, it is represented by t.

Car	Rate	Time	Distance
1	55	t	$55t$
2	65	t	$65t$

Now add together the two distances from the chart and set them equal to the total distance.

$$55t + 65t = 420$$

Solve for t

$$120t = 420$$

$$t = 3.5 \text{ hr}$$

Check:

$$55(3.5) + 65(3.5) = 420$$

$$192.5 + 227.5 = 420$$

$$420 = 420$$

2. **(A)** A diagram, a chart, and the formula $D = RT$ are used to solve this problem.

Let x represent the walking rate of the second camper.

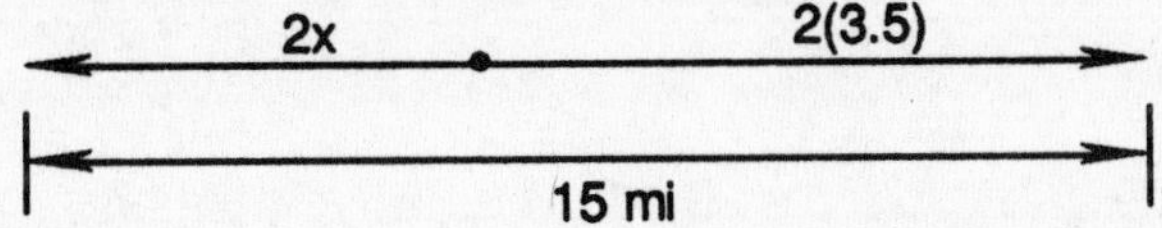

The diagram indicates that we need to add the two individual distances to equal the entire distance of 15 miles.

In the chart, we fill in the rate and the time for each camper. The formula $D = RT$ is used to find the value in the last column.

	Rate	Time	Distance
1st	3.5	2	7
2nd	x	2	$2x$

Now add the two individual distances together and set them equal to the total distance.

$$7 + 2x = 15$$

Solve for x.

$$7 + 2x = 15$$

$$2x = 8$$

$$x = 4 \text{ mph}$$

Check:

$$7 + 2(4) = 15$$

$$7 + 8 = 15$$

$$15 = 15$$

3. **(A)** Let r = the initial average rate and let t = the initial time. Then since $D = RT$, $75 = rt$.

If the rate is increased by 5 mph, it would be written $r + 5$. If the time is reduced by $^3/_4$, it becomes $^3/_4t$. Using the same formula, $D = RT$, $75 = (r + 5)\,(^3/_4t)$.

Use the distributive property in the second equation.

$$75 = (r + 5)\,(^3/_4t)$$

$$75 = {}^3/_4rt + {}^{15}/_4t$$

Multiply both sides of the equation by 4.

$$300 = 3rt + 15t$$

Since the first equation is $rt = 75$, substitute 75 for the expression rt.

$$300 = 3(75) + 15t$$

Solve for t.

$$300 = 225 + 15t$$

$$75 = 15t$$

$$5 = t$$

Since the problem asked for the rate, use t to find r.

$$rt = 75$$

$$r(5) = 75$$

$$r = 15 \text{ mph}$$

Check: $15(5) = 75$ $(15 + 5) \times {}^3/_4\,(5) = 75$

$75 = 75$ $20 \times 3.75 = 75$

$75 = 75$

Drill 3 – Work

1. **(B)** To solve this problem, decide on a convenient unit of time — here the hour is the easiest choice. Next, write the amount of work that each person can do in that amount of time (this is the *rate* of work):

In one hour, Louise can do $^1/_3$ of the job.

In one hour, Pat can do

$$\frac{1}{2\frac{1}{4}} \text{ or } \frac{1}{\frac{9}{4}} \text{ or } \frac{4}{9}$$

of the job.

The unknown in this problem is the amount of time it will take the two working together — call this unknown x. Then multiply each person's rate of work by the amount of time spent working together to obtain the portion of the total job each person did. Louise did $^x/_3$ and Pat did $^{4x}/_9$ of the work.

Then add each person's part of the work together and set it equal to 1; this represents one completed task. Now the equation looks like this:

$$\frac{x}{3}+\frac{4x}{9}=1$$

Find the Least Common Denominator (LCD) and multiply both sides of the equation by the LCD.

$$9\left(\frac{x}{3}+\frac{4x}{9}\right)=(1)\,(9)$$

$$3x+4x=9$$

$$7x=9$$

$$x=\frac{9}{7}\text{ hr or }1\frac{2}{7}\text{ hr}$$

2. **(D)** Let x represent the time it would take for the brother to mow the lawn alone.

Since Troy does the lawn in 3 hours, he does $^1/_3$ of the lawn in one hour. Since the brother takes x hours to mow the lawn, in one hour he does $^1/_x$ of the job. Both rates are multiplied by 2 since they complete the job in 2 hours.

	In One Hour	Time	Part of Job
Troy	$^1/_3$	2	$^2/_3$
Brother	$^1/_x$	2	$^2/_x$

Now add the part that each person does and set the sum equal to 1. The 1 represents one complete job.

$$^2/_3 + {}^2/_x = 1$$

Multiply by the LCD of $3x$.

$$(^2/_3)\,(3x) + (^2/_x)\,(3x) = 1(3x)$$

$$2x + 6 = 3x$$

Solve for x.

$$6 = x$$

It would take the little brother 6 hours to mow the lawn by himself.

Check: $^2/_3 + {}^2/_6 = 1$

$$^2/_3 + {}^1/_3 = 1$$

$$1 = 1$$

3. **(D)** Let x represent the time to fill the tank.

Since it takes 15 minutes for the inlet pipe to fill the tank, in one minute it can fill $^1/_{15}$ of the tank. Since the outlet pipe drains the tank in 75 minutes, in one minute it can drain $^1/_{75}$ of the tank. The amount done in one minute is multiplied by the time to get the part of the job done in x minutes.

	In One Minute	Time	Part of Job
Inlet	$^1/_{15}$	x	$^x/_{15}$
Outlet	$^1/_{75}$	x	$^x/_{75}$

In setting up the equation, the part of the job done by the outlet pipe must be *subtracted* from that part done by the inlet pipe. The difference is set equal to one to represent one completed job.

The equation is

$$\frac{x}{15} - \frac{x}{75} = 1$$

Multiply by the LCD, 75.

$$(75)\frac{x}{15} - (75)\frac{x}{75} = (75)1$$

$$5x - x = 75$$

$$4x = 75$$

$$x = 18\frac{3}{4} \text{ minutes}$$

Check: $$\frac{18.75}{15} - \frac{18.75}{75} = 1$$

$$1.25 - 0.25 = 1$$

$$1 = 1$$

Drill 4 – Mixture

1. **(C)** For each solution, fill in the chart with the amount of the solution, the percent of alcohol it contains, and the amount of alcohol it contains.

Solution	Amount of Solution	% of Alcohol	Amount of Alcohol
1st	x	.20	$.20x$
2nd	80	.50	.50(80)
Mix	$(x + 80)$	.45	$.45(x + 80)$

Since we don't know how much of the first solution there is, the amount of the first solution is represented by x.

Add the first two amounts of alcohol together and set the sum equal to the amount of alcohol in the mixture. Solve the equation for x.

$$.20x + .50(80) = .45(x + 80)$$

$$.20x + 40 = .45x + 36$$

$$4 = .25x$$

$$16 = x$$

So 16 liters of the 20% alcohol solution must be added to the 50% solution.

Check: $.20(16) + .50(80) = .45(16 + 80)$

$$3.2 + 40 = .45\ (96)$$

$$43.2 = 43.2$$

2. **(D)** Fill in the chart with the amount of each solution, the percent of salt each solution is, and the amount of salt contained in each solution. Let x represent the amount of water to be evaporated.

Solution	Amount	%	Amount of Salt
Original	50	0.10	0.10(50)
Water	x	0	0
New Sol.	$(50 - x)$	0.15	$0.15(50 - x)$

The amount of salt in the original solution less the amount of salt in the water evaporated (which is 0) equals the amount of salt in the new solution.

$$0.10(50) - 0 = 0.15(50 - x)$$

Solve for x.

$$5 - 0 = 7.5 - 0.15x$$

$$-2.5 = -0.15x$$

$$16\,{}^{2}/_{3} = x$$

$$16.\overline{66} = x$$

Sixteen and two-thirds kilograms of water must be evaporated from the original solution.

Check: $5 = 7.5 - 0.15(16\,{}^{2}/_{3})$

$$5 = 7.5 - {}^{15}/_{100} \times {}^{50}/_{3}$$

$$5 = 7.5 - 2.5$$

$$5 = 5$$

3. **(B)** Fill the chart in with the amount of each coffee, the price per pound of each coffee, and the total price.

Since the amount of coffee A is the unknown, call it x.

Coffee	Amount	Price/lb	Total Price
A	x	3.00	$3x$
B	2.5	4.20	2.5(4.2)
Mix	$(x + 2.5)$	3.75	$3.75(x + 2.5)$

Add the total prices of the two coffees together and set the sum equal to the total price of the mixture. Solve for x.

$$3x + 2.5(4.2) = (2.5 + x)\ (3.75)$$

$$3x + 10.50 = 9.375 + 3.75x$$
$$1.125 = 0.75x$$
$$1.5 = x$$

The amount of coffee *A* to be added to the mixture is 1.5 lb.

Check: $3(1.5) + 2.5(4.2) = (2.5 + 1.5)(3.75)$
$$4.5 + 10.5 = 4(3.75)$$
$$15 = 15$$

Drill 5 – Interest

1. **(B)** Let x = the amount invested at 8%. Then, since the total amount is \$3,000, the remaining part is $(3000 - x)$.

Multiply the amount invested by the % of interest and add these two amounts together to equal the total interest.

$$0.08x + 0.07(3{,}000 - x) = 220$$
$$0.08x + 210 - 0.07x = 220$$
$$0.01x = 10$$
$$x = 1{,}000$$

Therefore, $3{,}000 - x = 2{,}000.$

The amount invested in Bonds is \$2,000.

Check: $0.08(1{,}000) + 0.07(2{,}000) = 220$
$$80 + 140 = 220$$
$$220 = 220$$

2. **(C)**

Let x = the amount invested at 11%.

Let $4x$ = the amount invested at 7.5%.

Multiply the amount invested by the interest rate to determine the individual interest. Add these two individual interests together and set the sum equal to the total interest.

$$0.11x + 0.075(4x) = 1{,}025$$
$$0.11x + 0.3x = 1{,}025$$
$$0.41x = 1{,}025$$
$$x = 2{,}500$$

\$2,500 was invested at 11%.

Check: $0.11(2{,}500) + 0.075(4 \times 2{,}500) = 1{,}025$
$$275 + 750 = 1{,}025$$
$$1{,}025 = 1{,}025$$

3. **(B)** Use the simple interest formula, $I = PRT$, to find the interest earned on each account.

Bank: $I = \$1,500 \times 0.065 \times 3 = \$292.50$

Credit Union: $I = \$1,500 \times 0.072 \times 3 = \$324$

Subtract the amounts of interest to see how much more you would earn by keeping the money in the credit union.

$\$324 - \$292.50 = \$31.50$

Drill 6 – Discount

1. **(D)** Let x be the original price of the coat.
The original price minus 20% of the original price equals \$156.

$x - 0.20(x) = 156$

or $1.0(x) - 0.20(x) = 156$

or $0.80(x) = 156$

so $x = 156/0.80 = 195$

The coat originally cost \$195.

Check: $195 - 0.20(195) = 156$

$195 - 39 = 156$

$156 = 156$

2. **(C)** If x = the original price of the sofa, then $0.30x$ = the amount saved, which was \$225.

So, $0.30x = 225$

Then $x = 225/0.30 = \$750$

The original price of the sofa was \$750.

Check: $0.30(750) = 225$

$225 = 225$

3. **(B)** A good technique to use in this problem is the formula

$$\frac{\text{Percentage}}{\text{Base}} = \frac{\text{Rate}}{100}$$

In this problem you are asked for the percent of discount which is the same as the rate — call it r.

The percentage is \$9.66 and the base, or total amount, is \$276.

The equation becomes

$$\frac{9.66}{276} = \frac{r}{100}$$

Use cross products to solve.

$$9.66(100) = 276r \text{ so } r = 966/276 = 3.5$$

The percent of discount is 3.5%.

Drill 7 – Profit

1. **(B)** The profit is the sale price less the initial cost. The initial cost was \$50. The sale price is 15% off the advertised price.

The advertised price is marked up 40% over the initial price — or \$50 + 0.40 (\$50). This advertised price is \$70.

Then the sale price is the advertised price less 15% of the advertised price, or \$70 – 0.15(70), or \$59.50.

Finally, the profit is \$59.50 – 50 = \$9.50.

2. **(A)** The profit is 115% of the initial cost of the desk.

$P = 1.15(\$200) = \$230$

3. **(B)** The profit on the stocks is the new value less the original value.

Original value = \$27.50 × 100 = \$2,750

New value = \$2,750 + 0.08(2,750) = \$2,970

Profit = \$2,970 – \$2,750 = \$220

Drill 8 – Sets

1. **(A)** Draw two overlapping circles to represent the numbers of people in each group. If 96 take Biology and Tech. I and 83 take Chemistry and Tech. I, this gives a total of 179. But there are only 147 students in all, so subtract to find the number in Tech. I.

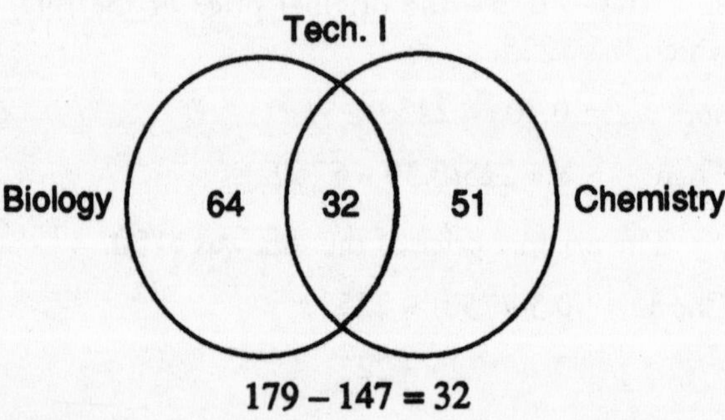

2. **(B)** Draw two overlapping circles and let one represent stocks and the other represent bonds.

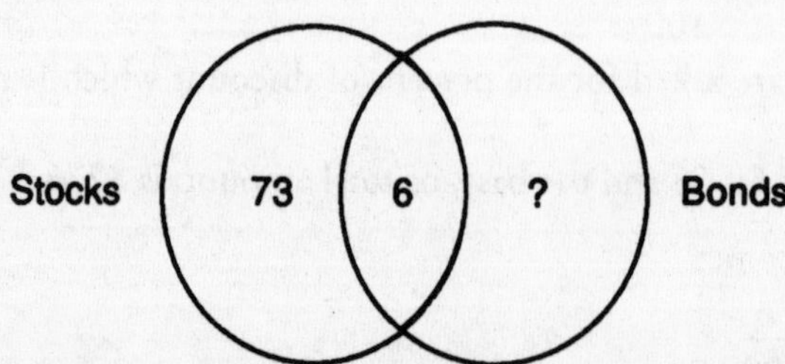

If 73 only own stocks and 6 own stocks and bonds, that leaves the remainder of the 100 people to own bonds only.

$$100 - (73 + 6) = 21$$

Twenty-one people own bonds only.

3. **(A)** Draw two overlapping circles to represent the orders — one for fries and the other for colas. The part of the cola circle outside the overlapping part represents 77 people. The part of the fries circle outside the overlapping part represents the 39 people ordering the fries only.

Add the two parts together and subtract the sum from 133 to get the number in the overlapping part.

$$133 - (77 + 39) = 17$$

There were 17 orders for both fries and cola.

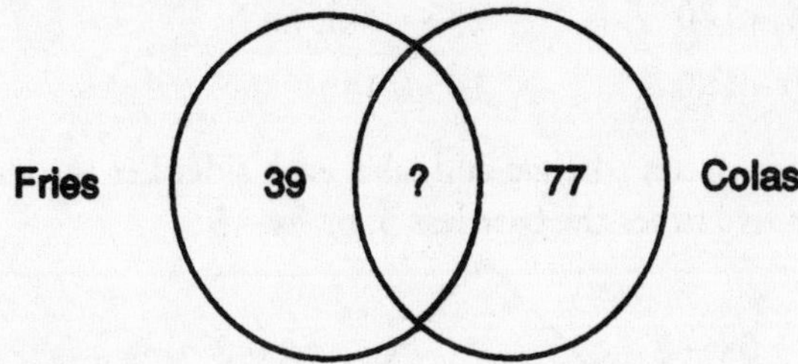

Drill 9 – Geometry

1. **(D)** Draw a sketch of the triangle and label the angles.

Two of the angles are compared to $\angle R$, so let x = the measure of $\angle R$. Then

$$\angle P = 2x + 8 \text{ and } \angle Q = 3x - 2$$

The sum of the measures of the angles of a triangle is 180°, so add the measures of all three angles and this will equal 180°.

$$x + (2x + 8) + (3x - 2) = 180$$
$$6x + 6 = 180$$
$$6x = 174$$
$$x = 29$$

The measure of $\angle R$ is 29° and the measure of $\angle Q$ is 3(29) – 2 or 85°.

Check: $29 + [2(29) + 8] + [3(29) - 2] = 180$

$$29 + 66 + 85 = 180$$
$$180 = 180$$

2. **(D)** Let A = the measure of angle A and let B = the measure of angle B. Since the two angles are supplementary, one equation is

$$A + B = 180$$

Since B is 5 more than four times the measure of angle A, either subtract 5 from the measure of angle B or add 5 to four times the measure of angle A. The equation becomes

$$B = 4A + 5$$

Now substitute the value of B into the first equation to get

$$A + (4A + 5) = 180$$

Solve the equation for A.

$$5A + 5 = 180$$

$$5A = 175$$

$$A = 35$$

Then $B = 4(35) + 5 = 145$.

Check: $35 + 145 = 180$ $\quad$ $145 = 4(35) + 5$

$180 = 180$ $\quad$ $145 = 145$

3. **(C)** Draw an isosceles triangle and label each side. Let the length of the base be x. Then each leg is five times the base less 3, or $5x - 3$.

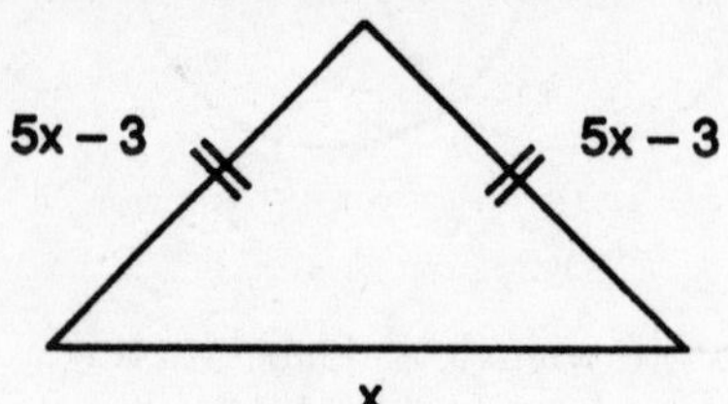

The perimeter is the sum of the sides, so the equation becomes

$$x + (5x - 3) + (5x - 3) = 60$$

Solve for x.

$$11x - 6 = 60$$

$$11x = 66$$

$$x = 6$$

and $\quad 5(6) - 3 = 27$

The length of each leg is 27.

Check: $6 + 27 + 27 = 60$

$60 = 60$

Drill 10 – Measurement

1. **(B)** Convert the measurements of the walkway to inches.

$3 \times 12 = 36$ inches and $11 \times 12 = 132$ inches

The area to be covered is 36 in × 132 in = 4,752 in^2.

Each brick has an area of 4 in × 6 in = 24 in^2.

Divide the area of the brick into the area to be covered to determine how many bricks are needed.

$4{,}752 \text{ in}^2 \div 24 \text{ in}^2 = 198$

There are 198 bricks needed to cover the walkway.

2. **(B)** Let x = the width of the wall.

The length of the wall is then $3x$.

The area of the wall is the length multiplied by the width, or

$x \times 3x = 192$

So, $3x^2 = 192$

Then $x^2 = 64$, so $x = 8$ ft

The width of the wall is $3 \times 8 = 24$ ft.

If a roll of paper is 2 feet wide, it will take 12 rolls to cover the wall.

3. **(D)** First change 2 kg into grams by multiplying by 1,000 (1 kg = 1,000 g). Then divide by 8 to determine the number of smaller containers that can be filled.

$(2 \times 1{,}000) \div 8 = 250$

Two hundred and fifty smaller bottles can be filled.

Drill 11 – Data Interpretation

1. **(D)** To determine the amount of scholarship money awarded in 1985, scan the bottom of the graph to find the year 1985. This is listed as "85." Then, draw a line with your eye up from 85 to the point where this line would intersect the plotted line (a "point" appears at this place on the line). From this point, draw a line with your eye to the left side of the graph where the amounts of money are listed. You will see that this falls halfway between \$150,000 and \$200,000. You will notice that the money amounts are listed in increments of \$50,000. Since half of \$50,000 is \$25,000, and since your point falls halfway between \$150,000 and \$200,000, then the amount of scholarship money awarded in 1985 was \$175,000.

\$150,000 + \$25,000 = \$175,000

2. **(C)** By using the same process described above, we can determine that the amount of scholarship money awarded in 1987 was \$75,000, and the amount of scholarship money awarded in 1988 was \$150,000. If we subtract \$75,000 from \$150,000, we can determine that the increase in scholarship money awarded between 1987 and 1988 was \$75,000.

3. **(B)** Since Car 2 received 32 mpg using regular unleaded gasoline and 38 mpg using unleaded gasoline with Super Treatment Plus, there was a 6 mpg increase when the new product was used.

4. **(A)** By using the same process as above, we can determine that Car 1 had an increase of 5 mpg while using the new product, and that Car 3 had an increase of 6 mpg while using the new product. In addition, we already know that Car 2 had an increase of 6 mpg while using the new product. Therefore, Cars 2 and 3 had the greatest mileage increase in this test.

5. **(B)** If your car averages 25 mpg (the same as Car 1), then you should expect the same mileage with the new product as Car 1, which is 30 mpg with the new product.

6. **(C)** To determine how much a family with an income of $1,500 a month would spend on housing, we must first look at the pie chart. Since the chart shows that 30% of the budget goes toward housing, we must determine 30% of $1,500.

$$\$1,500 \times .30 = \$450$$

7. **(B)** Since the amount spent on an automobile is 15% and the amount spent on housing is 30%, we can set up the proportion $^{15}/_{30}$. This can be factored down to $^{1}/_{2}$.

$$\frac{15}{30} = \frac{3 \times 5}{3 \times 10} = \frac{5}{10} = \frac{5 \times 1}{5 \times 2} = \frac{1}{2}$$

8. **(D)** A family with an income of $1,240 should spend 8% of this amount on clothing. Eight percent of $1,240 is $99.20. If the family spends $125 on clothing, they are over budget by $25.80.

$$\$125.00 - \$99.20 = \$25.80$$

9. **(C)** If dieter 1 eats 2 ounces of french bread, s/he has consumed 140 calories. If dieter 2 eats 2 ounces of bran bread, s/he has consumed 190 calories (note that the table lists the amount of calories for 2 ounces of french bread, while it lists the amount of calories for only 1 ounce of bran bread). Therefore, dieter 2 has consumed 50 calories more than dieter 1.

$$190 \text{ calories} - 140 \text{ calories} = 50 \text{ calories}$$

10. **(A)** There are 115 calories in 1 ounce of whole wheat bread. If 0.5 ounces of oatmeal bread has 55 calories, then a whole ounce of oatmeal bread would have twice as many calories.

$$2 \times 55 = 110 \text{ calories}$$

Subtract this amount from the amount of calories in 1 ounce of whole wheat bread.

$$115 - 110 = 5 \text{ calories}$$

Drill 12 – Combination of Mathematical Skills

1. **(D)** Let x represent the first integer and $x + 1$ represent the next integer. Three times an integer is represented by $3x$. Four times the next consecutive integer is $4(x + 1)$.

The equation is

$$3x + 4(x + 1) = -17$$

Using the distributive law on the left side of the equation, we get:

$$3x + 4x + 4 = -17$$

Combining like terms on the left side of the equation, we get:

$$7x + 4 = -17$$

Transposing the constant term + 4 to the right side of the equation:

$$\begin{array}{rcl} 7x + 4 & = & -17 \\ -4 & & -4 \\ \hline 7x & = & -21 \end{array}$$

To solve for x in the equation $7x = -21$, we divide both sides by 7 as follows:

$$\frac{7x}{7} = \frac{-21}{7}$$

$$x = -3$$

$$x + 1 = -3 + 1 = -2$$

Therefore, the product of the two numbers is $(-3)(-2) = 6$.

Answer choice (A) is incorrect since -5 is the sum of -3 and -2, not the product of the two numbers.

Answer choice (B) is one of the integers to be multiplied.

Answer choice (C) is one of the integers to be multiplied.

2. **(B)** Let x represent one number and $x + 14$ represent the other number—since more than represents addition. This means that x is the smaller number and $x + 14$ is the larger number.

The sum of three times the larger number is represented by $3(x + 14)$.

Twice the smaller number is represented by $2x$.

The equation is then

$$3(x + 14) + 2x = 87$$

Using the distributive law on the left side of the equation, we get:

$$3x + 42 + 2x = 87$$

Combining like terms on the left side of the equation, we get:

$$5x + 42 = 87$$

Transpose the constant term 42 to the right side of the equation as follows:

$$\begin{array}{rcr} 5x + 42 & = & 87 \\ -42 & = & -42 \\ \hline 5x & = & 45 \end{array}$$

To solve for x in the equation $5x = 45$, divide both sides by 5 as follows:

$$\frac{5x}{5} = \frac{45}{5}$$

$$x = 9$$

Then the larger number is

$$x + 14 = 9 + 14 = 23.$$

Once we have the larger number, we must find its square. To do this, multiply the number by itself.

$$23 \times 23 = 529$$

Choice (D) is incorrect because it is the square of the smaller number.

3. **(D)** Let x represent the width of the rectangle and $x + 12$ represent the length of the rectangle.

The formula for the perimeter of a rectangle is:

$$2(\text{length}) + 2(\text{width}) = \text{Perimeter}$$

$$2(x + 12) + 2(x) = 92$$

Using the distributive law on the left side of the equation, we get:

$$2x + 24 + 2x = 92$$

Combining like terms on the left side of the equation, we get:

$$4x + 24 = 92$$

Transposing the constant term 24 to the right side of the equation:

$$\begin{array}{rcr} 4x + 24 & = & 92 \\ -24 & & -24 \\ \hline 4x & = & 68 \end{array}$$

To solve for x in the equation $4x = 68$, we divide both sides by 4 as follows:

$$\frac{4x}{4} = \frac{68}{4}$$

$$x = 17$$

17 is the width of the rectangle and

$$x + 12 = 17 + 12 = 29$$

is the length of the rectangle.

To find the area of a rectangle, use the formula

length × width

We found the length of the rectangle to be 29 and the width to be 17.

Multiply the two together

$29 \times 17 = 493$ square inches.

4. **(B)** We use the formula

rate × time = distance

Let x represent the time it takes Lee to catch up to Jane, i.e., Jane has walked x hours by this time. Since Jane travels at the rate of 4 miles per hour, her distance after x hours is $4x$. Since Lee leaves the house two hours later than Jane, by the time he catches up to Jane and covers the same distance as Jane is $x - 2$. Since Lee jogs at 6 miles per hour, his distance covered is $6(x - 2)$. Since Lee and Jane cover the same distance the equation is:

Jane's distance = Lee's distance

$$4x = 6(x - 2)$$

Using the distributive law on the right side of the equation, we get:

$$4x = 6x - 12$$

Transposing the $6x$ to the left side of the equation, we get:

$$\begin{array}{rcr} 4x = & & 6x - 12 \\ -6x & & -6x \\ \hline -2x = & & -12 \end{array}$$

To solve for x in the equation $-2x = -12$, we divide both sides by -2 as follows:

$$\frac{-2x}{-2} = \frac{-12}{-2}$$

$$x = 6$$

Six equals Jane's time and Lee's time is $x - 2 = 6 - 2 = 4$ hours.

The question asks for the number of minutes it will take for Lee to catch Jane. Therefore, we need to multiply the number of hours, 4, by 60 because this is the number of minutes in an hour.

$4 \times 60 = 240$ minutes

5. **(A)** Let x represent the first integer, $x + 2$ represent the second integer, and $x + 4$ represent the third integer.

Twice the smallest integer is represented by $2x$; three times the largest integer is represented by $3(x + 4)$.

The equation is

$$2x + 3(x + 4) = 72.$$

Using the distributive law on the left side of the equation, we get:

$$2x + 3x + 12 = 72$$

Combining like terms on the left side of the equation, we get:

$$5x + 12 = 72$$

Transposing the constant term + 12 to the right side of the equation:

$$\begin{array}{rcr} 5x + 12 & = & 72 \\ -12 & = & -12 \\ \hline 5x & = & 60 \end{array}$$

To solve for x in the equation $5x = 60$, we divide both sides by 5 as follows:

$$\frac{5x}{5} = \frac{60}{5}$$

$$x = 12$$

12 is the smallest number and $x + 2 = 12 + 2 = 14$ is the middle number, and $x + 4 = 12 + 4 = 16$ is the largest integer. Therefore the sum of the first integer and the third integer is

$$12 + 16 = 28.$$

Answer choice (B) is incorrect since 26 is the sum of the first number and second number.

Answer choice (C) is incorrect since 30 is the sum of the second number and third number.

Answer choice (D) is incorrect since 12 is the first number.

REFERENCE TABLE

SYMBOLS AND THEIR MEANINGS:

Symbol	Meaning	Symbol	Meaning
$=$	is equal to	$\leq$	is less than or equal to
$\neq$	is unequal to	$\geq$	is greater than or equal to
$<$	is less than	$\parallel$	is parallel to
$>$	is greater than	$\perp$	is perpendicular to
$\approx$	approximately equal to	$\ngeq$	not greater than or equal to
$\pi \approx$	3.14	$\nleq$	not less than or equal to
$\sim$	similar to	$\angle$	angle
$\cong$	congruent to	$\llcorner$	right angle
$\overline{AB}$	line segment AB	$\pm$	plus or minus
$\overleftrightarrow{AB}$	line AB	$a{:}b$ or $\frac{a}{b}$	ratio of a to b

FORMULAS

DESCRIPTION	FORMULA
AREA (A) of a:	
square	$A = s^2$; where s = side
rectangle	$A = lw$; where l = length, w = width
parallelogram	$A = bh$; where b = base, h = height
triangle	$A = {}^1/_2\, bh$; where b = base, h = height
circle	$A = \pi r^2$; where $\pi = 3.14$, r = radius
PERIMETER (P) of a:	
square	$P = 4s$; where s = side
rectangle	$P = 2l + 2w$; where l = length, w = width
triangle	$P = a + b + c$; where a, b, and c are the sides
circumference (C) of a circle	$C = \pi d$; where $\pi = 3.14$, d = diameter
VOLUME (V) of a:	
cube	$V = s^3$; where s = side
rectangular container	$V = lwh$; where l = length, w = width, h = height
Pythagorean relationship	$c^2 = a^2 + b^2$; where c = hypotenuse, a and b are legs of a right triangle
distance (d) between two points in a plane	$d = \sqrt{(x_2 - x_1)^2 + (y_2 - y_1)^2}$; where (x_1, y_1) and (x_2, y_2) are two points in a plane
mean	**mean** $= \frac{x_1 + x_2 + \ldots + x_n}{n}$; where the x's are the values for which a mean is desired, and n = number of values in the series
median	**median** = the point in an ordered set of numbers at which half of the numbers are above and half of the numbers are below this value
simple interest (i)	$i = prt$; where p = principal, r = rate, t = time
distance (d) as function of rate and time	$d = rt$; where r = rate, t = time
total cost (c)	$c = nr$; where n = number of units, r = cost per unit

Writing Section Review

Chapter 4

WRITING SECTION REVIEW

Part I: Multiple-Choice

Part II: Writing Sample

Your first step in preparing for the TASP Writing Section is to study this review. The Writing Section consists of two parts: a Multiple-Choice Subsection and a Writing Sample Subsection. Our review covers all of the material you will need to know in order to pass both parts of the Writing Section. In addition, each review section is accompanied by drills that test your knowledge of the material covered. By studying our review, you will greatly increase your chances of achieving a passing score on the Writing Section of the TASP.

Part I of this review will assist you in preparing for the Multiple-Choice questions in the Writing Section. In this section, you are responsible for recognizing

- the writer's purpose and intended audience,
- the qualities of effective organization, including the unity, focus, and development of a piece, and
- effective and correct sentence structure and mechanics.

You will encounter between 40 and 50 questions in this part, although only 35 questions will be scored. The review will cover

- Recognizing the Writer's Purpose and Intended Audience,
- Recognizing Effective Organization, and
- Recognizing Effective Sentence Structure and Mechanics, including a Review of Standard Written English.

Part II of this review will prepare you for the Writing Sample. You will be responsible for writing an essay which employs all of the elements of good writing. This review will cover

- Essay Strategies,
- The Writing Process,
- Prewriting and Planning,
- Writing Your Rough Draft,

- Supporting Evidence,
- Reviewing and Organizing the Paragraphs, and
- Polishing and Editing the Essay.

As you study, and while you take the test, keep in mind that your score on the Writing Sample is more critical than your score on the Multiple-Choice questions. If you obtain a total score of 6, 7, or 8 on the Writing Sample, then you will automatically pass the Writing Section of the TASP, regardless of your score on the Multiple-Choice questions. If you receive a score of 5 on the Writing Sample, then you must obtain 25 correct answers out of the 35 scored Multiple-Choice items in order to pass the Writing Section. Anyone scoring a 4 or below on the Writing Sample automatically fails the Writing Section, regardless of the student's Multiple-Choice score.

The more familiar you are with the topics that will appear on this section, the more likely you are to do well. Even if you are sure you know all of the information provided in our review, you should still complete the included drills. These drills will help you become accustomed to the types of questions presented, as well as sharpen your overall thinking skills.

Part I: Multiple-Choice

I. **Strategies for the Multiple-Choice Subsection**

II. **Recognizing the Writer's Purpose and Intended Audience**

III. **Recognizing Effective Organization: Unity, Focus, and Development**

IV. **Recognizing Effective Sentence Structure and Mechanics**

V. **Review of Standard Written English**

Writing and reading for understanding and information are essential for success. You cannot compete in college or hold a decent job without these skills. Good students and good employees are also good readers and writers. This review will teach you what you need to know to be an effective reader and writer, and to succeed on the Multiple-Choice questions of the TASP Writing Section.

I. Strategies for the Multiple-Choice Subsection

To give yourself the best chance of success on the Multiple-Choice questions, follow these steps.

Before the test, this is your plan of attack:

➤ Step 1 Make sure you study our review to brush up on your skills. Read and study our review!

➤ Step 2 Learn and understand the directions, so you don't waste valuable time reading them on the day of the exam. This will allow you to just skim them when beginning the test. The directions will be similar to the following:

> **DIRECTIONS:** You will encounter 16 passages in this portion of the test. Each part of the passage will be numbered, with the questions that follow the passage referring to the numbered parts. Only **ONE** answer to each question is the **best** answer, although more than one answer may appear to be correct. There are between 40 and 50 multiple-choice questions in this portion. Choose your answers carefully and mark them on your answer sheet. Make sure that the space you are marking corresponds to the answer you have chosen.
>
> Note: The use of the term "nonstandard" in the questions means "does not follow standard written English."

When reading the passage, this is your plan of attack:

➤ Step 1 Identify the main idea and purpose of the passage. The main idea may be found within the first few sentences of the passage.

➤ Step 2 Uncover the main idea of each paragraph. It may be found in either the first or last sentence of the paragraph.

➤ Step 3 Skim over the detailed points of the passage, making sure to circle key words and phrases. These are words or phrases such as but, on the other hand, although, however, yet, and except.

When answering the questions, this is your plan of attack:

➤ Step 1 If a question requires you to change a numbered section and you cannot determine the answer, try plugging in the answer choices to see which works.

➤ Step 2 Save for last questions that require you to find specific information in the passage.

➤ Step 3 Answer immediately questions dealing with main idea or purpose.

➤ Step 4 Utilize the key words and phrases which you circled.

➤ Step 5 If you cannot determine an answer, use the process of elimination and then guess.

Additional Tips

- Attack each question one at a time. Read each carefully.
- Don't panic! Work naturally and quickly, but remember that you should have plenty of time in which to complete these questions. Rushing through can cause you to make careless mistakes, thus costing you valuable points.
- Study your vocabulary. If you do not know a word, use its root, prefix, and suffix to determine its meaning. If you know whether a word's connotation is negative or positive, you can eliminate choices with similar connotations.

II. Recognizing the Writer's Purpose and Intended Audience

Now that you know what you are being tested for in these exams, you should know what characteristics of prose passages or essays guide the reader to clear understanding. Listed below are some guidelines to help you become more alert to reading cues in writing that you may need to understand a given passage.

Analyzing a Passage for Purpose and Audience

Read the whole passage through once. On your first pass look for the following key items to comprehend the overall purpose of the passage and the audience it serves.

Determine What Essay Strategy the Writer Uses: Explain, Inform, or Persuade

All writing is organized to achieve a particular purpose, either implied or stated; all of an essay's organizational strategies may be used to argue. Writers use **seven basic strategies** to organize information and ideas in essays to help prove their point (thesis, or T) and achieve a particular purpose (to inform, explain, or persuade). All of the seven strategies might be useful in persuading a reader to see the issue the writer's way.

To prove a thesis, writers may

1. show how a *process* or a procedure does or should work step by step in time;
2. *compare or contrast* two or more things or ideas to show important differences or similarities;
3. *identify a problem* and then explain how to solve it;
4. *analyze* into its components, or *classify* by its types or categories an idea or thing to show how it is put together or how it works or how it is designed;
5. *explain* why something happens to produce a particular result or set of results;
6. *describe* the particular individual characteristics, beauty and features, of a place, person(s), time, or idea;
7. *define* what a thing is or what an idea means.

In a given essay, one pattern tends to dominate the discussion, depending on the object or idea in question. (For example, I might *describe* and *explain* in order to *define* the varied meanings of "love").

Consider Implications and Inferences

Writers sometimes *imply* things that would be a logical extension of what they actually say. For example, it would be unreasonable to suggest that the writer in the passage below is implying that he wants a liberated feminist career woman for his spouse. It doesn't logically fit the examples (E's) he offers in his paragraph. These examples don't support that idea.

> (E) I want a wife who will wash my clothes and iron my shirts. (E) I want a wife who will clean the house and do the dishes. (E) I want a wife who will change the babies' diapers and cook my meals. (E) I want a wife who will do the shopping and greet me with my favorite cocktail when I come home tired from work.

It is obvious that the writer wants a wife. Now, whatever you may think of the writer (never let your emotions cloud your feelings and get in the way of what was said), he is making a point about *what kind* of wife he wants. Notice that the paragraph is nothing but (E's) examples. All of the sentences show, or exemplify, characteristics of the "wife" this guy wants — but no one of them brings us to a firm conclusion. So, this writer *implies* in the paragraph, without actually stating, the kind of wife he wants. Yet we still get a pretty clear picture or idea of her:

[The writer] wants a traditional housekeeper wife. (T) This would probably be close to the T sentence of this writer's paragraph or passage if he had not implied it, but had stated it instead. Some of you may have been *feeling* that what he wants is a slave, not a wife — but be careful: that's what you may feel, not what the writer is implying. Don't confuse your feelings with the writer's facts or illustrations.

These tests will often require you to understand and recognize what a reader can *infer* from the passage once you have read it. Actually, implications and inferences are very similar; the only difference is who is making them: Writers imply, readers infer. For example, in this case, the reader could *infer* that the writer is a male who wants a conventional wife. He probably likes football, too. Probably — that's an **inference:** a reader's probable and reasonable conclusion or interpretation of an idea based upon what the writer has written. For example, it would be unreasonable to infer the writer was a woman — women generally have husbands, not wives.

Determine the Nature of the Audience

If you ask a series of questions about a given passage, you can determine the nature of the audience. As you read, keep in mind the writer's purpose as you understand it. Using the questions below, develop through your answers a mental picture of the audience (besides yourself) reading this passage.

1. What does the writer intend the readers of this passage to take away with them? The writer's point of view? Information?
2. How old are the readers?
3. What is their level of education?
4. What attitudes, prejudices, opinions, fears, experience, and concerns might the audience for this passage have?

Considerations of audience will directly affect the tone of a passage, and thus determine what level of usage or meaning is appropriate in a given paragraph or section of an essay. For example, if I am writing to a 13-year-old, should I write: "Please peruse with comprehension the tome offered," or "Please be sure to read and study what is in this book." The latter sentence, with its simple vocabulary, is the appropriate choice.

III. Recognizing Effective Organization: Unity, Focus, and Development

Look for Key Sections (T) and (*t*)

In reading a particular passage, you want to identify what portions or sections of a whole essay you confront. Depending upon which section of an essay is offered, you may decide whether you are reading the writer's main point (or thesis), purpose, or evidence. You will also need to know or recognize what sort of logic the writer is using, such as cause/effect, or problem/solution, and so on.

Key Sections to Recognize

Introduction: The introductory paragraph usually shows the writer's point of view, or thesis (T), about an issue and introduces that position with some lead-in or general data to support the thesis. The thesis of an essay is the writer's stated or implied position on a particular issue or idea; the writer's thesis (T) is the writer's stand on the subject under discussion. Identify the writer's purpose and point of view.

Development: Three middle paragraphs (or more) which prove the writer's position from different angles, using evidence from real life experience and knowledge. Evidence may take the form of facts, examples, statistics, illustrations, opinions, or analogies. For our purpose, we will call all such evidence **examples** (E's).

In addition, each paragraph within the development section will have a stated or implied main point (*t*) used to support the thesis (T) of the whole passage. The main point (*t*) of a paragraph in the development section will be used to support the essay's whole thesis (T). For example, my thesis might be, "Dogs are better than cats." Having said that, I might write a whole paragraph with supporting examples to show a main point (*t*) in support of that idea. The main point (*t*) of the paragraph that needs support, then, might be as follows:

First of all, dogs are more loyal than cats. (*t*)

The evidence (E) that I summon to support that point (*t*) which, in turn, supports my overall thesis (T), would therefore have to be either facts, statistics, expert testimony, or anecdotal knowledge that showed that dogs were indeed more loyal than cats. For example: "The A.S.P.C.A. reports that 99 out of 100 dogs cannot adjust to new owners after the death of their original masters, while only 2 out of 100 cats cannot adjust in the same situation." (E)

Conclusion: The last paragraph, or two, usually (but not always) sums up the writer's position (T) and may add some final reminder of what the issue was, some speculation, or some call to action that the writer suggests.

Determine the Type of Evidence (E)

To prove any thesis (T) that the writer maintains is true, s/he may employ any one of the seven strategies listed on page 293 to prove the idea. But s/he will call on evidence from one or all of the four following areas to support the thesis of the passage. Identify which kind of evidence the writer uses in the passage you are reading.

1. **Hard data** (facts, statistics, scientific evidence, research) — documented evidence that has been verified to be true. A fact is something that will always be true no matter who finds it out and reports it, e.g., a foot is a measurement of twelve inches.

2. **Anecdotal evidence** — stories from the writer's own experience and knowledge that illustrate a particular point or idea. For example, a writer might relate the story of a person he knows or has heard about who was terrified of dogs but who nonetheless saved her baby from a crazed Doberman, thereby illustrating what "courage" means.

3. **Expert opinions** — assertions, usually by authorities on the matter under discussion. For example, a writer uses the stated opinion of a great psychologist to prove or support a point about human behavior that the writer wants readers to believe.

4. **Analogies** — show a resemblance between one phenomenon and another. For example, a writer might state that growing up to maturity is like a flower coming into bloom. Just as a flower is most beautiful in full bloom, so at maturity, a person reaches the full bloom of wisdom, judgment, and civility. Notice the appearance of "like" to show the relationship between the two ideas. Writers use analogies to help the reader understand the perspective the writer has, not to prove anything. Analogies never prove anything. Analogies support probability when the reader can see the similarity of the relationships of the two ideas.

Check for Logic

Make sure the evidence proves the writer's point and not something else.

Be careful about conclusions. The writer may not have proven his point. An essay is essentially a syllogism that proves something by induction or deduction. Induction is that sort of reasoning which arrives at a general conclusion based on the relationship among the particular elements of a thing or idea. Deduction reasons from the general to the particular. For example, I may assert that all frogs croak before they jump, and then go on to find supporting evidence for that in frog ponds around the world. If I never find a frog that doesn't croak, I may assume that my deduction is correct.

Sometimes, however, the premises of an argument are false or unprovable. For example,

Premise One: Harry Jones has a beard.

Premise Two: All goats have beards.

Conclusion: Therefore, Harry is a goat.

The conclusion is incorrect, for it could be true only if *just* goats have beards. This is intuitively untrue because male human beings may have beards as well; therefore, the conclusion is insupportable. In this example, we lack sufficient information to draw a conclusion about what or who Harry is.

Here are typical traps that some writers fall into:

Either/Or: The writer assumes only two opposing possibilities apply. "Either we abolish cars, or the environment is doomed." Other factors may contribute to destroying the environment.

Oversimplification: "Only motivated athletes become champions." Maybe not; unfortunately, sometimes athletes with enhancing steroids become champions, too.

Begging the Question: The writer assumes as proven something which needs to be proven: "Faithful dogs never leave their masters." Dogs, however, may sometimes prove unfaithful.

Ignoring the Issue: An argument against the truth of a person's argument shifts from what the writer observed to how the testimony is no good because it is about a disgusting or repulsive topic.

Arguing Against a Person, Not an Idea: The writer argues that somebody's idea has no merit because s/he is immoral or personally stupid (this is called an *ad hominem* attack). "John can't prove anything about dogs being faithful; he can't even understand basic mathematics." One has nothing to do with the other.

Non Sequitur: Leaping to a wrong conclusion: "John is tall; he must know a lot about basketball."

Drawing the Wrong Conclusion from a Sequence: "He trained and then read and then trained some more and therefore won the match." Perhaps something else besides this sequence of events led to his winning the match.

Note the Transitions

As you review the passage a second time, look for and circle transitions that reveal the connections among the writer's ideas. Transitions show how the writer is reasoning to get to the point — perhaps it is a cause/effect pattern or a problem/solution discussion in which the writer provides the solution. S/he may use transitions either at the beginnings of paragraphs or to show connections among ideas within a single paragraph.

Here are some typical transitional words and phrases:

Linking similar ideas

For explanation, analogy, accruing factual evidence or opinions for a point of view.

again	for example	likewise

- also
- for instance
- moreover
- and
- further
- nor
- another
- furthermore
- of course
- besides
- in addition
- similarly
- equally important
- in like manner
- too

Linking dissimilar/contradictory ideas

To show comparison or contrast among similar or opposing notions.

- although
- however
- otherwise
- and yet
- in spite of
- provided that
- as if
- instead
- still
- but
- nevertheless
- yet
- conversely
- on the contrary
- even if
- on the other hand

Indicating cause, purpose, result

To show the solutions to a problem or the outcome of a certain series of causes. Causes may be immediate or remote: The immediate cause for my spilling the glass of water was that I knocked it over with my hand. The remote cause might be that I was trying to put on my hat, and in the process I lost my focus on the glass of water in line with my sweeping hand, which was reaching for my hat across the table.

- as for
- so
- as a result
- for this reason
- then
- because
- hence
- therefore
- consequently
- since
- thus

Indicating time or position

Used in process and procedure explanations or chronological narratives to show a sequence in time or place.

- above
- before
- meanwhile
- across
- beyond
- next
- afterward
- eventually
- presently
- around
- finally
- second
- at once
- first
- thereafter
- at the present time
- here
- thereupon

Indicating an example or summary

Used to point to supporting evidence or explanatory material and to complete an idea within a paragraph or within a whole essay.

as a result	in any event	in short
as I have said	in brief	on the whole
for example	in conclusion	to sum up
for instance	in fact	in any case
in other words		

IV. Recognizing Effective Sentence Structure and Mechanics

Test Your Skills

To prepare yourself for the questions you will encounter on this section of the TASP, test yourself with this grammar Diagnostic. After you have completed the test, check your answers against the Diagnostic Answer Key at the end of the test to determine your areas of weakness. As you will see, the Diagnostic Answer Key includes detailed explanations to all of the answers. At the end of each explanation is a section reference in brackets [. . .] that refers to our Review of Standard Written English which follows the test. If you get a particular item wrong, the section reference in brackets will be an area in which you need further review. For example, if you see [Section 1], then you should study Section 1: Sentence Fragments in our Review of Standard Written English.

Diagnostic

DIRECTIONS: Rewrite the following items so that they follow the rules of correct standard written English.

1. About the television.

   Rewrite:

2. I like television and I think people should watch it television is good because it is so real I think many people would die without it.

   Rewrite:

3. In my opinion, I believe that in order to be able to understand this issue many hours and a lot of time must be devoted to comprehending what the message is that the writer is trying to communicate with ideas due to the fact that s/he is so involved with them.

   Rewrite:

4. Since the car was so old, it was difficult for the mechanic to find the correct parts.

   Rewrite:

5. While waiting for the check, the doorbell rang in the living room.

   Rewrite:

6. I like eating fish and to go to the shore.

   Rewrite:

7. I bought a computer and some word processing software which was quick and inexpensive.

   Rewrite:

8. We cannot reimburse you for moving boats over 14 feet.

   Rewrite:

9. We could of been contenders in the contest, but the sweep of events make us losers in the end.

   Rewrite:

10. This book is more better than yours, but John's is the worse of all three that we read.

    Rewrite:

11. Each employee should take his paycheck to the counter. This is the first one you will see.

    Rewrite:

12. The doctor was ready and but he could not operate until dawn.

    Rewrite:

13. After the ball was over Scarlet went back to her plantation.

    Rewrite:

14. Captain Kirk Admiral of the Starfleet was also the Captain of the *Enterprise.*

    Rewrite:

15. The dog ate the bones and Richard punished him.

Rewrite:

16. I like inland woodland ducks, however, I prefer the silent white swans.

Rewrite:

17. The woman said she had never worked with a "gopher".

Rewrite:

18. The stores in Brooklyn had been terminated; the Harley Skull Gang had torched, or set fire, to them as an act of political revenge. Head Skull John Harley said, We were only protecting our own turf, as we call it.

Rewrite:

19. The boys couldnt find a way to get to the childrens pool over at the Jones house without the Harley boys gang knowing about it.

Rewrite:

20. the article about france, entitled "come to the heart of europe now" was cited by senator smith whom i had known as a Professor in sociology 101.

Rewrite:

DIAGNOSTIC

ANSWER KEY

1. This is a fragment; it has no subject or verb to complete it so you will have to choose your own subject and verb. In fact, it is merely a prepositional phrase. Notice that it has no action in it. Notice that the television, though a noun, is not doing anything. Correction: John knows nothing about television. [See Section 1.]

2. This is a run-on sentence. It has many subject and verb units not correctly separated by punctuation. Correction: I like television, and I think people should watch it. Television is good because it is so real. I think many people would die without it. [See Section 2.]

3. This is a wordy sentence. Rewrite this as one or two short sentences that convey the same idea. Correction: Readers must spend time to understand this issue since the writer is so involved with the ideas. [See Section 3.]

4. Though this sentence is correct grammatically, it is longer than necessary. The problems here are wordiness and effective usage. A better version of this sentence would read: "Since the car was so old, the mechanic had difficulty finding the right parts." [See Section 3.]

5. This is an example of a dangling modifier. Reading this sentence, one would think that the doorbell works for a living, i.e., who was really waiting for the check? Correction: While *I* was waiting for the check, the doorbell rang in the living room. [See Section 4.]

6. This sentence does not link up the phrases that begin "eating . . . ," and "to go . . ." They are not parallel. Correction: I like eat*ing* fish and go*ing* to the shore. [See Section 5.]

7. This sentence suggests that either the computer or the software is quick and inexpensive. Which is it? The reader can't be sure because s/he can't tell which word the phrase that begins with "which" refers to. Correction: I bought a computer, which was quick and inexpensive, and some word processing software. [See Section 6.]

8. This sentence is confusing because the meaning of "14 feet" seems ambiguous. Does the writer mean 14-foot long boats? Surely moving boats over 14 feet is not a costly proposition. Correction: For boats over 14 feet long, we cannot reimburse you for moving expenses. [See Section 6.]

9. This sentence has two major flaws: (1) "could of" should be "could have." "Of" is never part of a verb; (2) in the second half, "make" should be "makes" to agree with the real subject, "sweep." The trouble is the writer probably thought "events" was the subject during the writing of the sentence. Correction: We could have been contenders in the contest, but the sweep of events makes us losers in the end. [See Section 7.]

10. Here the writer uses two comparative forms (better/more) where only the one, "better," is appropriate. In English, comparative adjectives have three forms: relative, comparative, and superlative. To compare items that have relative degrees of "goodness" we may say that a single item (say a cookie) is good. But if we have two of the item and we compare them in terms of "good," then one is "better" than the other. If I decide to compare three or more, then I must describe one among them as "the best."

The sentence above also has an error in the use of "worse." The writer should have used the superlative form "worst." Know the comparatives of Standard English, especially the irregular ones. Below, for example, you might expect the comparative version of "worse" to be "worser." [See Section 8.]

relative	comparative	superlative
worse	worse	worst

Correction: This book is better than yours, but John's is the worst of all three that we read.

11. The mistake is with the word "This." What does it refer to — the counter or the paycheck? Make sure you know your pronouns are clear. [See Section 9.]

12. Conjunctions (and, but, so, or, nor, for, if, yet) join together units of syntax which would be independent sentences without them. Use only one to join together two independent thoughts or sentence units. Also, make sure that if you have written two independent sentences joined by a conjunction that you punctuate the place of joining (the conjunction of the two ideas) with a comma just before you begin the clause with the conjunction. In this case, the writer should have said "The doctor was ready, *but* he could not operate until dawn." [See Section 10.]

13. This sentence is incorrectly punctuated. There should be a comma after "over" and before "Scarlet." Any sentence that has words, phrases, or dependent clauses coming before the main independent subject and verb unit should have a comma separating that word, phrase, or dependent clause from the main event. Thus: *In the beginning,* John could not work alone. [See Section 11.]

14. Put a pair of commas around words, phrases, or clauses enclosed in an independent sentence unit. Thus above, "Admiral of the Starfleet" should be set off with a pair (not one) of commas on either side of it. The same thing would be true if

I inserted in the same place in the main sentence something like "who happened to be Admiral of the Starfleet," or simply, "however," [See Section 11.]

15. The dog ate the bones, *and* Richard punished him. Notice that on either side of the unit (, and) is a word group, or clause, that without the conjunction could be a sentence that could stand by itself. [See Section 11.]

16. This sentence is incorrectly punctuated with commas. It is actually two sentences on either side of the "however." Consequently, a semicolon [;] could be placed after "ducks." You might also use (.) or if you replace "however," you could use (, but). [See Section 12.]

17. All quotation marks, no matter how much is being quoted in a given sentence, are placed outside the punctuation associated with them. In this case, it ought to be "gopher." If the sentence demanded a comma after "gopher," it would appear as just shown.

The only exception is a semicolon. If something is placed in quotes in the first part of a sentence using a semicolon, the quotation mark stays inside the semicolon punctuation. Thus: The dog was "smart"; however, George hated him anyway. [See Section 13.]

18. When words are used in a special sense by the writer or speaker, not that of a Standard English meaning for the context, then the writer must put quotation marks around the specially used word or phrase. Also, if a word is quoted inside another quote, it should be set off by a single quotation mark ('turf') rather than two. So, these sentences should be punctuated as follows:

The stores in Brooklyn had been "terminated"; the Harley Skull Gang had "torched," or set fire to, them as an act of "political" revenge. Head Skull John Harley said, "We were only protecting our own 'turf,' as we call it." [See Section 13.]

19. Apostrophes are the problem here. The sentence should read: "The boys couldn't find a way to get to the children's pool over at the Jones' house without the Harley boys' gang knowing about its whereabouts." [See Section 14.]

20. Beware of faulty capitalization and weak mechanics. The sentence should read: *T*he article about *F*rance, entitled "*C*ome to the *H*eart of *E*urope *N*ow!" was cited by *S*enator *S*mith, whom *I* had known as a professor in *S*ociology 101. [See Sections 15, 16, and 17.]

Now that you know the areas in which you need improvement, study the following Review of Standard Written English.

V. Review of Standard Written English

Even though we are constantly surrounded by the English language, many of us are unsure of how to use Standard Written English properly. Students continually question their ability to recognize correct grammar and usage.

When answering TASP Writing questions, you must be careful not to repeat the common errors that exist in written English. This review will make you aware of these various errors.

The following pitfalls are the most common errors that are made in writing. By keeping these frequently repeated mistakes in mind when completing the multiple-choice questions in the Writing Section, you will be able to identify all the errors quickly and easily.

Section 1: Sentence Fragments

NO: A tree as old as your father.

This is just the opposite of a run-on sentence. A sentence fragment does not have enough in it to make it a complete thought. It is usually missing a subject or a verb.

YES: The tree is as old as your father.

Section 2: Run-on Sentences

NO: It was a pleasant drive the sun was shining.

A run-on sentence is a sentence with too much in it. It usually contains two complete sentences separated by a comma, or two complete sentences merged together.

YES: It was a pleasant drive because the sun was shining.

NO: Talk softly, someone is listening.

Sometimes a writer will try to correct a run-on sentence by inserting a comma between the clauses, but this creates another error, a comma splice. The following examples illustrate various ways to correct the comma splice.

YES: Talk softly; someone is listening.

or

Talk softly, because someone is listening.

☞ Drill: Sentence Fragments/Run-on Sentences

DIRECTIONS: The following sentences may be either run-on sentences or sentence fragments. Make any necessary corrections.

1. After the rain stopped.

2. Mow the lawn, it is much too long.

3. The settlement you reached it seems fair.

4. When I read, especially at night. My eyes get tired.

5. It was impossible to get through on the phone, the lines were down because of the storm.

6. Is this the only problem? The leaky pipe?

7. Everyone saw the crime, no one is willing to come forth.

8. The weather was bad, she played in the rain.

9. Ellen paced the floor. Worrying about her economics final.

10. Their season was over, the team had lost the playoffs.

Section 3: Short Sentences/Wordiness

Effective writing means concise writing. Wordiness, on the other hand, decreases the clarity of expression by cluttering sentences with unnecessary words. Of course, all short sentences are not better than long ones simply because they are brief. As long as a word serves a function, it should remain in the sentence. However, repetition of words, sounds, and phrases should be used only for emphasis or other stylistic reasons. Editing your writing will reduce its bulk. Notice the difference in impact between the first and second sentences in the following pairs.

NO: The medical exam that he gave me was entirely complete.

YES: The medical exam he gave me was complete.

NO: Larry asked his friend John, who was a good, old friend, if he would join him and go along with him to see the foreign film made in Japan.

YES: Larry asked his good, old friend John if he would join him in seeing the Japanese film.

NO: I was absolutely, totally happy with the present that my parents gave to me at 7 a.m. on the morning of my birthday.

YES: I was totally happy with the present my parents gave me on the morning of my birthday.

NO: It seems perfectly clear to me that although he went and got permission from the professor, he still should not have played that awful, terrible joke on the Dean.

YES: It seems clear to me that although he got permission from the professor, he still should not have played that terrible joke on the Dean.

NO: He went to England by means of a long boat.

YES: He went to England by boat.

NO: It will be our aim to ensure proper health care for each and every one of the people in the United States.

YES: Our aim will be to ensure proper health care for all Americans.

☞ Drill: Short Sentences/Wordiness

DIRECTIONS: Through revision, improve the following sentences.

1. He graduated college. In no time he found a job. Soon after he rented an apartment. He was very happy.

2. The book that she lent me was lengthy. It was boring. I wouldn't recommend it to anyone. There was nothing about the book that I enjoyed.

3. It was raining. We expected to go on a picnic. Now our plans are ruined. We have nothing to do.

4. Whenever anyone telephoned her to ask her for help with their homework she always obliged right away.

5. She liked to paint. She was quite good. Materials are expensive. She can't afford them.

6. Jane is just one of those people who you can't really describe with words.

7. It was time to leave. They hoped they packed everything. There was no time to think. The taxi was outside. It was waiting.

8. The candidate promised he would do what was necessary to lengthen prison terms. This was his major issue. He hoped he was elected.

9. *Long Days Journey Into Night* is a play. It is a dramatic play. Eugene O'Neill wrote it. The play is also autobiographical.

10. He could have still asked her for her approval.

Section 4: Misplaced Modifiers

NO: Harold watched the painter gaping in astonishment.

The dangling participle is an error that results in an unclear sentence. The participle should appear immediately before or after the subject of the sentence.

YES: Gaping in astonishment, Harold watched the painter.

NO: On correcting the test, his errors became apparent.

Many modifiers cause confusion when they are out of place.

YES: His errors became apparent when the test was corrected.

NO: Jane almost polished the plate until it shined.

Words such as *almost, only, just, even, nearly, hardly, not,* and *merely* must appear immediately before the word they modify or they will cause confusion.

YES: Jane polished the plate until it almost shined.

☞ Drill: Misplaced Modifiers

DIRECTIONS: The following group of sentences may contain misplaced modifiers. Make any necessary corrections.

1. I saw a stray dog riding the bus this afternoon.

2. The clothing was given to the poor in large packages.

3. I found five dollars eating lunch in the park.

4. We saw two girls riding bicycles from our car.

5. Reading my book quietly, I jumped up when the car crashed.

6. He ran the mile with a sprained ankle.
7. The history majors only were affected by the new requirements.
8. Running quickly to catch the bus, Susan's packages fell out of her arms onto the ground.
9. He just asked the man directions to make sure.
10. He discovered a new route driving home.

Section 5: Parallel Structure

NO: The janitor stopped, listened a moment, then he locked the door.

When ideas are similar, they should be expressed in similar forms. When elements of a sentence are similar, they too should appear in similar form.

YES: The janitor stopped, listened a moment, then locked the door.

☞ Drill: Parallel Structure

DIRECTIONS: The following group of sentences may contain errors in parallel structure. Make any necessary corrections.

1. In the summer I usually like swimming and to water-ski.
2. The professor explained the cause, effect, and the results.
3. Mary read the book, studied the examples, and takes the test.
4. Mark watched the way John started the car, and how he left the curb.
5. They bought the house because of location and its affordability.
6. The movie was interesting and had a lot of excitement.
7. Shakespeare both wrote beautiful sonnets and complex plays.
8. The painting is done either in watercolors or with oils.
9. The lecturer spoke with seriousness and in a concerned tone.
10. Either we forget those plans, or accept their proposal.

Section 6: Phrases and Clauses

Phrases

All this time the Guard was looking *at her,* first *through a telescope,* then *through a microscope,* and then *through an opera-glass. At last* he said, "You're travelling the wrong way," and shut up the window and went away.

"So young a child," said the gentleman *sitting opposite to her* (he was dressed *in white paper),* "ought to know which way she's going, even if she doesn't know her own name!"

A Goat, that was sitting *next to the gentleman in white,* shut his eyes and said in a loud voice, "She ought to know her way *to the ticket-office,* even if she doesn't know her alphabet!"

– Lewis Carroll, *Through the Looking Glass*

All the italicized groups of words are **phrases**. Phrases fill in many of the details that make a sentence interesting. For example, the sentence "We sat." could turn into any of the following by the addition of phrases:

We sat for hours, *looking at the painting.*

On the cliffs by the sea we sat, *watching the sunset.*

We sat by Amelia *at the restaurant.*

A **phrase** is a group of connected words without a subject or predicate. A **prepositional phrase** begins with a preposition, and contains a noun and its modifiers. Some examples are:

Take me *to the opera.*

I think Mark is *in his room.*

What is *in the box* that came *from Hawaii?*

George works best *under pressure.*

After the movie, let's drive *by the river.*

The noun in a prepositional phrase is called the **object of the preposition**. A prepositional phrase can be used as an adjective.

The woman *on the phone* is Jane.

The mysteries *of outer space* are waiting for us.

Henry felt like the Sword *of Damocles* was hanging over his head.

A prepositional phrase can also be used as an adverb.

Anthony was caught *between the horns of a dilemma.*

A large rabbit dove *under the ground.*

Carol lifted the weight *with apparent ease.*

Without doubt, the council decided *for the best.*

A prepositional phrase can be used as a noun as well.

In the evening is as good a time as any.

A **gerund phrase** contains a gerund and its modifiers. It is always used as a noun.

Reading blueprints is not as easy as it sounds.

Thoreau placed great value on *living simply.*

W*andering in and out of stores* is Harriet's favorite way of passing time.

Living well is the best revenge.

Leaving at night helped us avoid the traffic. (gerund phrase as subject)

They accused him of *robbing the bank.* (gerund phrase as the object of the preposition *of*)

Having missed the bus, we arrived at the party late. (participial phrase as modifier)

Exercising regularly is *seizing an opportunity to keep healthy.* (gerund phrase as subject and as predicate nominative)

An **infinitive phrase** contains an infinitive and its modifiers. It can also be used as a noun, adjective, or adverb.

To know him is *to know his brother.* (noun)

A waiter's job is *to serve a table.* (noun)

It's important to have good language *to suit the occasion.* (adjective)

Tom brought a book *to lend me.* (adjective)

We'll have to run *to catch the train.* (adverb)

No one had time *to complete the extra-credit problem.* (infinitive phrase used as an adjective modifying the noun *time*)

We managed *to arrive on time.* (infinitive phrase used as an adverb modifying the verb *manage*)

We hope *to win the race.* (infinitive phrase used as object of verb)

The **present infinitive** also expresses the future time.

We hope *now* to win the race *in the future.*

A **participial phrase** contains a participle and its modifiers. It is used as an adjective to modify a noun or a pronoun.

The gentleman *standing in the aisle* is the owner.

Having said his piece, he sat down.

The fisherman, *weathered by experience,* calmly took the line.

Walking the balance beam, she was extremely careful. (The participial phrase modifies *she. Balance beam* is the direct object of the participle *walking.*)

Missing the bus by a second, we decided to take a taxi. (The participial phrase modifies *we. Bus* is the object of the participle *missing.*)

Running into the house, Mary tripped on the rug. (*Running into the house* is the participial phrase. But the prepositional phrase *into the house* is also a part. It modifies the participle *running.* The participial phrase modifies *Mary. House* is the object of the preposition *into.*)

The incorrect use of the participial phrase results in a stylistic error called the **dangling modifier**. For further information on these phrases, see Section 4, "Misplaced Modifiers."

☞ Drill: Phrases

<u>DIRECTIONS</u>: In the following sentences, label the **prepositional phrase** (PR), the **infinitive phrase** (I), the **participle phrase** (P), and the **gerund phrase** (G). In the prepositional phrases, identify the **object of the preposition** (OP).

1. The police set out to solve the crime and to maintain justice.
2. The woman on the billboard over there is a famous athlete.
3. The man, having painted the house, took a rest.
4. Staying in shape is not as difficult as it appears.
5. James solved the problem with pure logic.
6. She found the time to help me with the job.
7. Having completed the mission, he filed a report.
8. The cake in the refrigerator should be saved for tomorrow.
9. Thinking about the future, she opened a savings account.

DIRECTIONS: Identify the kinds of phrases in each of the following. Also note what role the phrase plays in relation to the rest of the sentence.

10. Having parked the car we went into the theater.

11. Mary's screaming upset the entire family.

12. She hopes to have made a good impression on the interviewers.

13. Jogging is good exercise.

14. Tom wouldn't dare speak in her presence.

15. While I was reading the newspaper, the phone rang.

16. Mrs. Jones likes singing in the morning.

17. Gaining confidence, she sent them a letter.

18. Greta wanted to open the package.

19. Having forgotten my sweater at the movies, I returned there the next day.

20. Winning the game was all Carl cared to do.

Clauses

A **clause** differs from a phrase in that it has a subject and a predicate.

PHRASE: We're planning a trip *to the museum.*

CLAUSE: We're planning a trip *so we can see the museum.*

PHRASE: *After a swim,* we'll have lunch.

CLAUSE: *After we swim,* we'll have lunch.

PHRASE: Bill told them *during dinner.*

CLAUSE: Bill told them *while they were eating dinner.*

PHRASE: *In the box* he found some old letters.

CLAUSE: *When he looked in the box,* he found some old letters.

PHRASE: Harriet laughed *at the comedian.*

CLAUSE: Harriet laughed *whenever the comedian opened his mouth.*

Often a **relative pronoun** like *that, which, who, whom,* or *whoever* will act as the subject of a clause.

Tell me *who* was singing.

Everyone *who* signed the sheet is eligible.

Arnold knew something *that* was generally unknown.

Do you remember *which* kind is better?

Give it to *whoever* has the most need.

In introductory clauses, the use of *that* and *which* often presents a problem for the writer. The difference is simple: If the clause is essential to the meaning of the sentence, use *that.* If the clause is not essential to the meaning of the sentence, use *which* and set off the clause with commas.

THAT: The book that contained the formula was missing. (It is essential that the formula is in the missing book.)

WHICH: The book, which contained the formula, was missing. (It is only essential that the book is missing.)

THAT: We saw a movie that lasted two hours. (The length of the film is important.)

WHICH: We saw a movie, which lasted two hours. (The length of the film is less important.)

THAT: The car that Al was driving got a flat tire. (Out of several cars, Al's car was the one to get a flat tire.)

WHICH: The car, which Al was driving, got a flat tire. (This car got a flat tire and, incidentally, Al was driving.)

THAT: The titles that are underlined will be printed in italics. (Only the underlined titles will be printed in italics. The rest of the titles will not.)

WHICH: The titles, which are underlined, will be printed in italics. (All of the titles are underlined, and they will all be printed in italics.)

THAT: Alan owns a boat that sailed around the world. (Alan's boat sailed around the world.)

WHICH: Alan owns a boat, which sailed around the world. (The fact that it sailed around the world is incidental.)

☞ Drill: Clauses

DIRECTIONS: In the following sentences, determine whether the italicized portion is a **phrase** or a **clause.**

1. The girl *in the red dress* is my sister.
2. They left the house early *so they could get a good seat in the theater.*
3. John moved the dresser *next to the door.*
4. Everyone *who attended the meeting is a member.*
5. We all knew *that was the truth.*

Section 7: Subject-Verb Agreement

NO: The arrival of many friends promise good times.

Always remember to make the verb agree with the subject of the sentence. Be wary of the words that come between the subject and the verb. They may distract you.

YES: The *arrival* of many friends *promises* good times.

NO: Into the darkness stares her black cats.

Don't be fooled by sentences where the subject follows the verb. Be especially careful to determine the subject and make it agree with the verb.

YES: Into the darkness *stares* her black *cat.*

NO: Either the principal or the football coach usually attend the dance.

When singular subjects are joined by *either . . . or, neither . . . nor, or* or *nor,* the verb is also singular.

YES: Either the principal or the football *coach* usually *attends* the dance.

NO: Neither the *cat* nor the *dogs* is eating today.

If one of the subjects is plural and one is singular, make the verb agree with the subject nearest it.

YES: Neither the cat nor the *dogs are* eating today.

NO: Politics are a noun.

Remember that a word used as the title of a particular work, even if it is plural, requires a singular verb.

YES: Politics is a noun.

☞ Drill: Subject-Verb Agreement

DIRECTIONS: The following group of sentences may contain errors in subject-verb agreement. Make any necessary corrections.

1. Either her mother or her father usually drive her to school on rainy days.
2. There is, if I calculated right, two hundred dollars left in my bank account.
3. Mary, and her friends, was late for the test.
4. Economics are a major taught in many colleges.
5. The first years of high school is the most difficult.
6. Aristotle's *Poetics* have always been read widely.
7. The noise from all those fans were distracting.
8. Neither the chorus nor the actors knows their parts.
9. Each of us are going away for the weekend.
10. Neither the grass nor the flowers was growing well.

Section 8: Comparison of Adjectives

NO: That was the most bravest thing he ever did.

Do not combine two superlatives.

YES: That was the *bravest* thing he ever did.

NO: Mary was more friendlier than Susan.

Do not combine two comparatives.

YES: Mary was *friendlier* than Susan.

NO: I can buy either the shirt or the scarf. The shirt is most expensive.

The comparative should be used when only two things are being compared.

YES: I can buy either the shirt or the scarf. The shirt is *more* expensive.

☞ Drill: Comparison of Adjectives

DIRECTIONS: In the following sentences, make the changes indicated in the parentheses. Also indicate if the comparative or superlative form is an adverb or an adjective.

1. He was sad to leave. (superlative)
2. She ran as fast as the others on the team. (comparative)
3. Throughout school, they were good in math. (superlative)
4. This class is as interesting as the European history class. (comparative)
5. He arrived as soon as I did. (comparative)
6. The test was as hard as we expected. (superlative)
7. He responded to the interviewer as candidly as Tom. (comparative)
8. The beggar had less possessions than she. (superlative)
9. That answer is perfectly correct. (superlative)
10. She read the part best. (comparative)

Section 9: Pronouns

Pronouns are the simple, everyday words used to refer to people, places, or things that have already been mentioned, such as *him, she, me, it,* or to indefinite people, places, things, or qualities, such as *who, where, this,* or *somebody.* They usually replace some noun and make an expression concise. There are only about fifty pronouns in the English language and most are short words; however, they can be difficult to use correctly. One reason these words may be so difficult to use properly is their frequency of occurrence. Of the twenty-five most commonly used words in the English language, ten are pronouns.

Perhaps it is due to their frequent usage that pronouns have acquired a variety of distinctive functions. Although pronouns are dissimilar in the ways they may or may not be used, they have two things in common. The first is their ability to stand alone, or "stand in" for nouns. The second is that they all have little specific meaning. Whatever meaning they have derives from the context in which they are found. Some pronouns that modify other words are also adjectives. In this chapter, we will mainly speak of pronouns that stand alone — that take the place either of a definite noun or of an unknown or uncertain noun. When we use pronouns as adjectives in examples in this chapter, they are marked (a.).

Whom are *you* speaking to?

That is *my* (a.) hat *you* are holding in *your* (a.) hand.

Marsha *herself* (a.) told *them all* (a.) about *what* happened to *her when it* started to rain.

Somebody had to let the *others* know *that she* was not to blame.

Who, what, where, when, and *how* are the five words by *which you* can organize *this.*

This is a new kind of information for *me* and *I* regret to *some* (a.) degree *that I* can't be more in touch with *them.*

She doesn't agree with *me; that's* too bad, but *that's* the way *it* is.

I've had *enough*! If *no one* wants to take care of *it, I'll* do *it myself* (a.).

It is not *enough* to think of *me; you* should send *me* a letter *when you* do.

I wonder *what* is in *it.*

All the italicized words in the preceding sentences are pronouns. Traditionally, pronouns are divided into six groups; each group has its own name, definition, and special functions. These categories are helpful in learning how to recognize the different kinds of pronouns and how to use them correctly, since they come in such a wide variety of forms.

Personal Pronouns

Because of their many forms, this can be a troublesome group.

Case

NUMBER	PERSON	SUBJECT	OBJECT	POSSESSIVE	POSSESSIVE ADJECTIVE
Singular	1st person	*I*	*me*	*mine*	*my*
	2nd person	*you*	*you*	*yours*	*your*
	*3rd person				
	(masc.)	*he*	*him*	*his*	*his*
	(fem.)	*she*	*her*	*hers*	*her*
	(neuter)	*it*	*it*		*its*
Plural	1st	*we*	*us*	*ours*	*our*
	2nd	*you*	*you*	*yours*	*your*
	3rd	*they*	*them*	*theirs*	*their*
		_____*saw it.*	*Let*_____.	*That's*_____.	_____*house.*

*When a pronoun is used to refer to someone (other than the speaker or the person spoken to), the "third person" is used, and a different form of the pronoun is employed to show the gender of the person referred to. *His, her, him, his,* and *hers,* all indicate the masculine or feminine gender. *It* and *its* refer to something to which gender does not apply.

There are three forms of personal pronouns:

1. PERSON: to indicate whether the person is the speaker (1st person), the person being spoken to (2nd person), or the person being spoken about (3rd person).
2. CASE: to show the job the pronoun is performing in the sentence.
3. NUMBER: to indicate whether the word is plural or singular.

Examples of Personal Pronoun Use

I went yesterday to see *her.*

You have *my* (a.) hat, don't *you*?

Her car was formerly *theirs.*

Between *you* and *me,* I really don't want to go with *him.*

In *his* opinion, the boating dock is *ours,* not *yours.*

They say *you* can't take *it* with *you.*

Won't *you* walk down to *his* garden with *them*?

Errors to Avoid — Pronoun Case

When a compound subject or object includes a pronoun, be sure that the case chosen is in agreement with the pronoun's place in the sentence — a subject case pronoun is used as the subject of the verb, an object case pronoun is used as the object, etc. The same rule of agreement is true when using an appositive (a word or words with the same meaning as the pronoun); the pronoun must be in the same case form as the word it renames.

Compounds

Both Mary and *he* (NOT *him*) have seen that movie. (subject — "Mary and he")

Last year the team elected both Jane and *me* (NOT *I*). (object — "Jane and me")

Could you wait for my brother and *me* (NOT *I*)? (object of a preposition — "My brother and me")

A trip to Europe appealed to Susan and *him* (NOT *he*). (object of a preposition — "Susan and him")

There has always been a great friendship between you and *me* (NOT *I*). (object of a preposition — "You and me")

Mrs. Williams and *I* (NOT *me*) will direct the chorus. (subject — "Mrs. Williams and I")

Appositions

Words with the same meaning as the pronoun.

We Americans value freedom. (subject)

They invited *us* (NOT *we*) cheerleaders. (object)

Let's you and *me* (NOT *I*) go together. (object)

Both players, James and *he* (NOT *him*), could be stars. (subject)

Our school sent two delegates, Mark and *him* (NOT *he*). (object)

It is not for *we* writers to determine editorial policy. (subject)

Will you give your decision to *us* applicants soon? (object)

Relative Pronouns — Interior Sentences (Clauses)

Relative pronouns play the part of the subject or object in sentences within sentences (clauses). They often refer to nouns that have preceded them, making the sentence more compact.

NO: The flower — the flower was yellow — made her smile.

YES: The flower, *which* was yellow, made her smile.

NO: The girl — the girl lived down the block — loved him.

YES: The girl *who* lived down the block loved him.

Sometimes their reference is indefinite.

I wonder *what* happened. (The event that occurred is uncertain.)

I'll call *whomever* you want. (The people to be called are unknown.)

Who (for persons), *that* (for persons and things), and *which* (for things) are the most common pronouns of this type.

Who can cause problems because it changes form depending on the part it plays in the interior sentence (clause).

Subject	Object	Possessive
who	whom	whose

Mr. Jackson, *who* is my friend, called yesterday. (subject)

Mr. Jackson, *whom* I know well, called yesterday. (object)

Mr. Jackson, *whose* friendship is important to me, called yesterday. (possessive)

Interrogative Pronouns — Questions

These pronouns are easy to recognize because they always introduce either direct or indirect questions. The words just discussed as relative pronouns are called **interrogative pronouns** when they introduce a question: *who, what, that, which, whom, whose, whoever, whichever,* and *whatever.*

Who is at the door? (refers to a person)

What do you want from me? (refers to a thing)

Which (flavor) do you want? (refers to a thing)

Which (a.) boy won the match? (refers to a person)

Whatever you mean by "liberal education," I don't know.

Is *that* what you meant to say?

Whom did you telephone last night?

Sometimes an interrogative is not recognized when it is used indirectly inside another sentence.

She wondered *who* was at the door.

Samuel asked them *what* they wanted.

He didn't know if he would ever find out *what* happened.

I couldn't guess *which* they would choose.

Demonstrative Pronouns — Pointers

This, that, these, and *those* are the most common words used as pronouns to point to someone or something clearly expressed or implied.

That is the apple I wanted. (subject)

Bring me *those*, please. (object)

I must tell him *that.* (object)

These are the ones I've been looking for. (subject)

That really made me mad! (subject)

"*This* above all, to thine own self be true." (subject)

Give *this* to her for me. (object)

Such or *so* may also serve as pointing pronouns.

Such was his fate. (subject)

He resented Jerry and told him *so.* (object)

These same words are often used as adjectives, and at first glance it is easy to classify them only as adjectives, forgetting that they also take the place of nouns and serve as pronouns.

That apple is the one I want. (adjective describing "apple")

Bring me *those* books, please. (adjective describing "books")

I must tell him *that* story. (adjective describing "story")

It was *such* a tiring day. (adjective describing "day")

She was *so* happy. (adjective describing "happy")

Indefinite Pronouns

This group of pronouns acquired its name because the reference (the noun for which they are standing in) is indefinite.

Indefinite persons or things: (all singular pronouns)

everybody	everyone
somebody	someone
anybody	anyone
nobody	no one

Everybody joined in the chorus.

No one took less than he did.

Is *anyone* here?

I hope *someone* answers my calls.

Indefinite quantities:

each		either
another	all	some
several	both	few
least	less	little
lots	many	plenty
other	most	more

Much has been said on the subject of delinquency.

She took *several* for herself.

It is *less* than I'd bargained for.

Dallas or Houston — *either* would be fine for me.

There are *plenty* of people who want your job.

Many are called, but few are chosen.

The *most* we can expect is to see her next week.

Each must chart his own course.

The biggest problem encountered with these pronouns is in trying to decide if they are singular or plural. See "AGREEMENT" for a discussion of this problem.

Reflexive Pronouns

These are the pronouns that end in "*self*" or "*selves.*"

myself	yourself	yourselves
himself	herself	itself
ourselves	themselves	

Their main purpose is to reflect back on the subject of a sentence.

She cut *herself.* (object, refers to "she")

I bought *myself* a new dress. (object, refers to "I")

You are just not *yourself* today. (object, refers to "you")

They consider *themselves* lucky. (object, refers to "they")

Give *yourself* a treat; go to the ice cream shop. (object, refers to "you" understood)

After that dust storm I washed *myself* very well. (object, refers to "I")

They also provide emphasis. When they serve this purpose, they should appear at the end of the sentence.

We will triumph over this outrage *ourselves.*

I will go to the ticket office *myself.*

She will tell it to him *herself.*

You *yourself* must discover the meaning.

I suppose I will have to do it *myself.*

Errors to Avoid — Reflexive Pronouns

Do not use the reflexive in place of the shorter personal pronoun.

NO: Both Sandy and *myself* plan to go.

YES: Both Sandy and *I* plan to go.

NO: *Yourself* will take on the challenges of college.

YES: *You* will take on the challenges of college.

NO: Either James or *yourself* will paint the mural.

YES: Either James or *you* will paint the mural.

Watch out for careless use of the pronoun form.

NO: George *hisself* told me it was true.

YES: George *himself* told me it was true.

NO: They washed the car *theirselves.*

YES: They washed the car *themselves.*

Notice that the reflexive pronouns are not set off by commas.

NO: Mary, *herself,* gave him the diploma.

YES: Mary *herself* gave him the diploma.

NO: I will do it, *myself.*

YES: I will do it *myself.*

Case — The Function of the Pronoun in a Sentence

By far the pronouns with which we are apt to make the most mistakes are those that change their form when they play different parts in a sentence — the personal pronouns and the relative pronoun *who.* A careful study of the peculiarities of these changes is necessary to avoid the mistakes associated with their use.

Subject Case (used mainly when the pronoun is a subject)

Use the **subject case** (*I, we, you, he, she, it, they, who,* and *whoever*) for the following purposes:

1. *As a subject or a repeated subject:*

NO: Mrs. Jones and *me* left early yesterday.

YES: Mrs. Jones and *I* left early yesterday.

NO: I know *whom* that is.

YES: I know *who* that is. (subject of "is")

NO: *Us* girls always go out together.

YES: *We* girls always go out together. ("girls" is the subject; "we" repeats it)

Watch out for a parenthetical expression (an expression that is not central to the meaning of the sentence). It looks like a subject and verb when actually it is the pronoun that is the subject.

NO: Larry is the one *whom* we know will do the best job.

YES: Larry is the one *who* we know will do the best job. (Do not be misled by "we know"; *who* is the subject of the verb "will do.")

NO: It was Jim and Gretchen *whom* I think were there.

YES: It was Jim and Gretchen *who* I think were there. (Disregard "I think;" *who* is the subject of *were.*)

2. *Following the verb "to be" when it has a subject:*

This is a part of the language that appears to be changing. It is a good example of how the grammar of a language follows speech and not the other way around. The traditional guideline has been that a pronoun following a form of "be" must be in the same case as the word before the verb.

It is *I.* ("It" is the subject.)

I thought it was *she.* ("it" is the subject.)

Was it *they* who arrived late? ("it" is the subject.)

Our ear tells us that in informal conversation "It is I" would sound too formal, so instead we tend to say:

It is *me.* (in conversation)

I thought it was *her.* (in conversation)

Was it *them* who arrived late? (in conversation)

In written English, however, it is best to follow the standard of using the subject case after the verb "be" when "be" is preceded by a word in the subject case, even though the pronoun is in the position of an object.

Some more examples that might cause trouble:

NO: Last week, the best students were *you* and *me.*

YES: Last week, the best *students* were *you* and *I.* (refers to "students," subject of "were")

NO: Whenever I hear that knock, I know it must be *him.*

YES: Whenever I hear that knock, I know it must be *he.* (refers to "it," subject of "must be")

NO: The *leaders* of the parade were John, Susan, and *me.*

YES: The leaders of the parade were John, Susan, and *I.* (refers to "leaders," subject of "were")

NO: I am expecting my mother to call. Is that *her?*

YES: I am expecting my *mother* to call. Is that *she?* (refers to "mother," subject of "to call")

3. *As a subject when the verb is omitted* (often after *than* or *as*):

I have known her longer than *he.* ("has known her" is understood)

She sings as well as *I.* ("sing" is understood)

We do just as well in algebra as *they.* ("do" is understood)

He is much better than *I* at such calculations. ("than I am at such calculations" — "am" is understood)

To test whether the subject or the object form is correct, complete the phrase in your mind and it will be obvious.

Object Case (used mainly when the pronoun is an object)

Use the **object case** (*me, us, him, her, it, you, them, whom, whomever*) as follows:

1. *As the direct or indirect object, object of a preposition, or repeated object:*

   The postman gave *me* the letter. (indirect object)

   Mr. Boone appointed *him* and *me* to clean the room. ("him and me" is the object of "appointed")

   They told *us* managers to rewrite the first report. ("managers" is the indirect object of "told"; "us" repeats)

   My attorney gave *me* a letter giving *her* power of attorney. ("me" is the indirect object of "gave"; "her" is the indirect object of "giving")

   That package is from *me.* (object of "from")

   Between *you* and *me,* I'm voting Republican. (object of "between")

   Whom were you thinking about? (object of "about")

   I know *whom* you asked. (object of "asked")

   My teacher gave both of *us,* June and *me,* an 'A.' ("us" is the object of "of"; "June and me" repeats the object)

2. *As the subject of an infinitive verb:*

   I wanted *her* to come.

   Janet invited *him and me* to attend the conference.

   He asked *her* to duplicate the report for the class.

   Whom will we ask to lead the group? ("Whom" is the subject of "to lead")

3. *As an object when the verb or preposition is omitted:*

   Father told my sister June more about it than (he told) *me.*

   The telephone calls were more often for Marilyn than (they were for) *him.*

   Did they send them as much candy as (they sent) *us?*

   He always gave Susan more than (he gave) *me.*

4. *Following "to be":*

In point number 2, we learned that the subject of an infinitive verb form must be in the object case. The infinitive "to be" is an exception to this rule. Forms of "to be" must have the same case before and after the verb. If the word preceding the verb is in the subject case, the pronoun following must be in the subject case also. (For example, *It* is *I.*) If the word before the verb is an object, the pronoun following must be objective as well.

We thought the *author* of the note to be *her.*

You expected the *winner* to be *me.*

Mother did not guess *it* to be Julie and *me* at the door.

Had you assumed the *experts* to be *us*?

5. *Subject of a progressive verb form that functions as an adjective (participle — "ing" ending):*

Two kinds of words commonly end in "ing": a **participle**, or a word that looks like a verb but acts like an adjective, and a **gerund**, a word that looks like a verb but acts like a noun. When an "ing" word acts like an adjective, its subject is in the object case.

For example:

Can you imagine *him acting* that way? ("acting" refers to the pronoun and is therefore a participle which takes a subject in the object case, "him")

They watched *me smiling* at all the visitors. ("smiling" refers to the pronoun, which must be objective, "me")

Compare:

Can you imagine *his acting* in that part? (Here the emphasis is on "acting"; "his" refers to "acting" which is functioning as a noun (it is a **gerund**) and takes the possessive case.)

It was *my smiling* that won the contest. (Emphasis is on "smiling" — it is playing the part of a noun and so takes a possessive case pronoun, "my.")

Possessive Case

Use the **possessive adjective** case (*my, our, your, her, his, its, their, whose*) in the following situations:

1. *To indicate possession,* classification of something, or connection. Possession is the most common.

I borrowed *her* car. (The car belongs to her.)

Come over to *our* house. (The house belongs to us.)

That is Jane's and *my* report. (The report belongs to us.)

It is *anyone's* guess.

Whose coat is this?

The plant needs water; *its* leaves are fading.

2. *Preceding a verb acting as a noun (gerund):*

Our leaving early helped end the party.

Whose testifying will you believe?

His reading was excessive.

Don't you think *her* playing astounded them?

Since there are no possessive forms for the demonstrative pronouns *that, this, these,* and *those,* they do not change form before a gerund.

NO: What are the chances of *that's* being painted today?

YES: What are the chances of *that* being painted today?

Use the **possessive case** (*mine, ours, yours, hers, his, its, theirs, whose*) in the following situations:

In any role a noun might play — a subject, object, or complement with a possessive meaning.

Hers was an exciting career. ("Hers" is the subject of "was")

Can you tell me *whose* this is? ("whose" is the complement of "is")

He is a friend of *mine.* ("mine" is the object of the preposition "of")

We borrowed *theirs* last week; it is only right that they should use *ours* this week. ("theirs" is the object of the verb "borrowed"; "ours" is the object of the verb "use")

I thought that was Mary's and *his.* ("Mary's and his" is the complement of the verb "was")

It and There — Expletives

Dictionaries will tell you that *it* and *there* are pronouns, but they are somewhat different from pronouns. They have even less meaning than the sometimes vague or indefinite pronouns. Because they provide so little information, their sole function is to fill space, to provide a formal subject for a sentence.

It — Impersonal

It's cold outside. (what is "it"?)

It's March 3.

What is this? *It's* my comb.

It's ten after three.

It's a twenty-minute walk to the grocery store.

It seems warmer than yesterday.

I know *it* gets crowded here at noon.

It — Anticipatory

Sometimes *it* fills the subject position while the actual subject appears later in the sentence. The italicized sections of the following sentences are the actual subjects.

It's surprising *how handsome he is.*

It's interesting *to know your background.*

It's curious *that Mary paints so well.*

It's hard *to keep reading this.*

It's pleasant *to study words.*

It's good *knowing you are waiting for me.*

Notice how *there* has no meaning but only fills the space of the subject.

There are three of us watching you.

There is lightning outside.

There are many ways to peel an onion.

There are only a few teachers who teach well.

There's a sale at Gimbel's.

There shall come a time when all this will end.

There is also often used as an adverb. If *there* is an expletive (space-filler), it is likely to be accompanied by "a." If it is accompanied by "the," it is probably an adverb and not a space-filler.

There's a place I'd like to visit. (space-filler)

There's the place I'd like to visit. (adverb referring to "is")

There's a girl in the corner. (space-filler)

There's the girl in the corner. (adverb referring to "is")

Agreement Between the Pronoun and the Word(s) It Refers To

A pronoun usually takes the place of some noun. The noun (or group of words that works as a noun) for which the pronoun stands in is called the **antecedent**. It usually comes before the pronoun in the sentence or the paragraph. It is important to remember that the pronoun and the word(s) it refers to have to "agree." If the antecedent is plural, the pronoun should be plural; if the antecedent is singular, the pronoun must also be. The gender and person must also be consistent.

I heard *one dog* barking *his* loudest.

I heard *three dogs* barking *their* loudest.

The *woman* raised *her* hand.

The *children* raised *their* hands.

The *man* read *his* newspaper.

☞ Drill: Pronouns

A. Relative Pronouns

DIRECTIONS: Complete the following sentences with a relative pronoun.

1. The man, ______ is standing in line, is a famous author.
2. She looks sad. I wonder ______ news she received.
3. The house, ______ was white, has been abandoned.
4. ______ one you chose will satisfy me.
5. I'll sing ______ you want.
6. The dress, ______ I borrowed from Mary, was lost in the cleaners.
7. The only seat ______ is available is the corner one.

B. Relative Pronouns

DIRECTIONS: "Who and Whom." In the following sentences choose the correct form of the pronoun given in the parentheses.

1. It's Susan from (who, whom) I received the assignment.
2. I must see the teacher (who, whom) I spoke with last week.
3. She is a girl (who, whom) I know very well.
4. I can't remember (who, whom) I met yesterday.
5. If you know (who, whom) sent the letter, please give me a name and an address.
6. This book will go to (whoever, whomever) lost it.
7. John (who, whom) played the lead in the play, was a great success.

8. When they know (who, whom) won the election, let me know.

9. The club is entitled to choose (whoever, whomever) they want for president.

10. Was it he (who, whom) won the race?

C. Interrogative and Demonstrative Pronouns

DIRECTIONS: Write five sentences using different interrogative pronouns. Then do the same exercise for demonstrative pronouns. In some of your sentences try using the pronouns in their less common role. Use them indirectly inside a sentence (interrogative pronoun) and as adjectives (demonstrative pronoun).

D. Reflexive Pronouns

DIRECTIONS: Complete the following sentences with the appropriate reflexive pronoun. Also note which pronoun the "reflector" is an object of.

1. We found ______ out of money.

2. I ______ will complete the project.

3. Give ______ the time needed.

4. The play, by ______, was quite good.

5. They will give it to him ______.

E. Reflexive Pronouns

DIRECTIONS: In the following sentences make the necessary corrections.

1. Both James and themselves went to the beach.

2. Jack, himself, read the speech.

3. Myself will unload the car.

4. They finished the painting theirselves.

5. He mowed the lawn, hisself.

F. Personal Pronouns

DIRECTIONS: In the following sentences choose the correct form of the pronoun given in the parentheses.

1. Both Peter and (I, me) went to the movies.
2. They missed the train because of (he, him).
3. (We, Us) soldiers must be ready for combat at all times.
4. You and (I, me) have always understood each other.
5. I don't know if it was (she, her) who was in the theater yesterday.
6. Susan and (he, him) have met before.
7. Neither Jack nor (they, them) will be going on vacation this summer.
8. We sing just as well as (they, them).
9. Do (we, us) officers have to attend the convention?
10. I am older than (she, her).
11. Mr. Grey and (I, me) will paint the scenery for the play.
12. Paul questioned (she, her) and (I, me) about the accident.
13. Both students, Mark and (he, him) were suspended from school.
14. They told (us, we) to clean the house.
15. Was it (they, them) who stopped by yesterday afternoon?
16. Sometimes (we, us) voters feel powerless.
17. I believed the winner of the contest to be (he, him).
18. Boys like (they, them) could never make the football team.
19. Can you believe (I, me) doing that well?
20. Give (we, us) beginners a chance!

21. You expected the performer to be (he, him).

22. Did you receive as much as (me, I)?

23. It appears that Joan and (they, them) have left the club.

24. They selected (we, us) musicians.

25. They asked (he, him) to drive.

26. Joe and (I, me) attend every school concert.

27. I can't believe you selected Sylvia and (she, her).

28. Neither you nor (I, me) can wait till spring arrives.

G. Possessive Pronouns

DIRECTIONS: Complete the following sentences with an appropriate possessive pronoun.

1. ______ car is this?

2. That is ______ dress in the closet.

3. What are the chances of ______ being finished tomorrow?

4. ______ intelligence was staggering.

5. They are relatives of ______.

6. ______ was a beautiful house.

7. We didn't know that was James' and ______.

H. Expletives

DIRECTIONS: Complete the following sentences with the correct expletive.

1. ______ the first day of March.

2. ______ are only a few chances left.

3. ______time to finish the game.

4. ______ looks like rain.

5. ______ interesting to read history.

I. Pronouns

DIRECTIONS: Complete the following sentences with an appropriate pronoun.

1. The girl picked up ______ books

2. The detectives finished ______ case.

3. I saw a beaver building ______ nest.

4. The villagers had ______ meetings on Wednesdays.

5. John left ______ key at home.

Section 10: Conjunctions

NO: She loved him dearly but not his dog.

When using a conjunction, be sure that the sentence parts you are joining are in agreement.

YES: *She loved him dearly* but *she did not love his dog.*

NO: They complimented them both for their bravery and they thanked them for their kindness.

When using conjunctions, a common mistake that is made is to forget that each member of the pair must be followed by the same kind of construction.

YES: They both *complimented them for their bravery* and *thanked them for their kindness.*

NO: While I'm usually interested in Fellini movies, I'd rather not go tonight.

While refers to time and should not be used as a substitute for *although, and,* or *but.*

YES: *Although* I'm usually interested in Fellini movies, I'd rather not go tonight.

NO: We read in the paper where they are making great strides in DNA research.

Where refers to a place or location. Be careful not to use it when it does not have this meaning.

YES: We read in the paper *that* they are making great strides in DNA research.

☞ Drill: Conjunctions

DIRECTIONS: The following group of sentences may contain errors in the use of conjunctions. Make any necessary corrections.

1. John's best assets are his personality and swimming ability.
2. I heard on the radio where the play is closing this week.
3. I was reading the paper and the phone rang.
4. Susan ate vegetables often but not fruits.
5. Please send me an answer to the question or opinions on the project.
6. While I'm tired from the trip, I'll attend the concert tonight.
7. Mary's goal is to study hard and pass the test.
8. He produced the play while she directed it.
9. A good essay is where the ideas are clearly articulated.
10. The class wanted neither to read the book nor do the assignment.

Section 11: The Comma

Of all the marks of punctuation, the comma (,) has the most uses. Before you tackle the main principles that guide its usage, be sure that you have an elementary understanding of sentence structure. There are actually only a few rules and conventions to follow when using commas; the rest is common sense. The worst abuse of commas comes from those who overuse them, who place them illogically. If you are ever in doubt as to whether or not to use a comma, do not use it.

In a Series

When more than one adjective (an adjective series) describes a noun, use a comma to separate and emphasize each adjective.

the long, dark passageway

another confusing, sleepless night

an elaborate, complex plan

the beautiful, starry night

the haunting, melodic sound

the old, grey, crumpled hat

In these instances, the comma takes the place of "and." To test if the comma is needed, try inserting "and" between the adjectives in question. If it is logical, you should use a comma. The following are examples of adjectives that describe an adjective-noun combination that has come to be thought of almost as one word. In such cases the adjective in front of the adjective-noun combination needs no comma.

a stately oak tree

an exceptional wine glass

a successful garage sale

my worst report card

a borrowed record player

a porcelain dinner plate

If you insert "and" between the adjectives in the above examples, it will not make sense.

The comma is also used to separate words, phrases, and whole ideas (clauses); it still takes the place of "and" when used this way.

an apple, a pear, a fig, and a banana

a lovely lady, an indecent dress, and many admirers

She lowered the shade, closed the curtain, turned off the light, and went to bed.

John, Frank, and my Uncle Harry all thought it was a questionable theory.

The only question that exists about the use of commas in a series is whether or not one should be used before the final item. Usually "and" or "or" precedes the final item, and many writers do not include the comma before the final "and" or "or." When first learning, however, it is advisable to use the comma because often its omission can be confusing; in such cases as these, for instance:

NO: Would you like to shop at Sak's, Lord and Taylor's and Gimbels?

NO: He got on his horse, tracked a rabbit and a deer and rode on to Canton.

NO: We planned the trip with Mary and Harold, Susan, Dick and Joan, Gregory and Jean and Charles. (Is it Gregory and Jean, or Jean and Charles, or Gregory and Jean and Charles?)

With a Long Introductory Phrase

Usually if a phrase of more than five or six words precedes the subject at the beginning of a sentence, a comma is used to set it off.

> After last night's fiasco at the disco, she couldn't bear the thought of looking at him again.
>
> Whenever I try to talk about politics, my husband leaves the room.
>
> When it comes to actual facts, every generation makes the same mistakes as the preceding one.
>
> Provided you have said nothing, they will never guess who you are.

It is not necessary to use a comma with a short sentence.

> In January she will go to Switzerland.
>
> After I rest I'll feel better.
>
> At Grandma's we had a big dinner.
>
> During the day no one is home.

If an introductory phrase includes a verb form that is being used as another part of speech (a "verbal"), it must be followed by a comma. Try to make sense of the following sentences without commas.

NO: When eating Mary never looked up from her plate.

YES: When eating, Mary never looked up from her plate.

NO: Because of her desire to follow her faith in James wavered.

YES: Because of her desire to follow, her faith in James wavered.

NO: Having decided to leave Mary James wrote her a letter.

YES: Having decided to leave Mary, James wrote her a letter.

Above all, common sense is the best guideline when trying to decide whether or not to use a comma after an introductory phrase. Does the comma make the meaning more clear? If it does, use it; if not, there is no reason to insert it.

To Separate Sentences with Two Main Ideas (Compound Sentences)

To understand this use of the comma, you need to have studied sentence structure and be able to recognize compound sentences.

When a sentence contains more than two subjects and verbs (clauses), and the two clauses are joined by a connecting word (*and, but, or, yet, for, nor*), use a comma before the connecting word to show that another clause is coming.

> I thought I knew the poem by heart, but he showed me three lines I had forgotten.

Are we really interested in helping the children, or are we more concerned with protecting our good names?

He is supposed to leave tomorrow, but who knows if he will be ready to go.

Jim knows you are disappointed, and he has known it for a long time.

If the two parts of the sentence are short and closely related, it is not necessary to use a comma.

He threw the ball and the dog ran after it.

Jane played the piano and Charles danced.

Errors to Avoid

Be careful not to confuse a sentence that has a compound verb and a single subject with a compound sentence. If the subject is the same for both verbs, there is no need for a comma.

NO: Charles sent some flowers, and wrote a long letter explaining why he had not been able to come.

NO: Last Thursday we went to the concert with Julia, and afterwards dined at an old Italian restaurant.

NO: For the third time, the teacher explained that the literacy level of high school students was much lower than it had been in previous years, and, this time, wrote the statistics on the board for everyone to see.

To Set Off Interrupting Material

There are so many different kinds of interruptions that can occur in a sentence that a list of them all would be quite lengthy. In general, words and phrases that stop the flow of the sentence or are unnecessary for the main idea are set off by commas. Some examples are:

Abbreviations after names

Did you invite John Paul, Jr., and his sister?

Martha Harris, Ph.D., will be the speaker tonight.

Interjections: An exclamation added without grammatical connection

Oh, I'm so glad to see you.

I tried so hard, alas, to do it.

Hey, let me out of here.

No, I will not let you out.

Direct address

Roy, won't you open the door for the dog?

I can't understand, mother, what you are trying to say.

May I ask, Mr. President, why you called us together?

Hey, lady, watch out for the car!

Tag questions: A question that repeats the helping verb in a negative phrase

I'm really hungry, aren't you?

Jerry looks like his father, doesn't he?

You'll come early, won't you?

We are expected at nine, aren't we?

Mr. Jones can chair the meeting, can't he?

Geographical names and addresses

The concert will be held in Chicago, Illinois, on August 12.

They visited Tours, France, last summer.

The letter was addressed to Ms. Marion Heartwell, 1881 Pine Lane, Palo Alto, California 95824. (No comma is needed before the zip code because it is already clearly set off from the state name.)

Transitional words and phrases

On the other hand, I hope he gets better.

In addition, the phone rang six times this afternoon.

I'm, nevertheless, going to the beach on Sunday.

You'll find, therefore, no one is more loyal to me than you.

To tell the truth, I don't know what to believe.

Parenthetical words and phrases

You will become, I believe, a great statesman.

We know, of course, that this is the only thing to do.

In fact, I planted corn last summer.

The Mannes affair was, to put it mildly, a surprise.

Bathing suits, generally speaking, are getting smaller.

Unusual word order

The dress, new and crisp, hung in the closet. (Normal word order: The new, crisp dress hung in the closet.)

Intently, she stared out the window. (Normal word order: She stared intently out the window.)

Nonrestrictive Elements (Not Essential to the Meaning)

Parts of a sentence that modify other parts are sometimes essential to the meaning of the sentence and sometimes not. When a modifying word or group of words is not vital to the meaning of the sentence, it is set off by commas. Since it does not restrict the meaning of the words it modifies, it is called "nonrestrictive." Modifiers that are essential to the meaning of the sentence are called "restrictive" and are not set off by commas. *Compare the following pairs of sentences:*

The girl *who wrote the story* is my sister. (essential)

My sister, *the girl who wrote the story*, has always been drawn to adventure. (nonessential)

John Milton's famous poem "*Paradise Lost*" tells a remarkable story. (essential — Milton has written other poems)

Dante's great work, "*The Divine Comedy,*" marked the beginning of the Renaissance and the end of the Dark Ages. (nonessential — Dante wrote only one great work)

The cup *that is on the piano* is the one I want. (essential)

The cup, *which my brother gave me last year,* is on the piano. (nonessential)

My parakeet *Simian* has an extensive vocabulary. (essential — because there are no commas, the writer must have more than one parakeet)

My parakeet, *Simian,* has an extensive vocabulary. (nonessential — the writer must have only one parakeet whose name is Simian)

The people *who arrived late* were not seated. (essential)

George, *who arrived late,* was not seated. (nonessential)

She always listened to her sister *Jean.* (essential — she must have more than one sister)

She always listened to her husband, *Jack.* (nonessential — obviously, she has only one husband)

To Set Off Direct Quotations

Most direct quotes or quoted materials are set off from the rest of the sentence by commas.

"Please read your part more loudly," the director insisted.

"I won't know what to do," said Michael, "if you leave me now."

The teacher said sternly, "I will not dismiss this class until I have silence."

Mark looked up from his work, smiled, and said, "We'll be with you in a moment."

Be careful not to set off indirect quotations or quotes that are used as subjects or complements.

"To be or not to be" is the famous beginning of a soliloquy in Shakespeare's *Hamlet.* (subject)

Back then my favorite song was "*A Summer Place.*" (complement)

She said she would never come back. (indirect quote)

"Place two tablespoons of chocolate in this pan" were her first words to her apprentice in the kitchen. (subject)

To Set Off Contrasting Elements

Her intelligence, *not her beauty*, got her the job.

Your plan will take you further from, *rather than closer to*, your destination.

It was a reasonable, *though not appealing*, idea.

He wanted glory, *but found happiness instead.*

James wanted an active, *not a passive*, partner.

In Dates

Both forms of the date are acceptable.

She will arrive on April 6, 1981.

He left on 5 December 1980.

In January, 1967, he handed in his resignation.

In January 1967 he handed in his resignation.

☞ Drill: The Comma

DIRECTIONS: In the following sentences insert commas wherever necessary. You may also want to note the reason for your choice.

1. However I am willing to reconsider.

2. She descended the long winding staircase.

3. Whenever I practice the violin my family closes the windows.

4. While driving Francis never took his eyes off the road.

5. The car which I bought last year is in the garage.

6. "Answer the door" said his mother loudly.

7. Miss can I ask you for the time?

8. He was after all an ex-convict.

9. I'm so bored aren't you?

10. The old tall shady tree is wonderful during the summer.

11. George Gary and Bill were on line early this morning. They bought their tickets read the newspaper and spoke for a while.

12. The author James Grey was awarded the prize.

13. She attended school in London England last year.

14. They said they would do the job.

15. His weight not his height prevented him from competing in the race.

16. The family who won the lottery lives in New Jersey.

17. She got in the car turned on the ignition and left the curb.

18. Incidentally he called last night.

19. The kitten small and cute was adopted by the Brown family.

20. Mary did you see James Jr. at the party last night?

21. Lisa saw the mailman and gave him the letter.

22. Last night I finished my essay and started on my next assignment.

23. Really I can't believe that is the truth.

24. We thought it was time to leave but we arrived early.

25. Monday she will leave for Boston.

26. After he got home he read a magazine ate dinner and left for the movies.

27. If you pass the test you will graduate.

28. When she decided to leave everyone was disappointed.

29. Hey John it's time to go.

30. He seemed wrong for the part yet he turned out to be the best actor in the production.

Section 12: The Colon and Semicolon

The Colon

The colon (:) is the sign of a pause about midway in length between the semicolon and the period. It can often be replaced by a comma and sometimes by a period. Although used less frequently now than it was 50 to 75 years ago, the colon is still convenient to use, for it signals to the reader that more information is to come on the subject of concern. The colon can also create a slight dramatic tension.

It is used to introduce a word, phrase, or complete statement (clause) that emphasizes, illustrates, or exemplifies what has already been stated.

> He had only one desire in life: to play baseball.
>
> The weather that day was the most unusual I'd ever seen: It snowed and rained while the sun was still shining.
>
> In his speech, the president surprised us by his final point: The conventional grading system would be replaced next year.
>
> Jean thought of only two things the last half hour of the hike home: a bath and a bed.

Notice that the word following the colon can start with either a capital or a small letter. Use a capital letter if the word following the colon begins another complete sentence. But when the words following the colon are part of the sentence preceding the colon, use a small letter.

> May I offer you a suggestion: Don't drive without your seatbelts fastened.
>
> The thought continued to perplex him: Where will I go next?

When introducing a series that illustrates or emphasizes what has already been stated, use the colon.

> Only a few of the graduates were able to be there: Jamison, Mearns, Linkley, and Commoner.
>
> For Omar Khayyam, a Persian poet, three things are necessary for a paradise on earth: a loaf of bread, a jug of wine, and his beloved.

> In the basement, he kept some equipment for his experiments: the test tubes, some chemical agents, three sunlamps, and the drill.

Long quotes set off from the rest of the text by indentation rather than quotation marks are generally introduced with a colon.

> The first line of Lincoln's Gettysburg address is familiar to most Americans:
>
> > Fourscore and seven years ago our fathers brought forth on this continent a new nation, conceived in liberty and dedicated to the proposition that all men are created equal.
>
> I quote from Shakespeare's *Sonnets*:
>
> > When I do count the clock that tells the time,
> > And see the brave day sunk in hideous night;
> > When I behold the violet past prime,
> > And sable curls all silver'd o'er with white . . .

It is also customary to begin a business letter with a colon.

> Dear Senator Jordan:
>
> To Whom It May Concern:
>
> Gentlemen:
>
> Dear Sir or Madam:

But in informal letters, use a comma.

> Dear Mary,
>
> Dear Father,

The colon is also used in introducing a list.

> Please send the following:
>
> 1. 50 index cards,
> 2. 4 typewriter ribbons, and
> 3. 8 erasers.
>
> Prepare the recipe as follows:
>
> 1. Slice the oranges thinly.
> 2. Arrange them in a circle around the strawberries.
> 3. Pour the liqueur over both fruits.
>
> At least three ladies will have to be there to help:
>
> 1. Mrs. Goldman, who will greet the guests;
> 2. Harriet Sacher, who will serve the lunch; and
> 3. my sister, who will do whatever else needs to be done.

Finally, the colon is used between numbers when writing the time, between the volume and number or volume and page number of a journal, and also between the chapter and verse in the Bible.

4:30 P.M.

The Nation, 34:8

Genesis 5:18

The Semicolon

Semicolons (;) are sometimes called mild periods. They indicate a pause midway in length between the comma and the colon. Writing that contains many semicolons is usually in a dignified, formal style. To use them correctly, it is necessary to be able to recognize main clauses — complete ideas. When two main clauses occur in a single sentence without a connecting word (*and, but, or, nor, for*), the appropriate mark of punctuation is the semicolon.

It is not a good idea for you to leave the country right now; you should actually try to stay as long as you possibly can.

Music lightens life; literature deepens it.

In the past, boy babies were often dressed in blue; girls in pink. ("were often dressed" is understood in the second part of the sentence.)

Can't you see it's no good to go on alone; we'll starve to death if we keep traveling this way much longer.

Burgundy and maroon are very similar colors; scarlet is altogether different.

Notice how the use of the comma, period, and semicolon each gives a sentence a slightly different meaning.

Music lightens life; literature deepens it.

Just as music lightens life, literature deepens it.

Music lightens life. Literature deepens it.

The semicolon lends a certain balance to writing that would otherwise be difficult to achieve. Nonetheless, you should be careful not to overuse it. A comma can just as well join parts of a sentence with two main ideas; the semicolon is particularly appropriate if there is a striking contrast in the two ideas expressed.

Ask not what your country can do for you; ask what you can do for your country.

It started out as an ordinary day; it ended being the most extraordinary of her life.

Our power to apprehend truth is limited; to seek it, limitless.

If any one of the following words or phrases are used to join together compound sentences, they are generally preceded by a semicolon:

then	however	thus	furthermore
hence	indeed	so	consequently
also	that is	yet	nevertheless
anyhow	in addition	in fact	on the other hand
likewise	moreover	still	meanwhile
instead	besides	otherwise	in other words
henceforth	for example	therefore	at the same time
even now			

For a long time, people thought that women were inferior to men; *even now* it is not an easy attitude to overcome.

Being clever and cynical, he succeeded in becoming president of the company; *meanwhile* his wife left him.

Cigarette smoking has never interested me; *furthermore,* I couldn't care less if anyone else smokes or not.

Some say Bach was the greatest composer of all time; *yet* he still managed to have an ordinary life in other ways: he and his wife had 20 children.

We left wishing we could have stayed much longer; *in other words,* they showed us a good time.

When a series of complicated items are listed, or if there is internal punctuation in a series, the semicolon is sometimes used to make the meaning more clear.

You can use your new car for many things: to drive to town or to the country; to impress your friends and neighbors; to protect yourself from rain on a trip away from home; and to borrow against should you need money right away.

The scores from yesterday's games came in late last night: Pirates-6, Zoomers-3; Caterpillars-12, Steelys-8; Crashers-9, Links-8; and Greens-15, Uptowns-4.

In October a bag of potatoes cost 69¢; in December 99¢; in February $1.09; in April $1.39. I wonder if this inflation will ever stop.

The semicolon is placed outside quotation marks or parentheses, unless it is part of the material enclosed in those marks.

I used to call him "my lord and master"; it made him laugh every time.

The weather was cold for that time of year (I was shivering wherever I went); nevertheless, we set out to hike to the top of that mountain.

☞ Drill: The Colon and Semicolon

DIRECTIONS: Correctly place the colon and the semicolon in the following sentences.

1. I have only one thing to say don't do it.

2. They seemed compatible yet they did not get along.

3. She had only one goal in life to be a famous pianist.

4. He thought the problem was solved instead his solution proved to be entirely wrong.

5. By the end of the day there were only two things on her mind rest and relaxation.

6. Only a few members were able to attend the convention Henry, Karen, David, Mark, and Susan.

7. They were willing to accept the proposal he was not.

8. The art students were expected to supply the following brushes, paints, pallets, and pads.

9. The time is now the time is right.

10. The highest scores on the final exam are as follows Linda Jones 96 John Smith 94 Susan Green 90. These grades are unusually high they must have studied well.

Section 13: Quotation Marks

The proper use of quotation marks must be studied and learned, since some of their uses appear arbitrary and outside common sense.

The most common use of double quotation marks (" ") is to set off quoted words, phrases, and sentences.

> "If everybody minded their own business," said the Duchess in a hoarse growl, "the world would go round a great deal faster than it does."
>
> "Then you would say what you mean," the March Hare went on.
>
> "I do," Alice hastily replied: "at least — at least I mean what I say — that's the same thing, you know."

"Not the same thing a bit!" said the Hatter. "Why, you might just as well say that 'I see what I eat' is the same thing as 'I eat what I see'!"

Both quotes from Lewis Carroll's *Alice in Wonderland*

In the last quote, single quotation marks are used to set off quoted material within a quote. Other examples of correct use of single quotation marks are:

"Shall I bring 'Rime of the Ancient Mariner' along with us?" she asked her brother.

Mrs. Green said, "The doctor told me, 'Go immediately to bed when you get home.'"

"If she said that to me," Katherine insisted, "I would tell her, 'I never intend to speak to you again! Goodbye, Susan.'"

Writing a Dialogue

When writing a dialogue, begin a new paragraph each time the speaker changes.

"Do you know what time it is?" asked Jane. "I don't want to be late for my class."

"Can't you see I'm busy?" snapped Mary. "Go into the kitchen if you want the time."

"It's easy to see you're in a bad mood today," replied Jane.

Use quotation marks to enclose words used as words (sometimes italics are used for this purpose).

"Judgment" had always been a difficult word for me to spell.

Do you know what "abstruse" means?

I always thought "nice" meant "particular" or "having exacting standards," but I know now it has acquired a much more general and vague meaning.

"Horse and buggy" and "bread and butter" can be used as either adjectives or nouns.

If slang is used within more formal writing, the slang words or phrases should be set off with quotation marks.

The "old boy" system is responsible for most promotions in today's corporate world.

I thought she was a "knockout," which made it difficult to relate to her as the supervisor.

Harrison's decision to leave the conference and to "stick his neck out" by flying to Jamaica was applauded by the rest of the participants.

When words are meant to have an unusual or special significance to the reader, for instance irony or humor, they are sometimes placed in quotation marks. This is, however, a practice to be avoided whenever possible. The reader should be able to get the intended meaning from the context.

For years, women were not allowed to buy real estate in order to "protect" them from unscrupulous dealers. (The writer is using somebody else's word; the use of the quotation marks shows he or she does not believe women needed protection.)

The "conversation" resulted in one black eye and a broken arm.

Our orders were always given as "suggestions."

To set off titles of radio and TV shows, poems, stories, and chapters in a book use quotation marks. (Book, motion picture, newspaper, and magazine titles are underlined when written and italicized in text.)

The article "Moving South in the Southern Rain," by Jergen Smith in the *Southern News*, attracted the attention of our editor.

The assignment was "Childhood Development," chapter 18 of *Human Behavior.*

My favorite essay by Montaigne is "*On Silence.*"

"I'm Gonna Wash that Man Right Out of My Hair" was the big hit song from *South Pacific.*

Whitman's "Song of the Open Road" may be the most famous poem from his *Leaves of Grass.*

"Happy Days" led the TV ratings for years, didn't it?

Jackson Miller's "What's Your Opinion?" on WNYB stirs plenty of controversy every Thursday night.

"Jesu Joy of Man's Desiring" by J.S. Bach leaves you optimistic and glad to be alive.

I saw it in the "Guide" in the Sunday *Times.*

You will find Keats' "Ode to a Grecian Urn" in chapter 3, "The Romantic Era," in Lastly's *Selections from Great English Poets.*

Errors to Avoid

Be sure to remember that quotation marks always come in pairs. Do not make the mistake of using only one set.

NO: "You'll never convince me to move to the city, said Thurman. I consider it an insane asylum."

YES: "You'll never convince me to move to the city," said Thurman. "I consider it an insane asylum."

NO: "Idleness and pride tax with a heavier hand than kings and parliaments," Benjamin Franklin is supposed to have said. If we can get rid of the former, we may easily bear the latter."

YES: "Idleness and pride tax with a heavier hand than kings and parliaments," Benjamin Franklin is supposed to have said. "If we can get rid of the former, we may easily bear the latter."

When a quote consists of several sentences, do not put the quotation marks at the beginning and the end of each sentence; put them at the beginning and end of the entire quotation.

NO: "It was during his student days in Bonn that Beethoven fastened upon Schiller's poem." "The heady sense of liberation in the verses must have appealed to him." "They appealed to every German." — John Burke

YES: "It was during his student days in Bonn that Beethoven fastened upon Schiller's poem. The heady sense of liberation in the verses must have appealed to him. They appealed to every German." — John Burke

Instead of setting off a long quote with quotation marks, you may want to indent and single space it. If you do indent, do not use quotation marks.

> We are not enemies, but friends. We must not be enemies. Though passion may have strained, it must not break, our bonds of affection. The mystic chords of memory, stretching from every battlefield and patriot grave to every living heart and hearthstone all over this broad land, will yet swell the chorus of the Union when again touched, as surely they will be, by the better angels of our nature.
>
> — Abraham Lincoln *First Inaugural Address*

Be careful not to use quotation marks with indirect quotation:

NO: Mary wondered "if she would ever get over it."

YES: Mary wondered if she would ever get over it.

NO: The nurse asked "how long it had been since we had visited the doctor's office."

YES: The nurse asked how long it had been since we had visited the doctor's office.

NO: "My exercise teacher told me," Mary said, "'that I should do these back exercises fifteen minutes each day.'"

YES: "My exercise teacher told me," Mary said, "that I should do these back exercises fifteen minutes each day."

When you quote several paragraphs, it is not sufficient to place quotation marks at the beginning and ending of the entire quote. Place quotation marks at the *beginning of each paragraph*, but only *at the end of the last paragraph*. Here is an abbreviated quotation for an example:

> "Here begins an odyssey through the world of classical mythology, starting with the creation of the world, proceeding to the divinities that once governed all aspects of human life. . . .
>
> "It is true that themes similar to the classical may be found in almost any corpus of mythology . . . Even technology is not immune to the influence of Greece and Rome. . . .
>
> "We need hardly mention the extent to which painters and sculptors . . . have used and adapted classical mythology to illustrate the past, to reveal the human body, to express romantic or antiromantic ideals, or to symbolize any particular point of view."

Remember that commas and periods are always placed inside the quotation marks even if they are not actually part of the quote.

NO: "Life always gets colder near the summit", Nietzsche is purported to have said, "—the cold increases, responsibility grows".

YES: "Life always gets colder near the summit," Nietzsche is purported to have said, "—the cold increases, responsibility grows."

NO: "Get down here right away", John cried. "You'll miss the sunset if you don't".

YES: "Get down here right away," John cried. "You'll miss the sunset if you don't."

NO: "If my dog could talk", Mary mused, "I'll bet he would say, 'Take me for a walk right this minute' ".

YES: "If my dog could talk," Mary mused, "I'll bet he would say, 'Take me for a walk right this minute.' "

Other marks of punctuation, such as question marks, exclamation points, colons and semicolons, go inside the quotation marks if they are part of the quoted material. If they are not part of the quote, however, they go outside the quotation mark. Be careful to distinguish between the guidelines for the comma and period, which always go inside the quotation marks, and those for the other marks of punctuation.

NO: "I'll always love you"! she exclaimed happily.

YES: "I'll always love you!" she exclaimed happily.

NO: Did you hear her say, "He'll be there early?"

(The question mark belongs to the entire sentence and not to the quote alone.)

YES: Did you hear her say, "He'll be there early"?

NO: She called down the stairs, "When are you coming"?

(The question mark belongs to the quote.)

YES: She called down the stairs, "When are you coming?"

NO: "Ask not what your country can do for you"; said Kennedy, "ask what you can do for your country:" a statement of genius, I think.

(The semicolon is part of the quoted material; the colon is not part of the quote, but belongs to the entire sentence.)

YES: "Ask not what your country can do for you;" said Kennedy, "ask what you can do for your country": a statement of genius, I think.

NO: "Let me out"! he cried. "Don't you have any pity"?

YES: "Let me out!" he cried. "Don't you have any pity?"

Remember to use only one mark of punctuation at the end of a sentence ending with a quotation.

NO: She thought out loud, "Will I ever finish this paper in time for that class?".

YES: She thought out loud, "Will I ever finish this paper in time for that class?"

NO: "Not the same thing a bit!", said the Hatter. "Why, you might just as well say that 'I see what I eat' is the same thing as 'I eat what I see'!".

YES: "Not the same thing a bit!" said the Hatter. "Why, you might just as well say that 'I see what I eat' is the same thing as 'I eat what I see'!"

☞ Drill: Quotation Marks

DIRECTIONS: Correctly punctuate the following sentences.

1. Take an umbrella, said his mother, it looks like rain.

2. I haven't seen my old lady in five years, he exclaimed.

3. Can I write a comparative essay using To Autumn and Ode to a Nightingale for the assignment, asked the student.

4. My Favorite Things is a popular song from The Sound of Music, he remarked.

5. Do you understand the difference between overt and covert?

6. The washing machine went haywire this afternoon.

7. They wondered if they could do the job.

8. "Joseph locked the door"; said Andy "then, he put the key under the doormat".

9. You and Your Health is a popular show on WMCA.

10. Mary said "She is leaving for California tomorrow"!

11. "Don't ask any questions now", Susan exclaimed, "I'm trying to read".

12. "I can't believe it"! she exclaimed.

13. "Give me a match"!, she cried. "Don't you know it's dark in here?"

14. The article Iran After the Revolution appeared in last month's issue of The Middle East Journal.

15. "I can't begin to tell you what my day was like, said Karen. It all began when I missed the bus."

16. "My history teacher suggested," Joe said, "'that I read Sinclair Lewis' *Main Street.*' "

17. Sitting in the dark she wondered "Will the lights ever come back on?"

18. February is always a spelling problem for me.

19. "It was after his trip to Europe that he decided to enroll in college." "It had been many years since he had been in school, but he truly wanted to return".

20. My aunt wanted to know "how many years it had been since we met last."

21. "Come over here, said Charles, I have something to show you."

22. "If he were here this moment", Linda said, "I know he would say, What's for dinner?"

23. I agree"; said Mark "its time to take a stand".

24. Please read Robert Frost's The Most of It in Chapter 15, Modern Poetry, in Gray's Anthology of Poetry.

25. Joan realized "it was time to leave the house".

Section 14: The Apostrophe

Use the apostrophe to form contractions: to indicate that letters or figures have been omitted.

can't (cannot)	o'clock (of the clock)
I'll (I will)	it's (it is)
memories of '42 (1942)	won't (will not)
you've (you have)	they're (they are)

Notice that the apostrophe is *always* placed where a letter or letters have been omitted. Avoid such careless errors as writing wo'nt instead of won't, for example. Contractions are generally not used in formal writing. They are found primarily in speech and informal writing.

An apostrophe is also used to indicate the plural form of letters, figures, and words that normally don't take a plural form. In such cases it would be confusing to add only an "s."

He quickly learned his *r's* and *s's*.

Children have difficulties in remembering to dot their *i's* and cross their *t's*.

Most of the *Ph.D.'s* and *M.D.'s* understand the new technology they are using for anticancer drugs.

Her *2's* always looked like her *4's*.

Marion used too many *the's* and *and's* in her last paper for English literature.

Whenever possible, try to form plurals of numbers and of single or multiple letters used as words by adding only "s."

the ABCs	the 1940s
in threes and fours	three Rs

Placement of the Apostrophe to Indicate Possession

In spoken English, the same pronunciation is used for the plural, singular, possessive, and plural possessive of most nouns. It is only by the context that the listener is able to tell the difference in the words used by the speaker. In written English, the spelling as well as the context tells the reader the meaning of the noun the writer is using. The writer has only to master the placement of the apostrophe so that the meaning is clearly conveyed to the reader. These words are pronounced alike but have different meanings:

Plural	Singular Possessive	Plural Possessive
neighbors	neighbor's	neighbors'
doctors	doctor's	doctors'
weeks	week's	weeks'
sopranos	soprano's	sopranos'
civilizations	civilization's	civilizations'

If you aren't sure of the apostrophe's placement, you can determine it accurately by this simple test: change the possessive phrase into "belonging to" or an "of" phrase to discover the basic noun. You will find this a particularly useful trick for some of the more confusing possessive forms such as those on words that end in "s" or "es."

Keats' poem: The poem belonging to Keats. Base noun is *Keats*; possessive is Keats' or Keats's, not Keat's or Keats'es.

The Joneses' house: The house of the Joneses (plural of Jones). Base is *Joneses*; possessive is Joneses', not Jones' or Jones'es.

Four months' pay: The pay of four months. *Months* is base; possessive is months', not month's.

In two hours' time: In the time of two hours. *Hours* is base; possessive is hours', not hour's.

The lioness' strength: The strength of the lioness. *Lioness* is base; possessive is lioness' or lioness's, not lioness'es or liones's.

It is anybody's guess: The guess of anybody. *Anybody* is the base noun; possessive is anybody's, not anybodys' or anybodies'.

☞ Drill: The Apostrophe

Contractions

DIRECTIONS: Write the contractions of the following.

1. she will, ______
2. shall not, ______
3. Class of 1981, ______
4. does not, ______
5. they have, ______
6. We are, ______

DIRECTIONS: In the following sentences, make the necessary corrections. Also, note the reasons for your corrections.

7. This boat isnt yours. We sold our's last year to Roberts parents.
8. At 10 oclock theyll meet us at Macys department store.
9. Lindas sister was politically active in the 1960's.
10. In Ms. Greens first grade class, she had difficulty writing x's and learning her ABC's.
11. Wordsworths poem "the Solitary Reaper" was published in J. Mahoneys edition of *The Romantic Poet's.*
12. Many of the defense attorneys witness' were afraid to appear at Johns trial.
13. "Its time to eat dinner," called James mother.
14. Arent you going to see if John's home so you can find out the results of Mondays game.
15. "Ode on a Grecian Urn," written by John Keats' is very famous. Ive read it at least twenty times.
16. Isn't it a shame that Peters team lost the game. They should have remembered their three Rs.

Possession

DIRECTIONS: Write the possessive singular and the plural possessive of each of the following words.

1. lady, _______, _______
2. child, _______, _______
3. cashier, _______, _______
4. Filipino, _______, _______
5. country, _______, _______
6. James, _______, _______
7. knife, _______, _______
8. mouse, _______, _______
9. roof, _______, _______
10. attorney, _______, _______

Section 15: Stops

There are three ways to end a sentence:

1. a period
2. a question mark
3. an exclamation point

The Period

Periods end all sentences that are not questions or exclamations. In speech, the end of a sentence is indicated with a full pause. The period is the counterpart of this pause in writing.

> Go get me my paper. I'm anxious to see the news.
>
> Into each life some rain must fall. Last night some fell into mine.
>
> The moon is round. The stars look small.
>
> Mary and Janet welcomed the newcomer. She was noticeably happy.

When a question is intended as a suggestion and the listener is not expected to answer, or when a question is asked indirectly as part of a sentence, a period is also used.

Mimi wondered if the parade would ever end.

May we hear from you soon?

Will you please send the flowers you advertised.

We'll never know who the culprit was.

Periods also follow most abbreviations and contractions.

N.Y.	Dr.	Jr.	Sr.
etc.	Jan.	Mrs.	Mr.
Esq.	cont.	A.M.	A.D.

Periods (or parentheses) are also used after a letter or number in a series.

a. apples	1. president
b. oranges	2. vice president
c. pears	3. secretary

Errors to Avoid

Be sure to omit the period after a quotation mark preceded by a period. Only one stop is necessary to end a sentence.

She said, "Hold my hand." (no period after the final ")

"Don't go into the park until later."

"It's not my fault," he said. "She would have taken the car anyway."

After many abbreviations, particularly for organizations or agencies, no period is used (check your dictionary if in doubt).

AFL-CIO	NAACP	GM
FBI	NATO	IBM
TV	UN	HEW

The Question Mark

Use a question mark to end a direct question even if it is not in the form of a question. The question mark in writing is the same as the rising tone of voice used to indicate a question in speech. If you read the following two sentences aloud, you will see the difference in tone between a statement and a question composed of the same words.

Mary is here.
Mary is here?

Here are some more examples of correct use of question marks; pay special attention to the way they are used with other punctuation:

Where will we go next?

Would you like coffee or tea?

"Won't you," he asked, "please lend me a hand?"

"Will they ever give us our freedom?" the prisoner asked.

"To be or not to be?" was the question asked by Hamlet.

Who asked "When?"

Question marks indicate a full stop and lend a different emphasis to a sentence than do commas. Compare these pairs of sentences:

Was the sonata by Beethoven? or Brahms? or Chopin?

Was the sonata by Beethoven, or Brahms, or Chopin?

Did they walk to the park? climb the small hill? take the bus to town? or go skating out back?

Did they walk to park, climb the small hill, take the bus to town, or go skating out back?

Sometimes question marks are placed in parentheses. This indicates doubt or uncertainty about the facts being reported:

The bombing started at 3:00 A.M.(?)

She said the dress cost 200,000 (?) dollars.

Harriet Stacher (18(?)-1914) was well thought of in her time.

Hippocrates (460(?)-(?)377 B.C.) is said to be the father of modern medicine.

The Exclamation Point

An exclamation point ends an emphatic statement. It should be used only to express strong emotions such as surprise, disbelief, or admiration. If it is used too often for mild expressions of emotion, it loses its effectiveness.

Let go of me!

Help! Fire!

It was a wonderful day!

What a beautiful woman she is!

Who shouted "Fire!" (notice no question mark is necessary)

Fantastic!

"Unbelievable!" she gasped. (notice no comma is necessary)

"You'll never win!" he cried.

Where else can I go! (The use of the exclamation point shows that this is a strong statement even though it is worded like a question.)

Avoid Overuse

The following is an example of the overuse of exclamation points:

Dear Susan,

I was so glad to see you last week! You looked better than ever! Our talk meant so much to me! I can hardly wait until we get together again! Could you believe how long it has been! Let's never let that happen again! Please write as soon as you get the chance! I can hardly wait to hear from you!

Your friend,

Nora

☞ Drill: Stops

DIRECTIONS: In the following sentences correctly supply periods, question marks, and exclamation points.

1. "Good gracious" she said "Didn't you know that I was coming"
2. Mr. Morgan works for the CIA
3. Alexander wondered if it was time to go
4. Leave me alone Can't you see that I'm busy
5. "How many boxes did you buy" asked Dr. Jones
6. "Be careful" he shouted "Didn't you see the car coming"
7. Impossible I have never seen anything like that before
8. Lynn asked if anyone had the time
9. What else can I do I lost all my money
10. Who cried "Help"

Section 16: Interjections, Dashes, and Parentheses

Interjections

An interjection is a word or group of words used as an exclamation to express emotion. It need not be followed by an exclamation point. Often an interjection is followed by a comma (see "THE COMMA") if it is not very intense. Technically, the interjection has no grammatical relation to other words in the sentence, yet it is still considered a part of speech.

Examples:

Oh dear, I forgot my key's again.

Ah! Now do you understand?

Ouch! I didn't realize that the stove was hot.

Oh, excuse me. I didn't realize that you were next on line.

Dashes

Use the dash to indicate a sudden or unexpected break in the normal flow of the sentence. It can also be used in the place of parentheses or of commas if the meaning is clarified. Usually the dash gives the material it sets off special emphasis. (On a typewriter, two hyphens (--) indicate a dash.)

Could you — I hate to ask! — help me with these boxes?

When we left town — a day never to be forgotten — they had a record snowfall.

She said — we all heard it — "The safe is not locked."

These are the three ladies — Mrs. Jackson, Miss Harris, and Ms. Forrester — you hoped to meet last week.

The sight of the Andromeda Galaxy — especially when seen for the first time — is astounding.

That day was the longest in her life — or so it seemed to her.

A dash is often used to summarize a series of ideas that have already been expressed.

Freedom of speech, freedom to vote, and freedom of assembly — these are the cornerstones of democracy.

Carbohydrates, fats, and proteins — these are the basic kinds of food we need.

Jones, who first suggested we go; Marshall, who made all the arrangements; and Kline, who finally took us there — these were the three men I admired most for their courage.

James, Howard, Marianne, Angela, Catherine — all were displeased with the decision of the teacher.

The dash is also used to note the author of a quotation that is set off in the text.

Nothing is good or bad but thinking makes it so.

— William Shakespeare

Under every grief and pine
Runs a joy with silken twine.

— William Blake

Parentheses

To set off material that is only loosely connected to the central meaning of the sentence, use parentheses [( )].

Most men (at least most that I know) like wine, women, and song, but have too much work and not enough time for such enjoyments.

On Tuesday evenings and Thursday afternoons (the times I don't have classes), the television programs are not too exciting.

Last year at Vale (we go there every year), the skiing was the best I've ever seen.

In New York (I've lived there all my life and ought to know), you have to have a license for a gun.

What must be done to think clearly and calmly (is it even possible?) and then make the decision?

Watch out for other punctuation when you use parentheses. Punctuation that refers to the material enclosed in the parentheses occurs inside the marks. Punctuation belonging to the rest of the sentence comes outside the parentheses.

I thought I knew the poem by heart (boy, was I wrong!).

For a long time (too long as far as I'm concerned), women were thought to be inferior to men.

We must always strive to tell the truth. (Are we even sure we know what truth is?)

When I first saw a rose (don't you think it's the most beautiful flower?), I thought it must be man-made.

☞ Drill: Interjections, Dashes, and Parentheses

Interjections and Dashes

DIRECTIONS: Read the following sentences. What effect does the dash have on the writing, especially the tone and mood?

1. Can you? — I would be ever so grateful — I'm having so much difficulty.

2. Could it be — no it can't be — not after all these years.

3. Time and patience — two simple words — yet why are they so hard for me to remember?

4. Most of the paintings in the gallery — in fact all but one — were done in the 19th century.

5. According to John Locke, these are man's inalienable rights — life, liberty, and property.

Parentheses

DIRECTIONS: Read the following sentences. What effect does the use of parentheses have on the writing? Also, make any necessary corrections.

1. The choice (in my opinion,) was a good one.

2. Linda's comment ("Where did you get that dress")? wasn't intended to be sarcastic.

3. After today (and what a day it was!) I will begin to work harder.

4. Last summer in Cape Cod (this is the first year we went there,) we did a lot of sightseeing.

5. The first time I went driving (do you remember the day)?, I was so scared.

Section 17: Capitalization

When a letter is capitalized, it calls special attention to itself. This attention should be for a good reason. There are standard uses for capital letters as well as much difference of opinion as to what should and should not be capitalized. In general, capitalize 1) all proper nouns, 2) the first word of a sentence, and 3) a direct quotation.

Names of Ships, Aircrafts, Spacecraft, and Trains

(Abbreviations preceding names and designations of class or make are not italicized.)

Apollo 13	Mariner IV
DC-10	S.S. United States
Sputnik 11	Boeing 707

Names of Deities

God	Jupiter
Allah	Holy Ghost
Buddha	Diana
Jehovah	Shiva

Geological Periods

Neolithic age	Cenozoic era
late Pleistocene times	Age of Reptiles
Ice Age	Tertiary period

Names of Astronomical Bodies

Venus	Big Dipper
the Milky Way	Halley's comet
Ursa Major	North Star
Scorpio	Deneb
the Crab nebula	Pleiades

(Note that sun, moon, and earth are not capitalized unless they are used with other astronomical terms that are capitalized.)

Personifications

Reliable *Nature* brought her promise of Spring.

Bring on *Melancholy* in his sad might.

Morning in the bowl of night has flung the stone that set the stars to flight.

Historical Periods

the Middle Ages	World War I
Reign of Terror	Great Depression
Christian Era	Roaring Twenties
Age of Louis XIV	Renaissance

Organizations, Associations, and Institutions

Girl Scouts of America	North Atlantic Treaty Organization
Young Men's Christian Association	Kiwanis Club
New York Yankees	League of Women Voters
Unitarian Church	Common Market
the Illinois Central	New York Philharmonic
Franklin Glen High School	the Jaycees

Government and Judicial Entities

United States Court of Appeals	Committee on Foreign Affairs
Camden City Council	House of Commons
Senate	Parliament
Arkansas Supreme Court	House of Representatives
Peace Corps	Department of State
Municipal Court of Chicago	Iowa Board of Education
Census Bureau	the Library of Congress

A general term that accompanies a specific name is capitalized only if it follows the specific name. If it stands alone or comes before the specific name, it is put in lowercase. This rule does *not* apply, however, when the general term directly precedes a person's name, thus acting as part of their title.

Washington State	the state of Washington
Central Park	the park
Golden Gate Bridge	the bridge

Tropic of Capricorn	the tropics
Glen Brook High School	the high school in Glen Brook
Monroe Doctrine	the doctrine originated by Monroe
the Milky Way Galaxy	our galaxy, the Milky Way
the Mississippi River	the river
Easter Day	the day we celebrated Easter
Treaty of Versailles	the treaty signed at Versailles
Webster's Dictionary	a dictionary by Webster
Senator Dixon	the senator from Illinois
President Andrew Jackson	the president of the U.S.
Pope John XXIII	the pope
Queen Elizabeth I	the queen, Elizabeth I

Use a capital to start a sentence or a sentence fragment.

Our car would not start.

When will you leave? I need to know right away

Never!

Let me in! Right now!

When a sentence appears within a sentence, start it with a capital.

The main question is, Where do we start?

We had only one concern: When would we eat?

My sister said, "I'll find the Monopoly set."

He answered, "We can only stay a few minutes."

In poetry, it is usual practice to capitalize the first word of each line even if the word comes in the middle of a sentence.

When I consider everything that grows
Holds in perfection but a little moment,
That this huge stage produceth naught but shows,
Whereon the stars in secret influence comment.
— William Shakespeare

She dwells with Beauty — Beauty that must die;
And Joy, whose hand is ever at his lips
Bidding Adieu.
— John Keats

The most important words of titles are capitalized. Those words not capitalized are conjunctions (e.g., *and, or, but*), articles (e.g., *a, the, and*), and short prepositions (e.g., *of, on, by, for*). The first and last word of a title must always be capitalized.

A Man for All Seasons	*Crime and Punishment*
Of Mice and Men	"Let Me In"
Rise of the West	"What to Look For"
"Sonata in G-Minor"	"The Ever-Expanding West"
Strange Life of Ivan Osokin	"Rubaiyat of Omar Khayyam"
"All in the Family"	*Symphony No. 41*
"Ode to Billy Joe"	"Piano Concerto No. 5"

☞ Drill: Capitalization

DIRECTIONS: The following sentences contain errors in capitalization. Correct these sentences by making words capital where necessary, and other words lowercase where necessary.

1. Where is the crab Nebula?
2. The girl scouts of America sells delicious cookies.
3. This year, senator Burns will run for reelection.
4. Barbara said, "let me know when you are off the phone."
5. beth's new car is a black dodge daytona which she purchased at the dodge dealer in new york city.
6. mike and jackie are both graduates of edison high school.
7. glaciers from the ice age still exist.
8. Today in class, the Professor lectured on the Neolithic Age.
9. aunt stella will be visiting washington, d.c. during february of next year.
10. We will be spending easter day with our aunt clara who lives near the mississippi river.
11. Helen asked, "when will betty and Rich be returning from yellowstone park?"

12. our english teacher will be reviewing the first twenty pages of the book of mice and men with the class.

13. The case went as high as the United States court of appeals.

14. At the baseball game last night, the Los Angeles dodgers beat the New York yankees by Ten runs.

15. Eric asked the teacher, "do you have a Webster's dictionary?"

Now that you have brushed up on the skills needed to succeed on Part I of the Writing Section, you should take the following drill. This drill follows the form of the actual multiple-choice questions and will help you become accustomed to dealing with these types of questions.

☞ Drill: Writing Skills

The following passage is written in the form of a popular magazine. Read the text and answer the questions.

[1]The Lincoln Cent was first struck in 1909 to celebrate the 100th. Anniversary of the birth of Abraham Lincoln, our 16th. President. [2]Designed by Victor D. Brenner, the coin carried the motto "In God We Trust" — the first time it appeared on this denomination coin. [3]It is interesting that the law for the motto was passed during Lincoln's administration as President. [4]Though we might not think so at first glance, the lowly Cent is a fitting memorial for the great man whose profile graces this most common coin of the realm, and a tolerable symbol for the nation whose commerce it serves.

[5]The obverse has the profile of Lincoln as he looked during the trying years of the War Between the States. [6]Faced with the immense problems of a divided nation, the prevention of the split between North and South was difficult. [7]"A house divided against itself cannot stand," he warned the nation. [8]With the outbreak of war at Fort Sumter. Lincoln was saddened to see his beloved country caught up in the senseless war in which father fought against son, brother against brother. [9]Throughout America, war captured the attention of people: the woman who saved the lives of the wounded, the soldier waiting to go into battle, the bewildered child trying hard to understand the sound of guns. [10]Lincoln stood on the broad, silent battlefield at Gettysburg in 1863 to dedicate the site as a national cemetery. [11]Gettysburg had been the scene of some of the most bitter fighting of the war and had ended in a Union victory. [12]____. [13]In his special address at Gettysburg, he called upon the American people to end the war. [14]His words boomed out over the large audience before him:

[15]. . . It is rather for us [the living] to be here dedicated to the great task remaining before us — that from these honored dead we take increased devotion to that cause for which they gave the last full measure of devotion; that we here highly resolve that these dead shall not have died in vain; that this nation under God, shall have a new birth of freedom; and that government of the people, by the people and for the people, shall not perish from the earth."

[16]Barely a month before the end of the war, Lincoln took the oath of office a secondly time as President. [17]With the war still raging, his inaugural address took on added meaning:

. . . With malice toward none, with charity for all, with firmness in the right as God gives us to see the right, let us strive on to finish the work we are in, to bind up the nation's wounds, to care for him who shall have borne the battle and for his widow and his orphan, to do all which may achieve and cherish a just and lasting peace among ourselves and with all nations.

1. Which of the following sentences, used in place of the blank lines labeled Part 12, would **best** fit the writer's purpose and be consistent with the point in the paragraph?

   (A) Lincoln felt the victory was pyrrhic and worthless.

   (B) The President was elated over the victory and felt that this was an opportunity to encourage more young men to join the Union ranks.

   (C) Lincoln was pleased with the victory but deeply concerned over the deaths of so many soldiers.

   (D) Lincoln, depressed over the loss of so many young men in the Union, wanted to use the dedication speech to whip up hatred for the Confederate cause.

2. Which of the following changes is needed in the third paragraph?

   (A) Part 16: Change "end" to "climax."

   (B) Part 16: Change "secondly" to "second."

   (C) Part 17: Change "With" to "Of."

   (D) Part 17: Change "on" to "in."

3. Which of the following changes is needed in the second paragraph?

   (A) Part 5: Change "has" to "had."

   (B) Part 6: Change "the prevention of the split between North and South was difficult" to "Lincoln found it difficult to prevent the split between North and South."

(C) Part 9: Change "waiting" to "waited."

(D) Part 10: Change "site" to "sight."

4. Which of the following parts is a nonstandard sentence?

(A) Part 2

(B) Part 4

(C) Part 8

(D) Part 11

The following passage is written in the form of an educational textbook. Read the text and answer the questions.

[1]Dr. Robert Goddard at one time a physics professor at Clark University, Worcester, Massachusetts was largely responsible for the sudden interest in rockets back in the twenties. [2]When Dr. Goddard first started his experiments with rockets, no related technical information was available. [3]He started a new science, industry, and field of engineering. [4]Through his scientific experiments, he pointed the way to the development of rockets as we know them today. [5]The Smithsonian Institute agreed to finance his experiments in 1920. [6]From these experiments he wrote a paper titled "A Method of Reaching Extreme Altitudes," in which he outlined a space rocket of the step (multistage) principle, theoretically capable of reaching the moon.

[7]Goddard discovered that with a properly shaped, smooth, tapered nozzle he could increase the ejection velocity eight times with the same weight of fuel. [8]This would not only drive a rocket eight times faster, but sixty-four times farther, according to his theory. [9]Early in his experiments he found that solid-fuel rockets would not give him the high power or the duration of power needed for a dependable supersonic motor capable of extreme altitudes. [10]______________________________ ______________________________.

[11]It attained an altitude of 184 feet and a speed of 60 m.p.h. [12]This seems small as compared to present-day speeds and heights of missile flights, but instead of trying to achieve speed or altitude at this time, Dr. Goddard was trying to develop a dependable rocket motor.

[13]Dr. Goddard later was the first to fire a rocket that reached a speed faster than the speed of sound. [14]He was first to develop a gyroscopic steering <u>thing</u> for rockets. [15]The first to use vanes in the jet stream for rocket stabilization during <u>the initial phase</u> of a rocket flight. [16]And he was first to patent the idea of step rockets. [17]After proving on paper and in <u>actual</u> tests that a rocket can travel in a vacuum, he developed the mathematical theory of rocket propulsion and rocket flight, including basic designs for long-range rockets. [18]All of his information was available to military men before World War II, but evidently its immediate use did not seem applicable. [19]Near the end of World War II we started intense <u>work</u> on rocket-powered guided

missiles, using the experiments and developments of Dr. Goddard and the American Rocket Society.

5. Which of the following sentences, used in place of the blank line labeled Part 10, would **best** fit the writer's pattern of development in the second paragraph?

   (A) Consequently, Doctor Goddard was able to fire a rocket successfully.

   (B) On the other hand, Dr. Goddard fired a rocket successfully.

   (C) On 16 March 1926, after many trials, Dr. Goddard successfully fired, for the first time in history, a liquid-fuel rocket into the air.

   (D) Firing a rocket successfully was thus an enormous difficulty.

6. Which of the following should be changed to reflect correct punctuation in the first paragraph?

   (A) Part 1: Put commas in after "Goddard" and after "Massachusetts."

   (B) Part 2: Remove the comma after "rockets."

   (C) Part 4: Put a comma in after "rockets."

   (D) Part 6: Remove the comma after "principle."

7. Which of the following parts of the third paragraph is a nonstandard sentence?

   (A) Part 14

   (B) Part 15

   (C) Part 16

   (D) Part 17

8. Which of the underlined words in the third paragraph should be replaced by more precise or appropriate words?

   (A) thing

   (B) the initial phase

   (C) actual

   (D) work

The following passage is written in the form of a feature editorial. Read the text and answer the questions.

[1]We've grown accustomed to seeing this working woman hanging from the subway strap during commuting hours. [2]We may refer disparagingly to her tailored suit and little tie but we no longer visualize her in a house dress with her hair

uncombed. [3]The woman who leaves her children to go to work in the morning is no longer a pariah in her community or her family. [4]Her paycheck is more than pin money; it buys essential family staples and often supports the entire family. [5]____.

[6]The situation for men has also changed as a result of women's massive entry into the work force for the better. [7]Men who would once have felt unrelenting pressure to remain with one firm and climb the career ladder are often freed up by a second income to change careers in midlife. [8]They enjoy greatest intimacy and involvement with their children.

[9]The benefits for business are also readily apparent. [10]No senior manager in the country would deny that the huge generation of women who entered management seven or eight years ago has functioned superbly, often outperforming men.

[11]Yet the prevailing message from the media on the subject of women and business is one filled with pessimism. [12]We hear about women leaving their employers in the lurch when they go on maternity leave. [13]Or we hear the flip side, that women are overly committed to their careers and neglectful of their families. [14]And in fact, it is true that problems arising from women's new work force role do exist, side by side with the benefits.

[15]The problems hurt business as well as individuals and their families, affordable quality childcare, for one example, is still a distant dream. [16]Some women are distracted at work, and men who would have felt secure about their children when their wives were home are also anxious and distracted. [17]Distraction also impedes the productivity of some high-achieving women with the birth of their first child and causes some to depart with the birth of their second.

9. Which of the following sentences, if added in the blank lines for Part 5, would be MOST consistent with the writer's point, purpose, and audience?

   (A) The working woman is a rare and unexpected phenomenon.

   (B) The presence of women in the management ranks of corporations is a reality.

   (C) Women in business are the outcasts of the working world.

   (D) Taking the career woman seriously is like worrying about one more drop of rainwater in a barrelful.

10. Which of the following parts of the passage displays a nonstandard placement of a modifying phrase?

    (A) Part 1

    (B) Part 3

    (C) Part 6

    (D) Part 7

11. Which of the following parts of the passage displays a nonstandard use of a comparative form?

    (A) Part 4

    (B) Part 8

    (C) Part 10

    (D) Part 13

12. Which of the following parts of the passage is a nonstandard sentence?

    (A) Part 14

    (B) Part 15

    (C) Part 17

    (D) Part 18

> The following passage is written in the form of a student essay. Read the text and answer the questions.

[1]In the past thirty years, television has become a very popular pasttime for almost everyone. [2]From the time the mother places the baby in front of the television while she drinks her orange juice until the time the senior citizen in the retirement home watches the letters turn on "Wheel of Fortune," Americans spend endless hours in front of the "boob tube." [3] ______________________________.

[4]When my mother was a little girl, what did children do to entertain themselves? [5]They played. [6]Their games usually involved social interaction with other children as well as imaginatively creating entertainment for themselves. [7]They also developed hobbies like woodworking and sewing. [8]Today, few children really know how to play with each other or entertain themselves. [9]Instead, they sit in front of the television, glued to cartoons that are senseless and often violent. [10]Even if they watch educational programs like "Sesame Street," they don't really have to do anything but watch and listen to what the answer to the question is.

[11]Teenagers, also, use television as a way of avoiding doing things that will be helping them mature. [12]How many kids does much homework anymore? [13]Why not? [14]Because they work part-time jobs and come home from work tired and relax in front of the television.

13. Which of the following sentences, if added in the blanks allowed for Part 3, would best reflect the writer's point of view?

    (A) However, television is unimaginative as a form of entertainment.

    (B) Television takes up too much time in our daily lives.

(C) I believe that television can become an addiction that provides an escape from the problems of the world and from facing responsibility for your own life.

(D) Television is a demanding as well as educational national pasttime.

14. Which of the following sentences uses a nonstandard verb form?

(A) Part 4

(B) Part 7

(C) Part 8

(D) Part 12

15. Which of the following sentences in the passage is nonstandard?

(A) Part 2

(B) Part 7

(C) Part 10

(D) Part 14

16. Which of the following changes is needed in the first paragraph?

(A) Part 1: Change "has become" to "is."

(B) Part 2: Change "she" to "the mother" or "the baby."

(C) Part 2: Change "watches" to "watched."

(D) Part 4: Change "When" to "Being that."

WRITING DRILLS

ANSWER KEY

Drill – Sentence Fragments/Run-on Sentences

1. Fragment: We went out after the rain stopped.

2. Run-on: Mow the lawn. It is much too long.

3. Run-on: The settlement you reached seems fair.

4. Fragment: My eyes get tired when I read, especially at night.

5. Run-on: It was impossible to get through on the phone, since the lines were down because of the storm.

6. Fragment: Is the leaky pipe the only problem?

7. Run-on: Everyone saw the crime, but no one is willing to come forth.

8. Run-on: The weather was bad. She played in the rain.

9. Fragment: Eileen paced the floor and worried about her economics final.

10. Run-on: The team had lost the playoffs; their season was over.

Drill – Short Sentences/Wordiness

1. He graduated from college and, in no time, found a job and rented an apartment. He was happy.

2. The book she lent me was lengthy, boring, and unenjoyable. I wouldn't recommend it to anyone.

3. We have nothing to do because our plans to go on a picnic have been ruined by the rain.

4. She immediately obliged anyone who telephoned for help with their homework.

5. She liked to paint and was quite good; unfortunately, materials are expensive and she cannot afford them.

6. Jane cannot be described with words.

7. It was time to leave; the taxi was waiting outside for them. There was no time to think; they hoped everything was packed.

8. The candidate's promise to lengthen prison terms was his major issue. He hoped to be elected.

9. *Long Days Journey into Night* is a dramatic and autobiographical play by Eugene O'Neill.

10. He still could have asked for her approval.

Drill – Misplaced Modifiers

1. I saw a stray dog while I was riding the bus this afternoon.

2. The clothing was given in large packages to the poor.

3. I found five dollars while I was eating lunch in the park.

4. While we were in our car we saw two girls riding bicycles.

5. When the car crashed, I jumped up from quietly reading my book.

6. He ran the mile although his ankle was sprained.

7. Only the history majors were affected by the new requirements.

8. Susan's packages fell out of her arms onto the ground as she was running quickly to catch the bus.

9. He asked the man for directions just to make sure.

10. While driving home, he discovered a new route.

Drill – Parallel Structure

1. In the summer I usually like to swim and water-ski.

2. The professor explained the cause, the effect, and the results.

3. Mary read the book, studied the examples, and took the test.

4. Mark watched how John started the car, and how he left the curb.

5. They bought the house because of its location and its affordability.

6. The movie was both interesting and exciting.

7. Shakespeare wrote both (optional) beautiful sonnets and complex plays.

8. The painting is done with either watercolor or oils.

9. The lecturer spoke in a serious, concerned tone.

10. Either we forget those plans, or we accept their proposal.

Drill – Phrases

1. "to solve the crime": (I); "to maintain justice": (I)

2. "on the billboard" (PR); "billboard" (OP)

3. "having painted the house" (P)

4. "staying in shape" (G)

5. "with pure logic" (PR); "logic" (OP)

6. "to help me" (I); "with the job" (PR); job (OP)

7. "Having completed the mission" (P)

8. "in the refrigerator" (PR); "refrigerator" (OP)

9. "Thinking about the future" (P)

10. Having parked; gerund phrase, into the theater; prepositional phrase (adverb)

11. Mary's screaming; gerund phrase (noun)

12. to have made; infinitive (adverb), on the interviewers; prepositional phrase (indirect object)

13. Jogging; gerund phrase (noun)

14. in her presence; prepositional phrase (complements)

15. while I was reading; prepositional phrase (adverb)

16. singing in the morning; gerund phrase (direct object)

17. Gaining confidence; participial phrase (adjective)

18. to open the package; infinitive phrase (adverb)

19. Having forgotten my sweater; participial phrase (adjective), at the movies; prepositional phrase (adverb)

20. Winning the game; gerund phrase (subject)

Drill – Clauses

1. Phrase
2. Clause
3. Phrase
4. Clause
5. Clause

Drill – Subject-Verb Agreement

1. Either her mother or her father usually drives her to school on rainy days.
2. There are, if I calculated right, two hundred dollars left in my bank account.
3. Mary and her friends were late for the test.
4. Economics is a major taught in many colleges.
5. The first years of high school are the most difficult.
6. Aristotle's *Poetics* has always been read widely.
7. The noise from all those fans was distracting.
8. Neither the chorus nor the actors know their parts.
9. Each of us is going away for the weekend.
10. Neither the grass nor the flowers were growing well.

Drill – Comparison of Adjectives

1. He was *saddest* to leave. (adjective)
2. She ran *faster* than the others on the team. (adverb)

3. Throughout school, they were *the best* in math. (adjective)

4. This class is *more interesting* than European history class. (adjective)

5. He arrived *sooner* than I did. (adverb)

6. The test was the *hardest* we expected. (adjective)

7. He responded to the interviewer *more candidly* than Tom. (adverb)

8. This sentence (referring to "she") *cannot* be put in the superlative form.

9. The answer is *most perfectly* correct. (adverb)

10. She read the part *better*. (adjective)

Drill – Pronouns

A. Relative Pronouns

1. who
2. what
3. which
4. whichever
5. whatever
6. which
7. that

B. Relative Pronouns

1. whom
2. whom
3. who
4. who
5. who
6. whoever
7. who
8. who
9. whomever
10. who

C. Interrogative and Demonstrative Pronouns

Interrogatives

1. We wondered *who* would come to the party.

2. I asked Janet *what* she wanted to do tonight.

3. I had no idea *which* club she wanted to go to.

4. I said we would go to *whichever* one she wanted to.

5. I have fun with Janet *whatever* we do.

Demonstratives

1. *Those* are the red shoes I want.

2. I was too nervous to speak to *that* girl

3. He was *so* sick after his first gin and tonic that he never drank another.

4. It was *such* an exciting party.

5. I must buy her *that* watch.

D. Reflexive Pronouns

1. ourselves (object, refers to "we")

2. myself (object, refers to "I")

3. yourself (object, refers to "you" understood)

4. itself (object, refers to "play")

5. themselves (object, refers to "they")

E. Reflexive Pronouns

1. Both James and they went to the beach.

2. Jack himself read the speech.

3. I will unload the car.

4. They finished the painting themselves.

5. He mowed the lawn himself.

F. Personal Pronouns

1. I
2. him
3. we
4. I
5. she
6. he

7. they
8. they
9. we
10. she
11. I
12. her and me
13. he
14. us
15. they
16. we
17. him
18. they
19. me
20. us
21. him
22. I
23. they
24. us
25. him
26. I
27. her
28. I

G. Possessive Pronouns

1. whose
2. her
3. that
4. His
5. mine
6. Theirs
7. hers

H. Expletives

1. It's
2. There
3. It's
4. It
5. It's

I. Pronouns

1. her
2. their
3. its
4. their
5. his

Drill – Conjunctions

1. John's best assets are his personality and his swimming ability.
2. I heard on the radio that the play is closing this week.

3. I was reading the paper when the phone rang.

4. Susan often ate vegetables but not fruits.

5. Please send me either an answer to the questions or opinions on the project.

6. Although I'm tired from the trip, I'll attend the concert tonight.

7. Mary's goal is not only to study hard but also to pass the test.

8. He produced the play and she directed it.

9. A good essay is one in which the ideas are clearly articulated.

10. The class wanted neither to read the book nor to do the assignment.

Drill – The Comma

1. However, I am willing to reconsider.

   Reason: "However" is a transitional word and requires a comma after it.

2. She descended the long, winding staircase.

   Reason: A comma is used in a series to emphasize each adjective.

3. Whenever I practice my violin, my family closes the windows.

   Reason: Use a comma after a long introductory phrase.

4. While driving, Francis never took his eyes off the road.

   Reason: When the introductory phrase includes a "verbal," a comma is necessary.

5. The car, which I bought last year, is in the garage.

   Reason: The modifying group of words ("which I bought last year") is not vital to the meaning of the sentence and, therefore, is set off by commas.

6. "Answer the door," his mother said loudly.

   Reason: Use a comma to set off direct quotations.

7. Miss, can I ask you for the time?

   Reason: Use a comma to set off direct address.

8. He was, after all, an ex-convict.

   Reason: Use commas to set off parenthetical words and phrases.

9. I'm so bored, aren't you?

   Reason: Use a comma to set off tag questions.

10. The old, tall, shady tree is wonderful during the summer.

    Reason: When an adjective series describes a noun, use a comma to separate and emphasize each adjective.

11. George, Gary, and Bill were on line early this morning. They bought their tickets, read the newspaper, and spoke for a while.

    Reason: For both sentences use a comma to separate words, phrases, and whole ideas (clauses).

12. The author, James Grey, was awarded the prize.

    Reason: Use commas to set off nonrestrictive words.

13. She attended school in London, England, last year.

    Reason: Use commas to set off geographical names.

14. No correction necessary.

15. His weight, not his height, prevented him from competing in the race.

    Reason: Use commas to set off contrasting elements.

16. No correction necessary.

17. She got in the car, turned on the ignition, and left the curb.

    Reason: A comma is used to separate words, phrases, and whole ideas.

18. Incidentally, he called last night.

    Reason: Use a comma to set off parenthetical words and phrases.

19. The kitten, small and cute, was adopted by the Brown family.

    Reason: Use commas to set off nonrestrictive elements.

20. Mary, did you see James, Jr., at the party last night?

    Reason: (1) Use a comma to set off direct address. (2) Use a comma to set off abbreviations after names.

21. No change necessary.

22. No change necessary.

23. Really, I can't believe that is the truth.

    Reason: Use a comma to set off an interjection.

24. We thought it was time to leave, but we arrived early.

    Reason: Use a comma to set off sentences with two main ideas.

25. Monday, she will leave for Boston.

    Reason: Use a comma to set off parenthetical words and phrases.

26. After he got home he read a magazine, ate dinner, and left for the movies.

    Reason: The comma is used to separate words, phrases, and clauses.

27. No correction necessary.

28. When she decided to leave, everyone was disappointed.

    Reason: Use a comma to set off a long introductory phrase.

29. Hey, John, it's time to go.

    Reason: Use commas to set off direct address.

30. He seemed wrong for the part, yet he turned out to be the best actor in the production.

    Reason: Use a comma to separate sentences with two main ideas.

Drill – The Colon and Semicolon

1. I have only one thing to say: don't do it.

2. They seemed compatible; yet they did not get along.

3. She had only one goal in life: to be a famous pianist.

4. He thought the problem was solved; instead, his solution proved to be entirely wrong.

5. By the end of the day there were only two things on her mind: rest and relaxation.

6. Only a few members were able to attend the convention: Henry, Karen, David, Mark, and Susan.

7. They were willing to accept the proposal; he was not.

8. The art students were expected to supply the following: brushes, paints, pallets, and pads.

9. The time is now: the time is right.

10. The highest scores on the final exam are as follows: Linda Jones, 96; John Smith, 94; Susan Green, 90. These grades are unusually high: they must have studied well.

Drill – Quotation Marks

1. "Take an umbrella," said his mother: "It looks like rain."

2. "I haven't seen my 'old lady' in five years!" he exclaimed.

3. "Can I write a comparative essay using 'To Autumn' and 'Ode to Nightingale' for the assignment?" asked the student.

4. "'My Favorite Things' is a popular song from *The Sound of Music*," he remarked.

5. Do you understand the difference between "overt" and "covert"?

6. The washing machine went "haywire" this afternoon.

7. They wondered if they could do the job.

8. "Joseph locked the door," said Andy; "then, he put the key under the doormat."

9. "You and Your Health" is a popular show on WMCA.

10. Mary said, "She is leaving for California tomorrow!"

11. "Don't ask any questions now!" Susan exclaimed. "I'm trying to read."

12. "I can't believe it!" she exclaimed.

13. "Give me a match!" she cried. "Don't you know it's dark in here?"

14. The article "Iran After the Revolution" appeared in last month's issue of *The Middle East Journal.*

15. "I can't begin to tell you what my day was like," said Karen. "It all began when I missed the bus."

16. "My history teacher suggested," Joe said, "that I read Sinclair Lewis' *Main Street.*

17. Sitting in the dark, she wondered: "Will the lights ever come back on?"

18. "February" is always a spelling problem for me.

19. "It was after his trip to Europe that he decided to enroll in college. It had been many years since he had been in school, but he truly wanted to return."

20. My aunt wanted to know how many years it had been since we last met.

21. "Come over here," said Charles. "I have something to show you."

22. "If he were here this moment," Linda said, "I know he would say, 'what's for dinner?'"

23. "I agree," said Mark. "It's time to take a stand."

24. "Please read Robert Frost's 'The Most of It,' in chapter fifteen, 'Modern Poetry,' in Gray's *Anthology of Poetry.*"

25. Joan realized it was time to leave the house.

Drill – The Apostrophe

Contractions

1. she'll
2. won't
3. Class of '81
4. doesn't
5. they've
6. we're
7. This boat isn't yours. We sold ours last year to Robert's parents.
8. At 10 o'clock they'll meet us at Macy's department store.
9. Linda's sister was politically active in the 1960's.
10. In Ms. Green's first grade class, she had difficulty writing x's and learning her ABCs.
11. Wordsworth's poem "The Solitary Reaper" was published in J. Mahoney's edition of *The Romantic Poets.*

12. Many of the defense attorney's witnesses were afraid to appear at John's trial.

13. "It's time to eat dinner," called James' mother.

14. Aren't you going to see if John is home so you can find out the results of Monday's game?

15. "Ode on a Grecian Urn," written by John Keats, is very famous. I've read it at least twenty times.

16. Isn't it a shame that Peter's team lost the game? They should have remembered their three Rs.

Possession

1. lady's, ladies'
2. child's, children's
3. cashier's, cashiers'
4. Filipino's, Filipinos'
5. country's, countries'
6. James', Jameses'
7. knife's, knives'
8. mouse's, mice's
9. roof's, roofs'
10. attorney's, attorneys'

Drill – Stops

1. "Good gracious!" she said. "Didn't you know that I was coming?"
2. Mr. Morgan works for the CIA.
3. Alexander wondered if it was time to go.
4. Leave me alone! Can't you see that I'm busy?
5. "How many boxes did you buy?" asked Dr. Jones.
6. "Be careful!" he shouted. "Didn't you see that car coming?"
7. Impossible! I have never seen anything like that before.
8. Lynn asked if anyone had the time.
9. What else can I do? I lost all my money.
10. Who cried "Help!"

Drill – Interjections, Dashes, and Parentheses

Interjections and Dashes

1. The use of the dash makes the sentence more urgent.
2. The use of the dash helps to convey a feeling of disbelief.
3. The words set off by dashes emphasize and modify the key words, "Time and patience."
4. The dashes help to emphasize and clarify the subject.
5. The dash is used to set off specifics.

Parentheses

1. The choice (in my opinion) was a good one. The comma in the sentence is unnecessary. The choice, in my opinion, was a good one. The parentheses are unnecessary in the sentence. "In my opinion" is not very necessary, since the statements made in writing are usually considered to be the author's, unless otherwise indicated.
2. Linda's comment ("Where did you get that dress?") wasn't intended to be sarcastic. The parentheses are a clear, effective method for containing a quote.
3. The parentheses properly set off material that is loosely connected to the central meaning of the sentence.
4. Last summer in Cape Cod (that was the first year we went there) we did a lot of sightseeing. The parentheses effectively contain the additional information.
5. The first time I went driving (do you remember the day?) I was so scared. The parentheses smoothly incorporate an important aside from the speaker.

Drill – Capitalization

1. Where is the Crab nebula?
2. The Girl Scouts of America sells delicious cookies.
3. This year, Senator Burns will run for reelection.
4. Barbara said, "Let me know when you are off the phone."
5. Beth's new car is a black Dodge Daytona which she purchased at the Dodge dealer in New York City.

6. Mike and Jackie are both graduates of Edison High School.

7. Glaciers from the Ice Age still exist.

8. Today in class, the professor lectured on the Neolithic age.

9. Aunt Stella will be visiting Washington, D.C. during February of next year.

10. We will be spending Easter Day with our Aunt Clara who lives near the Mississippi River.

11. Helen asked, "When will Betty and Rich be returning from Yellowstone Park?"

12. Our English teacher will be reviewing the first twenty pages of the book *Of Mice and Men* with the class.

13. The case went as high as the United States Court of Appeals.

14. At the baseball game last night, the Los Angeles Dodgers beat the New York Yankees by ten runs.

15. Eric asked the teacher, "Do you have a Webster's Dictionary?"

Drill – Writing Skills

1. **(C)** Evidence for Lincoln's feelings suggests that he was "saddened" by the bitter fighting, and that he had "worked hard to prevent a split." In addition, he felt that these soldiers had not died "in vain," or uselessly. Consequently, only (C) could be correct.

2. **(B)** The adjectival form "second," not the adverbial form "secondly," is appropriate here, since it modifies a noun not a verb.

3. **(B)** The opening verbal phrase is a dangling modifier. "Prevention" is not "faced" with anything; Lincoln is. All the other choices are standard English sentences.

4. **(C)** "With the outbreak . . ." is a prepositional phrase that is stopped with a period[.]. It has no subject or verb and is not a standard English sentence. All the rest are correct English.

5. **(C)** Since the pattern of the paragraph is to show evidence for how Dr. Goddard developed his rocket technology over time, only (C) could be correct. Transitions that show logical connections ("consequently," "thus,") are not appropriate. Also, choices (A), (B), and (D) are all abstract statements, not evidence for

Goddard's developmental progress. Only (C) meets both these requirements of the chronological pattern using concrete evidence to show Goddard's progress.

6. **(A)** The phrase "at one time . . ." is a nonrestrictive unit that is not necessary to the basic meaning of the sentence; consequently, both commas are needed. The commas for (B) and (D) are necessary to set off introductory or qualifying phrases. No commas are needed in (B) since the phrase that follows is a direct adjectival qualification of what kind of rockets they are as we know them today. Thus, no comma of separation is needed.

7. **(B)** This is just a long phrase; it has no subject or verb. (C) is an atypical, but rhetorically correct and standard English sentence. Many sentences in English begin with "And." The other choices are standard subject/verb independent sentence units.

8. **(A)** This word is too general for such a specific informational context. (B) should remain because it is the exact, or first, phrase the writer discusses. (C) need not be changed because only a synonym such as "real" would be needed, but the meaning would remain the same. (D) is all right because the writer points not to any specific study, research, or development done, but to all that type of "work" in general.

9. **(B)** The writer uses evidence in the form of illustrative examples to demonstrate that the executive woman in business is everywhere. (A) is incorrect for this reason. (C) is incorrect because the writer clearly states that she is no longer the "pariah," or outcast, of the business world. (D) is clearly incorrect because it stands in direct contradiction to what the writer's examples demonstrate of the ubiquity of her presence and the value of her paycheck.

10. **(C)** It is not the work force that is "for the better," but the situation for men. This is also supported by the rest of the evidence offered in the paragraph. The other sentences have their modifying phrases directly related to the idea they qualify.

11. **(B)** The writer is comparing before and after the appearance of women in management; only two things — therefore the comparative form, not the superlative, is correct: "greater." (A), (B), and (D) are all incorrect responses; they have no comparative adjectives, just adverbs used as qualifiers, e.g., "overly." These are used in a standard way.

12. **(B)** It is a run-on sentence, incorrectly punctuated with a comma after "families" instead of a period or a semicolon. The rest of the choices are all standard sentences.

13. **(C)** (A) is not correct because although the writer states that watching television doesn't demand much imagination, s/he never says that the entertainment

itself is unimaginative. (B) is not correct because it is not the best representation of the writer's complete point of view, but only part of it. (D) is incorrect because the third paragraph clearly supports the notion that television is neither demanding nor very educational.

14. **(D)** Has an incorrect agreement between "kids" and "does." Kids (they) do (something). All the other sentences use standard English syntax.

15. **(D)** The sentence is a rhetorical clause that begins with a subordinating conjunction, "because." Consequently, it cannot stand alone as a complete standard sentence. The rest are standard.

16. **(B)** The writer has to specify with the correct noun who exactly is drinking the orange juice. Since there is a possibility that the baby is female like the mother, it is not clear to whom the word "she" refers.

Part II: Writing Sample

- **I. Strategies for the Writing Sample**
- **II. Appropriate, Unified, and Focused Essays**
- **III. Writing Your Essay**
- **IV. Polishing and Editing Your Essay**

This review is meant to help you become familiar with the skills you will need to pass the Writing Sample portion of the Writing Section. In writing your essay, you will be asked to produce ideas, rather than analyze ideas. Our review will guide you through a step-by-step process of how to write your essay, from writing strategies to budgeting your time during the exam. Even if you feel that you are a good writer, you should still study this review as it will help you become familiar with the type of essay you will be expected to write. By reading through this review and going through the included drill, you will increase your chances of doing well on this section of the test.

As you begin reading each section of this review, try not to become frustrated if you feel that you are not a good writer. The strategies included are provided to help you write an essay which is to the point, easily understood, properly structured, well supported, and correct according to the rules of grammar. You will not be expected to write a best-selling book in order to pass this test. Remember, the more you practice the strategies provided in this review, the easier it will be for you to write a passing essay.

I. Strategies for the Writing Sample

To give yourself the best chance of writing a passing essay, you should follow these steps.

Before the test, this is your plan of attack:

➤ **Step 1** Study the following review to enhance your ability to write an essay. Remember, the sharper your skills, the more likely you are to receive a passing grade on your writing sample.

➤ **Step 2** Practice writing an essay. The best way to do this is to complete the drill at the end of the review. Make sure to take this drill under the same types of conditions you will experience when taking the actual exam.

➤ **Step 3** Learn and understand the directions, so that you don't waste valuable time reading them on the test day. This will allow you to quickly review them before writing your essay. The directions appear similar to the following.

DIRECTIONS: In this section, you are required to write an essay of between 300 and 600 words on the writing topic which appears on the next page. You should expect to spend approximately 60 minutes on your writing sample. During this time, you should organize your ideas, write a rough draft, and proofread and revise your draft essay.

Make sure to read the topic carefully and consider what your position will be before you start to write the essay. After you are confident in what you have written, copy your essay onto the lined pages of the Writing Sample answer sheet.

Your essay will be scored against the following seven criteria:

1. Appropriateness (how well you explore the given topic and how suitably you address your audience)
2. Unity and Focus (the pointedness of your perspective and direction)
3. Development (the quality of evidence that you offer to support your argument)
4. Organization (the logical arrangement of your essay)
5. Sentence Structure (how successfully you use sentences and how varied your sentence forms are)
6. Usage (the effectiveness and proper implementation of your word usage)

7. Mechanical Conventions (your proper use of spelling, punctuation, and capitalization)

Your essay must be written on the topic given and must employ numerous paragraphs. Make sure it is legible — if it cannot be read, it cannot be graded.

When writing your essay, this is your plan of attack:

➤ **Step 1** Decide immediately what your position will be in regard to the writing topic and stick to it.

➤ **Step 2** Organize your thoughts and write them on the provided scratch paper. Make sure to decide what points you will cover in your essay. You may want to jot down a brief outline of what each paragraph will include.

➤ **Step 3** Develop your essay from the notes you have made. Present your position clearly and logically, making sure to provide adequate examples and/or support. Write your draft on the scratch paper.

After writing your essay, this is your plan of attack:

➤ **Step 1** Proofread your essay! Check every word for errors in spelling. Be sure that your sentences are concise and grammatically correct. Make any necessary revisions.

➤ **Step 2** Copy the final version of your essay onto the lined pages of the Writing Sample answer sheet.

Additional Tips

- Be sure that you have not strayed from your topic or introduced points that you have not explained.
- Vary your types of sentences so that your essay flows smoothly and is easy to read.
- Use vocabulary that suits your audience. Make sure not to insult your audience by using simple vocabulary, or by explaining things they already know. Likewise, do not alienate your audience by using complicated jargon, or by assuming that they are already familiar with the subject on which you are writing.

II. Appropriate, Unified, and Focused Essays: Recognizing Effective Writing

Why Essays Exist

People write essays for purposes other than testing. Some of our best thinkers have written essays which we continue to read from generation to generation. Essays offer the reader a logical, coherent, and imaginative written composition showing the nature or consequences of a single controlling idea when considered from the writer's unique point of view. Writers use essays to communicate their opinion or position on a topic to readers who cannot be present during their live conversation. Writers use essays to help readers understand or learn about something that readers should or might want to know or do. Essays always express more or less directly the author's opinion, belief, position, or knowledge (backed by evidence) about the idea or object in question.

Organization and Purposeful Development

For this test you will need to recognize and generate the elements of an "excellent" essay. In essence, you will be taking the principles covered in Part I of this review and utilizing them to create your own original essay. With that in mind, read carefully the standards and explanations below to prepare you for what to look for in your own essay response.

Essay Writing

In academic writing, two purposes dominate essays:

1. Persuasion through argumentation using one, some, or all of the logical patterns described below,
2. Informing and Educating through analysis and using one, some, or all of the logical patterns described below.

All of an essay's organizational strategies may be used to argue in writing. The author offers reasons and/or evidence so an audience will be inclined to believe the position that the author presents about the idea under discussion. Writers use seven basic strategies to organize information and ideas in essays to help prove their point (thesis). All of these strategies might be useful in arguing for an idea and persuading a reader to see the issue the writer's way. Your job is to use strategies that are appropriate to demonstrate your thesis. For example, you may wish to use comparison/contrast to demonstrate that one thing or idea is better or worse than another.

As mentioned in the Multiple-Choice review, the following seven steps can be used to prove a thesis.

Seven Steps to Prove a Thesis

1. Show how a *process* or procedure does or should work step by step in time.
2. *Compare or contrast* two or more things or ideas to show important differences or similarities.
3. *Identify a problem* and then explain how to solve it.
4. *Analyze* into its components, or *classify* by its types or categories an idea or thing to show how it is put together or how it works, or how it is designed.
5. *Explain* why something happens to produce a particular result or set of results.
6. *Describe* the particular individual characteristics, beauty and features, of a place, person(s), time, or idea.
7. *Define* what a thing is or what an idea means.

Depending upon the purpose of the essay, one pattern tends to dominate the discussion question. (For example, the writer might use *description* and *explanation* to define the varied meanings of "love.")

The Writing Process: Controlling Organization, Paragraph Development, Sentence Structure, Usage, and Mechanical Conventions

During this test you will be called upon to exercise control over your writing by using the writing process and by knowing the pitfalls of weak writing and correcting them. Using the steps outlined below, compose your essay in the order suggested and note the elements and qualities to correct during each stage of the process of composing your essay test response. Make any corrections you need during the appropriate stage of the writing process; to correct errors at the wrong stage may waste time and interfere with your producing the best essay response.

Composing Your Essay: Using the Writing Process

Most of us think (erroneously) that writers just sit down and churn out a wonderful essay or poem in one sitting in a flash of genius and inspiration. This is not true. Writers use the writing process from start to finish to help them to write a clear document. If you do not reflect on your composition in stages and make changes as you develop it, you will not see all the problems or errors in it. Don't try to write an essay just once and leave the room. Stay and look through it. Reflect upon it using the writing process in the following way.

The writing process has about four or five steps: (1) Prewriting or Planning time, (2) Rough Drafting, (3) Organizing and Revising the ideas (not the words or sentences themselves), (4) Polishing or Editing (making sure sentences themselves are sentences, that the words you use are the right words, and that the spelling and punctuation are correct), and (5) Proofreading to make sure no little mistakes are left.

Using this process does not mean that you have to write five drafts. Write *one* draft (*stages* 1 and 2), leaving space for corrections (e.g., writing on every other line) and then working on the existing draft through the rest of the *stages* (3 through 5). If time allows, you may want to do the whole process on scrap paper and then copy the finished product onto the allotted test paper. But if you do copy it, make sure you proofread your copy to see if while transcribing it you left anything out or said a word twice or made any other errors.

Out of the four hours in which you have to take the TASP, set aside 60 minutes for your Writing Sample. You might allocate your time for the five writing steps in this manner:

1. Prewriting, Planning: 5 minutes
2. Rough Draft: 20 minutes
3. Organizing, checking evidence, checking "flow," and paragraphing: 20 minutes
4. Polishing, Editing: 5–10 minutes
5. Proofreading: 2–5 minutes

If you have more time or less time, adjust this schedule proportionately. Practice this with someone timing you.

III. Writing Your Essay

Prewriting/Planning Time

Read the essay question and decide on your purpose. Do you want to persuade your reader? Would you rather explain something?

Sample: "Television is bad for people."

Do you agree or disagree with this statement? Decide. Take a stand. Don't be noncommittal. Write down the statement of your position.

Sample: I agree that television is bad for people.

or

Television is an excellent learning tool and is good for most people.

This is your thesis.

Consider Your Audience

The writer's responsibility is to write clearly, honestly, and cleanly for the reader's sake. Essays would be pointless without an audience. Why write an essay if no one wants or needs to read it? Why add evidence, organize your ideas, or correct bad grammar? The reason to do any of these things is that someone out there needs to understand what you mean or say. What would the audience need to know in order to believe you or to come over to your position? Imagine someone you know (visualize her — name him) listening to you declare your position or opinion and then saying, "Oh yeah? Prove it!"

In writing your essay, make sure to answer the following questions:

What evidence do you need to prove your idea to this skeptic?

What would s/he disagree with you about?

What does s/he share with you as common knowledge?

What does s/he need to be told by you?

Control Your Point of View

We may write essays from one of three points of view, depending upon the essay's audience. The points of view below are discussed from Informal to Formal.

1. Subjective/Personal Point of View:

   "I think

   "I believe . . . cars are more trouble than they are worth."

   "I feel

2. Second Person (We . . . You; I . . . You): "If *you* own a car, *you* soon find out that it is more trouble than it is worth."

3. Third Person Point of View: (focuses on the idea, not what "I" think of it): "*Cars* are more trouble than *they* are worth."

Stick with one or another; don't switch your "point of view" in the middle. Any one is acceptable.

Consider Your Support

Next, during prewriting, jot down a few phrases that show ideas and examples that support your point of view. Do this quickly on a separate piece of paper for about *five minutes.* Don't try to outline, simply *list things* that you think might be important to discuss. After you have listed several, pick at least three to five things you want or need to discuss, and number them in the order of importance that is relevant to proving your point.

Write Your Rough Draft

Spend about *20 minutes* writing your *rough draft.* Looking over at your prewriting list, write down what you think is useful to prove your point in the order you think best to convince the reader. Be sure to *use real evidence* from your life experience or knowledge to support what you say. You do not have to draw evidence from books; your own life is equally appropriate.

For example, don't write, "Cars are more trouble to fix than bicycles" and then not show evidence for your idea. Give *examples* of what you mean: "*For example,* my father's Buick needs two hundred parts to make one brake work, but my bicycle only has four pieces that make up the brakes, and I can replace those myself." Write naturally and quickly. Don't worry too much at this point about paragraphing, spelling, punctuation — just write down what you think or want to say in the order determined on your list.

Transitions

To help the reader follow the flow of your ideas, and to help unify the essay, use transitions to show the connections among your ideas. You may use transitions either at the beginnings of paragraphs, or you may use them to show the connections among ideas within a single paragraph.

Here again are some typical transitional words and phrases that you should use when writing your essay.

To link similar ideas, use the words:

again	for example	likewise
also	for instance	moreover
and	further	nor

another	furthermore	of course
besides	in addition	similarly
equally important	in like manner	too

To link dissimilar/contradictory ideas, use words such as:

although	however	otherwise
and yet	in spite of	provided that
as if	instead	still
but	nevertheless	yet
conversely	on the contrary	
even if	on the other hand	

To indicate cause, purpose, or result, use:

as	for	so
as a result	for this reason	then
because	hence	therefore
consequently	since	thus

To indicate time or position, use words like:

above	before	meanwhile
across	beyond	next
afterward	eventually	presently
around	finally	second
at once	first	thereafter
at the present time	here	thereupon

To indicate an example or summary, use phrases such as:

as a result	in any event	in short
as I have said	in brief	on the whole
for example	in conclusion	to sum up
for instance	in fact	
in any case	in other words	

Grammar

Correct use of grammar is also a very important element in writing a good essay. Therefore, you should make sure to correctly employ all of the rules of standard written English. If you feel that your grammar skills are not up to par, go back and restudy our Review of Standard Written English which appears in Part I of this chapter.

Providing Evidence in Your Essay

You may employ any one of the seven steps previously listed to prove any thesis that you maintain is true. But as explained in the Multiple-Choice review, you may call on evidence from one or all of the four following kinds of evidence to support the thesis of your essay. Identify which kind(s) of evidence you can use to prove the points of your essay. In test situations, most essayists use anecdotal evidence or analogy to explain, describe, or prove a thesis. But if you know salient facts or statistics, don't hesitate to call upon them.

1. **Hard data** (facts, statistics, scientific evidence, research) — documented evidence that has been verified to be true.

2. **Anecdotal evidence** — stories from the writer's own experience and knowledge that illustrate a particular point or idea.

3. **Expert opinions** — assertions, usually by authorities on the matter under discussion.

4. **Analogies** — show a resemblance between one phenomenon and another.

Organizing and Reviewing the Paragraphs

The unit of work for revising is the paragraph. After you have written what you wanted to say based on your prewriting list, spend about *20 minutes* revising your draft by looking to see if you need to indent for paragraphs anywhere. If you do, make a little proofreader's mark (¶) to indicate to the reader that you think a paragraph should start here. Check to see if you want to add anything that would make your point of view more convincing. Be sure to supply useful transitions to keep up the flow and maintain the focus of your ideas. If you don't have room on the paper, or if your new paragraph shows up out of order, add that paragraph and indicate with a number or some other mark where you want it to go. Check to *make sure* that you gave examples or illustrations for your statements. In the examples below, two paragraphs are offered: one without concrete evidence and one with evidence for its idea. Study each. Note the topic sentence (T) and how that sentence is or is not supported with evidence.

Paragraphing with No Evidence

(T) Television is bad for people. *Watching television takes time away from other things.* Programs on television are often stupid and depict crimes that people later copy. Television takes time away from loved ones, and it often becomes addictive. So, television is bad for people because it is no good.

Comment: In this example, the author has not give any concrete evidence for any of the good ideas presented. S/he just declares them to be so. Any one of the sentences above might make a good opening sentence for a whole paragraph. Take the second sentence for example:

Watching television takes time away from other things. (first piece of evidence) For example, all those hours people spend sitting in front of the tube, they could be working on building a chair or fixing the roof. *(second piece of evidence)* Maybe the laundry needs to be done, but because people watch television, they may end up not having time to do it. Then Monday comes around again and they have no socks to wear to work — all because they couldn't stand to miss that episode of "Everybody Loves Raymond." *(third piece of evidence)* Someone could be writing a letter to a friend in Boston who hasn't been heard from or written to for months. *(fourth piece of evidence)* Or maybe someone misses the opportunity to take in a beautiful day in the park because s/he had to see "Jerry Springer." They'll repeat "Jerry Springer," but this beautiful day only comes around once. Watching television definitely keeps people from getting things done.

The primary evidence the author uses here is that of probable illustrations taken from life experience, largely anecdotal. Always *supply evidence.* Three examples or illustrations of your idea per paragraph is a useful number. Four is OK, but stop there. Don't go on and on about a single point. You don't have time. In order for a typical test essay to be fully developed, it should have about five paragraphs, organized in the following manner:

Introduction: A paragraph which shows your point of view (thesis) about an issue and introduces your position with three general ideas which support your thesis.

Development: Three middle paragraphs which prove your position from different angles, using evidence from real life and knowledge. Each paragraph of the middle should support each of the three ideas you started out with in Paragraph 1.

Conclusion: The last paragraph, which sums up your position and adds one final reminder of what the issue was, perhaps points to a solution:

> So, television takes away from the quality of life and is therefore bad for human beings. We should be watching the sun, the sky, the birds, and each other, not the "boob tube."

Write a paragraph below using this sentence as your focus:

"Television takes valuable time away from our loved ones."

Check for Logic

Make sure that you present your argument in a logical manner. If you have not, you may not have proven your point. Your conclusion must follow from a logical set of premises.

Once again, here is a list of typical fallacies that writers may fall into.

- **Either/Or** — The writer assumes that only two opposing possibilities may be attained: "Either this . . . , or this . . . ."
- **Oversimplification** — The writer simplifies the subject: "Only the rich are happy."
- **Begging the question** — The writer assumes he has proved something which needs to be proven: "People who go to college always attain good jobs."
- **Ignoring the issue** — The writer argues against the truth of an issue due to its conclusion: "John is a good boy and therefore did not rob the store."
- **Arguing against a person, not an idea** — The writer argues that somebody's idea has no merit because s/he is immoral or personally stupid: "Eric will fail out of school because he is not doing well in gym class."
- **Non Sequitur** — The writer leaps to the wrong conclusion: "Jake is from Canada; he must play hockey."
- **Drawing the wrong conclusion from a sequence** — The author attributes the outcome to the wrong reasons: "Betty married at a young age to an older man and now has three children and is therefore a housewife."

IV. Polishing and Editing Your Essay

If the unit of work for revising is the paragraph, the unit of work for editing is the sentence. In *the last 5 to 10 minutes,* check your paper for mistakes in editing. To help you in this task, follow our checklist.

Polishing Checklist

- Are all your sentences *really* sentences, or have you written some fragments or run-on sentences?
- Are you using your vocabulary correctly?
- Have you used some word which seems colloquial or informal?
- Did you leave out punctuation anywhere? Did you capitalize correctly? Did you check for commas, periods, and quotation marks?

Proofreading

In the last three to five minutes, read your paper word for word, first forward and then backward, reading from the end to the beginning. Doing so can help you find errors that you may have missed by having read forwards only.

Now, try your hand at applying these techniques by completing the following drill.

☞ Drill: Writing Sample

DIRECTIONS: Write an essay on the following topic.

Many scholars note the decline of interest in literature written before the twentieth century. A diminishing number of students pursue studies in Classical, Medieval, and even Renaissance literature. In an essay written to an English teacher, argue whether you feel that the trend of studying modern versus past literature is commendable or contemptible. Reflect on modern culture and the effects of literature upon it. Discuss the advantages/disadvantages of a study that excludes or minimizes the literature of earlier periods. Finally, draw upon your own exposure to and attitude toward modern and past literatures, respectively.

ESSAY WRITING DRILLS

ANSWER KEY

Drill – Writing Sample

Writing Sample with a Score of 6, 7, or 8

(A student scoring a 6, 7, or 8 on his/her essay automatically passes the Writing Section of the TASP, without requiring the grading of his/her multiple-choice questions.)

The Literature of the Past

The direction of modern literary scholarship points toward an alarming conclusion. The depreciation of the literary study of bygone periods is a sign of two disturbing trends. First, scholars are avoiding more difficult study in preference to what seems light or facile. Furthermore, the neglect of the literature of former eras is a denial of the contribution that past authors have made toward modern literature. This is not to suggest that all scholars who study modern literature do so because they are either intimidated by past literature or do not appreciate its value. However, the shrinking minority of past literary scholarship is a clear indication that intimidation and awe of past conventions are deterrents to many students of literature.

The dread associated with past literature reflects poorly upon our society. The attempts to simplify literature to accommodate simpler audiences has resulted in a form of literary deflation. The less society taxes its audience's minds, the less comprehensive those unexercised minds become. Information and ideas are now transmitted to the average man through the shallow medium of television programming. Modern students are evolving from this medium, and the gap separating them from the complexity of the classics is continuing to grow.

Once more, it is important to stress that this essay does not seek to diminish students of modern literature. The only demand this argument makes upon modern students is that they supplement their study with significant portions of the classics from which all subsequent literature has been derived, whether consciously or unconsciously. Failure to do so is an act akin to denying the importance of history itself. Like history, literature exists as an evolutionary process; modern literature can only have come into existence through the development of past literature.

Concerning the relative complexity of the classics to modern literature, the gap is not so great as one may think. Surely, one who glances at the works of

Shakespeare or Milton without prior exposure will be daunted by them. However, a disciplined mind can overcome the comprehensive barriers erected over the past few centuries through persistence and perseverance.

Unfortunately, the ability to overcome the barriers to past literature may eventually become obsolete. The more frequently students select their courses of study through fear rather than interest, the wider the literary gap will become, until the pampered minds of all future readers will prove unequal to the task of reading the literature of our fathers. The more frequently students deny the usefulness of the literature antedating this century, the more frequently they deny their own literary heritage, the more probable it will become for modern literature's structure to crumble through lack of firm foundation.

Features of the Writing Sample Scoring 6, 7, or 8

Appropriateness

The paper's topic and the writer's viewpoint are both well laid out in the first paragraph. The two trends described by the author in the topic paragraph are explored in deeper detail throughout the essay. The language and style fit the writer's audience. The style is formal, but possesses a personalized voice.

Unity and Focus

The essay follows the course presented in the topic paragraph, reemphasizing major points such as the writer's reluctance to condemn all modern scholars. This emphasis is not straight repetition, but carries different viewpoints and evidence for the writer's argument. The digression on television in the second paragraph neatly rounds off the writer's overall concern for cultural consequences of past literature's depreciation.

Development

The writer follows the suggestions of the writing assignment closely, structuring his essay around the reflections and discussions listed therein. Each paragraph bears an example to lend authority to the writer's argument. The second paragraph uses the theory of television's vegetative influence. The third paragraph utilizes the evolutionary equality of history. The fourth paragraph evokes names that the reader can relate to in terms of comprehensive difficulty.

Organization

Many transitional conventions are utilized. "Once more . . ."; "Concerning the relative complexity . . ."; "Unfortunately . . ." The examples throughout the paragraphs have a pointed direction. The conclusion paragraph rounds off the argument with a premonition of future calamity should its warning go unheeded.

Sentence Structure

The sentences are standardized and vary in form, although some passive constructions ("will be daunted," "the more probable it will become") may have been avoided. The repetition of "the more frequently" in the final paragraph is particularly effective and pointed.

Usage

Words are chosen to offer variety. "Past literature" is supplemented by "literary study of bygone days" and "the literature of former eras." Phrasing is consistent and standard, although the third sentence of the second paragraph ("The less society taxes...the less comprehensive...") is slightly awkward, though the repetition does achieve some effect.

Mechanical Conventions

Spelling and punctuation are mostly standard throughout the essay. The sentences in the final paragraph might be divided and shortened, although this might diminish their effect.

Writing Sample with a Score of 5

(A student scoring a 5 on his/her essay must obtain 25 correct answers out of the 35 scored multiple-choice items in order to pass the Writing Section of the TASP.)

Modern Literature

It doesn't matter whether or not we read past literature. Past literature has been converted into what we now know as "modern literature." The elements of the past are therefore incorporated into the body of what we now have.

When we read a work of modern literature based upon the classics, such as Joyce's *Ulysses,* it doesn't matter whether or not we've read Homer's *Odyssey.* What matters is what Joyce made out of Homer's epic; not what Homer started out with.

When we see *West Side Story* in the movies, it doesn't matter whether or not we've read *Romeo and Juliet*: the end result is the same; therefore, we do not need to know the original source. I don't think it makes a difference whether or not we even recognize Tony and Maria as Romeo and Juliet. Tony and Maria are today's versions of Romeo and Juliet, and they match the culture that they are told in.

It has been said that all of the good plots have been used up by past ages, and that all we create now are variations of those plots. This statement is false. It is rather the case that these plots are universal variables that each age must interpret in its own unique way. I find it rather faseatious to study the interpretation of other cultures. We should be concerned only with our own.

Past literature is not necessary in a modern world that has reformed the mistakes of the past. Anything that hasn't carried over from the past is negligible: what was good for Shakespeare's audience may not be what we need. In conclusion, I would have to strongly conclude that the "trend of studying modern versus past literature" is commendable, and not contemptible.

Features of the Writing Sample Scoring 5

Appropriateness

The main topic is not supplied directly within the work. Though the reader is aware of the conflict between modern and past literature, there is no sense of scholarly consensus as suggested by the writing assignment. The writer's somewhat informal style is unbalanced throughout the work by his uncertainty with his audience.

Unity and Focus

Though the writer knows the point he is trying to promote, his evidence is presented haphazardly and without a logical design. However, his rather abrupt conclusion is somewhat supported by his points.

Development

The essay does not follow a logical pattern; one premise does not meld comfortably into another. Though the premises loosely support the conclusion, they do not support each other.

Organization

Transitions are slight, if any. The repetition of "when we" opening two paragraphs is noticeable. Each point should have been further developed. The writer assumes his reader is quite familiar with *West Side Story* and its characters.

Sentence Structure

Most sentences follow standard sentence structure, although some are very irregular. The first sentence of paragraph three expresses two or three independent thoughts and should be separated accordingly. The final sentence of the fourth paragraph contains an unclear modifier: "own" should read either "own interpretation" or "own culture."

Usage

Most words are used in their proper context, and an attempt has been made to use some erudite words. "End result" is redundant; "end" should have been excluded. The declaration that "this statement is false" in the fourth paragraph is not supported by logical evidence. In this case, the writer should have asserted that this was his own opinion. However, in other cases it is recommended that the writer be bold with assertions. A degree of proof is all that is required to make those assertions. "In conclusion" is redundant with "conclude" in the final sentence of the essay. Contractions such as "we've" and "don't" should be written out in their long forms.

Mechanical Conventions

Most words are spelled properly, although "faseatious" should be spelt "facetious." The period in the second sentence of the first paragraph should lie within the quotation marks. The comma after "commendable" in the final paragraph should be eliminated because it does not introduce a new clause.

Writing Sample with a Score of 4, 3, 2, or 1

(A student scoring a 4, 3, 2, or 1 on his/her essay automatically fails the Writing Section of the TASP.)

Modern literature is no better than past literature, and vice-versa. It is interest that matters. If people aren't interested in the past, then so be it. A famous man once said "To each his own". I agree.

For example, you can see that books are getting easier and easier to understand. This is a good thing, because more knowledge may be comunicated this way. Comunication is what literature is all about: Some people comunicate with the past, and others with the present.

I communicate with the present. I'm not saying we all should. It's all up to your point of view. When a scholer chooses past over present, or vice-versa, that's his perogative. It doesn't make him better or worse than anybody else. We should all learn to accept each other's point of view.

When I read someone like Fitzgerald or Tolkien, I get a different feeling than Shakespeare. Shakespeare can inspire many people, but I just don't get that certain feeling from his plays. "The Hobbit," "The Great Gatsby," "Catcher in the Rye," and "Of Mice and Men." These are all great classics from this century. We should be proud of them. However, some people prefer "The Trojan War" and "Beowulf." Let them have it. Remember: "To each his own."

Features of the Writing Sample Scoring 4, 3, 2, or 1

Appropriateness

The writer misconstrues the topic and writes about the relative worth of modern and past literature. The topic does not call for a judgment of period literatures; it calls for a study on the way in which they are studied. His personal style is too familiarized; it is unclear to whom the essay is addressed.

Unity and Focus

The writer seems to contradict his own points at times, favoring modern literature rather than treating the subject as objective as he had proposed. It is clear that the writer's train of thought shifted during the essay. This was covered up by ending with the catch phrase, "to each his own."

Development

The writer attempts to angle his argument in different ways by presenting such concepts as "communication" and "point of view." However, his thought processes are abrupt and underdeveloped.

Organization

There is neither direction nor logical flow in the essay. One point follows the next without any transition or connection. All three persons are used to prove his argument: the writer resorts to "I," "you," and "a famous man." It is clear there is no overall thesis guiding the essay.

Sentence Structure

Some sentences follow standard formation. Sentence three of the final paragraph is a fragment. The sentences are short and choppy, as is the thought they convey. Too many sentences are merely brief remarks on the preceding statements (e.g., "I agree"; "Let them have it"; etc.). These are not appropriate because they do not evoke new thought. The reference to Shakespeare in the first sentence of the final paragraph implies more than the writer intended. It should read: "than when I read Shakespeare."

Usage

Many words are repeated without any attempt to supply synonyms (e.g., "communication," "past"). Colloquial expressions are widespread, and should be avoided. *The Trojan War* is evidently an improper reference to Homer's *Iliad.*

Mechanical Conventions

There are many mechanical errors. Punctuation and spelling are inconsistent. "Comunication" and "comunicate" are spelt improperly in paragraph two, while "communicate" is spelt correctly in paragraph three. "Scholer" should be spelt "scholar." "Perogative" should be spelt "prerogative." In the fourth sentence of the first paragraph, the period should lie within the quotation marks as it does in the final sentence of the essay. The book titles in sentences three and six of the final paragraph should be underlined and not quoted.

TASP

Texas Academic Skills Program

Practice Test 1

READING SECTION

(ANSWER SHEETS APPEAR IN THE BACK OF THIS BOOK.)

DIRECTIONS: You will encounter eight passages in this section of the test, each followed by a number of questions. Only **ONE** answer to each question is the **best** answer, although more than one answer may appear to be correct. There are 45 multiple-choice questions in this section. Choose your answers carefully and mark them on your answer sheet. Make sure that the space you are marking corresponds to the answer you have chosen.

Read the passage and answer the questions that follow.

Adapted from: "South Dakota's Badlands: Castles in Clay," by John Madson

1 One of the most wonderful things about the North American continent is its diversity. And one of the most unusual extreme aspects of this diversity is located in South Dakota: the Badlands National Park. Located in a ***semi-arid*** area, this wonder of nature goes through long periods of drought followed by torrential rains. The result is erosion that continually shapes the landscape. Composed largely of volcanic ash, the terrain assumes amazing shapes that are formed by water. The rivers spread mud, sand, and gravel on the flatlands; the erosion that affects those deposits results in the spectacular scenery we see in South Dakota.

2 The geological history of the Badlands is fascinating. Millions of years ago on these plains, erosion took place much more slowly than the deposits accumulated. However, time has reversed the process.

3 Today, the buildup of these same deposits occurs at a much slower rate than the rate of erosion. The by-products of this wearing away are spires, pinnacles, and ridges that give the suggestion of castles in the clay. And today the heart of this picturesque site is the Badlands National Park.

4 Like the ever-changing face of sand dunes along the seashore, the complexion of the Badlands doesn't stay the same. Rain constantly eats away at surfaces, changing the shapes and reducing sizes. Old layers of sediment deposits peel off to reveal new sights. Fossils are among them. One may find an ancient tool from an earlier stage of man, a tooth from some now-extinct animal. One such important find in the Badlands is the oredont, a pig-shaped mammal. Other finds include saber-toothed cats, especially the Hyaenodon. This wolf-like creature was the size of a black bear.

5 Because of such revelations, fossil hunting is popular in the Badlands. However, only licensed paleontologists are allowed to remove fossils from the park. Officials insist that treasures uncovered by natural elements like rain remain in the park, except of course for those removed by licensed scientists. While officials acknowledge that the weather will eventually destroy these fossils, they also think that science and the general public will benefit more from them if they are left alone. And plenty of fossils remain. South Dakota, a main passageway for mammals that migrated here from Asia across the Bering Straits, has been a site for a large mammal population in the past — pronghorn antelope, grizzly bears, gray wolves, bighorn sheep, and coyotes.

6 Today the Badlands National Park protects the land, the animals, and the fossils alike. This protection can help to partially restore what has been lost in the past to early American settlers and miners who inhabited the area when the country was younger. However, the park area has not always been protected. In 1922 and 1928 efforts to create a national park failed. President Franklin Roosevelt did erect a Badlands National Monument, but a national park was not established until 1978.

As far as wild game is concerned, a resurgence in the number of species has taken place. In 1963, for example, twenty-eight bison were introduced into the area as well as twelve Rocky Mountain bighorn sheep. Since that time a wide variety of animals has flourished under the protection of the Badlands National Park.

1. Which of the following best defines the word ***semi-arid*** as it is used in the first paragraph of the selection?

   (A) Desolate and isolated

   (B) Dry

   (C) Containing shapes formed by rain

   (D) Desert

2. Which of the following best expresses the main idea of the selection?

   (A) The beauty of the South Dakota Badlands is in danger of being lost to natural erosion.

   (B) The South Dakota Badlands is now protected as a national park for its rich geological and biological history.

   (C) The government has failed to stop the loss of endangered species and items of scientific value in the South Dakota Badlands.

   (D) The South Dakota Badlands should become a national park in order to have its natural resources protected.

3. In the fifth paragraph the writer mentions that South Dakota was the main passageway for mammals as they migrated to this continent from Asia across the Bering Straits. The writer probably includes this information in order to

   (A) reinforce the idea that much of North American wildlife came from Asia.

   (B) identify the reason for the extinction of so many animals in the Badlands.

   (C) encourage people to visit the Badlands.

   (D) explain the presence of so many fossils in the Badlands.

4. According to the selection, which of the following occurred first in the formations found in the Badlands?

   (A) Land erosion

   (B) Formation of spires, pinnacles, and ridges

   (C) Sediment buildup caused by rivers

   (D) Formation of new shapes by rainfall

5. Which of the following sets of topics would best organize the information in the selection?

(A) I. Role of erosion in the formation of the Badlands
    II. Fossils as an effect of erosion in the Badlands
    III. Conservation of the Badlands

(B) I. Weather conditions in the Badlands
    II. Animal life in the Badlands
    III. Tourism in the Badlands

(C) I. Historical significance of the Badlands
    II. Federal regulations of the Badlands
    III. Future of the Badlands

(D) I. Effects of erosion on the Badlands
    II. Effects of animal migration on erosion in the Badlands
    III. Protection of the Badlands

Read the passage and answer the questions that follow.

Adapted from: "Religion Without Dogma," by C.S. Lewis

1 Professor Hostead, in his article "Modern Agnosticism Justified," argues that a) religion is basically belief in God and immortality, b) most religions consist of ***"accretions of dogma and mythology"*** that science has disproven, c) it would be desirable, if it were possible, to keep the basic religious belief without those accumulations of religious notions and legends, but that d) science has rendered even the basic elements of religion almost as incredible as the "accretions." For the doctrine of immortality involves the view that man is a composite creature, a soul in a state of symbiosis with a physical organism. But science can successfully regard man only monastically, as a single organism whose psychological characteristics all arise from his physical nature; the soul then becomes indefensible. In conclusion, Professor Hostead asserts that our only hope rests in empirical, observable evidence for the existence of the soul; in fact, in the findings of psychical research.

2 My disagreement with Professor Hostead starts at the beginning. I do not consider the essence of religion as simply the belief in God and immortality. Early Judaism, for example, didn't accept immortality. The human soul in Sheol (the afterworld) took no account of Jehovah, and God in turn took no account of the soul. In Sheol all things are forgotten. The religion revolved around the ritual and ethical demands of God and on the blessings people received from him. During earthly life these blessings were usually material in nature: happy life, many children, good health, and such. But we do see a more religious note also. The Jew hungers

for the living God; he obeys God's laws devoutly; he considers himself as impure and sinful in Jehovah's presence. God is the sole object of worship. Buddhism makes the doctrine of immortality vital, while we find little in the way of that which is religious. The existence of the gods is not denied, but it has no religious significance. In Stoicism again both the practice of religion and the belief in immortality are variables, not absolute traits of religion. Even within Christianity itself we find, as in Stoicism, the subordinate position of immortality.

6. Which of the following best defines the phrase ***accretions of dogma and mythology*** as it is used in the first paragraph?

   (A) Combinations of fact and fiction

   (B) Conflicts of sound principles and unsound theories

   (C) Implications and ideas of religion

   (D) Religious ideas and fables that have gradually accumulated to form accepted religious belief

7. What is the main idea of the entire passage?

   (A) Belief in God is scientifically valid.

   (B) Professor Hostead's assumption that the essence of religion is the belief in God and immortality is incorrect.

   (C) Neither Judaism, Buddhism, Stoicism, nor Christianity fit into Hostead's definition of religion.

   (D) Judaism, Buddhism, Stoicism, and Christianity are all valid ideologies in their regard for immortality and belief in God.

8. The writer's purpose in this passage is to

   (A) outline basic tenets of Judaism, Buddhism, Stoicism, and Christianity.

   (B) establish scientific credibility of four ideologies so as to undermine Hostead's positions.

   (C) attack Hostead's views by establishing the vulnerability of Hostead's first position.

   (D) define the essence of religion.

9. According to this selection, how does Judaism exemplify an error in Hostead's assertions?

   (A) Early Judaism emphasized earthly rewards from God instead of eternal life with God.

   (B) Judaism can be proven scientifically.

(C) The existence of gods is not religiously significant.

(D) Judaism emphasizes only a man's social behavior in this world as a prescription for earthly existence, not the worship of an actual supreme being.

10. The writer uses Judaism, Buddhism, Stoicism, and Christianity to illustrate

(A) the superiority of Christianity over the other three religions.

(B) that the essence of religion is not necessarily belief in God and immortality.

(C) empirical evidence for the soul, the psychical research, which Hostead requires as proof for the soul.

(D) the validity of religious thought over a scientific system devoid of religious, spiritual beliefs.

11. Which of the following lists of topics best organizes the information in this passage?

(A) I. Hostead's definition of religion
II. Writer's definition of religion
III. Illustrations to support new definition

(B) I. Hostead's definition of religion
II. Writer's definition of Judaism
III. Writer's comparison of other ideologies to Judaism

(C) I. Hostead's position regarding religion
II. Writer's problem with Hostead's position
III. Illustrations to support objections

(D) I. Hostead's definition of religion
II. Hostead's definition of science
III. Writer's position against Hostead's definition of religion and science

Read the passage and answer the questions that follow.

Economic Effects of the Depression

1 During the early months of the depression most people thought it was just an adjustment in the business cycle which would soon be over. Hoover repeatedly assured the public that prosperity was just around the corner. As time went on, the worst depression in American history set in, reaching its bottom point in early 1932.

The gross national product fell from $104.6 billion in 1929 to $56.1 billion in 1933. Unemployment reached about 13 million in 1933, or about 25 percent of the labor force excluding farmers. National income dropped 54 percent from $87.8 billion to $40.2 billion. Labor income fell about 41 percent, while farm income dropped 55 percent from $11.9 billion to $5.3 billion. Industrial production dropped about 51 percent. The banking system suffered as 5,761 banks, over 22 percent of the total, failed by the end of 1932.

UNEMPLOYMENT, 1929-1945

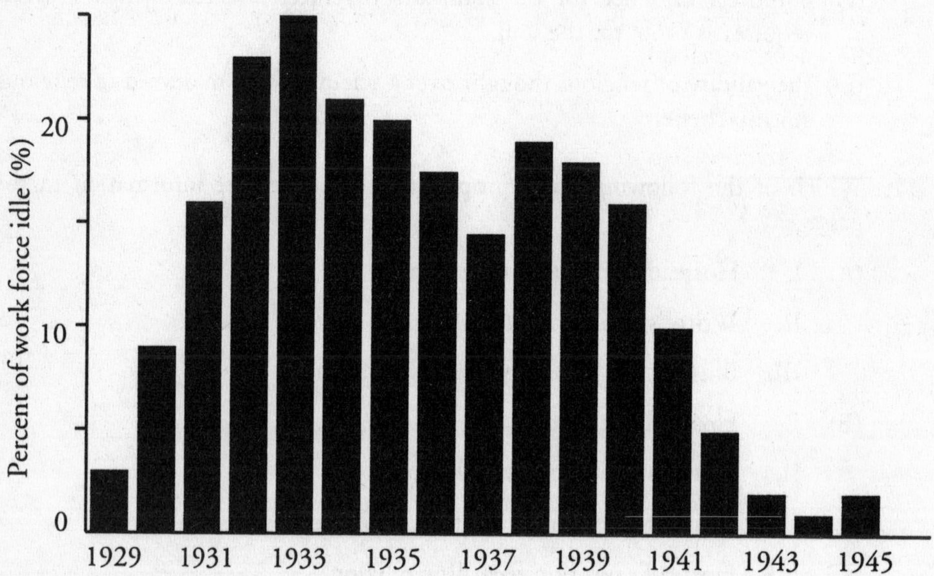

2 As the depression grew worse, more and more people lost their jobs or had their wages reduced. Many were unable to continue credit payments on homes, automobiles, and other possessions, and lost them. Families doubled up in houses and apartments. Both the marriage rate and the birth rate declined as people put off ***family formation.*** Hundreds of thousands became homeless and lived in groups of makeshift shacks called Hoovervilles in empty spaces around cities. Others traveled the country by foot and boxcar seeking food and work. State and local government agencies and private charities were overwhelmed in their attempts to care for those in need, although public and private soup kitchens and soup lines were set up throughout the nation. Malnutrition was widespread but few died of starvation, perhaps because malnourished people are susceptible to many fatal diseases.

12. The author's purpose for writing this passage was probably

    (A) to degrade Hoover's presidency.

    (B) to track the gross national product.

(C) to link Depression statistics to their effects in everyday life.

(D) to monitor the effects of the banking system.

13. Which of the following best explains the meaning of the last sentence?

(A) Many diseases can make people immune to starvation.

(B) Many diseases cause malnutrition.

(C) Few malnourished people survived diseases long enough to starve.

(D) Few died to the effects of malnutrition.

14. What is the meaning of the term ***family formation*** in the fourth sentence of the second paragraph?

(A) Family inception and growth

(B) Family statistics

(C) Rank and file of the family system

(D) Family census

15. According to the selection, which of the following provisions was made in accordance with the overwhelming of government agencies and private charities?

(A) Hoovervilles

(B) Two-family houses

(C) Private soup kitchens and soup lines

(D) Disease centers

16. According to the bar graph, the unemployment rate was highest in

(A) 1929.

(B) 1933.

(C) 1938.

(D) 1944.

17. According to the graph, the unemployment rate was lowest in

(A) 1929.

(B) 1933.

(C) 1938.

(D) 1944.

Read the passage and answer the questions that follow.

Natural Resources and Environment

1 *Objectives.* The Forest Service has the Federal responsibility for national leadership in forestry. Its mission is to provide a continuing flow of natural resource goods and services to help meet the needs of the Nation and to contribute to the needs of the international community. To accomplish this, it has adopted the following objectives:

1. provide a sustained flow of renewable resources — outdoor recreation, ***forage***, wood, water, wilderness, wildlife, and fish — in a combination that best meets the needs of society now and in the future;
2. administer the nonrenewable resources of the National Forest System to help meet the Nation's need for energy for the Nation's forests and rangeland;
3. develop and make available scientific and technological capabilities to advance renewable natural resource management, use, and protection; and
4. further natural resource conservation through cooperation with other Federal agencies and State and local governments.

2 *National Forest System.* The Forest Service manages 156 national forests, 19 national grasslands, and 17 land utilization projects on 191 million acres in 44 states, the Virgin Islands, and Puerto Rico under the principles of multiple-use and sustained yield. The Nation's tremendous need for wood and paper products is balanced with the other vital, renewable resources or benefits that the national forests and grasslands provide: recreation and natural beauty, wildlife habitat, livestock forage, and water supplies. The guiding principle is the greatest good to the greatest number in the long run.

3 *Cooperation with the States.* The Forest Service provides national leadership and financial and technical assistance to non-Federal forest landowners, operators, processors of forest products, and urban forestry interests. Through its cooperative State and private forestry programs, the Forest Service protects land, improves the quality of air, water, soil, and open space, and encourages uses of natural resources on non-Federal lands that best meet the needs of the Nation, while protecting the environment.

18. Based upon its use in the selection, what is the best definition for the word ***forage***?

(A) Nonrenewable forest products

(B) Products made commercially from forests

(C) Looking for food

(D) Food for horses and cattle

19. Which of the following would best describe the main idea of the selection?

    (A) The National Forest Service is designed to meet the Nation's various forest-related needs.

    (B) The National Forest System is the chief tool that the National Forest Service uses in monitoring our Nation's forests.

    (C) The purpose of the National Forest Service is to regulate State activity where U.S. forests are concerned.

    (D) The National Forest Service is designed to protect our Nation's forests and grasslands.

20. The writer's chief purpose in this selection is

    (A) to clarify what the agency's functions are and are not.

    (B) to identify the objectives of the National Forest Service, explain its role, and clarify the service's relationship with the states.

    (C) to explain how the National Forest System works.

    (D) to differentiate between the Federal and State responsibilities regarding forests and grasslands.

21. Ideas in this selection are most influenced by which of the following assumptions?

    (A) The State governments are not in the best position to monitor our forests.

    (B) Our forests are in danger of annihilation without correct supervision.

    (C) We are in a "catch-up" mode where our natural resources are concerned.

    (D) The delicate nature of our country's forests and grasslands, both private and public, requires supervision.

22. Based upon the phrase "multiple-use and sustained yield" in the second paragraph, we can assume that

    (A) many people should use the land and yield it then to the consumer.

    (B) all land can be used for many purposes.

    (C) the Federal government competes financially against states for producing a variety of products from the forests.

    (D) an aim of the National Forest Service is using forests and grasslands for a wide range of purposes with products coming from the land on a continual basis.

Read the passage and answer the questions that follow.

Adapted from: "The American Wedding," by Marcia Seligson

1 People of every civilization throughout the relentless timeline of the ages have celebrated the transmutation of life from one state to another. Birth, the arrival of adulthood, completion of our education at various levels, birthdays, weddings, funerals — each of these significant stages is proclaimed in some ceremonial fashion, always public, verified by the witness of others, testifying to life's perpetualness of some natural sequence of human history. Validating the uniqueness of the rite of passage, its separateness from the day's other occurrences, these rituals, by the norm, demand pageantry, elaborate dress, the giving of gifts, and eating and drinking. Funerals ask for our dark apparel, christenings and birthdays ask for our gifts, wakes give us the right to get stoned, and bar mitzvahs make gluttons of us all. Yet, of fundamental birth, marriage, and death, oddly enough, only one can claim our actual attendance completely and fully: the wedding, mankind's most vital rite of passage. And so it is that this indelible imprint is found engraved in civilization's foundation.

2 The wedding ceremony itself, which prepares an individual's move from one stage in life to another, is ***organic*** to the society from which the individual comes. In certain African tribes, a young adolescent male finds himself hurled headlong into a wilderness where he is expected to kill a lion with nothing but his hands and intellect. His society judges his value as a man on the basis of his success in meeting that challenge. In an odd way, American newlyweds experience a similar rite as they enter a consumer society; therefore, the dynamics of wedding ***hoo-hah*** appropriately testify to commercial, mercantile values. Not only the "witnesses" buy presents. Brides buy for grooms, grooms for brides, brides for bridesmaids, ushers for grooms, and on the procedure goes. Rehearsal dinners, last-fling dinners, showers. The spiraling carnival of splish-splash around the wedding itself. The American wedding celebrates in a raucous epicurean fashion a frenzied, gluttonous revelry unparalleled by any future event in the life of an American couple.

23. Which of the following best describes the word ***organic*** as the writer uses the term in the second paragraph?

    (A) That which occurs naturally and spontaneously

    (B) Healthy

    (C) Artificial and contrived

    (D) Fundamental and basic

24. Which of the following statements best expresses the central idea of this passage?

(A) The progression of humans from one stage in life to the next is marked by ceremony and ritual.

(B) Weddings are frenzied affairs.

(C) While the passage of an individual from one stage of life to another plays a vital role in civilization, the wedding is, of all such rituals, the most important.

(D) Weddings are important affairs in all cultures.

25. The selection includes the made-up word ***hoo-hah***. Which describes its most probable meaning as the writer uses it?

(A) The crass commercialism surrounding a wedding

(B) Bustling excitement surrounding the wedding

(C) Chaotic and meaningless

(D) Laughter and mirth

26. The writer includes the account of the African boy thrown into a wilderness to illustrate which idea?

(A) The incident contrasts sharply to the American ritual of the wedding ceremony.

(B) The incident serves to show the absurdity of the ritual, just as the wedding reflects an absurdity.

(C) The incident parallels the frenzy of the American wedding.

(D) The seriousness of a boy being thrown into a dangerous situation suggests the importance of the ceremony itself to the culture.

27. Which set of topics best organizes the information found in this selection?

(A) I. Significance of marriage in civilization

II. Significance of other key rituals

III. Significance of rituals around the world

IV. Significance of rituals in America

(B) I. Significance of ceremony and ritual in civilization

II. Significance of the wedding

III. Nature of the ceremony itself

(C) I. Religious rites

II. Nonreligious rites

III. Foreign rites

IV. Domestic rites

(D) I. Definition of rites of passage

II. Examples of rites of passage

III. Absurdity of the extent of the rites

IV. Absurdity of the American wedding

Read the passage and answer the questions that follow.

Excerpted from: "Resurrection," by Frederick Douglas

1 I have already intimated that my condition was much worse, during the first six months of my stay at Mr. Covey's, than in the last six. The circumstances leading to the change in Mr. Covey's course toward me form an ***epoch*** in my humble history. On one of the hottest days of the month of August, 1833, Bill Smith, William Hughes, a slave named Eli, and myself, were engaged in fanning wheat. Eli was turning, Smith was feeding, and I was carrying wheat to the fan. The work was simple, requiring strength rather than intelligence; yet, to one entirely unused to such work, it came very hard. About three o'clock of that day, I broke down; my strength failed me; I was seized with a violent aching of the head, attended with extreme dizziness . . . I nerved myself up, feeling it would never do to stop work. I stood as long as I could stagger to the hopper with grain. When I could stand no longer, I fell, and felt as if held down by an immense weight. The fan of course stopped; every one had his own work to do; and no one could do the work of the other, and have his own go on at the same time.

2 Mr. Covey was at the house . . . On hearing the fan stop, he immediately . . . came to the spot where we were. He hastily inquired what the matter was. Bill answered that I was sick. I had by this time crawled away under the side of the post and rail-fence, hoping to find relief by getting out of the sun. He then asked where I was. Told by one of the hands, he came to the spot, and, after looking at me for a while, asked me what the matter was. I told him as well as I could, for I scarce had the strength to speak. He then gave me a savage kick in the side, and told me to get up. I tried to do so, but fell back in the attempt. He gave me another kick, and again told me to rise. I again tried, and succeeded in gaining my feet; but I again staggered and fell. Mr. Covey took up the hickory slat with which Hughes had been striking off the half-bushel measure, and with it gave me a heavy blow upon the head, making a large wound, and the blood ran freely.

3 Mr. Covey had now left me to my fate. At this moment I resolved to go to my master, enter a complaint, and ask his protection. In order to do this, I must that afternoon walk seven miles; and this, under the circumstances, was truly a severe undertaking. I was exceedingly feeble by the kicks and blows I had received. While Covey was looking in the opposite direction, I succeeded in getting a considerable

distance on my way to the woods, when Covey discovered me, and called after me to come back, threatening what he would do if I did not come. I disregarded both his calls and threats.

4 This battle with Mr. Covey was the turning point in my career as a slave. It rekindled within me a sense of my own manhood. It recalled the departed self-confidence, and inspired me again with a determination to be free. My long-crushed spirit rose, cowardice departed, bold defiance took its place; and I now resolved that, however long I might remain a slave in form, the day had passed forever when I could be a slave in fact. I did not hesitate to let it be known of me, that the white man who expected to succeed in whipping, must also succeed in killing me.

28. Define the word ***epoch*** as it is used in the first paragraph of this selection.

    (A) Change of direction

    (B) Great event

    (C) Period of time

    (D) A blot or stain

29. Which of the following best sums up the writer's main idea in this selection?

    (A) Slavery was a more brutal thing than anyone who has never been a slave could know.

    (B) What began as a conflict with Mr. Covey resulted in a slave's new understanding of his own manhood and self-esteem.

    (C) Slavery made men out of people rather than crush their spirits.

    (D) White slave owners were generally an insensitive lot.

30. The content of paragraph two indicates the writer's belief that

    (A) freedom was within his grasp.

    (B) he had nothing to lose in fleeing Mr. Covey.

    (C) he would not live much longer.

    (D) he had some distinguishable right as a human being even though he was only a slave.

31. From the selection we can assume that the fan mentioned by the writer

    (A) was intended to provide some relief for the workers from the heat.

    (B) was used to blow impurities from the wheat.

    (C) was a source of constant danger to the slaves who worked around it.

    (D) was Mr. Covey's chief concern when he arrived to see what was wrong.

32. Which of the following statements best summarizes the selection?

    (A) The incident with fellow slaves began with my belief that I was no better than a slave. It caused me to see that Mr. Covey was unjust and cruel. It established my conviction that I was, in truth, no slave.

    (B) The incident with Mr. Covey resulted from what was bound to happen between us. When the inevitable incident — my illness at work — happened, I was prepared to act. And I left, once again certain of myself.

    (C) An important incident in my life occurred as I worked with other men on the wheat. Finding myself the humiliated object of my owner's unmerited wrath, I was pushed to a course of action which in turn reminded me of the man I was and the slave that I, in reality, wasn't.

    (D) The incident with Mr. Covey came as I was ill and at work with my co-workers, who would do nothing to help me. I felt I had to act on my own if I were to survive. I left, finding my self-esteem.

Read the passage and answer the questions that follow.

Adapted from: *History of the Theater*, by Oscar G. Brockett

1 While we can trace drama, as we know it since its emergence from the so-called Dark Ages, from its origin in the church, theater's move into secular circles was a significant move indeed. The earliest plays outside the church probably date back to the twelfth century; the first certain date of any such performance that we have is 1204. But an even more important question revolves around the reason for drama's exit from liturgical surroundings into the lives of the common man. We might assume that the clergy opposed the condition that drama had settled into; buffoonery abounded in the productions as plays that began with religious foundations focused on colorful antics of demons and devils, much to the delight of peasant audiences. Then, too, the productions may well have interfered with regular liturgical services. After all, mounting a sizable production would have required no small effort and would have levied much imposition on church facilities and personnel. Finally, the productions simply outgrew the churches; they had to move outside.

2 We have few plays from the transitional period between drama's tenure within the church and its subsequent home outside the church. However, we can be certain of changes that ensued the move. Spring and summer became "the season" of sorts, since weather was best at those times. One favorite time, the Corpus Christi festival, fell somewhere between May 23 and June 24. This gala event, conceived by Pope Urban IV in 1264, attempted, like others of its kind, to make church more meaningful to the common man. It was a perfect opportunity to present plays. Another change involved craft cycle plays or ***"cosmic"*** drama, which covered biblical themes from the Creation to Judgment Day. Instead of presenting all plays in a central location like the church, the plays went to the people on pageant wagons in "cycles," which depicted the story of Adam and Eve, Abraham and Isaac, Noah and the

Flood, and other biblical characters from both the Old and New Testaments. One of the most important changes involved the switch from the use of Latin, which was the language of liturgical dramas, to the use of the vernacular, the language of the people. At first, the plays mixed the two; *Play of Adam*, for instance, mixed Latin with French. This important change not only introduced nonclerical actors to the drama but changed the nature of drama from international to national. By the end of the fourteenth century, the change from liturgical to secular drama was fairly complete. Secular theater was in place.

33. The word ***cosmic*** as it is used in this selection is best defined as
    (A) artificial and cosmetic in nature.
    (B) satanic and irreligious.
    (C) universal and broad in scope.
    (D) religious.

34. The main idea of the second paragraph is that
    (A) changes took place when drama left the church.
    (B) drama took on a lower, less moral tone when it left the church.
    (C) the church had difficulty in maintaining theatrical productions and thus gave it over to laymen.
    (D) the drama moved from the church for a variety of reasons.

35. The writer of this selection would most likely agree with which of the following statements?
    (A) Drama could not have stayed in the church much longer had the church wanted to continue its responsibilities in the productions.
    (B) People enjoy secular drama more than they do liturgical drama.
    (C) The quality of drama dropped because of less literate playwrights.
    (D) The church could no longer afford the productions.

36. According to the selection, what is the primary reason that Corpus Christi was a popular time for drama?
    (A) Pope Urban IV, who conceived the festival, favored dramas at Corpus Christi.
    (B) The festival made church more meaningful for common man.
    (C) The time of year was favorable for outdoor presentations.
    (D) The church naturally would be in favor of such festivals serving as the occasion for religious dramas.

37. Which of the following lists of topics best organizes the selection?

    (A) I. Drama's removal from the church
        II. Reasons for the removal of drama
        III. Effects of the removal of drama from the church

    (B) I. Drama's unpopularity in the church
        II. Reasons for drama's popularity outside the church
        III. Results of drama's exit from the church

    (C) I. Drama's tenure in the church
        II. Nature of drama's exit from the church
        III. Nature of drama outside the church

    (D) I. Drama in the Dark Ages
        II. Drama after 1204 in the church
        III. Drama after 1204 outside the church

Read the passage and answer the questions that follow.

Adapted from: "The Aims of Education," by Jacques

1 Intelligence and will support a man. Man relies not merely on physical existence, for something beyond the physical resides within him. This "something" transcends the physical; it is a more rewarding existence. Through knowledge and love man has a ***"spiritual superexistence"*** which creates him more than a part of a whole but instead creates a microcosm, containing within himself the elements of the entire universe through knowledge. And the characteristic of love enables him to give freely to others whom he regards as other selves. Nowhere in the physical environment can we find such a unique relationship as this.

2 At the root of this phenomenon is the concept of the soul, which Aristotle described as the first principle of life in any organism and which he thought contained a superior intellect in man. Christianity maintains that the soul is the dwelling place of God and is therefore created for eternity. The human soul exists within our physical framework, amidst all the bones and tissue and internal organs, and has greater value than the entire universe. Though a man is subject to the slightest material accidents, his soul dominates time and death. The soul is the root of personality.

38. According to this selection, how could we best define the term ***spiritual superexistence***?

    (A) That quality that makes man more than simply another part of the universe

(B) That quality that lives forever

(C) Supreme intelligence

(D) Knowledge and love

39. Which of the following statements best sums up the central idea of this selection?

(A) Man's knowledge and love separate him from the lower animals.

(B) The human soul is the key factor that makes man a microcosm instead of simply another part of our universe.

(C) Both Aristotle and Christianity have placed tremendous importance on the human soul.

(D) The value of the soul is greater than that of the physical universe.

40. Which of the following statements represents an opinion of the writer rather than a fact?

(A) Christians maintain that the soul is the dwelling place of God.

(B) Aristotle dismissed the idea of the soul.

(C) Intelligence and will support a man.

(D) Man is subject to accidents.

Read the passage and answer the questions that follow.

Adapted from: "Troubled Odyssey of Vietnamese Fishermen," by Harvey Arden

1 Survivors are always extraordinary people. They seem to possess qualities that humans in their finest hour have. One particular group of wanderers from Vung Tau, Vietnam, fall into this category. As certainly as birds find their way to their winter homes, these people have a knack for finding a route to freedom. Originally natives of Southeast Asia, they were part of an exodus from their homeland to new places, and finally ended up in the United States. They consist mainly of fishermen and their families; altogether, they number about 1,300 in all. Their most outstanding trait is their ability to survive after having to flee their homes. They have done so through unity and togetherness.

2 Originally, these fishermen lived in North Vietnam. Because of the threat of communism, they fled their homes in 1954 and settled in Vung Tau, South Vietnam. However, their new home was not permanent. The Vietnam War broke out, and once again these people found themselves in a dangerous position. With the fall of South Vietnam came the need to relocate once more. In 1975 the group moved, this time half-way around the world to Biloxi, Mississippi. Actually, Biloxi was only

one of several Gulf Coast towns in which these Vietnamese people settled, perhaps because of the ***propinquity*** of the water. Although they were newcomers to a country with a chance to begin fresh, their troubles were not over. They faced a war of not being accepted by Americans.

3 A major source of income for the Vietnamese is the fishing industry. In Biloxi that industry resides along the Back Bay waterfront. While boats and ships are common sights in Biloxi, a Vietnamese vessel is different: it is a mixture of Oriental and American design. A visitor to the area can hear the hammers and saws and chatter of workers in chilly January weather putting together this strange-looking boat. The Vietnamese people, however, are proud of it because it is their boat. And as Ba Van Nguyen, the boat's owner, moves over the crushed oyster and barnacle shells that cover the ground here on the dockyard, he appears proud of his boat and his people.

4 In America, however, not everyone approves of these foreigners. One particular source of opposition is the American fisherman. The reason for the opposition is simple: competition for jobs. The Vietnamese people were so glad to be here that they would work at any job. A few have managed to survive here. As of 1981, some Vietnamese, like boat owner Ba Van Nguyen, actually owned part of a shipyard.

5 Yet many Vietnamese wanderers remain in refugee camps in Southeast Asia until a host country is found to take them. The wait for permission to leave for a better life is long and discouraging.

6 Today the wanderers from Vung Tau want more than menial labor along the docks. They want to compete as fishermen. Many of them have bought boats — at first, boats in poor condition, then better ones. Gradually, these people have enabled themselves to compete as commercial fishermen. But in the process they have angered American fishermen. Many Americans say that they simply minded their own business and that the Vietnamese moved into established fishing areas and hurt everyone else. Now and then, signs pop up with slogans such as "Vietnamese Go Home!" After all, the Americans said, it is difficult to buy and sell their catch with so many more fishermen around.

7 Still more problems exist. Physical harassment has occurred. In Seadrift, Texas, an American fisherman was killed, supposedly by a Vietnamese. Additionally, fishing styles differ. The Vietnamese fish from north to south while Americans fish east to west. Language is still another problem. It all adds up to even more problems for the wanderers from Vung Tau.

41. Which of the following best defines the word ***propinquity*** in paragraph two?

   (A) Nature of

   (B) Necessity

   (C) Turning motion

   (D) Nearness

42. Which of the following statements best expresses the main idea of the selection?

    (A) The Vung Tau survivors thrive and enjoy the challenges and danger that fill their lives.

    (B) Vietnamese people are, by tradition, nomadic by nature, destined never to have a home of their own.

    (C) The Vietnamese fishermen from Vung Tau have found survival, even here in America, to be a continuous challenge.

    (D) America is the land of opportunity for exiled people from all around the globe.

43. The material presented in this selection is most suitable for

    (A) provoking sympathy for those who must struggle against odds to have what others have.

    (B) entertaining readers who enjoy local color stories.

    (C) encouraging people to fight for equal rights of all races here in America.

    (D) persuading people to adopt foreign families who desire American citizenship.

44. In the selection, the writer attributes the survivors' continual moving to

    (A) war and political unrest.

    (B) the nomadic nature within them.

    (C) the need to find work.

    (D) a search for lost loved ones.

45. Which of the writer's following observations is an opinion?

    (A) Physical harassment has occurred to them since they came to Biloxi.

    (B) The outbreak of war in Vietnam placed these people into a dangerous situation as long as they remained there.

    (C) The Vietnamese survivors have managed to enter the field of commercial fishing here in America.

    (D) The survivors' most outstanding trait is the ability to survive after having to flee their homes.

MATHEMATICS SECTION

(ANSWER SHEETS APPEAR IN THE BACK OF THIS BOOK.)

<u>DIRECTIONS</u>: In this section, you will encounter 45 multiple-choice questions. Only **ONE** answer to each question is the **best** answer, although more than one answer may appear to be correct. Choose your answers carefully and mark them on your answer sheet. Make sure that the space you are marking corresponds to the answer you have chosen.

You may use the provided Reference Table in making your calculations.

REFERENCE TABLE

SYMBOLS AND THEIR MEANINGS:

Symbol	Meaning	Symbol	Meaning
$=$	is equal to	$\leq$	is less than or equal to
$\neq$	is unequal to	$\geq$	is greater than or equal to
$<$	is less than	$\parallel$	is parallel to
$>$	is greater than	$\perp$	is perpendicular to
$\approx$	approximately equal to	$\ngeq$	not greater than or equal to
$\pi \approx$	3.14	$\nleq$	not less than or equal to
$\sim$	similar to	$\angle$	angle
$\cong$	congruent to	$\llcorner$	right angle
$\overline{AB}$	line segment AB	$\pm$	plus or minus
$\overleftrightarrow{AB}$	line AB	$a{:}b$ or $\frac{a}{b}$	ratio of a to b

FORMULAS

DESCRIPTION	FORMULA
AREA (A) of a:	
square	$A = s^2$; where s = side
rectangle	$A = lw$; where l = length, w = width
parallelogram	$A = bh$; where b = base, h = height
triangle	$A = \frac{1}{2} bh$; where b = base, h = height
circle	$A = \pi r^2$; where $\pi = 3.14$, r = radius
PERIMETER (P) of a:	
square	$P = 4s$; where s = side
rectangle	$P = 2l + 2w$; where l = length, w = width
triangle	$P = a + b + c$; where a, b, and c are the sides
circumference (C) of a circle	$C = \pi d$; where $\pi = 3.14$, d = diameter
VOLUME (V) of a:	
cube	$V = s^3$; where s = side
rectangular container	$V = lwh$; where l = length, w = width, h = height
Pythagorean relationship	$c^2 = a^2 + b^2$; where c = hypotenuse, a and b are legs of a right triangle
distance (d) between two points in a plane	$d = \sqrt{(x_2 - x_1)^2 + (y_2 - y_1)^2}$; where (x_1, y_1) and (x_2, y_2) are two points in a plane
mean	**mean** $= \frac{x_1 + x_2 + \ldots + x_n}{n}$; where the x's are the values for which a mean is desired, and n = number of values in the series
median	**median** = the point in an ordered set of numbers at which half of the numbers are above and half of the numbers are below this value
simple interest (i)	$i = prt$; where p = principal, r = rate, t = time
distance (d) as function of rate and time	$d = rt$; where r = rate, t = time
total cost (c)	$c = nr$; where n = number of units, r = cost per unit

1. Which is the smallest?

   (A) $^2/_3$

   (B) $^7/_8$

   (C) $^5/_9$

   (D) $^3/_4$

2. What product is obtained from the roots of the equation

   $(x - 7)(x + 6) = 0$?

   (A) – 49

   (B) 42

   (C) – 42

   (D) – 36

3. The sum of three numbers is 90. The largest number is three times the smallest and the smallest is 10 less than the middle number. Find the area of a circle with a diameter equivalent to the middle number.

   (A) 216.52

   (B) 148.01

   (C) 530.66

   (D) 628.66

4. A piggy bank contains only nickels and dimes. In all there are 42 coins with a total value of $3.85. How many nickels are in the piggy bank?

   (A) 35

   (B) 17

   (C) 3

   (D) 7

5. Which is the best estimate of

   $11\ ^8/_9 \div 2\ ^{12}/_{13}$?

   (A) 4

   (B) 6

   (C) 22

   (D) 5

6. Perform the operations.

$$(-8x^4y^3 + 5x^3y^4 + 7x^2y) - (5x^4y^3 + x^3y^4 - 4x^2y)$$

(A) $-13x^4y^3 + 4x^3y^4 + 11x^2y$

(B) $-3x^4y^3 + 4x^3y^4 + 11x^2y$

(C) $-3x^4y^3 + 6x^3y^4 + 3x^2y$

(D) $-13x^4y^3 + 4x^3y^4 + 3x^2y$

7. $\dfrac{35 \times 10^9}{5 \times 10^4} =$

(A) 7×10^5

(B) 7×10^{13}

(C) 30×10^5

(D) 30×10^{13}

8. A clerk in a store receives $75 a week and 2% commission on items he sells that are above $100. One week he sold a TV for $350 and a radio for $175. How much did he earn that week?

(A) $78.50

(B) $85.50

(C) $82.00

(D) $180.00

9. Use this graph to answer the question.

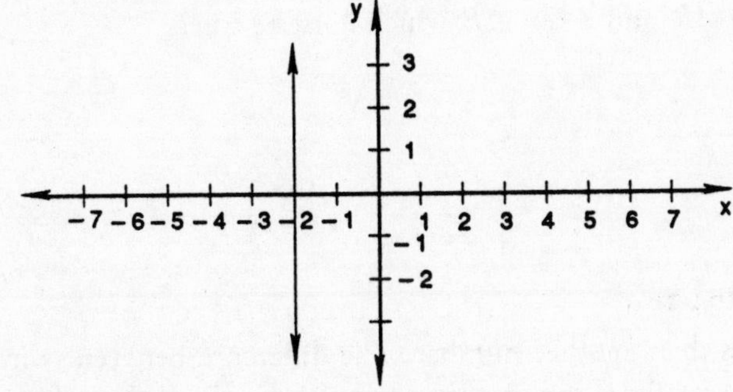

Which equation is represented above?

(A) $x = 2$

(B) $x = -2$

(C) $y = 2$

(D) $y = -2$

10. Use this diagram to answer the question.

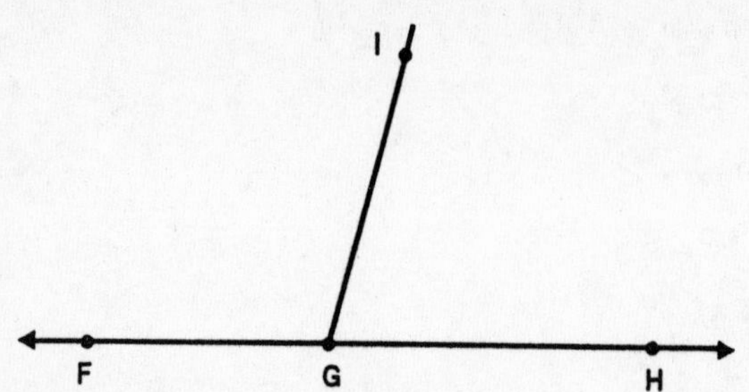

If segment $\overline{IG}$ meets line FH at point G, which is true?

(A) $\angle FGI$ and $\angle IGH$ are supplementary angles.

(B) Segment $\overline{IG}$ is perpendicular to line FH.

(C) $\angle FGI$ and $\angle IGH$ are complementary angles.

(D) $\angle FGI$ and $\angle IGH$ are vertical angles.

11. Use this diagram to answer the question.

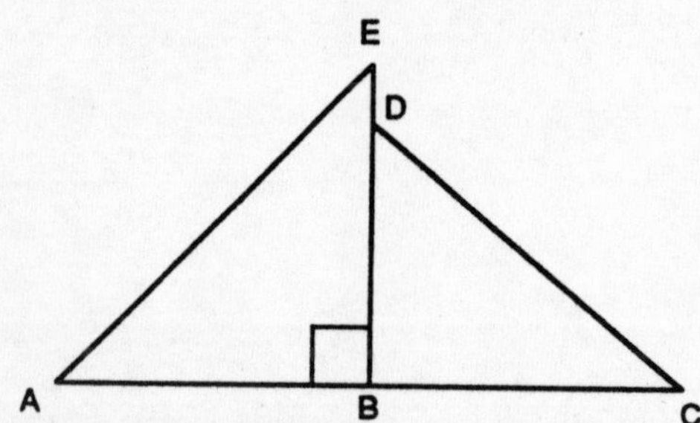

If $\overline{BE} \perp \overline{AC}$, $\overline{DB} \cong \overline{AB}$, and $\angle C = \angle E$, which must be true?

(A) $\overline{AB} = {}^1/_2\ \overline{AC}$

(B) $\overline{BE} \cong \overline{AE}$

(C) $\overline{DB} = {}^2/_3\ \overline{BE}$

(D) $\overline{BC} \cong \overline{BE}$

12. A number is five less than another number. The difference between twice the larger number and three times the smaller number is six. Find the cube of the smaller number.

(A) 64

(B) 16

(C) 729

(D) 205

13. Multiply.

$(5x^2 + 2)(4x^2 - 7)$

(A) $20x^4 - 27x^2 - 14$

(B) $20x^4 + 43x^2 - 14$

(C) $20x^4 - 14$

(D) $20x^4 - 35x^2 - 14$

14. Which equation expresses the relationship that the height (h) varies inversely as the square of the base (b)?

(A) $h = \frac{b^2}{k}$

(B) $kb^2 = h$

(C) $h = \frac{k}{b^2}$

(D) $kh = b^2$

15. Read the graph and answer the question.

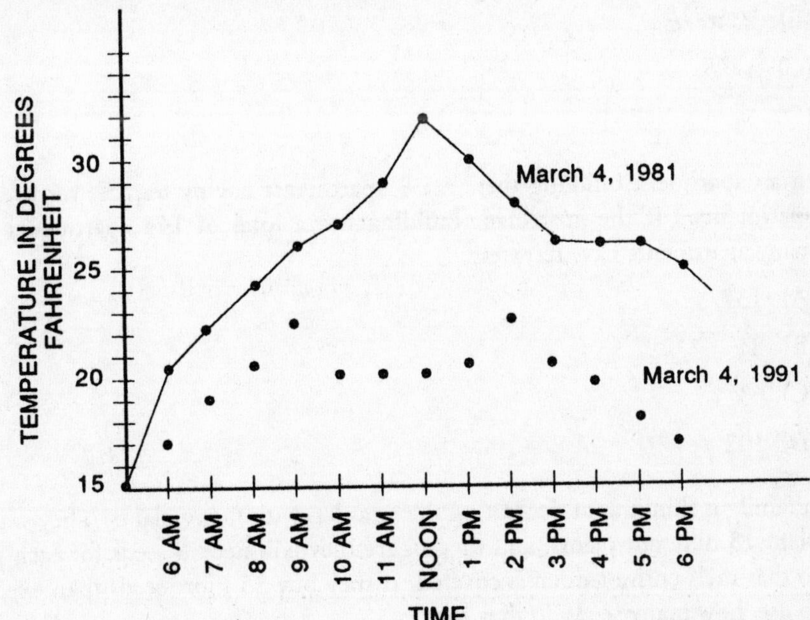

Which is true at 11 AM for the recorded temperatures on March 4, 1981 and March 4, 1991?

(A) Both temperatures recorded on March 4, 1981 and March 4, 1991 are increasing.

(B) Both temperatures recorded on March 4, 1981 and March 4, 1991 are decreasing.

(C) The temperature recorded on March 4, 1981 is increasing and the temperature recorded on March 4, 1991 is stable.

(D) The temperature recorded on March 4, 1981 is stable and the temperature recorded on March 4, 1991 is increasing.

16. The sum of 3 angles of a triangle is 180°. The second angle is 11° less than the first angle. The third angle is twice the measure of the first angle increased by 3. If x represents the number of degrees in the first angle, which equation correctly represents the relationship among the three angles?

(A) $x + (11 - x) + (2x + 3) = 180$

(B) $x + (x - 11) + 2(x + 3) = 180$

(C) $x + (x - 11) + (2x + 3) = 180$

(D) $x + (x - 11) + (2x - 3) = 180$

17. Which of the following can be used to determine the surface area of a cylindrical can that has a height of h meters and a radius of r meters?

(A) $2\pi rh + 2\pi r^2$

(B) $1/3\ \pi r^2 h$

(C) $\pi r^2 h$

(D) $4\pi r^2$

18. In an apartment building there are 9 apartments having terraces for every 16 apartments. If the apartment building has a total of 144 apartments, how many apartments have terraces?

(A) 137

(B) 81

(C) 63

(D) 102

19. A family is thinking of decorating their garden with many plants. They want to plant 15 different plants, and they figure they will need 8 seeds for each plant so that their entire garden is covered. If they buy 35 more seeds than expected to use, how many seeds do they buy?

(A) 120 seeds

(B) 85 seeds

(C) 155 seeds

(D) 645 seeds

20. $(4 \times 10^{15}) \times (2 \times 10^{8}) =$

(A) 8×10^{7}

(B) 2×10^{23}

(C) 8×10^{22}

(D) 8×10^{23}

21. Anita saves dimes and quarters so that she can go to the laundromat. She has six more quarters than twice the number of dimes. Altogether she has $6.90. Find the number of quarters she has and use it as the denominator of a fraction. If the numerator of the fraction is 5, what would this fraction added to $^{7}/_{80}$ equal?

(A) $^{27}/_{80}$

(B) $^{71}/_{240}$

(C) $^{5}/_{24}$

(D) $^{3}/_{26}$

22. A carpenter is building a big recreation room which is 625 square feet in area, and he must decide how to apportion each section of the room. He has decided to set aside 30% of the room for the Baby Grand Piano and an additional 46.7 square feet for a stage. How much of the room is set aside for the Baby Grand Piano and stage?

(A) 234.2 square feet

(B) 610.99 square feet

(C) 548.3 square feet

(D) 76.7 square feet

23. Given points A, B, C, and D as shown below, which two lines would intersect at a right angle?

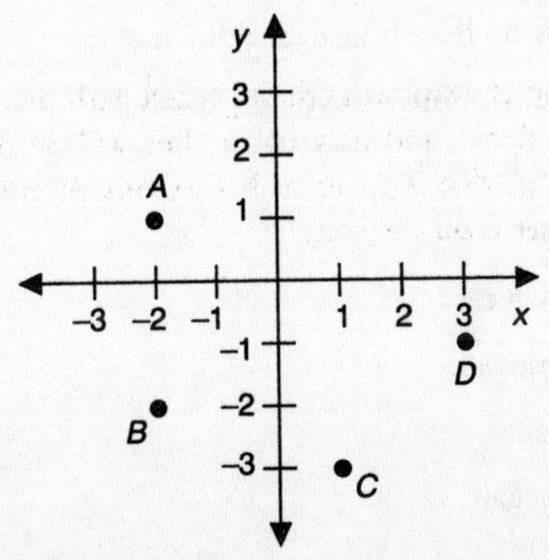

(A) $\overline{AB} \perp \overline{BD}$

(B) $\overline{AC} \perp \overline{BD}$

(C) $\overline{AC} \perp \overline{CD}$

(D) $\overline{BC} \perp \overline{CD}$

24. A rectangular box is to be filled with boxes of candy. The rectangular box measures 4 feet long, 3 feet wide, and $2^1/_2$ feet deep. If a box of candy weighs approximately 3 pounds per cubic foot, what will the weight of the rectangular box be when the box is filled to the top with candy?

(A) 10 pounds

(B) 90 pounds

(C) 12 pounds

(D) 36 pounds

25. If $8r = 5t - 4$, what does t equal?

(A) $t = \dfrac{8r + 4}{5}$

(B) $t = \dfrac{8r - 4}{5}$

(C) $t = \dfrac{8r}{5} + 4$

(D) $t = \dfrac{8r}{5} - 4$

26. Read the statements below and answer the question.

1. All people who exercise have blue eyes.
2. Some of the people have brown eyes.
3. All people who have blue eyes enjoy movies.
4. People who have brown eyes like baseball.
5. Sarah has blue eyes.

Which must be true?

(A) Sarah has brown eyes.

(B) Sarah enjoys movies.

(C) Sarah exercises.

(D) Sarah likes baseball.

27. Use the table to answer the question.

WORLD POPULATION AVERAGE

(Billions)

Year	Developed Countries	Undeveloped Countries
1950	0.8	1.8
1960	0.9	2.4
1970	1.2	2.9
1980	1.3	3.0
1990	1.37	4.2
2000 (projected)	1.4	5.2

Between 1960 and 2000 the average world population in undeveloped countries increased by

(A) 3.4 billion.

(B) .6 billion.

(C) .5 billion.

(D) 2.8 billion.

28. Approximately, what is the area of a circular swimming pool that has a 36-foot diameter?

(A) 108 square feet

(B) 980 square feet

(C) 3,888 square feet

(D) 500 square feet

29. Use the diagram to answer the question.

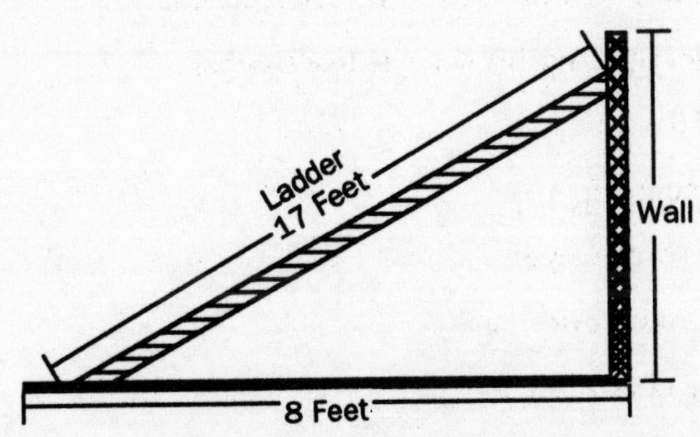

A 17-foot ladder leans against a wall. If the ladder is 8 feet from the base of the wall, how far is it from the bottom of the wall to the top of the ladder?

(A) 9 feet

(B) 5 feet

(C) 15 feet

(D) $2\sqrt{34}$ feet

30. Examine the pattern sequence and answer the question.

$1 \quad z \quad 3 \quad w \quad 9 \quad \underline{\ ?\ } \quad 27 \quad q \quad 81$

What is the missing symbol?

(A) 13

(B) *s*

(C) *t*

(D) *u*

31. Perform the operations.

$$\frac{10}{0.05} \times 0.003$$

(A) 0.006

(B) 0.6

(C) 600

(D) 60

32. The second side of a triangle is the same length as the first side. The third side is three feet longer than the second side. Find the area of the triangle if the perimeter is 18 feet.

(A) 50 sq. ft.

(B) 18 sq. ft.

(C) 16 sq. ft.

(D) 12 sq. ft.

33. What percent of 85 is 17?

(A) 5%

(B) 20%

(C) $14\,^{9}/_{20}\%$

(D) 68%

34. Sam finds that his monthly commission, C, in dollars can be calculated by the equation $C = 270g - 3g^2$, where g is the number of goods he sells for the company. In January, he sold 30 goods; and in February, he sold 40 goods. How much additional commission did Sam make in February over January?

    (A) \$11,400

    (B) \$600

    (C) \$5,400

    (D) \$6,000

35. If $-2p + 7 = -9p - 8$, what does p equal?

    (A) $p = \dfrac{-8-7}{-2+9}$

    (B) $p = \dfrac{-8-7}{-2-9}$

    (C) $p = \dfrac{-9-8-7}{-2}$

    (D) $p = \dfrac{-9-8}{-2+7}$

36. If $-{}^1/_5\,x - 4 = 17$, what is the value of $3x - 1$?

    (A) 62

    (B) -105

    (C) -316

    (D) -164

37. Find the slope of a line whose equation is

    $y = 14x + 7.$

    (A) $-{}^1/2$

    (B) 2

    (C) 7

    (D) 14

38. Three men worked a total of 53 hours to construct a cement patio for a house. John worked seven hours longer than Bill, and Sam worked twice as long as John. How much did John earn for the job if he makes $11 per hour and two of his hours were paid at time and a half?

(A) $165

(B) $176

(C) $143

(D) $167

39. Read the bar graph and answer the question.

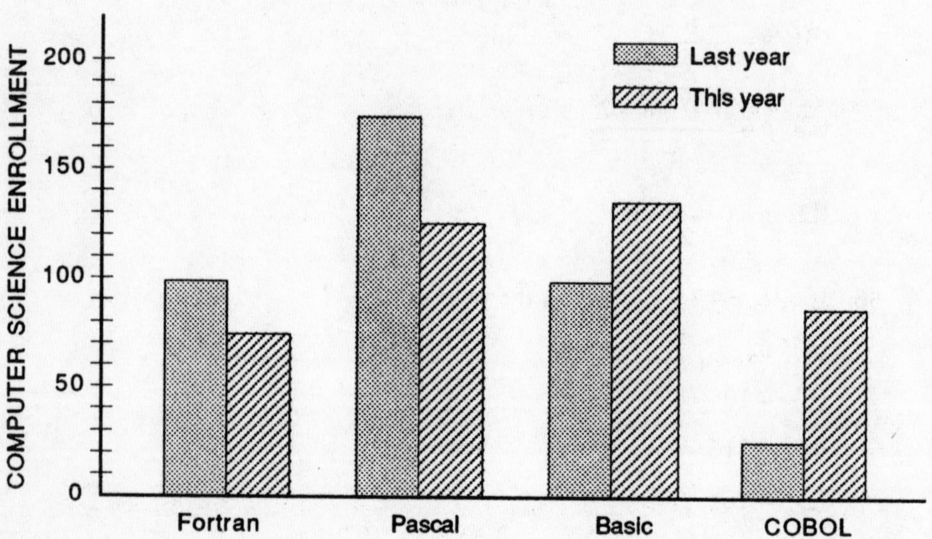

Which computer science course showed the greatest increase in enrollment between last year and this year?

(A) Fortran

(B) Pascal

(C) Basic

(D) COBOL

40. Read the graph and answer the question.

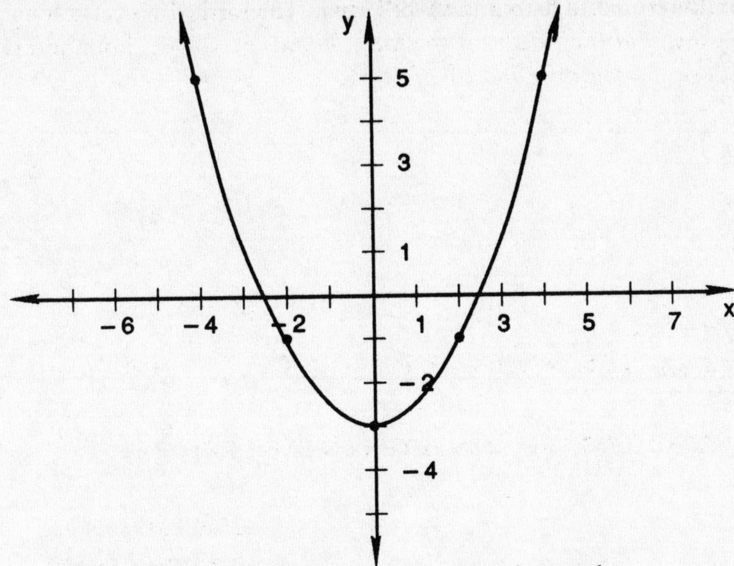

Which equation could be represented by the graph?

(A) $y = {}^1/_2x^2 + 3$

(B) $y = -{}^1/_2x^2 - 3$

(C) $y = {}^1/_2x^2 - 3$

(D) $y = -{}^1/_2x^2 + 3$

41. Which is a factor of

$6x^2 + 2x - 4$?

(A) $(3x - 4)$

(B) $(6x - 1)$

(C) $(x - 1)$

(D) $(3x - 2)$

42. Perform the operations.

$$\frac{9 \times 0.5}{0.03}$$

(A) 1,500

(B) 0.15

(C) 15

(D) 150

43. In 18 years, Jack will be 4 times as old as he is today. Which of the following equations could be used to determine Jack's age in 18 years?

(A) $4R - 18 = R$

(B) $4R - 72 = R$

(C) $R/4 = 18$

(D) $4R = 18$

44. Solve for x.

$$\begin{aligned} 5x + 2y &= -5 \\ -3x + y &= 3 \end{aligned}$$

(A) 0

(B) $-1/11$

(C) 1

(D) -1

45. Betty knows French and German.

Alice knows Swedish and Russian.

Sally knows Spanish and French.

Tanya knows German and Swedish.

If French is easier than German; and Russian is harder than Swedish; German is easier than Swedish; and Spanish is easier than French, which girl knows the most difficult languages?

(A) Betty

(B) Alice

(C) Sally

(D) Tanya

WRITING SECTION

MULTIPLE-CHOICE

(ANSWER SHEETS APPEAR IN THE BACK OF THIS BOOK.)

DIRECTIONS: You will encounter 16 passages in this portion of the test. Each part of the passage will be numbered, with the questions that follow the passage referring to the numbered parts. Only **ONE** answer to each question is the **best** answer, although more than one answer may appear to be correct. There are 45 multiple-choice questions in this portion. Choose your answers carefully and mark them on your answer sheet. Make sure that the space you are marking corresponds to the answer you have chosen.

Note: The use of the term "nonstandard" in the questions means "does not follow standard written English."

The following passage is written in the form of an anthropology textbook. Read the text and answer the questions.

[1]Actually, the term "Native American" is incorrect. [2]Indians migrated to this continent from other areas, just earlier than Europeans did. [3]The ancestors of the Anasazi — Indians of the four-state area of Colorado, New Mexico, Utah, and Arizona — probably crossed from Asia into Alaska. [4]About 25,000 years ago while the continental land bridge still existed. [5]This land bridge arched across the Bering Strait in the last Ice Age. [6]About A.D. 500 the ancestors of the Anasazi moved onto the Mesa Verde, a high plateau in the desert country of Colorado. [7]The Wetherills, five brothers who ranched in the area, are generally given credit for the first exploration of the ruins in the 1870s and 1880s. [8]There were some 50,000 Anasazi thriving in the four-corners area by the 1200s. [9]At their zenith, A.D. 700 to 1300, the Anasazi had established widespread communities and built thousands of sophisticated structures — cliff dwellings, pueblos, and kivas. [10]________________ [11]They even engaged in trade with Indians in surrounding regions by exporting pottery and other goods.

1. Which of the following is a nonstandard sentence?

   (A) Part 1

   (B) Part 2

   (C) Part 4

   (D) Part 5

2. Which of the following draws attention away from the main idea of the paragraph?

   (A) Part 3

   (B) Part 4

   (C) Part 7

   (D) Part 8

3. Which of the following, if used in place of the blank labeled Part 10, **best** supports the main idea of the paragraph?

   (A) Artifacts recovered from the area suggest that the Anasazi were artistic, religious, agricultural, classless, and peaceful.

   (B) By A.D. 1000-1200, some Indians had established their unique cultures in the Southwest.

   (C) The Navaho called their ancestors the Anasazi, the Ancient Ones.

(D) Before Columbus reached the New World, the Anasazi had virtually disappeared.

The following passage is written in the form of a student letter to a college newspaper. Read the text and answer the questions.

[1]The dismissal of Dr. Dennis Ruoff is a travesty of justice. [2]It is not a good feeling to know that a tenured professor can be hounded out of his post just because he disagrees with the board of regents. [3]True, his was the only negative vote on the curriculum issue pushed by the university board of regents. [4]However, since when has a dissenting opinion been the catalyst for persecution of faculty members on this campus? [5]_______________ [6]English professors, especially, have traditionally had the reputation of fighting courageously against blockhead thinking and against lockstep decision making. [7]They have also historically been the school's champions against injustice.

[8]There cannot be an issue closer to the basis of America's founding principles than this one because the foundation of America is based on freedom of speech. [9]The students of this university need to know whose to blame for the loss of Dr. Ruoff. [10]He is a stimulating speaker, an engaging person, and one of the finest teachers. [11]Where will this issue come to a halt? [12]Will other tenured professors now be even more intimidated and hesitate to express any view not consistent with the general consensus of opinion? [13]Will students receive a quality education from a university that infringes on freedom of speech?

4. Which of the following requires revision for unnecessary repetition?

   (A) Part 3

   (B) Part 6

   (C) Part 8

   (D) Part 12

5. Which of the following, if added between Parts 4 and 6, **best** supports the writer's purpose and audience?

   (A) We should allow teachers to express their own opinions regardless of what we ourselves think.

   (B) This university has always prided itself on teachers who are rather maverick in their thinking, to say the least.

   (C) Don't you think this is a pitiful way to treat a fine teacher?

   (D) One must acknowledge that university professors, as a whole, should support the opinions of fellow faculty members.

6. Which one of the following changes is needed?

   (A) Part 8: Change "closer" to "closest."

   (B) Part 9: Change "whose" to "who's."

   (C) Part 10: Change "finest" to "finer."

   (D) Part 11: Change "Where" to "When."

The following passage is written in the form of a student essay. Read the text and answer the questions.

Note: In the second paragraph, a paragraph organization error is purposely included.

[1]A growing number of businesses are providing day care facilities for the children of their employees. [2]Some companies charge a standard fee, but most provide the day care free or at a nominal cost. [3]These care programs provide services that continue through the early teens of the children. [4]Many companies are trying to decide if they should help with day care at all. [5]In the event parents need to work overtime, centers are even open on weekends, and some companies showing special initiative in building company loyalty of each employee <u>makes</u> arrangements for special field trips to zoos and museums. [6]Is this kind of care really necessary? [7]Should businesses really be in the business of day care?

[8]Experts in the field cite many advantages for this system. [9]Therefore, loyalty to the company is built, so morale climbs. [10]Studies show that when a company helps its employees blend parent and worker roles, absenteeism and tardiness drop. [11]In addition, workers feel the company has taken more of a personal interest in them. [12]Turnover becomes a much less significant factor for managers. [13]Human resource managers also estimate that every $1 spent on these programs returns $2 or more in increased productivity.

7. Which of the following improves the first paragraph?

   (A) Change the conjunction from "but" to "and" in Part 2.

   (B) Delete the phrase "in the event parents need to work overtime" from Part 5.

   (C) Delete Part 4.

   (D) Change Part 6 from an interrogative to a declarative sentence, as in "This kind of care is."

8. Which of the following should be substituted for the underlined word in Part 5?

   (A) make

(B) is making

(C) should make

(D) making

9. Which of the following improves the sequence of ideas in the second paragraph?

   (A) Reverse the order of Parts 8 and 9.

   (B) Place Part 12 before Part 9.

   (C) Delete Part 13.

   (D) Place Part 9 after Part 11.

The following passage is written in the form of an education textbook. Read the text and answer the questions.

[1]It is important for a teacher to select appropriate reading materials for students in the classroom. [2]Because students vary widely in their ability to read, the first step should be to assess each child's reading level and assign reading material appropriately. [3]Teachers who instruct from materials above the child's reading level are significantly decreasing that child's chance at educational success. [4]The child who reads at a first grade level will have difficulty with a book on the third grade level. [5]__________________ [6]Even if the child reading at the second grade level enjoys and even appreciates stories from a sixth grade reader, for example, he or she will likely learn few skills and the child's reading will not be facilitated by being far below grade level in the reading text.

[7]Unfortunately, it is a problem which is difficult to correct. [8]______________ a teacher may be well aware of the child's specific reading level, finding a book appropriate for their level may pose some difficulties. [9]Textbook publishers sometimes include materials from varied reading levels within the same text. [10]__________________, two books designated for the same grade level, because of nonstandard labeling procedures, may vary widely in reading difficulty.

10. Which of the following, if used in the blank labeled Part 5, **best** fits the writer's pattern of development?

    (A) A wide range of reading skills is evident at every grade level.

    (B) Parents should be involved in the process of selecting reading texts.

    (C) Standardized tests are available to help teachers assess reading levels for their students.

    (D) The disparity of reading levels increases with each grade level until the child may vary as many as ten years by the time he or she reaches the sixth grade.

11. Which of the following is needed in the second paragraph?

    (A) Part 7: Change "it is" to "its."

    (B) Part 8: Change "their" to "his or her."

    (C) Part 9: Change "varied" to "a variety of."

    (D) Part 10: Change "designated" to "designates."

12. Which of the following would, if inserted *in order* into the blanks in the second paragraph, improve the logical sequence of ideas?

    (A) In addition; However

    (B) As a result; For example

    (C) Even though; Also

    (D) In spite of this; In conclusion

The following is written in the form of a science textbook.
Read the text and answer the questions.

[1]Polar bears, so named because they live near the North Pole, are called "Nanook" by the Eskimo. [2]Living along the cold waters and ice floes of the Arctic Ocean, some polar bears spend time along the coastal areas of northern Canada, Alaska, Norway, Siberia, and Greenland, although some bears live on the islands of the Arctic Ocean and never come close to the mainland. [3]Most of these areas lie north of the Arctic circle, and about 85% of Greenland is always covered with ice. [4]To protect them from the arctic cold and ice, polar bears have water-repellant fur and a pad of dense, stiff fur on the soles of their snowshoe-like feet. [5]In addition, the bears have such a thick layer of fat that infrared photos show no detectable heat, except for their breath.

[6]Polar bears are the largest land-based carnivores. [7]__________________ [8]Because their fur is white with a tinge of yellow, they are difficult to spot on ice floes, their favorite hunting ground. [9]Polar bears have a small head, a long neck, and a long body, so they make efficient swimmers. [10]Polar bears have no natural enemy except man, and since increased human activity in the Arctic region has put pressure on polar bear populations, the Polar Bear Specialist Group was formed to conserve and manage this unique animal. [11]An increase in the number of polar bears is due to cooperation between five nations. [12]In 1965, there were 8,000 to 10,000 bears reported, but that population is estimated at 25,000 at the present time.

13. Which of the following would help the focus of the main idea in the first paragraph?

    (A) Delete the phrase "so named" in Part 1.

(B) Change the comma after "Greenland" to a semicolon in Part 2.

(C) Delete Part 3.

(D) Change Part 5 by placing the phrase "except for their breath" after "In addition."

14. Which of the following, used in place of the blank labeled Part 7, **best** fits the writer's pattern of development?

    (A) Full-grown polar bears may be about nine feet long and weigh between 1,000 and 1,600 pounds.

    (B) These bears have keen eyesight and are not sensitive to snow blindness.

    (C) In the winter the female polar bear enters a cave in an iceberg and gives birth to one or two cubs.

    (D) Polar bears can swim great distances with a speed of approximately six miles an hour.

15. Which of the following changes is needed?

    (A) Part 6: Change "largest" to "larger."

    (B) Part 10: Change "was" to "is."

    (C) Part 11: Change "between" to "among."

    (D) Part 12: Change "but" to "and."

The following passage is written in the form of a science article. Read the text and answer the questions.

[1]Physicians are now emphasizing that health-conscious citizens pay attention to triglyceride levels in the body. [2]Triglycerides are another form of fat in the bloodstream, and high triglyceride levels are associated with increased risk of heart disease. [3]In considering health risks, people should consider the levels of triglycerides, along with high-density lipoproteins (HDLs) — the "good" cholesterol — and low-density lipoproteins (LDLs) — the "bad" cholesterol. [4]____________________ [5]For most Americans, a normal triglyceride level falls below 200, and the medical community now recommends that anyone with levels above 200 mg/dl should get further testing and attention.

[6]There are several ways high triglycerides can be treated, a mild aerobic exercise, such as swimming, bicycling, or walking, is recommended. [7]Also, alcohol consumption should be restricted, and caloric intake should be reduced. [8]The diet should be adjusted so that no more than 30 percent of calories should come from fat, and no more than 10 percent of calories should come from saturated fats.

16. Which of the following, if used in the blank labeled Part 4, **best** fits the pattern of development in the second paragraph?

    (A) In the sixties, triglycerides received much publicity.

    (B) Particularly dangerous is a combination of high triglycerides and low HDL.

    (C) Many people think only the LDLs are important.

    (D) Women do not have as high a risk factor of developing heart disease as men do.

17. Which of the following is a nonstandard sentence?

    (A) Part 2

    (B) Part 5

    (C) Part 6

    (D) Part 8

The following passage is written in the form of a sociology textbook. Read the text and answer the questions.

Note: In the second paragraph, a paragraph organization error is purposely included.

[1]A significant development during the Paleolithic period was the emergence of modern man. [2]During this time, one million years ago to 12,000 B.C., man's brain became much larger. [3]There are two suggested reasons for the rapid evolutionary development of man's brain. [4]First, meat eating led to big-game hunting, an activity that necessitated group planning and cooperation; and second, the use of speech to facilitate planning and coordination of group activities. [5]Tool making was once thought to be a major factor in the development of a large brain for man, but it is now known that many animals use tools and even make tools. [6]Otters will balance a rock on their stomachs as an anvil for breaking open mollusks.

[7]There are two other factors which have greatly influenced the emergence of modern man. [8]Also, food supplies increased significantly after the retreat of the great glaciers about 12,000 years ago. [9]It seems that about 100,000 years ago, genetic evolution became less important than cultural evolution as man developed the ability to pass on accumulated knowledge. [10]This increase in food supplies may have contributed to the ability of man to increase his own numbers, thus ensuring the survival of his species.

18. Which of the following would help the focus of the main idea in the first paragraph?
    (A) Delete Part 1.
    (B) Reverse the order of Parts 1 and 2.
    (C) Add a sentence after Part 2 describing the measurements and configurations of brains.
    (D) Delete Part 6.

19. Which of the following makes the sequence of ideas clearer in the second paragraph?
    (A) Delete Part 7.
    (B) Reverse the order of Parts 7 and 8.
    (C) Reverse the order of Parts 8 and 9.
    (D) Delete Part 10.

20. Which one of the following is needed?
    (A) Part 4: Change "to facilitate" to "facilitated."
    (B) Part 7: Delete "other."
    (C) Part 9: Change "less" to "least."
    (D) Part 10: Change "ensuring" to "ensured."

The following passage is written in the form of a college history textbook. Read the text and answer the questions.

[1]Alexander the Great was a general and ruler who changed the world. [2]His boyhood was shaped by two strong parents. [3]Alexander's father, King Philip of Macedonia, was an <u>excellent general</u> whose armies conquered Greece and made Macedonia a powerful force in the ancient world. [4] ____________________ [5]Taught before he was ten to read, sing, and debate in Greek, Alexander was later encouraged by the philosopher Aristotle to be curious about foreign lands.

[6]Alexander was <u>fearless and showed great promise</u>. [7]He observed a horse that no one had been able to touch, much less ride. [8]After noticing that the horse <u>shied</u> every time it saw its own shadow Alexander concluded that the horse was afraid. [9]He mounted the horse, rode it only into the sun at first, and thus tamed Bucephalus. [10]Alexander grew up in a military environment and became accustomed to the hardships of a soldier's life. [11]He enjoyed combat and at a <u>very early age</u> commanded some cavalry in battle, defeating the Greeks at Chaeronea. [12]However, his father seldom took Alexander with him on his campaigns. [13]News of his father's conquests prompted the ambitious son to complain that his father would leave nothing great for Alexander to do.

21. Which of the following, used in the blank labeled Part 4, **best** fits the pattern of development in the first paragraph?

 (A) The great philosopher Aristotle became Alexander's tutor and taught him a respect for Greek ideals and way of life.

 (B) When Alexander was 20, he became king of Macedonia.

 (C) Always carrying with him a copy of the *Iliad*, Alexander took Achilles for his role model.

 (D) Alexander's mother, Olympias, was a brilliant and temperamental woman who taught her son that he was descended from Achilles and Hercules.

22. Which of the following, underlined in the passage, needs to be replaced by more precise words?

 (A) excellent general

 (B) fearless and showed great promise

 (C) shied

 (D) very early age

23. Which of the following is needed?

 (A) Part 7: Change "that" to "who."

 (B) Part 8: Place a comma after the phrase "every time it saw its own shadow."

 (C) Part 12: Move "However" after the word "seldom."

 (D) Part 13: Change "to complain" to "in complaining."

The following passage is written in the form of a college economics textbook. Read the text and answer the questions.

[1]Consumers who believe a company is well run and shows promise of doing well in the stock market will invest in that company's stock. [2]If the company shows a profit, the investor will receive a dividend check. [3]Buying United States Savings Bonds is another well-known way of investing money. [4]Some companies offer a dividend reinvestment plan: the profits, instead of being sent to the investor in the form of a check, can be reinvested automatically in the company's stock. [5]To encourage this practice, companies offer several incentives. [6]________________, if the dividend is too small to buy a whole share, most companies allow the investor to purchase part of a share until enough dividends accumulate for a whole share. [7]________________, some companies offer shareholders a discount off the market price of their stock. [8]A five percent discount is the usual rate. [9]________________, about 70 percent of companies charge no fee if the stockholder wishes to purchase more shares for cash.

[10]There are several advantages to reinvestment in this manner. [11]There are no brokerage commissions or service fees for most dividend reinvestment plans. [12]Further, there is the benefit of compounding the profits, similar to earning interest on the interest earned from a traditional savings account. [13]Also, dividend reinvestment enables the consumer to dollar-cost average. [14]By steadily purchasing stock at fixed intervals, the investor ends up buying more shares when the price goes down and fewer shares when the price goes up.

24. Which of the following, if added between Parts 11 and 12, **best** fits the writer's purpose and intended audience?

    (A) Therefore, the system is a relatively inexpensive way to build a strong portfolio of stock in reliable companies.

    (B) Doesn't this form of investment sound like a smart idea?

    (C) Some people question the fiscal policy of reinvesting and prefer to have control over when to buy and sell extra stocks.

    (D) Personally, I think automatic reinvestment of dividends is a sound idea.

25. Which of the following draws attention away from the first paragraph?

    (A) Part 1

    (B) Part 2

    (C) Part 3

    (D) Part 4

26. Which of the following, if inserted *in order* into the blanks in the third paragraph, help clarify the sequence of ideas?

    (A) Although; Moreover; In contrast

    (B) Eventually; First; Second

    (C) In other words; As a result; Later

    (D) For example; In addition; Finally

The following is written in the form of a college fine arts textbook. Read the text and answer the questions.

Note: In the first paragraph, a paragraph organization error is purposely included.

[1]Medieval literature and art, despite the predominance of religious themes, was greatly varied. [2]In literature, for example, the chivalric tradition embodied in such words as the Arthurian legends, as well as the Anglo-Saxon epic *Beowulf* and the

French epic *Song of Roland*, showed the richness of themes. [3]Originating in France during the mid-1100s, the Gothic style spread to other parts of Europe. [4]However, it was in Gothic architecture that the Medieval religious fervor best exhibited itself. [5]Gothic cathedrals were the creation of a community, many artisans and craftsmen working over many generations. [6]Most of the populace could not read or write, so donating funds or working on the building and its furnishings became a form of religious devotion as well as a means of impressing neighboring areas and attracting tourism. [7]The first Gothic structures were parts of an abbey and a cathedral. [8]Later, during the twelfth and thirteenth centuries, Gothic architecture reached its peak in the great cathedrals of Notre Dame in Paris, Westminster Abbey in England, and Cologne Cathedral in Germany.

[9]Gothic architecture strives to emphasize height and light. [10]Characteristic internal structures are the ribbed vault and pointed arches. [11]Thick stone walls give way to stained glass windows depicting religious scenes, and the masonry is embellished with delicate tracery. [12]Outside, slender beams called *flying buttresses* provides support for the height of the building. [13]Great spires complete the illusion of rising to the sky.

27. Which of the following makes the sequence of ideas clearer in the first paragraph?

    (A) Place Part 3 after Part 7.

    (B) Reverse the order of Parts 2 and 4.

    (C) Reverse the order of Parts 7 and 8.

    (D) Delete Part 6.

28. Which of the following, if added between Parts 10 and 11, is the MOST consistent with the writer's purpose and audience?

    (A) Often, you can find gargoyles, grotesque demonic-looking creatures carved on the outside of the building.

    (B) Particularly impressive to me are the carvings of realistic animals and plants on the pulpits.

    (C) Tall, thin columns reach to the ceiling and help to support the roof.

    (D) These buildings were designed to impress everyone who saw them.

29. Which of the following is needed?

    (A) Part 2: Change "as" to "like."

    (B) Part 4: Move "best" to the end of the sentence.

    (C) Part 8: Replace the commas after "Paris" and "England" with semicolons.

    (D) Part 12: Change "provides" to "provide."

The following passage is written in the form of a popular magazine. Read the text and answer the questions.

[1]Dalmatians have an interesting history. [2]Of the 131 breeds that the American Kennel Club recognizes, Dalmatians have risen in popularity from 24th to 19th. [3]Although unsure of the exact origin, the breed may have originated in Dalmatia, a district of Yugoslavia. [4]Dalmatia, a narrow strip of land along the Adriatic Sea, is populated mostly by Croatians. [5]Most people believe that when bands of Gypsies traveling westward to settle in Yugoslavia, the dogs traveled with them.

[6]Alert, curious, clean, and useful, Dalmatians have proved their worth as draft dog, shepherd, and hunting dog. [7]Their greatest fame, however, is as a coach dog. [8]A running mate for the horses of a phaeton or brougham, the Dalmatian would clear stray farm animals from the road. [9]The dog is known for its calm temper and would settle the nerves of a skittish horse. [10]____________________ [11]Although the advent of the horseless carriage cut the necessity of the Dalmatian for firemen, the breed is still regularly chosen as a fire station mascot.

30. Which of the following is LEAST relevant to the main idea of the first paragraph?
    - (A) Part 1
    - (B) Part 2
    - (C) Part 3
    - (D) Part 4

31. Which of the following, if used in the line labeled Part 10, **best** develops the main idea of the second paragraph?
    - (A) Many horses such as the Clydesdale don't have a nervous temperament.
    - (B) Dalmatians are also known to be good trackers and pointers.
    - (C) For this reason, perhaps the Dalmatian's greatest fame is as the coach dog for horse-drawn fire trucks in the nineties.
    - (D) One thing to watch out for when selecting a Dalmatian is their genetic predisposition to kidney trouble.

32. Which of the following should be substituted for the underlined word in Part 5 of the first paragraph?
    - (A) traveled
    - (B) is traveling
    - (C) had traveled
    - (D) will travel

The following passage is written in the form of a college writing textbook for first-year students. Read the text and answer the questions.

[1]Unlike fiction writing, newspaper writing is based on factual reporting of events and observable conditions. [2]News reports must be concise. [3]Articles in a newspaper are presented in what is known as an "inverted pyramid"; that is, the most important information appears first, with the less important details covered later in the article. [4]I think this makes a lot of sense, don't you? [5]Many people don't have much time to sit down and read the paper in a leisurely fashion, so essential details must be set forth in the first sentence or two.

[6]The rest of the article fills in important details of the story. [7]Excerpts of an interview with the main participant or opinions of an expert are certain to be included in a well-written, interesting news article. [8]____________________ [9]However, the writer must avoid inserting his or her own opinion or including an extremely biased and unsubstantiated opinion.

[10]A news story does not have to be boring, and there are several techniques used to make news reports more interesting. [11]Whenever possible, the writer should use present tense in order to make the news appear up-to-date. [12]No one wants to read old news, anyway. [13]Paragraphs should be kept short, so three or four sentences for most are sufficient. [14]Another technique to make the news story more interesting is to accompany the article with a relevant photograph. [15]News reports are not subtle compositions. [16]They emphasize clarity and are meant to be read easily because today's news is often perishable.

33. Which of the following would help the focus of the main idea in the third paragraph?
    - (A) Delete "there are" from Part 10.
    - (B) Add a clause to Part 11 explaining the form of present tense and giving some examples.
    - (C) Delete Part 12.
    - (D) Combine Parts 15 and 16 by changing the period after "compositions" to a comma.

34. Which of the following is LEAST consistent with the author's purpose and audience?
    - (A) Part 1
    - (B) Part 2
    - (C) Part 3
    - (D) Part 4

35. Which of the following, if used in place of the blank labeled Part 8, **best** fits the development of the second paragraph?

    (A) Consequently, many reporters take along a photographer so the article can be supplemented with action photographs.

    (B) A direct quotation makes the information seem more immediate and lively, not to mention authoritative.

    (C) Direct quotations from any eyewitness make the news article unbiased.

    (D) Simply summarizing the events is, in fact, the best way to catch a busy reader's attention.

The following passage is written in the form of a college communication textbook. Read the text and answer the questions.

[1]Wading through the mud of a political campaign can be a tedious and messy affair. [2]Frequently, issues become buried under a landslide of name-calling and personal attacks, innuendoes, and allegations. [3]The most frequently used fallacy in political campaigns is an attack on the opponent's personality. [4]Attempting to discredit the opponent's views by attacking his or her character is known as the *ad hominem* fallacy. [5]Literally, a Latin phrase, "to the man."

[6]Casting aspersions can divert voters from the facts of the case. [7]For example, if one of the major issues of a campaign year is inflation, voters might hear how a legislator is so rich and has so many tax shelters that he pays less taxes than the average American. [8]The implication, of course, is that the legislator is dishonest, or, at the very least, uncaring about the concerns of his potential constituents. [9]____________________ [10]A politician who has proved to have a conflict of interests in awarding a lucrative government contract to a previous business partner should be challenged when another government contract is going to be awarded. [11]However, a past record of dishonesty does not preclude honesty now or in the future. [12]Also, politicians are only human, and it is to be expected that some will have personal problems. [13]Will these problems affect their record of public service? [14]Do we really need to know all the faults of each public figure running for political office?

36. Which of the following focuses attention on the main idea of the passage?

    (A) Combine Parts 4 and 5 by changing the period after "fallacy" to a comma.

    (B) Omit the comma after "inflation" in Part 7.

    (C) Change the comma after "dishonest" in Part 8 to a semicolon.

    (D) Rephrase Part 11 so that it reads, "Honesty now or in the future cannot be predicted by a past record of dishonesty."

37. Which of the following, if used in place of the blank labeled Part 9, **best** supports the main idea of the second paragraph?

    (A) Politicians should be given more freedom in deciding how to spend our money.

    (B) Every crooked politician should be kicked out of office.

    (C) On the other hand, sometimes it is necessary to question a person's intentions or integrity.

    (D) The American public is tired of all these accusations and name-calling.

The following passage is written in the form of a popular magazine. Read the text and answer the questions.

[1]Recycling helps the environment. [2]Most people now are aware of the need to recycle materials such as newspapers and aluminum cans. [3]City sanitation departments have begun to make recycling easier by providing bags or bins for recyclable materials. [4]Encouraging well-meaning but lazy people to participate in saving the environment. [5]Also, many people do not live close to a recycling collection point or are elderly or handicapped, so the curbside pickup is convenient for everyone.

[6]The most common recyclable materials are newspapers and aluminum cans, but plastic and glass are joining that list. [7]Manufacturers pay more for aluminum cans, and in 1989 it was estimated that Americans recycled about 60 percent of the aluminum cans they used. [8]That's a statistic to be proud of! [9]Plastic is one of the newer recyclables. [10]Although plastic containers cannot be melted down and re-formed as new plastic containers, recycled plastic is used to create such diverse recycled plastic products as park benches and roads.

[11]Tin cans are seldom recycled because manufacturers do not pay very much for the used cans, but this is starting to change. [12]If we only recycled one-third of the ones we now throw away, we'd save about 10 billion cans a year. [13]Think about the savings to our pocketbook and to our environment! [14]Even though recycling centers don't pay consumers for tin cans yet, they often accept the cans and recycle them, anyway. [15]Contact your city hall, city sanitation service, or your nearest recycling center to encourage the recycling of tin cans.

38. Which of the following, if added between Parts 11 and 12, is MOST consistent with the writer's purpose and audience?

    (A) Actually, tin cans are 99 percent steel with just a thin coating of tin added to prevent rusting.

    (B) Tin cans can be melted down and reused just as easily as aluminum cans.

    (C) Let's face it: tin cans are harder to recycle than aluminum ones.

(D) Actually, most people now prefer frozen vegetables rather than canned ones.

39. Which of the following requires revision for unnecessary repetition?

    (A) Part 5

    (B) Part 10

    (C) Part 11

    (D) Part 13

40. Which of the following is a nonstandard sentence?

    (A) Part 4

    (B) Part 8

    (C) Part 14

    (D) Part 15

The following passage is written in the form of a world geography textbook. Read the text and answer the questions.

[1]Ecuador lies on the west coast of South America, between Colombia on the north and Peru on the south. [2]Because the equator crosses the country, Ecuador derives its name from the Spanish word *ecuador,* meaning *equator.* [3]The country of Ecuador is divided into three regions: the coastal lowlands, the Andes highlands, and the eastern lowlands. [4]In addition, Ecuador owns the Galapagos Islands.

[5]Comprising about one-fourth of the area of Ecuador, the coastal lowlands are a flat plain lying along the Pacific coast. [6]Abundant rains and rich soil, particular in the central area of the lowlands, provide an excellent climate for crops. [7]About one-half of Ecuadorians live in the lowlands. [8]The Andes highlands, or *altiplano,* <u>lies</u> at an elevation between 8,000 and 10,000 feet above sea level and provides a cool climate for crops. [9]Some of the highest mountains in South America, Chimborazo (20,561 feet) and Cotopaxi (19,347 feet), are in the Andes mountains, or *Sierra,* which run from north to south through Ecuador. [10]Ecuador's capital city, Quito, lies almost on the equator at an altitude of over 9,300 feet. [11]Most of Ecuador's land is in the *Oriente,* the thick tropical rainforest east of the Andes highlands. [12]This area is largely undeveloped and is populated by native Indians. [13]About 600 miles off the mainland, the Galapagos Islands were made famous by the naturalist Charles Darwin. [14]The Galapagos contain many rare and unusual species of animals and plants. [15]Although it is a tourist attraction, the Galapagos area is a fragile habitat and more stringent safeguards are now being applied to protect it.

41. Which of the following changes is needed?

    (A) Part 3: Put quotation marks around the phrase, "the coastal lowlands, the Andes highlands, and the eastern lowlands."

    (B) Part 6: Change "particular" to "particularly."

    (C) Part 7: Delete "of Ecuadorians."

    (D) Part 14: Delete either "rare" or "unusual."

42. Which of the following should replace the underlined word in Part 8?

    (A) lie

    (B) lay

    (C) will lie

    (D) have lain

The following passage is written in the form of a student essay. Read the text and answer the questions.

[1]Most teenagers do not get in trouble on a regular basis, and few commit crimes. [2]Many of us, however, do good works for which we receive little or no publicity in newspapers. [3]The news media should give teenagers the good publicity we deserve.

[4]Three recent activities in my home town of Greenhill illustrate this point. [5]Neighbors and other town residents have been repairing the home of an elderly couple, James and Pauline Martin. [6]In another example, a local youth church group visited a retirement home in order to give presents and sing songs one afternoon. [7]Although the youths were mentioned in the story, this story is buried on the back page of the paper, and part of the story the publicity chairman submitted was cut. [8]My final example concerns the Eagle Scout project of a teenager named Sharad Amtey, who made beautiful signs for the city to denote locations of public buildings such as city hall, the library, the police station, and so on. [9]No one from the news showed up for the dedication of the signs, but a reporter was across town gathering information of a traffic accident. [10]The story of the accident caused by a teenaged driver made the front page of the next edition, of course, while a report on the signs has yet to be mentioned in the paper. [11]Obviously, <u>these kind of conduct</u> by the news media is unfair and shows that adults really don't respect people our age. [12]I think these three examples show how good works by teens are passed over. [13]Truly, we deserve recognition for our positive contributions to society.

43. Which of the following, if added between Parts 5 and 6, is MOST consistent with the writer's purpose and audience?

(A) Reports vary as to the amount of money needed to buy supplies for the repairs.

(B) Don't you think it's kind of neat to know that teenagers were among the helpers?

(C) Over half the volunteer construction workers were teenagers, but only adults were mentioned in the news story or pictured in accompanying photographs.

(D) Their home was damaged after being hit by lightning, and because they have had so many medical bills recently, the Martins had not renewed their homeowner's insurance.

44. Which of the following would help the focus of the main idea in the passage?

(A) Add a clause after Part 1 naming some examples of teenagers who have committed crimes.

(B) Reverse the order of Parts 7 and 8.

(C) Delete Part 11.

(D) Combine Parts 12 and 13 by changing the period after "over" to a comma.

45. Which of the following should replace the underlined phrase in Part 11 of the second paragraph?

(A) these kinds of conduct

(B) this kind of activities

(C) those kind of activities

(D) this kind of conduct

WRITING SAMPLE

(ANSWER SHEETS APPEAR IN THE BACK OF THIS BOOK.)

DIRECTIONS: In this section, you are required to write an essay of between 300 and 600 words on the writing topic which appears on the bottom of this page. You should expect to spend approximately 60 minutes on your writing sample. During this time, you should organize your ideas, write a rough draft, and proofread and revise your draft essay.

Make sure to read the topic carefully and consider what your position will be before you start to write the essay. After you are confident in what you have written, copy your essay onto the lined pages of the Writing Sample answer sheet.

Your essay will be scored against the following seven criteria:

1. Appropriateness (how well you explore the given topic and how suitably you address your audience)
2. Unity and Focus (the pointedness of your perspective and direction)
3. Development (the quality of evidence that you offer to support your argument)
4. Organization (the logical arrangement of your essay)
5. Sentence Structure (how successfully you use sentences and how varied your sentence forms are)
6. Usage (the effectiveness and proper implementation of your word usage)
7. Mechanical Conventions (your proper use of spelling, punctuation, and capitalization)

Your essay must be written on the topic given and must employ numerous paragraphs. Make sure it is legible — if it cannot be read, it cannot be graded.

Writing Sample Topic

States today observe Dr. Martin Luther King's birthday because of his contributions to the Civil Rights movement of the sixties. However, observance of this holiday still causes controversy. Write an essay, to be read by a peer who has recently immigrated to this country, explaining the various sides of the issue.

PRACTICE TEST 1

ANSWER KEY

Reading Section

1. (B)	10. (B)	19. (A)	28. (C)	37. (A)
2. (B)	11. (C)	20. (B)	29. (B)	38. (A)
3. (D)	12. (C)	21. (D)	30. (D)	39. (B)
4. (C)	13. (C)	22. (D)	31. (B)	40. (C)
5. (A)	14. (A)	23. (D)	32. (C)	41. (D)
6. (D)	15. (C)	24. (C)	33. (C)	42. (C)
7. (B)	16. (B)	25. (B)	34. (A)	43. (A)
8. (C)	17. (D)	26. (D)	35. (B)	44. (A)
9. (A)	18. (D)	27. (B)	36. (C)	45. (D)

Mathematics Section

1. (C)	10. (A)	19. (C)	28. (B)	37. (D)
2. (C)	11. (D)	20. (D)	29. (C)	38. (B)
3. (C)	12. (A)	21. (B)	30. (C)	39. (D)
4. (D)	13. (A)	22. (A)	31. (B)	40. (C)
5. (A)	14. (C)	23. (A)	32. (D)	41. (D)
6. (A)	15. (C)	24. (B)	33. (B)	42. (D)
7. (A)	16. (C)	25. (A)	34. (B)	43. (B)
8. (B)	17. (A)	26. (B)	35. (A)	44. (D)
9. (B)	18. (B)	27. (D)	36. (C)	45. (B)

Writing Section (Multiple-Choice)

1. (C)	10. (D)	19. (C)	28. (C)	37. (C)
2. (C)	11. (B)	20. (A)	29. (D)	38. (B)
3. (A)	12. (C)	21. (D)	30. (B)	39. (B)
4. (C)	13. (C)	22. (D)	31. (C)	40. (A)
5. (B)	14. (A)	23. (B)	32. (A)	41. (B)
6. (B)	15. (C)	24. (A)	33. (C)	42. (A)
7. (C)	16. (B)	25. (C)	34. (D)	43. (C)
8. (A)	17. (C)	26. (D)	35. (B)	44. (C)
9. (D)	18. (D)	27. (A)	36. (A)	45. (D)

DETAILED EXPLANATIONS OF ANSWERS

Reading Section

1. **(B)** The context suggests little rain for much of the year. (A) is incorrect; the context doesn't connect isolation with the term. (C) is incorrect; the context doesn't suggest shapes in connection with the word. (D) is incorrect; the paragraph clearly indicates that the area is not completely devoid of rain.

2. **(B)** The selection cites such a history and government's attempts to protect it. (A) is incorrect; the writer views erosion as a natural cause of the Badlands' beauty, not as a threat. (C) is incorrect; the opposite is true. (D) is incorrect; the selection says that we already have a national park in the Badlands.

3. **(D)** The central idea of the paragraph deals with fossils in the Badlands. This comment suggests why such fossils exist and why there are so many. (A) is incorrect; the point of the paragraph is not that many of our mammals came from Asia. (B) is incorrect; the paragraph's purpose is not to investigate the cause of extinction. (C) is incorrect; while the writer would want visitors to come, he doesn't give this idea in an attempt to entice them.

4. **(C)** The first paragraph explains how the buildup began. (A) is incorrect; erosion was slower initially than the buildup. Erosion formed the shapes only after the terrain was built up. (B) is incorrect; these shapes were formed as one of the latter stages. (D) is incorrect because this formation is going on today with new rains; it would hardly be the first step.

5. **(A)** The first paragraph establishes erosion's role in the Badlands' formation as the central idea and the next paragraphs show how erosion reveals fossils; the final part deals with the formation of a national park to protect the Badlands. (B) is incorrect; while weather is referred to, it isn't the central idea. (C) is incorrect; the selection doesn't deal with the Badlands' historical significance but rather with its geological significance. The second section doesn't deal with federal regulation. (D) is incorrect; the selection doesn't discuss the effects of animal migration on erosion.

6. **(D)** Item (C) in the first paragraph refers to this term with a correct definition: "those accumulations of religious notions and legends." (A) is incorrect; the first paragraph doesn't suggest that these "accretions" are anything but "incredible" and fiction. (B) is incorrect; the first paragraph maintains that Hostead's position rejects any soundness in such accretions. (C) is incorrect; again, "accretions," according to contextual clues, doesn't mean "implications," but rather "accumulations."

7. **(B)** Hostead's first assumption makes that statement about the essence of religion while the second sentence in paragraph two disputes it. (A) is incorrect; paragraph one defines Hostead's position, while the second paragraph addresses the first position, which doesn't deal with scientific validity of any belief in God. (C) is incorrect; these four ideologies are simply used to illustrate that immortality is not necessarily the essence of a religion, but the central idea of the passage is not the defense of these ideologies. (D) is incorrect; the writer is not defending the validity of those ideologies, but using them to attack one of Hostead's points.

8. **(C)** The first two sentences of the second paragraph state this purpose exactly. (A) is incorrect; the writer only touches on one aspect of each of these beliefs to disprove Hostead's first point. (B) is incorrect; the writer touches only the first position, which does not deal with scientific credibility. (D) is incorrect; the writer disputes Hostead's definition of essence of religion rather than provide his own definition.

9. **(A)** The writer points out that early Judaism had no belief in immortality, that benefits from God are often merely worldly benefits. (B) is incorrect; the writer in no way addresses this issue. (C) is incorrect; this is a statement made about Buddhism, not Judaism. (D) is incorrect; the Jew hungers for the living God.

10. **(B)** The writer states this in the second sentence of the second paragraph, and proceeds to illustrate his point with those four beliefs. (A) is incorrect; the writer makes no statement or inference of that nature; he treats the four equally. (C) is incorrect; the writer doesn't address a psychical approach. (D) is incorrect; the writer is not testifying to the validity of any of these ideologies, but using them to illustrate the error of Hostead's first contention.

11. **(C)** Paragraph one itemizes Hostead's positions and a conclusion while paragraph two begins with the writer's objection to Hostead's position followed by illustrations from four main streams of religious thought. (A) is incorrect; neither Hostead nor the writer defines religion. (B) is incorrect; Hostead doesn't define religion; the writer neither defines Judaism nor uses it as a basis of comparison. (D) is incorrect; again, Hostead defines neither religion nor science while the writer never addresses science.

12. **(C)** This fits the entire framework of the passage (i.e., first the statistics, then their effects). Though the passage tracks the gross national product (B), this is by no means central to the entire passage. The passage nowhere degrades Hoover's presidency (A) nor does it monitor the actual *effects* of the banking system, though it does show how the banking system was *affected;* yet even so, this is by no means central to the passage.

13. **(C)** Due to the inherent logic of the sentence, (C) is correct. The diseases do make people immune to *starvation* (A), because the victims of the disease die

before they can starve. The sentence nowhere implies that the diseases cause malnutrition (B); rather, it is the malnutrition that creates disease susceptibility. Although few died of starvation, many died of disease, which is indirectly caused by malnutrition; therefore, (D) is incorrect.

14. **(A)** Because new families are lessening in number, (A) is correct. The marriage and birth rates are not listed in the sentence, so *family formation* has little to do with those statistics (B). The word *formation* does not imply either *rank and file* (C) or an informational census (D).

15. **(C)** The passage directly links the two ideas in the same sentence (second to last sentence in the final paragraph). Hoovervilles (A) have no association with any government or private agencies. Two-family houses (B) and disease centers (D) are not directly mentioned in the passage.

16. **(B)** The 1933 bar is highest, and the graph measures the percent of unemployment by the height of the bars. The bars for 1929 (A), 1938 (C), and 1944 (D) are all lower than the bar for 1933, in which year unemployment was the highest.

17. **(D)** 1944 (the bar between 1943 and 1945) is the shortest bar on the graph. As mentioned above, the graph measures the percentage of unemployment on the length of the bars. The bars for 1929 (A), 1933 (B), and 1938 (C) are all higher than the bar for 1944, which is the lowest bar on the graph.

18. **(D)** The term "livestock forage" used in the passage suggests this definition. (A) is incorrect; the term is not necessarily used in relationship to the forest alone; additionally, the first paragraph calls forage a renewable product. (B) is incorrect; the second paragraph calls it something that forests and grasslands, not commercial industry, provide. (C) is incorrect; the term is used strictly as a noun in the selection, not as a verb.

19. **(A)** The objectives tell us this. (B) is incorrect; while this statement may be true, the selection does not say or imply this. (C) is incorrect; the third section of the selection, which doesn't suggest such as the chief purpose of the service, doesn't indicate that state activity is regulated. (D) is incorrect; the central idea of this selection goes beyond simple protection of the environment.

20. **(B)** Each of the three sections do exactly that. (A) is incorrect; the selection at no point states what the functions are not. (C) is incorrect; the forest system plays a partial role here, and how it functions really isn't addressed. (D) is incorrect; the states' role is never outlined.

21. **(D)** The objectives aim at supervising. The last sentence in paragraph two suggests this answer; and the final sentence of paragraph three also suggests it. (A) is

incorrect; this statement may be true, but it is not necessarily the chief assumption behind the selection; simply the need to monitor forests is primary. (B) is incorrect; rather than suggest a fear of what disaster may happen, the selection rests on the positive results of good supervision. (C) is incorrect; the article doesn't imply that we've passed a danger point in our forests by mismanagement or by any other unfortunate thing.

22. **(D)** "Multiple-use" suggests a range of uses for the land, while "sustained yield" suggests a perpetual reaping of various products. (A) is incorrect; "yield" doesn't refer to those that use the land but to the land itself. (B) is incorrect; it would be a mistake to infer from this statement that the service thinks all land can produce all things; rather all land collectively can produce many products. (C) is incorrect; who benefits from the land is not the important thing here; instead, the emphasis lies in the land's productivity.

23. **(D)** "Organic" means of a fundamental nature; the ceremony itself is fundamentally important, the writer says. (A) is incorrect; in the context of the selection, the ceremony does not have to occur, nor is it spontaneous. (B) is incorrect; neither physical nor mental health is implied by the term's usage here. (C) is incorrect; the term's meaning suggests the opposite, just as the opposite is suggested here in this article.

24. **(C)** The first paragraph establishes the first clause of this answer; the next-to-last sentence in that paragraph states the idea found in the main clause of the statement. (A) is incorrect; while this statement is true of the article, it does not constitute the main point of the writer. (B) is incorrect; again this statement is true and occurs in the selection; however, the article's meaning goes beyond the idea. (D) is incorrect; the point of the article is not so much a look at weddings around the world, but rather an emphasis on weddings per se, especially in comparison to other rites of passage.

25. **(B)** The passage that follows the term pinpoints such bustling activity as buying, partying, etc. (A) is incorrect; the writer's tone is not necessarily demeaning. (C) is incorrect; the term may suggest chaos but not meaninglessness. (D) is incorrect; mirth may be implicit in the passage, but the context in which the term appears does not focus on the mirth of the occasion but on the excitement of it.

26. **(D)** The writer is making the point, as stated in the first sentence, that the ceremony is "organic" and thereby serious business to the culture. (A) is incorrect; the two are depicted as parallel, not in contrasting terms. (B) is incorrect; the writer's intent is not to show absurdity; she shows instead the seriousness. (C) is incorrect; the incident is not developed sufficiently to reflect the idea of frenzy; however, the incident does reflect a seriousness in the ceremony.

27. **(B)** The first paragraph discusses various rites of passage before finally

zeroing in on the wedding; the second introduces the organic nature of the ceremony, then examines the American wedding in light of the opening. (A) is incorrect; the selection does not address marriage at all, only the wedding ceremony; nor does the selection begin with the significance of weddings in general. (C) is incorrect; there is not emphasis on religion or foreign or domestic rites at all. (D) is incorrect; the article doesn't define "rites of passage" and does not ridicule the extent of rites.

28. **(C)** The context in which this word is used at the beginning of the paragraph suggests this meaning. (A) is incorrect; there exists no indication that the change in Mr. Covey refers to "epoch." (B) is incorrect; the selection doesn't imply that the event is a great event as such; the term would then contradict the writer's "humble history." (D) is incorrect; the writer gives no indication that what follows is a demeaning thing.

29. **(B)** The writer expresses this in the last paragraph. (A) is incorrect; this may be a true assertion, but this point is never made or hinted at by the writer. (C) is incorrect; this statement would be an unfair generalization about a singular incident about one man. (D) is incorrect; the writer speaks of a single owner and makes no inferences about slave owners as a whole.

30. **(D)** When the writer decides to register a complaint and ask for protection, he assumes that he, as any other human being, not only had the right to protection but stood a chance of receiving it. (A) is incorrect; the writer clearly makes no insinuation that his aim was freedom as he sets out from Mr. Covey's. (B) is incorrect; he certainly does not indicate that belief. Quite the contrary, he seems bent on leaving in spite of the consequences. (C) is incorrect; while he was not in good physical shape, he expresses no suspicion that he will die soon, either from his injuries or from any future action. He may well have thought that, but we don't gain that insight from paragraph two.

31. **(B)** While not stated explicitly, we can assume that the fan was used to process wheat. (A) is incorrect; the slaves' comfort was not considered; moreover, we're told that one was involved in "fanning the wheat." (C) is incorrect; no suggestion to this effect is made in the selection, nor does the fan injure the narrator. (D) is incorrect; Mr. Covey heard the fan stop, but his concern was the general stoppage of work, not the fan itself.

32. **(C)** Mr. Covey's mistreatment insulted the writer's dignity and spurred him to walk off; it resulted in the realization that we read in the last paragraph. (A) is incorrect; the writer's initial belief was not that he was no better than a slave; his self-esteem, he says, was "rekindled." (B) is incorrect; the writer expresses no preconceived notion about Mr. Covey before the incident; the incident doesn't appear to be the crowning blow. (D) is incorrect; it would be unfair to summarize this selection by placing any responsibility on the writer's fellow workers, who were also slaves subject to Covey's wrath.

33. **(C)** The text here uses it to show the range in the plays from the beginning (Creation) to the end (Judgment). (A) is incorrect; there is no suggestion in the passage that cosmic dramas were artificial. (B) is incorrect; while many of the plays, according to the writer, involved the subject of devils, this term doesn't necessarily suggest this. (D) is incorrect; while the plays did deal with religious topics, this term does not refer to the religious nature of the plays.

34. **(A)** The paragraph says this in sentence two and gives three major changes. (B) is incorrect; the changes drama experienced, according to the selection, went beyond a moral nature. (C) is incorrect; the church did have such difficulty, but this paragraph goes beyond this to other factors as well. (D) is incorrect; this is the central idea of paragraph one.

35. **(B)** As the language of drama changed from Latin to the vernacular, the level of enjoyment would have increased; moreover, the increased buffoonery, a trait of the vernacular, suggests that the people were already anxious for nonliturgical drama. (A) is incorrect; the selection points out increased buffoonery, which implies that church control over people and their taste in drama was not strong. (C) is incorrect; the writer doesn't imply such a change and doesn't address the quality of drama, just the taste of the people. (D) is incorrect; again there's no hint of such an idea; in fact, the wealth of the church could have produced more extravagant productions than laymen could have.

36. **(C)** The text says the festival was held in spring when weather was good. (A) is incorrect; the selection does not say or imply that. (B) is incorrect; this true statement does not affect the timing of the dramas. (D) is incorrect; again, this assumption is irrelevant to the question.

37. **(A)** Paragraph one opens with references to drama's exit, with several reasons; paragraph two itemizes three effects. (B) is incorrect; while I. may have validity and III. is valid, II. is incorrect; the selection does not develop such reasons. (C) is incorrect; while paragraph one discusses why drama left the church, the nature of its exit isn't discussed. (D) is incorrect; the selection does not use 1204 as a pivot for discussing drama.

38. **(A)** The fourth sentence of the selection states this. (B) is incorrect; the selection does not say that "spiritual super-existence" lives forever; the soul does. (C) is incorrect; the writer doesn't say man doesn't have "supreme" intelligence; he says that Aristotle felt the human soul had a superior intellect. (D) is incorrect; man has spiritual super-existence through his knowledge and love, but the writer doesn't say knowledge and love are the essence of spiritual super-existence.

39. **(B)** The first paragraph establishes man as a microcosm while the second paragraph attributes that condition to the human soul. (A) is incorrect; perhaps this is a statement with which the writer would agree, but it's only by inference that this statement would be considered true. (C) is incorrect; this true statement doesn't

summarize the central idea of the passage; it only supports it. (D) is incorrect; this statement, which reflects the writer's opinion, doesn't constitute the main idea of the selection.

40. **(C)** This is not a factual statement; many would argue that man has no more will than any other creature. (A) is incorrect; while not all agree with this statement, it is a fact that Christians believe this. (B) is incorrect; this is the opposite of what the writer says. (D) is incorrect; we can all agree that man is indeed subject to accidents, as the writer maintains; this is not an opinion.

41. **(D)** The context indicates that the Gulf Coast is near the water. (A) is incorrect; the specific nature of the water doesn't appear to be an issue. (B) is incorrect; the context doesn't suggest that water is a necessity, even though the Vietnamese might prefer it. (C) is incorrect; the water's motion is not relevant.

42. **(C)** The selection reflects on the struggles of the Vietnamese — including those here in the U.S. — for a life of their own. (A) is incorrect; the selection doesn't focus on the enjoyment that the Vietnamese gain. If anything, the experience annoys them. (B) is incorrect; however nomadic these people are, their wandering nature is not the main idea of the article. (D) is incorrect; America is not the focal point of the selection, and it is certainly not depicted in this light.

43. **(A)** We indeed see what it's like to struggle for things that we often take for granted. (B) is incorrect; the account is not quite entertaining, nor does it contain local color. (C) is incorrect; the focus of the story is not on equal rights in the U.S.; the issue never comes up. (D) is incorrect; a pitch is not made about such adoption, nor is one implied.

44. **(A)** Conflicts in North and South Vietnam caused them to flee more than once. (B) is incorrect; Vietnamese are not pictured as nomadic by nature. They desire to stay in one place. (C) is incorrect; they are able to fish in Southeast Asia. Work is not the motivation behind their move to Biloxi. (D) is incorrect; no reference is made to any kind of search for loved ones.

45. **(D)** Another writer might say a different trait was their most outstanding. (A) is incorrect; the selection sufficiently supports this observation as a fact. (B) is incorrect; the selection establishes clearly that communism besieged the country and endangered people. That would be a fairly observable fact. (C) is incorrect; this statement is verified within the article by fact.

Mathematics Section

1. **(C)**

$$\frac{2}{3} = 3\overline{)2.00}^{\,.66\frac{2}{3}} \quad \frac{7}{8} = 8\overline{)7.00}^{\,.87\frac{1}{2}} \quad \frac{5}{9} = 9\overline{)5.00}^{\,.55\frac{5}{9}} \quad \frac{3}{4} = \overline{)3.00}^{\,.75}$$

Then $\frac{5}{9} < \frac{2}{3} < \frac{3}{4} < \frac{7}{8}$

since $.55\frac{5}{9} < .66\frac{2}{3} < .75 < .87\frac{1}{2}$.

Answer (A) is incorrect because division of 2 by 3 = $.6\bar{6}$ which is more than $.5\bar{5}$. Answer (B) is incorrect because

$$\frac{7}{8} = 8\overline{)7.000} = .875$$

which is more than $.5\bar{5}$. Answer (D) is also incorrect because

$$\frac{3}{4} = 4\overline{)3.00} = .75$$

which is greater than $.5\bar{5}$.

2. **(C)**

To solve $(x-7)(x+6) = 0$, set each of the factors equal to zero and solve each equation.

$$\begin{array}{rcl|rcl} (x-7) & = & 0 & (x+6) & = & 0 \\ +7 & & +7 & -6 & & -6 \\ \hline x & = & 7 & x & = & -6 \end{array}$$

Therefore, the two roots are 7 and – 6; and their product (7) (– 6) = – 42.

Answer choice (A) is wrong because only one root was multiplied by itself and the sign was also reversed.

$$\begin{aligned} (x-7)(x+6) &= 0 \\ x-7 &= 0 \\ x &= 7 \\ (x)(x) = (7)(7) &= 49 = -49 \end{aligned}$$

Answer choice (B) is wrong due to an error in multiplication of a negative number.

$$\begin{aligned} (x-7)(x+6) &= 0 \\ x-7 = 0,\ x+6 &= 0 \\ x = 7,\ x &= -6 \\ (7)(6) &= 42 \end{aligned}$$

Answer choice (D) is wrong because it only uses one root and multiplies it incorrectly.

$$(x-7)(x+6) = 0$$

$$x+6 = 0$$

$$x = -6$$

$$(x)(x) = (-6)(-6) = -36$$

3. **(C)**

Let x represent the smallest number.

The largest number is $3x$. Since the smallest number is 10 less than the middle number or the smallest number is the middle number minus 10, then the smallest number plus 10 is the middle number. So the middle number is $x + 10$.

The first number	+	second number	+	third number	=	90
(smallest)		(middle)		(largest)		
x	+	$x + 10$	+	$3x$	=	90

Combining like terms on the left side, we get:

$$5x + 10 = 90$$

Transposing the constant term + 10 to the right side of the equation:

$$\begin{array}{rcr} 5x + 10 & = & 90 \\ -10 & = & -10 \\ \hline 5x & = & 80 \end{array}$$

To solve for x in the equation $5x = 80$, we divide both sides by 5 as follows:

$$\frac{5x}{5} = \frac{80}{5}$$

$$x = 16$$

So	$x = 16$	is the smallest number.
	$3x = 3(16) = 48$	is the largest number
	$x + 10 = 16 + 10 = 26$	is the middle number

The diameter of the circle would then be 26.

To find the area of a circle we must use the formula

$$\pi \times \text{radius}^2.$$

The radius is half the diameter, so the radius would be

$$26 \div 2 = 13.$$

Multiply the radius by itself:

$$13 \times 13 = 169$$

Multiply the radius squared by $\pi(3.14)$:

$$169 \times 3.14 = 530.66$$

4. **(D)**

Let x = number of nickels, then

$.05x$ = monetary value of the number of nickels

Let y = number of dimes, then

$.10y$ = monetary value of the number of dimes

Since there are 42 coins in the bank, and the bank contains only nickels and dimes, then

number of nickels	+	number of dimes		42 coins
↓	or	↓	=	
x	+	y	=	42

Since the total monetary value of the coins in the bank is \$3.85, then

monetary value of nickels	+	monetary value of dimes	=	\$3.85
↓	or	↓		
$.05x$	+	$.10y$	=	\$3.85

Since the problem asks us to determine the number of nickels written in terms of x, we want the equation

$$.05x + .10y = \$3.85$$

(or multiplying through by 100, each term, in order to move the decimal points two places to the right, we get)

$$5x + 10y = 385$$

to be written in terms of x, so that "y" is replaced by the term $10y$.

Solving for y in the equation $x + y = 42$, we subtract x from both sides to get

$$\begin{array}{rcl} x + y &=& 42 \\ -x & & -x \\ \hline y &=& 42 - x \end{array}$$

Substitute $y = 42 - x$ in the equation

$$5x + 10y = 385$$

This gives us

$$y = 42 - x$$

$$5x + 10y = 385$$

$$5x + 10(42 - x) = 385 \quad \text{substituting for } y$$

$$5x + 420 - 10x = 385 \quad \text{use distributive law}$$

$$-5x + 420 = 385 \quad \text{combine like terms}$$

$$\begin{array}{rl} -420 & -420 \\ \hline -5x = & -35 \quad \text{transpose the constant} \end{array}$$

$$\frac{-5x}{-5} = \frac{-35}{-5} \quad \text{divide by the coefficient of } x \text{ on the left side of the equation}$$

$$x = 7$$

Answer choice (A) is incorrect because it refers to the number of dimes.

$$(42 - x)(.05) + x(.10) = 3.85$$

$$2.10 - .05(x) + .10(x) = 3.85$$

$$.05x = 1.75$$

$$x = 35 = \text{\# of dimes}$$

Answer choice (B) is incorrect based on a guess of 30 dimes making \$3.00 and 17 nickels making a total of \$3.85, but with a wrong total number of coins.

$$30(.10) + 17(.05) = \$3.85, \quad 30 + 17 \neq 42$$

Answer choice (C) is incorrect because the total number of coins was changed to 40.

$$(x)(.05) + (40 - x)(.10) = \$3.85$$

$$(.05x) + 4.00 - (.10x) = \$3.85$$

$$-.05x = -.15$$

$$x = 3$$

5. **(A)**

$11^8/_9$ is approximately 12.

$2^{12}/_{13}$ is approximately 3.

Then $11^8/_9 \div 2^{12}/_{13}$ is approximately $12 \div 3 = 4$.

Answer choice (B) is incorrect because $2^{12}/_{13}$ is rounded to 2.

$12 \div 2 = 6$

Answer choice (C) is incorrect because of a mistake in rounding $11^8/_9$ to 11 and $2^{12}/_{13}$ to 2 followed by an error in computation.

$$11 \times 2 = 22$$

Answer choice (D) is incorrect because $11^8/_9$ is rounded to 11.

$$11 \div 2 = 5^1/2 \approx 5$$

6. **(A)**

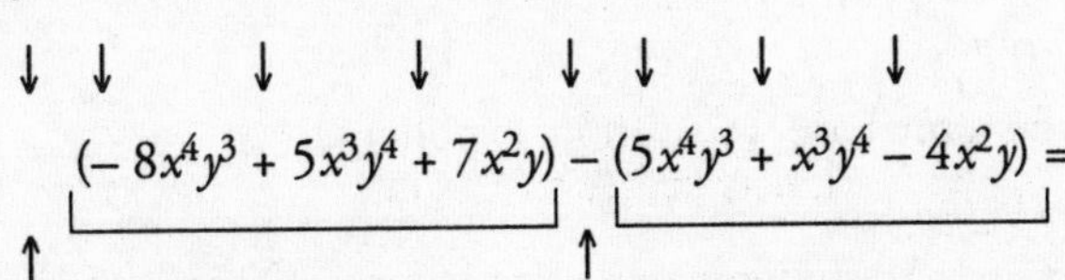

$$(-8x^4y^3 + 5x^3y^4 + 7x^2y) - (5x^4y^3 + x^3y^4 - 4x^2y) =$$

drop parentheses since no sign on the outside means positive, which does not change the signs of the coefficients of each term on the inside of these parentheses

change signs of the coefficients of each term on the inside of these parentheses because of the minus sign outside the parentheses

$$-8x^4y^3 + 5x^3y^4 + 7x^2y - 5x^4y^3 - x^3y^4 + 4x^2y =$$

Combine like terms — terms having the same variables and same exponents.

$$-8x^4y^3 + 5x^3y^4 + 7x^2y - 5x^4y^3 - 1x^3y^4 + 4x^2y =$$

$$-13x^4y^3 + 4x^3y^4 + 11x^2y$$

neg + neg = neg

coefficient of $-x^3y^4$ is a -1

Answer choice (B) is incorrect due to an error in adding negative numbers.

$$\begin{array}{r} -8x^4y^3 + 5x^3y^4 + 7x^2y \\ -(5x^4y^3 + x^3y^4 - 4x^2y) \\ \hline 3x^4y^3 + 4x^3y^4 + 11x^2y \end{array} \qquad -8x^4y^3 - 5x^4y^3 = 3x^4y^3$$

Answer choice (C) is incorrect because the signs in the second parentheses were not changed.

$$\begin{array}{r} -8x^4y^3 + 5x^3y^4 + 7x^2y \\ -(5x^4y^3 + x^3y^4 - 4x^2y) \\ \hline -3x^4y^3 + 6x^3y^4 + 3x^2y \end{array}$$

Answer choice (D) is incorrect due to an error in subtracting a negative number.

$$\begin{array}{l} -8x^4y^3 + 5x^3y^4 + 7x^2y \\ -(5x^4y^3 + x^3y^4 - 4x^2y) \\ \hline -13x^4y^3 + 4x^3y^4 + \underline{3x^2y} \end{array} \qquad 7x^2y - (-4x^2y) = 3x^2y$$

7. **(A)**

$$\frac{35 \times 10^9}{5 \times 10^4} = \frac{35}{5} \times \frac{10^9}{10^4}$$

$$= 7 \times 10^{9-4}$$

In division of terms with the same base we subtract exponents.

$$= 7 \times 10^5$$

Answer choice (B) is incorrect because during a division of exponential numbers the exponents are subtracted, not added.

$$\frac{35 \times 10^9}{5 \times 10^4} = \left(\frac{35}{5}\right) \times \left(\frac{10^9}{10^4}\right) = 7 \times (10^{9+4}) = 7 \times 10^{13}$$

Answer choice (C) is incorrect because the values of 35 and 5 are subtracted instead of the exponents only.

$$\frac{35 \times 10^9}{5 \times 10^4} = (35 - 5) \times (10^{9-4}) = 30 \times 10^5$$

Answer choice (D) is incorrect because the exponents should not be added and 35 and 5 should not be subtracted.

$$\frac{35 \times 10^9}{5 \times 10^4} = (35 - 5) \times (10^{9+4}) = 30 \times 10^{13}$$

8. **(B)**

The salary for the week = \$75 + .02 (sales above \$100)
= \$75 + .02 (\$350 + \$175)
= \$75 + .02 (\$525)
= \$75 + \$10.50
= \$85.50

We add the sales of \$350 + \$175, which are above \$100, change 2% to .02 and multiply .02(\$525) first, by order of operations, before adding on the \$75.

Answer choice (A) is incorrect because it only takes 2% of \$175.

.02 × \$175 = \$3.50

\$3.50 + \$75.00 = \$78.50

Answer choice (C) is incorrect because it only takes 2% of \$350.

.02 × \$350 = \$7.00

$7.00 + $75.00 = $82.00

Answer choice (D) is incorrect because it multiples 2% of $525 incorrectly and does not add on the base pay of $75.00.

.02 × $525 = $10.50 → $105.00

9. **(B)**

The graphs of the equations represented by the other choices are as follows.

Answer choice (A): $x = 2$

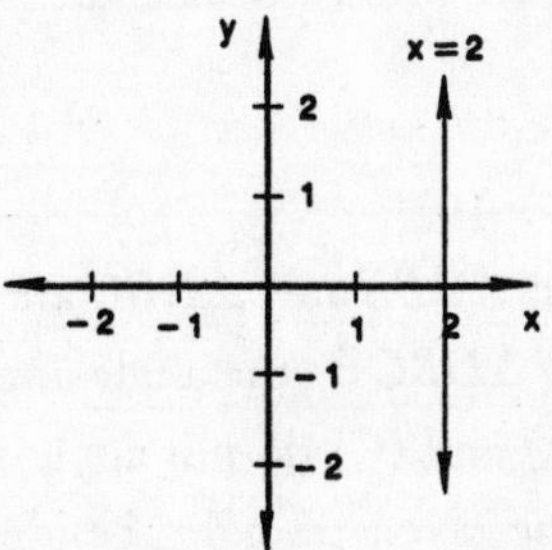

Answer choice (C): $y = 2$

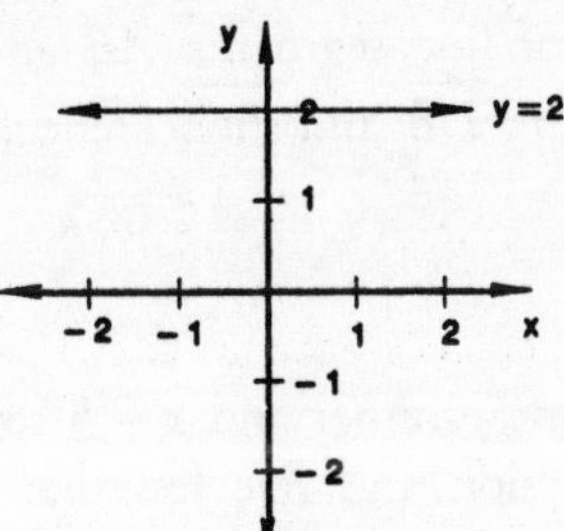

Answer choice (D): $y = -2$

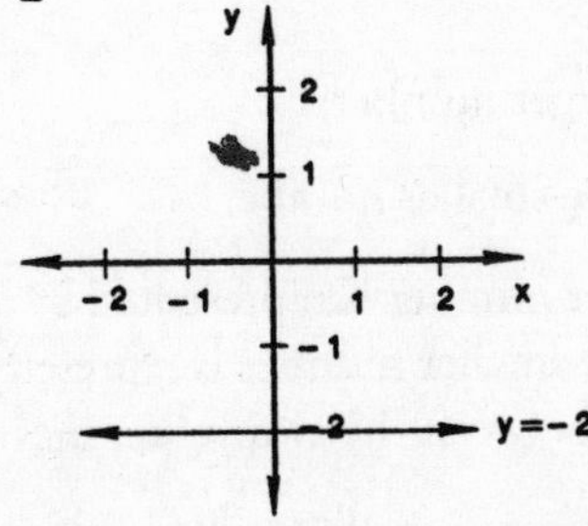

The graph of $x = -2$ is parallel to the y-axis and passes through the point $(-2, 0)$.

10. **(A)**

$\angle FGH$ is a straight angle. The number of degrees in a straight angle is 180°. When the sum of two angles is 180°, the angles are said to be supplementary. In the diagram,

$$\angle FGI + \angle IGH = \angle FGH$$

Therefore, $\angle FGI + \angle IGH = 180°$ and $\angle FGI$ and $\angle IGH$ are supplementary angles.

Answer choice (B) is incorrect because $\angle FGI \neq \angle IGH \neq 90°$ in the diagram. Answer choice (C) is incorrect because complementary angles have a sum of 90°.

$$\angle FGI + \angle IGH = 180° \neq 90°$$

Answer choice (D) is incorrect because vertical angles are opposite angles formed when two lines cross each other.

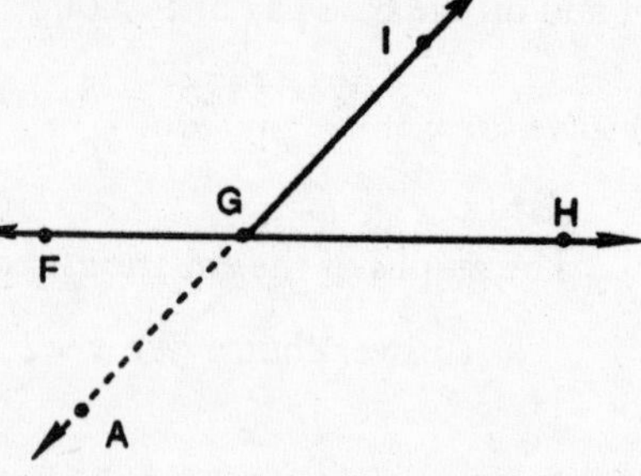

$\angle AGH$ would be $\angle FGI$'s vertical angle.

11. **(D)**

If $\overline{BE} \perp \overline{AC}$ then $\angle ABE$ and $\angle DBC$ are both 90°. In addition, if $\angle C = \angle E$, then ΔABE is similar to ΔDBC by the angle-angle correspondence. Therefore, $\angle A = \angle D$. Answer choices (A) and (C) do not apply since there are relationships between the line segments in the given triangles besides those relationships resulting from similar triangles. Particularly, we see then that in addition to $\overline{DB} \cong \overline{AB}$, the right angle $\angle ABE$ consists of line segments $\overline{AB}$ and $\overline{BE}$, and the right angle $\angle DBC$ consists of line segments $\overline{DB}$ and $\overline{BC}$. Hence, $\overline{BE} \cong \overline{BC}$, and answer choice (B) does not apply.

12. **(A)**

Let x represent one number and $x - 5$ represent the other number since less than represents subtraction and five less than another number means the other number minus five.

This means:

x is the larger number;

$x - 5$ is the smaller number.

Twice the larger number is represented by $2x$.
Three times the smaller number is represented by $3(x - 5)$.
The difference between the two values means

larger value	–	smaller value	is	6
$2x$	–	$3(x-5)$	=	6

Using the distributive law on the left side of the equation, we get:

$$2x - 3x + 15 = 6$$

Combining like terms, $2x - 3x$, on the left side of the equation, we get:

$$-1x + 15 = 6$$

Transpose the constant term, + 15, to the right side of the equation as follows:

$$\begin{array}{rcr} -1x + 15 & = & 6 \\ -15 & = & -15 \\ \hline -1x & = & -9 \end{array}$$

To solve for x in the equation $-1x = -9$ divide both sides by -1 as follows:

$$\frac{-1x}{-1} = \frac{-9}{-1}$$

$$x = 9$$

and substituting $x - 5 = 9 - 5 = 4$ gives the smaller number.

To find the cube of a number, multiply it by itself three times:

$$4 \times 4 \times 4 = 64$$

Choice (B) is the square of the number, not the cube.
Choice (C) is the cube of the larger number.

13. **(A)**

Multiplication of binomials assumes that for

$$(5x^2 + 2)(4x^2 - 7) =$$

(first: $5x^2$ and $4x^2$; outer: $5x^2$ and -7; inner: 2 and $4x^2$; last: 2 and -7)

we multiply the first terms $(5x^2)(4x^2)$ in the parentheses; then we multiply the outer terms $(5x^2)(-7)$ in the parentheses; then we multiply the inner terms $(2)(4x^2)$ in the parentheses; and then we multiply the last terms $(2)(-7)$ in the parentheses. This means

$$(5x^2 + 2)(4x^2 - 7) =$$

$$(5x^2)(4x^2) + (5x^2)(-7) + (2)(4x^2) + (2)(-7) =$$

$$20x^4 - 35x^2 + 8x^2 - 14 =$$

multiplying each pair of terms and adding exponents in the first term

Combine the like terms $-35x^2 + 8x^2$ and we get

$$20x^4 - 27x^2 - 14$$

Answer (B) is incorrect due to an error in multiplying by a negative number.

$$\begin{aligned} (5x^2 + 2)(4x^2 - 7) &= (5x^2)(4x^2) + (2)(4x^2) + (5x^2)(-7) + (2)(-7) \\ &= 20x^4 + 8x^2 + (-35x^2) - 14 \\ &= 20x^4 + 8x^2 + 35x^2 - 14 \\ &= 20x^4 + 43x^2 - 14 \end{aligned}$$

Answer (C) is incorrect because the product of inner and outer terms were not added.

$$(5x^2 + 2)(4x^2 - 7) = (5x^2)(4x^2) + (2)(-7)$$
$$= 20x^4 - 14$$

Answer (D) is also incorrect because the inner product was not added to the outer product.

$$(5x^2 + 2)(4x^2 - 7) = (5x^2)(4x^2) + (5x^2)(-7) + (2)(-7)$$
$$= 20x^4 - 35x^2 - 14$$

14. **(C)**

If x and y vary inversely as each other and k is the constant of variation, then $xy = k$. So if height (h) varies inversely as the square of the base (b^2) then $hb^2 = k$. Solving for h, we divide both sides of the equation $hb^2 = k$, by b^2 as follows:

$$\frac{hb^2}{b^2} = \frac{k}{b^2}$$

$$h = \frac{k}{b^2}$$

Answer (A) is incorrect because h varies directly as the square of the base,

$$h = \frac{b^2}{k},$$

if h increases then b^2 must also increase. Answer (B) is incorrect because h also varies directly as the square of the base,

$$kb^2 = h,$$

if h increases then b^2 must also increase. Answer (D) is incorrect because it takes the same form as answer (A) so the reasons are the same.

$$kh = b^2$$

$$h = \frac{b^2}{k}$$

15. **(C)**

In the interval of 10 AM to 12 Noon one observes on the graph that for March 4, 1981 the temperature in degrees Fahrenheit is increasing from 27° to 32° as follows: (10, 27), (11, 29), (Noon, 32); while for March 4, 1991 the temperature in degrees Fahrenheit is stable at 20° as follows: (10, 20), (11, 20), (Noon, 20).

Answer choice (A) is incorrect because there is no change in temperature for March 4, 1991 from 10 AM to Noon.

Time	Temperature
10 AM	20°
11 AM	20°
Noon	20°

Answer choice (B) is incorrect because there is an increase in temperature on March 4, 1981 between 10 AM and a stable, horizontal leveling of the temperature for March 4, 1991 between 10 AM and Noon:

Time	Temp. on March 4, 1991	Temp. on March 4, 1981
10 AM	20°	27°
11 AM	20°	29°
Noon	20°	32°

Answer choice (D) is incorrect because the dates are reversed.

16. **(C)**

x = number of degrees in the first angle. The second angle is **11°** less than the **first angle**; so the second angle = $x - 11$, where less than signifies subtraction (switching around), and the first angle (x) is the first term and 11° (11) is the second term.

The third angle is twice **the measure of the first angle** increased by 3; so the third angle = $2x + 3$, where twice represents multiplication by 2 and increased by means addition.

Since the **sum** of the angles of a triangle equals 180°, then

$$\text{first angle} + \text{second angle} + \text{third angle} = 180°$$

$$\downarrow \quad \text{and} \downarrow$$

$$x + (x - 11) + (2x + 3) = 180°$$

Answer choice (A) is wrong because of an error in interpretation of 11 less than x.

$$\angle 2 = (11 - x)$$

Answer choice (B) is wrong because of an error in interpretation of twice x increased by 3.

$$\angle 3 = 2(x + 3)$$

Answer choice (D) is wrong because of an error in interpretation of twice x increased by 3.

$$\angle 3 = (2x - 3)$$

17. **(A)**

The surface area of a cylinder consists of the area of both circular bases ($\pi r^2 + \pi r^2 = 2\pi r^2$) and the area of the side

$$\left\{ \begin{array}{l} = \text{circumference of base} \times \text{height} \\ = 2\pi r \times h \end{array} \right\}$$

Therefore, the surface area of a cylinder equals

$2\pi r^2 + 2\pi rh$ or $2\pi rh + 2\pi r^2$

Answer choice (B) is incorrect because it is the formula for the volume of a cone.

$V = {}^1/_3\, \pi r^2 h$

Answer choice (C) is incorrect because it is the formula for the volume of a cylinder.

$V = \pi r^2 h$

Answer choice (D) is incorrect because it is the formula for the surface area of a sphere.

$A = 4\pi r^2$

18. **(B)**

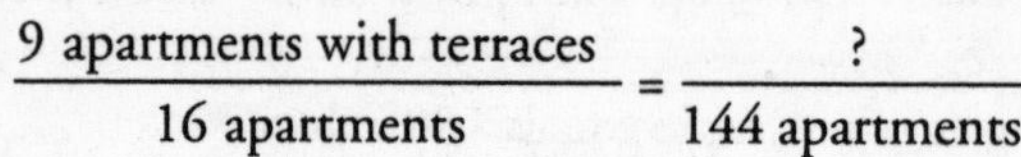

$$\frac{\text{9 apartments with terraces}}{\text{16 apartments}} = \frac{?}{\text{144 apartments}}$$

Solving this proportion for the "?"

$$? = \frac{\text{9 apartments} \times \text{144 apartments}}{\text{16 apartments}} = \frac{\text{1296 apartments}}{\text{16 apartments}} = \text{81 apartments}$$

Answer (A) is incorrect because the apartments were subtracted.

$144 - (16 - 9) = 144 - 7 = 137$ apartments

Answer (C) is incorrect because the number of apartments with terraces is 9 not $16 - 9$.

$(144 \div 16) \times (16 - 9) = 9 \times 7 = 63$

Answer (D) is incorrect due to a multiplication factor guess of 6.

$144 - [(16 - 9) \times 6] = 102$

19. **(C)**

8 seeds / ~~plant~~ × 15 ~~plants~~ = 120 seeds total needed

120 seeds total needed + 35 extra seeds = 155 seeds

Answer (A) is incorrect because the additional seeds were not added on to the total seeds needed.

$8 \times 15 = 120$ seeds

Answer (B) is incorrect because the additional seeds were subtracted from the total seeds needed.

$8 \times 15 = 120$ seeds, $120 - 35 = 85$ seeds

Answer (D) is incorrect because the number of types of plants was multiplied by the sum of seeds per plant type and the additional number of seeds.

$35 + 8 = 43$ seeds, $43 \times 15 = 645$ seeds

20. **(D)**

$$(4 \times 10^{15}) \times (2 \times 10^{8}) = (4 \times 2) \times (10^{15} \times 10^{8})$$
$$= 8 \times 10^{15+8}$$

In multiplication of terms with the same base, we add exponents.

$$= 8 \times 10^{23}$$

Answer choice (A) is incorrect because exponents were subtracted.

$$(4 \times 10^{15}) \times (2 \times 10^{8}) = (4 \times 2) \times (10^{15} \times 10^{8})$$
$$= 8 \times (10^{15-8})$$
$$= 8 \times 10^{7}$$

Answer choice (B) is incorrect due to a subtraction of the values 4 and 2.

$$(4 \times 10^{15}) \times (2 \times 10^{8}) = (4 - 2) \times (10^{15} \times 10^{8})$$
$$= 2 \times (10^{15+8})$$
$$= 2 \times 10^{23}$$

Answer choice (C) is incorrect because the exponents were incorrectly added.

$$(4 \times 10^{15}) \times (2 \times 10^{8}) = (4 \times 2) \times (10^{15} \times 10^{8})$$
$$= 8 \times (10^{15+8})$$
$$= 8 \times 10^{22}$$

21. **(B)**

Let x represent the number of dimes, then $10x$ represents the amount of dimes in cents.

Six more quarters than twice the number of dimes is represented by $6 + 2x$, and then $25(6 + 2x)$ represents the amount of quarters in cents. Altogether she has 690 cents. The equation is

$$10x + 25(6 + 2x) = 690$$

Using the distributive law on the left side of the equation, we get:

$$10x + 150 + 50x = 690$$

Combining like terms on the left side of the equation, we get:

$$\begin{array}{rcr} 60x + 150 & = & 690 \\ -150 & & -150 \\ \hline 60x & = & 540 \end{array}$$

To solve for x in the equation $60x = 540$, we divide both sides by 60 as follows:

$$\frac{60x}{60} = \frac{540}{60}$$
$$x = 9$$

Nine is the number of dimes. Then the number of quarters is

$6 + 2x = 6 + 2(9) = 6 + 18 = 24.$

Using this as the denominator and 5 as the numerator, we get a fraction of $^5/_{24}$.

Adding this to $^7/_{80}$ we get:

$$\frac{5}{24} + \frac{7}{80}$$

Remember, in order to add fractions, you must have a common denominator. The lowest common multiple of 24 and 80 is 240.

5 must be multiplied by 10 because this is now many times 24 goes into 240.

$5 \times 10 = 50$

Our first fraction is $^{50}/_{240}$.

7 must be multiplied by 3 because this is how many times 80 goes into 240.

$7 \times 3 = 21$

The second fraction is $^{21}/_{240}$. We can now add the fractions together.

$$\frac{50}{240} + \frac{21}{240} = \frac{71}{240}$$

22. **(A)**

625 square feet × .30 room for Baby Grand Piano = 187.5 square feet

187.5 square feet for Baby Grand Piano + 46.7 square feet for stage

= 234.2 square feet

Answer (B) is wrong because of incorrect multiplication followed by a subtraction step.

$46.7 \times .30 = 14.01$

$625 - 14.01 = 610.99$ square feet

Answer (C) is wrong because of incorrect usage of a subtraction step.

$625 - 30 - 46.7 = 548.3$ square feet

Answer (D) is also wrong because addition was incorrectly used.

$30 + 46.7 = 76.7$ square feet

23. **(A)**

Since the slopes of perpendicular lines are the negative reciprocal of each other you can determine the slope of each possible line. Any 2 lines meeting these criteria will meet perpendicularly.

$$\text{slope} = M = \frac{\Delta y}{\Delta x} = \frac{y_2 - y_1}{x_2 - x_1}$$

$$M_{AB} = \frac{-2-1}{-3+3} = \emptyset \quad \text{undefined slope}$$

$$M_{AD} = \frac{-1-1}{3+3} = \frac{-2}{6} = \frac{-1}{3}$$

$$M_{AC} = \frac{-3-1}{1+3} = -\frac{4}{4} = -1$$

$$M_{BC} = \frac{-3+2}{1+3} = -\frac{1}{4}$$

$$M_{BD} = \frac{-1+2}{3+3} = \frac{1}{6}$$

$$M_{CD} = \frac{-1+3}{3-1} = \frac{2}{2} = 1$$

$M_{AC} = -1$ and $M_{CD} = 1$, meeting the criteria; therefore $\overline{AC} \perp \overline{CD}$.

24. **(B)**

The volume of the rectangular box

= (length) (width) (height)

= (4) (3) ($2^1/_2$)

(12) ($2^1/_2$)

Writing quantities in fractional form:

$$= \frac{12}{1} \times \frac{5}{2}$$

Cancel and multiply numerators:

$$= \frac{6}{1} \times \frac{5}{1} = 30 \text{ cubic feet}$$

If each box of candy weighs approximately 3 pounds per cubic foot and there are 30 cubic feet in the rectangular box, the weight of the rectangular box is

(30 ~~cubic feet~~) (3 pounds/~~cubic foot~~) = 90 pounds

when the box is filled to the top with candy.

Answer (A) is wrong due to an error in computation.

4 ft × 3 ft × $2^1/_2$ ft × $ft^3/3$ pounds = 10 pounds

Answer (C) is wrong because it only considers the length of the box in the computation.

4 ft × 3 pounds/cubic foot = 12 pounds

Answer (D) is wrong because it deletes the height (deepness) from the computation.

4 ft × 3 ft × 3 pounds/cubic foot = 36 pounds

25. **(A)**

To solve for t means to get t to be on one side by itself. Since there are no t terms on the left side, do the additions (add +4 to both sides of the equation), before the divisions (divide both sides by 5; the coefficient of t) i.e.,

$$\begin{array}{rcl} 8r & = & 5t-4 \\ +4 & & +4 \\ \hline 8r+4 & = & 5t \end{array}$$

$8r$ and 4 are unlike terms so place +4 a little to the right of the $8r$.

$$\frac{8r+4}{5} = \frac{5t}{5}$$

$$\frac{8r+4}{5} = t$$

Answer choice (B) is incorrect because the – 4 is incorrectly transposed.

$$8r = 5t-4$$

$$8r-4 = 5t$$

$$\frac{8r-4}{5} = t$$

Answer choice (C) is incorrect because of an error in order of operations where division came first.

$$8r = 5t-4$$

$$\frac{8r}{5} = t-4$$

$$\frac{8r}{5}+4 = t$$

Answer choice (D) is incorrect due to an order of operation error followed by an incorrect transposition.

$$8r = 5t-4$$

$$\frac{8r}{5} = t-4$$

$$\frac{8r}{5}-4 = t$$

26. **(B)**

Statement 1 implies people who exercise have blue eyes. Statement 3 implies people who have blue eyes enjoy movies. If Sarah has blue eyes, then Sarah enjoys movies.

Answer (A) is wrong because it contradicts statement 5. Answer (C) is wrong because statement 1 says "All people who exercise have blue eyes," not "All people with blue eyes exercise." Answer (D) is wrong because "People who have brown eyes like baseball," so this has no bearing on Sarah.

27. **(D)**

The world population average in undeveloped countries in 1960 was 2.4 billion. The world population average in undeveloped countries in 2000 will be 5.2 billion. Therefore, the average world population in undeveloped countries increased by

$$5.2 \text{ billion} - 2.4 \text{ billion} = 2.8 \text{ billion}$$

Answer (A) is wrong because the data from 1950 was used: 5.2 – 1.8 = 3.4 billion. Answer (B) is wrong because the data was taken from 1950 and 2000 of developed countries: 1.4 – .8 = .6 billion. Answer (C) is wrong because data from developed countries was used: 1.4 billion – .9 billion = .5 billion.

28. **(B)**

The diameter is double the radius. If the diameter is 36 feet, then diameter = 2 × radius means the radius is 18 feet. The formula for the area of a circle

$$\cong 3.14 \times r^2 \cong 3.14 \times 18^2 = 3.14 \times 324 = 1{,}017.36$$

The closest answer choice is

$$3 \times 324 = 972 \cong 980 \text{ square feet}$$

Answer choice (A) is incorrect because it solves for the circumference of the pool.

$$C = \pi\, d \cong (3)\,(36) = 108$$

Answer choice (C) is incorrect because it substitutes the diameter for the radius.

$$A = \pi\, r^2 = (3)\,(36^2) = 3{,}888 \text{ square feet}$$

Answer choice (D) is incorrect because it is an improperly chosen educated guess: ? = A = 500 square feet.

29. **(C)**

The triangle in the diagram is a right triangle. If the triangle is a right triangle, the lengths of the sides satisfy the Pythagorean property, namely $a^2 + b^2 = c^2$, where a, b are the lengths of the legs of the right triangle and c is the length of the hypotenuse. Therefore,

$a^2 + b^2 = c^2$ translates to

(length of base)^2 + (length of wall)^2 = (length of ladder)^2

or

$$\begin{aligned} 8^2 + b^2 &= 17^2 \\ 64 + b^2 &= 289 \quad \text{Solving for } b^2, \\ -64 \quad &\quad -64 \\ \hline b^2 &= 225 \end{aligned}$$

and $b^2 = 225$ means to take the positive square root of both sides which yields $b = 15$ feet.

Answer choice (A) is incorrect due to the improper use of the Pythagorean property.

17 feet – 8 feet = 9 feet

Answer choice (B) is incorrect due to the improper use of the Pythagorean property.

17 feet + 8 feet = 25 feet

$\sqrt{25} = 5$ feet

Answer choice (D) is also incorrect due to the improper use of the Pythagorean property.

$$\sqrt{(17)(8)} = \sqrt{136} = \sqrt{4}\sqrt{34} = 2\sqrt{34}$$

30. **(C)**

The sequence alternates numbers with letters. Particularly, the number sequence represents powers of three, namely,

$3^0 = 1, 3^1 = 3, 3^2 = 9, 3^3 = 27, 3^4 = 81$

The letter sequence starts with the last letter of the alphabet, *z*, then deletes two letters preceding *z* — namely *x*, *y*. The next letter on the list is *w*; delete the two letters preceding *w* — namely *u*, *v*. Following this pattern, the next letter in the sequence is *t*, because, after deleting the two letters preceding *t*, we get the letter *q*.

Diagrammatically, we start with *q*, deleting two subsequent letters until we end at the letter *z*:

q r s t u v w x y z

↑

missing symbol in sequence

Since the sequence alternates numbers first, letters second, the missing symbol is a letter and must be *t*.

Answer (A) is incorrect because the symbol needs to be a letter of the alphabet. Answer (B) is incorrect because the symbol should be evenly separated by a number of letters so it falls into the midpoint of *w* and *q*.

$$\overbrace{\quad x_1 \quad}\overbrace{\quad x_1 \quad}$$
$$w \underset{?}{\rule{6cm}{0.4pt}} q$$

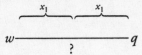

Answer (D) is also incorrect because it does not fall evenly spaced between w and q.

31. **(B)**

To solve this problem, divide the numerator by the denominator in the fraction.

$$\frac{10}{0.05}$$

First move the decimal point two places to the right in both the numerator and the denominator, so that the denominator, 0.05, will become a whole number, 005. In this way,

$$\frac{10.}{0.05} = \frac{1000}{005} = 200$$

Then, multiply 200 × 0.003, counting the number of places the decimal point moved from right to left in the problem.

$$200 \times 0.003 = .6$$

Answer choice (A) is incorrect because of incorrect placement of the decimal point in the denominator.

$$\frac{10}{0.05} = \frac{10}{5.} = 2 \times .003 = .006$$

Answer choice (C) is incorrect because of incorrect placement of the decimal point when multiplying.

$$\frac{10}{0.05} = \frac{1000}{005} = 200 \times 3 = 600$$

Answer choice (D) is also incorrect because of incorrect placement of the decimal point when multiplying.

$$\frac{10}{0.05} = \frac{100}{5} = 20 \times 3 = 60$$

32. **(D)**

If the second side is the same length as the first, it is an isosceles triangle. The third side is three feet longer than the second side. If we let x represent the first side, we can use the equation:

$$x + x + x + 3 = 18$$

The perimeter of a triangle is the sum of its three sides. The first and second side are equivalent, so they both are represented by x.

Adding like terms in our equation, we get:

$$3x + 3 = 18$$

Subtract 3 from both sides to get:

$$3x = 15$$

Divide both sides by 3.

$$\frac{3x}{3} = \frac{15}{3}$$

$$x = 5$$

The three sides of the triangle are 5, 5, and 3 + 5 = 8.

The area of the triangle is found by using the formula

$$^1/_2 \times \text{base} \times \text{height}$$

We must find the height of the triangle to solve the problem. Our triangle should look like this:

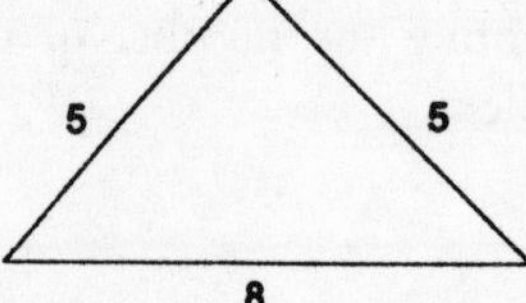

If we draw a line which bisects the top angle and is perpendicular to the longest side, we can create the height and two right triangles.

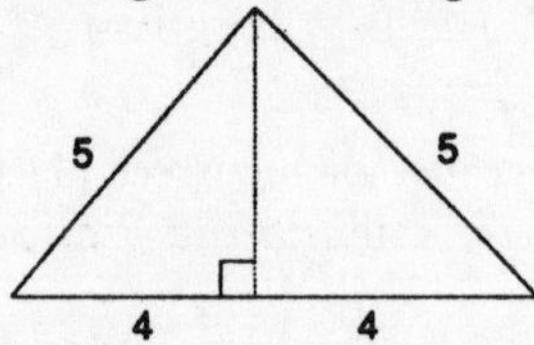

Using the Pythagorean Theorem, we get:

$$4^2 + b^2 = 5^2$$

$$16 + b^2 = 25$$

Subtract 16 from both sides.

$$b^2 = 9$$

Take the square root of both sides.

$$b = \sqrt{9} = 3$$

The height is 3. If we go back to the formula $^1/_2 \times$ base $\times$ height and insert the numbers, we get

$$^1/_2\,(8) \times 3$$

$$^1/_2\,(8) = 4$$

$$4 \times 3 = 12$$

33. **(B)**

What percent of 85 is 17?

translates to	↓		↓		is means "="
?	×	85	=	17	of means "×"

Solving this equation for "?" we divide both sides by 85 as follows:

$$\frac{? \times \not{85}}{\not{85}} = \frac{17}{85}$$

The 85 in both the numerator and denominator on the left side cancel, and we are left with

$$? = \frac{17}{85}$$

Writing $^{17}/_{85}$ as a percent and moving the decimal point two places to the right in the quotient and attaching the percent sign, we get:

$$85 \overline{)17.00} \quad .20.\%$$

Answer choice (A) is incorrect due to a swap of numerator and denominator.

$^{85}/_{17} = 5 \cong 5\%$

Answer choice (C) is incorrect because multiplication was used instead of division.

$85 \times 17 = 1{,}445 \cong 14^{9}/_{20}\%$

Answer choice (D) is incorrect because division and not subtraction should be used.

$85 - 17 = 68 \cong 68\%$

34. **(B)**

When $g = 30$

$C = 270g - 3g^2$	becomes
$C = 270(30) - 3(30)^2$	substituting $g = 30$
$C = 8{,}100 - 3(900)$	multiplying through
$C = 8{,}100 - 2{,}700$	
$C = 5{,}400$	

The monthly commission in January is \$5,400.

When $g = 40$

$C = 270g - 3g^2$	becomes
$C = 270(40) - 3(40)^2$	substituting $g = 40$

$C = 10{,}800 - 3(1{,}600)$ multiplying through

$C = 10{,}800 - 4{,}800$

$C = 6{,}000$

The monthly commission in February is \$6,000.

To determine Sam's commission in January and in February we consider:

Change in commission	=	Commission in February	–	Commission in January
	=	\$6,000	–	\$5,400
Change in commission	=	\$600		

Answer choice (A) is incorrect because the two commissions were added together, giving a total, not a difference.

$$[270(30) - 3(30^2)] + [270(40) - 3(40^2)] = \$11{,}400$$

Answer choice (C) is incorrect because it consists of only the January commission.

$$270(30) - 3(30^2) = \$5{,}400$$

Answer choice (D) is incorrect because it accounts for only the February commission.

$$270(40) - 3(40^2) = \$6{,}000$$

35. **(A)**

To solve for p:

$$-2p + 7 = -9p - 8$$

Transpose your variable terms to one side of the equation, say the left side, as follows:

$$\begin{array}{rcl} -2p + 7 & = & -9p - 8 \\ +9p & & +9p \\ \hline -2p + 9p + 7 & = & -8 \end{array}$$

Then transpose your constant terms to the other side of the equation, i.e., the right side, as follows:

$$\begin{array}{rcl} -2p + 9p + 7 & = & -8 \\ -7 & & -7 \\ \hline -2p + 9p & = & -8 - 7 \end{array}$$

Then factor p from the left side of the equation as follows:

$$-2p + 9p = (-2 + 9)\,p$$

This means $(-2 + 9)p = -8 - 7$ from the above statement.

To solve for p in $(-2 + 9)p = -8 - 7$, we divide both sides of this equation by the constant in parentheses $(-2 + 9)$ as follows:

$$\frac{(-\not{2}+\not{9})p}{(-\not{2}+\not{9})} = \frac{-8-7}{(-2+9)}$$

So that $$p = \frac{-8-7}{-2+9}$$

Answer choice (B) is incorrect because $-9p$ is added to both sides.

$$\begin{aligned} -2p + 7 &= -9p - 8 \\ -9p \quad & \quad -9p \\ \hline -2p - 9p + 7 &= -8 \\ -2p - 9p &= -8 - 7 \\ p(-2 - 9) &= -8 - 7 \\ p &= \frac{-8-7}{-2-9} \end{aligned}$$

Answer choice (C) is incorrect because it does not solve for p correctly and deletes p in $-9p$ term.

$$\begin{aligned} -2p + 7 &= -9p - 8 \\ -7 \quad & \quad -7 \\ \hline -2p \quad &= -9p - 8 - 7 \\ p &= \frac{-9-8-7}{-2} \end{aligned}$$

Answer choice (D) is incorrect because the coefficient and constant on the right side was divided by the coefficient and constant on the left side with a p incorrectly factored out each time.

$$\begin{aligned} -2p + 7 &= -9p - 8 \\ p(-2 + 7) &= p(-9 - 8) \\ p &= \frac{-9-8}{-2+7} \end{aligned}$$

36. **(C)**

To solve for x in:

$$\begin{aligned} -{}^{1}/_{5}x - 4 &= 17 \\ +4 \quad &\quad +4 \qquad \text{Add } +4 \text{ to both sides} \\ \hline \end{aligned}$$

$$-{}^{1}/_{5}x = 21$$

Since the x term is on the left side, we transpose the constant term (– 4) on the left side to the right side.

Then continue to solve for x in $-{}^{1}/_{5}\,x = 21$ by multiplying both sides of the equation by (– 5). In this way the 5's on the left side will cancel to yield the result.

$$-{}^{1}/_{5}x = 21$$

$$(-5)\,(-{}^{1}/_{5})x = (-5)\,(21)$$

$$x = -105$$

Now continue to substitute $x = -105$ in the expression $3x - 1$ as follows:

$$3(-105) - 1 = -315 - 1 = -316$$

Answer choice (A) is incorrect because a multiplication step was skipped in solving for x.

$$-{}^{1}/_{5}x - 4 = 17$$

$$-{}^{1}/_{5}x = 17 + 4$$

$$x = 17 + 4 = 21$$

$$\therefore\ 3x - 1 = 3(21) - 1 = 62$$

Answer choice (B) is incorrect because x was not substituted into the equation $3x - 1$.

$$-{}^{1}/_{5}x - 4 = 17$$

$$-{}^{1}/_{5}\,x = 17 + 4 = 21$$

$$x = 21x(-5)$$

$$x = -105$$

No substitution $3x - 1 = -105$. Answer choice (D) is incorrect because of an error in subtraction.

$$-{}^{1}/_{5}x - 4 = 17$$

$$\underline{\quad -4 \quad -4}$$

$$-{}^{1}/_{5}x = 11$$

$$x = -55$$

$$3x - 1 = -164$$

37. **(D)**

In general a linear equation is represented by the form $y = mx + b$, where m = slope and b = y-intercept (the point at which $x = 0$).

Since $y = 14x + 7$ is of the form

$$y = mx + b$$

we see $m = 14$ = slope.

Answer choice (A) is incorrect because a slope of $-^1/_2$ corresponds to the general equation: $y = -^1/_2x + b$. Answer choice (B) is incorrect because a slope of 2 reflects the equation: $y = 2x + b$. Answer choice (C) is also incorrect because a slope of 7 reflects the equation: $y = 7x + b$.

38. **(B)**

Let x represent the number of hours that Bill worked. John worked 7 hours longer than Bill means $x + 7$ represents the number of hours that John worked. Sam worked twice as long as John means $2(x + 7)$ represents the number of hours that Sam worked.

Bill's hours	+	John's hours	+	Sam's hours	=	53
x	+	$x + 7$	+	$2(x + 7)$	=	53

Using the distributive law on the left side of the equation, we get:

$$x + x + 7 + 2x + 14 = 53$$

Combining like terms on the left side of the equation, we get:

$$4x + 21 = 53$$

Transposing the constant term + 21 to the right side of the equation:

$$\begin{array}{rcr} 4x + 21 & = & 53 \\ -21 & = & -21 \\ \hline 4x & = & 32 \end{array}$$

To solve for x in the equation $4x = 32$, we divide both sides by 4 as follows:

$$\frac{4x}{4} = \frac{32}{4}$$

$$x = 8$$

This is the number of hours Bill worked. Therefore, John worked 7 hours longer than Bill, i.e., $8 + 7 = 15$ hours.

Subtract two hours off of the total to account for his two hours' time and a half pay.

$$15 - 2 = 13 \text{ hours}$$

Multiply the remaining hours by his wages, \$11 per hour:

$$13 \times 11 = \$143$$

If John makes time and a half, take his original pay, divide it in half, and take this amount and add it to the original pay.

$$11 \div 2 = 5.5 \rightarrow 11 + 5.5 = \$16.50 \text{ per hour}$$

Multiply this amount by 2.

$$16.50 \times 2 = \$33$$

Add the two amounts together to get John's total pay for the job.

$$\$33 + \$143 = \$176$$

Choice (A) is incorrect because it is the amount John would have made without time and a half.

Choice (C) is incorrect because it is the amount John would have made working only 13 hours.

39. **(D)**

The Fortran course **decreased** from 100 students to 75 students. The Pascal course **decreased** from 175 students to 125 students. The Basic course **increased** from 100 students to 137 students, and

$$137 - 100 = 37$$

student increase. The COBOL course **increased** from 25 students to 87 students, and

$$87 - 25 = 62$$

student increase.

Answer (A) is wrong because the number decreased from 100 to 75 students.

$$75 - 100 = -25 < 62$$

Answer (B) is wrong because the number decreased from 175 to 125 students.

$$125 - 175 = -50 < 62$$

Answer (C) is wrong because the increase in students was less than 62.

$$137 - 100 = 37 < 62$$

40. **(C)**

The graph passes through the points (0, – 3), (2, – 1), (– 2, – 1), (4, 5), and (4, – 5). Also, the graph is a parabola which faces upward and, therefore, the coefficient of the x^2-term must be positive. These conditions are only satisfied by

$$y = {}^1/_2 x^2 - 3$$

and, therefore, answer choices (A), (B), and (D) are incorrect.

41. **(D)**

$$6x^2 + 2x - 4 = 2(3x^2 + x - 2),$$

factoring out a 2 from each term. The $(3x^2 + x - 2)$ is further factored by finding the terms which multiply to $3x^2$, namely, $3x$ and x; and by finding the terms which multiply to -2, namely, -2 and 1 or $+2$ and -1. Here are the possibilities. Check the product of the inner terms and the product of the outer terms for each factor. We are looking for the middle term of $3x^2 + x - 2$, i.e., $+1x$.

$$3x^2 + x - 2 =$$

$(3x + 2)(x - 1)$: outer $-3x$, inner $+2x$, sum $-1x$ ×

$(3x - 2)(x + 1)$: outer $+3x$, inner $-2x$, sum $+1x$ ✓

$(3x + 1)(x - 2)$: outer $-6x$, inner $+1x$, sum $-5x$ ×

$(3x - 1)(x - 2)$: outer $+6x$, inner $-1x$, sum $+5x$ ×

This says

$$3x^2 + x - 2 = (3x - 2)(x + 1).$$

Therefore,

$$6x^2 + 2x - 4 = 2(3x - 2)(x + 1),$$

and the factor which appears as one of the choices is $(3x - 2)$.

Answer choice (A) is incorrect because of a wrong use of the distributive law.

$$6x^2 + 2x - 4$$

$$2(3x^2 + x - 2) = 2(3x - 2)(x + 1)$$

$$2(3x - 2) = 3x - 4$$

Answer choice (B) is incorrect because of improper factoring out using a "F.O.I.L." method.

$$6x^2 + 2x - 4 = (6x - 1)(x + 4)$$

Answer choice (C) is also incorrect because of a change in sign.

$$6x^2 + 2x - 4 = 2(3x - 2)(x + 1),\ (x + 1) = (x - 1)$$

42. **(D)**

$$\frac{9 \times 0.5}{0.03} =$$

Multiply the numerator, counting the number of places the decimal point moved from right to left in the problem.

$$\frac{4.5}{0.03} =$$

Divide the numerator by the denominator, moving the decimal point two places to the right in both the numerator and the denominator, so that the denominator, 0.03, will become a whole number, 003.

$$\frac{450.}{003.} = 150$$

Answer choice (A) is incorrect because of incorrect placement of the decimal point in the numerator.

$$\frac{9 \times 0.5}{0.03} = \frac{45}{.03} = 1{,}500$$

Answer choice (B) is incorrect because of incorrect placement of the decimal point in the numerator.

$$\frac{9 \times 0.5}{0.03} = \frac{.0045}{0.03} = \frac{.45}{3.0} = .15$$

Answer choice (C) is incorrect because of incorrect placement of the decimal point in the numerator.

$$\frac{9 \times 0.5}{0.03} = \frac{.45}{0.03} = \frac{45}{3} = 15$$

43. **(B)**

$$R = \text{Jack's age in 18 years}$$

$$R - 18 = \text{Jack's age now}$$

$$4(R - 18) = \text{Jack's age in 18 years}$$

Then $4(R - 18) = R \Rightarrow 4R - 72 = R$

Answer choice (A) is wrong because of wrong usage of the distributive law.

$$4(R - 18) = R$$

$$4R - 18 = R$$

Answer choice (C) is wrong because "times" refers to multiplication not division.

$$4(R - 18) = R$$

$$R/4 = R + 18 = 18$$

Answer choice (D) is wrong because of an error in the use of the distributive law and a transposition error deletes an *R*.

$$4(R - 18) = R$$

$$4R - 18 = R$$

$$4R = 18$$

44. **(D)**

$$\begin{aligned} 5x + 2y &= -5 \\ -3x + y &= 3 \end{aligned}$$

Multiply the bottom equation by -2 so that the terms in the y-column will cancel as follows (in this way if the y-terms cancel you will be solving for x).

$$\begin{aligned} 5x + 2y &= -5 & \qquad & 5x + \cancel{2y} = -5 \\ -2(-3x + y) &= -2(3) & \Rightarrow \qquad & 6x - \cancel{2y} = -6 \end{aligned}$$

$$\frac{11x}{11} = \frac{-11}{11}$$

$$x = -1$$

Add the coefficients/terms in the x-column and the constants on the right side. Then divide both sides by 11, the coefficient of the x-term.

Answer choice (A) is incorrect because it solved for the variable y.

$$\begin{aligned} 3(5x + 2y = -5) &= \quad 15x + 6y = -15 \\ 5(-3x + y = 3) &= \quad -15x + 5y = 15 \end{aligned}$$

$$11y = 0$$

$$y = 0$$

Answer choice (B) is incorrect because of an error in adding 2 negative numbers.

$$\begin{aligned} 5x + 2y &= -5 \\ 6x - 2y &= -6 \end{aligned}$$

$$11x = -1, \quad x = -1/11$$

Answer choice (C) is incorrect because of an error in signs.

$$\begin{aligned} 5x + 2y &= -5 \\ -6x - 2y &= -6 \end{aligned}$$

$$x = 1$$

45. **(B)**

You construct a diagram as follows:

Betty: Fr & G

Alice: Sw & R

Sally: Sp & Fr

Tanya: G & Sw

Since French is easier than German, you will write

Fr < G

(where the symbol, <, "less than" means "is easier than"). Since Russian is harder than Swedish, then Swedish **is easier than** Russian and you will write

Sw < R

Since German **is easier than** Swedish, you will write

G < Sw

Since Spanish **is easier than** French, you will write

Sp < Fr

So you have the following series of four inequalities:

(1) Fr < G

(2) Sw < R

(3) G < Sw

(4) Sp < Fr

Inequalities (1) and (3) imply

Fr < G < Sw

by transitivity. Inequality (2) will now imply

Fr < G < Sw < R

by transitivity. Inequality (4) will now imply

Sp < Fr < G < Sw < R

by transitivity. The most difficult languages are Swedish and Russian, and Alice knows Swedish and Russian. Therefore, answer choices (A), (C), and (D) do not apply.

Writing Section

Multiple-Choice Subsection

1. **(C)** Choice (C) is a prepositional phrase, "About 25,000 years ago," which is followed by a subordinate clause. This part should be linked to the previous sentence as it is integral to the migration of the Anasazi. Choices (A), (B), and (D) are all complete sentences.

2. **(C)** Choice (C) has to do with the later history of the Mesa Verde area, after the Anasazi had abandoned it. Since this is so far removed chronologically, Part 7 should be deleted or further developed in a third paragraph. Choices (A) and (B) discuss the very early history of the Indians. Choice (D) follows the chronological time order from A.D. 500 and leads into a discussion of the height of the Anasazi civilization.

3. **(A)** Choice (A) fits naturally into a discussion of the Anasazi culture, between the dwellings mentioned in Part 9 and the trade mentioned in Part 11. Choice (B) is too vague; at this point in the paragraph, the discussion has narrowed to the Anasazi. Choice (C) could have come earlier in the paragraph but is out of place at this point. Choice (D) belongs in a discussion of the disappearance of the Anasazi.

4. **(C)** Choice (C) unnecessarily repeats the words "basis," "based," "founding," and "foundation." These forms need not be repeated and the sentence should be condensed. Choice (A) repeats the phrase "board of regents," found in the previous sentence, but it is needed for transition of thought. Choice (B) and choice (D) are well worded sentences.

5. **(B)** Choice (B) fits between Part 4 and Part 6. Part 4 mentions the topic of dissenting opinion, and Part 6 elaborates by stating the position that English professors have always been outspoken. This idea is continued in Part 7. Choice (A) changes voice to "we," which is out of place in this letter. Choice (C) is too casual. Choice (D) directly contradicts the thesis of the letter.

6. **(B)** Choice (B) contains an inappropriate use of words. The contraction for "who is" should be used to make the sentence correct. The possessive "whose" is not correct in this context. Choice (A) correctly uses the comparative degree. Choice (C) correctly uses the superlative degree. Choice (D) does not make a needed change.

7. **(C)** Choice (C), delete Part 4, is the correct choice. The sentence labeled Part 4 introduces a new topic — the fact that some companies are not committed to a day care program. Since the paragraphs are both discussing companies that have already made this decision, and the advantages of having made this decision, Part 4

is out of place. Choice (A) would make a contradictory statement. Choice (B) would delete a needed phrase. Choice (D) would destroy the parallelism created with Parts 6 and 7 that lead naturally as a transition into the next paragraph.

8. **(A)** Choice (A) is needed for correct subject and verb agreement. The plural subject "companies" should be followed by the plural verb "make." Confusion is caused by an intervening phrase, "showing special initiative in building company loyalty of each employee." Because the phrase ends with a singular noun, it is a common error to make the verb singular also. Choice (B), present progressive, and choice (C), future, are incorrect tenses for the context of the sentence and the paragraph. Choice (D) needs a helping verb and cannot stand alone.

9. **(D)** Part 9 begins with the transition word "Therefore," so it is best placed after a sentence that would state a reason for building company loyalty and morale. Part 11 gives a compelling reason — the company's personal interest in each employee. Choice (A) would remove the topic sentence to a less prominent position, as well as have Part 9 clearly out of order with no idea before it in the paragraph. Choice (B) does not place a sentence with a clear reason before the transition "therefore." Choice (C) would weaken the paragraph.

10. **(D)** Choice (D) fits between the two parts. Part 4 concerns a child who may read two years below grade level. Part 6 concerns a child who reads five years below grade level. The answer choice stating that a child may be as many as five or more years behind in reading ability is the best choice for the paragraph. Choice (A) is far too broad. Choices (B) and (C) introduce extraneous ideas to the paragraph.

11. **(B)** Choice (B) contains the solution to the agreement problem: "the child" should be followed by a singular pronoun, "his or her." The pronoun "their" is plural and would be appropriate to refer to a plural noun such as "children." Choice (A) would insert an incorrect possessive pronoun. Choice (C) would not improve the sentence. Choice (D) is not a correct solution because it makes the verb tense incorrect.

12. **(C)** Choice (C) contains the correct transition words, "Even though" and "Also." Choice (A) is incorrect because "In addition" indicates another example has just been named. As the first sentence is the topic sentence, it does not contain a specific example. Choices (B) and (D) are incorrect because they indicate contrast, and nothing that follows contrasts or is a negative example to the topic sentence.

13. **(C)** Choice (C) contains irrelevant information, so it should be eliminated. Choice (A) contains a phrase essential to the sentence. Choice (B) would create a fragment after the semicolon because the clause beginning with "although" is a subordinate clause, and only an independent clause would be appropriate after the semicolon. Choice (D) would create a misplaced modifier; "except for their breath" would be taken to modify the layer of fat on polar bears.

14. **(A)** Choice (A) fits the development of the paragraph by describing how large polar bears are, a concept introduced in the previous sentence. Choice (B) and choice (D), although related to hunting, do not fit well in this place. Choice (C) introduces an extraneous topic.

15. **(C)** Choice (C) is correct because "between" should be used to compare two things; "among" should be used to compare three or more things. Since there are five countries, "among" is the correct form. Choice (A) would create an error in comparison, since there are more than two types of land-based carnivores. Choice (B) makes no improvement. Choice (D) deletes the necessary idea of contrast shown by "but" in contrasting the two levels of polar bear population.

16. **(B)** Choice (B) is a transition between the discussion of lipoproteins and triglycerides. Part 3 introduces HDL and Part 5 discusses the normal triglyceride level. Choice (A) changes the topic slightly by introducing history. Choice (C) might be a good choice but does not contain mention of triglycerides, so there is no transition. Choice (D) introduces a new topic — the chances of men and women developing heart disease.

17. **(C)** Choice (C) is a type of run-on sentence. The technical name for this sentence is a comma splice since two independent clauses are joined by only a comma; they should be joined by a semicolon (as in this explanatory sentence). The comma after "treated" should be a semicolon. Choices (A), (B), and (D) are correctly punctuated compound sentences because they contain a comma followed by a conjunction to link the two independent clauses.

18. **(D)** Choice (D) discusses the tool-making abilities of an otter, not man, so it should be deleted. Choice (A) would delete the topic sentence from the paragraph. Choice (B) is incorrect because Part 2 begins with "During this time," and there would be no antecedent for "this" if the two parts are reversed. Choice (C) is incorrect because the suggested addition does not pertain to the development of man during this time period.

19. **(C)** Parts 8 and 9 need to be reversed. Part 8 begins with the transition word "Also" which clearly introduces a second feature, not a first as the position would indicate. Choice (A) would delete the topic sentence from the paragraph. Choice (B) would put the second factor after the topic sentence which introduces it. Choice (D) is the concluding sentence and should not be eliminated.

20. **(A)** Choice (A) eliminates the fragment in the second half of Part 4. The subject is "the use of speech," so the verb should be "facilitated" and not the infinitive "to facilitate." Choice (B) would delete the necessary transition word "other," needed to link developments discussed in the first paragraph with developments discussed in the second paragraph. Choice (C) changes the comparative degree "less," needed to compare two items in Part 9, to the superlative

degree needed to compare three or more things. Choice (D) changes the present participle "ensuring" to the past participle "ensured." This change is incorrect because the present participle is necessary to show that survival is still going on; the past participle would indicate that survival has stopped.

21. **(D)** Choice (D) is correct because Part 2 mentions two parents, and Part 3 discusses his father. Therefore, discussing Alexander's mother is an appropriate topic. Choice (A) is the next best choice, because it ties in with Aristotle in Part 5, but it is not as good for the reason that Alexander's other parent is the logical topic. Choices (B) and (C) introduce extraneous topics and topics out of chronological order.

22. **(D)** Choice (D) is the choice because we need to know if Alexander was a child, a teenager, or a young man. Choice (A) has an example in the sentence. Choice (B) is followed by several examples of Alexander's fearlessness and promise. Choice (C) is a very specific verb describing the behavior of horses.

23. **(B)** Choice (B) is correct because a comma is needed after introductory adverbial clauses. Choice (A) is incorrect because "who" is a personal pronoun to describe people, not animals or objects. Choices (C) and (D) do not make any appreciable improvements in the sentence.

24. **(A)** Choice (A) shows clear cause-and-effect sequence begun by Parts 10 and 11. The tone of choices (B) and (D) are far too casual because they introduce the contraction "doesn't" and the personal pronoun "I." Choice (C) directly contradicts the thesis.

25. **(C)** Choice (C) introduces an extraneous topic, another form of investment savings — savings bonds. Choice (A) is necessary because it is the topic sentence. Choice (B) explains the reason people buy a company's stock. Choice (D) is essential as it introduces the next part of the paragraph, dividend reinvestment.

26. **(D)** Choice (D) has correct transition words for three main ideas: "For example" introduces the first idea; "In addition" indicates a second idea; "Finally" indicates the last idea. Choice (A) introduces transition words for contrasting ideas, "Although" and "In contrast." The first transition word, "Eventually," in choice (B) is not appropriate for a first idea or example. The other two transition words are out of order: "First" leads in the second idea, and "Second" leads in the third idea. Choice (C) incorrectly introduces the idea of cause-and-effect, "As a result," and chronological sequence, "Later."

27. **(A)** Part 3 discusses Gothic style spreading to other parts of Europe; therefore, it should be placed just before Part 8 which lists the other places in Europe where the Gothic style spread. Choice (B) would remove the example for Part 1 of the passage, the variety of Medieval art and literature. Choice (C) gets ideas

out of sequence by moving the idea in Part 7, the first Gothic structures, after the spread of the Gothic style of architecture. Choice (D) removes the reason why Gothic cathedrals were a community project and therefore so popular.

28. **(C)** Choice (C) adds a detail supporting the topic in Part 9, height of the cathedrals. Choice (A), although a legitimate part of Gothic architecture, is an extraneous idea for the second paragraph. Choice (B) breaks the formal tone of this passage with the insertion of a personal pronoun, "me." Choice (D) is certainly a true statement, but it would be better added at the end of the passage because it interrupts the discussion of height and light.

29. **(D)** Choice (D) corrects the subject-verb agreement error of Part 12. The subject, "beams," is plural and needs a plural verb, "provide." The presence of an intervening phrase, "called *flying buttresses,*" should not affect the choice of the verb form. Choice (A) "as" is correct; "like" should be used for unusual comparisons called similes. Choice (B) makes no improvement. Choice (C) is not necessary. Commas are strong enough to connect this series of cathedrals.

30. **(B)** Choice (B) is least important because it does not relate to the history of Dalmatians. Choice (A) is the topic sentence. Choices (C) and (D) directly relate to the location of the probable origin of Dalmatians.

31. **(C)** Choice (C) provides a smooth flow of ideas by showing the effect of the Dalmatians' calm temperament. Choice (A) introduces an extraneous topic, Clydesdale horses with calm natures. Choices (B) and (D), although true facts, break the flow of ideas.

32. **(A)** Choice (A) is past tense, the appropriate tense for a discussion of historical events. Choice (B) incorrectly indicates the migration is still in progress. Choice (C) incorrectly changes the form of past tense so it is not parallel with the second part of the sentence, "the dogs traveled"; dogs and man traveled together, not separately. Choice (D) incorrectly changes the time of the action to the future.

33. **(C)** The tone of Part 12 is too casual to fit in with the overall formal tone of the essay. Besides, the logic is flawed; all news in a newspaper is "old" because it takes time to process the news into a newspaper. Choice (A) would create an incoherent sentence. Choice (B) would introduce items that are too technical and do not tie in directly with the thesis. Choice (D) would create a comma splice because a comma is insufficient to join two independent clauses.

34. **(D)** Choice (D) is written in an informal tone and shifts the person: "I" speaking to "you." This shift is incorrect as voice should be consistent throughout an essay. Choices (A), (B), and (C) all maintain a formal, detached tone.

35. **(B)** Choice (B) has a logical flow of ideas: it follows the idea of including a

quotation discussed in Part 7 and precedes the careful exclusion of bias discussed in Part 9. Choice (A) introduces a new idea, the photographer. Choices (C) and (D) directly contradict the information and ideas presented in the selection.

36. **(A)** Choice (A) will eliminate the fragment found in Part 5. Choice (B) contains a comma necessary to mark an introductory adverbial clause. Choice (C) creates a fragment in the second half of the sentence if the semicolon is used since "uncaring" is a participle used as the compound completer: "the legislator is dishonest . . . or uncaring." Choice (D) does not change the meaning to any extent.

37. **(C)** Choice (C) fits in with the flow of ideas and prepares the way for Part 10, an example of when it is a good idea to question a politician's motives. Choice (A) directly contradicts the thesis. Choice (B) is too casual, "kicked out of office." Choice (D) introduces new ideas associated with campaign tactics, "accusations and name-calling."

38. **(B)** Choice (B) gives the reason why the recycling of tin cans is gaining momentum. Choice (A) is true, but it does not have anything to do with recycling. Choice (C) contradicts the essay's information. Choice (D) has nothing to do with recycling.

39. **(B)** Choice (B) can be revised to get rid of the unnecessary repetition of "plastic," "containers," and "recycled." Choices (A), (C), and (D) are all concise sentences.

40. **(A)** Choice (A) is a fragment which can be corrected by linking it to Part 3 with a comma. Choice (B) is an exclamatory sentence. Choice (C) is a complex sentence. Choice (D) is a command, an imperative sentence.

41. **(B)** Choice (B) is the correct choice because the adjective "particular" should be changed to "particularly" in order to indicate a condition. Choice (A) is incorrect because quotation marks are not needed. Choice (C) is necessary for clarity; otherwise, the subject "one-half" would refer to "crops" in the previous sentence. Choice (D) needs both "rare" and "unusual" to describe the living things on the famous Galapagos islands.

42. **(A)** Choice (A) is correct; the subject "highlands" needs a plural verb "lie." Choices (B) and (D) both indicate past tense. Choice (C) is future tense. Since the location and elevation of the Ecuadorian Andes highlands have not shifted in our lifetime, and probably will not shift for many thousands of years to come, present tense is correct usage.

43. **(C)** Choice (C) is an example of the topic sentence of Part 4. Choice (C) is needed between the mention of the neighbors and Part 6, which begins with "In another example." Choices (A) and (D) might be logical, but they do not mention

contributions of teenagers; also, both stray slightly from the topic by focusing on cost of supplies or insurance problems. Choice (B) changes voice, "you," and introduces slang, "kind of neat."

44. **(C)** Choice (C) shows weak wording. "Unfair" is a word to be avoided in persuasive writing, and the sentence contains a sweeping generality, "adults don't really respect people our age." Choice (A) would detract from the thesis by adding negative examples to refute the thesis. Choice (B) would place ideas out of order. Choice (D) would create a comma splice as a comma is not strong enough to join two independent clauses.

45. **(D)** Choice (D) contains all three main words in the singular form. Choices (A), (B), and (C) mix plural and singular forms of words. In order to have correct agreement in a phrase such as this, all three words must be singular or all must be plural: "this kind of conduct" or "these kinds of activities."

Writing Sample Subsection

Writing Sample with a Score of 6, 7, or 8

The Dream: A Holiday for Dr. King

Perhaps no one person more influenced the sixties Civil Rights movement than the Rev. Dr. Martin Luther King of Atlanta, Georgia. Assassinated April, 1968 by James Earl Ray, Dr. King contributed time, energy, sincerity, and, literally, life for the cause of racial and economic equality and opportunity. That admirers would want to commemorate Dr. King and his achievements on an annual basis is a very logical conclusion. First, President Ronald Reagan signed legislation that proclaimed King's birthday as a national holiday, then state legislatures of Texas, New York, and California, for example, later proclaimed King's birthday a state holiday as well. While many Americans agreed that Dr. King made undeniable inroads to racial toleration and equality, not all agreed on just how his memory should be celebrated.

One concern among King holiday supporters was when to celebrate — on Dr. Kings birthday January 15 or on the first Monday following his birthday. Federal workers supported the latter date, stating that it would provide a logical weekend holiday concept. Others supported the actual birth date because it was more accurate. The federal government decided to commemorate Dr. King's birth and civic contributions the following Monday after the 15th. State governments also decided to follow the same pattern. This decision created, however, disagreement among some city council members when state budgets and economic lay-offs increased. Their primary concern was that the states had very little extra money to absorb the added expense of another paid holiday. Supporters of the King holiday countered that argument by recalling that no other African-American had ever been so honored and the time was now at hand. Both sides agreed to put the issue before the people for a vote. As a result of this action, state after state voted to honor the slain civil rights leader with an "official" annual date.

Another concern for honoring Dr. King was the issue of school children and their teachers. Little did people realize that this would touch off another sensitive issue — how does a person observe such a day. This problem was especially a concern when many states allowed students to be out of school but not their teachers. In other words, teachers were not "working," technically; they were not teaching students but they were at school on work days or in-service. Some teachers, particularly those who wanted to observe the holiday, argued that because they were required to attend school, they were prohibited from participating in many of the day's events. Others argued that only the students needed to be out of school, because if Dr. King were alive, he probably would not agree to have a holiday at all if it meant closing school for an entire day.

While I can't possibly tell you of all the controversial concerns that have surrounded the King holiday, I feel that the two that I have explained are sufficient to give you a sense of how important an issue this has been to this country. What I find most interesting about the question of whether or not to support a holiday for Dr. King has always been the general consensus of all Americans that Dr. Martin Luther King was a great man, a man who represented nonviolence even in the face of his own death. It seems that this idea by itself suggests that this person was a great man who in some way realized his dream.

Features of the Writing Sample Scoring 6, 7, or 8

Appropriateness

The paper's topic is clearly defined in the first paragraph. The writer's voice and style are appropriate for his audience. The many details provided are necessary for developing the argument.

Unity and Focus

The essay follows a logical progression throughout its development. The reader must infer her/his opinion at the outset, although her/his objective account of the relevant facts presents a clear picture of the situation. Her/his final opinion is offered in the conclusion.

Development

The author's viewpoint is developed gradually. The many examples and details lend a steady progression of authenticity to the argument. Because the author's opinion is suppressed until the end, the audience is permitted to make its own inferences based upon this crucial data.

Organization

Paragraph arrangement presents a simple but effective framework for dealing with the issue. Transitions are somewhat weak, as in the opening of the third paragraph: "Another concern..." Some other transitional conventions may have been used.

Sentence Structure

The sentences are mostly standard and varied in form. However, there are many instances of an overabundance of prepositional phrases; this should be avoided. The second sentence of the final paragraph should have been cut into two sentences to reduce its run-on features.

Usage

There is little repetition, and some effort has been made to use a variety of terms. Some frequently repeated words, such as "holiday," should have had substitutes intermittently placed.

Mechanical Conventions

Spelling and punctuation are mostly standard throughout the essay. The second sentence of the third paragraph should have ended in a "?". This is a common error with questions posed after declarative statements such as the clause preceding the "—".

Writing Sample with a Score of 5

Martin Luther King and the Controversial Holiday

I don't know if you have state and federal holidays in your country, but in the United States we have. Some of our holidays are for all of us so that we don't have to go to work or school like on Independence Day while others are for some not to go to work and for us to go to school like on George Washington's Birthday. He was our first president, you know. On days like President Washington's birthday us school kids have special programs in school and maybe have to even remember special facts about him and what he did. And then we have holidays like that of Dr. Martin Luther King that we all get to celebrate, sort of. But while everybody agrees that America's Independence Day should be celebrated by everyone and that everyone should be given the opportunity to be off not all agree so readily on celbrating Dr. Martin Luther King's birthday in the same way.

To make things fair for everyone, the Congress sought views from around the country from the voters. City and state governments were doing the same thing, too. The result was that the majority of people everywhere decided that Dr. King did deserve his very own day on the calender. This process as you can probably imagine was a long, drawn out issue. People wrote letters to thier Congressman, Representative, and city councilman. They also signed petitions and mailed them to Washington and they staged non-violent marches and demonstrations. I really believe that it was the non-violent marches and demonstrations that eventually persuaded the federal and finally state governments to agree because Dr. King stood for non-violence.

So I guess you understand now why we celebrate Dr. Martin Luther King's birthday with parades, speakers, speacial readings, speacial entertainment, other events.

Features of the Writing Sample Scoring 5

Appropriateness

The essay does not clearly define the areas of controversy and reasons for both sides as detailed in the assignment. The author's style is loose and inconsistent.

Unity and Focus

The writer's argument provides the background information of the debate, not the issues discussed therein. However, this one-sided opinion of the affair is maintained steadily throughout.

Development

There is little sense of overall development of thought, other than a step-by-step relation of the happenings surrounding the main action excluded from the essay's narrative.

Organization

Paragraph breaks and arrangement are completely arbitrary. The informal style makes it difficult to make clean transitions without resorting to colloquialisms, which pervade the essay.

Sentence Structure

There are some examples of nonstandard sentence formation, particularly in the use of run-on sentences such as the second and last sentences of the first paragraph. There is little variety in basic sentence forms.

Usage

There is little attempt to use a wide variety of words to avoid repetition. The first sentence of the first paragraph ends without the anticipated object. Several sentences begin with conjunctions, which should be avoided in general and infrequently used as a rule.

Mechanical Conventions

There are some examples of nonstandard spelling and punctuation. Misspelled words include "celbrating," "thier," and "speacial," In the third sentence of the first paragraph, "us school kids" should read "we school kids."

Writing Sample with a Score of 4, 3, 2, 1, or 0

Martin Luther King: Holiday or No?

Whether your from this country or not you have probably heard about Dr. King. He's real popular all over the world. But what you probably don't know is that we haven't always had a holiday that celebrated his birthday. I think that those people who don't want to recognoze Dr. King's contributions to this country are people who realy don't care about this country. Or about its minorties at least. Everybody should support the King holiday if they live in America.

And now that your going to be an American you too can support King's holiday. He died for your right to come here. He died for everyone no matter what race or religion or nationality to do or to become what ever they want to be. Some people say that he was not a president or some one rely important but I say he was. I remember he said that he dreamed of the day when all children of all colors would be accepted for themselves for who they are and not for what they look like or where they came from. How can you not like a man like that? When you think about it a holiday is the lest thing that they could of given him. You know he won the pulitzer prize once because he was such an important man of peace.

So when some one comes up to you and asks you if you know of any important Americans yet be sure to say yes Dr. Martin Luther King, Jr. I know him and of his holiday that he deserves.

Features of the Writing Sample Scoring 4, 3, 2, 1, or 0

Appropriateness

There is no central thought governing the essay, nor does it present any of the issues concerning the controversy it only alludes to. The author's tone is highly opinionated and his statements are overly exaggerated and generalized. His style is extremely informal.

Unity and Focus

That the author favors Dr. King is maintained firmly throughout the essay, although his focus is blurred. Statements and examples do not follow a central thought.

Development

The essay has no direction; it is merely an amalgamation of various opinions. There is no logical progression from premise to premise within the author's argument.

Organization

Sentences are arbitrarily placed within a loose paragraph structure. The openings to the three paragraphs use "Whether," "And," and "So," which are weak beginnings for sentences not to mention paragraphs.

Sentence Structure

Several sentences are nonstandard in form. The third sentence of the second paragraph uses gerunds ("to do or to become") where conjunctions should have been employed. The fourth sentence of the same paragraph ends without receiving its anticipated predicate.

Usage

Little attempt has been made to use a variety of terms. Colloquialisms and informal writing slur the writer's ideas into a loose assemblage.

Mechanical Conventions

There are many examples of nonstandard spelling, including words such as "recognoze," "rely," "lest," "what ever," and "some one." Words are placed without regard to punctuation, such as "yes Dr. Martin Luther King, Jr." in the final paragraph, which should have been quoted; a colon should have been placed after "yes," which should have been capitalized. The term "pulitzer prize" should be capitalized. The word "of" in the second to last sentence of the second paragraph should have been replaced by "have."

TASP

Texas Academic Skills Program

Practice Test 2

READING SECTION

(ANSWER SHEETS APPEAR IN THE BACK OF THIS BOOK.)

DIRECTIONS: You will encounter eight passages in this section of the test, each followed by a number of questions. Only **ONE** answer to each question is the **best** answer, although more than one answer may appear to be correct. There are 45 multiple-choice questions in this section. Choose your answers carefully and mark them on your answer sheet. Make sure that the space you are marking corresponds to the answer you have chosen.

Read the passage and answer the questions that follow.

Adapted from: "A letter to Martin Van Buren, President of the United States," by Ralph Waldo Emerson

1 Sir, my communication concerns the evil rumors that fill this part of the country concerning the Cherokee people. The interests always felt in the Indian population has been heightened in regard to this tribe. Even in our distant state some good rumor of their worth and civility has arrived. We have learned with joy their improvements in the ***social arts.*** We have read their newspapers. We have seen some of them in our schools and colleges. Along with the great body of the American people, we have witnessed with sympathy the painful labors of these red men to rescue their own race from the threat of feelings of eternal inferiority, and to include in their tribe the arts and customs of the white race.

2 The newspapers now inform us that, in December 1835, a treaty calling for the sale of all the Cherokee territory was pretended to be made by an agent on the part of the United States with some persons appearing on the part of the Cherokees; afterwards the fact surfaced that these deputies did not by any means represent the will of the nation. Out of 18,000 souls composing the Cherokee nation, 15,668 have protested against the so-called treaty. It now appears the government of the United States chooses to hold the Cherokees to this sham treaty. Almost the entire Cherokee nation stands up and says, "This is not our act. Behold us. Here are we. Do not mistake that handful of deserters for us."

3 The principle that is left in the United States — if only in its roughest form — forbids us to entertain this rumor as a fact. Such a failure of all faith and virtue, such a denial of justice, and such deafness to screams for mercy were never heard of in times of peace and in the dealing of a nation with its own allies since the Earth was made. Sir, does this government think that the people of the United States have become savage and mad? From our minds are the feelings of love and a good nature wiped out? The soul of man, the justice, the mercy that is the hearts of all men, from Maine to Georgia, abhors this business.

4 You will not do us the injustice of connecting this plea with the feelings and convictions of any political party. It is the simplest commandment of brotherly love. We will not have this great claim upon human justice brushed aside under the flimsy plea of being the act of a political party. Sir, the questions which have aggravated both the government and the people during the past year — those of the economy — are mild issues compared to this one. Times are hard indeed, but above these hard times rings an important question: Will a civilized people such as those in these United States do injustice to a race of savage men? Will the American people put aside reason, civility, justice, and mercy in their dealings with the Cherokee?

1. Which of the following best defines the term ***social arts*** as it appears in the selection?

   (A) Ability to be friendly and make friends

   (B) How to publish newspapers

   (C) Communication with those outside the Indian community

   (D) Artwork that is performed by several people

2. Which of the following statements from the selection best expresses the main idea of the final paragraph?

   (A) We as a nation are not acting out of brotherly love in our dealings with the Cherokees.

   (B) The issue that concerns the plight of the Cherokees is more than a political question or more pressing than a current, temporary problem.

   (C) Our present actions regarding the Cherokees have become political issues.

   (D) The president should rethink America's position regarding the Cherokees.

3. The writer's main purpose in this selection is to

   (A) suggest ways of repairing relationships with the Indians.

   (B) warn the president against possible injustices against the Cherokee people.

   (C) inquire if rumors about injustices against the Cherokee people are true.

   (D) commend the president for looking into injustices against the Cherokees.

4. Which of the following assumptions most influences ideas presented in the selection?

   (A) Americans are cruel to minorities, particularly Indians.

   (B) The president is insensitive to the entire issue regarding the Indians.

   (C) The president is responsible for the unfair actions taken against the Indians.

   (D) The rumors about the treatment of the Indians are true.

5. According to the selection, what current issue had apparently claimed the attention of the people in recent times?

   (A) Foreign trade problems

   (B) Diplomatic relations with other countries

   (C) The economy

   (D) Civil war

Read the passage and answer the questions that follow.

Adapted from: "The Wonder of Gravity," by Hans C. von Baeyer

1 Three simple questions can sum up three areas that mystified the great Albert Einstein in his lifetime: what is space, what is time, what is gravity. Neither he nor any other human will answer these mind-bogglers. However, Einstein discovered unsuspected connections among these questions. One of those connections concerned a common part of everyday life for everyone on the face of the Earth: gravity. Even today Einstein's theory of gravity remains the profoundest of concepts where logic in natural philosophy is concerned. In fact, gravity itself is one of science's more intriguing puzzlements.

2 Gravity is unique in that it possesses traits that other natural forces don't have. Gravity, like time, cannot be turned off or on as, say, our electricity can. We can control the path of an electrical current with switches. Even magnetism can be shielded with a surface between the magnet and the object it attracts. However, gravity ***abnegates*** its effects to no force, passing through absolutely anything and everything. Regardless of where we are on Earth, we are subject to it. We cannot escape its effects. No force opposes it.

3 Since gravity always exists on Earth, and exists unaffected, we usually pay no attention to it. Even so, it touches our lives in every way. We might even think of our relationship with gravity as a daily competition. We manage to triumph over it each time a baby lifts its head, each time he rises to his feet, each time he takes a step. We win when we ride a bike, climb a tree, throw a football. But gravity wins when we fall down steps, slide down a snow bank, plunge over the side of the pool. And an airplane crash is a sad testimony to the power and victory of gravity.

4 Our encounters with gravity form a never-ending cycle. They begin as we rise each morning and feel an almost unsurmountable pull as we strive to get rolling on a new day. At times, gravity wins. Perhaps the more industrious among us will taunt gravity with knee bends, push-ups, and jogging. Then we'll spend the day climbing stairs, moving equipment, raising and lowering things. As we do, the blood in our veins works against gravity as it moves upward through our bodies. This battle occurs each day of our lives until finally we die and give in to the gravity in the grave.

5 Gravity works not only in our lives but in the natural processes in the world around us. It provides the adhesive that holds our globe together. It propels streams and rivers while pulling water from the sky and leaves from trees. As a result of gravity's effects, the lower parts of animals differ from the upper parts. It shapes the stars and galaxies, the planets' orbits, the expanding universe itself.

6. Which of the following best defines the word ***abnegates*** as it is used in the second paragraph?
   (A) Yields
   (B) Creates
   (C) Replaces
   (D) Destroys

7. Which of the following best expresses the main idea of the selection?
   (A) Gravity may serve as man's ally or his chief enemy.
   (B) One of Einstein's greatest achievements was his theory concerning the nature of gravity.
   (C) All life forms must in some way learn to adapt to the force of gravity in order to live.
   (D) Gravity, of all nature's forces, is perhaps the most unique because of its effects on the Earth itself and all forms of life on Earth.

8. The writer's purpose in writing this selection is to
   (A) convince us of the need to study more about gravity.
   (B) identify the components of Einstein's theory.
   (C) show ways in which gravity's unique features affect the Earth and forms of life.
   (D) explain how gravity works.

9. According to the selection, how does gravity differ from other natural forces of our universe?
   (A) Gravity is more dangerous than other forces.
   (B) Gravity's effects cannot be controlled as other forces can.
   (C) Gravity is more productive for us than other forces.
   (D) We know less about gravity than we do about other forces.

10. In referring to Einstein's accomplishments in the first paragraph of the selection, the writer wishes to
   (A) establish Einstein's contribution to the study of gravity.
   (B) introduce the idea that gravity is a profound natural force.
   (C) praise Einstein as a leading scientist.
   (D) explain how we know what we know about gravity.

11. Which of the following lists of topics best organizes the information in the selection?

    (A) I. Einstein as the brilliant scientist

    II. Gravity: how it works

    III. Gravity: how it affects us all

    IV. Gravity: how it affects the planets

    (B) I. Gravity's importance to all of us

    II. Gravity's relationship to magnetism and electricity

    III. Gravity's role as ally and enemy to mankind

    IV. Gravity: how we use it in the world around us

    (C) I. Impact of Einstein on the study of gravity

    II. Understanding where gravity comes from

    III. Coping with the negative effects of gravity

    IV. Explaining how gravity affects animal life

    (D) I. Gravity as a unique natural force

    II. Gravity vs. other natural forces

    III. Gravity's effects on human life

    IV. Gravity's effects on the Earth, universe, and life forms

Read the passage and answer the questions that follow.

Adapted from: "The Human Environment," by Theodore Roszak

1 A rock-solid consensus of opinion exists in urban-industrial society regarding the correct means of measuring our progress beyond the primal, the period when human civilization was in its infancy. The prevailing conclusion is that we measure progress by examining how artificial our environment becomes, either by ridding ourselves of nature's presence or by controlling natural forces. Without much doubt, human environment must always maintain an artificial flair about it. In fact, we might almost say that the human space is destined to possess an ***"artificial naturalness"*** in that people spontaneously fill their universe with artifacts and man-made, non-natural institutions. Humans invent and scheme, devise and intricately thread a finished product: ***culture,*** a buffer zone conceived by and intended for man where man may live legitimately as plant and animal inhabit their environment of instinct, reflex, and roteness. But as we acknowledge human culture, we must also acknowledge natural environment — the mountain and the shore, the fox and its flora, the heavenly bodies — and the close relationship primitives had with this natural habitat

for millennia. These people used as their clocks the seasonal rhythms, timing their own activities to these smooth organic cycles. They learned from the plants and animals that surrounded them, spoke with them, worshipped them. Primitives considered their destiny tied inherently to the non-humans, allies and foes alike, and created places of honor for them in their culture.

2 We cannot possibly exaggerate the importance of this intimacy between human and nature to the growth of human awareness. This inadequate, sterile term "nature" that we use to categorize the non-human world has regretfully lost its impact through the simple connotation we give it today: a designated area of random physical things and events outside and other than ourselves. We may think of "nature poetry" as poems that touch on daisies and sunsets, one possible topic out of myriad possibilities, many of which are irrelevant to polluted city streets and the asphalt aura of modern life. We overlook the universal view of nature, which includes us. Nature, however, has brought us into existence and will outdistance us; from it we have learned of our destiny. It mirrors who we are. Whatever our culture produces that severs humans from a vibrant tie with nature, that removes us from or alienates nature is — strictly speaking — a sick delusion. What culture produces unmindful of the natural world doesn't merely lack ecological soundness; more alarmingly it lacks psychological completeness. It remains devoid of a truth our primitive counterparts learned from an infant world of nature: the reality of spiritual being.

12. Which of the following best defines ***culture*** as the writer uses the term?

    (A) The result of mankind changing his otherwise natural environment to an artificial one

    (B) The condition of being destructive to the forces of nature

    (C) The condition of being literate and articulate in the ways of human life

    (D) Man's recognition of nature's elements

13. For what purpose does the writer use the phrase ***artificial naturalness***?

    (A) To show how man should treat nature

    (B) To suggest an insincere attitude on man's part

    (C) To suggest man's integral tie to nature

    (D) To demonstrate man's natural tendency to create an artificial environment

14. According to this passage, what caused primitive peoples to place importance on elements of nature?

    (A) The belief that their fates were intricately entwined with the natural world

    (B) Simply their primitive, superstitious ignorance

(C) Their lack of an artificial environment

(D) Their ecological concerns

15. Which of the following paraphrases from the selection expresses an opinion held by the writer, not a fact?

    (A) Nature is considered by moderns as "a designated area of random physical things and events outside and other than ourselves."

    (B) Severing ourselves from nature is a "sick delusion."

    (C) Nature is a system that includes people.

    (D) Plant and animal existence is marked by instinct, reflex, and roteness.

16. The first means used to tell time, according to the passage, was

    (A) plants and animals.

    (B) human instinct, reflex, and roteness.

    (C) the awareness of spiritual being, which man derived from his awareness of nature.

    (D) seasonal rhythms.

Read the passage and answer the questions that follow.

Architect of the Capitol

1 The first architect of the Capitol was appointed in 1793 by the President of the United States. During the period of the construction of the Capitol (1793-1865), appointments were made to the position of Architect at such times and for such periods as the various stages of the construction of the work required. The office of Architect has, however, been continuous from 1851 to date.

2 The functions of the office have changed materially through the years in accordance with the increased activities imposed on it by Congress, due principally to the addition of new buildings and grounds. Originally, the duties of the Architect of the Capitol were to plan and construct the Capitol Building, and later, to supervise its care and maintenance.

3 Permanent authority for the care and maintenance of the Capitol Building is provided by an act of August 15, 1876. This act has been amended from time to time to provide for the care and maintenance of the additional buildings and grounds placed under the jurisdiction of the Architect of the Capitol by Congress in subsequent years.

4 The Architect of the Capitol, acting as an agent of Congress, is in charge of the structural and mechanical care of the United States Capitol Building and making

arrangements with the proper authorities for ceremonies held in the building and on the grounds; is responsible for the care, maintenance, and improvement of the Capitol Grounds, comprising approximately 208.7 acres of landscaping, parks, streets, and parking; is responsible for the ***structural*** and mechanical care of the Library of Congress Buildings and the United States Supreme Court Building; and under the direction of the Senate Committee on Rules Land Administration, and the Committee on House Administration, respectively, is charged with the operation of the United States Senate and House restaurants.

5 The Architect of the Capitol also is charged with planning and construction of such buildings as may be committed to his care by Congress from time to time. Current projects include extension, reconstruction, alteration, and improvement of the United States Capitol; construction and improvements under the additional House Office Building projects; and expansion, modification, and enlargement of the facilities of the Capitol Power Plant.

17. Which of the following best expresses the purpose of the selection?

    (A) To persuade us of the necessity of the role of the Architect of the Capitol

    (B) To examine the areas of concern about the Architect of the Capitol

    (C) To identify a brief background and duties of the Architect of the Capitol

    (D) To review the history and office of the Architect of the Capitol

18. According to the selection, who is primarily responsible for determining the exact duties and responsibilities of the office of Architect of the Capitol?

    (A) The President of the United States

    (B) Congress

    (C) The Office of the Architect itself

    (D) The Constitution

19. Which would best sum up the nature of the work included in ***structural*** care referred to in paragraph four?

    (A) Lawn and garden, or grounds, maintenance

    (B) Repairs and necessary work on buildings

    (C) Supervision and machinery

    (D) Designing and building new structures

Read the passage and answer the questions that follow.

Adapted from: "The Pine Barrens," by John McPhee

1 One can usually see undisturbed territory for about twelve miles standing on the fire tower on Bear Swamp Hill, located in Washington Township, Burlington County, New Jersey. Primarily one sees pines and oaks. Here and there stand long, dark patches of Atlantic white cedars, tall and close to each other so that they appear to line the ridges. As a matter of fact, they are sprinkled along the streams that meander through the forests. Looking eastward, one finds a similar view, but there he finds, if he looks closely enough — most folks who aren't natives to this area don't look that closely, though — miles of dwarf trees, forests in which a man can stand and be seen above tree tops for miles. To the west one can see Apple Pie Hill; to the south his view is disturbed by a lake and a cranberry bog.

2 Of course, this view of New Jersey is a far cry from the one that most people have of the state. And so it is that this area called the Pine Barrens is so beautiful yet so different from the transportation corridor situated beside it. There the traffic of people and cargo is more congested than it is anywhere on Earth. One finds along this corridor the sounds of industry as well as the affected air that accompanies such progress. He finds thousands and thousands of houses cobbled along the miles. Railroads and highways tie up this area like string about a package. One day we'll find one continuous city that stretches from Boston to Richmond; this section of that urban area has already been filled in along this route.

3 The Pine Barrens covers about 650,000 acres, making it nearly the size of Yosemite. And it exceeds the size of such places as Sequoia and Great Smoky Mountains National Parks. New Jersey has a population of about a thousand people per square mile; no other state in the Union has so great a density. However, in the central Pine Barrens the land carries about fifteen people per square mile. Those fifteen people per square mile usually bunch up in small forest towns so that in one particular area of more than 100,000 acres, you'll find twenty-one people.

4 Today the Pine Barrens is not nearly so large as the original wilderness area that it once was. Over the years various development companies have moved into the area, reducing the amount of acreage that is still wild. The line that divides the developed property from the undeveloped is, in some places, so abrupt that forests sit beside industrial sites or residential areas. Indeed, the signs of civilization are moving into the area so that a person may be in the Pine Barrens but close to a metropolis. In fact, on a clear night a person standing atop the Empire State Building in New York City could see a light in the middle of the Pine Barrens. And if a person drew on a map a straight line from Boston to Richmond, the epicenter of this sprawling ***megalopolis*** would fall, if you can believe it, in the northern part of these very woods, some twenty miles from Bear Swamp Hill.

20. Which of the following best describes the word ***megalopolis*** as it is used in the final paragraph of the selection?

    (A) Wilderness

    (B) Highway

    (C) Large, heavily populated, city-like area

    (D) Forest

21. For what purpose does the writer cite population figures for the various areas in and around the Pine Barrens?

    (A) To show the sharp difference between the wilderness areas and the populated areas that lie beside each other

    (B) To illustrate the need to preserve the Pine Barrens

    (C) To explain that industry needs the wilderness area for expansion

    (D) To show how nature hinders industrial progress

22. According to the information given, what would the writer say is the greatest threat to the wilderness area of the Pine Barrens?

    (A) The progressive advance of urban and industrial development

    (B) The careless attitudes of industry

    (C) Harmful pollutants from automobiles and industry

    (D) The increasing need for timber

23. Which of the following statements from the selection expresses an opinion held by the writer rather than a fact?

    (A) A person standing at the top of the Empire State Building on a clear night can see a light in the Pine Barrens.

    (B) Industry and residential areas stand side by side with the Pine Barrens today.

    (C) The population density in the wilderness areas is considerably less than that of the rest of the state.

    (D) In the future we can expect a long, continuous urban area to stretch from Boston to Richmond.

24. According to the selection, the size of the Great Smokey Mountains National Park is

    (A) smaller than Sequoia National Park.

    (B) larger than the Pine Barrens.

(C) less than 650,000 acres.

(D) larger than Yosemite National Park.

Read the passage and answer the questions that follow.

The Slave Trade

1 The most significant demographic shift in these decades was the movement of blacks from the Old South to the new Southwest. Traders shipped servants by the thousands to the newly opened cotton lands of the gulf states. A prime field hand fetched an average price of $800, as high as $1500 in peak years. Families were frequently split apart by this miserable traffic. Planters freely engaged in this trade, but assigned very low status to the traders who carried it out.

BLACK SOCIAL STRUCTURE IN THE OLD SOUTH, 1860

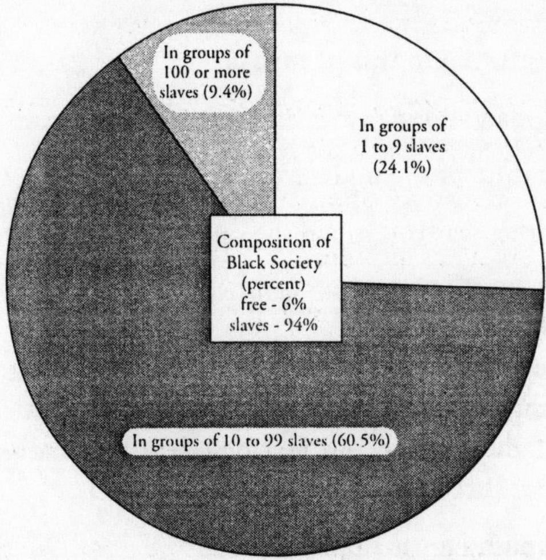

2 Although the importation of slaves from abroad had been outlawed by Congress since 1808, they continued to be smuggled in until the 1850s. The import ban kept the price up and encouraged the continuation of the internal trade.

3 Blacks in bondage suffered varying degrees of repression and deprivation. The harsh slave codes were comprehensive in their restrictions on individual freedom, but they were unevenly applied, and so there was considerable variety in the severity of life. The typical slave probably received a rough but adequate diet and enjoyed crude but sufficient housing and clothing.

4 But the loss of freedom and the injustice of the system produced a variety of responses. Many ***"soldiered"*** on the job, and refused to work hard, or they found ways to sabotage the machinery or the crops. There was an underground system of ridicule toward the masters which was nurtured, as reflected in such oral literature as the "Brer Rabbit" tales.

5 Violent reaction to repression was not uncommon. Gabriel Prosser in Richmond (1800), Denmark Vesey in Charleston (1822), and Nat Turner in coastal Virginia (1831) all plotted or led uprisings of blacks against their white masters. Rumors of such uprisings kept whites in a state of constant apprehension.

6 The ultimate rebellion was to simply leave, and many tried to run away, some successfully. Especially from the states bordering the North, an ever increasing number of slaves fled to freedom, many with the aid of the "underground railroad" and smugglers such as Harriet Tubman, who led over 300 of her family and friends to freedom after she herself had escaped.

7 Most of those in bondage, however, were forced to simply adapt, and they did. A rich culture was developed within the confines of the system, and included distinctive patterns of language, music, and religion. Kinship ties were probably strengthened in the face of the onslaughts of sale and separation of family members. In the face of incredible odds, the slaves developed a distinctive network of tradition and interdependence, and they survived.

25. The main idea portrayed in this passage is

(A) Harriet Tubman and many slaves escaped bondage.

(B) the oral literature of the underground ridiculed white slavemasters.

(C) the slave market was run much the same way as other markets.

(D) black society in the nineteenth century endured despite great hardship.

26. At the end of the first paragraph, the author writes, "Planters freely engaged in this trade, but assigned very low status to the traders who carried it out." What is the purpose of the clause, "but assigned very low status to the traders who carried it out"?

(A) To gain sympathy for the planters

(B) To expose the planters' hypocrisy

(C) To explain the lifestyle of slave traders

(D) To show who engaged in slave trading

27. In what way is the word ***soldiered*** used in the second sentence of paragraph 4?

(A) Took up arms

(B) Labored

(C) Undercut their labor

(D) Were uniformed

28. Which of the following best expresses the main idea of the third paragraph?
    (A) While a violation of human freedom, slave treatment did not always include inhumane living conditions.
    (B) Insufficient housing and diet were typical with slave treatment.
    (C) Most slaves received the same degree of abuse as their fellows.
    (D) Poor living conditions often forced escape attempts by slaves.

29. According to the graph,
    (A) 100% of all blacks in the Old South were slaves of some sort.
    (B) the majority of slave groups consisted of 100 or more persons.
    (C) more than half the slaves were in groups of 10 to 99 slaves.
    (D) more than half the slaves were in groups of 1 to 9 slaves.

Read the passage and answer the questions that follow.

Adapted from: "That Lean and Hungry Look," by Suzanne Britt Jordan

1 You can take it from Julius Caesar: you've got to watch people. I've watched them for a long time, and it's not a pretty sight. I shake at lean men around me. You find all sorts of these "leanies" about if you look long enough: the condescending lean man, the "he's got it all together" lean man, the efficiency expert lean man — all lean, all a social nuisance.

2 Leanies are funless. They don't mess around in the fat way. Their messing leads somewhere, amounts to something, proves constructive in some way. That's not true messing. Five minutes with nothing to do but drink coffee will get you an empty cup, cleaned and washed and put back on the rack along with the coffee spoon spotless and in the drawer, the cream and sugar nowhere in sight. Full of industry as they are, leanies say things like, "I need a twenty-five-hour day to get everything done." Fat people consider the day too confounded long as it is.

3 Also, leanies are tiringly energetic to the point of being unhealthy. On "slow" they're in a dead run. There's always that executive briskness in their walk, as if they are always on their way to an important meeting with the board when all they're really headed for is the bathroom. They're always ready to "tackle" and "meet head-on." But fat people say, "Give me your sluggish, your ***inert***, your 'give me a minute, will ya!' type who intelligently conclude: mop it today, they just track it up tomorrow."

4 Mostly, the leanies oppress. They always have good intentions. What happened to the nice, healthy attitude, "I wasn't gonna do it anyway"? Or they parade around with bony trunks, ship shapes, alert eyes, straight posture — the kind a mugger

never hits in the parking lot. Their shirt tails are never out; they never sit back on the sofa, always on the edge. They always keep their left hands in their laps at lunch. Fat people keep it loose, comfortable, spread out, soft. They can fearlessly slouch to their cars in parking lots because crooks see immediately they probably spent all their money inside on popcorn and pizza. They don't keep their hands in their laps when they eat. That's where the napkin goes.

5 And leanies are stupidly logical. There's that condescending shake of the head before they start to tell you how stupid you are. There's the index finger that counts off on the other hand the list of things so you won't lose track. They know the TV schedule — those that even watch TV — when it comes to news programs, educational programs, and prerecorded exercise shows. They know about cholesterol and smoking, body fats, and safe sex. And always, always they are financially responsible and sound.

6 Fat people, on the other hand, are comfortably illogical — not stupid, you understand. But we tend to see the other side of "smart" and "with it." We don't know the TV schedule because we don't have a TV schedule. Not only that, but having a TV schedule implies planning ahead. Planning ahead to watch a show you watch each week whether you plan to or not somehow takes the fun out of it; it removes the spontaneity of life. And while fat people aren't into keeping up with their cholesterol or triglycerides, they are aware that chances are you'll die in a car accident before your arteries kill you.

30. Which of the following best defines ***inert*** in the third paragraph of this selection?

    (A) Unintelligent

    (B) Helpless

    (C) Ignored

    (D) Not active

31. Which of the following statements best expresses the main idea of paragraph two?

    (A) Fat people don't have a productive purpose in life.

    (B) Thin people can take any situation in life and convert it into a productive experience.

    (C) The approach that thin people have toward life is lifeless and boring because everything has to be productive.

    (D) Thin people should learn how to mess around in a fat way.

32. Which of the following statements would the writer of the selection most likely agree with?

    (A) Happy people are more likely to be fat people.

    (B) Fat people will usually outlive thin people.

    (C) Thin people aren't as successful as they appear.

    (D) Happy people actually have more intelligence than thin people.

33. Which of the following, according to the selection, would best sum up the writer's point in the third paragraph about the "executive briskness" in the thin person's walk?

    (A) Much of the energy of a thin person is "put on."

    (B) Fat people don't know how to walk fast.

    (C) Executives are more likely to be thin and energetic.

    (D) Thin people are better workers.

34. Which of the following lists of topics best organizes information presented in the selection?

    (A) I. Ways thin people approach life

        II. Ways fat people approach life

        III. Superiority of the "fat" approach

    (B) I. Lean people are unsocial

        II. Lean people are unhealthy

        III. Lean people are stupid

    (C) I. Lessons that lean people could learn from fat people

        II. How to conserve energy

        III. How to stay healthy

        IV. How to view life

    (D) I. Problems with thin people

        II. A perspective of fat people.

Read the passage and answer the questions that follow.

Adapted from: "Reflections on Horror Movies," by Robert Brustein

1 Because they engage the feelings and not the mind, horror movies, which have always had a special place in the lives of theater-goers, have enjoyed a recent revival. And when we examine the makeup of this brand of film, we find just beneath the surface assumptions about science. First, the major horror types in question here are the Interplanetary Monster, the Atomic Beast, and the Mad Doctor. More exist, to be sure, but these types contain doctor and beast, creator and creature. And the attitudes toward these two reveal changes that are taking place.

2 Probably the oldest of the three would be the Mad Doctor. Rooted in European folklore, this figure sprang from Balkan legends about vampires and werewolves. The Frankenstein monster can be traced back to Golem, a figure that the Jews created from clay to lead them from oppression. Coupled with crude religious overtones, superstitions give these films a medieval flavor. However, those superstitions now have moved to the area of science — at least science that has been distorted somewhat. Where old horror movies would convert humans into perverted lower forms of life — monsters and beasts — newer horror movies have now converted them to mad scientists. Whereas Dr. Faustus, that figure in Christopher Marlowe's play about black magic, was a church scholar, his later counterpart, Dr. Frankenstein, is the research physician. The black arts that call up evil and demonic spirits now give way to test tubes and electrical equipment.

3 In Marlowe's play and in movies patterned after it, Dr. Faustus stepped beyond natural bounds by conjuring up demonic spirits. *Frankenstein* similarly steps too far by exploring taboo areas for humans. Dr. Frankenstein assumes the role of the villain, the mad doctor whose chief concern is no longer the good of humanity but the experiment, which occupies his total attention. And as he is absorbed in his work among the network of complex machinery in his laboratory, he presents the picture of an immoral being whose complete madness is ***commensurate*** with his great intelligence.

4 Essentially, Dr. Frankenstein represents the victory of his intellect over the conscience of those who oppose him. He is convinced of his own correctness and soundness. And as he becomes increasingly aware of the total opposition to his work of those about him, he becomes set on revenge. He victimizes the surrounding countryside in a mad rage of violence. Ultimately, the rage turns on the scientist himself and destroys him. And as the movie-goer views the superior intellect self-destruct on film, he rests in the comfort that even though he himself is not as intelligent as Dr. Frankenstein, he is still loved by God.

5 A fairly recent trend in horror movies that also employs the Mad Scientist idea is the Teenage Monster film. We have such examples as *Blood of Dracula, I Was a Teenage Werewolf,* and *Teenage Monster.* At first one might regard these films as jokes not actually intended as serious horror movies. However, the opposite is true.

In these movies the Mad Scientist is not a shabbily dressed maniac doctor whose hair goes in all directions. Now he is a well-dressed member of society who attends the local high school and enjoys the good opinion by his peers. Behind such outer appearances, however, there lurks an evil mind that desires to kill and hurt. He may be emotionally troubled but becomes much more threatening as the film progresses. The end result is a monster every bit as terrifying as the older, more traditional monster.

35. Which of the following best defines the word ***commensurate*** at the end of paragraph three?

    (A) Having the same measure or degree as

    (B) Inappropriate

    (C) Coming before

    (D) Separated by time and/or distance

36. Which of the following statements from the selection best expresses the main idea of the fourth paragraph?

    (A) The story of Dr. Frankenstein reflects the struggle in which man's intelligence fights against man's moral awareness and conscience.

    (B) The theme of the Frankenstein story reveals to movie patrons the idea that they are less intelligent than Dr. Frankenstein.

    (C) In the end of these old horror movies, the love of God ultimately triumphs over evil and man's intellect.

    (D) The theme of old horror movies serves to show the futility of man's intellect in the eyes of God.

37. The content of the last paragraph of the selection indicates the writer's belief that

    (A) today's horror films have lost some of their horror because of their modern settings.

    (B) young people make better villains in horror films than older people did in the past.

    (C) today's move toward younger horror film villains can be seen in some of the earlier monster movies.

    (D) a true horror movie doesn't have to contain the old traditional horror film characteristics in order to be horrifying.

38. According to the selection, what is the chief contribution of ancient folklore to the horror movie?

    (A) Modern horror films depend upon ancient folklore for plot ideas.

    (B) Most key figures in modern horror films have been taken directly from ancient folklore.

    (C) It has provided horror films with moral, religious, and supernatural elements.

    (D) We get the science theme from ancient folklore.

39. Which of the following assumptions most influence the views expressed by the writer in this selection?

    (A) Horror movies are second rate entertainment.

    (B) Horror movies represent a legitimate type of film which attracts a sizable audience and deserves attention.

    (C) Theatergoers are naturally inquisitive about the background of horror monsters such as Frankenstein.

    (D) All horror movies have a rich history from a variety of cultures that dates far back.

40. Which of the following statements best summarizes the information presented in the selection?

    (A) There exist three major types of horror film villains, and each one has an illustrious history. All three may be traced back to Dr. Faustus, through Frankenstein, and up to the modern teenage monster.

    (B) Of all the horror movie types, the Mad Doctor probably came first, having gone through a lengthy evolution to its present-day status. These old films carefully treat the villain as a troubled mind gone bad, even to the point of violating moral boundaries. Today's version of the old horror type is no less horrible, in spite of his familiar setting.

    (C) We can trace the history of horror films back to the Balkan countries and their superstitions. In fact, the Dr. Faustus and Frankenstein stories have their roots in the legends of those areas. The most recent product of that Balkan tradition is the teenage monster.

    (D) Horror movies are rooted in religion. We can trace them back to religious beliefs. Whether we speak of Dr. Faustus, Frankenstein, or a modern teenage monster, we look to old legends, myths, and religions for their origins.

Read the passage and answer the questions that follow.

Adapted from: "Who's Afraid of Math, and Why?", by Sheila Tobias

1 Myth has it that a person either has or has not a mathematical mindset. While we might conclude that research of a complex nature requires such traits as mathematical imagination and intuition, people who can perform college-level functions in other areas should be able to handle math as well. True, one may learn faster or slower than another; the pressure of time may affect some more than others; low self-esteem may hamper a few at times. However, we'd be hard-pressed to find evidence that says a "mathematical mind" is a necessity to learn math.

2 The effects of this "math myth" are reasonably evident. Supposedly, only a handful of us possess the adequate intelligence for math; that means the rest of us are living on "borrowed time" till we botch up and reveal our mathematical incompetency to the rest of the world. We go into the whole ordeal already defeated. Or parents, especially girls' parents, assume that their offspring will experience as much difficulty in learning math as they themselves did. They unintentionally pass along the negative mindset.

3 For what it's worth, we might observe some interesting things connected with "mathephobia." Girls are more likely than boys to drop out of math. According to a Berkeley survey in 1972, about eight percent of the incoming freshmen girls had four years of math; fifty-seven percent of the boys had. What does this mean? It means the girls are already hampered by the lack of mathematical training and are consequently behind their male counterparts where job competition is concerned.

4 As we examine the differences in girls' and boys' abilities in math, we might consider several additional interesting tidbits of information: 1. Girls are better at computation than boys from elementary school on. 2. Word problems, long considered the girls' area of achievement, are solved better by boys than girls from about age thirteen on. 3. Boys, from about sixteen, will take more courses in math than girls. 4. Girls will develop a hate for math at an earlier age than boys will. Obviously these observations reveal that standard arguments that girls excel in word problems while boys excel in math do not always hold true.

5 So why the turnaround? Why is it that as they grow older, boys do, in fact, excel more in math than girls? Consider these observations: 1. Math becomes increasingly difficult and demanding as it progresses. 2. Somewhere around age ten, boys and girls encounter social pressure not to excel in domains that are reserved for the other sex. 3. Girls then have a socially accepted reason for not doing well in math, but boys don't. Society expects boys to perform better in math than girls.

6 The search for concrete, biological reasons for the differences between boys' and girls' abilities in math continues, but few results surface. After all, it is difficult to determine with research if there is a measurable, solid way of locating a math ability somewhere in the human body. But as we consider that only about seven percent of

all Ph.D.'s in mathematics go to women, we have to conclude either that these women have genes, hormones, and brain organization that differ from those of other women, or that these women have not had the negative experiences with math that other women have. Can we conclude then that males and females are different in a mathematical sense? The fact of the matter is that the connection between genetics and mathematics is not supported by good, solid evidence.

41. Which of the following best expresses the central idea of the fifth paragraph of this selection?

    (A) The primary reason for girls' greater difficulty with math lies in social conditioning and pressures.

    (B) As females mature, natural biological processes decrease the math ability.

    (C) Society tries unsuccessfully to push girls into math.

    (D) Boys have a greater in-born math ability.

42. The writer's main purpose in this selection is to

    (A) determine why boys are born with more natural ability for math than girls.

    (B) explain why girls shouldn't pursue math.

    (C) show that society doesn't want girls in math-related fields.

    (D) show that math ability doesn't depend upon one's sex.

43. According to the selection, what is a main reason that girls do poorly as they grow older?

    (A) Girls have a natural tendency not to like math.

    (B) Girls are slower at math early in life and thus do worse as they grow older.

    (C) Society provides them with a good reason to avoid a difficult area.

    (D) Girls have an inadequate background for math.

44. Which of the following facts from the selection best supports the writer's argument that society's notions about math hurt girls' chances in their training and careers?

    (A) Girls in the younger grades in school often outperform boys in math.

    (B) A Berkeley survey shows that girls, on the average, have less math training coming into college than boys.

    (C) Society doesn't want girls in math fields.

    (D) Boys, contrary to myth, can excel in word-related areas.

45. Which of the following best summarizes the information presented in the selection?

    (A) Society, notably women, defeats itself with its attitude toward math abilities. However, women do in fact experience difficulties because abilities reverse as sexes mature. Boys don't excel in math until later years while girls are better in math in their early years; however, they lose their natural math ability as they mature.

    (B) Society suffers from its myth about math by producing a generation of girls who don't succeed as well as boys. In spite of the myth, girls actually demonstrate math aptitude early in their development, while boys show signs of strength in verbal power, a "girl-oriented" area. The reasons for the later reversal lie not in genetics but in social attitudes that accompany more complex math concepts and allow girls to "drop out."

    (C) In response to the math-related myths, we are on the verge of finding evidence that the varying ability of the sexes to work difficult math problems lies in the areas of sexual differences. We need to find such evidence soon because of the negative effects imposed on girls.

    (D) All people are equally capable of doing math. Math is no different from verbal communication in terms of difficulty. However, since girls excel in verbal areas from the lower grades on, they miss out on complex math backgrounds and never develop math aptitudes.

MATHEMATICS SECTION

(ANSWER SHEETS APPEAR IN THE BACK OF THIS BOOK.)

DIRECTIONS: In this section, you will encounter 45 multiple-choice questions. Only **ONE** answer to each question is the **best** answer, although more than one answer may appear to be correct. Choose your answers carefully and mark them on your answer sheet. Make sure that the space you are marking corresponds to the answer you have chosen.

You may use the provided Reference Table in making your calculations.

REFERENCE TABLE

SYMBOLS AND THEIR MEANINGS:

Symbol	Meaning	Symbol	Meaning
$=$	is equal to	$\leq$	is less than or equal to
$\neq$	is unequal to	$\geq$	is greater than or equal to
$<$	is less than	$\parallel$	is parallel to
$>$	is greater than	$\perp$	is perpendicular to
$\approx$	approximately equal to	$\ngeq$	not greater than or equal to
$\pi \approx$	3.14	$\nleq$	not less than or equal to
$\sim$	similar to	$\angle$	angle
$\cong$	congruent to	$\llcorner$	right angle
$\overline{AB}$	line segment *AB*	$\pm$	plus or minus
$\overleftrightarrow{AB}$	line *AB*	$a{:}b$ or $\frac{a}{b}$	ratio of *a* to *b*

FORMULAS

DESCRIPTION	FORMULA
AREA (A) of a:	
square	$A = s^2$; where s = side
rectangle	$A = lw$; where l = length, w = width
parallelogram	$A = bh$; where b = base, h = height
triangle	$A = \frac{1}{2}bh$; where b = base, h = height
circle	$A = \pi r^2$; where $\pi = 3.14$, r = radius
PERIMETER (P) of a:	
square	$P = 4s$; where s = side
rectangle	$P = 2l + 2w$; where l = length, w = width
triangle	$P = a + b + c$; where a, b, and c are the sides
circumference (C) of a circle	$C = \pi d$; where $\pi = 3.14$, d = diameter
VOLUME (V) of a:	
cube	$V = s^3$; where s = side
rectangular container	$V = lwh$; where l = length, w = width, h = height
Pythagorean relationship	$c^2 = a^2 + b^2$; where c = hypotenuse, a and b are legs of a right triangle
distance (d) between two points in a plane	$d = \sqrt{(x_2 - x_1)^2 + (y_2 - y_1)^2}$; where (x_1, y_1) and (x_2, y_2) are two points in a plane
mean	**mean** $= \frac{x_1 + x_2 + \ldots + x_n}{n}$; where the x's are the values for which a mean is desired, and n = number of values in the series
median	**median** = the point in an ordered set of numbers at which half of the numbers are above and half of the numbers are below this value
simple interest (i)	$i = prt$; where p = principal, r = rate, t = time
distance (d) as function of rate and time	$d = rt$; where r = rate, t = time
total cost (c)	$c = nr$; where n = number of units, r = cost per unit

1. $(-3 \times 10^{25}) \times (4 \times 10^{7}) =$

(A) -12×10^{18}

(B) 1×10^{32}

(C) -12×10^{31}

(D) -12×10^{32}

2. Solve.

$$\frac{20 \times 0.03}{0.005}$$

(A) 12

(B) 120

(C) 1,200

(D) 1.2

3. Estimate.

$15\ ^{3}/_{4} \div 2\ ^{5}/_{6}$

(A) 7

(B) 8

(C) 5

(D) 30

4. 23% of 460 is what?

(A) 105.8

(B) 20

(C) 10.58

(D) 2,000

5. Which is the smallest?

(A) $^{1}/_{3}$

(B) $^{2}/_{5}$

(C) $^{3}/_{20}$

(D) $^{2}/_{7}$

6. Solve.

   $8 - 7(-4 + 6)$

   (A) 22

   (B) 3

   (C) 6

   (D) -6

7. In a school building there are 10 rooms having fire escapes for every 20 rooms total. If the school building has a total of 150 rooms, how many rooms have fire escapes?

   (A) 140

   (B) 75

   (C) 135

   (D) 80

8. An owner of a delicatessen is thinking of constructing a parking lot in back of his store. He would like to have 35 parking spaces, and will need 2 pounds of cement for each parking space. If he buys 40 more pounds of cement than he expects to use, how many pounds of cement does he buy?

   (A) 110 pounds

   (B) 70 pounds

   (C) 30 pounds

   (D) 1,470 pounds

9. A gardener wishes to decorate a garden which is 576 square feet in area, and he must decide how to apportion each section of the garden with specific plants. He has decided to set aside 20% of the garden with roses and an additional 32.9 square feet for a tomato patch. How much of the garden is set aside for the roses and tomatoes?

   (A) 569.42 square feet

   (B) 523.1 square feet

   (C) 148.1 square feet

   (D) 52.9 square feet

10. Read the graph below, then answer the question.

A runner has her heartbeat recorded for two 10.1 miles races run in the same park near her home, held on different days, and both starting at 6 AM.

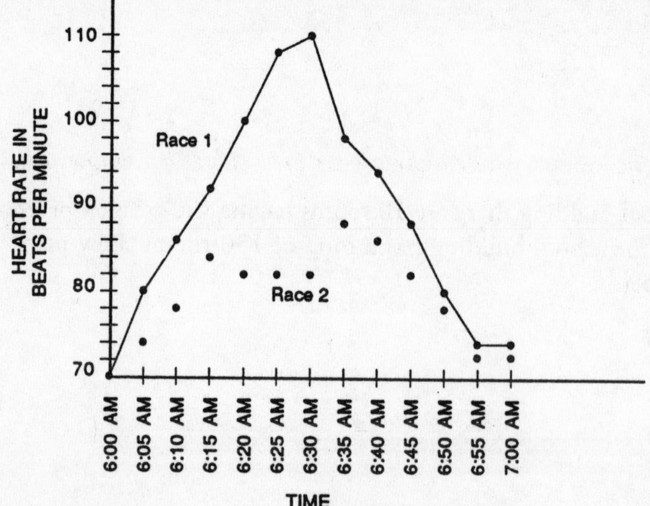

Which of the following is true at 6:20 AM for the recorded heartrates for Race #1 and Race #2.

(A) Both recorded heartrates are increasing.

(B) Both recorded heartrates are decreasing.

(C) The recorded heartrate for Race #1 is increasing, and the recorded heartrate for Race #2 is stable.

(D) The recorded heartrate for Race #1 is stable, and the recorded heartrate for Race #2 is increasing.

11. Read the table and answer the question which follows.

Charles kept a six-month record of his income for the years 1989 and 1990 as follows:

INCOME

Month	1989	1990
January	$398	$423
February	$452	$457
March	$356	$399
April	$321	$372
May	$376	$401
June	$364	$392

Between February and June, Charles' income for 1990 decreased by

(A) \$31.

(B) \$34.

(C) \$88.

(D) \$65.

12. Which two points would connect to give the slope whose absolute value is lowest?

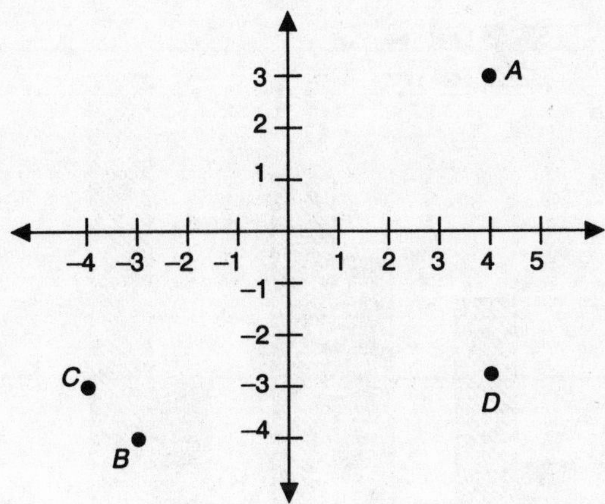

(A) $\overline{AD}$

(B) $\overline{BD}$

(C) $\overline{BC}$

(D) $\overline{CD}$

13. Read the graph, then answer the question.

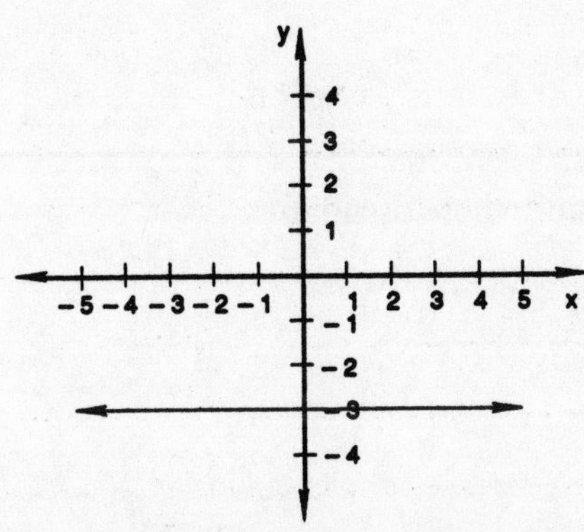

Which equation is represented above?

(A) $y = 3$

(B) $y = -3$

(C) $x = 3$

(D) $x = -3$

14. Read the graph, then answer the question.

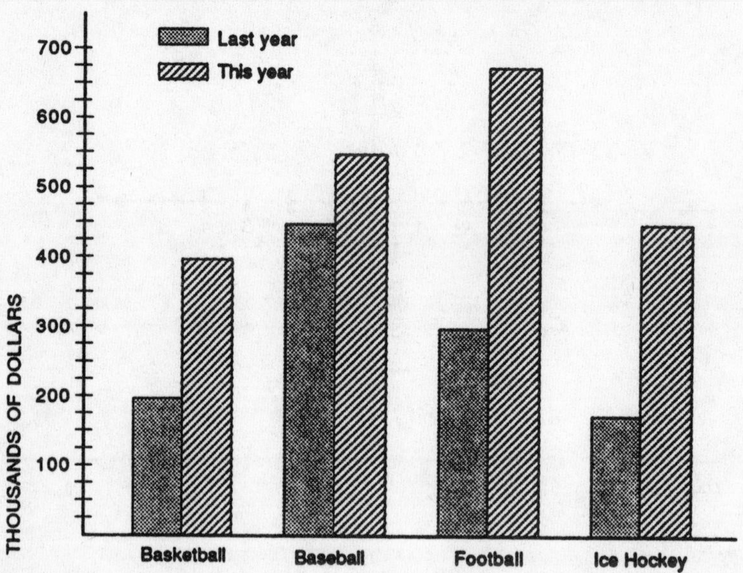

Which sport showed the greatest increase in average salary between last year and this year?

(A) Basketball

(B) Baseball

(C) Football

(D) Ice Hockey

15. Find the slope of a line whose equation is

$y = -6x + 3.$

(A) $-1/6$

(B) 6

(C) 3

(D) -6

16. Solve for x.

$$5x - 2y = 20$$
$$2x + 3y = 27$$

(A) 5

(B) $^6/_{19}$

(C) 6

(D) $^6/_{11}$

17. If $-\,^1/_7x - 6 = 34$, find the value of $-2x + 3$.

(A) -77

(B) -280

(C) 563

(D) 395

18. If $9r = 4t + 3$, find the value of t.

(A) $t = \dfrac{9r+3}{4}$

(B) $t = \dfrac{9r-3}{4}$

(C) $t = \dfrac{9r}{4} - 3$

(D) $t = \dfrac{9r}{4} + 3$

19. The sum of three consecutive odd integers are arranged such that twice the middle integer is equal to 9 more than the largest. Find the sum of the three integers.

(A) 9

(B) 11

(C) 13

(D) 33

20. A car salesman receives \$575 a week in addition to 3% commission on all cars whose sticker price is above \$4,500. One week he sold a Ford for \$8,785 and a Buick for \$5,832. How much did he earn that week?

(A) \$1,013.51

(B) \$838.55

(C) \$749.96

(D) \$4,385.10

21. A child's bank contains only pennies and nickels. In all there are 64 coins with a total value of \$2.44. How many nickels are in the child's bank?

(A) 45

(B) 19

(C) 40

(D) 46

22. The sum of the 3 angles of a triangle is 180°. The first angle is 5° more than twice the measure of the second angle. The third angle is 10° less than twice the measure of the first angle. If n represents the number of degrees in the second angle, which equation correctly represents the relationship among the three angles?

(A) $(2n + 5) + n + (-4n) = 180$

(B) $(2n + 5) + n + 4n = 180$

(C) $2(n + 5) + n + 4n = 180$

(D) $(2n - 5) + n + 4n = 180$

23. In 23 years, John will be 5 times as old as he is today. If R = John's age in 23 years, which of the following equations could be used to determine John's age in 23 years?

(A) $5R - 23 = R$

(B) $R/5 = 23$

(C) $5R - 115 = R$

(D) $5R = 23$

24. $\dfrac{7}{35x + 42} =$

(A) $\dfrac{1}{5x + 42}$

(B) $\dfrac{1}{35x + 6}$

(C) $\dfrac{1}{5x + 6}$

(D) $\dfrac{0}{5x + 6}$

25. Read the graph, then answer the question.

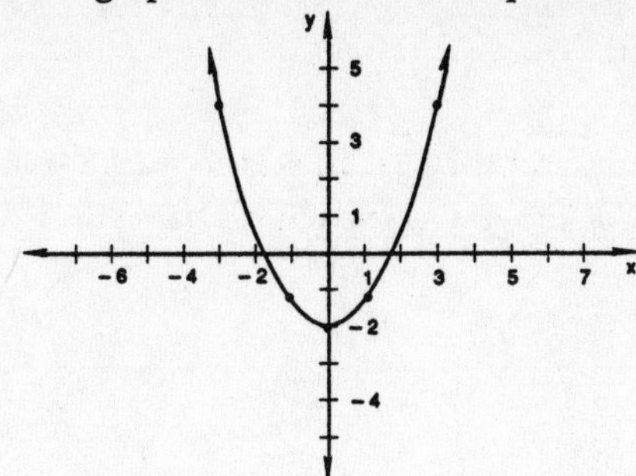

Which of the following could be represented by the graph above?

(A) $y = {}^1/_3x^2 + 2$

(B) $y = -{}^1/_3x^2 - 2$

(C) $y = -{}^1/_3x^2 + 2$

(D) $y = {}^1/_3x^2 - 2$

26. Joe finds that his monthly commission, C, in dollars can be calculated by the equation $C = 360s - 4s^2$, where s is the number of sales he makes for his company. In June, he made 60 sales; and in July, he made 50 sales. How much marginal profit did Joe make in these 2 months?

(A) \$15,200

(B) \$7,200

(C) \$8,000

(D) \$800

27. Which of the following shows that the length (L) varies inversely as the cube of the width (w)?

(A) $L = \dfrac{w^3}{k}$

(B) $kw^3 = L$

(C) $L = \dfrac{k}{w^3}$

(D) $kL = w^3$

28. Which of the following is a factor of $10x^2 - 5x - 50$?

(A) $(2x - 25)$

(B) $(10x - 1)$

(C) $(2x - 5)$

(D) $(x - 2)$

29. Perform the following operations.

$$(-9x^5y^4 + 6x^4y^5 + 8x^3y^2) - (6x^5y^4 + x^4y^5 - 5x^3y^2)$$

(A) $-3x^5y^4 + 5x^4y^5 + 13x^3y^2$

(B) $-3x^5y^4 + 7x^4y^5 + 3x^3y^2$

(C) $-15x^5y^4 + 7x^4y^5 + 3x^3y^2$

(D) $-15x^5y^4 + 5x^4y^5 + 13x^3y^2$

30. Solve.

$$(7x^2 - 5)(6x^2 + 11)$$

(A) $42x^4 + 47x^2 - 55$

(B) $42x^4 - 47x^2 - 55$

(C) $42x^4 - 55$

(D) $42x^4 + 77x^2 - 55$

31. An excavation for a building is 30 yards long, 10 yards wide, and $20^1/_2$ yards deep. If a cubic yard of earth weighs approximately 9 pounds per cubic yard, what will the weight of the earth (that fills the excavation) be when the excavation is filled to the top?

(A) $683^1/_3$ pounds

(B) 270 pounds

(C) 2,700 pounds

(D) 55,350 pounds

32. Answer the question based on the following diagram.

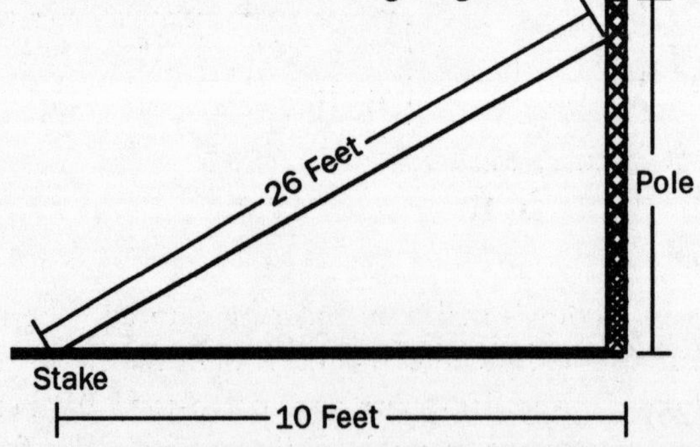

A 26-foot wire reaches from the top of a pole to a stake in the ground. If the distance from the base of the pole to the stake is 10 feet, how high is the pole?

(A) 24 feet

(B) 16 feet

(C) 6 feet

(D) $2\sqrt{65}$ feet

33. Answer the question based on the following:

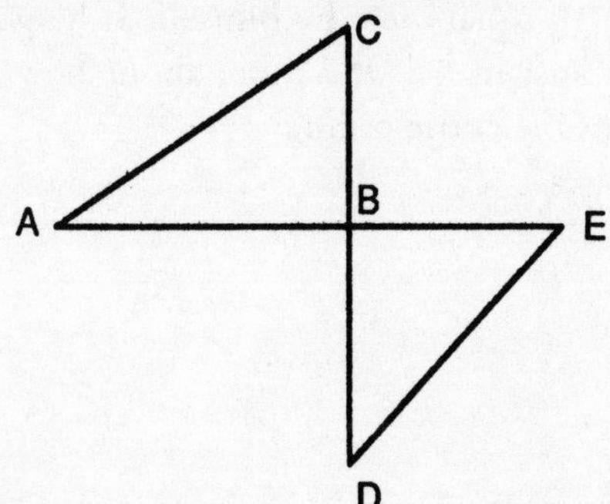

If $\overline{BC} \perp \overline{AE}$, $\overline{DB} \cong \overline{AB}$, and $\angle E = \angle C$, which of the following must be true?

(A) $\overline{AB} = 2\,\overline{BE}$

(B) $\overline{BC} \cong \overline{AC}$

(C) $\overline{BC} = {}^{2}/_{3}\,\overline{BD}$

(D) $\overline{BC} \cong \overline{BE}$

Questions 34–36 refer to the following diagram. All lines are parallel or perpendicular.

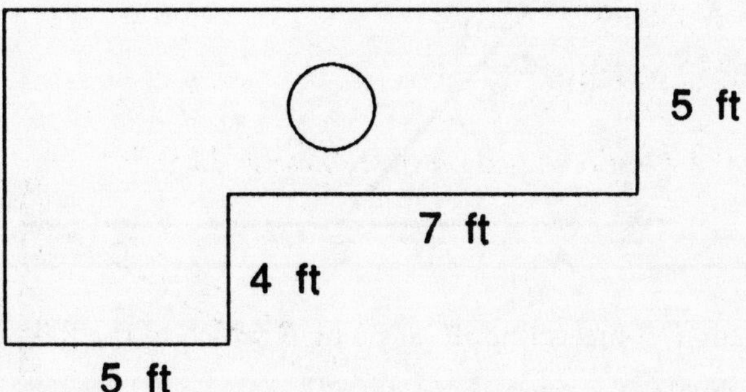

34. The ceiling of George's bedroom must be painted. The diagram above represents his bedroom and includes a circular light fixture with a diameter of 2 feet. A gallon of paint covers 16 square feet and costs $8.95. How much will George have to spend on paint to cover the entire ceiling except for the light fixture?

(A) $44.75

(B) $50.20

(C) $35.80

(D) $42.99

35. George takes off the light fixture and decides to paint underneath it. It takes George 2 hours to paint 10 square feet by himself. If he gets a friend to help, who can paint the same area in half the time, about how many hours will it take both of them to paint the entire ceiling?

(A) 7

(B) $5\,^1/_2$

(C) 8

(D) 4

36. George would like to paint a trim around the edge of the ceiling. If the cost to paint the trim is $.86 per foot, how much will he need to spend to put the trim around the ceiling?

(A) $66.10

(B) $36.12

(C) $68.80

(D) $35.12

37. Answer the question based on the following diagram.

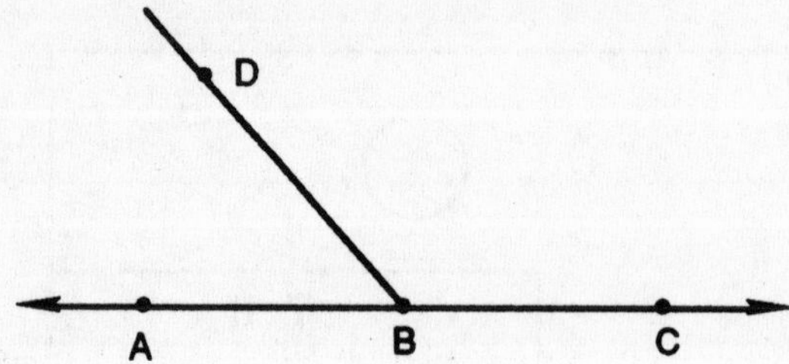

If segment $\overline{DB}$ meets line AC at point B, which of the following is true?

(A) $\angle ABD$ and $\angle DBC$ are supplementary angles.

(B) Segment $\overline{DB}$ is perpendicular to line AC.

(C) $\angle ABD$ and $\angle DBC$ are complementary angles.

(D) $\angle ABD$ and $\angle DBC$ are vertical angles.

38. Read the information which follows and answer the question below.

    1. All bears are beautiful.
    2. Some bears are hairy.
    3. All bears which are beautiful live up North.
    4. Bears who are hairy fight a lot.
    5. Wanda is a bear.

    Which must be true?

    (A) Wanda is hairy.

    (B) Wanda lives up North.

    (C) Wanda is not a bear.

    (D) Wanda fights a lot.

39. Examine the pattern sequence and answer the question below.

    284 280 140 136 68 64 32 ___

    What number is missing in the sequence?

    (A) 8

    (B) 16

    (C) 28

    (D) 30

40. Which is the largest?

    (A) $^1/_5$

    (B) $^3/_4$

    (D) $^1/_2$

    (D) $^{18}/_{25}$

41. A student is building a porch on his family's house. He will use 20 boards for the porch floor and will need 15 nails for each board. If he buys 25 more nails than he expects to use, how many nails does he buy?

    (A) 300 nails

    (B) 325 nails

    (C) 275 nails

    (D) 800 nails

42. A town planning committee must decide how to use a 135-acre piece of land. The committee sets aside 40% of the land for watershed protection and an additional 27.8 acres for recreation. How much of the land is set aside for watershed protection and recreation?

    (A) 123.88 acres

    (B) 67.2 acres

    (C) 67.8 acres

    (D) 81.8 acres

43. Michael, George, Bob, and Sam differ in height. Their last names are Jones, Wong, Bell, and Smith, but not necessarily in that order.

    I. George is taller than Michael, shorter than Bob, and shorter than Sam.

    II. Bob is taller than Sam.

    III. Smith is the tallest of the four, and Bell is the shortest of the four.

    IV. Wong is taller than Jones.

    What is Sam's last name?

    (A) Jones

    (B) Wong

    (C) Bell

    (D) Smith

44. At a hotel, 7 out of every 15 rooms have balconies. If the hotel has a total of 195 rooms, how many rooms have balconies?

    (A) 139

    (B) 114

    (C) 67

    (D) 91

45. If you plot the reflections of the given points about the line $y = -x$, then what would the radius of the circle that contains all the points be?

    (A) 5

    (B) 29

    (C) $\sqrt{29}$

    (D) 58

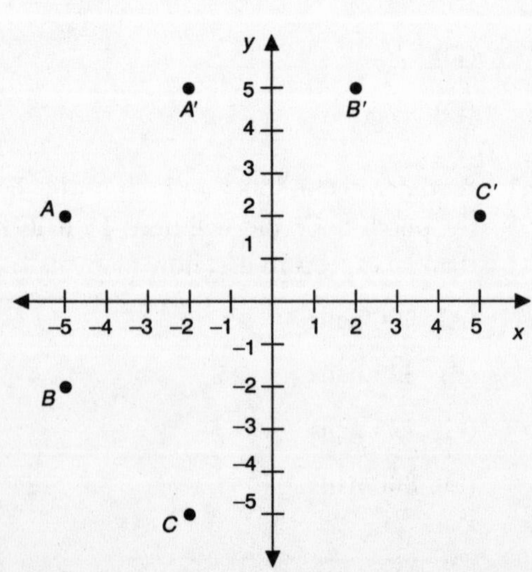

WRITING SECTION

MULTIPLE-CHOICE

(ANSWER SHEETS APPEAR IN THE BACK OF THIS BOOK.)

DIRECTIONS: You will encounter 16 passages in this portion of the test. Each part of the passage will be numbered, with the questions that follow the passage referring to the numbered parts. Only **ONE** answer to each question is the **best** answer, although more than one answer may appear to be correct. There are 45 multiple-choice questions in this portion. Choose your answers carefully and mark them on your answer sheet. Make sure that the space you are marking corresponds to the answer you have chosen.

Note: The use of the term "nonstandard" in the questions means "does not follow standard written English."

The following passage is written in the form of a student essay. Read the text and answer the questions.

Note: In the second paragraph, a paragraph organization error is purposely included.

[1]By the end of the decade, it will be easier for manufacturers to be more concerned about the environment. [2]Consumers are putting increasing pressure on manufacturers to emphasize environmentally safe products. [3]In making their concerns known, consumers are influencing the corporate world to transform the way it produces and markets goods. [4]There are people who are not concerned with production and care only that the product be cheap and reliable.

[5]Soon, it will be the rare business that does not use "being green" as a promotional device. [6]Thereafter, its impossible to know with any certainty if the product is recyclable or environmentally safe. [7]Some companies are now beginning to display a seal that purports to verify their claims of being environmentally safe. [8]These "seals of approval" are being given by nonprofit or volunteer organizations, not the federal government, so there are problems with this system. [9]For example, the degree of safety and protection of the environment *varies.* [10]Although the government polices deceptive advertising claims, there are no set standards to which a company must comply before meriting a seal of approval.

1. Which of the following focuses attention on the main idea of the first paragraph?

   (A) Delete the phrase "By the end of the decade" from Part 1.

   (B) Change Part 2 from a declarative sentence to an interrogative sentence by beginning the sentence, "Why are consumers."

   (C) Change the pronoun in Part 3 from "their" to "our."

   (D) Delete Part 4.

2. Which of the following changes makes the sequence of ideas in the second paragraph clearer?

   (A) Reverse the order of Parts 5 and 6.

   (B) Place Part 6 after Part 9.

   (C) Reverse the order of Parts 7 and 8.

   (D) Delete Part 10.

3. Which of the following is needed in the second paragraph?

   (A) Part 5: Change "does not use" to "uses."

(B) Part 6: Change "its" to "it is."

(C) Part 7: Change "now beginning to display" to "beginning to now display."

(D) Part 8: Change "not" to "as well as."

The following passage is written in the form of an archaeology textbook. Read the text and answer the questions.

[1]The Dead Sea Scrolls are considered the archaeological find of the century. [2]The scrolls, about 800 different documents, are written on leather and papyrus. [3]_______________ [4]The manuscripts are believed to have been written between 200 B.C. and A.D. 50 by the Essenes, members of an ascetic Jewish sect. [5]Most of the Old Testament books (except Esther) appear in the scrolls, and some of the scrolls are multiple copies of these books written by different scribes. [6]Other scrolls are books of the Apocrypha, such as Jubilees, Tobit, and the Wisdom of Solomon, as well as hymns, prayers, prophecies, and biblical commentaries.

[7]For nearly 2,000 years this priceless cache of sacred writings lay hidden in the desert of Judah along the Dead Sea. [8]The first find was in 1947 when a Bedouin shepherd boy discovered the scrolls in a rocky cave of Qumran, ten miles from Jerusalem on the edge of the Dead Sea. [9]Shortly after, other manuscripts were uncovered nearby in different caves. [10]The larger group of scrolls was found in 1952.

[11]Four photographic copies of the scrolls were distributed, and these photographic copies were kept under the strict supervision of a group of 40 scholars dedicated to studying the photographs and analyzing the copies. [12]In December 1990, however, the Huntington Library in San Marino, California, began granting access to anyone who wants to view and study the photographs. [13]This move is hailed by those who have felt left out of the elite cadre of 40 scroll scholars.

4. Which of the following, if used in the blank labeled Part 3, **best** fits the writer's pattern of development?

   (A) Some of the manuscripts are fragments, a few about the size of a dime.

   (B) Only a select group of scholars have been allowed to view the manuscripts.

   (C) In 1951 archaeologists excavated the ruins of a building believed to be a library.

   (D) Many people think information in some of the unstudied scrolls will destroy or undermine many tenets of the Christian faith.

5. Which of the following changes is needed?

   (A) Part 4: Change "between" to "among."

   (B) Part 7: Change "lay" to "have lain."

(C) Part 10: Change "larger" to "largest."

(D) Part 12: Change "who" to "whom."

6. Which of the following requires revision for unnecessary repetition?

   (A) Part 5

   (B) Part 7

   (C) Part 8

   (D) Part 11

The following passage is written in the form of a college economics textbook. Read the text and answer the questions.

[1]Most banks require that they be responsible for paying hazard insurance premiums and real estate taxes on houses they are financing. [2]The reason is that if the insurance premium or taxes are not paid, the bank's interest in the property may be jeopardized. [3]Therefore, the mortgage servicer sets up a special account called an escrow account to handle these expenses.

[4]A mortgage loan is usually set up so that the homeowner pays to the bank each month an amount that will eventually pay for taxes and insurance when these expenses come due. [5]Each month's house payment, then, is principal and interest plus 1/12 of the estimated total amount due each year for interest and taxes. [6]Because the amount of taxes levied by the county may vary, and because sometimes insurance rates rise, the bank will sometimes collect more then it will actually pay out. [7]The overage is applied toward the next year's payments, so the house payment reflects a lower amount due each month. [8]If the bank has underestimated the taxes and insurance, there will be a shortage in the escrow account, so the house payments will rise in order that the bank may recoup its loss.

7. Which of the following, if added between Parts 4 and 5, is MOST consistent with the writer's purpose and audience?

   (A) This money is put into a special account called a mortgage escrow account.

   (B) Some folks resent the fact that the bank hangs on to a part of their money in an interest-free account.

   (C) Most mortgage servicers do not set up an escrow account.

   (D) How anybody can fail to see that banks are going out of their way to protect clients is beyond me.

8. Which of the following is needed in the second paragraph?

    (A) Part 4: Change "set" to "sit."

    (B) Part 6: Change "then" to "than."

    (C) Part 7: Change "so" to "but."

    (D) Part 8: Change "rise" to "raise."

The following passage is written in the form of a popular magazine. Read the text and answer the questions.

[1]Many people think of Ransom Eli Olds as the actual founder of the automobile industry. [2]He built the first automobile factory and was the first to mass produce cars with an assembly-line method. [3]In the late 1800s he experimented with steam engines; the first steam-powered four-wheeled vehicle came out in 1883. [4]This car was sold to a company in India. [5]In 1896 he built his first gasoline-powered car. [6]He helped found the Olds Motor Works in 1899, which produced gasoline engine automobiles.

[7]However, it was in 1901 that he introduced the method that turned out the "curved dash" Oldsmobile in an assembly-line or "stage" production. [8]Assembled in a process using jigs and machine tools, the vehicle was a light-weight, one-cylinder model. [9]This car sold for $650, about one-half the price of similar vehicles from competitors. [10]Many were sold by 1906. [11]In 1904, for example, 5,000 cars, more than three times that of its larger competitor, Peugeot.

[12]Later, in 1914, Henry Ford revolutionized the automotive industry at the Ford Motor Co. plant. [13]This plant used the first moving assembly production line and could turn out a complete vehicle in 90 minutes.

9. Which of the following underlined words in the second paragraph should be replaced by more precise wording?

    (A) assembly-line

    (B) process

    (C) about one-half

    (D) Many

10. Which of the following is a nonstandard sentence?

    (A) Part 3

    (B) Part 7

    (C) Part 11

    (D) Part 12

11. Which of the following is LEAST relevant to the main idea of the first paragraph?

    (A) Part 1

    (B) Part 2

    (C) Part 3

    (D) Part 4

The following passage is written in the form of a popular magazine. Read the text and answer the questions.

[1]Sandra Davis and her two children are finding out just how cold life can be when you're poor. [2]It's the beginning of Fall, and a chill wind briskly tosses red and gold leaves into a pile by the front door of the Davis home on Rand Street. [3]But, the inside of the house is cold, too, because the gas has just been turned off for non-payment of the bill. [4]Sandra is out of a job. [5]She suffers, but her children will suffer as much or more.

[6]In fact poor children across America are suffering. [7]According to the stereotype, we believe that poor children are born into large families in big cities, and these families are headed by minority, welfare mothers. [8]Nothing could be further from the truth. [9]More poor children live outside cities. [10]Nearly two-thirds of all poor families have only one or two children. [11]Most poor families' income comes from the wages of one or more workers. [12]Most shocking of all is that even if every single-parent family was to disappear, the United States would still have one of the highest child poverty rates among industrialized nations. [13]This problem is a disgrace in a country as great as ours, but the government cannot legislate a solution. [14]The people of the United States must become concerned about child poverty and commit to a personal involvement before there can be an effective solution.

12. Which of the following, if added between Parts 6 and 7, is MOST consistent with the writer's purpose and audience?

    (A) Who can blame Sandra for being angry about being laid off her job?

    (B) However, many of the stereotypes about poor children to which most Americans subscribe are not on target.

    (C) A study on child poverty made newspaper headlines on the front pages of American newspapers.

    (D) Frankly, I am shocked by the poverty that still exists in the United States.

13. Which of the following is needed?

    (A) Part 1: Delete the word "out."

    (B) Part 3: Change the comma after "too" to a semicolon.

(C) Part 6: Place a comma after the phrase "In fact."

(D) Part 7: Place a colon after the word "stereotype."

14. Which of the following uses a nonstandard verb form?

(A) Part 11

(B) Part 12

(C) Part 13

(D) Part 14

The following passage is written in the form of a student essay. Read the text and answer the questions.

[1]Summer is upon us, and many students are going out to "catch some rays." [2]In order to keep themselves beautiful and healthy, these sun worshipers should show respect for the power of old Sol. [3]Frequent or prolonged exposure to the sun can cause skin cancer, the deadliest form of which is malignant melanoma, and incidences of this disease are rising faster than any cancer. [4]Ninety percent of skin cancer is caused by overexposure to the sun.

[5]While most Americans believe application of sun screen helps prevent cancer, less than ten percent of us use it when we go out. [6]Also, we tend to go out during the most dangerous part of the day, between 10 a.m. and 2 p.m. in the summer. [7]This is the time when the sun emits peak ultraviolet radiation in the Northern Hemisphere. [8]Even hiding under an umbrella near a pool or beach is insufficient to protect us from the damaging effects of the sun because the UV rays are reflected off the surface of sand and water.

[9]Wearing sunscreen may protect us a little, but sweat or swimming washes the lotion off, so the sunscreen really doesn't help protect us very much. [10]____________________ [11]It's hard to use self-control in a nation that worships the rich, the thin, and the tan, but the burning rays of the sun can give cancer to anyone who wants a dark tan every summer. [12]We'd be better off trying to get rich and thin.

15. Which of the following is needed?

(A) Part 3: Add "other" between "any" and "cancer."

(B) Part 5: Change "application" to "applying."

(C) Part 8: Change "to protect us" to "in protecting us."

(D) Part 9: Delete "off."

16. Which of the following requires revision for unnecessary repetition?
    (A) Part 2
    (B) Part 3
    (C) Part 8
    (D) Part 9

17. Which of the following, if used in the blank labeled Part 10, **best** fits the writer's pattern of development in the first paragraph?
    (A) There is some evidence that propensity for skin cancer is a genetic inheritance.
    (B) Skin cancer is usually not linked to other forms of cancer.
    (C) People with all shades of skin color can burn, but fair-skinned people with freckles tend to burn the easiest.
    (D) The best protection is staying indoors during midday or wearing a long-sleeved shirt and a hat.

The following passage is written in the form of an economics textbook. Read the text and answer the questions.

Note: In the second paragraph, a paragraph organization error is purposely included.

[1]When interest rates decrease, home mortgage rates also drop. [2]Homeowners who bought a house when rates were high seek to refinance their mortgage loans in order to take advantage of the cheaper rates. [3]Lower interest rates <u>results</u> in lower monthly payments.

[4]A person who owns a $100,000 home with a fixed interest rate of 11 percent for 30 years pays almost $1,000 in monthly principal and interest. [5]However, there is a fee of $1,800 to $2,400 for refinancing. [6]The same home with a 30 year loan, but with a 9 percent loan, pays about $850 a month. [7]Obviously, it is to the consumer's advantage to refinance his home. [8]The "rule of thumb" in the mortgage industry is that the homeowner is wise to refinance if he can get a loan at two or more percentage points lower than his current rate. [9]Therefore, if the homeowner is planning to move within a year or two, refinancing is not considered a wise choice of action.

18. Which of the following should be used to replace the underlined word in Part 3?
    (A) result
    (B) resulted

(C) is resulting

(D) had resulted

19. Which of the following makes the sequence of ideas clearer in the second paragraph?

    (A) Place Part 5 after Part 8.

    (B) Reverse the order of Parts 4 and 5.

    (C) Reverse the order of Parts 7 and 9.

    (D) Delete Part 6.

20. Which of the following is a nonstandard sentence?

    (A) Part 4

    (B) Part 6

    (C) Part 8

    (D) Part 9

The following passage is written in the form of an architecture article. Read the text and answer the questions.

[1]Although most new homes across the United States are finished in brick, stucco is an old finish that is becoming increasingly popular. [2]Stucco finishes, applied with a trowel, <u>is</u> composed of sand, water, and a cementing mixture. [3]The first coat or two is thicker, about 3/8 of an inch, with the final coat about 1/4 to 1/8 of an inch thick.

[4]Stucco has many advantages. [5]One of the most attractive selling features is that stucco is energy efficient. [6]In addition, a waterproof, low maintenance exterior is produced by coating the final application with a clear acrylic finish. [7]Since stucco finishes are mixed with color homeowners and designers can select from a wide range of shades. [8]Also, stucco is lightweight and quite inexpensive. [9]By substituting stucco for brick veneer, the typical home gains about 200 square feet of living space.

21. Which of the following, if added between Parts 2 and 3, is MOST consistent with the writer's purpose and audience.

    (A) Personally, I know people who think stucco is an ugly finish for a home.

    (B) Sometimes, Spanish and Indian style homes in the Southwest are finished with stucco on the interior walls.

    (C) Indeed, stucco creates a California ambiance many wish to emulate.

    (D) The plasterlike stucco is applied in two or three thin coats.

22. Which of the following is needed in the second paragraph?
    (A) Part 5: Delete the second "is."
    (B) Part 6: Move "in addition" after "finish."
    (C) Part 7: Place a comma after "color."
    (D) Part 8: Move "quite" after "is."

23. Which of the following should be used in place of the underlined verb in Part 2?
    (A) are
    (B) will be
    (C) being
    (D) should be

The following passage is written in the form of a natural history article. Read the text and answer the questions.

Note: In the second paragraph, a paragraph organization error is purposely included.

[1]There are more things to recycle than tin, plastic, aluminum, and newsprint. [2]One type of recycling that is gaining in popularity is Christmas tree recycling. [3]Most of the 34 million Christmas trees that Americans buy every year end up in landfills. [4]This is an expensive waste of organic material and valuable space in the landfills. [5]Many communities have bought wood chippers so the trees can be turned into mulch for the garden. [6]Some areas dump the trees on the bottoms of lakes to supply habitat for fish and other organisms, and along the coastlines, states are tying Christmas trees into large bundles for use in coastline reclamation projects. [7]Eventually covered by sand and coastal vegetation, the trees become dunes which keep valuable beaches from being washed away.

[8]In Texas, along the Gulf Coast, there are people who recycle used oil rigs. [9]Following a master plan designed by a special advisory commission, this self-sustaining program encouraged the use of petroleum rigs for the development of underwater recreational areas. [10]Since it is cheaper to topple a rig rather than tow it back to shore, participating companies topple their tall offshore petroleum drilling platforms and give half the money saved to the Artificial Reef Fund. [11]The state has an Artificial Reef Fund, a program which does not use the taxpayers' money. [12]These offshore rigs have already become underwater fish habitats because the rig's barnacle-encrusted legs provide protection against larger predators. [13]Often, undersea sport fishers and divers already know the locations of these platforms and come there even while drilling is in progress. [14]Once the rig is toppled, new organisms will inhabit the structure, and new types of fish will find a home there. [15]The toppled rigs become an artificial reef.

24. Which of the following, if added between Parts 4 and 5, is MOST consistent with the writer's purpose and audience?

    (A) It makes more sense to recycle the trees.

    (B) Some people think the trees provide a useful function in the landfill by adding organic material.

    (C) A big problem is that people often don't take off the tinsel and artificial icicles.

    (D) How could anyone get out in the cold of late December?

25. Which of the following makes the sequence of ideas clearer in the second paragraph?

    (A) Delete Part 8.

    (B) Delete Part 10.

    (C) Reverse the order of Parts 8 and 15.

    (D) Place Part 11 before Part 9.

26. Which one of the following is needed?

    (A) Part 8: Change "who" to "which."

    (B) Part 9: Change "encouraged" to "encourages."

    (C) Part 10: Change "cheaper" to "cheapest."

    (D) Part 13: Add a comma after "platforms."

The following passage is written in the form of a fine arts textbook. Read the text and answer the questions.

[1]A French composer, the bolero inspired Anton Ravel to create the ballet *Bolero.* [2]The sister of the legendary Russian dancer Vaslav Nijinsky choreographed the ballet created by Ravel. [3]A popular and well-known folk dance in Spain, the bolero as we know it is credited to Anton Bolsche and Sebastian Cerezo around the mid 1700s. [4]Although almost no one has seen the ballet, the music from *Bolero* has retained immense popularity and is performed on a regular basis around the world.

[5]The center and driving force of this musical composition is a snare drum. [6]The percussionist begins by playing a rhythmic pattern lasting two measures and six beats, the rhythm of the bolero dance, as quietly as possible. [7]At the beginning, other instruments pick up the rhythm as the frenzy builds. [8]The first flute then introduces the melody, the second important part of *Bolero*; different instruments, such as the clarinet, bassoon, and piccolo, play individual parts. [9]The buildup of the music occurs in two ways: the individual musicians play their instrument louder

and louder, and more and more instruments begin to play together. [10]For most of the 15 to 17 minutes of the performance, *Bolero* is played in an unrelenting harmony of C Major. [11]The end is signaled by a brief shift to E Major, and then a strong return to C Major.

27. Which of the following is LEAST relevant to the main idea of the first paragraph?
    (A) Part 1
    (B) Part 2
    (C) Part 3
    (D) Part 4

28. Which of the following, if added between Parts 6 and 7 of the second paragraph, is MOST consistent with the writer's purpose and audience?
    (A) Doesn't that sound kind of boring?
    (B) It's pretty obvious why this piece is not currently popular.
    (C) It would be helpful to see the ballet, as bolero dancers use facial expressions and wave their arms to express emotions.
    (D) This rhythm does not change during the entire performance, but the music becomes gradually louder until the final crescendo.

29. Which of the following contains a misplaced modifier?
    (A) Part 1
    (B) Part 3
    (C) Part 6
    (D) Part 10

The following passage is written in the form of a science textbook. Read the text and answer the questions.

[1]One of the world's most valuable gems, pearls are valued for their luminous beauty. [2]Pearls are formed when an irritant, like a few grains of sand or a parasite, enters a mollusk. [3]Nacre-forming cells begin to cover the intruder with smooth layers of calcium carbonate until the irritant assumes the same appearance as the inside of the mollusk. [4]Only rarely, and after many years, do the layers of nacre form a pearl.

[5]____________________ a cut pearl is examined under a microscope, concentric layers of nacre are revealed. [6]Tiny crystals of the mineral aragonite, held in place

by a cartilage-like substance called conchiolin, reflect light in an iridescent rainbow effect. [7]Jewelers call this iridescence *orient.* [8]Most mollusks do not make iridescent pearls ______________________ their aragonite crystals are too large.

[9]Perfectly round pearls are quite rare in natural occurrence. [10]Most pearls now are cultured. [11]A young oyster receives both a piece of mantle from a donor oyster and a seeding bead of mussel shell. [12]These are tucked into a carefully-made incision in an oyster. [13]Which is then lowered into the ocean in a wire cage so it can be cleaned and periodically x-rayed to check on progress. [14]Since the oyster is a living organism, and not a machine in a factory, the oyster may choose to spit out the introduced nucleus, or the resulting pearl may be full of lumps and stains. [15]Minor stains and imperfections, however, may be eliminated by carefully grinding down the surface of the pearl in order to produce a smaller, but more valuable, perfect pearl.

30. Which of the following is needed in the first paragraph?
    (A) Part 1: Delete "One of."
    (B) Part 2: Change "like" to "such as."
    (C) Part 3: Change "until" to "because."
    (D) Part 4: Change "and after" to "and then."

31. Which of the following, if inserted in order into the blanks of the second paragraph, helps a reader understand the logical sequence of ideas?
    (A) When; because
    (B) If; so
    (C) Until; as a result of
    (D) For example; later

32. Which of the following focuses attention on the main idea of the third paragraph?
    (A) Hyphenate "Perfectly round" in Part 9.
    (B) Combine Parts 12 and 13 by changing the period after "oyster" to a comma.
    (C) Delete Part 14.
    (D) Add a sentence between Parts 14 and 15 to give examples of defects.

The following passage is written in the form of a history textbook. Read the text and answer the questions.

[1]One thing is certain: Christopher Columbus was a real person who left real logs of his journey from Spain on August 3, 1492, to the Bahamas and back. [2]____________________ [3]To the Spanish he is Cristobal Colon, but the Italians call him Cristoforo Colombo. [4]The Italians insist he is a native of Genoa, but some claim he was a Jew born in Spain, or born in Spain but not a Jew. [5]One version has touted Columbus as a Norwegian.

[6]Contrary to the popular myth, most educated people of the 1400s believed the world was round. [7]Columbus didn't have to sell most anyone on that idea. [8]What he was trying to sell was a faster route to India. [9]Trade with India went by the centuries-old overland routes or the newer route by ship around the southern tip of Africa. [10]Also, another common myth is that Isabella had to sell her jewels in order to provide financing; actually, her husband had to approve all expenses, and funding was taken from the royal treasury.

[11]Even the original landing site is not known for certain, but most scholars agree that it is probably San Salvador Island in the Bahamas. [12]After his voyage, Columbus sent his handwritten logs to Isabella. [13]The copy the queen had made is known as the Barcelona log. [14]The original handwritten one has disappeared, as has all but a fragment of the Barcelona log copied by a Dominican friar named Bartolome de las Casas.

33. Which of the following, if used in the blank labeled Part 2, **best** supports the main idea of the first paragraph?

    (A) Supposedly, Columbus began his sailing career as a boy 13 years old.

    (B) Because he wanted the lifetime annuity offered by Ferdinand and Isabella, Columbus falsely claimed to be the first to see land.

    (C) Columbus apparently sailed a course different from the one officially recorded in his log.

    (D) Almost everything else about him, including his name and place of birth, is controversial or uncertain.

34. Which of the following is needed in the second paragraph?

    (A) Part 6: Change "Contrary to" to "Opposing."

    (B) Part 7: Delete the word "most."

    (C) Part 9: Change "by" to "around."

    (D) Part 11: Change "probably" to "probable."

The following passage is written in the form of an editorial in a college newspaper. Read the text and answer the questions.

Note: In the first paragraph, a paragraph organization error is purposely included.

[1]The recent contretemps over the <u>proposed</u> hike in the student parking fee has provided a test for the new administration. [2]After a proposed doubling of the current $40 per semester parking fee, students threatened a walkout and planned demonstrations. [3]The fees were intended to cut down on the incidents of vandalism and potential assaults in campus parking lots. [4]Faced with these threats, the director of student services, the provost, and several other administrators met with the president of the student body and heads of several student organizations. [5]The increased fees, already approved by the board of regents, were to pay the salary of additional parking lot attendants. [6]<u>Some</u> students viewed the rate increase as a means of subsidizing more campus minor bureaucrats and petty disciplinarians. [7]Although our university has not had much trouble with vandalism in the past, and no reported incidents of assault, such incidents are rising in surrounding areas and are a growing problem in universities across the States.

[8]<u>After</u> the two groups met, complaints and fears were exchanged. [9]The administration listened <u>attentively</u>. [10]Rather than just paying "lip service" to the process of negotiation, the administration agreed to a compromise on the service fee in exchange for a well-organized student patrol which will be trained and monitored by the town's police force. [11]____________________ [12]It is hoped that the presence of these students, who will wear an identifying arm band, will deter potential criminal activity.

35. Which of the following makes the sequence of ideas clearer in the first paragraph?

    (A) Reverse the order of Parts 1 and 2.

    (B) Delete Part 2.

    (C) Place Part 3 after Part 6.

    (D) Delete Part 7.

36. Which of the following, if used in the blank labeled Part 11, **best** supports the main idea of the second paragraph?

    (A) It is a relief that the administration has been responsive, but it is even more of a relief to know there will be additional coverage of the lots.

    (B) Don't worry about your safety; there is adequate protection for people in the parking lots right now.

(C) When the new administration came in, students were concerned that the new administration would not be responsive to the needs of the students.

(D) Similar to citizens' Crime Watch program in the town, this patrol will not be allowed to interfere but will report suspicious activities.

37. Which of the following, underlined in the above passage, should be replaced by a more precise word?

(A) proposed

(B) Some

(C) After

(D) attentively

The following passage is written in the form of a letter to a college newspaper. Read the text and answer the questions.

[1]Dena may die soon. [2]For 21 years, all Dena has ever known is captivity. [3]How would you like to spend your entire life in captivity? [4]Even though Dena is not a human, but an orca, a killer whale, don't you think Dena deserves to be released into her natural habitat? [5]Orcas are much too intelligent and too delicate to be confined in tanks. [6]Dena's owners, Sea Habitat, Inc., claim she is displaying geriatric signs normal for an orca 25 years old. [7]Orcas are not meant to be caged, no matter how kind the jailer who holds the keys.

[8]We don't know enough about orcas and how they interact. [9]Who are we to confine a species that may be as intelligent as humans? [10]True, Dena may be rejected by her original pod, members of which stay together for life. [11]____________________ [12]Maybe she is too old to live much longer. [13]However, we should at least allow Dena to die with dignity in her natural surroundings. [14]And, if Dena succeeds in surviving in the wild, maybe we can pressure other zoos and marine institutions around the world to release these beautiful animals back to the wild, where they can have longer, healthier lives. [15]I urge everyone to write a letter to their local senator and congressman demanding the return of all orcas to the oceans of the Earth.

38. Which of the following, if added between Parts 6 and 7, is MOST consistent with the writer's purpose and audience?

(A) Some say leave her where she is because there's no use in crying over spilled milk.

(B) People attempt to obfuscate the issue by ignoring the fact that orcas have no natural enemy other than man.

(C) Did you know that orcas have an average of 40-48 teeth?

(D) However, the high death rate of orcas in captivity clearly indicates that Dena may be sick from having been confined.

39. Which of the following, if used in the blank labeled Part 11, **best** develops the main idea of the second paragraph?

(A) Another problem to be overcome is training Dena to hunt live fish, instead of depending on being fed dead fish by her human captors.

(B) As a matter of fact, it is now against the law to capture orcas in the wild and sell them to zoos.

(C) As we all know, the breeding of captive orcas has not been successful.

(D) Since orcas live an average of 20-30 years, Dena should not be released because she is clearly too old to adapt to the wild.

40. Which of the following displays nonstandard pronoun usage?

(A) Part 3

(B) Part 7

(C) Part 14

(D) Part 15

The following is written in the form of an education textbook. Read the text and answer the questions.

[1]Consultative teaching models have gained much popularity lately. [2]The Content Mastery program is one such model designed to assist students who have been identified as learning disabled to achieve their maximum potential in normal classroom environments. [3]Learning disabled students are intelligent but need extra skills in order to overcome their disabilities. [4]A learning disabled student who is mainstreamed may have difficulties in a class where the teacher may not have the training necessary to help students with different disabilities. [5]The student who needs extra help can go to the Content Mastery classroom and work on an individualized basis under the guidance of the special programs teacher with the materials available there. [6]Students needing the Content Mastery program exhibit the following characteristics consistently low grades, poor performance, and gaps in skills.

[7]__________________, Content Mastery is not just "a little extra help." [8]It also is not designed to "give" students the answers to worksheets and tests. [9]What Content Mastery does is offer increased stimulus variation in the form of many different strategies. [10]__________________, the Content Mastery materials include taped textbooks, hi-lighted books and worksheets, and supplementary materials (such as laminated charts to practice labeling), as well as small study groups, individual counseling, sessions on test-taking strategies, and other types of problem-solving skills.

41. Which of the following, if inserted between Parts 4 and 5, is MOST consistent with the writer's purpose and audience?

(A) Also, since class sizes vary, some classes may be too large for the teacher to give individualized instruction necessary for the success of these students.

(B) I think some students use the Content Mastery classroom as a cop-out for getting out of work.

(C) It has been clearly demonstrated that students below grade level in their psychomotor development benefit most from practicing tactile kinesthetic skills activities in Content Mastery.

(D) Even though it is a problem-solving model, Content Mastery is not successful with all students.

42. Which of the following is needed?

(A) Part 1: Change "much" to "a lot."

(B) Part 3: Change "their" to "his or her."

(C) Part 6: Add a colon after "characteristics."

(D) Part 7: Remove the quotation marks around "a little extra help."

43. Which of the following, if used in order in the blanks of the second paragraph, **best** help the transition of ideas?

(A) On one hand; In contrast

(B) However; For example

(C) Later; In addition

(D) Furthermore; As long as

The following passage is written in the form of a college fine arts textbook. Read the text and answer the questions.

[1]Born Domenikos Theotokopoulos in Crete in 1541, El Greco became one of the world's great painters. [2]He earned his name, *El Greco*, meaning "The Greek," when he moved to Spain around 1577 after several frustrating years in Venice and Rome. [3]Probably because El Greco was unable to obtain important commissions during his years in Italy, he left for Spain in his mid-30s. [4]However, he had no better luck in Spain. [5]At that time, paintings were supposed to inspire prayer and teach religious doctrine, but El Greco did not always adhere to scripture. [6]For example, he put three Marys in *The Disrobing of Christ,* set biblical scenes in Toledo, Spain, and painted Roman soldiers in 16th century armor. [7]As a result, he lost the patronage of the Toledo Cathedral. [8]Later, he was able to gain the respect and patronage of Toledo's intellectuals who admired and supported El Greco. [9]This wide audience probably left the artist more freedom in developing his own style.

[10]El Greco's painting style is based on his early Venetian training. [11]The Venetian style, called *mannerism,* characterized by elongated forms, graceful lines, and metallic colors with white highlights. [12]El Greco's works show humans and animals such as horses extremely elongated, and his landscapes distorted. [13]Although some critics attribute these characteristics to a peculiar brand of mysticism, probably they show more freedom of experimentation, a freedom not allowed those artists painting politically correct scenes. [14]With loose brushstrokes and sharp contrasts in light and shadow, he anticipated the Expressionist style and profoundly influenced those painters in the 1900s.

44. Which of the following, if placed between Parts 4 and 5, **best** supports the writer's purpose and audience?

    (A) He sought work under King Philip of Spain, the most powerful monarch in Europe at that time.

    (B) El Greco sought to show the difference between the mundane and the supernatural by making his figures seem to glow with an inner radiance.

    (C) In his masterpiece, *The Burial of Count Orgaz,* El Greco created a realistic lower, earthly half to contrast with abstract forms and distorted proportions in the upper, heavenly half.

    (D) The painter from Crete failed to win King Philip's favor with the painting *Martyrdom of St. Maurice.*

45. Which of the following is a nonstandard sentence?

    (A) Part 3

    (B) Part 8

    (C) Part 11

    (D) Part 13

WRITING SAMPLE

(ANSWER SHEETS APPEAR IN THE BACK OF THIS BOOK.)

DIRECTIONS: In this section, you are required to write an essay of between 300 and 600 words on the writing topic which appears on the bottom of this page. You should expect to spend approximately 60 minutes on your writing sample. During this time, you should organize your ideas, write a rough draft, and proofread and revise your draft essay.

Make sure to read the topic carefully and consider what your position will be before you start to write the essay. After you are confident in what you have written, copy your essay onto the lined pages of the Writing Sample answer sheet.

Your essay will be scored against the following seven criteria:

1. Appropriateness (how well you explore the given topic and how suitably you address your audience)
2. Unity and Focus (the pointedness of your perspective and direction)
3. Development (the quality of evidence that you offer to support your argument)
4. Organization (the logical arrangement of your essay)
5. Sentence Structure (how successfully you use sentences and how varied your sentence forms are)
6. Usage (the effectiveness and proper implementation of your word usage)
7. Mechanical Conventions (your proper use of spelling, punctuation, and capitalization)

Your essay must be written on the topic given and must employ numerous paragraphs. Make sure it is legible — if it cannot be read, it cannot be graded.

Writing Sample Topic

Because of increased crime involving teenagers at area malls and other places of recreational activity, local city councils and many concerned citizens have recently proposed curfews, hoping to stem the tide of teen crime. Write an essay, to be read by the city council and concerned citizens, approving or disapproving of the proposed curfews for teenagers.

PRACTICE TEST 2

ANSWER KEY

Reading Section

1. (C)
2. (B)
3. (B)
4. (D)
5. (C)
6. (A)
7. (D)
8. (C)
9. (B)
10. (B)
11. (D)
12. (A)
13. (D)
14. (A)
15. (B)
16. (D)
17. (C)
18. (B)
19. (B)
20. (C)
21. (A)
22. (A)
23. (D)
24. (C)
25. (D)
26. (B)
27. (C)
28. (A)
29. (C)
30. (D)
31. (C)
32. (A)
33. (A)
34. (D)
35. (A)
36. (A)
37. (D)
38. (C)
39. (B)
40. (B)
41. (A)
42. (D)
43. (C)
44. (B)
45. (B)

Mathematics Section

1. (D)
2. (B)
3. (C)
4. (A)
5. (C)
6. (D)
7. (B)
8. (A)
9. (C)
10. (C)
11. (D)
12. (D)
13. (B)
14. (C)
15. (D)
16. (C)
17. (C)
18. (B)
19. (D)
20. (A)
21. (A)
22. (B)
23. (C)
24. (C)
25. (D)
26. (D)
27. (C)
28. (C)
29. (D)
30. (A)
31. (D)
32. (A)
33. (D)
34. (A)
35. (B)
36. (B)
37. (A)
38. (B)
39. (C)
40. (B)
41. (B)
42. (D)
43. (B)
44. (D)
45. (C)

Writing Section (Multiple-Choice)

1. (D)
2. (B)
3. (B)
4. (A)
5. (C)
6. (D)
7. (A)
8. (B)
9. (D)
10. (C)
11. (D)
12. (B)
13. (C)
14. (B)
15. (A)
16. (D)
17. (D)
18. (A)
19. (A)
20. (B)
21. (D)
22. (C)
23. (A)
24. (A)
25. (D)
26. (B)
27. (C)
28. (D)
29. (A)
30. (B)
31. (A)
32. (B)
33. (D)
34. (B)
35. (C)
36. (D)
37. (C)
38. (D)
39. (A)
40. (D)
41. (A)
42. (C)
43. (B)
44. (D)
45. (C)

DETAILED EXPLANATIONS OF ANSWERS

Reading Section

1. **(C)** The context refers to those social activities that demand Indian interaction with whites as well as communication — newspapers and colleges. (A) is incorrect; the term goes far beyond simply being friendly. (B) is incorrect; while this may be partly correct, the term "social arts" goes beyond just this activity. (D) is incorrect; the term doesn't relate at all to artwork.

2. **(B)** The paragraph begins with references to these areas, then says that the issue deals with an "important question." (A) is incorrect; this may reflect the writer's attitude, but it doesn't sum up his central idea in this paragraph. (C) is incorrect; the writer says the Cherokee problem is greater than politics, not just another political problem. (D) is incorrect; this idea may be implicit in the entire selection, but it isn't the point in this particular paragraph.

3. **(B)** The writer assumes what he has heard is true and cautions the president. (A) is incorrect; the writer doesn't suggest any alternative. (C) is incorrect; the writer seems to assume the rumors are true; he doesn't ask if rumors are true. (D) is incorrect; he is critical of the president.

4. **(D)** While the writer refers to "rumor," he clearly speaks as if the rumor is true. (A) is incorrect; the opposite is true. He maintains that people are against such a thing. (B) is incorrect; he in no way implies such a thing. The letter itself testifies to the opposite. (C) is incorrect; the writer explicitly says that others are responsible.

5. **(C)** We find this in the final paragraph. (A) is incorrect; such a suggestion is never made. (B) is incorrect for the same reason. (D) is likewise incorrect.

6. **(A)** The context of the sentence suggests that gravity doesn't give up its powers for anything else. (B) is incorrect; gravity doesn't create at all; thus the word is irrelevant. (C) is incorrect; the context simply doesn't suggest the idea of replacement. (D) is incorrect; here, as in the case of (B) and (C), the context doesn't allow for such a meaning and none of the words gives the sentence a logical reading.

7. **(D)** The last sentence of the first paragraph establishes this as the central idea; the following paragraphs illustrate the idea. (A) is incorrect; the passage doesn't serve to illustrate how gravity works against man, in spite of the end of the third paragraph, but rather the effect of gravity on life. (B) is incorrect; Einstein's theory is only alluded to and not discussed. (C) is incorrect; this statement is true but the

passage's intent is not to show that life forms must adapt. That might serve as an assumption but is not the central idea.

8. **(C)** The developmental paragraphs do, in fact, show how gravity affects everything. (A) is incorrect; the selection isn't persuasive, nor does the writer encourage us to study gravity more. (B) is incorrect; the writer never touches on the elements of Einstein's theory. (D) is incorrect; the writer doesn't tell us how gravity works.

9. **(B)** The second paragraph says this. (A) is incorrect; the selection doesn't say this, and it's not necessarily true. (C) is incorrect; again, the selection doesn't say this. (D) is incorrect; the passage doesn't tell us this.

10. **(B)** The selection is not about Einstein but about something that Einstein touched on. (A) is incorrect; the paragraph says little about Einstein's contribution. (C) is incorrect; Einstein's general scientific contributions are not discussed. (D) is incorrect; the paragraph neither says nor implies this idea.

11. **(D)** Each item represents the central idea of a paragraph in the order of appearance in the selection. (A) is incorrect; the writer doesn't dwell on Einstein's work and doesn't tell how gravity works. (B) is incorrect; the selection doesn't cover how we use gravity or how important gravity is, although these might be implications in the selection. (C) is incorrect; the writer doesn't examine Einstein's impact. Generally, each answer except (D) contains obviously incorrect items.

12. **(A)** The writer says humans make their environment artificial and the result of their efforts is culture. (B) is incorrect; the writer does not suggest that culture in and of itself is a bad or destructive thing. (C) is incorrect; the writer doesn't allude to erudition or intelligence; even primitive, illiterate man had culture. (D) is incorrect; culture is an artificial element while nature's elements are not.

13. **(D)** Sentences three and four say this outright. (A) is incorrect; the writer introduces this term early in the passage before he even touches on man's relationship with nature. (B) is incorrect; the word "artificial" doesn't connote lack of sincerity; it suggests "not occurring in nature." (C) is incorrect; the passage does say man is inherently a part of nature, but this term is not used by the writer to describe that relationship.

14. **(A)** The final sentence in the first paragraph states that. (B) is incorrect; the writer calls them primitive but not ignorant; in fact, the passage suggests enlightenment on their part. (C) is incorrect; the writer doesn't suggest that primitive man had no culture; their worship of nature didn't take the place of an artificial environment. (D) is incorrect; their concerns were not ecological but more theological; they may have acted in "ecologically correct" fashion, but the writer doesn't emphasize any ecological concerns.

15. **(B)** Severance may be unwise, but such a pronouncement is not fact, just as one's opinion of "sick delusion" is not fact since some might consider the act neutral. (A) is incorrect; this is, in fact, what we generally consider nature to be: an all-inclusive term. (C) is incorrect; in its broad sense, nature includes humankind, regardless of narrower definitions. (D) is incorrect; this is fact since nonhumans function by these impulses.

16. **(D)** The sentence that begins with this phrase in paragraph one makes this statement. (A) is incorrect; while one may infer that organic cycles prompt plants and animals to act in clock-like fashion, the writer does not say that early humans used them as clocks. (B) is incorrect; these are qualities that the writer ascribes to nonhuman aspects of nature and animals. (C) is incorrect; the writer's reference to the spiritual being is not related to his discussion of primitive man's methods of telling time.

17. **(C)** The opening gives a background and the remaining paragraphs detail the various duties. (A) is incorrect; the selection doesn't appear to be persuasive. It simply rests on the assumption that we have such an office and sets about to describe it. (B) is incorrect; concerns *about* simply are not covered. Concerns *of* are covered. (D) is incorrect; while a reference to the history of this office occurs early, the reference is brief and in no way constitutes the main idea of the selection.

18. **(B)** The second paragraph states this. (A) is incorrect; the only mention of the president is in paragraph one. (C) is incorrect; no reference to such autonomy is even hinted. (D) is incorrect; again, we find no hint of Constitutional provision.

19. **(B)** "Structural" suggests structures or the buildings. The sentence implies as much with reference to care "of the United States capitol building." (A) is incorrect; such maintenance is mentioned separately in the context, suggesting that grounds are not included in structural care. (C) is incorrect; these items would fall into the mechanical care, not structural care. (D) is incorrect; no provisions are made in this paragraph for designing new buildings.

20. **(C)** The idea contained in the phrase "from Boston to Richmond" and in the entire preceding paragraph suggests a heavily populous urban area. Paragraph two also assists in defining this word. (A) is incorrect; the Pine Barrens is a wilderness, but the context clearly suggests that the megalopolis and the Pine Barrens are two different things, that the latter is the epicenter of the former. (B) is incorrect; nothing except possibly "a straight line" would suggest this. (D) is incorrect for the same reason as (A).

21. **(A)** The writer's point here is that civilization and wilderness are juxtaposed side by side. (B) is incorrect; the writer never "sells" a viewpoint. (C) is incorrect; the writer doesn't touch upon industry's need for additional land. (D) is incorrect; the writer does not display any unsympathetic views about the wilderness area.

22. **(A)** The selection points to urban advancement, which is already threatening the area. (B) is incorrect because attitudes are not the subject of the selection. (C) is incorrect; pollutants don't seem to concern the writer. The problem is larger in scope. (D) is incorrect; the need for timber is not the subject nor the implied concern. Generally, the threat is an implicit thing and therefore more general than items (B) through (D).

23. **(D)** Even though it is a widely accepted and probable opinion, it remains conjecture. (A) is incorrect; one can either see or not. According to the selection, one can. (B) is incorrect; the writer makes a literal observation of this fact. (C) is incorrect; the population density is a matter of record. Unless the writer is lying or misinformed, the figures represent fact.

24. **(C)** The selection says that Smoky Mountains Park is smaller than the Pine Barrens' 650,000 acres. (A) is incorrect; the selection doesn't say which of the two is larger. (B) is incorrect; the opposite is true. (D) is incorrect; it would be smaller than Yosemite.

25. **(D)** This message either underlies or is explicitly stated in every part of the passage. Though the statements regarding Harriet Tubman (A), the oral literature (B), and the slave market (C) are all true, they are only important in the respective paragraphs in which they appear.

26. **(B)** This is implied by the overall mood of the passage. The author's perspective hardly allows for sympathy toward the planters (A) or interest in the actual slave traders (C). The unitalicized part of the sentence shows who engaged in slave trading (D), not the clause in question.

27. **(C)** This is evident from the results of "soldiering" in the rest of the sentence (i.e., refusing to work hard, sabotaging the machinery and crops). It could not mean "labored" (B), because this is incompatible with the remainder of the sentence. The sentence does not imply armed resistance to oppression (A), nor certainly does it mention anything to do with uniforms (D).

28. **(A)** Both the violation of human freedom and the less severe living conditions experienced by some slaves are emphasized in the paragraph. (B) is incorrect, because "adequate diet" and "sufficient housing" are both mentioned in the paragraph as being afforded to typical slaves. (C) is incorrect, because the paragraph clearly states the varying degrees of slave hardship. Although (D) may be true, it is not mentioned in the paragraph.

29. **(C)** The dark area labeled "In groups of 10 to 99 slaves (60.5%)" is not only larger than half the circle graph, but also is clearly greater than 50% (60.5%). (B) is clearly not correct, because the 9.4% slice of the circle graph hardly represents the majority of slaves. (D) is incorrect, because the group representing 1 to 9 slaves

is 24.1%, obviously less than a half of the slaves represented on the graph. (A) is incorrect, because, as stated on the key to the graph in the center, only 94% of Black Society in the Old South consisted of slaves. The total percentages of the graph itself only equal 94%.

30. **(D)** The word "sluggish" provides a key clue. (A) is incorrect; the sentence containing the word has nothing to do with intelligence. (B) is incorrect; the writer is not referring to those who can't help themselves but to those who don't care to act. (C) is incorrect; the writer's concern is not with those who receive no attention. Generally, only (D) reflects the context clue given in the paragraph.

31. **(C)** Sentence one contains this idea as a topic concept while the rest of the paragraph shows how dull the "thin" approach is and how different it is from the "fat" approach. (A) is incorrect; the writer neither says nor implies such a conclusion. (B) is incorrect; while this statement may be true, it misses the writer's intent: the productive approach is "funless," dull. (D) is incorrect; the writer may think this, but he doesn't say it and his intent is not to say what thin people should do but what they actually do (or do not do).

32. **(A)** When the author asserts that thin people are funless, she in essence agrees with this; the entire selection implies it clearly. (B) is incorrect; the writer in no way tries to argue that fat people live longer, just happier. (C) is incorrect; if anything, she thinks they are every bit as successful as they appear. (D) is incorrect; she doesn't argue about intelligence in the selection.

33. **(A)** According to the context, the thin person walks as if to convey executive urgency when in fact the situation is otherwise. (B) is incorrect; the writer might say this humorously, but the point is not a fat person's walking speed. (C) is incorrect; the writer implies that brisk walkers are not true executives. (D) is incorrect; if anything, the opposite here would be true, although the point isn't whether thin people are good or poor in their performance.

34. **(D)** Paragraphs two through five discuss a different aspect of life as leanies see it; the final sentence alludes to the fat counterperspective. Paragraph four addresses the fat viewpoint in slightly more depth. Paragraph six then looks at the fat viewpoint. (A) is incorrect; the selection doesn't focus on the ways fat people approach life but on the ways lean people approach it. (B) is incorrect; although the three key words in the answer may appear in the selection, they do not reflect the main ideas of the respective paragraphs. (C) is incorrect; the point of the selection is not to teach lessons to lean people; the paragraphs' intentions are not to do such things as teach how to conserve energy or to stay healthy.

35. **(A)** The sentence suggests that intelligence is equal to madness in amount. (B) is incorrect; the context doesn't suggest that intelligence and madness are inappropriate in their relationship. (C) is incorrect; there exists no implied chrono-

logical relationship. (D) is incorrect; again, we find no spatial or chronological relationship in the context.

36. **(A)** The first sentence summarizes this point fairly well. (B) is incorrect; this idea is mentioned fleetingly in the last sentence but doesn't serve as the guiding idea in the paragraph. (C) is incorrect; this idea simply doesn't exist in the paragraph. (D) is incorrect; the paragraph doesn't attempt to explain how God views man's intellect.

37. **(D)** The last sentence of the paragraph especially corroborates this view. (A) is incorrect; if anything, the writer feels otherwise. (B) is incorrect; the writer may feel that the old and new are equal, but he doesn't suggest one is better. (C) is incorrect; in no way does the writer suggest such a trend.

38. **(C)** The second paragraph tells us of the role of ancient religion and superstition in horror stories. (A) is incorrect; nothing is said of plots or modern films' dependency on folklore for plots. (B) is incorrect; while a film may have a vampire or werewolf, the paragraph doesn't suggest that such characters are antiquity's chief contribution to horror films. (D) is incorrect; the science theme is relatively new and has been added to ancient elements.

39. **(B)** The writer's enthusiastic attitude clearly assumes that the history of horror movies merits discussion. (A) is incorrect; the opposite may well be true, and the writer's enthusiasm for the subject does not suggest such an attitude. (C) is incorrect; theater-goers may be inquisitive, but that trait doesn't appear to be the writer's chief motive behind this selection. (D) is incorrect; some horror movies may be rooted in such a tradition — but only some.

40. **(B)** Each statement takes either a paragraph or section of the selection and sums it up. (A) is incorrect; the selection deals primarily with one type, not all three. (C) is incorrect; we may trace some of the horror monsters and types back to Balkan origins but not horror films as a whole. (D) is incorrect; while religion and superstition provided some material for some of the horror movie stories, the selection doesn't suggest that horror movies as a whole are rooted in religion.

41. **(A)** The paragraph itemizes observations suggesting that society gives girls reasons to give up math while encouraging boys to continue. (B) is incorrect; the paragraph does not say anything about biological processes. (C) is incorrect; the opposite is true. (D) is incorrect; boys' inborn ability is not mentioned.

42. **(D)** The selection ends with this thesis and presents a case showing how the sexes defy socially accepted myths about math-oriented sexes. (A) is incorrect; the selection maintains boys don't have more ability. (B) is incorrect; while the selection touches on this question, the purpose of the selection is broader. (C) is incorrect; the article maintains that society discourages girls from math-related fields, but the point is not the central issue.

43. **(C)** Because society pushes boys into math and expects girls to perform poorly, then it's "all right" for girls to drop out. (A) is incorrect; the article simply doesn't say this. (B) is incorrect; the opposite may well be true, according to the article. (D) is incorrect; the selection looks at boys and girls with the same training as younger children and investigates what happens to cause the turnaround.

44. **(B)** By coming to college with less training, girls are less likely than boys to succeed. (A) is incorrect; this idea is irrelevant to the question at hand. (C) is incorrect; this isn't a fact, but an opinion. (D) is incorrect; this is irrelevant.

45. **(B)** Each sentence reflects the major idea of a paragraph or group of paragraphs in the order they appear in the selection. (A) is incorrect; the writer doesn't say that abilities reverse. Other things cause the turnaround. (C) is incorrect; we have no evidence of genetic differences and the writer doesn't imply that we are on the verge of finding such evidence. (D) is incorrect; the selection doesn't develop the idea that verbal and math areas are of the same level of difficulty. And girls' later difficulties do not result from the cause cited in this passage.

Mathematics Section

1. **(D)**

$$(-3 \times 10^{25}) \times (4 \times 10^{7}) = (-3 \times 4) \times (10^{25} \times 10^{7})$$
$$= -12 \times 10^{25+7}$$

In multiplication of terms with the same base, we add exponents.

$$= -12 \times 10^{32}$$

Answer choice (A) is incorrect because the exponents should be added, **not** subtracted.

$$(-3 \times 10^{25}) \times (4 \times 10^{7}) = (-3)(4) \times 10^{25-7} = -12 \times 10^{18}$$

Answer choice (B) is incorrect because 4 and – 3 should be multiplied, **not** added.

$$(-3 \times 10^{25}) \times (4 \times 10^{7}) = (4 + (-3)) \times 10^{25+7} = 1 \times 10^{32}$$

Answer choice (C) is incorrect because the exponents are improperly added.

$$(-3 \times 10^{25}) \times (4 \times 10^{7}) = (-3 \times 4) \times 10^{25+7} = -12 \times 10^{31}$$

2. **(B)**

$$\frac{20 \times 0.03}{0.005} =$$

Multiply the numerator 20 × 0.03 = 0.60, moving the decimal point two places from right to left in the answer to 20 × 0.03. Then we have

$$\frac{0.60}{0.005} = \frac{60}{.5} = \frac{600}{5} = 120$$

since we move the decimal point three places to the right in both the numerator and the denominator, so that the denominator, 0.005, will become a whole number.

Answer choice (A) is incorrect because it shows

$$\frac{0.60}{0.005} = \frac{60}{5} = 12$$

Answer choice (C) is incorrect because it shows

$$\frac{0.60}{0.005} = \frac{6,000}{0005} = 1,200$$

Answer choice (D) is incorrect because it shows

$$\frac{0.60}{0.005} = \frac{.6}{.5} = \frac{6}{5} = 1.2$$

3. **(C)**

$15^{3}/_{4}$ is approximately 16.

$2^5/_6$ is approximately 3.
Then $16 \div 3$ is approximately 5.
Answer choice (A) is incorrect because it shows

$$15^3/4 \div 2^5/6 \approx 15 \div 2 \approx 7$$

Answer choice (B) is incorrect because it shows

$$15^3/4 \div 2^5/6 \approx 16 \div 2 = 8$$

Answer choice (D) is incorrect because it shows

$$15^3/4 \div 2^5/6 \approx 15 \times 2 = 30$$

4. **(A)**

	23%	of	460	is	what?	
translates to	↓	↓	↓	↓	↓	is means "="
	.23	×	460	=	?	of means "×"

and 23% = .23; to go from percent to decimal drop the percent sign and move the decimal point two places to the left.

Solving this equation for "?" we multiply $.23 \times 460$ to get 105.8.
Answer choice (B) is incorrect because it shows

$$\frac{460}{23} = 20$$

Answer choice (C) is incorrect because it shows

$$.23 \times 460 = .23 \times 46.0 = 10.58$$

Answer choice (D) is incorrect because it shows

$$\frac{460}{.23} = \frac{46{,}000}{23} = 2{,}000$$

5. **(C)**

$$\frac{1}{3} = 3\overline{)1.00}\ \ .33\tfrac{1}{3} \qquad \frac{2}{5} = 5\overline{)2.00}\ \ .40 \qquad \frac{3}{20} = 20\overline{)3.00}\ \ .15 \qquad \frac{2}{7} = 7\overline{)2.00}\ \ .28\tfrac{4}{7}$$

Then $\frac{3}{20} < \frac{2}{7} < \frac{1}{3} < \frac{2}{5}$

since $.15 < .28\frac{4}{7} < .33\frac{1}{3} < .40$

Answer choice (A) is incorrect because it shows

$$1/3 = 1 \div 3 = 33^1/3 \text{ and } .33^1/3 > .15$$

Answer choice (B) is incorrect because it shows

$$2/5 = 2 \div 5 = .40 \text{ and } .40 > .15$$

Answer choice (D) is incorrect because it shows

$^{2}/_{7} = 2 \div 7 = .28^{4}/_{7}$ and $.28^{4}/_{7} > .15$

6. **(D)**

$8 - 7(-4 + 6) =$

Add the – 4 + 6 first in parentheses.

$8 - 7\,(2) =$

Then do the multiplication next considering that negative × positive = negative.

$8 - 14 = -6$

Answer choice (A) is incorrect because it shows

$8 - 7\,(-4 + 6) = 8 - 7\,(-2) = 8 + 14 = 22$

Answer choice (B) is incorrect because it shows

$8 - 7\,(-4 + 6) = 8 - 7 - 4 + 6 = 3$

Answer choice (C) is incorrect because it shows

$8 - 7\,(-4 + 6) = -8 + 7(2) = -8 + 14 = 6$

7. **(B)**

$$\frac{\text{10 rooms total having fire escapes}}{\text{20 rooms}} = \frac{?}{\text{150 rooms}}$$

Solving this proportion for the "?"

$$? = \frac{\text{10 rooms} \times \text{150 rooms}}{\text{20 rooms}} = \frac{\text{1,500 rooms}}{\text{20 rooms}} = \text{75 rooms}$$

Answer choice (A) is incorrect because it shows

150 total rooms – (20 rooms – 10 rooms) = 140 rooms

Answer choice (C) is incorrect because it shows

20 rooms – (150 rooms ÷ 20 rooms) = 13.5 rooms

and 13.5 rooms × 10 rooms = 135 rooms

Answer choice (D) is incorrect because it shows

20 rooms – 10 rooms = 10 rooms with no fire escape

Assume 7 rooms/floor and 7 rooms/floor × 10 rooms = 70 rooms

and 150 rooms – 70 rooms = 80 rooms

8. **(A)**

2 pounds of cement/parking space × 35 parking spaces
= 70 pounds of cement

70 pounds of cement + 40 extra pounds of cement
= 110 pounds of cement

Answer choice (B) is incorrect because it does not add on the 40 extra pounds of cement.

2 pounds of cement/parking space × 35 parking spaces = 70 pounds

Answer choice (C) is incorrect because it subtracts the 40 extra pounds of cement.

(2 pounds of cement/parking space × 35 parking spaces) – 40 pounds
= 30 pounds

Answer choice (D) is incorrect because it shows

(40 pounds + 2 pounds) × 35 parking spaces = 1,470 pounds

9. **(C)**

576 square feet × .20 garden for roses = 115.2 square feet

32.9 square feet for tomato patch + 115.2 square feet for roses
= 148.1 square feet

Answer choice (A) is incorrect because it shows

32.9 square feet × .20 = 6.58 square feet

and 576 – 6.58 = 569.42 square feet

Answer choice (B) is incorrect because it shows

576 square feet – 20 square feet – 32.9 square feet = 523.10 square feet

Answer choice (D) is incorrect because it shows

20 square feet + 32.9 square feet = 52.9 square feet

10. **(C)**

In the interval of 6:20 AM to 6:30 AM, one observes on the graph that for Race #1 the heartrate in beats per minute is increasing from 100 beats/minute to 110 beats/minute, as follows: (6:20, 100), (6:25, 108), (6:30, 110); while for Race #2 the heartrate in beats per minute is stable at 82 beats/minute, as follows: (6:20, 82), (6:25, 82), (6:30, 82).

Answer choice (A) is incorrect because the heartrate for Race #2 is steady. Answer choice (B) is incorrect because the heartrate for Race #1 is increasing, and the heartrate for Race #2 is steady. Answer choice (D) is incorrect because the answers are reversed: Race #2 is stable, and Race #1 is increasing.

11. **(D)**

Charles' 1990 income in February was $457. Charles' 1990 income in June was $392. Therefore, Charles' income decreased by

$457 – $392 = $65

Answer choice (A) is incorrect because it shows the difference between January and June of 1990.

$\$423 - \$392 = \$31$ decrease

Answer choice (B) is incorrect because it shows the difference between January and June of 1989.

$\$398 - \$364 = \$34$ decrease

Answer choice (C) is incorrect because it shows the difference between February and June of 1989.

$\$452 - \$364 = \$88$ decrease

12. **(D)**

$$M = \text{slope} = \frac{\Delta y}{\Delta x} = \frac{y_2 - y_1}{x_2 - x_1}$$

$$M_{AD} = \frac{-3-3}{4-4} = \varnothing \quad \text{undefined slope}$$

$$M_{BC} = \frac{-3+4}{-4+3} = -1 \quad |-1| = 1$$

$$M_{BD} = \frac{-3+4}{4+3} = \frac{1}{7}$$

$$M_{CD} = \frac{-3+3}{4+4} = 0$$

$$M_{AC} = \frac{-3-3}{-4-4} = \frac{6}{8} = \frac{3}{4}$$

$$M_{AB} = \frac{-4-3}{-3-4} = 1$$

Since zero is the lowest possible value, $\overline{CD}$ has the slope that is least steep.

13. **(B)**

The graph of $y = -3$ is parallel to the x-axis and passes through the point $(0, -3)$.

Answer choice (A) is incorrect because $y = 3$ represents the graph:

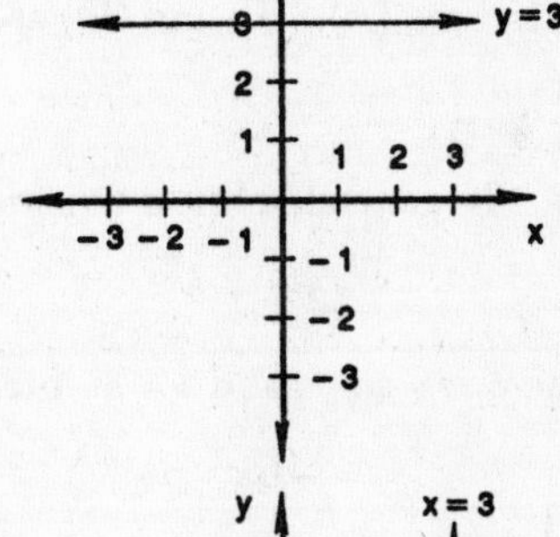

Answer choice (C) is incorrect because $x = 3$ represents the graph:

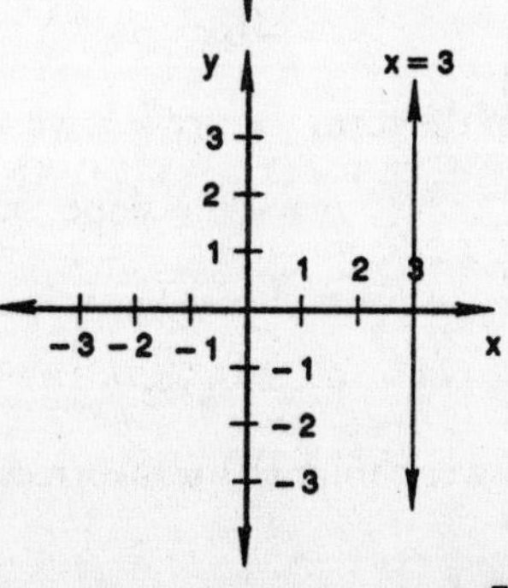

Answer choice (D) is incorrect because $x = -3$ represents the graph:

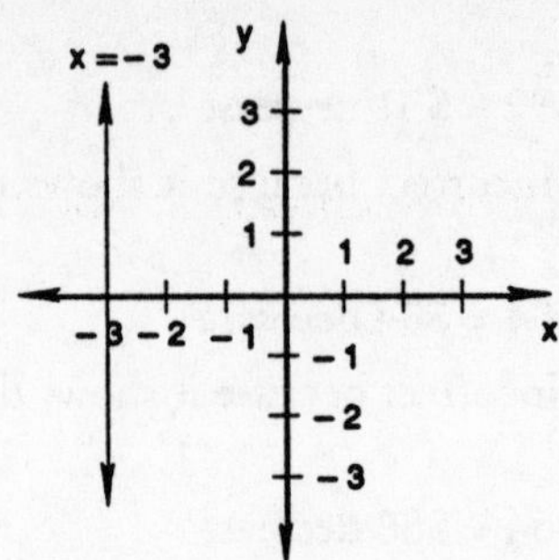

14. **(C)**

The average salary for basketball players increased from

$200,000 to $400,000

and $400,000 – $200,000 = $200,000 increase

The average salary for baseball players increased from

$450,000 to $550,000

and $550,000 – $450,000 = $100,000 increase

The average salary for football players increased from

$300,000 to $675,000

and $675,000 – $300,000 = $375,000 increase

The average salary for ice hockey players increased from

$175,000 to $450,000

and $450,000 – $175,000 = $275,000 increase

Football players' salaries increased by $375,000, which is the highest increase. Therefore, (A), (B), and (D) are incorrect.

15. **(D)**

In general, a linear equation is represented by the form

$$y = mx + b$$

where m = slope and b = y-intercept (the point at which $x = 0$). Since

$$y = -6x + 3$$

is of the form $y = mx + b$, we see

$$m = -6 = \text{slope}$$

Answer choice (A) is incorrect because it reflects the equation

$$y = -{}^{1}/{6}x + b$$

Answer choice (B) is incorrect because it reflects the equation

$$y = 6x + b$$

Answer choice (C) is incorrect because it reflects the equation

$$y = 3x + b$$

16. **(C)**

$$\begin{aligned} 5x - 2y &= 20 \\ 2x + 3y &= 27 \end{aligned}$$

Multiply the bottom equation by 2 and the top equation by 3, so that the terms in the *y*-column will cancel as follows (in this way if the *y*-terms cancel you will be solving for *x*):

$$\begin{aligned} 3(5x - 2y) &= 3(20) & 15x - 6y &= 60 \\ 2(2x + 3y) &= 2(27) \quad \Rightarrow & 4x + 6y &= 54 \\ & & \frac{19x}{19} &= \frac{114}{19} \\ & & x &= 6 \end{aligned}$$

Add the coefficients/terms in the *x*-column and the constants on the right side. Then divide both sides by 19, the coefficient of the *x*-term.

Answer choice (A) is incorrect because it solves for *y*.

$$\begin{aligned} 2(5x - 2y = 20) &= & 10x - 4y &= 40 \\ 5(2x + 3y = 27) &= & -(10x + 15y &= 135) \\ & & -19y &= -95 \\ & & y &= 5 \end{aligned}$$

Answer choice (B) is incorrect because it solves the equation incorrectly.

$$\begin{aligned} 15x - 6y &= 60 \\ 4x + 6y &= 54 \\ 19x &= 6 \\ x &= 6/19 \end{aligned}$$

Answer choice (D) is incorrect because it assumes errors in signs.

$$\begin{aligned} 15x - 6y &= 60 \\ 4x + 6y &= 54 \\ 11x &= 6 \\ x &= 6/11 \end{aligned}$$

17. **(C)**

To solve for x in:

$$-\frac{1}{7}x - 6 = 34$$
$$+6 \quad +6$$
$$-\frac{1}{7}x = 40$$

Add + 6 to both sides; since the x term is on the left side, we transpose the constant term (– 6) on the left side to the right side.

Then continue to solve for x in $-\frac{1}{7}x = 40$ by multiplying both sides of the equation by (– 7). In this way the 7's on the left side will cancel to yield the result.

$$-\frac{1}{7}x = 40$$
$$(-7)(-\frac{1}{7})x = (-7)(40)$$
$$x = -280$$

Now continue to substitute $x = -280$ in the expression $-2x + 3$ as follows:

$$-2(-280) + 3 =$$
$$560 + 3 = 563$$

Answer choice (A) is incorrect because it shows

$$-\frac{1}{7}x - 6 = 34 \Rightarrow -\frac{1}{7}x = 40 \text{ (Step 1)}$$
$$+6 \quad +6$$

Then $\quad -2x + 3 = -2(40) + 3 = -80 + 3 = -77$

Answer choice (B) is incorrect because it forgets to substitute $x = -280$ above in the expression $-2x + 3$. Answer choice (D) is incorrect because it shows

$$-\frac{1}{7}x - 6 = 34$$
$$-6 \quad -6$$
$$-\frac{1}{7}x = 28$$
$$x = -196 \quad \text{(Step 1)}$$

Then Step 2 takes $x = -196$ and substitutes it in the expression

$$-2x + 3 =$$
$$-2(-196) + 3 =$$
$$392 + 3 = 395 \quad \text{(Step 2)}$$

18. **(B)**

To solve for t means to get t on one side by itself. Since there are no t terms on the left side, do the additions (add – 3 to both sides of the equation), before the divisions (divide both sides by 4; the coefficient of t), i.e.,

$$\begin{array}{rcl} 9r & = & 4t + 3 \\ -3 & & -3 \\ \hline 9r - 3 & = & 4t \end{array}$$

$9r$ and -3 are unlike terms so place -3 a little to the right of the $9r$.

$$\frac{9r-3}{4} = \frac{4t}{4}$$

$$\frac{9r-3}{4} = t$$

Answer choice (A) is incorrect because it shows the +3 being transposed incorrectly.

$$\begin{array}{rcl} 9r & = & 4t + 3 \\ +3 & & +3 \\ \hline 9r + 3 & = & 4t \end{array}$$

Answer choice (C) is incorrect because it rewrites t.

$$\begin{array}{rcl} 9r & = & 4t + 3 \\ -3 & & -3 \\ \hline 9r - 3 & = & 4t \end{array}$$

and $t = \dfrac{9r-3}{4} = \dfrac{9r}{4} - 3.$

Answer choice (D) is incorrect because it rewrites t.

$$\begin{array}{rcl} 9r & = & 4t + 3 \\ +3 & & +3 \\ \hline 9r + 3 & = & 4t \end{array}$$

and $t = \dfrac{9r+3}{4} = \dfrac{9r}{4} + 3.$

19. **(D)**

Let x represent the first integer; $x + 2$ represent the second integer; and $x + 4$ represents the third integer.

Twice the middle integer is represented by $2(x + 2)$.

Nine more than the largest is represented by $9 + (x + 4)$.

The equation is

$$2(x + 2) = 9 + (x + 4)$$

Using the distributive law on the left side of the equation, we get:

$$2x + 4 = 9 + x + 4$$

Combining like terms on the right side of the equation, we get:

$$2x + 4 = 13 + x$$

Transposing the variable x on the right side of the equation to the left side of the equation, we get:

$$\begin{array}{r} 2x + 4 = 13 + x \\ -x \qquad\quad -x \\ \hline x + 4 = 13 \end{array}$$

Then transposing the constant term + 4 to the right side of the equation:

$$\begin{array}{rcl} x + 4 & = & 13 \\ -4 & & -4 \\ \hline x & = & 9 \end{array}$$

$$x + 2 = 9 + 2 = 11$$

$$x + 4 = 9 + 4 = 13$$

Therefore, the sum of the three consecutive odd integers is

$$9 + 11 + 13 = 33.$$

Answer choice (A) is incorrect since 9 is one of the integers to be added.
Answer choice (B) is incorrect since 11 is one of the integers to be added.
Answer choice (C) is incorrect since 13 is one of the integers to be added.

20. **(A)**
The salary for the week

= \$575 + .03 (cars sold above \$4,500)

= \$575 + .03 (\$8,785 + \$5,832)

= \$575 + .03(\$14,617)

= \$575 + \$438.51

= \$1,013.51

We add the sales of \$8,785 + \$5,832, which are prices of cars sold above \$4,500, change 3% to .03 and multiply .03 (\$14,617) first, by order of operations before adding on the \$575.

Answer choice (B) is incorrect because it takes 3% of \$8,785 only and adds this to his base pay.

\$8,785 × .03 = \$263.55 + \$575 = \$838.55

Answer choice (C) is incorrect because it takes 3% of \$5,832 only and adds this to his base pay.

$\$5,832 \times .03 = \$174.96 + \$575 = \$749.96$

Answer choice (D) is incorrect because it takes 3% of $14,617 incorrectly.

$.03 \times \$14,617 = \$438.51 = \$4,385.10$

21. **(A)**

Let x = number of nickels, then

$.05x$ = monetary value of the number of nickels

Let y = number of pennies, then

$.01y$ = monetary value of the number of pennies

Since there are 64 coins in the child's bank, and the bank contains only nickels and pennies, then

number of nickels	+	number of pennies	=	64 coins
↓	or	↓		
x	+	y	=	64

Since the total monetary value of the coins in the bank is $2.44, then

monetary value of nickels	+	monetary value of pennies	=	$2.44
	or			
$.05x$	+	$.01y$	=	$2.44

Since the problem asks us to determine the number of nickels written in terms of x, we want the equation

$$.05x + .01y = \$2.44$$

(or multiplying through by 100, each term, in order to move the decimal points two places to the right, we get)

$$5x + 1y = 244$$

to be written in terms of x, so that y is replaced in the term $1y$.

Solving for y in the equation $x + y = 64$, we subtract x from both sides to get

$$\begin{array}{rcl} x + y & = & 64 \\ -x & & -x \\ \hline y & = & 64 - x \end{array}$$

Substitute $y = 64 - x$ in the equation

$$5x + 1y = 244$$

This gives us

$$5x + 64 - x = 244$$

$5x + 1(64 - x) = 244$		substituting for y
$5x + 64 - x = 244$		use distributive law
$4x + 64 = 244$		combine like terms
$-64 \quad -64$		transpose the constant
$\frac{4x}{4} = \frac{180}{4}$		divide by the coefficient of x on the left side of the equation
$x = 45$		

Answer choice (B) is incorrect because it refers to the number of dimes. Answer choice (C) is incorrect because it assumes \$.44 in pennies and \$2.00 in nickels or 40 nickels. Answer choice (D) is incorrect because it assumes $y = 60 - x$.

22. **(B)**

n = number of degrees in the second angle.

The first angle is 5 degrees more than twice the second angle; so the first angle =

$$5 + 2n$$

where twice represents multiplication by 2 and more than means addition.

The third angle is 10 degrees less than twice the first angle; so the third angle =

$$2(5 + 2n) - 10$$

where less than signifies subtraction (switching around) and first angle $(5 + 2n)$ comes first and 10° (10) comes second. Particularly, twice the first angle is

$$2(5 + 2n) = 10 + 4n$$

This means the third angle =

$$2(5 + 2n) - 10 = \cancel{10} + 4n - \cancel{10} = 4n$$

Since the **sum** of the angles of a triangle equals 180° then

first angle	+	second angle	+	third angle	=	180°
$(2n + 5)$	+	n	+	$4n$	=	180°

(addition is commutative).

Answer choice (A) is incorrect because it uses the wrong interpretation of 10° less than twice the measure of the first angle. Answer choice (C) is incorrect because it uses the wrong interpretation of 5° more than twice the measure of the second angle. Answer choice (D) is incorrect because it uses a minus sign in the interpretation of 5° more than twice the measure of the second angle.

23. **(C)**

$$R = \text{John's age in 23 years}$$
$$R-23 = \text{John's age now}$$
$$5(R-23) = \text{John's age in 23 years}$$

Then $5(R-23) = R \Rightarrow 5R-115 = R$

Answer choice (A) is incorrect because it shows wrong use of the distributive law. Answer choice (B) is incorrect because it asserts "times" refers to division, not multiplication. Answer choice (D) is incorrect because the equation should be rewritten as $R+23 = 5R$ when R represents John's age now.

24. **(C)**

$$\frac{7}{35x+42} = \frac{7}{7(5x+6)}$$

when you factor a 7 out of the denominator. Then the 7's cancel in both the numerator (top) and the denominator (bottom) to leave

$$\frac{1}{5x+6}$$

since $\frac{7}{7(5x+6)} \div \frac{7}{7} = \frac{1}{5x+6}$

Answer choice (A) is incorrect because it did not factor out a 7 from the + 42. Answer choice (B) is incorrect because it did not factor out a 7 from the 35. Answer choice (D) is incorrect because it shows $7 \div 7 = 0$ incorrectly.

25. **(D)**

The graph passes through the points $(0, -2)$, $(1, -1^2/_3)$, $(-1, -1^2/_3)$, $(3, 4)$, $(-3, +4)$. Also, the graph is a parabola which faces upward and, therefore, the coefficient of the x^2-term must be positive. These conditions are only satisfied by $y = {}^1/_3x^2 - 2$, and, therefore, answer choices (A), (B), and (C) are incorrect.

26. **(D)**

When $s = 60$

$C = 360s - 4s^2$	becomes
$C = 360(60) - 4(60)^2$	substituting $s = 60$
$C = 21,600 - 4(3,600)$	multiplying through
$C = 21,600 - 14,400$	
$C = 7,200$	

The monthly commission in June is \$7,200.

When $s = 50$

$C = 360s - 4s^2$	becomes
$C = 360(50) - 4(50)^2$	substituting $s = 50$
$C = 18{,}000 - 4(2{,}500)$	multiplying through
$C = 18{,}000 - 10{,}000$	
$C = 8{,}000$	

The monthly commission in July is \$8,000.

To determine Joe's profit from his commission in June and in July, we consider:

Profit from commission	=	commission in July	–	commission in June
	=	\$8,000	–	\$7,200
Profit from commission	=	\$800		

Answer choice (A) is incorrect because it adds the two commission values.

$$360(50) - 4(50^2) + 360(60) - 4(60^2) = \$15{,}200$$

Answer choice (B) is incorrect because it only gives the June commission.

$$360(60) - 4(60^2) = \$7{,}200$$

Answer choice (C) is incorrect because it only gives the July commission.

$$360(50) - 4(50^2) = \$8{,}000$$

27. **(C)**

If x and y vary inversely as each other and k is the constant of variation, then $xy = k$. So if length (L) varies inversely as the cube of the width (w^3) then

$$Lw^3 = k$$

Solving for L, we divide both sides of the equation $Lw^3 = k$ by w^3 as follows:

$$\frac{L\cancel{w^3}}{\cancel{w^3}} = \frac{k}{w^3}$$

$$L = \frac{k}{w^3}$$

Therefore, answer choices (A), (B), and (D) are incorrect.

28. **(C)**

$$10x^2 - 5x - 50 = 5(2x^2 - x - 10),$$

factoring out a 5 from each term. The $(2x^2 - x - 10)$ is further factored by finding the terms which multiply to $2x^2$, namely, $2x$ and x; and by finding the terms which multiply to -10, namely, $+5$ and -2, -5 and $+2$, $+10$ and -1, or -10 and $+1$. Here are the possibilities. Check the product of the inner terms and the product of the outer terms for each factor. We are looking for the middle term of $2x^2 - x - 10$, i.e., $-1x$.

$2x^2 - x - 10 =$

Factors	Outer	Inner	Sum		Factors	Outer	Inner	Sum	
$(2x - 10)(x + 1) =$	$+2x$	$-10x$	$-8x$	×	$(2x + 10)(x - 1)$	$-2x$	$+10x$	$+8x$	×
$(2x - 1)(x + 10)$	$+20x$	$-1x$	$+19x$	×	$(2x + 1)(x - 10)$	$-20x$	$+1x$	$-19x$	×
$(2x + 5)(x - 2)$	$-4x$	$+5x$	$+1x$	×	$(2x - 5)(x + 2)$	$+4x$	$-5x$	$-1x$	✓
$(2x + 2)(x - 5)$	$-10x$	$+2x$	$-8x$	×	$(2x - 2)(x + 5)$	$+10x$	$-2x$	$+8x$	×

This says

$$2x^2 - x - 10 = (2x - 5)(x + 2)$$

Therefore, $10x^2 - 5x - 50 = 5(2x - 5)(x + 2)$,

and the factor which appears as one of the choices is $(2x - 5)$.

Answer choice (A) is incorrect because it shows improper use of the distributive law.

$$5(2x - 5) = 2x - 25$$

Answer choice (B) is incorrect because it represents

$$(10x - 1)(x + 50) = 10x^2 - x + 500x - 50 = 10x^2 - 5x - 50$$

Answer choice (D) is incorrect because it incorrectly states the factor $x + 2$ as $x - 2$.

29. **(D)**

$$(-9x^5y^4 + 6x^4y^5 + 8x^3y^2) - (6x^5y^4 + x^4y^5 - 5x^3y^2) =$$

drop the parentheses since no sign on the outside means positive, which does not change the signs of the coefficients of each term on the inside of these parentheses

change signs of the coefficients of each term on the inside of these parentheses because of the minus sign outside the parentheses

$$-9x^5y^4 + 6x^4y^5 + 8x^3y^2 - 6x^5y^4 - x^4y^5 + 5x^3y^2 =$$

Combine like terms — terms having the same variables and same exponents.

$$-9x^5y^4 + 6x^4y^5 + 8x^3y^2 - 6x^5y^4 - x^4y^5 + 5x^3y^2 =$$

$$-15x^5y^4 + 5x^4y^5 + 13x^3y^2$$

neg + neg = neg

coefficient of $-x^4y^5$ is a -1

Answer choice (A) is incorrect because it shows

$$-9x^5y^4 - 6x^5y^4 = -3x^5y^4$$

Answer choice (B) is incorrect because it shows that the signs of the terms in the second parentheses were not changed. Answer choice (C) is incorrect because it shows

$$8x^3y^2 - (-5x^3y^2) = 3x^3y^2$$

30. **(A)**

Multiplication of binomials assumes that for

$$(7x^2 - 5)(6x^2 + 11) =$$

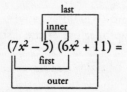

(last, inner, first, outer)

we multiply the first terms $(7x^2)(6x^2)$ in the parentheses; then we multiply the outer terms $(7x^2)(11)$ in the parentheses; then we multiply the inner terms $(-5)(6x^2)$ in the parentheses; and then we multiply the last terms $(-5)(11)$ in the parentheses. This means

$(7x^2 - 5)(6x^2 + 11) =$

$(7x^2)(6x^2) + (7x^2)(11) + (-5)(6x^2) + (-5)(11) =$

$42x^4 + 77x^2 - 30x^2 - 55 =$ { multiplying each pair of terms and adding exponents in the first term

Combine the like terms, $77x^2 - 30x^2 = 47x^2$, and we get

$42x^4 + 47x^2 - 55$

Answer choice (B) is incorrect because it shows

$(7x^2)(11) + (-5)(6x^2) = 77x^2 - 30x^2 = -47x^2$

Answer choice (C) is incorrect because it forgot to add the product of the inner terms and the product of the outer terms. Answer choice (D) is incorrect because it forgot to add the product of the inner terms.

$(7x^2)(11) = 77x^2$

31. **(D)**

The volume of the rectangular excavation for the building

= (length) (width) (height)

= (30) (10) ($20^1/_2$)

= (300) × ($20^1/_2$)

$= \frac{300}{1} \times \frac{41}{2} = \frac{150}{1} \times \frac{41}{1}$

(writing quantities in fractional form)

= 6,150 cubic yards,

cancelling and multiplying numerators.

If a cubic yard of earth weighs approximately 9 pounds per cubic yard and there are 6,150 cubic yards in the excavation, the weight of the earth that fills the space produced by the excavation is

(6,150 ~~cubic yards~~) (9 pounds/~~cubic yard~~) = 55,350 pounds

when the excavation is filled with earth.

Answer choice (A) is incorrect because it divides by the weight per volume.

(30 × 10 × $20^1/_2$) ÷ 9 pounds/cubic yard = $683^1/_3$

Answer choice (B) is incorrect because it deletes the width and height from the computation.

30 yards × 9 pounds/cubic yard = 270 pounds

Answer choice (C) is incorrect because it deletes the height from the computation.

(30 yards × 10 yards) × 9 pounds/cubic yard = 2,700 pounds

32. **(A)**

The triangle in the diagram is a right triangle. If the triangle is a right triangle, the lengths of the sides satisfy the Pythagorean property, namely $a^2 + b^2 = c^2$, where a, b are the lengths of the legs of the right triangle and c is the length of the hypotenuse.

Therefore, $a^2 + b^2 = c^2$ translates to

$$(\text{length of base})^2 + (\text{length of pole})^2 = (\text{length from stake to pole})^2$$

$$
\begin{aligned}
10^2 + b^2 &= 26^2 \\
100 + b^2 &= 676 \quad \text{Solving for } b^2 \\
-100 \quad & \quad -100 \\
\hline
b^2 &= 576
\end{aligned}
$$

and $b^2 = 576$ means to take the positive square root of both sides. Doing so yields $b = 24$.

Answer choice (B) is incorrect because it incorrectly uses the Pythagorean property.

$$26 \text{ feet} - 10 \text{ feet} = 16 \text{ feet}$$

Answer choice (C) is incorrect because it incorrectly uses the Pythagorean property.

$$\sqrt{26+10} = 6$$

Answer choice (D) is incorrect because it incorrectly uses the Pythagorean property.

$$\sqrt{(26)(10)} = \sqrt{260} = \sqrt{4}\sqrt{65} = 2\sqrt{65}$$

33. **(D)**

If $\overline{BC} \perp \overline{AE}$, then $\angle ABC$ and $\angle DBE$ are both 90°. In addition, if $\angle E = \angle C$, then ΔABC is similar to ΔDBE by the angle-angle correspondence. Therefore, $\angle A = \angle D$. Answer choices (A) and (C) do not apply since there are relationships between the line segments in the given triangles besides those relationships resulting from similar triangles. Particularly, we see then that in addition to $\overline{DB} \cong \overline{AB}$, the right angle $\angle ABC$ consists of line segments $\overline{AB}$ and $\overline{BC}$, and the right angle $\angle DBE$ consists of line segments $\overline{DB}$ and $\overline{BE}$. Hence, $\overline{BC} \cong \overline{BE}$, and answer choice (B) does not apply.

34. **(A)**

In order to solve this problem, we must determine the area of the ceiling. This is accomplished by drawing a line that creates two rectangles as shown in the accompanying figure.

Determine the area of both rectangles using the formula

$$A = \text{length} \times \text{width}$$

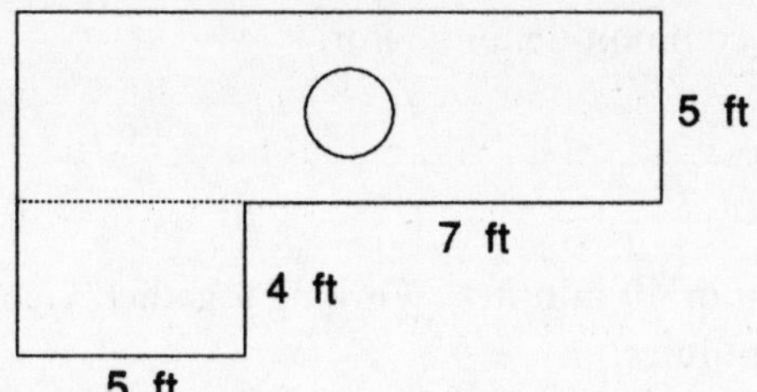

The smaller rectangle will have an area of 5 × 4 or 20 sq. ft.

To find the length of the larger rectangle, use the information provided on the diagram. The lengths given on the bottom of the diagram are 7 and 5 which add up to 12.

Use the area formula and multiply 12 by 5 which yields 60 sq. ft.

Add the two areas together to obtain 60 + 20 = 80.

Do not forget about the area of the light fixture. George does not want to paint over the fixture, so we must subtract the area of the light fixture from the total area of the ceiling.

The area of a circle is determined by the formula π times the radius squared.

We are given the diameter of the circle, 2 feet. The radius is half of the diameter, so our radius is 1 foot. Squaring this number leaves us with 1 still. So our formula is now π times 1. This will give us π which is equivalent to about 3.14.

Subtract the area of the light from the total area.

$$80 - 3.14 = 76.86$$

Next, determine how many times 16 (the number of square feet one gallon of paint covers) divides into 76.86.

$$76.86 \div 16 = 4.8.$$

To determine the cost of the project, multiply the number of gallons it will take to paint the ceiling by the price per gallon, \$8.95.

Since the number of gallons did not come out to an even number, we must round this number up because you cannot buy $^8/_{10}$ of a gallon.

4.8 rounds up to 5.

5 gallons × \$8.95 = \$44.75

35. **(B)**

Let x equal the number of hours it would take for both men working together to complete the job.

Then $^x/_2$ equals the part of the job done by George and $^x/_1$ equals the part of the job done by his friend. The relationship used in setting up the equation is

Part of job done by George + Part of job done by his friend = 1 job

$$\frac{x}{2} + \frac{x}{1} = 1$$

Multiply by 2 to get a common denominator.

$$x + 2x = 2$$

$$3x = 2$$

$x = {}^2/_3$ of an hour or 40 minutes. Working together, George and his friend can paint 10 sq. ft. in 40 minutes.

We know from the previous problem that the total area of ceiling is 80 sq. ft. including the light fixture.

The problem states that George wants to paint all of the ceiling, so we need to divide the total area of the ceiling by the amount that was determined that the two of them can paint.

$$80 \div 10 = 8$$

Multiply 8 times the amount of time they spend painting 10 sq. ft.

$$8 \times 40 = 320 \text{ minutes}$$

All of the possible answer choices are given in hours. To determine the number of hours, divide 320 by 60 (the number of minutes in an hour).

$$320 \div 60 = 5.333\overline{3}$$

The question uses the word "about," so we can estimate the amount of time. 5.33 is about $5^1/_2$ hours.

36. **(B)**

To determine the answer to this problem, find the perimeter and multiply this with the cost per foot, $.86.

To find the perimeter, add up all of the sides of the figure. We are given four of the sides. We know the top of the figure is equal to 12 ft. The left side of the figure can be determined by adding the two dimensions from the right side of the figure together.

$$5 + 4 = 9 \text{ ft.}$$

We now have all of the dimensions and can add them all together.

$$9 + 12 + 5 + 4 + 7 + 5 = 42 \text{ ft.}$$

Multiply 42 with .86.

$$42 \times .86 = \$36.12$$

37. **(A)**

$\angle ABC$ is a straight angle. The number of degrees in a straight angle is 180°. When the sum of two angles is 180°, the angles are said to be supplementary. In the diagram

$\angle ABD + \angle DBC = \angle ABC$. Therefore,

$$\angle ABD + \angle DBC = 180°$$

and $\angle ABD$ and $\angle DBC$ are supplementary angles.

Answer choice (B) is incorrect because it assumes

$$\angle ABD = \angle DBC = 90°$$

Answer choice (C) is incorrect because it assumes

$$\angle ABD + \angle DBC = 90°$$

Answer choice (D) is incorrect because $\angle ABD$ and $\angle DBC$ are adjacent angles, not vertical angles.

38. **(B)**

Statement 1 implies all bears are beautiful. Statement 3 implies all bears who are beautiful live up North. If Wanda is a bear, then Wanda lives up North.

Answer choice (A) is incorrect because only some bears are hairy, so Wanda may or may not be hairy. Answer choice (C) is incorrect because it contradicts statement 5. Answer choice (D) is incorrect because only hairy bears fight a lot, but Wanda may or may not be hairy.

39. **(C)**

The sequence is decreasing; subtracts four, then divides by two. Particularly,

$$284 - 4 = 280;\ 280 \div 2 = 140$$

$$140 - 4 = 136;\ 136 \div 2 = 68$$

$$68 - 4 = 64;\ 64 \div 2 = 32$$

Therefore, the next number in the sequence is $32 - 4 = 28$.

Answer choice (A) is incorrect because it considers

$$32 \div 4 = 8$$

Answer choice (B) is incorrect because it considers

$$32 \div 2 = 16$$

Answer choice (D) is incorrect because it considers

$$32 - 2 = 30$$

40. **(B)**

$$1/5 = 1 \div 5 = .20 \qquad 3/4 = 3 \div 4 = .75$$

$$1/2 = 1 \div 2 = .50 \qquad 18/25 = 18 \div 25 = .72$$

Then $.20 < .50 < .72 < .75$

Answer choice (A) is incorrect because

$$1/5 = 1 \div 5 = .20 \text{ and } .20 < .75$$

Answer choice (C) is incorrect because

$^1/_2 = 2 \div 2 = .50$ and $.50 < .75$

Answer choice (D) is incorrect because

$^{18}/_{25} = 18 \div 25 = .72$ and $.72 < .75$

41. **(B)**

15 nails/~~board~~ × 20 ~~boards~~ = 300 nails total needed

300 nails total needed + 25 extra nails = 325 nails

Answer choice (A) is incorrect because it does not add on the 25 extra nails.

15 nails/board × 20 boards = 300 nails

Answer choice (C) is incorrect because it subtracts the 25 extra nails.

15 nails/board × 20 boards = 300 nails

300 nails – 25 extra nails = 275 nails

Answer choice (D) is incorrect because it adds 25 extra nails to each board.

25 extra nails + 15 nails/board = 40 nails/board

40 nails/board × 20 boards = 800 nails

42. **(D)**

135 acres × .40 land for watershed protection = 54 acres

54 acres for watershed protection + 27.8 acres for recreation = 81.8 acres

Answer choice (A) is incorrect because of improper multiplication.

27.8 acres × .40 land for watershed = 11.12 acres

135 acres – 11.12 acres = 123.88 acres

Answer choice (B) is incorrect because subtraction was improperly used.

135 acres – 40 acres – 27.8 acres = 67.2 acres

Answer choice (C) is incorrect because it incorrectly uses an addition step.

40 acres + 27.8 acres = 67.8 acres

43. **(B)**

You construct a diagram as follows:

Statement I implies George (G) is taller than Michael (M) so

$G > M$

George (G) is shorter than Bob (B) so

$G < B$

George (G) is shorter than Sam (S) so

$G < S$

Statement II implies Bob (B) is taller than Sam (S) so

$B > S$

Putting this together we have

$$G > M, G < B, \quad G < S, B > S$$

or $$\underbrace{M < G, G < B}, \quad \underbrace{S < B, G < S}$$

or $$M < G < B, G < S < B$$

or $$\underset{\text{(shortest)}}{M} < G < S < \underset{\text{(tallest)}}{B}$$

Statement III implies Smith is the tallest, corresponding to Bob (B). Bell is the shortest, corresponding to Michael (M).

Statement IV implies Wong is taller than Jones, implying Wong corresponds to Sam (S) and Jones corresponds to George (G). Therefore, Sam's last name is Wong and answer choices (A), (C), and (D) do not apply.

44. **(D)**

$$\frac{7 \text{ rooms with balconies}}{15 \text{ rooms}} = \frac{?}{195 \text{ rooms}}$$

Solving this proportion for the "?"

$$? = \frac{7 \text{ rooms} \times 195 \text{ rooms}}{15 \text{ rooms}} = \frac{1{,}365 \text{ rooms}}{15 \text{ rooms}} = 91 \text{ rooms}$$

Answer choice (A) is incorrect because it shows

15 rooms – 7 rooms = 8 rooms (no balcony)

8 rooms × 7 rooms = 56 rooms (no balcony)

195 rooms total – 56 rooms (no balcony) = 139 rooms

Answer choice (B) is incorrect because it shows

195 rooms total ÷ 15 rooms = 13 rooms

15 rooms – 7 rooms = 8 rooms (no balcony)

13 rooms × 8 rooms (no balcony) = 114 rooms

Answer choice (C) is incorrect because it shows

15 rooms – 7 rooms = 8 rooms (no balcony)

8 rooms (= 2^3) × 16 rooms (= 2^4) = 128 rooms (no balcony)

195 rooms total – 128 rooms (no balcony) = 67 rooms

45. **(C)**

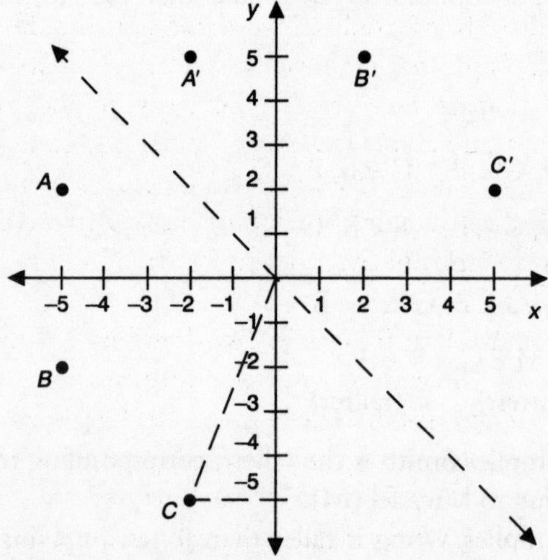

As you can see, when you plot the reflections of *A*, *B*, and *C*, the resulting circle is centered on the origin. Hence, *C* and *B'* and *B* and *C'* would be endpoints of diameters. Since you know the center, by using the Pythagorean theorem or the distance formula and the coordinates of any of the points, you can determine the radius. Therefore, using point *C* it becomes

Pythagorean theorem or distance formula

$$a^2 + b^2 = c^2$$
$$\sqrt{a^2 + b^2} = c$$
$$\sqrt{(-5)^2 + (-2)^2} = c$$
$$\sqrt{29} = c$$

$$d = \sqrt{(x_2 - x_1)^2 + (y_2 - y_1)^2}$$
$$d = \sqrt{(-2 - 0)^2 + (-5 - 0)^2}$$
$$d = \sqrt{(-2)^2 + (-5)^2}$$
$$d = \sqrt{29}$$

Writing Section

Multiple-Choice Subsection

1. **(D)** Part 4 directly contradicts the thesis and should be eliminated. Since the author of the essay is promoting business concern for recycling brought about by consumer pressure, it does not benefit the essay to include a sentence about consumers who do not care about recycling. Choice (A) contains a clause necessary for time frame reference. Choice (B) creates an illogical sentence. Choice (C) would create an informal tone by changing "their" to "our." Although the author may be a concerned consumer, the tone of the article is formal and should not be broken.

2. **(B)** In choice (B), Part 6 logically fits after Part 9. This sequence is marked by the transition word "Therefore" and the continuation of the subject of not knowing the safety of any product due to the lack of government standards of labeling. Choice (A) would move the topic sentence, Part 5, to an unsatisfactory position. Choice (C) reverses the logical order of ideas: first, the seals are introduced in Part 7; then, the seals are referred to in Part 8 with the transition "These seals." Choice (D) completes the idea of lack of government standards and, therefore, should not be deleted.

3. **(B)** In choice (B), the correct form of the subject and verb combination is "it is" or "it's." The form "its" is a possessive pronoun. Choice (A) creates a negative statement that contradicts the thesis. Choice (C) forms a split infinitive, "to now display." The adverb "now" should be placed before or after the infinitive "to display," because infinitives should never be split by an adverb. Choice (D) would form an inaccurate sentence.

4. **(A)** Choice (A) gives details on the condition of the manuscripts. Choice (B) introduces an idea that best belongs in the third paragraph. Choice (C), although accurate, is an extraneous idea. Choice (D), although a fear of some people, does not fit into a discussion of the discovery and history of the scrolls.

5. **(C)** Choice (C) is the correct answer. The comparative degree is used for comparing two things, so "larger" should be changed to the superlative degree, "largest," because more than two caves were discovered containing scrolls. Choice (A) correctly uses "between" to indicate something falling between two dates; "among" is used for more than two things. In choice (B) the use of "lay" is correct; the past tense is required for a condition no longer in effect. In choice (D) "who" is correct as the subject of the subordinate clause with the verb "wants." "Whom" is the objective case and cannot be a subject.

6. **(D)** Choice (D) should be revised to eliminate unnecessary repetition of "photographic" and "copies." Choices (A), (B), and (C) are concise sentences.

7. **(A)** Choice (A) contains the transition "This money," a phrase which clearly refers to "amount" in Part 4. Also, the repetition of "mortgage" indicates the correct flow of ideas. Choice (B) is too casual in using "folks," and choice (D) changes voice, "me," as well as being too causal in phrasing. Choice (C) is contradicted by information in the passage.

8. **(B)** Choice (B) changes "then," a word indicating passage of time in a narrative, to "than," a word indicating contrast. Choice (A) correctly uses "set" in meaning that the bank's account has been set up, or arranged deliberately. Choice (C) incorrectly changes the transition "so" which shows cause-and-effect, to the transition word "but" which shows contrast. Choice (D) correctly uses "rise" to indicate something going up.

9. **(D)** Choice (D) should be made more precise. It would add a needed specific, concrete detail to bolster the interest of the passage. Choice (A) is readily understood as it is. Choice (B) does not really need clarification because it can be inferred that the "process" is an assembly-line method. Choice (C) is a common and simple concept.

10. **(C)** Choice (C) is a fragment lacking a verb for the apparent subject, "5,000 cars." Part 11 should probably be combined with Part 10. Choices (A), (B), and (D) are all standard sentences.

11. **(D)** In choice (D), although it is interesting to note that India bought steam-powered vehicles from Ransom Eli Olds, the information is really not essential and is the least relevant. Choice (A) is the topic sentence. Choice (B) and choice (C) are proof to substantiate the pioneering Olds did in the automobile industry.

12. **(B)** Choice (B) contains the continuation of the topic "poor children" with the addition of "stereotype." Therefore, choice (B) would be the logical sentence to tie together Parts 6 and 7. Choice (A) is a question best asked in the first paragraph. Choice (C) might be a logical choice, but there is no transition included to tie together Parts 6 and 7. Choice (D) shifts voice, "I."

13. **(C)** In choice (C) a comma is indicated for the introductory phrase "In fact." Choice (A) creates no difference. Choice (B) would create a fragment in the second half of the sentence by isolating the subordinate clause beginning with "because." Choice (D) is incorrect because no colon should be used after the introductory phrase.

14. **(B)** Choice (B) has an incorrect verb form. The subjunctive mood "were" is needed in conditions contrary to fact. Thus, the sentence should read, "even if every single-parent family were to disappear" because the clause beginning with "if" signals condition contrary to fact. Choices (A), (C), and (D) are all correct.

15. **(A)** Choice (A) is correct because any time one item is being compared or contrasted with other items in the same category or group, it is necessary to include the word "other" or "else." Choice (B) creates an awkward construction, "applying of." Choice (C) creates a bit of an awkward wording and does not improve the sentence. In choice (D) the word "off" is necessary to the meaning of Part 9.

16. **(D)** Choice (D) has unnecessary repetition of the phrase "protect us." Choices (A), (B), and (C) are tightly-worded sentences.

17. **(D)** Choice (D) is the best selection because it mentions two forms of protection from the sun, and these require the self-control mentioned in Part 11. Choice (A) is too formal and would be better placed in the first paragraph. Choice (B) should be in paragraph one. Choice (C), although true, is an extraneous detail in this paragraph.

18. **(A)** Choice (A) is correct use of present tense. Choices (B) and (D) incorrectly use past tense. Choice (C) is incorrect use of present progressive.

19. **(A)** Choice (A) places Part 5 before Part 9. This creates a logical flow of ideas because Part 9 is the explanation of the drawback of the refinancing fee mentioned in Part 5. Choice (B) is incorrect because a sentence beginning with "However," needs to follow a contrasting idea. Choice (C) is incorrect because Part 7 is a sentence concluding the advantages and train of thought presented in Parts 4 and 6. Choice (D) would delete a vital piece of information.

20. **(B)** Choice (B) is missing a clear subject, a person paying the money. It is obvious that a home cannot pay a loan. Choices (A), (C), and (D) are clear sentences.

21. **(D)** Choice (D) is the logical transition between Part 2 which describes the composition of stucco and Part 3 which describes how the finish is applied. Choice (A) contradicts the thesis and breaks voice, "I." Choice (B) and choice (C), although true facts, introduce extraneous ideas.

22. **(C)** In choice (C) a comma is necessary to set off the introductory adverbial clause that begins with "Since." Choice (A) would create an incoherent sentence. Choice (B) is incorrect as the transition "In addition" needs to be placed close to the beginning of a sentence, or at least in the middle, but not at the end. Choice (D) changes the meaning of the sentence since the cheapness is the main emphasis, not the weight.

23. **(A)** Choice (A) is correct because the plural verb "are" agrees with the plural subject "finishes." An intervening phrase, "applied with a trowel," does not affect the choice of verb, even if the phrase ends with a singular word, "trowel." Choice (B) is incorrect because future tense is not needed. Choice (C) would create a

fragment. Choice (D) is conditional tense and inappropriate because the composition for a stucco finish is clearly defined, not subject to condition.

24. **(A)** Choice (A) is correct because it introduces the idea of recycling the trees. Choice (B) detracts from the thesis. Choice (C) introduces extraneous information. Choice (D) changes tone and detracts from support for the thesis.

25. **(D)** Choice (D) would move Part 11, which names the Artificial Reef Fund, before Part 9, which makes reference to the "self-sustaining program." Choice (A) deletes the topic sentence. Choice (B) would delete a vital piece of information, how the program works. Choice (C) reverses the topic sentence introducing the topic with the concluding sentence summarizing the usefulness of the rigs.

26. **(B)** Choice (B) is correct because present tense is needed to show this program is still operational. Choice (A) is incorrect because "who" can be used only for people, and "which" is used only for objects. Choice (C) changes the correct comparative degree used for two options to the superlative degree used for more than two options. Choice (D) would include an unnecessary comma, needed to form a compound sentence only if there were a subject after "and." Part 13 has a compound verb: "sport fishers and divers already know . . . and come."

27. **(C)** Choice (C) indicates that information about the originators of the folk dance is not necessary in a paragraph about the ballet. Choice (A) introduces the topic of the ballet and its composer. Choice (B) tells who choreographed the ballet. Choice (D) gives further information on the ballet and its music.

28. **(D)** Choice (D) is the only choice containing information about the rhythm discussed in Parts 6 and 7. Choice (A) and choice (B) both break the formal tone and use contractions. Choice (C), although a possible choice, has nothing to do with rhythm and introduces information on the folk dance.

29. **(A)** Choice (A) contains the phrase, "A French composer," which does not modify "the bolero." The phrase should be placed after "Anton Ravel" to correct the error. Choices (B), (C), and (D) are all correct sentences.

30. **(B)** Choice (B) is correct because "such as" is used to introduce an example; "like" signals unequal comparisons. Choice (A) changes the meaning of the sentence; pearls are not the most valuable gems. In choice (C) the change would omit the correct transition "until" which shows time sequence. Choice (D) would create an incoherent sentence.

31. **(A)** Choice (A) is correct because the first blank needs a time indicating word such as "When," and the second blank needs a cause-and-effect word such as "because." In choice (B) the first transition word is plausible, but the second one is not. Choices (C) and (D) produce incoherent sequences of ideas.

32. **(B)** Choice (B) combined the fragment in Part 13 with the complete sentence in Part 12. Choice (A) is not a necessary addition. Choice (C) would delete a necessary sentence, one which provides the lead into the idea of grinding down imperfections. Choice (D) is unnecessary because examples of defects have already been listed in Part 14, "lumps and stains."

33. **(D)** Choice (D) is the thesis for the passage: Christopher Columbus is covered in controversy. Part 1 introduces the contrast to choice (D) by stating that it is certain Columbus existed and went on the voyage. Choice (A) is a true but unnecessary fact in this blank. Choice (B) is supposition but not appropriate in this blank. Choice (C) would be more appropriate in the third paragraph.

34. **(B)** Choice (B) would delete the unnecessary pronoun "most." Choice (A) creates a poorly worded transition. Choice (C) creates a sentence that is self-contradictory, making the traders appear to avoid the route they actually took. Choice (D) changes the correct adverb "probably," meant to modify the verb "is," to the incorrect adjective "probable."

35. **(C)** Choice (C) would move the sentence discussing the reason for the fees, avoiding vandalism and assaults, to the end of the paragraph. Part 5 introduces the use for the fees, and Part 6 presents student objections to the attendants. Part 3 should be placed before Part 7 which further explains the problem of vandalism and assaults. Choice (A) would move Part 2, introducing the idea of threatened demonstrations and walkouts, away from Part 4 which contains reference to "these threats." Choice (B) would eliminate the crucial cost of the fees. Choice (D) would eliminate the overriding reason for the fee hike.

36. **(D)** Choice (D) contains important information about the student patrol group mentioned in Parts 10 and 12. Choice (A) would best serve as a summary sentence at the end of the article. Choice (B) is too casual in tone. Choice (C) would be best placed as a lead sentence to the entire article.

37. **(C)** In choice (C) the incorrect word "After" should be replaced with the correct word "When." It is unlikely that fears and complaints were not exchanged until after the meeting between administration and students. Choice (A) is shown with concrete details in Part 2. Choice (B) is not necessary as inclusion of the protestors' names would be irrelevant and counterproductive to the conciliatory tone of the article. Choice (D) needs no elaboration because the administration has shown its responsiveness with a compromise.

38. **(D)** Choice (D) contains the idea of Dena's failing health, mentioned in Part 6, and the idea of captivity, followed up on in Part 7. Choice (A) uses a cliche, "no use crying over spilled milk." Choice (B) is too formal in tone and does not fit logically. Choice (C) introduces irrelevant information.

39. **(A)** Choice (A) is a logical choice because the beginning of the second paragraph deals with obstacles to returning Dena to the wild. Choice (B) and choice (C) introduce topics which are true but would be better used elsewhere in the passage, perhaps in the opening paragraph which mentions the idea of captivity, or deleted altogether. Choice (D) refutes the thesis of the letter.

40. **(D)** Choice (D) is correct because Part 15 contains an error in pronoun and antecedent agreement. The indefinite pronoun "everyone" is always singular and should be followed by the singular pronouns "his or her," not the plural pronoun "their." Choices (A), (B), and (C) all contain correct pronoun usage.

41. **(A)** Choice (A) contains the transition word "Also" and another reason why the pull-out program, Content Mastery, is necessary. Choice (B) contains slang, "cop-out," as well as a negative attitude not displayed in the rest of the passage. Choice (C) is far too formal in tone. Choice (D) refutes the thesis of the passage and the reason for instituting a Content Mastery program.

42. **(C)** In choice (C) a colon is necessary before a list introduced by "the following." Choice (A) creates a grammar usage error; "a lot" is a parcel of land, not a unit of measurement. Choice (B) would change a correct plural pronoun "their," referring to a plural antecedent "students," to an incorrect singular one. Choice (D) would incorrectly remove necessary quotation marks around a commonly repeated phrase that breaks the tone of the essay.

43. **(B)** Choice (B) makes the clearest transitions. The word "However" indicates the argument that is the detractors' main objection. "For example" connects with an idea in the previous sentence, "many different strategies," and leads into examples of Content Mastery materials. In choice (A), the first transition may be viable, but the second, "In contrast," is clearly inappropriate for examples unless they are negative examples. Choice (C) is incorrect because the first transition listed, "Later," is used for chronological sequence. In choice (D) the second transition is incorrect.

44. **(D)** Choice (D) is logical because it gives a specific example of El Greco's failure to win the patronage of an influential person, the king. Choice (A) may appear logical at first, but it does not show the result of the attempt to become employed by the king; therefore, it does not continue the idea of "no better luck in Spain." Choices (B) and (C), although true, deal with El Greco's style, not his failure to seek employment in Spain.

45. **(C)** Choice (C) is a fragment. The subject "Venetian style" needs to be completed by the verb phrase "is characterized by." Choices (A), (B), and (D) are complete sentences.

Writing Sample Subsection

Writing Sample with a Score of 6, 7, or 8

Life, Liberty, and Curfews

In a way we all are subject to a variety of curfews. Some curfews are self-imposed, while others are imposed on us by others. Parents, for example, sometimes impose their own curfews on us and even themselves, especially if they have young children that they can't find babysitters for. Students who participate in extra-curricular activities and attend out of town functions have curfews imposed upon them by chaperons and coaches. Curfews like these are okay because they are enforced by relatives or by people standing in for relatives. But city-wide curfews that will be imposed on teenagers not even known by these officials are unfair and unconstitutional.

Local support of these curfews stereotype all teenagers as participants in crimes such as theft, harassment, loitering, and drug abuse. And although supporters state that curfews actually protect teenagers from being victims themselves and therefore do not lump all teens into one category, the majority of citizens first think about teenagers as juvenile delinquents. As a result every teenager at area malls who is not accompanied by a parent or guardian generally represents, to the curfew supporter, a potential act of violence about to occur.

Stereotyping is not the only negative result that occurs from imposed curfews. Class and race stereotyping also occurs. Kids who dress differently or wear their hair differently or are of a minority race are most often targets for adult harassment, especially at malls. Some managers and security guards at these places like Red Bird Mall or West End Marketplace say that they really aren't discriminating against any class or race, but the kids that are most often asked to leave or are even ticketed are kids from lower socio-economic levels and/or a minority. Curfews would not only make this problem worse, but it would punish many teens who fit these physical and social categories but not the crime-related one.

Since America functions on the idea that all people are created equal with equal rights and protection under the law, instituting any type of curfew, regardless of how well-intentional, represents an unconstitutional act targeted at an entire group of people — teenagers. Just as our government has always been there to stop unlawful acts against a group or race of people, it should be here now for us teens. We are just like the African-Americans of the Civil Rights movement, the women of the suffragist/feminist movement, the Hispanic, Asians, and any other group or culture seeking fairness, equality, and respect. Just because we are under the age of 21, though, adults sometimes feel that they don't have to ask us how we feel, what solutions we could recommend, or how we'd handle certain situations.

So what is the best solution? Rather than instituting city-wide curfews that would punish, stereotype, and alienate all teenagers — criminals and victims — I suggest that if teenagers find themselves in trouble, their parents should bear the responsibility. If, for example, I am creating a disturbance at a mall and am reprimanded by the manager, the manager should notify the police, and they in turn will notify and fine my parents. Needless to say, my parents will not long abide my getting into trouble, especially since they have to pay. By using this plan instead of a city-wide curfew, only those teens who are committing the crime or disturbance will actually pay the consequences. The tide of teen crime, consequently, would decrease considerably. Teens who work late or whose dates run later than the curfew will not be punished. And most importantly, parents will have to take an active and responsible role in their children's actions.

Features of the Writing Sample Scoring 6, 7, or 8

Appropriateness

The essay topic is clearly introduced in the first paragraph. The language fits the writer's perspective: one teen speaking for many. Though the style is informal, it reflects maturity and rationality in its author.

Unity and Focus

The essay systematically addresses the question in mind, without unnecessary tangents. The appeal to using family-centric authority to impose curfews is suggested in the first paragraph, and neatly completed in the conclusion. The examples given, though centering frequently on mall activity, all coordinate with the main topic.

Development

The author is careful about leaping to conclusions, and controls the limits of forceful language. Each paragraph builds upon the argument, with appeals to government and local authorities for justice. The conclusion ends with a suggestion for improvement, which helps soften the otherwise negative drift of the argument.

Organization

Paragraphs end and begin whenever new ideas surface. Transitional features, such as the opening question of paragraph five, help ease the shift from one element of the argument into another. Examples are both frequent and necessary to sustain the argument.

Sentence Structure

Sentences are mostly standardized, although occasional sentences begin with conjunctions. However, though irregular, this is not improper if not abused. Sentence forms vary throughout the essay to break up any potential for monotony.

Usage

Though the words chosen are not particularly extravagant, the variety of the argument prevents frequent repetition. However, words such as "teens" and "curfew," which are central to the argument and therefore requiring some repetition, should have occasionally been substituted with words like "young adult" and "time limit."

Mechanical Conventions

Spelling and punctuation are standard throughout the essay.

Writing Sample with a Score of 5

Curfews Are No Way Out From Violence

I wish to adress the city council and all of the concerned citizens who are concerned about the teen violence in our city. I am a teenager who does enjoy going out on the weekends and I also enjoy staying out late. Since I am 17 years old I don't think that I need a chaperonne or a curfew to try to prevent me from getting into trouble. Because if a kid is going to get into trouble, he is going to get in trouble and vice versa without a chaperonne or a curfew. So the city council should not vote to support a teen curfew.

If you support the teen curfew, who will decide the time cut-off? Will you allow teenagers to make reccommendations and suggestions? And will you act on some of those reccommendations and suggestions? I think not. All you really want to do, it seems to me, is push forward some kind of rule that will punish everybody — the good with the bad.

And what if you do pass this rule? Will you succeed in stopping the violence downtown? And will you succeed in making sure teenagers are at home at "respectable hours"? As I said when I began, I stay out late because I want to stay out late and not because I ask anyone's special permission. I and other teenagers will continue to stay out and go anywhere we want, anytime we want, anyplace we want.

So I urge you to vote against this rule or risk angering teenagers everywhere. We will not allow our civil rights to be abused by you or anyone else.

Features of the Writing Sample Scoring 5

Appropriateness

The topic must be inferred from the passage. The style is extremely informal. The paper's mode of operating is intimidation, which would only force its audience to take even more drastic measures.

Unity and Focus

The author's single-minded intent allows him to keep on track of his viewpoint. However, little attempt is made to unite the entire work with a controlling pattern of thought.

Development

The essay develops from mildly hostile to overtly hostile. There are little or no examples offered to help clarify the author's point. No logical argument is coherently presented within the essay.

Organization

Although transitional usage is frequent, paragraph separation is completely arbitrary. Because the essay is commanded by one narrow viewpoint, there also seems to be little reason for the arrangement of the paragraphs.

Sentence Structure

There are many examples of irregular sentence formation. Many sentences begin with conjunctions, and many sentences are run-on without any sense of style intended. The "I-you" relationship of the essay is not broken up by any variety in sentence structure. "Concerned citizens who are concerned" in the opening sentence of the essay is redundant. The final sentence of the third paragraph is one of the worst examples of nonstandard sentence formation. "I and other teenagers" should be reversed to "Other teenagers and I"; the final three phrases, though presented for emphasis, make the sentence a run-on sentence.

Usage

There is no attempt to approach the argument with new words or phrases. Most of the language employed in the essay is colloquial.

Mechanical Conventions

There are many incorrectly spelled words, such as "adress," "chaperonne," and "reccommendations." The "?" after "respectable hours" in the third sentence of the third paragraph belongs inside the quotation marks.

Writing Sample with a Score of 4, 3, 2, 1, or 0

Just Say No

Well here we go agin. It seems like govment is always trying to tell you to do something. Pay this, go there, stop, turn around, pay more. No one wants to let the citizen alone. They say this country is founded on life, liberty and the pursuit of happiness but wher's the happiness for teenagers? We have absolutely no rights whatsoever. We have to follow more rules than any other group in the whole world. We can't smoke, we can't drink, we can't vote, and now we can't go out unless you tell us to, when you tell us to, and where you tell us to. Wher's the freedom and justice in this? But we can go to war and die We can keep on going to school until were fourty. No one says no then. Just like when you have those 16 and 17 year old kids going to colege and they aren't even old enough to realy see straight. But thats okay thats allright. I say no. This kind of unfairness is not allright. If we can die and go to war and go to colege early then we can go wher we want when we want. So I say you should just say no.

Features of the Writing Sample Scoring 4, 3, 2, 1, or 0

Appropriateness

The author's style is hardly appropriate to his audience. There is no attempt at rationalization or persuasive points. The author's use of exaggeration is sarcastic and pointless.

Unity and Focus

The topic is very difficult to eke out. Although the author seems to have a viewpoint, his thoughts are disorganized and incoherent.

Development

The single paragraph presented makes no topic at developing a logical argument. The premises of his argument do not build on anything whatsoever.

Organization

Examples and points of debate cited by the author are arranged haphazardly, with no attempt to progress the argument or surprise its audience.

Sentence Structure

Sentence formation, though irregular, seems to mostly follow "subject-verb" agreement, though this is strained at the very least. Sentence two is completely incoherent and muddled. Sentence seven is an example of a run-on sentence. Sentence thirteen ("But thats okay thats allright.") should have been separated into two sentences or omitted altogether.

Usage

There is no attempt to vary word usage to enlighten the salient points of the argument.

Mechanical Conventions

There are many examples of nonstandard spelling, such as "agin," "govment," "wher's," "fourty," "realy," and "colege." Nonstandard punctuation is frequent. Many apostrophes are missing in contractions (thats okay = that's okay), and sentence eight is missing a period to divide its two properly capitalized clauses. A comma belongs after "happiness" in sentence five.

TASP

Texas Academic Skills Program

Answer Sheets

Answer Sheet — TASP Test 1

Reading Section

1. Ⓐ Ⓑ Ⓒ Ⓓ
2. Ⓐ Ⓑ Ⓒ Ⓓ
3. Ⓐ Ⓑ Ⓒ Ⓓ
4. Ⓐ Ⓑ Ⓒ Ⓓ
5. Ⓐ Ⓑ Ⓒ Ⓓ
6. Ⓐ Ⓑ Ⓒ Ⓓ
7. Ⓐ Ⓑ Ⓒ Ⓓ
8. Ⓐ Ⓑ Ⓒ Ⓓ
9. Ⓐ Ⓑ Ⓒ Ⓓ
10. Ⓐ Ⓑ Ⓒ Ⓓ
11. Ⓐ Ⓑ Ⓒ Ⓓ
12. Ⓐ Ⓑ Ⓒ Ⓓ
13. Ⓐ Ⓑ Ⓒ Ⓓ
14. Ⓐ Ⓑ Ⓒ Ⓓ
15. Ⓐ Ⓑ Ⓒ Ⓓ
16. Ⓐ Ⓑ Ⓒ Ⓓ
17. Ⓐ Ⓑ Ⓒ Ⓓ
18. Ⓐ Ⓑ Ⓒ Ⓓ
19. Ⓐ Ⓑ Ⓒ Ⓓ
20. Ⓐ Ⓑ Ⓒ Ⓓ
21. Ⓐ Ⓑ Ⓒ Ⓓ
22. Ⓐ Ⓑ Ⓒ Ⓓ
23. Ⓐ Ⓑ Ⓒ Ⓓ
24. Ⓐ Ⓑ Ⓒ Ⓓ
25. Ⓐ Ⓑ Ⓒ Ⓓ
26. Ⓐ Ⓑ Ⓒ Ⓓ
27. Ⓐ Ⓑ Ⓒ Ⓓ
28. Ⓐ Ⓑ Ⓒ Ⓓ
29. Ⓐ Ⓑ Ⓒ Ⓓ
30. Ⓐ Ⓑ Ⓒ Ⓓ
31. Ⓐ Ⓑ Ⓒ Ⓓ
32. Ⓐ Ⓑ Ⓒ Ⓓ
33. Ⓐ Ⓑ Ⓒ Ⓓ
34. Ⓐ Ⓑ Ⓒ Ⓓ
35. Ⓐ Ⓑ Ⓒ Ⓓ
36. Ⓐ Ⓑ Ⓒ Ⓓ
37. Ⓐ Ⓑ Ⓒ Ⓓ
38. Ⓐ Ⓑ Ⓒ Ⓓ
39. Ⓐ Ⓑ Ⓒ Ⓓ
40. Ⓐ Ⓑ Ⓒ Ⓓ
41. Ⓐ Ⓑ Ⓒ Ⓓ
42. Ⓐ Ⓑ Ⓒ Ⓓ
43. Ⓐ Ⓑ Ⓒ Ⓓ
44. Ⓐ Ⓑ Ⓒ Ⓓ
45. Ⓐ Ⓑ Ⓒ Ⓓ

Mathematics Section

1. Ⓐ Ⓑ Ⓒ Ⓓ
2. Ⓐ Ⓑ Ⓒ Ⓓ
3. Ⓐ Ⓑ Ⓒ Ⓓ
4. Ⓐ Ⓑ Ⓒ Ⓓ
5. Ⓐ Ⓑ Ⓒ Ⓓ
6. Ⓐ Ⓑ Ⓒ Ⓓ
7. Ⓐ Ⓑ Ⓒ Ⓓ
8. Ⓐ Ⓑ Ⓒ Ⓓ
9. Ⓐ Ⓑ Ⓒ Ⓓ
10. Ⓐ Ⓑ Ⓒ Ⓓ
11. Ⓐ Ⓑ Ⓒ Ⓓ
12. Ⓐ Ⓑ Ⓒ Ⓓ
13. Ⓐ Ⓑ Ⓒ Ⓓ
14. Ⓐ Ⓑ Ⓒ Ⓓ
15. Ⓐ Ⓑ Ⓒ Ⓓ
16. Ⓐ Ⓑ Ⓒ Ⓓ
17. Ⓐ Ⓑ Ⓒ Ⓓ
18. Ⓐ Ⓑ Ⓒ Ⓓ
19. Ⓐ Ⓑ Ⓒ Ⓓ
20. Ⓐ Ⓑ Ⓒ Ⓓ
21. Ⓐ Ⓑ Ⓒ Ⓓ
22. Ⓐ Ⓑ Ⓒ Ⓓ
23. Ⓐ Ⓑ Ⓒ Ⓓ
24. Ⓐ Ⓑ Ⓒ Ⓓ
25. Ⓐ Ⓑ Ⓒ Ⓓ
26. Ⓐ Ⓑ Ⓒ Ⓓ
27. Ⓐ Ⓑ Ⓒ Ⓓ
28. Ⓐ Ⓑ Ⓒ Ⓓ
29. Ⓐ Ⓑ Ⓒ Ⓓ
30. Ⓐ Ⓑ Ⓒ Ⓓ
31. Ⓐ Ⓑ Ⓒ Ⓓ
32. Ⓐ Ⓑ Ⓒ Ⓓ
33. Ⓐ Ⓑ Ⓒ Ⓓ
34. Ⓐ Ⓑ Ⓒ Ⓓ
35. Ⓐ Ⓑ Ⓒ Ⓓ
36. Ⓐ Ⓑ Ⓒ Ⓓ
37. Ⓐ Ⓑ Ⓒ Ⓓ
38. Ⓐ Ⓑ Ⓒ Ⓓ
39. Ⓐ Ⓑ Ⓒ Ⓓ
40. Ⓐ Ⓑ Ⓒ Ⓓ
41. Ⓐ Ⓑ Ⓒ Ⓓ
42. Ⓐ Ⓑ Ⓒ Ⓓ
43. Ⓐ Ⓑ Ⓒ Ⓓ
44. Ⓐ Ⓑ Ⓒ Ⓓ
45. Ⓐ Ⓑ Ⓒ Ⓓ

Writing Section

1. Ⓐ Ⓑ Ⓒ Ⓓ
2. Ⓐ Ⓑ Ⓒ Ⓓ
3. Ⓐ Ⓑ Ⓒ Ⓓ
4. Ⓐ Ⓑ Ⓒ Ⓓ
5. Ⓐ Ⓑ Ⓒ Ⓓ
6. Ⓐ Ⓑ Ⓒ Ⓓ
7. Ⓐ Ⓑ Ⓒ Ⓓ
8. Ⓐ Ⓑ Ⓒ Ⓓ
9. Ⓐ Ⓑ Ⓒ Ⓓ
10. Ⓐ Ⓑ Ⓒ Ⓓ
11. Ⓐ Ⓑ Ⓒ Ⓓ
12. Ⓐ Ⓑ Ⓒ Ⓓ
13. Ⓐ Ⓑ Ⓒ Ⓓ
14. Ⓐ Ⓑ Ⓒ Ⓓ
15. Ⓐ Ⓑ Ⓒ Ⓓ
16. Ⓐ Ⓑ Ⓒ Ⓓ
17. Ⓐ Ⓑ Ⓒ Ⓓ
18. Ⓐ Ⓑ Ⓒ Ⓓ
19. Ⓐ Ⓑ Ⓒ Ⓓ
20. Ⓐ Ⓑ Ⓒ Ⓓ
21. Ⓐ Ⓑ Ⓒ Ⓓ
22. Ⓐ Ⓑ Ⓒ Ⓓ
23. Ⓐ Ⓑ Ⓒ Ⓓ
24. Ⓐ Ⓑ Ⓒ Ⓓ
25. Ⓐ Ⓑ Ⓒ Ⓓ
26. Ⓐ Ⓑ Ⓒ Ⓓ
27. Ⓐ Ⓑ Ⓒ Ⓓ
28. Ⓐ Ⓑ Ⓒ Ⓓ
29. Ⓐ Ⓑ Ⓒ Ⓓ
30. Ⓐ Ⓑ Ⓒ Ⓓ
31. Ⓐ Ⓑ Ⓒ Ⓓ
32. Ⓐ Ⓑ Ⓒ Ⓓ
33. Ⓐ Ⓑ Ⓒ Ⓓ
34. Ⓐ Ⓑ Ⓒ Ⓓ
35. Ⓐ Ⓑ Ⓒ Ⓓ
36. Ⓐ Ⓑ Ⓒ Ⓓ
37. Ⓐ Ⓑ Ⓒ Ⓓ
38. Ⓐ Ⓑ Ⓒ Ⓓ
39. Ⓐ Ⓑ Ⓒ Ⓓ
40. Ⓐ Ⓑ Ⓒ Ⓓ
41. Ⓐ Ⓑ Ⓒ Ⓓ
42. Ⓐ Ⓑ Ⓒ Ⓓ
43. Ⓐ Ⓑ Ⓒ Ⓓ
44. Ⓐ Ⓑ Ⓒ Ⓓ
45. Ⓐ Ⓑ Ⓒ Ⓓ

TASP Test 1 Writing Section — Writing Sample Subsection

Answer Sheet — TASP Test 2

Reading Section

1. Ⓐ Ⓑ Ⓒ Ⓓ
2. Ⓐ Ⓑ Ⓒ Ⓓ
3. Ⓐ Ⓑ Ⓒ Ⓓ
4. Ⓐ Ⓑ Ⓒ Ⓓ
5. Ⓐ Ⓑ Ⓒ Ⓓ
6. Ⓐ Ⓑ Ⓒ Ⓓ
7. Ⓐ Ⓑ Ⓒ Ⓓ
8. Ⓐ Ⓑ Ⓒ Ⓓ
9. Ⓐ Ⓑ Ⓒ Ⓓ
10. Ⓐ Ⓑ Ⓒ Ⓓ
11. Ⓐ Ⓑ Ⓒ Ⓓ
12. Ⓐ Ⓑ Ⓒ Ⓓ
13. Ⓐ Ⓑ Ⓒ Ⓓ
14. Ⓐ Ⓑ Ⓒ Ⓓ
15. Ⓐ Ⓑ Ⓒ Ⓓ
16. Ⓐ Ⓑ Ⓒ Ⓓ
17. Ⓐ Ⓑ Ⓒ Ⓓ
18. Ⓐ Ⓑ Ⓒ Ⓓ
19. Ⓐ Ⓑ Ⓒ Ⓓ
20. Ⓐ Ⓑ Ⓒ Ⓓ
21. Ⓐ Ⓑ Ⓒ Ⓓ
22. Ⓐ Ⓑ Ⓒ Ⓓ
23. Ⓐ Ⓑ Ⓒ Ⓓ
24. Ⓐ Ⓑ Ⓒ Ⓓ
25. Ⓐ Ⓑ Ⓒ Ⓓ
26. Ⓐ Ⓑ Ⓒ Ⓓ
27. Ⓐ Ⓑ Ⓒ Ⓓ
28. Ⓐ Ⓑ Ⓒ Ⓓ
29. Ⓐ Ⓑ Ⓒ Ⓓ
30. Ⓐ Ⓑ Ⓒ Ⓓ
31. Ⓐ Ⓑ Ⓒ Ⓓ
32. Ⓐ Ⓑ Ⓒ Ⓓ
33. Ⓐ Ⓑ Ⓒ Ⓓ
34. Ⓐ Ⓑ Ⓒ Ⓓ
35. Ⓐ Ⓑ Ⓒ Ⓓ
36. Ⓐ Ⓑ Ⓒ Ⓓ
37. Ⓐ Ⓑ Ⓒ Ⓓ
38. Ⓐ Ⓑ Ⓒ Ⓓ
39. Ⓐ Ⓑ Ⓒ Ⓓ
40. Ⓐ Ⓑ Ⓒ Ⓓ
41. Ⓐ Ⓑ Ⓒ Ⓓ
42. Ⓐ Ⓑ Ⓒ Ⓓ
43. Ⓐ Ⓑ Ⓒ Ⓓ
44. Ⓐ Ⓑ Ⓒ Ⓓ
45. Ⓐ Ⓑ Ⓒ Ⓓ

Mathematics Section

1. Ⓐ Ⓑ Ⓒ Ⓓ
2. Ⓐ Ⓑ Ⓒ Ⓓ
3. Ⓐ Ⓑ Ⓒ Ⓓ
4. Ⓐ Ⓑ Ⓒ Ⓓ
5. Ⓐ Ⓑ Ⓒ Ⓓ
6. Ⓐ Ⓑ Ⓒ Ⓓ
7. Ⓐ Ⓑ Ⓒ Ⓓ
8. Ⓐ Ⓑ Ⓒ Ⓓ
9. Ⓐ Ⓑ Ⓒ Ⓓ
10. Ⓐ Ⓑ Ⓒ Ⓓ
11. Ⓐ Ⓑ Ⓒ Ⓓ
12. Ⓐ Ⓑ Ⓒ Ⓓ
13. Ⓐ Ⓑ Ⓒ Ⓓ
14. Ⓐ Ⓑ Ⓒ Ⓓ
15. Ⓐ Ⓑ Ⓒ Ⓓ
16. Ⓐ Ⓑ Ⓒ Ⓓ
17. Ⓐ Ⓑ Ⓒ Ⓓ
18. Ⓐ Ⓑ Ⓒ Ⓓ
19. Ⓐ Ⓑ Ⓒ Ⓓ
20. Ⓐ Ⓑ Ⓒ Ⓓ
21. Ⓐ Ⓑ Ⓒ Ⓓ
22. Ⓐ Ⓑ Ⓒ Ⓓ
23. Ⓐ Ⓑ Ⓒ Ⓓ
24. Ⓐ Ⓑ Ⓒ Ⓓ
25. Ⓐ Ⓑ Ⓒ Ⓓ
26. Ⓐ Ⓑ Ⓒ Ⓓ
27. Ⓐ Ⓑ Ⓒ Ⓓ
28. Ⓐ Ⓑ Ⓒ Ⓓ
29. Ⓐ Ⓑ Ⓒ Ⓓ
30. Ⓐ Ⓑ Ⓒ Ⓓ
31. Ⓐ Ⓑ Ⓒ Ⓓ
32. Ⓐ Ⓑ Ⓒ Ⓓ
33. Ⓐ Ⓑ Ⓒ Ⓓ
34. Ⓐ Ⓑ Ⓒ Ⓓ
35. Ⓐ Ⓑ Ⓒ Ⓓ
36. Ⓐ Ⓑ Ⓒ Ⓓ
37. Ⓐ Ⓑ Ⓒ Ⓓ
38. Ⓐ Ⓑ Ⓒ Ⓓ
39. Ⓐ Ⓑ Ⓒ Ⓓ
40. Ⓐ Ⓑ Ⓒ Ⓓ
41. Ⓐ Ⓑ Ⓒ Ⓓ
42. Ⓐ Ⓑ Ⓒ Ⓓ
43. Ⓐ Ⓑ Ⓒ Ⓓ
44. Ⓐ Ⓑ Ⓒ Ⓓ
45. Ⓐ Ⓑ Ⓒ Ⓓ

Writing Section

1. Ⓐ Ⓑ Ⓒ Ⓓ
2. Ⓐ Ⓑ Ⓒ Ⓓ
3. Ⓐ Ⓑ Ⓒ Ⓓ
4. Ⓐ Ⓑ Ⓒ Ⓓ
5. Ⓐ Ⓑ Ⓒ Ⓓ
6. Ⓐ Ⓑ Ⓒ Ⓓ
7. Ⓐ Ⓑ Ⓒ Ⓓ
8. Ⓐ Ⓑ Ⓒ Ⓓ
9. Ⓐ Ⓑ Ⓒ Ⓓ
10. Ⓐ Ⓑ Ⓒ Ⓓ
11. Ⓐ Ⓑ Ⓒ Ⓓ
12. Ⓐ Ⓑ Ⓒ Ⓓ
13. Ⓐ Ⓑ Ⓒ Ⓓ
14. Ⓐ Ⓑ Ⓒ Ⓓ
15. Ⓐ Ⓑ Ⓒ Ⓓ
16. Ⓐ Ⓑ Ⓒ Ⓓ
17. Ⓐ Ⓑ Ⓒ Ⓓ
18. Ⓐ Ⓑ Ⓒ Ⓓ
19. Ⓐ Ⓑ Ⓒ Ⓓ
20. Ⓐ Ⓑ Ⓒ Ⓓ
21. Ⓐ Ⓑ Ⓒ Ⓓ
22. Ⓐ Ⓑ Ⓒ Ⓓ
23. Ⓐ Ⓑ Ⓒ Ⓓ
24. Ⓐ Ⓑ Ⓒ Ⓓ
25. Ⓐ Ⓑ Ⓒ Ⓓ
26. Ⓐ Ⓑ Ⓒ Ⓓ
27. Ⓐ Ⓑ Ⓒ Ⓓ
28. Ⓐ Ⓑ Ⓒ Ⓓ
29. Ⓐ Ⓑ Ⓒ Ⓓ
30. Ⓐ Ⓑ Ⓒ Ⓓ
31. Ⓐ Ⓑ Ⓒ Ⓓ
32. Ⓐ Ⓑ Ⓒ Ⓓ
33. Ⓐ Ⓑ Ⓒ Ⓓ
34. Ⓐ Ⓑ Ⓒ Ⓓ
35. Ⓐ Ⓑ Ⓒ Ⓓ
36. Ⓐ Ⓑ Ⓒ Ⓓ
37. Ⓐ Ⓑ Ⓒ Ⓓ
38. Ⓐ Ⓑ Ⓒ Ⓓ
39. Ⓐ Ⓑ Ⓒ Ⓓ
40. Ⓐ Ⓑ Ⓒ Ⓓ
41. Ⓐ Ⓑ Ⓒ Ⓓ
42. Ⓐ Ⓑ Ⓒ Ⓓ
43. Ⓐ Ⓑ Ⓒ Ⓓ
44. Ⓐ Ⓑ Ⓒ Ⓓ
45. Ⓐ Ⓑ Ⓒ Ⓓ

TASP Test 2 Writing Section — Writing Sample Subsection

Additional Answer Sheet — TASP Test __

Reading Section

1. (A) (B) (C) (D)
2. (A) (B) (C) (D)
3. (A) (B) (C) (D)
4. (A) (B) (C) (D)
5. (A) (B) (C) (D)
6. (A) (B) (C) (D)
7. (A) (B) (C) (D)
8. (A) (B) (C) (D)
9. (A) (B) (C) (D)
10. (A) (B) (C) (D)
11. (A) (B) (C) (D)
12. (A) (B) (C) (D)
13. (A) (B) (C) (D)
14. (A) (B) (C) (D)
15. (A) (B) (C) (D)
16. (A) (B) (C) (D)
17. (A) (B) (C) (D)
18. (A) (B) (C) (D)
19. (A) (B) (C) (D)
20. (A) (B) (C) (D)
21. (A) (B) (C) (D)
22. (A) (B) (C) (D)
23. (A) (B) (C) (D)
24. (A) (B) (C) (D)
25. (A) (B) (C) (D)
26. (A) (B) (C) (D)
27. (A) (B) (C) (D)
28. (A) (B) (C) (D)
29. (A) (B) (C) (D)
30. (A) (B) (C) (D)
31. (A) (B) (C) (D)
32. (A) (B) (C) (D)
33. (A) (B) (C) (D)
34. (A) (B) (C) (D)
35. (A) (B) (C) (D)
36. (A) (B) (C) (D)
37. (A) (B) (C) (D)
38. (A) (B) (C) (D)
39. (A) (B) (C) (D)
40. (A) (B) (C) (D)
41. (A) (B) (C) (D)
42. (A) (B) (C) (D)
43. (A) (B) (C) (D)
44. (A) (B) (C) (D)
45. (A) (B) (C) (D)

Mathematics Section

1. (A) (B) (C) (D)
2. (A) (B) (C) (D)
3. (A) (B) (C) (D)
4. (A) (B) (C) (D)
5. (A) (B) (C) (D)
6. (A) (B) (C) (D)
7. (A) (B) (C) (D)
8. (A) (B) (C) (D)
9. (A) (B) (C) (D)
10. (A) (B) (C) (D)
11. (A) (B) (C) (D)
12. (A) (B) (C) (D)
13. (A) (B) (C) (D)
14. (A) (B) (C) (D)
15. (A) (B) (C) (D)
16. (A) (B) (C) (D)
17. (A) (B) (C) (D)
18. (A) (B) (C) (D)
19. (A) (B) (C) (D)
20. (A) (B) (C) (D)
21. (A) (B) (C) (D)
22. (A) (B) (C) (D)
23. (A) (B) (C) (D)
24. (A) (B) (C) (D)
25. (A) (B) (C) (D)
26. (A) (B) (C) (D)
27. (A) (B) (C) (D)
28. (A) (B) (C) (D)
29. (A) (B) (C) (D)
30. (A) (B) (C) (D)
31. (A) (B) (C) (D)
32. (A) (B) (C) (D)
33. (A) (B) (C) (D)
34. (A) (B) (C) (D)
35. (A) (B) (C) (D)
36. (A) (B) (C) (D)
37. (A) (B) (C) (D)
38. (A) (B) (C) (D)
39. (A) (B) (C) (D)
40. (A) (B) (C) (D)
41. (A) (B) (C) (D)
42. (A) (B) (C) (D)
43. (A) (B) (C) (D)
44. (A) (B) (C) (D)
45. (A) (B) (C) (D)

Writing Section

1. (A) (B) (C) (D)
2. (A) (B) (C) (D)
3. (A) (B) (C) (D)
4. (A) (B) (C) (D)
5. (A) (B) (C) (D)
6. (A) (B) (C) (D)
7. (A) (B) (C) (D)
8. (A) (B) (C) (D)
9. (A) (B) (C) (D)
10. (A) (B) (C) (D)
11. (A) (B) (C) (D)
12. (A) (B) (C) (D)
13. (A) (B) (C) (D)
14. (A) (B) (C) (D)
15. (A) (B) (C) (D)
16. (A) (B) (C) (D)
17. (A) (B) (C) (D)
18. (A) (B) (C) (D)
19. (A) (B) (C) (D)
20. (A) (B) (C) (D)
21. (A) (B) (C) (D)
22. (A) (B) (C) (D)
23. (A) (B) (C) (D)
24. (A) (B) (C) (D)
25. (A) (B) (C) (D)
26. (A) (B) (C) (D)
27. (A) (B) (C) (D)
28. (A) (B) (C) (D)
29. (A) (B) (C) (D)
30. (A) (B) (C) (D)
31. (A) (B) (C) (D)
32. (A) (B) (C) (D)
33. (A) (B) (C) (D)
34. (A) (B) (C) (D)
35. (A) (B) (C) (D)
36. (A) (B) (C) (D)
37. (A) (B) (C) (D)
38. (A) (B) (C) (D)
39. (A) (B) (C) (D)
40. (A) (B) (C) (D)
41. (A) (B) (C) (D)
42. (A) (B) (C) (D)
43. (A) (B) (C) (D)
44. (A) (B) (C) (D)
45. (A) (B) (C) (D)

TASP Additional Test Writing Section — Writing Sample Subsection
Test _____

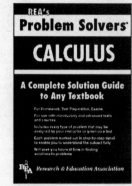

REA's Test Prep Books Are The Best!

(a sample of the hundreds of letters REA receives each year)

"I am writing to congratulate you on preparing an exceptional study guide. In five years of teaching this course I have never encountered a more thorough, comprehensive, concise and realistic preparation for this examination."

Teacher, Davie, FL

"I have found your publications, *The Best Test Preparation...*, to be exactly that."

Teacher, Aptos, CA

"I used your *CLEP Introductory Sociology* book and rank it 99% – thank you!"

Student, Jerusalem, Israel

"Your GMAT book greatly helped me on the test. Thank you."

Student, Oxford, OH

"I recently got the French SAT II Exam book from REA. I congratulate you on first-rate French practice tests."

Instructor, Los Angeles, CA

"Your AP English Literature and Composition book is most impressive."

Student, Montgomery, AL

"The REA LSAT Test Preparation guide is a winner!"

Instructor, Spartanburg, SC

(more on front page)